Communications in Computer and Information Science 467

T0215136

Jaime Lloret Mauri   Sabu M. Thampi
Danda B. Rawat   Di Jin (Eds.)

Security in Computing and Communications

Second International Symposium, SSCC 2014
Delhi, India, September 24-27, 2014
Proceedings

 Springer

Volume Editors

Jaime Lloret Mauri
Polytechnic University of Valencia, Spain
E-mail: jlloret@dcom.upv.es

Sabu M. Thampi
Indian Institute of Information Technology and Management
Trivandrum, Kerala, India
E-mail: smthampi@ieee.org

Danda B. Rawat
Georgia Southern University
Statesboro, GA, USA
E-mail: drawat@georgiasouthern.edu

Di Jin
Chrysler Group LLC
Auburn Hills, MI, USA
E-mail: djin@ieee.org

ISSN 1865-0929   e-ISSN 1865-0937
ISBN 978-3-662-44965-3   e-ISBN 978-3-662-44966-0
DOI 10.1007/978-3-662-44966-0
Springer Heidelberg New York Dordrecht London

Library of Congress Control Number: 2014948938

Typesetting: Camera-ready by author, data conversion by Scientific Publishing Services, Chennai, India

Printed on acid-free paper

Springer is part of Springer Science+Business Media (www.springer.com)

Preface

The International Symposium on Security in Computing and Communications (SSCC) aims to provide the most relevant opportunity to bring together researchers and practitioners from both academia and industry to exchange their knowledge and discuss their research findings. The second event of the Symposium (SSCC 2014) was hosted by Galgotias College of Engineering & Technology, Greater Noida, Delhi, India during September 24–27, 2014. SSCC 2014 was co-located with the Third International Conference on Advances in Computing, Communications and Informatics (ICACCI 2014).

In response to the call for papers, 132 papers were submitted to the symposium. These papers were evaluated on the basis of their significance, novelty, and technical quality. Each paper was reviewed by at least three members of the Program Committee and 30 regular papers and 12 work-in-progress papers were accepted.

There is a long list of people who volunteered their time and energy to put together the conference and who warrant acknowledgment. We would like to thank the authors of all the submitted papers, especially the accepted ones, and all the participants who made the symposium a successful event. Thanks to all members of the Technical Program Committee, and the external reviewers, for their hard work in evaluating and discussing papers.

We are grateful to the members of the Steering Committee for their support. Our most sincere thanks go to all keynote speakers who shared with us their expertise and knowledge. Special thanks to members of the Organizing Committee for their time and effort in organizing the conference.

Finally, we thank Alfred Hofmann and his team at Springer-Verlag for their excellent support in bringing out the proceedings on time.

September 2014

Jaime Lloret Mauri
Sabu M. Thampi
Danda B. Rawat
Di Jin

Organization

Technical Program Committee

Program Chairs

Jaime Lloret Mauri   Polytechnic University of Valencia, Spain
Di Jin   Chrysler Group LLC, USA
Danda B. Rawat   Georgia Southern University, USA

TPC Members

Afrand Agah   West Chester University of Pennsylvania, USA
Agusti Solanas   Rovira i Virgili University, Spain
Ai-Chun Pang   National Taiwan University, Taiwan
Ali Al-Sherbaz   The University of Northampton, UK
Aniruddha Bhattacharjya   Amrita School of Engineering, India
Ankit Chaudhary   MUM, USA
Apostolos Fournaris   University of Patras, Greece
Ashok Kumar Das   IIIT Hyderabad, India
Asrul Izam Azmi   Universiti Teknologi Malaysia, Malaysia
Azza Elaskary   Atomic Energy Authority, Egypt
Bernd Becker   University of Freiburg, Germany
Bing Wu   Fayetteville State University, USA
Binod Kumar   Jayawant Technical Campus, India
Bo Tan   Qualcomm Research, USA
Chandika Wavegedara   University of Moratuwa, Sri Lanka
Chih-Yu Wen   National Chung Hsing University, Taiwan
Chin-Chen Chang   Feng Chia University, Taiwan
Christos Bouras   University of Patras CTI&P-Diophantus, Greece
Christos Dimitrakakis   Chalmers University of Technology, Switzerland
Claudio Ardagna   Università degli Studi di Milano, Italy
Cristina Alcaraz Tello   University of Malaga, Spain
Deepthi P.P   NIT Calicut, India
Dezun Dong   National University of Defense Technology, China
Dimitrios Karras   Sterea Hellas Institute of Technology, Greece
Dimitrios Stratogiannis   National Technical University of Athens, Greece
Eduardo Fernandez   Florida Atlantic University, USA
Edward Moreno   UFS - Federal University of Sergipe, Brazil
Eva Ibarrola   University of the Basque Country, Spain

Falk-Moritz Schaefer	TU Dortmund University, Germany
Feng Cheng	University of Potsdam, Germany
Flavio Lombardi	University di Roma Tre, Italy
Francesca Paradiso	University of Florence, Italy
George Papadopoulos	Aristotle University of Thessaloniki, Greece
Gheorghita Ghinea	Brunel University, UK
Giacomo Verticale	Politecnico di Milano, Italy
Gregorio Martinez Perez	University of Murcia, Spain
Ha Duyen Trung	Hanoi University of Science and Technology, Vietnam
Hao Liang	University of Alberta, Canada
Harikrishnan Ramiah	Universiti Malaya, Malaysia
Harry Skianis	University of the Aegean, Greece
Indrakshi Ray	Colorado State University, USA
Iwannis Stamatiou	University of Iwannina/CTI, Greece
Jerzy Konorski	Gdansk University of Technology, Poland
Jiankun Hu	University of New South Wales, Australia
Jiannong Cao	Hong Kong Polytechnic University, Hong Kong
Joachim Schonowski	Deutsche Telekom Laboratories, Germany
Kai Bu	Zhejiang University, China
Karima Boudaoud	University of Nice Sophia Antipolis, France
Kejie Lu	University of Puerto Rico at Mayaguez, Puerto Rico
Keyurkumar Patel	Department of Defence, Australia
Khoi-Nguyen Le-Huu	University of Information Technology, Vietnam
Kira Kastell	Fachhochschule Frankfurt am Main - University of Applied Sciences, Germany
Lau Cheuk Lung	Federal University of Santa Catarina, Brazil
Luca Vollero	Università Campus Bio-Medico (Roma), Italy
Malamati Louta	University of Western Macedonia, Greece
Marek Klonowski	TU Wroclaw, Poland
Marius Marcu	Politehnica University of Timisoara, Romania
Marjan Naderan	Shahid Chamran University of Ahwaz, Iran
Mauricio Papa	The University of Tulsa, USA
Maurizio Aiello	National Research Council, Italy
Mercy Shalinie	Thiagarajar College of Engineering, India
Michele Pagano	University of Pisa, Italy
Mohamed Hussien	Misr University for Science and Technolgy, Egypt
Nattapong Kitsuwan	Trinity College Dublin, Ireland
Nicolas Sklavos	Technological Educational Institute of Western Greece, Greece

Wojciech Mazurczyk	Warsaw University of Technology, Poland
Xiaofei Cheng	Institute for Infocomm Research, Singapore
Xiaoqi Jia	Institute of Information Engineering, Chinese Academy of Sciences, China
Yanjiang Yang	Institute for Infocomm Research, Singapore
Yiming Ji	University of South Carolina Beaufort, USA
Yong Wang	Dakota State University, USA
Young-Long Chen	National Taichung University of Science and Technology, Taiwan
Youssef Said	Tunisie Telecom, Tunisia
Zbigniew Kotulski	Warsaw University of Technology, Poland
Zhongxiang Wei	University of Liverpool, UK

Additional Reviewers

Aditya Vempaty	Syracuse University, USA
Amadou Bagayoko	Institut National Polytechnique Toulouse- ENSEEIHT, France
Amit Gautam	SP College of Engineering, India
Amrita Manjrekar	Shivaji University, India
Ankita Wadhawan	DAV Institute of Engineering and Technology, India
Ankur Dumka	UPES, India
Balwant Ram	Lovely Professional University, India
Deepa Krishnan	Pillai Institute of Information Technology, India
Deepti Theng	G.H. Raisoni College of Engineering, India
Geetika Narang	SIT College, India
Harmeet Khanuja	University of Pune, India
Himani Goel	CDAC Noida, India
Jagruti Shah	Nagpur University, India
Jignesh Doshi	L.J. Institute of Management Studies, India
Jinesh K	Amrita Vishwa Vidyapeetham, India
Kishore Ravi	Anna University, India
Manisha Joshi	M G M 's College of Engineering, India
Maxwell Christian	Gujarat Technological University, India
Mumtaz Khan	JMI Central University, India
Musheer Ahmad	Jamia Millia Islamia, India
Nadana Ravishankar	Valliammai Engineering College, India
Neera Batra	M. M. Engineering College, M. M. University, India
Nikunj Domadiya	Gujarat Technological University, India
Prashant Menghal	MCEME, India
Pravin Chandra	Guru Gobind Singh Indraprastha University, India

Preeti Shivach   Gurukul Kangri Vishwavidyalaya Haridwar,
                              India
Premanand Ghadekar   Vishwakarma Institute of Technology,
                              India
Rafael Campos   UFRJ - Universidade Federal do Rio de Janeiro,
                              Brazil
Rahul Hans   D.A.V. Institute of Engineering and Technol-
                              ogy,
                              India
Ravi Kodali   National Institute of Technology, India
Rekha Bhatia   Punjabi University, India
Remya Ajai A S   Amrita Vishwa Vidyapeetham, India
S. Vijaykumar   6th Sense Advanced Research Foundation,
                              India
Sandeep Thorat   Shivaji University, India
Saumya Batham   ABES Engineering College, India
Taranand Mukhopadhyay   VIT University, India
Umer Abbasi   Universiti Teknologi PETRONAS, Malaysia
Vaseem Ghada   Assistant Proffesor, India
Vikas Pardesi   Lovely Professional University, India
Virendra Yadav   ABES Engineering College, India

Steering Committee

Antonio Puliafito   MDSLab - University of Messina, Italy
Axel Sikora   University of Applied Sciences Offenburg,
                              Germany
Bharat Bhargava   Purdue University, USA
Chandrasekaran K.   NITK, India
Deepak Garg, Chair   IEEE Computer Society Chapter,
                              IEEE India Council, India
Dilip Krishnaswamy   IBM Research - India
Douglas Comer   Purdue University, USA
El-Sayed M. El-Alfy   King Fahd University of Petroleum and
                              Minerals, Saudi Arabia
Gregorio Martinez Perez   University of Murcia, Spain
Hideyuki Takagi   Kyushu University, Japan
Jaime Lloret Mauri   Polytechnic University of Valencia, Spain
Jianwei Huang   The Chinese University of Hong Kong,
                              Hong Kong
John F. Buford   Avaya Labs Research, USA
Manish Parashar   Rutgers, The State University of New Jersey,
                              USA
Mario Koeppen   Kyushu Institute of Technology, Japan
Nallanathan Arumugam   King's College London, UK

Nikhil R. Pal   Indian Statistical Institute, India
Pascal Lorenz   University of Haute Alsace, France
Raghuram Krishnapuram   IBM Research - India
Raj Kumar Buyya   University of Melbourne, Australia
Sabu M. Thampi   IIITM-K, India
Selwyn Piramuthu   University of Florida, USA
Suash Deb, President   International Neural Network Society (INNS),
                                       India Regional Chapter

ICACCI Organizing Committee

Chief Patron

Suneel Galgotia, Chairman   GEI, India

Patrons

Dhruv Galgotia, CEO   GEI, India
R. Sundaresan, Director   GCET, India

General Chairs

Sabu M. Thampi   IIITM-K, India
Demetrios G. Sampson   University of Piraeus, Greece
Ajith Abraham   MIR Labs, USA & Chair, IEEE SMCS TC on
                                       Soft Computing

Program Chairs

Peter Mueller   IBM Zurich Research Laboratory, Switzerland
Juan Manuel Corchado
   Rodriguez   University of Salamanca, Spain
Javier Aguiar   University of Valladolid, Spain

Industry Track Chair

Dilip Krishnaswamy   IBM Research Labs, India

Workshop and Symposium Chairs

Axel Sikora   University of Applied Sciences Offenburg,
                                       Germany
Farag Azzedin   King Fahd University of Petroleum and
                                       Minerals, Saudi Arabia
Sudip Misra   Indian Institute of Technology, India

Special Track Chairs

Amit Kumar   BioAxis DNA Research Centre, India
Debasis Giri   Haldia Institute of Technology, India

Demo/Posters Track Chair

Robin Doss   Deakin University, Australia

Keynote/Industry Speakers Chairs

Al-Sakib Khan Pathan   IIUM, Malaysia
Ashutosh Saxena   Infosys Labs, India
Shyam Diwakar   Amrita Vishwa Vidyapeetham Kollam, India

Tutorial Chairs

Sougata Mukherjea   IBM Research, India
Praveen Gauravaram   Tata Consultancy Services Ltd., India

Doctoral Symposium Chairs

Soura Dasgupta   The University of Iowa, USA
Abdul Quaiyum Ansari   Jamia Millia Islamia, India
Praveen Ranjan Srivastava   Indian Institute of Management (IIM), India

Organizing Chair

Bhawna Mallick   Galgotias College of Engineering & Technology
                                    (GCET), India

Organizing Secretaries

Sandeep Saxena   GCET, India
Rudra Pratap Ojha   GCET, India

Publicity Chairs

Lucknesh Kumar   GCET, India
Dharm Raj   GCET, India

Table of Contents

Security and Privacy in Networked Systems

Authentication and Access Control Systems

Encryption and Cryptography

System and Network Security

Work-in-Progress

Cryptanalysis of an Efficient Biometric Authentication Protocol for Wireless Sensor Networks

Ashok Kumar Das

Center for Security, Theory and Algorithmic Research,
International Institute of Information Technology, Hyderabad 500 032, India
iitkgp.akdas@gmail.com, ashok.das@iiit.ac.in

Abstract. In 2013, Althobaiti et al. proposed an efficient biometric-based user authentication scheme for wireless sensor networks. We analyze their scheme for the security against known attacks. Though their scheme is efficient in computation, in this paper we show that their scheme has some security pitfalls such as (1) it is not resilient against node capture attack, (2) it is insecure against impersonation attack, (3) it is insecure against man-in-the-middle attack, and (4) it is also insecure against privileged insider attack. Finally, we give some pointers for improving their scheme so that the designed scheme needs to be secure against various known attacks.

Keywords: Wireless sensor networks, User authentication, Smart cards, Biometrics, Cryptanalysis.

1 Introduction

In a wireless sensor network (WSN), a large number of tiny computing nodes, also called sensors or motes, are scattered in an area (called the deployment field or target field) for the purpose of sensing some important information and transmitting those sensing information to the nearby *base stations* for further processing. Sensor nodes are generally deployed densely in a close proximity to the phenomenon to be monitored. A sensor node is a node in a WSN that is capable of performing some processing, gathering sensory information and communicating with other connected sensor nodes in that network. Sensor nodes communicate among each other by short range radio communications. The base station is usually a computationally well-equipped node in the network, whereas the sensor nodes are extremely resource-starved. The sensor nodes are scattered in a *sensor field* (i.e., deployment area or target field) and each of the scattered nodes has the capability to collect data and route data back to the base station via a multi-hop infrastructure-less communication through other sensor nodes.

Sensor networks are widely deployed in a variety of applications ranging from military to environmental and medical research. In many applications, such as target tracking, battlefield surveillance and intruder detection, WSNs often operate in hostile and unattended environments. Therefore, there is a strong need

J. Lloret Mauri et al. (Eds.): SSCC 2014, CCIS 467, pp. 1–9, 2014.

for protecting the sensing data and sensing readings. In wireless environments, an adversary not only can eavesdrop the radio traffic, but also has the ability to intercept or interrupt the exchanged messages. Thus, many protocols and algorithms do not work in hostile environments without adequate security measures. Hence, security becomes one of the major concerns when there are potential attacks against sensor networks. A survey on wireless sensor networks and the security issues could be found in [1], [3], [4], [6], [18].

Critical applications in wireless sensor network (WSN) are real-time based applications. Therefore, users are generally interested in accessing real-time information [9]. This is possible, if the users (called the external parties) are allowed to access the real-time data directly from the nodes inside WSN and not from the base station. The sensory information from nodes are gathered periodically in the base station and so, the gathered information may not be real-time. In order to get the real-time information from the nodes, the user needs to be first authorized to the nodes as well as the base station so that illegal access to nodes do not happen. As a result, the user authentication problem becomes a very important topic in research of WSN security in recent years.

Several password-based user authentication schemes have been proposed in the literature [5], [12], [13], [14], [16], [20], [22]. However, most of these schemes are insecure against various known attacks. Das et al. [9] proposed a novel and efficient password-based user authentication scheme for the hierarchical wireless sensor networks. Their scheme was shown to be secure against various known attacks including the replay and man-in-the-middle attacks with the help of formal security verification [7]. Further, an improved version of Das et al.'s scheme [9] has been proposed in [21] in the literature. Recently, biometric-based user authentication in WSNs has drawn a considerable research attention. Thus, the biometric-based user authentication in WSN becomes inherently more reliable and secure than usual traditional password-based user authentication schemes. Yuan et al.'s biometric-based user authentication scheme [23] provides better security as compared to that for M. L. Das's scheme [10] because the former scheme uses biometrics verification along with the password verification of the user. Yuan et al.'s scheme [23] has same drawbacks as in M. L. Das's scheme [10]. However, their scheme cannot resist denial-of-service attack and node compromise attack. Das et al. proposed a new secure biometric-based user authentication scheme in hierarchical wireless body area sensor networks [8]. Althobaiti et al. [2] proposed an efficient biometric-based user authentication scheme for WSNs. Unfortunately, we show that their scheme has several security pitfalls and as a result, their scheme is not practical to use for the real-life WSN applications.

The roadmap of this paper is sketched as follows. In Section 2, we describe the Althobaiti et al.'s scheme [2]. We then show that Althobaiti et al.'s scheme is insecure against four attacks in Section 3. In Section 4, we point out some suggestions to improve Althobaiti et al.'s scheme in order to withstand those security pitfalls. Finally, we conclude the paper in Section 5.

2   Review of Althobaiti et al.'s Scheme

In this section, we briefly review the recently proposed Althobaiti et al.'s biometric based user authentication scheme in wireless sensor networks [2]. The different phases of their scheme are discussed in the following subsections. We use the notations listed in Table 1 for describing and analyzing Althobaiti et al.'s scheme.

Table 1. The notations used in this paper

Symbol	Explanation
U_i	i^{th} user
SN_j	Identity of the jth sensor node SN_j
X	Secret information shared by GW–node and all deployed sensor nodes
$E_k(\cdot)$	Symmetric encryption using the key k
$D_k(\cdot)$	Symmetric decryption using the key k
$MAC_k(m)$	Message authentication code of m using the key k
$h(\cdot)$	Secure one-way collision-resistant hash function
$A\|\|B$	Data A concatenates with data B
$A \oplus B$	Data A is bitwise XORed with data B

2.1   Registration Phase

For the registration of a user U_i, the system randomly selects an encryption key, say ek_i, and it is saved in the GW-node or the base station (BS) as a key of U_i. The features of U_i's biometric (for example, iris) are extracted and then hashed by the one-way hash function $h(\cdot)$ (for example, SHA256 [19]). After that the hash digest is XORed with the key ek_i in order to generate BE template, which is then saved in U_i's device. In this phase, the user U_i's data (identity ID_i, name, etc.) and ek_i are saved in the GW-node's database. The GW-node computes $F_i = h(ID_i \oplus X)$, where X is a secret parameter generated by the GW-node and it is also saved in all the sensor nodes SN_j (the sensor login-nodes) before the deployment of those sensor nodes in a particular target field. Finally, the GW-node sends the registration message $\langle ID_i, F_i \rangle$ to the user U_i via a secure channel. In this scheme, as in M. L. Das's scheme [10], all the deployed sensor nodes SN_j are responsible to respond to the data/query that the users U_i are looking for and know the secret parameter X. Note that U_i's device contains the information $\{ID_i, F_i, h(ek_i), BE\}$, where $BE = h(biometric\_feature) \oplus ek_i$.

2.2   Login Phase

The user U_i first inputs his/her identity ID_i and personal biometric, iris by camera in the device. The biometric features of U_i's iris are extracted, corrected by error correcting code, and then hashed by SHA256. After that the hashed value is XORed with saved BE template in the U_i's device in order to regenerate the encryption key ek_i as $ek_i' = BE \oplus h(biometric\_feature)$. Then ek_i' is hashed and $h(ek_i)$ stored in the device is compared with $h(ek_i')$. If there is a match, a login request $\langle ID_i, request \rangle$ is sent to the GW-node along with ID_i via a public channel. Otherwise, the login phase is terminated immediately.

2.3   Authentication Phase

After receiving the login request from U_i, the GW-node replies to the user U_i with the authentication request $\langle R \rangle$, where R is a random challenge. When U_i receives the message from the GW-node, U_i encrypts R and T_1 with the encryption key ek_i derived in the login phase, where T_1 is the current timestamp of U_i's device, and sends the message $\langle E_{ek_i}(R, T_1) \rangle$ to the GW-node via a public channel.

After receiving the message from U_i, the GW-node decrypts the message using the encryption key ek_i stored in the GW-node and checks if $|T_1 - T_2| < \Delta T$, where ΔT denotes the interval of the expected time for the transmission delay in WSN and T_2 the time when the message was received. If it is invalid, the authentication phase is terminated immediately.

The GW-node computes $F_i = h(ID_i \oplus X)$ and $Y_i = MAC_{F_i}(ID_i || SN_j || T_3)$, where SN_j denotes the sensor node which is supposed to reply to the query made by the user U_i, and T_3 is the GW-node's current timestamp. The GW-node then sends the message $\langle ID_i, Y_i, T_3 \rangle$ to SN_j via a public channel.

When SN_j receives the message from the GW-node, SN_j checks the validity of T_3 by verifying the condition $|T_3 - T_4| < \Delta T$, where T_4 is the time when the message was received. If the condition is valid, SN_j computes $F_i = h(ID_i \oplus X)$, $Y_i' = MAC_{F_i}(ID_i || SN_j || T_3)$ and checks if $Y_i' = Y_i$. If it holds, SN_j responds to the U_i's query (RM), computes $V_i = h(ID_i || F_i || T_5)$, $C_i = h(RM)$ and $L = E_{V_i}(RM, C_i)$, and then sends the message $\langle L, T_5 \rangle$ to the user U_i via a public channel, where T_5 is the SN_j's current timestamp.

Finally, when the user U_i receives the message from SN_j at time T_6, U_i first validates by checking whether $|T_5 - T_6| < \Delta T$, and if it is valid then U_i computes $V_i = h(ID_i || F_i || T_5)$. After that U_i decrypts L to retrieve RM and C_i as $(RM', C_i') = D_{V_i}(L)$, and then computes $C_i^* = h(RM')$. If $C_i^* = C_i'$, U_i accepts RM as a valid query response from SN_j. Otherwise, U_i rejects RM. Note that in this scheme $V_i = h(ID_i || F_i || T_5)$ is considered as a session key between U_i and SN_j.

The summary of the login phase and authentication phase of Althobaiti et al.'s scheme is provided in Table 2.

3   Cryptanalysis of Althobaiti et al.'s Scheme

In this section, we first give a threat model in Section 3.1 under which the security of WSN is generally evaluated. After that we show that Althobaiti et al.'s scheme is insecure against four attacks, which are described in Section 3.2.

Table 2. Summary of exchanged messages in the login and authentication phases

User U_i	GW-node	Sensor SN_j
Login phase		
$\langle ID_i, request \rangle$		
$\longrightarrow$		
Authentication phase		
	$\langle$A random challenge, $R \rangle$	
	$\longleftarrow$	
$\langle E_{ek_i}(R, T_1) \rangle$		
$\longrightarrow$		
	$\langle ID_i, Y_i, T_3 \rangle$	
	$\longrightarrow$	
Receives $\langle L, T_5 \rangle$ from SN_j		$\langle L, T_5 \rangle$
		$\longleftarrow$

3.1 Threat Model

For evaluating the security analysis of Althobaiti et al.'s scheme, we use the threat model as follows. In most applications, sensor networks operate in the hostile environments. We assume that sensor nodes can be physically captured by an attacker. Sensor nodes are not usually equipped with tamper-resistant hardware due to cost constraints and as a result, once a node is captured by an attacker, all the sensitive data as well as cryptographic information stored in its memory are revealed to the attacker. Even if the sensor nodes are tamper-resistant, an attacker can still know all the sensitive information stored in their memory by monitoring the power consumption of the captured sensor nodes [15], [17]. However, we assume that in any case, the base station or gateway node (GW) will not be compromised by an attacker. As in [10], we make use of the Dolev-Yao threat model [11] in which two communicating parties (nodes) communicate over an insecure public channel. We adopt the similar threat model for WSNs where the channel is insecure and the end-points (sensor nodes) cannot in general be trustworthy. Finally, we assume that an attacker can eavesdrop on all traffic, inject packets and reply old messages previously delivered.

3.2 Attacks on Althobaiti et al.'s Scheme

In this section, we show that Althobaiti et al.'s scheme is insecure against the following attacks.

Resilience against Node Capture Attack. As described in [9], the resilience against node capture attack of a user authentication scheme in WSN is measured by estimating the fraction of total secure communications that are compromised by a capture of c sensor nodes *not including* the communication in which the compromised nodes are directly involved. In other words, we want to find out the effect of c sensor nodes being compromised on the rest of the network. For example, for any non-compromised sensor node SN_j, we need to find out the probability that the adversary can decrypt the secure communication between

SN_j and a user U_i, when c sensor nodes are already compromised by the adversary. If we denote this probability by $P_e(c)$, and $P_e(c) = 0$, we call such user authentication scheme as *unconditionally secure against node capture attack*.

Suppose an adverasry (attacker) captures a login-sensor node, say SN_j. Then the adversary knows the secret parameter X stored in the sensor SN_j's memory and the GW-node. Intercepting the messages $\langle ID_i, Y_i, T_3 \rangle$ and $\langle L, T_5 \rangle$ during the authentication phase, the adversary can compute $F_i = h(ID_i \oplus X)$ and $V_i = h(ID_i \| F_i \| T_5)$, which is the session key between a user U_i and the sensor SN_j. Hence, the adversary knows the session key V_i. We now show that the adversary has the ability to compromise all the session keys between U_i and any other non-compromised sensor node SN_j' as follows. Let the GW-node send the message $\langle ID_i, Y_i', T_3' \rangle$ to SN_j' and the sensor SN_j', which is a non-compromised node, send the message $\langle L', T_5' \rangle$ during the authentication phase, where $F_i = h(ID_i \oplus X)$, $Y_i' = MAC_{F_i}(ID_i \| SN_j' \| T_3')$, $C_i' = h(RM)$, $V_i' = h(ID_i \| F_i \| T_5')$ and $L' = E_{V_i'}(RM, C_i')$. Since the adversary knows X, ID_i and T_5', so he/she can easily derive the session key $V_i' = h(ID_i \| F_i \| T_5')$. It is then clear that the adversary can derive all the session keys between U_i and any non-compromised sensor node SN_j' even if a single login-sensor node is already compromised in WSN. As a result, compromise of a single sensor node leads to comprmise the successful decryptions of all secure communications between U_i and any non-compromised sensor SN_j'. Thus, we have $P_e(c) = 1.0$. Hence, Althobaiti et al.'s scheme is not at all resilient against node capture attack.

Impersonation Attack. In this attack, we show that an adversary $\mathcal{A}$ can impersonate the GW-node to a login sensor node. The detailed description is as follows. Suppose $\mathcal{A}$ physically captures a login-sensor node, say SN_j. $\mathcal{A}$ then knows the secret parameter X from the catured node SN_j. $\mathcal{A}$ also intercepts the message $\langle ID_i, Y_i, T_3 \rangle$ during the authentication phase. Let $\mathcal{A}$ wish to impersonate the GW-node to another non-compromised login-sensor node SN_j'. For this purpose, $\mathcal{A}$ can compute $F_i' = h(ID_i \oplus X)$ and $Y_i' = MAC_{F_i'}(ID_i \| SN_j' \| T_3')$, where SN_j' denotes the sensor node from which the user U_i is expecting the reponse of the query, and T_3' is the current timestamp of the adversary $\mathcal{A}$'s system. $\mathcal{A}$ then sends the message $\langle ID_i, Y_i', T_3' \rangle$ to SN_j' via a public channel. After receiving the message, SN_j' checks checks the validity of T_3'. If it is valid, SN_j' computes $F_i = h(ID_i \oplus X)$, $Y_i^* = MAC_{F_i}(ID_i \| SN_j' \| T_3')$ and checks the condition $Y_i^* = Y_i'$. If it holds, SN_j' responds to the user U_i's query (RM'), computes the session key $V_i' = h(ID_i \| F_i \| T_5')$, $C_i' = h(RM')$ and $L' = E_{V_i'}(RM', C_i')$, where T_5' is the current timestamp of SN_j', and finally sends the message $\langle L', T_5' \rangle$ to U_i via a public channel. Note that in this case, $\mathcal{A}$ can also derive the session key V_i' using X, ID_i and T_5'. As a result, Althobaiti et al.'s scheme fails to protect the impersonation attacks.

Man-in-the-Middle Attack. In this attack, an adversary $\mathcal{A}$ tries to modify, delete or change the contents of the messages in such a way that the login-sensor nodes as well as the user U_i can not detect them. Assume that $\mathcal{A}$ captures a login-sensor node and then he/she knows the secret parameter X from its memory. Suppose the GW-node sends the message $\langle ID_i, Y_i, T_3 \rangle$ to a login-sensor node SN_j from which the user U_i wants to get the response of the query. The adversary $\mathcal{A}$ intercepts this message, computes $F_i^* = h(ID_i \oplus X)$ using ID_i and extracted X, $Y_i^* = MAC_{F_i^*}(ID_i||SN_j||T_3^*)$, where T_3^* is the current timestamp of the adversary $\mathcal{A}$'s system, and sends the modified message $\langle ID_i, Y_i^*, T_3^* \rangle$ to the sensor node SN_j instead of the original message $\langle ID_i, Y_i, T_3 \rangle$ via a public channel.

After receiving the message from $\mathcal{A}$, SN_j believes that the message comes from the GW-node and proceeds to validate the timestamp T_3^* and if it is valid, SN_j computes $F_i = h(ID_i \oplus X)$, $Y_i^{**} = MAC_{F_i}(ID_i||SN_j||T_3^*)$ and checks the condition $Y_i^{**} = Y_i^*$. If it holds, SN_j responds to the U_i's query (RM^*) by computing the session key shared with the user U_i as $V_i^* = h(ID_i||F_i||T_5^*)$, $C_i^* = h(RM^*)$ and $L^* = E_{V_i^*}(RM^*, C_i^*)$, and then sendsing the message $\langle L^*, T_5^* \rangle$, where T_5^* is the current timestamp of U_i's device. $\mathcal{A}$ again intercepts the message $\langle L^*, T_5^* \rangle$. $\mathcal{A}$ computes $V_i^{**} = h(ID_i||F_i^*||T_5^*)$ and decrypts L^* to retrive RM^* and C_i^*. Note that $\mathcal{A}$ now knows the reponse to the query, RM^* which is intended for U_i only. However, $\mathcal{A}$ can create a totally face response RM^{**} to the query instead of the original RM^*, and compute $C_i^{**} = h(RM^{**})$ and $L^{**} = E_{V_i^{**}}(RM^{**}, C_i^{**})$. Finally, $\mathcal{A}$ can send the modfied message $\langle L^{**}, T_5^* \rangle$ to the user U_i. It is noted that this message is successfully authenticated by the user U_i, and hence U_i treats RM^{**} as a valid response to his/her query. Thus, it is clear that Althobaiti et al.'s scheme fails to protect the man-in-the-middle attack.

Privileged Insider Attack. During the registration phase of Althobaiti et al.'s scheme, the GW-node generates a random encryption key ek_i for a registered user U_i, which is stored directly in the GW-node's database. Note that ek_i is used to encrypt a random challenge R and timestamp T_1. As a result, an insider attacker of the GW-node can easily use ek_i to forge the user U_i. Thus, Althobaiti et al.'s scheme fails to preserve the privileged insider attack.

4   Discussions

From the cryptanalysis of Althobaiti et al.'s scheme discussed in Section 3.2, it is clear that their scheme becomes insecure due to the fact that the master secret parameter X is stored in every deployed sensor node, which is also shared with the GW-node as in M. L. Das's scheme [10]. As a remedy, one solution could be to generate a unique random master key MK_{SN_j} for each sensor node SN_j in WSN by the GW-node in offline, and then only MK_{SN_j} needs to be preloaded in the sensor node SN_j's memory prior to its deployment in the target field and also in the GW-node as pointed out in Das et al.'s scheme [9]. This strategy will certainly help to improve significantly the resilience against node capture attack, because compromise of a sensor node only reveals its master key, not the master keys of any other non-compromised sensor nodes. As a consequence, other attacks will also be eleminated. To avoid the privileged insider attack, the user U_i must not share the encryption key ek_i with the GW-node. In future, we aim to propose an improvement on Althobaiti et al.'s scheme in order to withstand the security waeknesses found in their scheme.

5 Conclusion

In this paper, we have first reviewed the recently proposed Althobaiti et al.'s scheme suited for WSNs. Althobaiti et al.'s scheme is efficient in computation. Unfortunately, we have shown that their scheme is insecure against several known attacks. Thus, their scheme is not suitable for practical application in WSNs. In addition, we have suggested some strategies in order to remedy the security weaknesses found in their scheme.

References

1. Akyildiz, I.F., Su, W., Sankarasubramaniam, Y., Cayirci, E.: Wireless sensor networks: A Survey. Computer Networks 38(4), 393–422 (2002)
2. Althobaiti, O., Al-Rodhaan, M., Al-Dhelaan, A.: An efficient biometric authentication protocol for wireless sensor networks. International Journal of Distributed Sensor Networks 2013, Article ID 407971, 1–13 (2013), http://dx.doi.org/10.1155/2013/407971
3. Chatterjee, S., Das, A.K., Sing, J.K.: Analysis and Formal Security Verification of Access Control Schemes in Wireless Sensor Networks: A Critical Survey. Journal of Information Assurance and Security 8(1), 33–57 (2013)
4. Chatterjee, S., Das, A.K., Sing, J.K.: A survey on user access control in wireless sensor networks with formal security verification. International Journal of Trust Management in Computing and Communications (in press, 2014)
5. Chen, T.-H., Shih, W.-K.: A Robust Mutual Authentication Protocol for Wireless Sensor Networks. ETRI Journal 32(5), 704–712 (2010)
6. Das, A.K.: A Survey on Analytic Studies of Key Distribution Mechanisms in Wireless Sensor Networks. Journal of Information Assurance and Security 5(5), 526–553 (2010)
7. Das, A.K., Chatterjee, S., Sing, J.K.: Formal Security Verification of a Dynamic Password-Based User Authentication Scheme for Hierarchical Wireless Sensor Networks. In: Thampi, S.M., Atrey, P.K., Fan, C.-I., Perez, G.M. (eds.) SSCC 2013. CCIS, vol. 377, pp. 243–254. Springer, Heidelberg (2013)
8. Das, A.K., Chatterjee, S., Sing, J.K.: A New Biometric-Based Remote User Authentication Scheme in Hierarchical Wireless Body Area Sensor Networks. Ad Hoc & Sensor Wireless Networks (in press, 2014)
9. Das, A.K., Sharma, P., Chatterjee, S., Sing, J.K.: A dynamic password-based user authentication scheme for hierarchical wireless sensor networks. Journal of Network and Computer Applications 35(5), 1646–1656 (2012)
10. Das, M.L.: Two-Factor User Authentication in Wireless Sensor Networks. IEEE Transactions on Wireless Communications 8(3), 1086–1090 (2009)
11. Dolev, D., Yao, A.: On the security of public key protocols. IEEE Transactions on Information Theory 29(2), 198–208 (1983)

12. Fan, R., Ping, L.-D., Fu, J.-Q., Pan, X.-Z.: A Secure and Efficient User Authentication Protocol for Two-Tieres Wireless Sensor Networks. In: Second Pacific-Asia Conference on Circuits, Communications and System (PACCS 2010), pp. 425–428 (2010)
13. He, D., Gao, Y., Chan, S., Chen, C., Bu, J.: An Enhanced Two-Factor User Authentication Scheme in Wireless Sensor Networks. Ad Hoc & Sensor Wireless Networks 10(4), 361–371 (2010)
14. Khan, M.K., Alghathbar, K.: Cryptanalysis and Security Improvements of 'Two-Factor User Authentication in Wireless Sensor Networks'. Sensors 10, 2450–2459 (2010)
15. Kocher, P.C., Jaffe, J., Jun, B.: Differential power analysis. In: Wiener, M. (ed.) CRYPTO 1999. LNCS, vol. 1666, pp. 388–397. Springer, Heidelberg (1999)
16. Lee, C.-C., Li, C.-T., Chen, S.-D.: Two Attacks on a Two-Factor User Authentication in Wireless Sensor Networks. Parallel Processing Letters 21(1), 21–26 (2011)
17. Messerges, T.S., Dabbish, E.A., Sloan, R.H.: Examining smart-card security under the threat of power analysis attacks. IEEE Transactions on Computers 51(5), 541–552 (2002)
18. Perrig, A., Stankovic, J., Wagner, D.: Security in wireless sensor networks. Communications of the ACM 47(6), 53–57 (2004)
19. Secure Hash Standard. FIPS PUB 180-1, National Institute of Standards and Technology (NIST), U.S. Department of Commerce (April 1995)
20. Vaidya, B., Makrakis, D., Mouftah, H.T.: Improved Two-Factor User Authentication in Wireless Sensor Networks. In: Second International Workshop on Network Assurance and Security Services in Ubiquitous Environments, pp. 600–606 (2010)
21. Wang, D., Wang, P.: Understanding security failures of two-factor authentication schemes for real-time applications in hierarchical wireless sensor networks. Ad Hoc Networks (in press, 2014), http://dx.doi.org/10.1016/j.adhoc.2014.03.003
22. Wong, K., Zheng, Y., Cao, J., Wang, S.: A dynamic user authentication scheme for wireless sensor networks. In: Proceedings of IEEE International Conf. Sensor Networks, Ubiquitous, Trustworthy Computing, pp. 244–251. IEEE Computer Society (2006)
23. Yuan, J., Jiang, C., Jiang, Z.: A Biometric-Based User Authentication for Wireless Sensor Networks. Wuhan University Journal of Natural Sciences 15(3), 272–276 (2010)

Security Analysis of an Adaptable and Scalable Group Access Control Scheme for Managing Wireless Sensor Networks

Vanga Odelu[1], Ashok Kumar Das[2], and Adrijit Goswami[3]

[1] Department of Mathematics,
Indian Institute of Technology, Kharagpur 721 302, India
odelu.phd@maths.iitkgp.ernet.in, odelu.vanga@gmail.com
[2] Center for Security, Theory and Algorithmic Research,
International Institute of Information Technology, Hyderabad 500 032, India
iitkgp.akdas@gmail.com, ashok.das@iiit.ac.in
[3] Department of Mathematics,
Indian Institute of Technology, Kharagpur 721 302, India
goswami@maths.iitkgp.ernet.in

Abstract. Recently, Wu et al. proposed an adaptable and scalable group access control scheme (GAC) for managing wireless sensor networks (WSNs) [Telematics and Informatics, 30:144-157, 2013], and they claimed that their proposed GAC mechanism provides forward secrecy and backward secrecy, and it also prevents man-in-the-middle attack. However, in this paper, we revisit Wu et al.'s scheme and show that Wu et al.'s scheme fails to provide the forward secrecy as well as the backward secrecy and also their scheme does not prevent the man-in-the-middle attack. As a result, Wu et al.'s scheme is not suitable for practical applications.

Keywords: Cryptanalysis, Group access control, SGC, Adaptability, Scalability, WSNs.

1 Introduction

Wireless sensor networks will be widely deployed in the near future. While much research has focused on making these networks feasible and useful, security has received little attention. Increased employment of WSN in real life applications and their hostile and remote locations accelerate demand of security in WSN [4], [7].

In a WSN, several tiny computing nodes, called sensors, are deployed in an area, called the deployment area or target field, for the purpose of sensing some important data from their surroundings and transmitting those data to nearby *base stations* for further processing. A sensor node has the ability of performing some processing, gathering sensory information and communicating with other connected nodes in the network. The transmission between the sensors take place by short range radio wireless communications. The base station is assumed to be

J. Lloret Mauri et al. (Eds.): SSCC 2014, CCIS 467, pp. 10–19, 2014.

computationally resource-rich, whereas the sensor nodes are extremely resource-starved. Each deployed sensor node has the capability to collect data and route data back to the base station, where data are routed back to the base station by a multi-hop infrastructure-less adhoc architecture through sensor nodes. A survey on WSN and its security aspects can be found in [1], [4], [6], [7].

Now a days, secure group communications (SGCs) are widely used for the efficient group-oriented applications in wireless sensor networks such as military and health care applications [3], [5], [8], [10], [11], [12], [14]. Thus, protecting the sensitive data from unauthorized accesses is an important security issue in SGCs. In this scenario, security is specific to the group access key (GAK). Hence, the group access control mechanism should ensure that the GAK can be neither revealed nor modified (unauthorized) during the distribution. Furthermore, when changing occurs in the entities' relationship, the group access control mechanism should preserve both forward secrecy and backward secrecy of GAK. In addition, it should prevent from unauthorized modifications of GAK.

The rest of the paper is organization as follows. In next section, we provide some basic mathematical preliminaries required to review and analyze Wu et al.'s scheme. In Section 3, we list the requirements needed for a GAC protocol in WSNs. In Section 4, we review Wu et al.'s scheme. In Section 5, we analyze Wu et al.'s scheme from security point of view and show that Wu et al.'s scheme is insecure against various attacks. Finally, in Section 6, we conclude the paper and make future research direction on this work presented in the paper.

2   Mathematical Preliminaries

In this section, we briefly describe some mathematical preliminaries, which are useful for analyzing Wu et al.'s scheme.

As given in [2], [9], there is an efficient probabilistic algorithm for finding all the roots of a given n-degree polynomial $f(x) \in GF(q)[x]$, where $n \in GF(q)$, the Galois field (finite field) of order q and another efficient probabilistic algorithm for factoring a given n-degree polynomial $f(x) \in GF(q)[x]$. We discuss the root finding and the factorization of given n-degree polynomial for convenience of our security analysis on Wu et al.'s GAC scheme. For more details, refer [2] and [9].

2.1   Root Finding of n-Degree Polynomial in Finite Field $GF(q)$

Suppose for a given polynomial $f(x) \in GF(q)[x]$ of degree n ($deg \cdot f = n$) in the finite field $GF(q)$, we want to find all the roots $a \in GF(q)$ of the equation $f(x) = 0$. Let q be odd. According to [2], [9], finding all the roots of the equation $f(x) = 0$ is as follows. First, we compute the greatest common divisor (gcd) as $f_1(x) = gcd(f(x), x^q - x)$. If $f_1(x) = 1$, then $f(x)$ has no roots in $GF(q)$. Otherwise, in general, we have, $f_1(x) = (x - a_1)(x - a_2) \cdots (x - a_k)$, $k \leq n$, where a_i's are all pairwise distinct roots of the equation $f(x) = 0$ in the field $GF(q)$. M. Ben-Or [2] showed that the expected number of operations required for the root finding algorithm in order to find all the roots of the equation

$f(x) = 0$ is $O(n \cdot log(n) \cdot L(n) \cdot log(q))$, where $L(n) = log(n) \cdot log(log(n))$. In other words, the expected running time is polynomial in n.

2.2   Factorization of n-Degree Polynomial in Finite Field $GF(q)$

Assume that we want to factor a polynomial $f(x) \in GF(q)[x]$ of degree n into its irreducible factors. Assume that the polynomial $f(x)$ has no repeated factors and we want to factor the polynomial $f(x)$ as $f(x) = g_1(x) \cdot g_2(x) \cdots g_n(x)$, where $g_d(x)$ is the product of irreducible factors of $f(x)$ of degree d. M. Ben-Or proposed the algorithm [2] for computing factors of the n-degree polynomial $f(x)$. Further, M. Ben-Or also discussed how to factor $g_i(x)$ into irreducible factors of equal degree in [2]. M. Ben-Or proved that the expected number of operations required to factor an n-degree polynomial $f(x)$ is $O(n^2 \cdot L(n) \cdot log(q))$.

3   Requirements of a GAC Scheme in WSNs

In this section, we list the requirements needed for an idle group access control (GAC) scheme in WSNs:

- **Adaptability** means that group access control should sustain heterogeneous, peer-to-peer, and hierarchical structures for managing the entities.
- **Efficiency** indicates that group access control should be efficient in terms of cryptographic parameters generation and distribution, and management of GAK.
- **Scalability** refers to the ability to manage the large number of sensor nodes that are arranged initially or incrementally in WSNs.
- **Security** is specific to the GAK, that is, group access control mechanism should ensure that the GAK can be neither revealed nor modified (unauthorized) during the distribution.
- **Forward secrecy** ensures that although an adversary knows the contiguous subset of the old GAKs, he/she cannot derive the subsequent keys, GAKs.
- **Backward secrecy** ensures that even if an adversary knows the contiguous subset of the existing GAKs, the adversary cannot derive the preceding GAKs.
- **Man-in-the-the-middle attack** refers that an access control mechanism should prevent unauthorized modifications of GAKs.

As defined in [13], [15], a sound and secure group access control mechanism should satisfy all the security properties including forward secrecy and backward secrecy of GAKs. Moreover, the group access control scheme must prevent unauthorized modification of the GAKs, called man-in-the-middle attack.

4   Review of Wu et al.'s GAC Scheme

In 2013, Wu et al. [15] proposed an adaptable and scalable group access control mechanism for managing WSNs based on Advanced Encryption Standard (AES) and Elliptic Curve public key cryptosystem.

We use the notations listed in Table 1 for describing and analyzing Wu et al.'s scheme. Wu et al.'s GAC scheme works as follows. In the first step, using symmetric-key cryptosystem AES, the task manager TM generates the group access key GAK_{C_i} to each sensor node R_n in the cluster C_i. In the second step, the task manager TM encrypts GAK_{C_i} using the secure filter function $f_{C_i}(x)$, which is protected by the public key cryptosystem ECC. In the third step, the task manager TM distributes the secure filter function $f_{C_i}(x)$ to the entities assigned in that group. Finally, the authorized entities can derive the group access key GAK_{C_i} using the secure filter function and their secret key sk_{R_n}.

Wu et al.'s scheme consists of two phases, namely the distribution of group access key phase and the management of group access key phase, which are discussed in the following subsections.

Table 1. The notations used in this paper

Symbol	Explanation
C_i	i^{th} cluster in WSN
$C_i M_j$	j^{th} cluster-member node of the ith cluster C_i
$C_i H$	Cluster-head node of ith cluster C_i
TM	Task manager
R	An entity (it may be a node or base station or task manager)
sk_R	Secret key of the entity R
PK_R	Public key of entity R which corresponds to sk_R
Sig_R	Digital signature signed by the entity R using secret key sk_R.
GAK_{C_i}	Group access key, which is generated by TM
$E_k(\cdot)$	Encryption function using the key, k
$D_k(\cdot)$	Decryption function using the key, k
$h(\cdot)$	Secure one-way collision-resistant hash function
$f_{C_i}(\cdot)$	Secure filter function
$A\|\|B$	Data A concatenates with data B

4.1 Distribution of Group Access Key

In Wu et al.'s scheme, the task manager TM initially configures the crypto-parameters into each sensor node R_n separately, including its hash value $h(ts_{R_n} \|\| sk_{R_n})$, public and secret key pair (PK_{R_n}, sk_{R_n}), ts_{R_n} denotes the timestamp of R_n, and the TM's public key is PK_{TM}. After initial configuration, the TM distributes these nodes into the WSN. In order to share the group access key GAK_{C_i} to each sensor node R_n in the cluster C_i, the task manager TM constructs the secure filter function $f_{C_i}(x)$ for the cluster C_i as follows:

$$f_{C_i}(x) = \begin{cases} GAK_{C_i}, & \text{if } \prod_{n=1}^{m}(x - h(ts_{R_n}\|\|sk_{R_n})) = 0 \\ \text{undefined value}, & \text{if } \prod_{n=1}^{m}(x - h(ts_{R_n}\|\|sk_{R_n})) \neq 0, \end{cases}$$

where the positive integers n and m respectively represent the initial and the final number of entities.

Example 1 (Distribution of group access keys). Assume that there is one task manager TM, one cluster head C_1H, and two cluster-member nodes C_1M_1 and C_1M_2. Initially, the task manager TM separately configures the crypto-parameters into each sensor node (including its hash value, public and secret key pair, and the TM's public key). After that the TM constructs the secure filter function for the cluster C_1 as follows:

$$f_{C_1}(x) = \prod_{n=1}^{3}(x - h(ts_{R_n}\|sk_{R_n})) + GAK_{C_1}$$
$$= (x - h(ts_{C_1H}\|sk_{C_1H}))(x - h(ts_{C_1M_1}\|sk_{C_1M_1}))(x - h(ts_{C_1M_2}\|sk_{C_1M_2})) + GAK_{C_1}.$$

Then, each authorized cluster-member node R_n can derive the group access key GAK_{C_1} by computing the value $f_{C_1}(h(ts_{R_n}\|sk_{R_n}))$. In this example, the node C_1M_1 in the cluster C_1 derives the key GAK_{C_1} as follows:

$$f_{C_1}(h(ts_{C_1M_1}\|sk_{C_1M_1})) = (h(ts_{C_1M_1}\|sk_{C_1M_1}) - h(ts_{C_1H}\|sk_{C_1H}))(h(ts_{C_1M_1}\|sk_{C_1M_1}) - h(ts_{C_1M_1}\|sk_{C_1M_1}))(h(ts_{C_1M_1}\|sk_{C_1M_1}) - h(ts_{C_1M_2}\|sk_{C_1M_2})) + GAK_{C_1}$$
$$= 0 + GAK_{C_1}$$
$$= GAK_{C_1}.$$

Finally, all these configured sensor nodes are deployed into WSN.

For some security reasons, an entity in the cluster may need to update its GAK. In addition, it is also important to ensure that the authorization of each entity before issuing the updated GAK. The details of the update process of GAK is described in the following protocol. As discussed above, initially each entity in the cluster is preloaded with its crypto-parameters (such as hash value, GAK, and public and secret key pair) and then they are deployed into WSN. Moreover, it is assumed that all the entities deployed in WSN are successfully installed and operating in WSN.

Protocol: Updating GAK in WSNs

In this protocol, the TM ensures the authorization of each entity R's identity before issuing the updated group access key to them. The following steps are required to successfully complete this task:

Step 1. Each entity R computes the ciphertext C through the following steps and sends it to TM.

> **Step 1.1.** R attaches a signature Sig_R to its identity id_R using its secret key sk_R. Let it be denoted by $(id_R)_{Sig_R}$.
>
> **Step 1.2.** R combines id_R, $(id_R)_{Sig_R}$ and the hash value $h(ts_R\|sk_R)$.
>
> **Step 1.3.** R encrypts the information id_R, $(id_R)_{Sig_R}$ and $h(ts_R\|sk_R)$ using the public key PK_{TM} of the task manager TM as $C = E_{PK_{TM}}[id_R, (id_R)_{Sig_R}, h(ts_R\|sk_R)]$.

Step 1.4. Finally, R sends the ciphertext C to the TM via a public channel.

Step 2. After receiving the ciphertext C from each entity R, the task manager TM verifies the validity of R's identity id_R through the following steps.

Step 2.1. TM decrypts the ciphertext C using its own secret key sk_{TM} as $D_{sk_{TM}}(C) = (id_R, (id_R)_{Sig_R}, h(ts_R \| sk_R)$.

Step 2.2. TM decrypts the signature $(id_R)_{Sig_R}$ using the public key PK_R of R to retrieve id_R as $id'_R = D_{PK_R}[(id_R)_{Sig_R}]$.

Step 2.3. TM verifies whether the derived identity id'_R matches with the original identity id_R or not. If it matches, the TM maintains $h(ts_R \| sk_R)$; otherwise, the TM rejects this application.

Step 3. For each cluster C_i in WSN, the TM constructs the secure filter function $f_{C_i}(x)$ as follows:

$$f_{C_i}(x) = \prod_{\forall R \in C_i} (x - h(ts_R \| sk_R)) + GAK_{C_i}.$$

Step 4. The TM then multicasts the secure filter function $f_{C_i}(x)$ to each entity R in the cluster C_i.

Step 5. Upon receiving the secure filter function $f_{C_i}(x)$, each entity R in C_i derives GAK_{C_i} using its own secret key sk_R as $GAK_{C_i} = f_{C_i}(h(ts_R \| sk_R))$.

4.2   Management of Group Access Key

In this section, we discuss the dynamic properties of Wu et al.'s scheme, such as joining of a new entity into the cluster and leaving an existing entity from the cluster. For security purposes, a WSN should have an efficient and secure mechanism to ensure both forward secrecy and backward secrecy when an entity leaves and joins the cluster, respectively.

Consider the following two examples to illustrate the process of joining and leaving an entity in Wu et al.'s scheme.

Example 2 (Executing the joining process). Assume that a cluster C_1 has three nodes $C_1 H$, $C_1 M_1$ and $C_1 M_2$. Let a new node R join into the cluster C_1. The following steps successfully complete the joining process of the newly added node R:

Step 1. R computes the ciphertext $C = E_{PK_{TM}}[id_R, (id_R)_{Sig_R}, h(ts_R \| sk_R)]$ using the public key PK_{TM} of TM and then sends C it to TM via a public channel.

Step 2. After receiving the ciphertext C from the new node R, the TM decrypts it using its secret key sk_{TM}. The TM then verifies whether the identity id_R is valid. If the identity is valid, TM gives the new identity $C_1 M_3$ to the newly joining node R. The TM generates the new secure filter function $f_{C'_1}(x)$ for the updated group access key $GAK_{C'_1}$. The secure filter functions before joining and after joining of the node respectively

$$f_{C_1}(x) = (x - h(ts_{C_1H}||sk_{C_1H}))(x - h(ts_{C_1M_1}||sk_{C_1M_1}))$$
$$(x - h(ts_{C_1M_2}||sk_{C_1M_2})) + GAK_{C_1},$$
$$f_{C_1'}(x) = (x - h(ts_{C_1H}||sk_{C_1H}))(x - h(ts_{C_1M_1}||sk_{C_1M_1}))$$
$$(x - h(ts_{C_1M_2}||sk_{C_1M_2})(x - h(ts_{C_1M_3}||sk_{C_1M_3})) + GAK_{C_1'}.$$

Step 3. Finally, the TM multicasts the newly computed $f_{C_1'}(x)$.

Example 3 (Executing the leaving process). Suppose that the cluster C_2 has three nodes C_2H, C_2M_1 and C_2M_2, and the cluster C_3 has three nodes C_3H, C_3M_1 and C_3M_2. Then, the secure filter function of C_2 and C_3 are respectively

$$f_{C_2}(x) = (x - h(ts_{C_2H}||sk_{C_2H}))(x - h(ts_{C_2M_1}||sk_{C_2M_1}))$$
$$(x - h(ts_{C_2M_2}||sk_{C_2M_2})) + GAK_{C_2},$$
$$f_{C_3}(x) = (x - h(ts_{C_3H}||sk_{C_3H}))(x - h(ts_{C_3M_1}||sk_{C_3M_1}))$$
$$(x - h(ts_{C_3M_2}||sk_{C_3M_2})) + GAK_{C_3}.$$

Assume that the node C_2M_2 wants to leave the cluster C_2 and join the cluster C_3. The new secure filter functions of C_2 and C_3 are then respectively

$$f_{C_2'}(x) = (x - h(ts_{C_2H}||sk_{C_2H}))(x - h(ts_{C_2M_1}||sk_{C_2M_1})) + GAK_{C_2'},$$
$$f_{C_3'}(x) = (x - h(ts_{C_3H}||sk_{C_3H}))(x - h(ts_{C_3M_1}||sk_{C_3M_1}))(x - h(ts_{C_3M_2}||sk_{C_3M_2}))$$
$$(x - h(ts_{C_3M_3}||sk_{C_3M_3})) + GAK_{C_3'},$$

where the new hash value $h(ts_{C_2M_2}'||sk_{C_2M_2})$ refers to $h(ts_{C_3M_3}||sk_{C_3M_3})$. Thus, only the timestamp $ts_{C_2M_2}$ needs to change, but the secret key $sk_{C_2M_2}$ remains same.

5   Cryptanalysis of Wu et al.'s Scheme

In this section, we show that Wu et al.'s scheme fails to preserve forward secrecy as well as backward secrecy. In addition, we show that Wu et al.'s scheme does not prevent the man-in-the-middle attack. For these security analysis, we consider Example 2 and Example 3, which are given in Section 4.2.

5.1   Wu et al.'s Scheme Fails to Provide Forward Secrecy

Consider Example 2 (joining process) in Section 4.2. Let a new sensor node C_1M_3 join into the cluster C_1. Then the old and updated secure filter functions, say $f_{C_1}(x)$ and $f_{C_1'}(x)$ are given in Example 2. Assume that an attacker $\mathcal{A}$ knows the old group access key GAK_{C_1} of the cluster C_1. The attacker can now compute the group access key $GAK_{C_1'}$ using the two secure filter functions $f_{C_1}(x)$ and $f_{C_1'}(x)$, and the old group access key GAK_{C_1} as follows.

Step 1. Using the root finding algorithm (described in Section 2), the attacker $\mathcal{A}$ computes all the roots $h(ts_{C_1H}||sk_{C_1H})$, $h(ts_{C_1M_1}||sk_{C_1M_1})$ and $h(ts_{C_1M_2}||sk_{C_1M_2})$ of the equation $f_{C_1}(x) - GAK_{C_1} = 0$.

Step 2. Since the derived roots in Step 1 are also roots of the equation $f_{C_1'}(x) - GAK_{C_1'} = 0$, the attacker $\mathcal{A}$ simply computes the new group access key $GAK_{C_1'}$ as $GAK_{C_1'} = f_{C_1'}(h(ts_R||sk_R))$, where $R \in \{C_1H, C_1M_1, C_1M_2\}$, using the derived roots.

Similarly, from the secure filter functions $f_{C_2}(x)$ and $f_{C_2'}(x)$, and $f_{C_3}(x)$ and $f_{C_3'}(x)$ given in Example 3 (leaving process), if an attacker $\mathcal{A}$ knows the old group access keys GAK_{C_2} and GAK_{C_3} of the clusters C_2 and C_3 respectively, he/she can compute the new group access keys $GAK_{C_2'}$ and $GAK_{C_3'}$ using the same argument given in Steps 1 and 2. Thus, it is clear that Wu et al.'s scheme does not provide the forward secrecy to the group access key.

5.2   Wu et al.'s Scheme Fails to Provide Backward Secrecy

Again consider Example 2 (joining process). Assume the sensor node C_1M_3 joins into the cluster C_1. Then the old and updated secure filter functions $f_{C_1}(x)$ and $f_{C_1'}(x)$ are given in Example 2. Further assume that an attacker $\mathcal{A}$ knows the new group access key $GAK_{C_1'}$ of the cluster C_1. The attacker then computes the old group access key GAK_{C_1} using two secure filter functions $f_{C_1}(x)$ and $f_{C_1'}(x)$, and the new group access key $GAK_{C_1'}$ as follows.

Step 1. Using root finding algorithm (described in Section 2), the attacker $\mathcal{A}$ computes all roots $h(ts_{C_1H}||sk_{C_1H})$, $h(ts_{C_1M_1}||sk_{C_1M_1})$, $h(ts_{C_1M_2}||sk_{C_1M_2})$ and $h(ts_{C_1M_3}||sk_{C_1M_3})$ of the equation $f_{C_1'}(x) - GAK_{C_1'} = 0$.

Step 2. The derived roots in Step 1 are again the roots of the equation $f_{C_1}(x) - GAK_{C_1} = 0$. The attacker $\mathcal{A}$ simply computes the old group access key GAK_{C_1} as $GAK_{C_1} = f_{C_1}(h(ts_R||sk_R))$, where $R \in \{C_1H, C_1M_1, C_1M_2\}$, using the derived roots except the roots $h(ts_{C_1M_3}||sk_{C_1M_3})$.

Similarly, from the secure filter functions $f_{C_2}(x)$ and $f_{C_2'}(x)$, and $f_{C_3}(x)$ and $f_{C_3'}(x)$ in Example 3 (leaving process), if an attacker $\mathcal{A}$ knows the new group access keys $GAK_{C_2'}$ and $GAK_{C_3'}$ of clusters C_2 and C_3 respectively, he/she can compute the old group access keys GAK_{C_2} and GAK_{C_3} using the same argument given in Steps 1 and 2. As a result, Wu et al.'s scheme does not provide the backward secrecy to the group access key.

5.3   Man-in-the-Middle Attack

In Wu et al.'s scheme, even if an attacker $\mathcal{A}$ arbitrarily modifies the secure filter function $f_{C_i}(x)$, no entity in the cluster can identify the modification since Wu et al.'s scheme does not provide any authentication mechanism to the group access key GAK_{C_i} of a cluster C_i to verify the validity of GAK_{C_i}. For example, the task manager TM sends the filter function, say $f_{C_i}(x)$ to the member-nodes in the cluster C_i. But, the member-nodes receives the modified filter function $f'_{C_i}(x)$ instead of original filter function $f_{C_i}(x)$. Therefore, in this case every entity in the cluster obtains the group access key, say GAK'_{C_i} from $f'_{C_i}(x)$, which is not equal to the original key. Since there is no signature mechanism to verify whether the derived key GAK'_{C_i} is valid key or not, the entity assumes that the derived key GAK'_{C_i} is the valid group access key. As a result, the entities in the cluster can use the invalid key. In this way, Wu et al.'s scheme does not prevent the man-in-the-middle attack.

6   Conclusion and Future Work

In this paper, we have shown that the recently proposed Wu et al.'s scheme does not preserve the forward secrecy and backward secrecy. Further, their scheme does not prevent the man-in-the-middle attack. In future work, we aim to propose an improvement on Wu et al.'s scheme, which needs to be more secure and efficient than Wu et al.'s scheme.

Acknowledgements. The authors would like to acknowledge the anonymous reviewers for their helpful comments and suggestions.

References

1. Akyildiz, I.F., Su, W., Sankarasubramaniam, Y., Cayirci, E.: Wireless sensor networks: A Survey. Computer Networks 38(4), 393–422 (2002)
2. Ben-Or, M.: Probabilistic algorithms in finite fields. In: Proceedings of 22nd Annual Symposium on Foundations of Computer Science (IEEE FOCS 1981), pp. 394–398 (1981)
3. Chatterjee, S., Das, A.K., Sing, J.K.: A secure and effective access control scheme for distributed wireless sensor networks. International Journal of Communication Networks and Distributed Systems (in press, 2014)
4. Chatterjee, S., Das, A.K., Sing, J.K.: Analysis and Formal Security Verification of Access Control Schemes in Wireless Sensor Networks: A Critical Survey. Journal of Information Assurance and Security 8(1), 33–57 (2013)
5. Chatterjee, S., Das, A.K., Sing, J.K.: An enhanced access control scheme in wireless sensor networks. Ad Hoc & Sensor Wireless Networks 21(1-2), 121–149 (2014)
6. Das, A.K.: Design and Analysis of Key Distribution Mechanisms in Wireless Sensor Networks. PhD thesis, Department of Computer Science and Engineering, Indian Institute of Technology Kharagpur, India (June 2008)
7. Das, A.K.: A Survey on Analytic Studies of Key Distribution Mechanisms in Wireless Sensor Networks. Journal of Information Assurance and Security 5(5), 526–553 (2010)
8. Das, A.K., Chatterjee, S., Sing, J.K.: A novel efficient access control scheme for large-scale distributed wireless sensor networks. International Journal of Foundations of Computer Science 24(05), 625–653 (2013)
9. Das, A.K., Paul, N.R., Tripathy, L.: Cryptanalysis and improvement of an access control in user hierarchy based on elliptic curve cryptosystem. Information Sciences 209, 80–92 (2012)

10. Du, X., Chen, H.H.: Security in wireless sensor networks. IEEE Wireless Communications 15(4), 60–66 (2008)
11. Huang, H.F.: A novel access control protocol for secure sensor networks. Computer Standards & Interfaces 31(2), 272–276 (2009)
12. Kim, Y., Perrig, A., Tsudik, G.: Group key agreement efficient in communication. IEEE Transactions on Computers 53(7), 905–921 (2004)
13. Perrig, A., Stankovic, J., Wagner, D.: Security in wireless sensor networks. Communications of the ACM 47(6), 53–57 (2004)
14. Sorniotti, A., Molva, R., Gomez, L., Trefois, C., Laube, A., Scaglioso, P.: Efficient access control for wireless sensor data. International Journal of Wireless Information Networks 16(3), 165–174 (2009)
15. Wu, F., Pai, H.T., Zhu, X., Hsueh, P.Y., Hu, Y.H.: An adaptable and scalable group access control scheme for managing wireless sensor networks. Telematics and Informatics 30, 144–157 (2013), http://dx.doi.org/10.1016/j.tele.2012.03.011

Secure Hierarchical Routing Protocol (SHRP) for Wireless Sensor Network

Sohini Roy and Ayan Kumar Das

Calcutta Institute of Engineering and Management,
Kolkata, India
roysohini266@gmail.com, ayandas24114057@yahoo.co.in

Abstract. Wireless Sensor Network (WSN) has emerged as an important supplement to the modern wireless communication systems due to its wide range of applications. The communication of sensitive data and working in hostile environmental condition needs security. The energy constraints, limited computational ability and low storage capacity of the sensor nodes have made the implementation of security more challenging. The proposed scheme adopts a level based secure hierarchical approach to maintain the energy efficiency. It incorporates light-weight security mechanisms like, nested hash based message authentication codes (HMAC), Elliptic-Curve Diffie-Hellman (ECDH) key exchange scheme and Blowfish symmetric cipher. Simulation results show that the scheme performs better than existing secure routing protocols FBSR and ATSR.

Keywords: Wireless Sensor Network, Hierarchical, Cluster Head, Trust value, One-way Hash Chain, Data Aggregation, Energy Efficiency, Network Lifetime.

1 Introduction

A wireless sensor network consists of many small sensor nodes, deployed very densely over a remote place with harsh environmental conditions. These sensor nodes are solely devoted to the task of sensing devastating information from the environment and sending that to the base station in a secure energy efficient way, so that necessary actions can be taken. Energy constraint, added with a number of security threats and attacks, increases challenges of wireless sensor network. In a dense network many nodes can sense the same event and send that information to the base station through multiple paths, which leads to a huge amount of energy consumption. Hierarchical routing can meet this energy constraint to some extent.

Although, several advancements are made in securing the wireless communications, wireless sensor network still faces a number of intricacies with respect to secure data transmission. Insecure nature of the radio links, presence of malicious nodes, network jamming and repeating messages are the major problems in wireless sensor network. The three main prerequisites of secure data transmission are: privacy, authenticity and integrity of the transmitted data. Secure routing again consumes more energy. Some of the common attacks in sensor network are Spoofing, Selective Forwarding, Sinkhole

J. Lloret Mauri et al. (Eds.): SSCC 2014, CCIS 467, pp. 20–29, 2014.

Attack, Sybil Attack, Wormhole Attack, Hello Flood attack, Denial of Service attack [1] etc.

The SHRP scheme proposes a secure hierarchical routing to route the information of devastating events to the base station in a secure energy efficient way. This scheme adopts light-weight security mechanisms like one-way-hash chains (OHC) for authentication purpose, hash-based Message Authentication Codes (HMAC) for authentication and verification of integrity of the messages, Elliptic-Curve Diffie-Hellman (ECDH) [2] key exchange scheme and symmetric key cryptography (Blowfish) [3] for confidentiality. The proposed protocol focuses on securing both the upstream and downstream flow of data. Detection of malicious nodes and sidestepping most of the common attacks on wireless sensor network are the main goals of SHRP. The hierarchical approach to route the devastating information to the base station saves lot of energy and increases network lifetime.

The rest of the paper is organized as follows: section 2 describes the related works. Section 3 discusses the network architecture and the threat model in brief. A detailed description of SHRP protocol is given in section 4, followed by performance analysis and simulation results in section 5. Section 6 is the concluding part.

2   Related Works

The secure hierarchical routing protocols have several pros and cons. The main drawback of existing protocols is that more stress is given on securing the upstream flow of data packets. Some of the secure routing protocols overlook the energy constraints. This section gives a brief discussion on the various secure routing protocols in practice.

On the Security of Cluster-based Communication Protocols for Wireless Sensor Networks [4] proposes a security solution for a homogeneous network like LEACH [5] where the clusters are formed dynamically and periodically. This security protocol concentrates only on the avoidance of outsider's attack and assumes the base station to be trust worthy. A Key Management Scheme for Cluster Based Wireless Sensor Networks [6] uses public key management scheme based on ECC [7] and Diffie-Hellman [8] key exchange scheme. The gateway nodes are preloaded with public keys of sensor nodes, their own public keys and the public key of the base station. Each sensor node is loaded with a private and a public key and also with the public keys of the gateways of the network. A low cost ECDSA [9] signature is used for the broadcast authentication of the gateways. Encryption and decryption of messages exchanged between the gateways and the sensor nodes is done using the public key of the gateways. In FBSR [10], feedback of the current computing capacity from neighboring nodes serves as dynamic information of the current network. This helps in decision making of which nodes will take part in the routing in a secured and energy efficient manner. The feedback from the base station is utilized to identify the malicious nodes. This scheme is well protected against sinkhole attack, selective forwarding and Sybil attack. ATSR [11] calculates the trust value of a node on the basis of multiple attributes like packet forwarding, network layer acknowledgements, message integrity, node authentication etc. Monitoring these attributes help in recognizing various misbehaviors of the nodes and help in avoiding certain attacks.

3   Network Framework and Threat Model

The SHRP protocol considers a network size of 100 x100 m^2 and the number of nodes range from 100 to 150. The following assumptions are made in designing the network architecture of SHRP.

1. All the nodes are static or slightly mobile and each node has an initial trust value.
2. The base station is trustworthy and is of high configuration with enough memory, high computation capability, and more energy. It is situated at a controllable place outside the network region.
3. Each node shares a global key G_k with the base station that is used to avoid outsider's attack. It is also assumed that even if a node gets compromised the global key is not revealed to the attacker.
4. Each node is preconfigured with a hash function F(x), an initial one-way hash chain number S_0 generated by the base station and a set of elliptic curves for the purpose of key generation. They agree upon all the domain parameters of the elliptic curves, with the base station for the purpose of ECDH [7] key exchange.

It is assumed that the adversary can pose the following attacks in the SHRP network model:

*   A malicious node can launch a flooding attack by broadcasting request messages to the nodes of the network.
*   Node compromise attack can be induced by physically capturing a node and reprogramming it. However, it is assumed that this attack requires a minimum time to be launched.
*   Compromised nodes of the network can launch a wormhole attack on the messages exchanged between a node and its neighbors.
*   Packet eavesdropping can be done by an intruder's node while sending the aggregated data to the base station.
*   Sybil attack can be propelled by a compromised node of the network making an illusion to the other nodes that it is present in more than one location at a time. Thus, can compel a node to forward its data to a fake node.
*   Sinkhole attack can be launched by a laptop-class attacker by advertising its high quality link and a high weight value based on which next-hop nodes are selected in SHRP.

4   Proposed Work

The proposed scheme SHRP is divided into five modules namely: level formation, cluster formation, key set up, data sensing and aggregation, and routing of aggregated data to the base station.

4.1   Level Formation

In the level formation module the base station broadcasts a request message (REQ) for initiating level formation, to the nodes within two-hop distance, the format of which is:

$$BS \rightarrow *: REQ\|BS\|OHC\|MAC(G_k; REQ\|BS\|OHC)$$

A One-way Hash Chain (OHC) is used to authenticate the base station to the nodes of the network. A hash chain is a sequence of keys generated using a hash function $F(x)$, such that, $y=F(x)$ can be calculated easily and $x=F^{-1}(y)$ is computationally infeasible to generate within a finite time. BS is the id of the base station. A MAC is generated on the REQ using the global key G_k, the base station id and the OHC to verify the authenticity of the message and prevent it from being eavesdropped. The hash chain is generated in the order: $S_n \rightarrow S_{n-1} \rightarrow ... \rightarrow S_4 \rightarrow S_3 \rightarrow S_2 \rightarrow S_1 \rightarrow S_0$. Base station first uses S_1, then S_2 and so on. Once a sequence number is used it is not reused in the lifetime of the network. The request is be verified by MAC generation and OHC computation by the receiving nodes. The request will be acceptable when the output of $F(F(...F(S_i)))=S_0$, i.e., by i times execution of the function $F(x)$ on S_i will be S_0. The nodes accepting the request will be included in level one. The base station being at level zero acts as the SUPERVISOR. The role of which is to monitor the behavior of the nodes of the next level and to assign a trust value to them. The trust value is increased depending on number of successful message delivered. If a node forwards less than 30% of the messages, it is marked as a suspicious node. Each node of level one calculates a status value for itself. The status value ($Stat_i$) is calculated as—

$$Stat_i = E_{Ri} * N_{ng} * TV_i \qquad (1)$$

where E_{Ri} is the remaining energy of that node, N_{ng} is the number of neighbor nodes of the next level it can sense and TV_i is the current trust value of the node. The nodes of level one rebroadcast the request to the nodes within two-hop distance from them to form the next level. Each node i of level one replace the id of the base station in the request with its own id before forwarding it. A nested MAC is generated over the received MAC from the base station using the global key (G_k), ID of the sender and the OHC. The nested MAC acts as a countermeasure against wormhole attack. The node forwarding the request, also append the status value of itself with the request. The format of the request is:

$$node_i \rightarrow *: REQ\|Stat_i\|ID_i\|OHC\|MAC(G_k; ID_i\|OHC\|(MAC\_of\_parent))$$

The nodes receiving the request of level formation from the nodes of level one, mark themselves as nodes of level two and the sender as their parent. Each node of level two selects its SUPERVISOR from the nodes of level one, within its sensing region, on the basis of the $Stat_i$ value of the forwarding nodes. Thus, there can be more than one SUPERVISOR in each level. The SUPERVISOR nodes of level one assigns the current trust value two the nodes of level two after monitoring them. The same process is repeated to form all the levels covering the network area. The level formation occurs only once and is not repeated in the lifetime of the network.

4.2   Cluster Formation

In the cluster formation phase, SHRP introduces energy efficiency by adopting an event-based cluster formation scheme, where the node that first senses the occurrence of an event initiates the cluster formation. This initiator node broadcasts request for cluster formation to the nodes of the same level at a two hop distance. The format of the request packet is:

$$\text{Initiator}_i \rightarrow * : \text{Clus\_REQ} \| \text{ID}_i \| \text{TV}_i \| \text{MAC}(G_k; \text{Clus\_REQ} \| \text{ID}_i \| \text{TV}_i)$$

where Clus_REQ is the request for cluster formation, ID_i is the ID of the initiator node and TV_i is the current trust value of the initiator. A node joins the cluster if it receives the request. In case, two nodes sense the event at the same time, the node with higher residual energy will act as the initiator.

Now each node of the cluster calculates a competition bid value for itself. The competition bid is calculated as:

$$CV_i = (E_{Ri} * TV_i * N_{adj})/D_{avg} \tag{2}$$

where E_{Ri} is the remaining energy of the node i, TV_i is the current trust value, N_{adj} is the number of nodes in the cluster adjacent to the node and D_{avg} is the average distance of node i from all its adjacent nodes in the cluster. The node with the highest competition bid value is selected as the cluster head node.

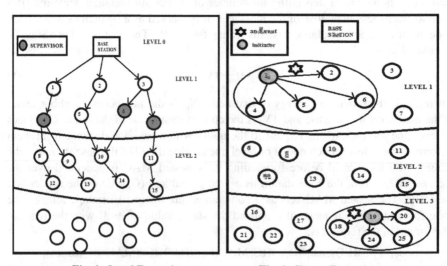

Fig. 1. Level Formation   Fig. 2. Cluster Formation

The cluster formation phase is repeated only when a new event takes place in the network region. However, the role of cluster head is rotated among the nodes of an existing cluster only when the remaining energy of the current cluster head node goes below the average residual energy of the cluster. The cluster head of a cluster takes up the role of SUPERVISOR in this phase and periodically monitors the member nodes to assign them their current trust value. The member node with the highest trust value in turn supervises the cluster head to assign its current trust value, at a particular interval. This both-way monitoring avoids assuming any of the nodes in a cluster to be trusted.

4.3   Key Set Up

The next phase is key set up phase. Each cluster head requests a session key from the base station. The request packet is forwarded to the base station following a route in which the next-hop node from the next lower level is chosen on the basis of a weight value W_t. The weight value is calculated as—

$$W_t=(TV_i*E_{Ri})/d_{ij} \tag{3}$$

where d_{ij} is the distance between the sender and the receiver. The packet format is:

$$CH_i \rightarrow BS: Key\_REQ\|ID_{CHi}\|TV_i\|MAC(G_k; Key\_REQ\|ID_{CHi}\|TV_i)$$

where Key_REQ is the request for a session key, ID_{CHi} is the ID of the cluster head sending the request and TV_i is the trust value of that cluster head.

The base station then uses Elliptic Curve Diffie-Hellman (ECDH) [2] key exchange scheme to establish a secure channel with each of the cluster heads separately. ECDH [2] is a key-agreement protocol that allows two nodes, each having an elliptic curve public and private key pair to establish a shared secret over an insecure channel. This shared secret can be used as a key for encryption-decryption purpose using a symmetric key cipher. In SHRP, the base station generates a private point d_B and a public point Q_B using Elliptic Curve Cryptography [7]. The base station forwards the public point to the cluster head in level one, if no cluster head is found in that level; it selects an active node of level one with the highest weight value (W_t). The packet format is:

$$BS \rightarrow CH_x \text{ or node}_x : Q_B\|BS\|ID_{CHx}\|OHC\|MAC(G_k; Q_B\|BS\| ID_{CHx}\|OHC)$$

where OHC is the new one-way hash chain sequence number appended by the base station and ID_{CHx} is the id of destination cluster head. If the node that received the public point is not the intended cluster head, then it will forward the packet to the next level, until it reaches the cluster head with ID_{CHx}. The packet format is:

$$CH_l \rightarrow CH_{l+1} : Q_B\|ID_l\|ID_{CHx}\|OHC\|MAC(G_k; ID_l\|ID_{CHx}\|OHC\|MAC\_of\_parent)$$

where ID_l is the id of the sender node of level l. Once the cluster head received the public point (Q_B), will generate a private and public key pair (d_{Cx}, Q_{Cx}) and follows the reverse path to send the public point (Q_{Cx}) to the base station. The base station then computes (x_k,y_k)=$d_B Q_{Cx}$ for each of the received public points of the different cluster heads. Each cluster head CH_x also computes (x_k,y_k)=$d_{Cx} Q_B$. This x_k (the x co-ordinate of the point in the elliptic curve) is the shared secret or the session key between the base station and the cluster head CH_x. The shared secret calculated by both the parties is equal since, $d_B Q_{Cx}=d_B d_{Cx}G=d_{Cx}d_B G=d_{Cx}Q_B$; where G is the generator of the elliptic curve. The cluster head CH_x then unicasts the same public point (Q_{Cx}) generated by it to each of its member nodes for MAC generation.

4.4   Data Sensing and Aggregation

After sensing of data each of the member nodes sends a MAC-ed data to the cluster head. The format of the message sent by each member node to the cluster head is:

$$v \rightarrow CH_x : R_v \| ID_v \| MAC(G_k; MAC(Q_{Cx};R_v \| ID_v \| C_v))$$

where R_v is the reading of the member node v, ID_v is the id of node v, C_v is a counter value that is incremented each time a new packet is forwarded to the cluster head in order to avoid replay attack. The cluster head then performs data aggregation to remove the redundant data and compress it.

4.5   Routing of Aggregated Data to the Base Station

The last phase is routing. The aggregated and compressed data is then encrypted using the session key K_S with the help of Blowfish symmetric cipher [3]. The cluster head sends it to the base station followed by a route, in which the next hop node is selected on the basis of weight values (W_t). The message format is:

$$CH_x \rightarrow BS : ARG_x \| ID_{CHx} \| Suspectlist \| MAC(G_k; MAC(K_S;ARG_x \| ID_{CHx} \| C_x))$$

where ARG_x is the aggregated and encrypted data from cluster head CH_x, ID_{CHx} is the id of that cluster head, K_S is the secret session key and C_x is a counter value. Suspect list contains the IDs of the member nodes of the cluster head CH_x whose trust value decrease considerably due to malicious behavior. The base station verifies the authenticity of the message received from cluster head CH_x and then uses Blowfish symmetric cipher to decrypt the message using the session key for that cluster head.

5   Performance Analysis and Simulation Result

The performance analysis of SHRP can be summed up as in the following—

1. In SHRP, the base station uses hash functions like MD5 or SHA-1 to generate a chain of numbers such that $S_i = F(S_{i+1})$ and appends a sequence number to every message it forwards. If any malicious node tries to launch a flooding attack, it will not be able to generate the same sequence number as the base station and thus its request will be discarded.
2. The nested message authentication code (MAC) is used as a countermeasure against the wormhole attack as the eavesdropper cannot crack it.
3. While monitoring the nodes of each level by the SUPERVISORs, the suspicious nodes are detected. Thus Sybil attack can be prevented by avoiding those nodes.
4. The aggregated data is encrypted with the secret session key, which is shared only between the base station and the cluster head. An intruder node trying to overhear the aggregated data, while sending to the base station, will not be able to decrypt it.
5. The compromised nodes will not be able to generate valid MACs as they don't have the global key. It will also not be able to generate the secret session key, as it requires private points which are never shared. The counter value in the message tries to avoid replay attack.

6. To conserve energy SHRP uses a light weight mechanism ECDH, which consumes less energy than the other ECC-based cryptographic methods. Blowfish symmetric cipher is also more energy aware than many other symmetric ciphers.
7. The event-driven cluster formation, weight value based path selection and rotation of the role of cluster head makes SHRP more energy efficient.

The parameters used to simulate the performance of SHRP are given in Table 1.

Table 1. Parameter List

Parameters	Description
Network size	100 nodes
Initial energy	50J per node
MAC Protocol	IEEE 802.15.4
Sensor Node	Imote2
Radio Frequency	13 MHz

NS2 is used as a simulation tool. Figure 3 shows the number of nodes alive in the network for SHRP, FBSR [10] and ATSR [11] with the increase in time.

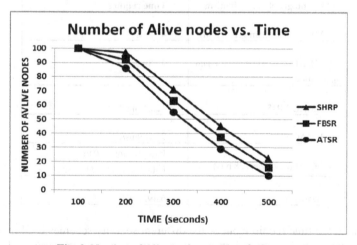

Fig. 3. Number of Alive nodes vs. Time in Seconds

It is observed in Figure 3 that even after 500 seconds more nodes are alive for SHRP in comparison to FBSR [10] and ATSR [11]. Thus SHRP is energy efficient and can prolong the network lifetime.

Figure 4 shows the number of packets lost in presence of malicious nodes by SHRP, FBSR [10] and ATSR [11]. It is perceived from the graph that the number of packets lost is lesser in case of SHRP even in presence of 25 malicious nodes. Thus, SHRP has better resistance to security threats in wireless sensor network and it can defend well against the different kinds of attacks.

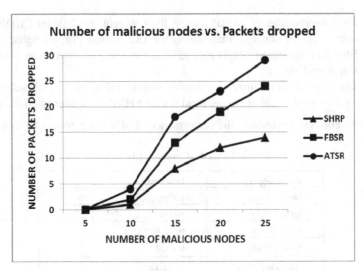

Fig. 4. Number of malicious nodes vs. Packets dropped

Table 2. Time Required

Cryptographic Mechanism	Time required
MD5 (Hash chain generation)	4.18ms
SHA-1 (Hash chain generation)	4.18ms
HMAC-MD5	12.217ms/KB
HMAC-SHA-1	21.959ms/KB
ECDH (key size=128 bits)	Initialization- 0.04ms Establishment- 2718.31ms
Blowfish	6.49ms/KB

In Table 2, the time requirement of the different security schemes used in SHRP is given. The table shows that together with energy awareness the proposed protocol also offers time efficiency. Thus, it is also guaranteed from the performance evaluation results that the devastating information sensed by the sensor nodes can reach the base station within a short span of time and also in a secured way.

6   Conclusions

The level-based approach adopted by SHRP protocol helps in partitioning the network region which helps in region-wise monitoring of the intent area. Even-driven cluster formation brings energy efficiency by avoiding the unnecessary formation of clusters, when no event is there in the network. Network lifetime is also prolonged by rotating the role of cluster head among the nodes of the cluster considering the residual energy of the nodes. Using the light-weight security mechanisms helps in conserving energy as well. In terms of security, SHRP can prevent attacks like sinkhole, wormhole, Sybil attack, packet eavesdropping and flooding attack.

References

[1] Karlof, C., Wagner, D.: Secure routing in wireless sensor networks: attacks and countermeasures. Ad Hoc Networks 1, 293–315 (2003), doi:10.1016/S1570-8705(03)00008-8

[2] Kumar, S., Girimondo, M., Weimerskirch, A., Paar, C., Patel, A., Wander, A.S.: Embedded end-to-end wireless security with ECDH key exchange. Published in: IEEE 46th Midwest Symposium on Circuits and Systems, vol. 2, pp. 786–789 (2003)

[3] Thakur, J., Kumar, N.: DES, AES and Blowfish: Symmetric Key Cryptography Algorithms Simulation Based Performance Analysis. International Journal of Emerging Technology and Advanced Engineering 1(2) (December 2011)

[4] Ferreira, A.C., Vilaça, M.A., Oliveira, L.B., Habib, E., Wong, H.C., Loureiro, A.A.F.: On the Security of Cluster-Based Communication Protocols for Wireless Sensor Networks. In: Lorenz, P., Dini, P. (eds.) ICN 2005. LNCS, vol. 3420, pp. 449–458. Springer, Heidelberg (2005)

[5] Heinzelman, W.B., et al.: An application-specific protocol architecture for wireless microsensor networks. IEEE Transactions on Wireless Communications 1(4), 660–670 (2002)

[6] Azarderakhsh, R., Reyhani-Masoleh, A., Abid, Z.-E.: A Key Management Scheme for Cluster Based Wireless Sensor Networks. In: IEEE/IFIP International Conference on Embedded and Ubiquitous Computing (2008)

[7] Mishra, A.R., Singh, M.: Elliptic Curve Cryptography (ECC) for Security in wireless Sensor Network. International Journal of Engineering Research & Technology (IJERT) 1(3) (May 2012)

[8] Boneh, D.: The Decision Diffie-Hellman Problem. In: Buhler, J.P. (ed.) ANTS 1998. LNCS, vol. 1423, pp. 48–63. Springer, Heidelberg (1998)

[9] Wang, H., Wu, Z., Tan, X.: A New Secure Authentication Scheme Based Threshold ECDSA For Wireless Sensor Network. In: Arabnia, H.R., Aissi, S. (eds.) Security and Management, pp. 129–133. CSREA Press (2006)

[10] Cao, Z., Hu, J., Chen, Z., Xu, M., Zhou, X.: FBSR: Feedback based Secure Routing Protocol for Wireless Sensor Networks. J. Pervasive Comput. & Comm. 1(1)

[11] Zahariadis, T., Leligou, H.C., Voliotis, S., Maniatis, S., Trakadas, P., Karkazis, P.: Energy-aware Secure Routing for Large Wireless Sensor Networks. WSEAS Transactions on Communications 8(9) (September 2009)

A Review on Mobile Sensor Localization

Jeril Kuriakose[1], V. Amruth[2], A.G. Sandesh[3], V. Abhilash[4],
G. Prasanna Kumar[5], and K. Nithin[6]

[1] School of Computing and IT, Manipal University Jaipur, India
jeril@muj.manipal.edu
[2] Department of Information Science and Engineering,
Bearys Institute of Technology, Mangalore, India
[3] Associate Consultant, Einsys Consulting Pvt. Ltd., Bangalore, India
[4] Freelancer, Electrical Engineer
[5] Department of Computer Science and Engineering,
National Institute of Engineering, Mysore, India
[6] Department of Electronics and Communication Engineering,
Bearys Institute of Technology, Mangalore, India

Abstract. Wireless sensor networks (WSNs) are on a steady rise in the current decade because of its progressions in hardware design, resource efficiency, communication and routing protocols, and other aspects. Recently, people started preferring mobile nodes in the place of static nodes, which brought mobile sensor network into focus. Location information always plays a key role in Mobile wireless sensor network (MWSN) and precise localization has always been a challenge for mobile sensor nodes. Deploying GPS receivers for each node would render network deployment cost for a dense network. The unavailability of GPS in indoor and underground environment has also put the installation of GPS into question. This makes the sensor nodes to identify its location coordinates or location reference without using GPS, and is achieved with the help of a special node that knows its location coordinates and protocols, called beacon node. This paper's goal is to confer different localization techniques used by mobile sensor nodes to identify their location information. Problems and future issues have also been discussed.

1 Introduction

Wireless sensor network is a broad area in wireless networking, which is specifically designed to measure small amounts of data, mostly sensed data and transmit the little information to a central server or an aggregation point. Recently, mobility became conventional and forced WSN to make the MWSN to be a part of it. The use of off-the-shelf materials and low power sensor nodes was made possible because of the advancements in communication protocols. Initially localization of mobile devices was considered to be more difficult; whereas [1] exploited mobility to achieve precise and accurate localization. Although mobility has few limitations, the introduction of mobility has benefited the network performance in terms of packet delay, coverage, and scalability [2].

J. Lloret Mauri et al. (Eds.): SSCC 2014, CCIS 467, pp. 30–44, 2014.
© Springer-Verlag Berlin Heidelberg 2014

Whenever a sensor node transmits the sensed data to the central server, the latter identifies the packet origin with the help of the location coordinates sent by the node. Location information is the heart of various solicitations like routing, surveillance and monitoring, fault identification, and defence. Location-based routing [3] and location-aided routing [4] avail location information of nodes to enhance the performance of routing in an ad hoc environment. Ubiquitous computing and smart environments [5] necessitate location information to satisfy the involvement of individuals from every environment. This paper reviews the different localization techniques used to identify the location coordinates of mobile sensor nodes. In this paper, the node that does not know its location coordinates are termed as 'unidentified nodes.'

During deployment each sensor node is made available with its location information with the help of manual or automatic configuration. Manual configuration involves a lot of physical work and is not encouraged for a colossal network, and installing a GPS receiver for each sensor node would also surge the deployment cost of the network. This engendered the sensor nodes to identify its location without any affluent approaches, like using GPS receiver. Several localization and ranging techniques such as lateration, angulation, Angle of Arrival (AoA) [6], [7], Time of Arrival (ToA) [6], [8], Time Difference of Arrival (TDoA) [6], [9], Received Signal Strength Indicator (RSSI) [6], [10], DV hop based localization [6], [11], and proximity based localization [6], [12] are used by the mobile sensor nodes to identify its location coordinates.

Most of the localization techniques are carried out with the help of neighbouring anchor or beacon nodes [13]. Beacon node is a special node that knows its present location coordinates (i.e., either manually or using GPS). Initially, during deployment few nodes are made as beacon nodes, and the remaining nodes identify their location coordinates with the help of the beacon nodes. A minimum of three beacon nodes must be accessible for a unidentified node to get localized. This technique is called cooperative localization [14]. Cooperative localization when extended to the mobile environment, suffers some problems like deprivation of estimation accuracy, reduced battery life, and high utilization of network resources [15]. The two key problems in mobile localization like local position tracking and global position estimation were subjugated by using sample-based techniques [16]. Several approached like dynamic localization protocols [17], dynamic reference protocol [18], and fusion techniques [19] helps in reducing the communication cost, and accumulated error.

Organization of paper - Section 2 studies the concepts and properties of mobile sensor network; section 3 provides the taxonomy of mobile localization techniques; section 4 covers the problems faced during localization; section 5 discusses the future research and section 6 concludes the paper.

2 Concepts and Properties of Mobile Wireless Sensor Network

The mobile wireless sensor network is a part of the wireless sensor network, in which most or all of the sensor nodes are mobile. The deployment of mobile wireless sensor network can be done on any scenario, thus making it more versatile than static wireless sensor network. A mobile sensor node is made up of off-the-shelf materials like micro-controller, battery, radio transceiver, and the parts that make the node mobile. And they are mostly used to sense temperature, heat, seismic waves, moving objects, and humidity.

The deployment of sensor network always is governed by the application. The nodes are placed randomly or in a grid or in the proximity of an object of interest. Optimal deployment might not be possible in many circumstances, and rearranging nodes position might not be simple for a fixed network. Conversely, redeployment and reorganizing would be simple and smooth when the sensor nodes are mobile. Mobility also reduces the drawbacks of a sparse network. Integrating mobile nodes in a network will improve coverage and reduce communication overhead [20]. Quince [21], the mobile robot was used in the surveillance missions for the Fukushima Daiichi Nuclear Power Station disaster. Fig. 1 shows the rescue and surveillance missions carried out by Quince.

Fig. 1. Quince is engaging in rescuing and surveillance missions

2.1 Challenges in Mobile Node Deployment

In a MWSN computation, sensing, and communication capabilities are identical for each sensor node. The mobility of each sensor node might change based on the requirements and surroundings. During node deployment, each sensor node must be made available with its location coordinates to successfully carry out its endeavours. This is carried out with the help of GPS or iterative multilateration [6]. The up-to-date location coordinates is required by each mobile node to make decisions regarding its next crusade. Mobile nodes can cause a concern during exploration, when multiple mobile nodes head towards the same objective. This was reduced by using global maps, adapting a heuristic approach for location exploration, and explicit communication between mobile nodes [22].

2.2 Environmental Challenges

The varying topology and shared medium cause a concern for the MWSN. Channel access mechanisms, such as CDMA, FDMA, TDMA, and CSMA must be regulated in order to reduce the shared medium problem. A varying topology gives rise to a couple of problems like sensor coverage and sensor connectivity in MWSN. Various schemes have been discussed in table 1, which uses location information to overcome the varying topology problem in mobile sensor network.

Table 1. Location information and varying topology problem

Technique Used	Premise Considered	Attributes	Approach
Potential Fields [22]	Location information and range	Balanced deployment with the help of repulsive mechanism, when in proximity to obstacles	Virtual forces
DSS Algorithm [23]	Location information	A profitable scheme to conserve energy during deployment of a WSN divided into clusters	
Co-Fi [24]	Location information	Distributed scheme to conserve energy and provide regulated coverage fidelity	Computational geometry
VEC, VOR, Minmax [25]	Location information	Identify coverage holes and enabling sensors to move away from dense area	

2.3 Hardware Challenges

The two hardware challenges that pose a threat are power consumption and cost requirements. Algorithms must be designed in such a way that it does not consume more power during computation. The ranging techniques like ToA, TDoA, RSSI, and AoA requires special hardware and time synchronization to accomplish the localization process, thus adding the cost and size complexity in nodes. However, hardware complexity must also be brought into contemplation when considering an economical network. Table 1 discuss few techniques that uses location information to improve energy efficiency.

3 Concepts and Properties of Mobile Localization

Identification of the exact locality or position where a node resides is called localization. GPS is the widely used technique for outdoor location identification, whereas it is not suitable for an indoor or underground environment. When deploying a dense and large wireless network, GPS is not desired because of its cost and power constrain. This bring about a circumstance where the unidentified nodes are supposed to determine its location by itself or with the help of neighbouring nodes. Typically, localization process is categorized into three phases [26], [27] namely: (1) Requesting phase, (2) ranging phase, and (3) localization phase.

Initially during deployment few nodes are made the beacon nodes, either manually or by installing a GPS receiver. Assistance from three or more beacon nodes is required for a unidentified node to identify its location. Fig. 2a, b, c shows a typical example of how unidentified nodes get localized with the help

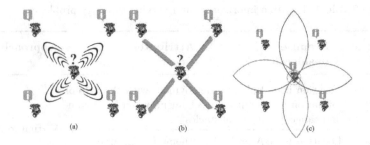

Fig. 2. Phases in localization. (a) Requesting phase. (b) Ranging phase. (c) Localization phase.

of beacon nodes. The node that wants to get localized requests its neighbouring beacon nodes for assistance and identifies its location by employing certain localization algorithms.

3.1   Phases in Localization

A mobile node needs to undergo three phases in order to get its location coordinates. The phases are as follows:

Requesting Phase: Whenever a mobile node wants to update its new location, it commences with a requesting phase, where it searches for neighbouring beacon nodes. A minimum of three beacon nodes is required for a node to get localized. This is done by sending a hello packet to the neighbouring beacon nodes, which then acknowledges the packet. Nowadays coordination techniques [28] encapsulate both time synchronization and node notification message in a single packet, in order to cut the non-deterministic latency involved in time harmonization. The reference broadcast synchronization (RBS) [29] and elapsed time on arrival (ETA) [30] have a very high accuracy in terms of a microsecond. Once the beacon node receives the request from any of the neighbouring nodes, it proceeds further to ranging phase. In fig. 2a the unidentified node sends a localization request to its neighbouring beacon nodes.

Ranging Phase: In the ranging phase, the beacon nodes identify the distance or bearing between the unidentified node and the beacon node. To achieve precise localization, signal modality must be taken into consideration. The dependence on the environment, node hardware and application requirement also hinder the signal modality. Different environments give different location accuracy, which turns out to be a burden in estimating the future position of the mobile node. Selecting environment aware signal propagation method would reduce the localization error occurred, like opting for acoustic signals instead of radio signals for moist environment, since the absorption and reflection of high frequency waves are more in moisture. Acoustic waves can also be preferred for indoor applications in order to avoid multipath propagation of radio signals.

Cricket [31] location support system uses ultrasound and radio frequency waves to evaluate the distance between beacon node and unidentified node. Initially RF signals are transmitted followed by ultrasound signals, and the difference in arrival time is used to measure the distance. Fig. 3a shows a typical example of Cricket location support system. A power optimized mobile localization for ad hoc network has been carried out using Bluetooth technology [32]. It cut down the power penalties through an efficient coordination phase by removing service discovery and potential pairing. Indoor mobile localization can be made economical and error tolerant when considering Bluetooth technology [33] for the application. Localization based on ZigBee technology [34] can very efficient in the outdoor and long range application requirements. ZigBee technology is always preferred when the localization is for expensive moving objects.

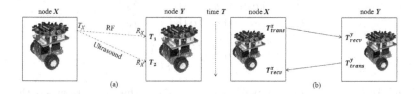

Fig. 3. (a) A typical Cricket location support system. (b) Measurement using ToA.

Once the signal is selected for our application, we need to choose a ranging technique that would suit our application. The ranging techniques can be grouped into range based and range free techniques. An additional hardware is required for range based techniques; whereas it is not required for range free techniques. Although range based techniques are mostly preferred because of its accuracy and reduced runtime. Fig. 2b shows the range measurement between the beacon nodes and the unidentified node. The range based techniques are as follows:

Received Signal Strength Indicator: Received Signal Strength Indicator (RSSI) [6], [10] uses the signal strength of the received signal to identify the distance or range. As a node moves far apart from another node the signal strength decreases. Whenever a node request for localization, the beacon node responds with its RSSI measurements; and the former identifies the distance with the received RSSI measurements.

Time of Arrival: Time of Arrival (ToA) [6], [8] identifies the distance between the sender and receiver by using the transmitted and received time. Fig. 3b shows the ToA range measurement technique. Calculation of distance using ToA is as follows [6]:

$$d_{xy} = \frac{1}{2} \left[(T^x_{recv} - T^x_{trans}) - (T^y_{trans} - T^y_{recv}) \right]$$

where, d_{xy} is the distance between node X and node Y, T_{recv}^x is the received power of node X, T_{trans}^x is the transmitted power of node X, T_{recv}^y is the received power of node Y, T_{trans}^y is the transmitted power of node Y.

Time Difference of Arrival: Time Difference of Arrival (TDoA) [6], [9] uses two or more receivers to identify the difference in arrival of the signals. The accuracy of TDoA is slightly higher than ToA, and it does not require any special hardware or chip-set, and software to be installed on the mobile client device. Fig. 4a shows a typical example of how TDoA works with a mobile node. The differences in the arrival of signals at different receivers are calculated by a central sever which has a TDoA equipment, to identify the distance. Estimation of distance using TDoA is as follows [9]:

$$\delta d_{i,j} = h(x, t, D)$$

$$D = \sqrt{(Y_i - Y_j)^2 + (X_i - X_j)^2}$$

$$\begin{bmatrix} x \\ y \end{bmatrix} = \begin{bmatrix} cos(\alpha) & sin(\alpha) \\ -sin(\alpha) & cos(\alpha) \end{bmatrix} \begin{bmatrix} X - X_0 \\ Y - Y_0 \end{bmatrix}$$

$$\alpha = arctan\left(\frac{Y_i - Y_j}{X_i - X_j}\right)$$

Angle of Arrival: Angle of Arrival (AoA) [6], [7] is the angle between the received signal to some reference direction. The reference direction is some fixed direction against which AoA is calculated. AoA current applications include geographic location identification of mobile devices. Fig 4b shows the consideration of angular measurements for AoA ranging.

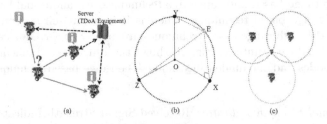

(a)   (b)   (c)

Fig. 4. (a) Ranging using TDoA. (b) Ranging using AoA. (c) Trilateration.

Hop based: This is a range free technique that uses hop count to identify the distance between two nodes [11]. Prior to the range measurement, the hop is identified with the help of few beacon nodes present in the network. The average hop distance is calculates as follows [11]:

$$H_d = \frac{\sum \sqrt{(A_i - A_j)^2 + (B_i - B_j)^2}}{\sum h}$$

where, H_d is average distance for one hop, $\sum h$ is the total number of hops, $(A_i, B_i)\&(A_j, B_j)$ are the location co-ordinates of the anchor nodes.

Localization Phase: From the ranging phase, the distance between the beacon node and the requesting node is identified. The same process is carried out with three or more different beacon nodes. Once three or more distances are obtained, localization procedure is carried out. The localization techniques differs for different applications and the most widely used localization technique is trilateration [35]. The techniques used to identify the position of mobile nodes are as follows:

Multilateration: If the localization procedure is carried out using multilateration [36], distances from two beacon nodes are sufficient. This technique uses the difference in distance between two beacon nodes to identify the location coordinates. Multilateration requires TDoA measurement to identify the position of moving objects like aircraft, and ship.

Trilateration: Trilateration is the method of identifying the approximate location coordinates with the help three or more distance measurements. The geometry of circles has been utilized in this scheme to identify the moving object. Fig. 4c shows the mobile node identification using trilateration. The intersection point of the three circles is the present location coordinates of the mobile node. The accuracy can be marginally increased by using four different distance measurements.

Triangulation: Triangulation [37] technique identifies the location coordinates of a unidentified mobile node with the help of angles. In contrast to trilateration, it does not associate distance measurements. Fig. 5a shows how trilateration is used to identify the distance and the location coordinates of a mobile node, in a bi-dimensional space.

RF Fingerprinting: Radar [38] uses an RF-based fingerprinting method to localize moving objects. It maintains a data set containing the signal strength (SS) of different locations, which is used in the location identification of the mobile nodes. Signal-to-noise data set is correlated with SS data sets in order to reduce the localization error caused due to noise disturbances.

Dead Reckoning: Dead reckoning [39] is an extensively used technique in many applications related to mobile localization. It estimates the mobile nodes current location with the help of formerly determined position. Fig. 5b shows how the location coordinates are identified for a mobile node. Many modern inertial surveillance and navigational systems are based upon dead reckoning.

Proximity based Localization: The unidentified mobile nodes determine its position with the help of any one neighbouring beacon node. The unidentified mobile node that comes under the coverage area of any beacon, acquires the location coordinates of that particular beacon node. Proximity based localization [12], works without the need for any special hardware or ranging technique and is suitable for an economical network. In contrast to other localization schemes, proximity based localization does not suffer fading [12]. Fig. 5c shows an example of proximity based localization. The proximity threshold is calculated as follows [12]:

$$Q_{x,y} = \begin{cases} 1, & P_{x,y} \geq P_1 \\ 0, & P_{x,y} < P_1 \end{cases}$$

where:

$P_{x,y}$ is the measured received power at node X transmitted by node Y.

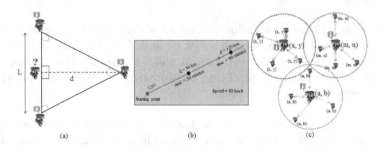

Fig. 5. (a) Estimation TDoA. (b) Dead reckoning technique. (c) Proximity based localization.

Estimation based localization: Estimation based localization techniques are mostly preferred scheme for mobile networks, because of their insensitivity towards measurement noise. The different categories of estimation based localization techniques are as follows:

Kalman Filter: Filtering based localization provides a recursive elucidation to remove the noise or disturbances present in the signal. Kalman filter [40] minimizes the mean square error by providing a recursive computational scheme. It has a powerful filter that can be used to precisely predict the future position of mobile nodes. Fig. 6a shows how Kalman filter observes a mobile node.

Extended Kalman Filter: Kalman filter was optimally intended to support linear system, whereas most of the engineering use non-linear systems. This brought Extended Kalman Filter (EKF) [41] into existence, to localize mobile nodes. EKF requires 'a priori' information to predict the future position of the mobile node. In the absence of such statistical parameters, Adaptive Extended Kalman Filter [42] uses an adaptive technique to estimate the unknown 'a priori' information.

Markov Localization: Markov localization [43] identifies the future location by retaining a position probability density in a probabilistic framework. Uniform distribution is maintained over all position in order to represent the state of uncertainty, and the initial position of the mobile node is not necessary to be known while using Markov localization.

Sequential Monte Carlo localization: Sequential Monte Carlo (SMC) localization [44] or particle filter exploits posterior probability to identify the future location. A highly sophisticated methodology is used in SMC to identify the samples from the given distribution, eliminating the need of presumptions. Each samples relates the posterior density and is identifies as particles which follows a grid based technique.

Monte Carlo Localization: Monte Carlo localization [16] initially begins with a uniform random distribution of samples or particles over the given map. Because of this the unidentified mobile node does not have any information about its current location. The movements of the particles or samples are used to identify the unidentified mobile nodes position.

Maximum Likelihood: Maximum likelihood expectation (MLE) uses statistical techniques to identify the most probable location of the mobile node [45]. MLE requires measured data and does not perform well with the help of prior data. From the given samples, MLE identifies the most likely sample, thus backing in recognizing the future position of the mobile node.

Mahalanobis Distance: Mahalanobis distance [46] applies posterior probability to identify the outliers or unwanted samples. When two beacon nodes in space are demarcated by two or more associated location coordinates, Mahalanobis distance can be used to find the distance measure between the two beacon nodes. Mahalanobis distance identifies the mobile nodes by comparing the location coordinates of the beacon nodes with respect to a centroid value.

Whenever a mobile localization is carried out, the network is categorized into three scenarios:

Nodes are still, beacon nodes are mobile: A mobile beacon node installed with a GPS device travels through the entire network enabling the static nodes to identify its location coordinates. Fig 6b shows how a mobile beacon node localizes static nodes.

Nodes are mobile, beacon nodes are still: Widely used in cellular network where the mobile identifies its proximity location with the help of fixed base stations.

Nodes and beacon nodes are mobile: Used in armed forces where group of soldiers enter a new territory with few soldiers having GPS devices with them, which is used by the rest of the soldiers to identify their location reference.

4   Limitations of Mobile Localization

Mobile localization tends to accept a borderline increase in error when compared with static localization. For faster moving mobile nodes, Doppler shift will add

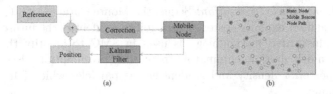

(a)   (b)

Fig. 6. (a) Kalman filter. (b) Nodes are static and beacon node is moving.

a significant increase in localization error. Centralized localization schemes like convex optimization [47] increases the communication cost and delay. Distributed localization schemes like range based techniques tend to increase the hardware cost such as time synchronization for ToA, need of ultrasound equipment for TDoA, special aerials like array antenna to support AoA technique.

In a static network the localization process need not be performed very often. Whereas mobile network requires a frequent update of location coordinates, which lays way to energy efficiency problems. Frequent update of the routing table is also required, engendering an increase in security. There are chances of data loss to happen when the sensed data is transferred to the sink. Signal modality plays a vital role in localization accuracy and it's necessary to choose an appropriate signal that suits the environment and application.

The accuracy of proximity based localization depends on the range of the beacon node, smaller the range, the larger is the accuracy. Hop based localization is not suitable for a dense environment. GPS receiver installed in a beacon node does not provide efficient localization in indoor and underground surroundings. Multipath propagation caused due to interferences such as walls, and furniture's, reduces the accuracy of localization in indoor environments.

Availability of beacon nodes is always necessary where both the unidentified nodes and beacon nodes are moving. Markov localization suffers from high computational overhead, and requires 'a priori' fixed state space. Dynamic information gathering is not possible in the traditional Monte Carlo simulation. A large of channels is required in Kalman filter which makes the computation part very complex and the Observation process, and the state process cannot be manipulated without a linear system. EKF does not provide an optimal estimation for linear system. The entire simulation might go wrong if the initial state estimation is erroneous.

5   Discussion and Future Events

Mobile localization will play a crucial function for the Internet of Things. MWSNs are being used in many applications such as PAN, wildlife monitoring, defence purpose, and pollution monitoring. Mobile vacuum cleaners and pool cleaners provide an unsupervised housekeeping service. Making use MWSNs for environmental monitoring provides a greater understanding of the Earth [48]. Hydro robot has been deployed in the lakes of Minnesota, to monitor the harmful effects of Carp fish. Mobile nodes are deployed in the battlefield to identify and to diffuse the landmine, thus preventing a lot of causalities.

Security is an important factor to be considered during localization. False location coordinates can be easily provided by a malicious beacon node. Resilient schemes to overcome vulnerability in MWSNs can be considered as a future event. Providing an energy efficient localization algorithm is always a conundrum. The localization techniques discussed in this paper are based on a 2-D scenario, and analysing its difference with 3-D scenario will be a significant effort.

6   Conclusion

In this paper we have discussed several types of localization techniques used in MWSNs. Location information is an essential requirement for the mobile nodes to move further with its locomotion. In contrast to lateration techniques, estimation techniques uses 'a priori' or 'posterior' information to predict the future position of the mobile node. The accuracy can be further improved by increasing the frequency of identification, but leading to a trade-off in energy management. Energy efficiency and security must be always considered while designing a localization technique. The applications of MWSNs are growing in a steady pace because of its applicability and user-friendliness. Few challenges and future issues have been discussed.

References

1. Hu, L., Evans, D.: Localization for mobile sensor networks. In: Proceedings of the 10th Annual International Conference on Mobile Computing and Networking, pp. 45–57. ACM (2004) 30
2. Munir, S.A., Ren, B., Jiao, W., Wang, B., Xie, D., Ma, J.: Mobile wireless sensor network: Architecture and enabling technologies for ubiquitous computing. In: 21st International Conference on Advanced Information Networking and Applications Workshops, AINAW 2007, vol. 2, pp. 113–120. IEEE (2007) 30
3. Füßler, H., Mauve, M., Hartenstein, H., Käsemann, M., Vollmer, D.: Mobicom poster: location-based routing for vehicular ad-hoc networks. ACM SIGMOBILE Mobile Computing and Communications Review 7(1), 47–49 (2003) 31
4. Ko, Y.-B., Vaidya, N.H.: Location-aided routing (lar) in mobile ad hoc networks. Wireless Networks 6(4), 307–321 (2000) 31
5. Garrido, J.E., Penichet, V.M.R., Lozano, M.D.: Integration of collaborative features in ubiquitous and context-aware systems using distributed user interfaces. In: Distributed User Interfaces: Usability and Collaboration, pp. 69–83. Springer (2013) 31
6. Kuriakose, J., Joshi, S., Vikram Raju, R., Kilaru, A.: A review on localization in wireless sensor networks. In: Thampi, S.M., Gelbukh, A., Mukhopadhyay, J. (eds.) Advances in Signal Processing and Intelligent Recognition Systems. AISC, vol. 264, pp. 599–610. Springer, Heidelberg (2014) 31, 32, 35, 36

7. Peng, R., Sichitiu, M.L.: Angle of arrival localization for wireless sensor networks. In: 2006 3rd Annual IEEE Communications Society on Sensor and Ad Hoc Communications and Networks, SECON 2006, vol. 1, pp. 374–382. IEEE (2006) 31, 36

8. H Schau and A Robinson. Passive source localization employing intersecting spherical surfaces from time-of-arrival differences. *Acoustics, Speech and Signal Processing, IEEE Transactions on*, 35(8):1223–1225, 1987. 31, 35

9. Gustafsson, F., Gunnarsson, F.: Positioning using time-difference of arrival measurements. In: Proceedings of the 2003 IEEE International Conference on Acoustics, Speech, and Signal Processing (ICASSP 2003), vol. 6, p. VI–553. IEEE (2003) 31, 36

10. Luo, X., O'Brien, W.J., Julien, C.L.: Comparative evaluation of received signal-strength index (rssi) based indoor localization techniques for construction jobsites. Advanced Engineering Informatics 25(2), 355–363 (2011) 31, 35

11. Niculescu, D., Nath, B.: Ad hoc positioning system (aps) using aoa. In: Twenty-Second Annual Joint Conference of the IEEE Computer and Communications, IEEE Societies, INFOCOM 2003, vol. 3, pp. 1734–1743. IEEE (2003) 31, 36

12. Patwari, N., Hero III, A.O.: Using proximity and quantized rss for sensor localization in wireless networks. In: Proceedings of the 2nd ACM International Conference on Wireless Sensor Networks and Applications, pp. 20–29. ACM (2003) 31, 37, 38

13. Want, R., Hopper, A., Falcao, V., Gibbons, J.: The active badge location system. ACM Transactions on Information Systems (TOIS) 10(1), 91–102 (1992) 31

14. Minami, M., Fukuju, Y., Hirasawa, K., Yokoyama, S., Mizumachi, M., Morikawa, H., Aoyama, T.: DOLPHIN: A practical approach for implementing a fully distributed indoor ultrasonic positioning system. In: Mynatt, E.D., Siio, I. (eds.) UbiComp 2004. LNCS, vol. 3205, pp. 347–365. Springer, Heidelberg (2004) 31

15. Higuchi, T., Higashino, T., Fujii, S., Yamaguchi, H.: Mobile node localization focusing on stop-and-go behavior of indoor pedestrians. IEEE Transactions on Mobile Computing, 1 (2014) 31

16. Dellaert, F., Fox, D., Burgard, W., Thrun, S.: Monte carlo localization for mobile robots. In: Proceedings of the 1999 IEEE International Conference on Robotics and Automation, vol. 2, pp. 1322–1328. IEEE (1999) 31, 39

17. Tilak, S., Kolar, V., Abu-Ghazaleh, N.B., Kang, K.-D.: Dynamic localization protocols for mobile sensor networks. arXiv preprint cs/0408042 (2008) 31

18. Hsieh, Y.-L., Wang, K.: Efficient localization in mobile wireless sensor networks. In: IEEE International Conference on Sensor Networks, Ubiquitous, and Trustworthy Computing, vol. 1, 5 p. IEEE (2006) 31

19. Wang, Z., et al.: Manet localization via multi-node toa-doa optimal fusion. In: IEEE Military Communications Conference, MILCOM 2006, pp. 1–7. IEEE (2006) 31

20. Liu, B., Brass, P., Dousse, O., Nain, P., Towsley, D.: Mobility improves coverage of sensor networks. In: Proceedings of the 6th ACM International Symposium on Mobile Ad Hoc Networking and Computing, pp. 300–308. ACM (2005) 32

21. Nagatani, K., Kiribayashi, S., Okada, Y., Tadokoro, S., Nishimura, T., Yoshida, T., Koyanagi, E., Hada, Y.: Redesign of rescue mobile robot quince. In: 2011 IEEE International Symposium on Safety, Security, and Rescue Robotics (SSRR), pp. 13–18. IEEE (2011) 32

22. Howard, A., Matarić, M.J., Sukhatme, G.S.: Mobile sensor network deployment using potential fields: A distributed, scalable solution to the area coverage problem. In: Distributed Autonomous Robotic Systems 5, pp. 299–308. Springer (2002) 32, 33

23. Heo, N., Varshney, P.K.: An intelligent deployment and clustering algorithm for a distributed mobile sensor network. In: IEEE International Conference on Systems, Man and Cybernetics, vol. 5, pp. 4576–4581. IEEE (2003) 33

24. Ganeriwal, S., Kansal, A., Srivastava, M.B.: Self-aware actuation for fault repair in sensor networks. In: Proceedings of the 2004 IEEE International Conference on Robotics and Automation, ICRA 2004, vol. 5, pp. 5244–5249. IEEE (2004) 33

25. Wang, G., Cao, G., La Porta, T.: Movement-assisted sensor deployment. IEEE Transactions on Mobile Computing 5(6), 640–652 (2006) 33

26. Girod, L., Lukac, M., Trifa, V., Estrin, D.: The design and implementation of a self-calibrating distributed acoustic sensing platform. In: Proceedings of the 4th International Conference on Embedded Networked Sensor Systems, pp. 71–84. ACM (2006) 33

27. Moore, D., Leonard, J., Rus, D., Teller, S.: Robust distributed network localization with noisy range measurements. In: Proceedings of the 2nd International Conference on Embedded Networked Sensor Systems, pp. 50–61. ACM (2004) 33

28. Hamza, A., Khalifa, S., Hamza, H., Elsayed, K.: A survey on inter-cell interference coordination techniques in ofdma-based cellular networks 34

29. Elson, J., Girod, L., Estrin, D.: Fine-grained network time synchronization using reference broadcasts. ACM SIGOPS Operating Systems Review 36(SI), 147–163 (2002) 34

30. Kusy, B., Dutta, P., Levis, P., Maroti, M., Ledeczi, A., Culler, D.: Elapsed time on arrival: a simple and versatile primitive for canonical time synchronisation services. International Journal of Ad Hoc and Ubiquitous Computing 1(4), 239–251 (2006) 34

31. Priyantha, N.B., Chakraborty, A., Balakrishnan, H.: The cricket location-support system. In: Proceedings of the 6th Annual International Conference on Mobile Computing and Networking, pp. 32–43. ACM (2000) 35

32. Johnson, T.A., Seeling, P.: Localization using bluetooth device names. In: Proceedings of the Thirteenth ACM International Symposium on Mobile Ad Hoc Networking and Computing, pp. 247–248. ACM (2012) 35

33. Fernandes, T.: Indoor localization using bluetooth. In: 6th Doctoral Symposium in Informatics Engineering, pp. 480–483 (2011) 35

34. Wisitpongphan, N.: Wireless sensor network planning for fingerprint based indoor localization usng zigBee: Empirical study. In: Meesad, P., Unger, H., Boonkrong, S. (eds.) IC2IT2013. AISC, vol. 209, pp. 83–92. Springer, Heidelberg (2013) 35

35. Manolakis, D.E.: Efficient solution and performance analysis of 3-D position estimation by trilateration. IEEE Transactions on Aerospace and Electronic Systems 32(4), 1239–1248 (1996) 37

36. Savvides, A., Park, H., Srivastava, M.B.: The bits and flops of the n-hop multilateration primitive for node localization problems. In: Proceedings of the 1st ACM International Workshop on Wireless Sensor Networks and Applications, pp. 112–121. ACM (2002) 37

37. Hartley, R.I., Sturm, P.: Triangulation. Computer vision and image understanding 68(2), 146–157 (1997) 37

38. Bahl, P., Padmanabhan, V.N.: Radar: An in-building rf-based user location and tracking system. In: Proceedings of the Nineteenth Annual Joint Conference of the IEEE Computer and Communications Societies, INFOCOM 2000, vol. 2, pp. 775–784. IEEE (2000) 37

39. Kleeman, L.: Optimal estimation of position and heading for mobile robots using ultrasonic beacons and dead-reckoning. In: Proceedings of the 1992 IEEE International Conference on Robotics and Automation, pp. 2582–2587. IEEE (1992) 37

40. Kalman, R.E.: A new approach to linear filtering and prediction problems. Journal of Basic Engineering 82(1), 35–45 (1960) 38

41. Curran, A., Kyriakopoulos, K.J.: Sensor-based self-localization for wheeled mobile robots. Journal of Robotic Systems 12(3), 163–176 (1995) 38

42. Jetto, L., Longhi, S., Venturini, G.: Development and experimental validation of an adaptive extended kalman filter for the localization of mobile robots. IEEE Transactions on Robotics and Automation 15(2), 219–229 (1999) 38

43. Fox, D., Burgard, W., Thrun, S.: Active markov localization for mobile robots. Robotics and Autonomous Systems 25(3), 195–207 (1998) 38

44. Handschin, J.E.: Monte carlo techniques for prediction and filtering of non-linear stochastic processes. Automatica 6(4), 555–563 (1970) 39

45. Howard, A., Matark, M.J., Sukhatme, G.: Localization for mobile robot teams using maximum likelihood estimation. In: IEEE/RSJ International Conference on Intelligent Robots and Systems, vol. 1, pp. 434–439. IEEE (2002) 39

46. Mahalanobis, P.C.: On the generalized distance in statistics. Proceedings of the National Institute of Sciences (Calcutta) 2, 49–55 (1936) 39

47. Doherty, L., El Ghaoui, L., et al.: Convex position estimation in wireless sensor networks. In: Proceedings of the Twentieth Annual Joint Conference of the IEEE Computer and Communications Societies, INFOCOM 2001, vol. 3, pp. 1655–1663. IEEE (2001) 40

48. Dunbabin, M., Marques, L.: Robots for environmental monitoring: Significant advancements and applications. IEEE Robotics & Automation Magazine 19(1), 24–39 (2012) 40

Power Aware and Secure Dynamic Source Routing Protocol in Mobile Ad Hoc Networks

Mohit Miglani[1], Deepika Kukreja[2],
Sanjay Kumar Dhurandher[3], and B.V.R. Reddy[4]

[1] Associate Application Developer, CSC, India
[2] Assistant Professor, MAIT, GGSIP University, Delhi, India
[3] Associate Professor, NSIT, Delhi University, Delhi, India
[4] Professor and Dean, USICT and USET, GGSIP University, Delhi, India

Abstract. Mobile Ad Hoc Networks (MANETs) show better and valuable performance in the circumstances where the generally used wireless networks fail to work. In order to make routing in MANETs secure, number of security based routing protocols have been proposed in the literature but none of them is compliant with the MANETs environment. We propose a protocol, termed as Power aware Secure Dynamic Source Routing (PS-DSR) that makes the standard Dynamic Source Routing protocol secure by using power aware trust based approach. The monitoring operation is distributed among a few set of nodes called monitor nodes. The set of monitor nodes is selected sporadically which makes the proposed method adaptable to the two focal concerns of MANETs: dynamic network topology and energy constraint devices. The method detects malicious packet dropping and packet modification attacks. It ensures the trustworthy and authentic selection of routes by the PS-DSR protocol and improves the overall performance of the protocol in presence of malicious nodes.

Keywords: Mobile Ad Hoc Networks, DSR,security, trust, routing, attacks, power.

1 Introduction

Mobile Ad Hoc Networks (MANETs) are infrastructure less networks, in which there is no central authority and each node functions as a host as well as a router. There are two focal concerns of MANETs: dynamic network topology and energy constraint devices. MANETs have dynamic network topology which means that mobile nodes are not fixed, they are free to move, and they may leave or join the network at any time. MANETs consist of nodes that are mainly battery operated hand held devices. Battery power is a limited resource which adds energy constraint problem to MANETs. Power aware Secure Dynamic Source Routing (PS-DSR) focuses on power saving and dynamic network topology which makes it complaint with MANETs environment. There are varied routing protocols in the literature, some of them are "proactive" and the others are "reactive" protocols. Dynamic Source Routing (DSR) protocol is a reactive protocol, which

J. Lloret Mauri et al. (Eds.): SSCC 2014, CCIS 467, pp. 45–56, 2014.

means it is source initiated and it will search for routes on demand and store them in its cache. PS-DSR is a power saving trust based protocol that ensures the trustworthy and authentic selection of routes thereby enhances the security and improves the performance of DSR in MANETs. The working of Power Aware Secure Dynamic Source Routing (PS-DSR) is divided into four phases: Maintenance of trust table, Selection of monitor nodes, Detection of nodes behaviors with updation of trust values and Route selection.

The organization of the paper is as follows. Section 2 gives the literature review on security based routing protocols. In sec. 3, the proposed security scheme is covered in detail. Section 4 presents our simulation results and their analysis. Finally, the conclusions are drawn in section 5.

2   Literature Review

Dynamic Source Routing was developed and proposed for Mobile Ad Hoc networks by Broch, Johnson and Maltz [1]. There are a number of routing protocols in the literature that were proposed and implemented to secure MANETs [2]. Marti et al. designed Watchdog and Pathrater method [3] to optimize and improve the technique of packet forwarding in the Dynamic Source Routing (DSR) protocol. It has two major components: Watchdog and Pathrater. Watchdog component is used to detect selfish nodes and Pathrater then uses this information and helps routing protocols to avoid the detected nodes. Watchdog fails to detect a misbehaving node in the presence of: Ambiguous collisions, false misbehavior, Receiver collisions, Partial dropping and Limited transmission power. CONFIDANT (Cooperation Of Nodes, Fairness In Dynamic Ad hoc NeTworks) [4] enhances [3] and adds two other components to it: trust manager and reputation system. In [5], Pirzada et al. proposed a method for establishing trust based routing in MANETs without requiring a trust infrastructure. Node's trust in [5] is calculated taking in view the packet forwarding behavior. C. Wang et al. [6] proposed a routing algorithm tr-DSR, which is an extension of DSR and is based on nodes' trust and path's trust. The method used in the paper selects the highest trust path used for data transmission. Pirzada et al. [7] modified the DSR protocol such that intermediary nodes act as Trust Gateways that keeps track of trust levels of the nodes in order to detect and avoid malicious nodes. In Pirzada et al. [8] a trust-based model based on direct experience rather than trusted third party is proposed. In this, trust agents that reside on each node perform three functions: Trust Derivation, Quantification, and Computation. Huang Chuanhe et al. [9] proposed a trusted routing protocol called Dynamic Mutual Trust based Routing protocol (DMTR), based on DSR protocol that secures the network using the Trust Network Connect (TNC), and improves the path security which is selected by barrel theory. P. Narula [10] introduces a method of message security using trust-based multi-path routing. It uses soft encryption techniques and avoids introducing large overheads. The whole message is divided into parts and the parts are self-encrypted. S. K. Dhurandher and V. Mehra [11] proposed a trust based routing for Ad Hoc networks which protects the message against modification. In this, trust is calculated in a dynamic way and a path is used to transmit data based on the security requirement of the message. S.K. Dhurandher et al. [12] proposed FACES, in this trust of the nodes is determined by sending challenges and sharing friends' lists. In PS-DSR only few selected nodes works in the promiscuous mode, this approach for detection of malicious nodes differs PS-DSR from the existing models.

3   Power Aware Secure Dynamic Source Routing Protocol

In standard DSR protocol, the routes are selected on a first come first serve basis, however route shortening is done whenever there is a shorter route to the destination, but there is no process to detect malicious nodes present in the path. In order to surmount this shortcoming, we employ a power aware trust based scheme to secure DSR. The proposed method detects malicious packet dropping and packet modification attacks. It also ensures the trustworthy and authentic selection of routes. Malicious nodes present in the network are observed and detected by a set of nodes called monitor nodes. Monitor nodes monitor the behavior of their neighboring nodes and based on behavior, the trust of the neighboring nodes is updated. The set of monitor nodes is chosen from time to time to make PS-DSR adaptable to the two central problems of MANETs: dynamic network topology and energy constraint devices. PS-DSR follows the standard DSR strategy to obtain the network topology information, it constructs forwarding routes when the source node broadcasts the RREQ packets to its neighbors and then destination node or an intermediate replies with RREP packet containing the path to the destination node, and those routes are stored in the cache. However our proposed scheme PS-DSR differs from DSR such that when the PS-DSR searches the routes from the cache it selects whose trust values are greater than Mal_threshold. Power Aware Secure Dynamic Source Routing (PS-DSR) is divided into four phases as follows:

1. Maintenance of trust table
2. Selection of monitor nodes
3. Detection of nodes' behaviors and updation of trust values
4. Route selection

Route selection is based on the trust values of the hops in the route. In order to accommodate the trust values for all the nodes in the network, a trust table is maintained, which stores the trust values of all the network nodes. The source node checks the trust table, accesses the trust values and according to the route selection strategy explained in section D, it selects the most suitable route. The route selected by the proposed protocol is shortest trustworthy route.

3.1   Maintenance of Trust Table

The trust model maintains a trust table regularly updated by a set of nodes in the network, called the Monitor Nodes (MNs); these nodes constantly work in promiscuous mode and overhear packets in its neighborhood. These nodes are selected by using the algorithm given in [13]. The trust table is accessed by only few nodes in the network: Monitor Nodes and the source. These monitor nodes detect two types of attacks, first is the packet dropping attack, and second is the packet modification attack. Whenever a node in the network drops or modifies a packet, its neighboring monitor node decreases the trust value of that node, similarly when a node forwards a packet; its neighbor monitor node increases the trust value of that node. Since a node may have more than one neighboring monitor node that are working in promiscuous mode and overhearing the packets, there must be only one trust update for node's activity. In order to avoid multiple updates, the algorithm given in sect. 3.3, detects the packet forwarding behavior and ensures that only one monitor node will update the trust table according to its behavior.

3.2   Selection of Monitor Nodes

There are two main reasons for executing the algorithm for selection of monitor nodes set periodically and on demand. The first reason is the dynamic network topology. As MANETs consist of mobile nodes which are free to move. The second is the energy as mobile nodes mainly are battery powered devices. The periodic selection of monitor nodes ensures complete network coverage and these nodes observe the behavior of each network node and hence do not leave any malicious node undetected. The time interval for periodic selection of monitor nodes depends on the network stability. The on demand selection of monitor nodes ensures distributed loss of energy and prevents any node from becoming energy deficient and thus prevents the induction of selfish behavior, in which an energy deficient node does not forward the packets which it was supposed to forward, in order to save its own energy. All the monitor nodes are continuously checked for energy and if any monitor node is found to be deficient in energy, program for selecting a new set of monitor nodes is called [13]. In this state, algorithm [13] does not consider energy deficient nodes and hence new set of monitor nodes that have enough remaining energy are selected. The algorithm first computes the node degree of all the wireless nodes in a given network and then checks for the circular links of the nodes one by one. By the checking of circular links we mean that the node arranges its neighbors in increasing order of their node ID's and check if that particular set of nodes are connected by 1 hop or 2 hops, if all the circular links are not present then the node is marked as the monitor node, otherwise it checks for the log links and for that we take the floor value of the logarithm of node degree for that node, supposedly it comes "n" then we check the connectivity of nodes (either connected by 1 hop or 2 hops) at a distance of n hops away from that node in the circular fashion that was previously taken. If all the log links are present then the node is marked as the regular node, otherwise it is marked as the monitor node. If monitor node lies in the vicinity of the route selected for data forwarding, then that monitor node operates in promiscuous mode.

3.3   Algorithm to Detect Packet Forwarding Behavior and Prevent Multiple Updates

Terminology Used in Algorithm

1. tap(Packet P): Packets overheard in promiscuous mode enter tap() function, P carries the reference of the packet overheard.
2. node_id: It is the ID of the node currently executing the tap function.
3. monitors[i to j]: It is the array of node IDs of monitor nodes executing the tap function, index values lie in the range from i to j.
4. nexthop.access(P) : It is a function which returns the address (node ID) of next hop from the source route field of the packet P.
5. prevhop.access(P): It is a function which returns the address (node ID) of previous hop from the source route field of the packet P.
6. next_hop: This variable contains the address (node ID) of the next hop returned by function nexthop.access(P).
7. previous_hop: This variable contains the address (node ID) of the previous hop returned by function prevhop.access(P).
8. isNeighbor(monitors[k], next_hop): This function returns TRUE if its input integer arguments are within communication range of each other, otherwise it returns FALSE.
9. received[n]: This counter counts the packets received by the node n.
10. forward[n]:This counter counts the packets forwarded by the node n.
11. D represents the difference of packets received and packets forwarded by a node, i.e. number of packet drops.
12. destination_node: It is the ID of the destination node in the network
13. sequence.access(P): It is a function which returns the sequence number of the packet P.

Algorithm to Detect Packet Drops and Prevent Multiple Update of Trust Values

1. tap(Packet P) //packets overheard in promiscuous mode enter this function
2. {
3. Initialize integer seqno with -1;
4. Initialize integer ph with -1;
5. Initialize int next_hop with the next hop of the packet;
   // function nexthop.access(P);
6. Initialize int prev_hop with the previous hop of the packet;
   //function prevhop.access(P);
7. IF node_id is not present in the array monitors[i] to monitors[j] THEN RETURN;
8. ELSE IF next_hop is the neighbor of the monitor node THEN Increment the received packet counter of the next_hop by one AND Increment the forward counter of the prevhop by one one in the table of monitor node currently executing the tap function.

// Using monitors[k].received[next_hop]++; and
monitors[k].forward[previous_hop]++; Where monitors[k] corresponds to
node_id i.e. the ID of the node currently executing the tap function.

9. IF integer ph is not equal to the previous hop of the packet THEN Increment
the trust of the previous hop of the packet and THEN Initialize ph with
current previous hop of the packet

10. IF next_hop of the packet is not the destination node THEN calculate the
difference between packets received and sent by the next_hop
// Using D(difference)=monitors[k].received[next_hop]- monitors[k].
forward[next_hop];

11. IF that packet difference is greater than C AND IF integer seqno is not
equal to the sequence number of the packet THEN decrease the trust of the
next_hop in the table of the monitor node AND Initialize seqno with the
current sequence number of the packet.
//Where C is a constant and function used is dec_trust(next_hop , dec_amt);

Explaination of Algorithm. In the above algorithm, monitor nodes update
the trust table of their neighbors depending on the packet forwarding behavior.
The trust value of a node is incremented by an amount inc_amt, if a node shows
benevolent behavior by forwarding the packet that it was supposed to forward.
If a node drops a packet, the neighboring monitor node decrements its trust
value by an amount dec_amt. In above algorithm we took two variables "seqno"
and "ph" which contains sequence number and the previous hop of the packet
respectively. We took the sequence number as the parameter to differentiate
between the packets, for instance if a trust value is decreased on a particular
sequence number by a monitor node, then other monitor nodes cannot decrease
the value of trust on the same sequence number, it has to be another sequence
number as multiple monitor nodes come across the activity of same packet drop
or packet modification. A similar logic is applied when there is a need to increase
the trust values in case a node forwards a packet without any malicious, in such
a case variable "ph" prevents multiple updates to the trust table. As multiple
monitor nodes overhear the packets forwarded by the nodes in the path, therefore
there must be some mechanism to control multiple updates hence, for a particular
forwarding hop i.e. previous hop ("ph") if trust is increased by a particular
monitor node, then other monitors cannot increase the trust for the same hop
and the same packet forward.

3.4 Route Selection

Source node computes the route trust of a route as:

$$RT_i = \frac{\sum T_i}{n_i} \qquad (1)$$

Where RT_i is the route trust of route i, $\sum T_i$ is the sum of trust values of all
the nodes in route i and n_i is the number of hops in route i and n_i. The route

trust is directly proportional to the average trust of the nodes in the route and inversely proportional to the number of hops. The source node makes use of two threshold values for the selection of most trustworthy path between source and destination. The thresholds are termed as Mal_threshold and RT_threshold as elucidated below:

1. Mal_threshold: It is a value at or below which a node is declared as malicious.
2. RT_threshold: It is a value below which route is not considered as optimum.

If the trust values of all the nodes in the network surpass the Mal_threshold then the route trust for that route is now checked for RT_threshold. If the route satisfies these two criteria, then that route is selected for packet forwarding, otherwise route is rejected.

4   Simulation

4.1   Setup

We used Network Simulator NS-2.34 to evaluate the effectiveness of the proposed security scheme. We simulated and compared the results of the proposed protocol PS-DSR with standard DSR routing protocol. The simulation parameters are listed in Table 1.

Table 1. Simulation parameters

Parameter	Simulation Value
Simulator	NS-2.34
Examined Protocol	DSR and EESDSR
Simulation time	140 seconds
Simulation area	1500 x 300 m
Number of nodes	60
Transmission range	250 m
Movement model	Random Waypoint
Maximum speed	20 m/s
Pause time	0 seconds
Traffic type	CBR (UDP)
CBR rate	0.2 Mbps
Packet size	1000 bytes
Maximum malicious nodes	25
Initial energy	160 J
rxPower	1 W
txPower	1 W
idlePower	1 W

4.2   Metrics

The following metrics are used to evaluate the performance of the proposed security scheme through simulations:

1. Packet Delivery Ratio (PDR): It is the ratio of the total number of data packets received by the destination node to the total number of data packets sent by the source node.
2. Packet Loss Percentage: It is the percentage of the packets that were dumped by malevolent nodes to the total number of packets.
3. Average end-to-end latency: It is the average of time (including buffer delays during route discovery, queuing delays at interface queues, re-transmission delays at MAC layer and propagation time) taken by the data packets from source to destination.
4. Routing packet overhead: It is the fraction of the total number of control packets to the total number of data packets.
5. Path optimality: It is the proportion of the total number of hops in the shortest route to the total number of hops in the route selected by the protocol for transmitting data packets.

4.3   Trust Parameters

The values of the trust parameters taken for the simulation are listed in Table 2.

Table 2. Trust parameters

Parameter	Simulation Value
Trust Range	0.0 to 8.0
Mal_threshold	4.0
Initial trust value	6.0
inc_amt	0.02
dec_amt	0.05
RTh	1.05

4.4   Results and Analysis

In this section, we present the performance results for the proposed PS-DSR and that of the standard DSR protocol, in the presence of varying number of malicious nodes. Figure 1 shows a network scenario chosen for the implementation of PS-DSR and standard DSR. Green coloured nodes depict the nodes having high remaining energy, yellow coloured nodes represent the nodes having moderate energy and red coloured nodes represent the nodes having low remaining energy.

Figure 2 shows the number of monitor nodes selected by PS-DSR at different times, indicating periodic and on demand selection of monitor nodes. As shown in the graph, new set of monitor nodes are selected after every 50 seconds. The time interval of 50 seconds has been taken as it has been observed that the topology of the network changes drastically within 50 seconds and this requires the selection of new set of monitor nodes as previous monitor nodes do not cover the whole network. The set of 10 new monitor nodes selected at time 120 seconds is on demand as remaining energy of few monitor nodes fall below the required energy to work as a monitor node. The monitor node set selection algorithm does not consider energy deficient nodes and hence new set of monitor nodes that have enough remaining energy are selected to observe all network nodes in their neighborhood. The size of the MN set depends upon the density of the network and the communication range. For our simulations, we considered 250m communication range and the size of MN set varies, as the density of the mobile network varies with time. Figure 3 show that, the packet delivery ratio using the proposed scheme PS-DSR is higher than the standard DSR in the presence of 25 malicious nodes. This can be attributed to the fact that the later does not take into account the routes free from malicious nodes.

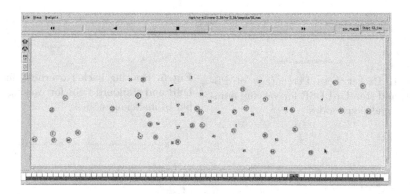

Fig. 1. Network topology of 60 nodes taken for the simulation

Figure 4 show that, the packet loss percentage using the proposed scheme PS-DSR is less than the standard DSR. PS-DSR selects the most trustworthy path avoiding the malicious nodes. This deviation from the routes selected by standard DSR leads to a raise in the packet overhead as shown in figure 5.

The average end to end delay of PS-DSR is more than the standard DSR, this can attributed to the delay in the route discovery process and the buffer delays. Average end to end delay is shown in figure 6. The path optimality presented in figure 7 for PS-DSR and the standard DSR comes out to be same in our simulation results.

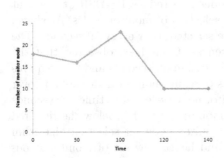

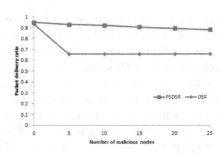

Fig. 2. Size of MN set selected by PS-DSR at different time intervals

Fig. 3. Packet Delivery Ratio of PS-DSR and standard DSR for varying number of malicious nodes

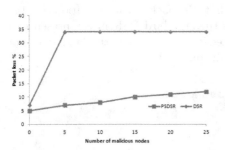

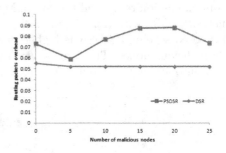

Fig. 4. Packet Loss Percentage of PS-DSR and standard DSR for varying number of malicious nodes

Fig. 5. Routing packet overhead for PS-DSR and standard DSR for varying number of malicious nodes

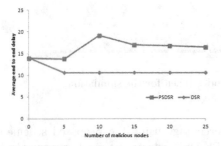

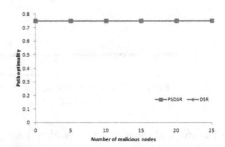

Fig. 6. Average end to end delay for PS-DSR and standard DSR for varying number of malicious nodes

Fig. 7. Path optimality for PS-DSR and standard DSR for varying number of malicious nodes

5   Conclusion

PS-DSR selects a more reliable path as compared to standard DSR. A monitor node cannot intentionally abuse its neighbors as each monitor is also being monitored by its neighboring monitor node.There is a significant increase in the packet delivery ratio, hence packet loss is less, and moreover, there is a marginal increase in the routing overhead. Using PS-DSR, the source node selects a new route free from malicious nodes without any delay after the detection of malicious node/s in the current route. PS-DSR is a power saving protocol as nodes working as monitoring nodes change their status from monitor to regular nodes and vice versa as and when required. PS-DSR is adaptable to dynamic topology of the network as new monitor nodes are selected from time to time. PS-DSR is using a completely innovative approach for detection of packet drops, the algorithm is designed from the scratch and PS-DSR considers energy factor as well as Trust factor during its operation.

References

1. Johnson, D.B., Maltz, D.A.: Dynamic Source Routing in Ad-Hoc Wireless Networks. In: Imielinski, T., Korth, H. (eds.) Mobile Computing, pp. 153–181. Kluwer (1996)
2. Kukreja, D., Singh, U., Reddy, B.V.R.: A Survey of Trust Based Routing Protocols in MANETs. In: Fourth International Conference on Electronics Computer Technology (ICECT 2012), pp. 537–542. IEEE Press (2012)
3. Marti, S., Giuli, T.J., Lai, K., Baker, M.: Mitigating routing misbehavior in mobile ad hoc networks. In: Proceedings of Sixth Ann. Int'l Conf. Mobile Computing and Networking (MobiCom), pp. 255–265 (2000)
4. Buchegger, S., Boudec, J.: Performance Analysis of the CONFIDANT Protocol: Cooperation of Nodes-Fairness in Distributed Ad Hoc NeTworks. In: Proceedings of IEEE/ACM Workshop Mobile Ad Hoc Networking and Computing (MobiHOC), pp. 226–236 (2002)
5. Pirzada, A.A., Datta, A., McDonald, C.: Trust-Based Routing for Ad-Hoc Wireless Networks, pp. 326–330. IEEE (2004)
6. Wang, C., Yang, X., Gao, Y.: A Routing Protocol Based on Trust for MANETs. In: Zhuge, H., Fox, G.C. (eds.) GCC 2005. LNCS, vol. 3795, pp. 959–964. Springer, Heidelberg (2005)
7. Pirzada, A.A., McDonald, C.: Deploying trust gateways to reinforce dynamic source routing. In: Proceedings of the 3rd International IEEE Conference on Industrial Informatics, pp. 779–784. IEEE Press (2005)
8. Pirzada, A.A., McDonald, C.: Trust Establishment In Pure Ad-hoc Networks. Wireless Personal Communications 37, 139–163 (2006)
9. Chuanhe, H., Yong, C., Wenming, S., Hao, Z.: A Trusted Routing Protocol for Wireless Mobile Ad hoc Networks. In: IET Conference on Wireless, Mobile and Sensor Networks (CCWMSN 2007), pp. 406–409 (2007)
10. Narula, P., Dhurandher, S.K., Misra, S., Woungang, I.: Security in mobile ad-hoc networks using soft encryption and trust based multipath routing. Sci. Direct Comput. Commun. 31, 760–769 (2008)
11. Dhurandher, S.K., Mehra, V.: Multi-path and message trust-based secure routing in ad hoc networks. In: Int. Conf. Advances in Computing, Control and Telecommunication Technologies (ACT 2009), pp. 189–194 (2009)

12. Dhurandher, S.K., Obaidat, M.S., Verma, K., Gupta, P., Dhurandher, P.: FACES: Friend-Based Ad Hoc Routing Using Challenges to Establish Security in MANETs Systems. IEEE Systems Journal 5(2), 176–188 (2011)
13. Li, Y., Peng, S., Chu, W.: An Efficient Algorithm for Finding an Almost Connected Dominating Set of Small Size on Wireless Ad Hoc Networks, pp. 199–205. IEEE (2006)
14. Kukreja, D., Miglani, M., Dhurandher, S.K., Reddy, B.V.R.: Security enhancement by detection and penalization of malicious nodes in wireless networks. In: International Conference on Signal Processing and Integrated Networks, pp. 275–280. IEEE (2014)

Quantifying the Severity of Blackhole Attack in Wireless Mobile Adhoc Networks

Satria Mandala[1,2], Kommineni Jenni[1,2], Md Asri Ngadi[2],
Maznah Kamat[2], and Yahaya Coulibaly[1,2]

[1] UTM-IRDA Digital Media Centre,
Media and Games Innovation Centre of Excellence,
Universiti Teknologi Malaysia, Malaysia
satriamandala@hotmail.com, jenni.k.507@gmail.com, coulibaly@utm.my
[2] Network Security Laboratory,
Faculty of Computing,
Universiti Teknologi Malaysia, Malaysia
{satria,jenni.k.507,dr.asri,kmaznah,coulibaly}@utm.my

Abstract. Blackhole attack is one of the severe attacks in MANET routing protocols. Generation of this attack is simple, which does not require specific tools or sophisticated attack techniques. However, this attack seriously corrupts the routing tables of nodes in the network. Even worse, the attack could increase the chances of losing confidential data and deny network services. Many researchers have proposed a variety of solutions to prevent this Conventional Blackhole Attack (CBA). Unfortunately, none of them has measured the severity of this attack. Filling gaps in measuring the severity of this attack, this research proposes a new security metrics, namely Corruption Routing Table (CRT), Compromising Relay Node (CRN) and Compromising Originator Node (CON). In addition, this research also introduces a new blackhole attack, namely Hybrid Black Hole Attack (HBHA) with two variants — Independent and Cooperative HBHAs. The proposed metrics proved effective in measuring the severity of both CBA and HBHAs. Simulation using Java in Time Simulator/Scalable Wireless Adhoc Network Simulator (JiST/SWANS) showed that Independent HBHA is the most severe attack compared to Cooperative HBHA and CBA. In addition, Cooperative HBHA is the most efficient attack than Independent HBHA and CBA.

Keywords: MANET Security, Hybrid Blackhole Attack, Severity of Attack.

1 Introduction

In recent years, Mobile Adhoc Networks (MANET) has been continuously developed and used in many applications, such as search and rescue missions, ad hoc communication in virtual classrooms and data tracking of environmental conditions. The setting up of such a network can be performed with or without human intervention or existence of infrastructure. Unfortunately, MANET is more vulnerable than wired network due to its open medium, mobility and unavailability

J. Lloret Mauri et al. (Eds.): SSCC 2014, CCIS 467, pp. 57–67, 2014.

of a central administration. As such many attacks are easily generated to cripple the operations of the network.

Blackhole attack is one of the severe attacks in MANET routing protocols [12, 19]. It causes corruption to routing tables, separates network into several small networks, and contributes to the unbalance route of network traffics. In the worst case scenario, the attack increases the possibility of losing confidential data and denying the network services. Many works have been proposed to contain this attack such as in [4, 10, 11, 15, 17–19]. Interestingly, none of these works have quantified the severity of the blackhole attacks on MANET. Moreover, study on network severity in general is almost non-existence.

This research aims to propose new security metrics to quantify the severity of the attack in nodes of the network. It also introduces a new blackhole attack, namely Hybrid Black Hole Attack (HBHA) with two variants — Independent and Cooperative HBHAs. The severity of these blackhole attacks is quantified using the proposed severity metrics, i.e., Corruption of Routing Table (CRT), Compromising Relay Node (CRN) and Compromising Originator Node (CON) metrics.

2   Attacks in MANET

Wu et al. [20] differentiated attacks in MANET into simple and sophisticated attacks based on the simplicity in triggering the attacks. Simple attacks are easily generated by a single attacker without the need of any special hardware or advanced technique of attacking. Meanwhile, the sophisticated attacks are defined as attacks that require special techniques, additional hardware or should be performed by a group of attackers.

Simple attacks do not imply less dangerous than sophisticated attacks. They could cause complicated problems to the network and the communicating nodes. These include stealing of confidential data, misinterpretation of network topology and causes a bottleneck at several parts of the network. In the case of the sophisticated attacks, the impact could be as severe as, or more severe than, the simple attacks. Even worse, the attacks are normally difficult to be identified if without proper advanced detection scheme. Simple attacks include selfish attack [3],blackhole attacks [5], fabrication attack [14], replay Attack [23], flooding attack (also known as Denial of Service - DoS - attack) [21] and spoofing attack [22]. Meanwhile, sophisticated attacks are sybil attack [6], wormhole attack [8], rushing attack [9] and jellyfish attack [1].

3   Hybrid Blackhole Attacks

This section presents new and specific class of blackhole attack, called as Hybrid Blackhole Attacks (HBHAs). In addition, starting from this section, the blackhole attack as described in [5] and [16] is called as a Conventional Blackhole Attack (CBA).

Generation of HBHAs in the network is simple because these attacks do not require any special hardware or advanced technique. However, these attacks seriously damage the nodes routing tables and potentially deny the network services because the attackers flood excessive number of false routing packets (malicious packets). In the case of AODV routing protocol, attackers effectively exploit the limitation of the protocol for attacking their targets. They use two critical events in the protocol as the starting point to perform the attacks. The critical events are the receiving of Route Request (RREQ) and the receiving Route Reply (RREP). Algorithm 3.1 and Algorithm 3.2 show both critical events, which have been modified for the purpose of generating HBHAs.

Algorithm 3.1. Attack Generation in Receiving Route Request

```
/*Initialization for external blackhole attack                              */
Input: RREQ_recv
Output: RREQ_out; MaliciousRREP_out
```

$$
\begin{array}{ll}
1 & \textbf{begin} \\
2 & \quad \textbf{if } (RREQBuffNum = 0) \parallel (\exists RREQ \in RREQBuffer : RREQ \neq RREQ_{recv} \textbf{ then} \\
3 & \quad\quad RREQBuffer \xleftarrow{save} RREQ_{recv} \\
4 & \quad \textbf{end} \\
5 & \quad \textbf{while } RREQBuffNum \neq 0 \textbf{ do} \\
6 & \quad\quad \textbf{if } (\exists RREQ \in RREQBuffer : RREQ \neq RREQ_{recv}) \textbf{ then} \\
7 & \quad\quad\quad \textbf{if } \textbf{Attack} = Cooperative \textbf{ then} \\
8 & \quad\quad\quad\quad \textbf{while } AtckAddrListNum \neq 0 \textbf{ do} \\
9 & \quad\quad\quad\quad\quad \textbf{if } (\exists Addr \in AtckAddrList : Addr \neq OrigAddrInRREQ_{recv}) \textbf{ then} \\
  & \quad\quad\quad\quad\quad\quad \texttt{/*Cooperative HBHA}\qquad\qquad\qquad\texttt{*/} \\
10 & \quad\quad\quad\quad\quad\quad \textbf{Generate } MaliciousRREP_{out} \textbf{ and SendTo } PreviousHop \\
11 & \quad\quad\quad\quad\quad \textbf{end} \\
12 & \quad\quad\quad\quad \textbf{end} \\
13 & \quad\quad\quad \textbf{else} \\
  & \quad\quad\quad\quad \texttt{/*Independent HBHA}\qquad\qquad\qquad\texttt{*/} \\
14 & \quad\quad\quad\quad \textbf{Generate } MaliciousRREP_{out} \textbf{ and SendTo } PreviousHop \\
15 & \quad\quad\quad \textbf{end} \\
16 & \quad\quad \textbf{end} \\
17 & \quad\quad \textbf{Forward } RREQ_{out} \text{ to the } NextHop \\
18 & \quad \textbf{end} \\
19 & \textbf{end}
\end{array}
$$

The attackers use Algorithm 3.1 for performing external blackhole attacks. Meanwhile, Algorithm 3.2 is used in generating internal blackhole attacks. This research calls such attacks as Hybrid Blackhole Attacks (HBHAs), due to the capability of attackers in exploiting both kinds of attacks algorithms in performing new attacks.

Referring to both algorithms, there are two scenarios of attacks in HBHA. They are Independent and Cooperative HBHA scenarios. Line 7-15 of Algorithm 3.1 describes Independent attack while line 2-12 of Algorithm 3.2 describes Cooperative attack. In Independent HBHA (IHBHA) scenario, a blackhole attacker strikes all nodes without considering if the victims are benign nodes or other attackers.

Algorithm 3.2. Attack Generation in Receiving Route Reply

```
/*Initialization for internal blackhole attack                          */
Input: RREP_recv;
       TTLForRREP_recv
Output: MaliciousRREP_out
1 begin
2 |   if Attack = Cooperative then
3 |   |   while AtckAddrListNum ≠ 0 do
4 |   |   |   if (∃ Addr ∈ AtckAddrList : Addr ≠ OrigAddrOfRReqNodeInRREP_recv)
  |   |   |   then
  |   |   |   |   /*Cooperative HBHA                                     */
5 |   |   |   |   if TTLForRREP_recv > 0 then
6 |   |   |   |   |   Send MaliciousRREP_out to the NextHop
7 |   |   |   |   end
8 |   |   |   end
9 |   |   end
10 |   else
   |   |   /*Independent HBHA                                           */
11 |   |   Send MaliciousRREP_out to the NextHop
12 |   end
13 end
```

In contrast, Cooperative HBHA (CHBHA) considers that among attackers are friends. Since they are friends, attacking among friends does not occur. The attacks are targeted only for the benign nodes. The implementation of CHBHA can be achieved by providing information about the list of friends for the attacker at initialization phase of simulation.

4   HBHA Simulation

This research simulates all the scenarios of the blackhole attacks (CBA and HBHAs) in JiST/SWANS simulator [2]. In the blackhole attacks simulation, a total of 50 nodes, which consists of attackers and benign nodes, is deployed into an area of size 3000x3000 m^2. The nodes move in the specified area using random point mobility model [7]. In addition, the simulation will be repeated 15 times for each PA. The repetition is required in order to achieve high confidence level results due to random selection of attackers and dynamic network topology. Most researchers [11, 13, 17, 19] repeat their simulations for 10 times. The detail of a simulation parameter is presented in Table 1.

5   Techniques, Symbols and Assumptions

5.1   Techniques for Analysis

This research proposes three security metrics to assess the severity of the blackhole attacks. They are corruption of routing table (CRT), compromising relay node (CRN), and compromising originator node (CON) metrics. CRT measures

Table 1. Simulation Parameters **Table 2.** Notations

Simulation Parameters	Description
Field dimension	3000x3000
Placement model	grid 10x10
Spatial propagation	hierarchy:5
Traffic	non cbr
Rate of sending messages on each node	1 message/minutes
Total Number of Nodes	50
Percentage of Attackers (Number of Attackers/Total Number of Nodes)	2% - 20%
Nodes Mobility/Timings (pause-time, precision, minimum speed, maximum speed)	Random Waypoint/10,30,2,10
Timings (start/stop/precisions)	0/2000/60
Transmission range	300 m
Attack Scenarios	Conventional Blackhole Attack
	Independent HBHA
	Cooperative HBHA
Experiment Repetition	15 times

RP	RREP
W	Without attack
I	Independent HBHA
C	Collaborative HBHA
$(.)_A$	All nodes
$(.)_G$	Good Node (Benign Node)
$(.)_O$	Originator Node
$(.)_B$	Bad Node (Attacker)
$(.)_R$	Relay Node
$(.)^1$	Attack Period Level 1 (APL1)
$(.)^2$	Attack Period Level 2 (APL2)
$(.)^3$	Attack Period Level 3 (APL3)
-	Malicious Packet
+	Legitimate Packet
$\hat{f}$	Fitting function

the number of route entries in the routing tables that have been corrupted by malicious packets. CRN computes numbers of malicious packets forwarded by relay nodes to spread the attacks. Meanwhile, CON quantifies the number of malicious packets received by the originator nodes due to these attacks.

Thus, based on these three metrics, a point of intersection between the increasing of the malicious packets and the decreasing of the legitimate packets for a group of nodes or all nodes in the network can be determined as the Intersection Point of CRT (IPCRT), Intersection Point of CRN (IPCRN) and Intersection Point of CON (IPCON). IPCRT refers to the equality between the number of corrupted route entries and the number of legitimate routes. IPCRN is a condition in which both numbers of malicious packets and legitimate packets forwarded by relay nodes are equal. Forwarding malicious packets can be used for indicating that the relay nodes are compromised. Finally, IPCON is defined as a condition, which the number of malicious packet and legitimate packet received by the originator nodes are equal. It should be noted that IPCRT, IPCRN and IPCON assume that plotting curve of the malicious packet must have an upward trend, and legitimate packet must have a downward trend. Other trends are irrelevant to be described using the intersection point of security metrics.

5.2 Symbols

Table 2 shows the symbols used for this research which can be used to compose a new symbol. For example, the meaning of symbol $RP_{A+}C$ is total number of legitimate RREP packets updated by all nodes in the network under CHBHA. Then $RP_{O-}I$ refers to the total number of malicious RREP packets received by originator nodes under IHBHA.

5.3 Assumptions

Each node in the network is equipped by a tool for identifying malicious packets. However, the tool does not have any mechanism to counter or to remove detected malicious packet detected. Worst, it cannot distinguish whether malicious packets belong to internal or external blackhole attacks. In addition, the tool has been configured for recording and detecting the events from RREP packet. As such it can detect and record 'RREP packet forwarding', 'RREP packet receiving', and updating routing table due to incoming of RREP packet.

To accelerate the identification of malicious packets, this research introduces a new field in RREP packet structure. The malicious RREP will have a value '1' on the new field of RREP, whiles the legitimate RREP will have a value '0'. Thus, whenever the malicious RREP is either generated or falsified by an attacker, the value of the new field will be set to '1', otherwise the new field will be set to '0'. Using this technique, the tool as described in previous paragraph easily distinguish whether the incoming packets are malicious packets or not.

6   Impact of Blackhole Attacks

Figure 1 shows the impact of malicious RREP packets flooding in the network under CBA and HBHAs. As depicted in the figure, CBA is used as a reference to plot the curves of malicious RREP packets in the network under HBHAs. As a result, the percentage of malicious RREP packets in the network under CBA is absolutely steady, i.e, 1 (100%) over all PAs (2% to 20%). In contrast, the percentage of malicious RREP packets in the network under HBHAs rapidly climbs to 2 (200%) at 20% of PAs.

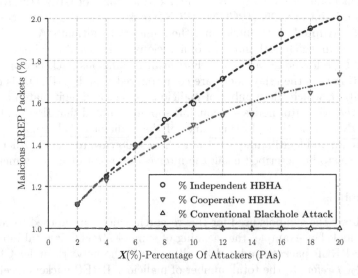

Fig. 1. The Flooding of Malicious RREPs Under Blackhole Attacks

As shown in Figure 1, 2% of PAs in HBHAs (Independent and Cooperative HBHAs) increases the malicious RREP packets to be 10% larger than CBA. At this number of PAs, the percentage of malicious RREP packets is 1.1 (110%).

However, the situation soon changes with the increasing of PAs. Under IHBHA, 20% of PAs has doubled the malicious RREP packets to 2 (200%). Meanwhile, with CHBHA, the same number of PAs has increased the malicious RREP packets to 1.7 (170%). These clearly indicate the severity of HBHAs attacks, which intensively flood the network with a large number of malicious packets.

7 Severity Analysis of Blackhole Attacks in MANET

The number of malicious RREP packets in the network under three blackhole attacks (CBA, IHBHA and CHBHA) will be analyzed to reveal the severity of these attacks. Figure 2 depicts the severity of these attacks using three security metrics as described in Sub Section 5.1. Meanwhile, Table 3 shows the mathematical models of these metrics in MANET under the blackhole attacks.

Table 3. Mathematical Models of the Proposed Security Metrics

Metrics	Fitting Equations	r_{xy}	R^2	Adj R^2	RMSE	Malicious RREP rate (packet/attacker)
CRT	$RP_A I = 29.89 + 342.24x - 7.01x^2$	0.9996	0.9991	0.9989	26.956	$\frac{dRP_A I}{dx} = -14.02x + 342.24$
CRN	$RP_A I = 0.50 + 296.39x - 6.43x^2$	0.9993	0.9986	0.9982	28.751	$\frac{dRP_A I}{dx} = -12.86x + 296.39$
CON	$RP_A I = -5.4 + 133.55x - 3.11x^2$	0.9998	0.9995	0.9994	8.677	$\frac{dRP_A I}{dx} = -6.22x + 133.55$
CRT	$RP_A C = 91.66 + 284.66x - 10.74x^2$	0.9984	0.9968	0.9959	32.753	$\frac{dRP_A C}{dx} = -21.48x + 284.66$
CRN	$RP_A C = 56.48 + 247.31x - 8.99x^2$	0.9980	0.9960	0.9949	32.615	$\frac{dRP_A C}{dx} = -17.98x + 247.31$
CON	$RP_A C = 27.78 + 108.33x - 3.61x^2$	0.9988	0.9977	0.9970	11.487	$\frac{dRP_A C}{dx} = -7.22x + 108.33$
CRT	$RP_A N = 154.98 + 190.02x - 2.65x^2$	0.9973	0.9946	0.9930	37.461	$\frac{dRP_A N}{dx} = -5.30x + 190.02$
CRN	$RP_A N = 79.59 + 178.28x - 3.04x^2$	0.9947	0.9894	0.9864	46.435	$\frac{dRP_A N}{dx} = -6.08x + 178.28$
CON	$RP_A N = 49.34 + 86.63x - 1.65\,x^2$	0.9984	0.9968	0.9958	10.233	$\frac{dRP_A N}{dx} = -3.30x + 86.63$

As depicted from Figure 2a, the route entries corrupted by these attacks have upward trends over all the values of PAs, albeit by varying degrees. In these attacks, 2% of PAs corrupts almost 370 route entries of routing tables. However, 20% of PAs in IHBHA corrupts almost 8 times greater than the aforementioned corrupted route entries, i.e., 2800 route entries. In CHBHA, the same number of PAs corrupts fewer route entries than ICHBHA, around 1910 route entries. Meanwhile, attackers in CBA corrupt only 1800 route entries at 20% of PAs. All curves of CRT in Figure 2a are then fitted and presented in Table 3 as mathematical models. CRT models under IHBHA, CHBHA and CBA, are $29.89 + 342.24x - 7.01x^2$, $91.66 + 284.66x - 10.74x^2$ and $154.98 + 190.02x - 2.65x^2$, respectively. In these models, x is the percentage of attackers. Figure 2b and Figure 2c show the number of RP_{A-} forwarded by relay nodes and the number of RP_{A-} received by the originator nodes, respectively. Clearly, both figures presents similar trends of RP_{A-} as in Figure 2a. In other words, CRN and CON

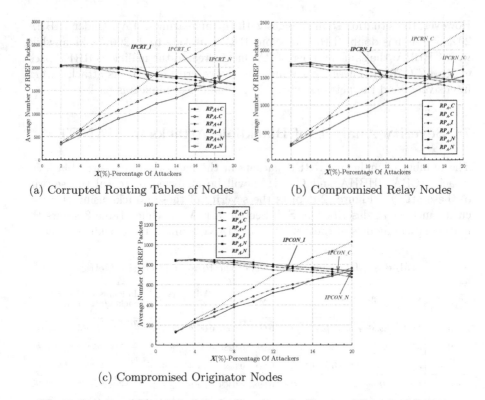

(a) Corrupted Routing Tables of Nodes   (b) Compromised Relay Nodes

(c) Compromised Originator Nodes

Fig. 2. Severity of Blackhole Attacks Based on the Proposed Security Metrics

Table 4. Intersection Point of Security Metrics

Metrics	Independent Attack (PA;Number of Packets)	Cooperative Attack (PA;Number of Packets)	Conventional Blackhole Attack (PA;Number of Packets)
IPCRT	(11%;1760)	(17%;1723)	(18%;1690)
IPCRN	(12%;1516)	(16%;1479)	(19%;1460)
IPCON	(13%;745)	(18%;725)	(20%;740)

metrics in these figures have upward trends over all the values of PAs. In addition, the mathematical models of these metrics are also presented in Table 3.

As can be seen in Figure 2a, Figure 2b and Figure 2c, the increasing RP_{A-} directly decreased the legitimate RREP packets (RP_{A+}). However, the degree of decreasing RP_{A+} is at a slightly slower pace than the degree of increasing RP_{A-}. In addition, the point of intersection between increased RP_{A-} and decrease RP_{A+} can be used for indicating that a dangerous situation is occurring in the network. For example, since RP_{A-} and RP_{A+} in the network are equal, most of route entries in the network become inaccurate because they have been corrupted by RP_{A-}. At this condition, most of the relay nodes and originator nodes have also been compromised by the attackers.

Figure 2a, Figure 2b and Figure 2c show IPCRT, IPCRN and IPCON. Numerical of these intersection points are given in column 2, 3 and 4 of Table 4. As shown from these figures, IHBHA outperforms both CHBHA and CBA in achieving IPCRT, IPCRN and IPCON. In IHBHA, IPCRT can be achieved with 11% of nodes in the network are attackers. In addition, IPCRN and IPCON requires 12% and 13% of nodes are attackers. IPCRT, IPCRN and IPCON in CHBHA can be achieved with larger value of PAs, i.e.,17%, 16% and 18%, respectively. Finally, the highest PAs to achieve IPCRT, IPCRN and IPCON, ie, 18%, 19% and 20%, occurs in CBA. These results indicate that the most severe attacks is IHBHA because it requires the least amount of PAs to achieve intersection points of the security metrics.

Rate of RP_{A-} ($\alpha_{CRT}, \alpha_{CRN}, \alpha_{CON}$) are presented in Figure 3. Meanwhile their mathematical models are shown in the last column of Table 3. As depicted in Figure 3, CHBHA outperforms compared to other two blackhole attacks (IHBHA and CBA) because all gradient of curves in $\alpha_{CRT}, \alpha_{CRN}, \alpha_{CON}$ are larger than others. These facts indicate that CHBHA is the most efficient attack than IHBHA and CBA because the node targets are benign nodes.

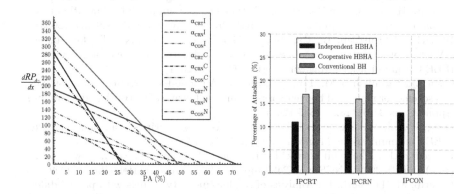

Fig. 3. Rate of Malicious RREP   **Fig. 4.** Severity of HBHAs in MANET

8   Discussion and Conclusion

Ramaswami and Upadhyaya [13] proposed a collaborative blackhole attack, while the implementation through a simulation are done by Weerasinghe and Fu in [19]. In this simulation, Weerasinghe and Fu [19] demonstrated the impact of two colluding attackers striking AODV routing protocol and proposed a data routing information (DRI) to prevent from the attack. They concluded that the protocol reduced packet loss to be 45% less compared to AODV under the attack for the same ratio of attackers. Tamilselvan and Sankaranarayanan [17] also proposed prevention of the collaborative blackhole attack [13]. However, they use different technique in analyzing this attack, i.e., a packet delivery ratio and routing overhead. Unfortunately, all these researchers did not measure the severity of the attack. Instead they show the performance metrics of MANET based on their proposed protocol.

Filling gaps in measuring the severity of this attack, this research proposes a new security metrics, namely Corruption Routing Table (CRT), Compromising Relay Node (CRN) and Compromising Originator Node (CON). This research also introduces a new blackhole attack, namely Independent Hybrid Black Hole Attack (IHBHA) and Cooperative Hybrid Black Hole Attack (CHBHA); and then measures the severity of both CBA and HBHAs. The simulation results showed that the proposed metrics are effective in measuring CBH and HBHAs. IHBHA is the most severe attack compared to Cooperative HBHA and CBA, see Figure 4. As shown in the figure, IHBHA requires the least amount of PAs to achieve intersection points of the security metrics. In addition, Cooperative HBHA is the most severe attack compared to HBHA and CBA.

References

1 Aad, I., Hubaux, J.P., Knightly, E.W.: Impact of denial of service attacks on ad hoc networks. IEEE/ACM Transactions on Networking 16(4), 791–802 (2008)
2 Barr, R., Haas, Z.J., van Renesse, R.: Jist: an efficient approach to simulation using virtual machines: Research articles. Softw. Pract. Experience 35, 539–576 (2005)
3 Blazevic, L., Buttyan, L., Capkun, S., Giordano, S., Hubaux, J.P., Le Boudec, J.Y.: Self organization in mobile ad hoc networks: the approach of terminodes. IEEE Communications Magazine 39(6), 166–174 (2001)
4 Chen, Q., Fadlullah, Z.M., Lin, X., Kato, N.: A clique-based secure admission control scheme for mobile ad hoc networks (manets). Journal of Network and Computer Applications 34(6), 1827–1835 (2011)
5 Deng, H., Li, W., Agrawal, D.P.: Routing security in wireless ad hoc networks. IEEE Communications Magazine 40(10), 70–75 (2002)
6 Douceur, J.R.: The sybil attack. In: Druschel, P., Kaashoek, M.F., Rowstron, A. (eds.) IPTPS 2002. LNCS, vol. 2429, pp. 251–260. Springer, Heidelberg (2002)
7 Garetto, M., Leonardi, E.: Analysis of random mobility models with partial differential equations. IEEE Transactions on Mobile Computing 6(11), 1204–1217 (2007)
8 Hu, Y.C., Perrig, A., Johnson, D.B.: Packet leashes: a defense against wormhole attacks in wireless networks. In: Proceedings of the INFOCOM 2003, pp. 1976–1986 (April 2003)
9 Hu, Y.C., Perrig, A., Johnson, D.B.: Rushing attacks and defense in wireless ad hoc network routing protocols. In: Proceedings of the 2nd ACM Workshop on Wireless Security, pp. 30–40. ACM, New York (2003)
10 Li, Z., Garcia-Luna-Aceves, J.: Non-interactive key establishment in mobile ad hoc networks. Ad Hoc Networks 5(7), 1194–1203 (2007)
11 Lu, S., Li, L., Lam, K.Y., Jia, L.: Saodv: A manet routing protocol that can withstand black hole attack. In: Proc. Int. Conf. Computational Intelligence and Security, CIS 2009, vol. 2, pp. 421–425 (2009)
12 Mandala, S., Ngadi, M.A., Abdullah, A.H., Ismail, A.S.: A variant of merkle signature scheme to protect AODV routing protocol. In: Özcan, A., Chaki, N., Nagamalai, D. (eds.) WiMo 2010. CCIS, vol. 84, pp. 87–98. Springer, Heidelberg (2010)

13 Ramaswami, S.S., Upadhyaya, S.: Smart handling of colluding black hole attacks in manets and wireless sensor networks using multipath routing. In: Proc. IEEE Information Assurance Workshop, pp. 253–260 (June 2006)

14 Sanzgiri, K., LaFlamme, D., Dahill, B., Levine, B., Shields, C., Belding-Royer, E.: Authenticated routing for ad hoc networks. IEEE Journal on Selected Areas in Communications 23(3), 598–610 (2005)

15 Su, M.Y.: Prevention of selective black hole attacks on mobile ad hoc networks through intrusion detection systems. Computer Communications 34(1), 107–117 (2011)

16 Sun, B., Guan, Y., Chen, J., Pooch, U.: Detecting black-hole attack in mobile ad hoc networks. In: Proceeding of Personal Mobile Communications, pp. 490–495 (April 2003)

17 Tamilselvan, L., Sankaranarayanan, V.: Prevention of co-operative black hole attack in manet. Journal of Networks 3, 13–20 (2008)

18 Wang, J., Liu, Y., Jiao, Y.: Building a trusted route in a mobile ad hoc network considering communication reliability and path length. Journal of Network and Computer Applications 34(4), 1138–1149 (2011)

19 Weerasinghe, H., Fu, H.: Preventing cooperative black hole attacks in mobile ad hoc networks: Simulation implementation and evaluation. International Journal of Software Engineering and Its Applications 2(3), 39–54 (2008)

20 Wu, B., Chen, J., Wu, J., Cardei, M.: A survey of attacks and countermeasures in mobile ad hoc networks. In: Wireless Network Security, pp. 103–135. Springer US (2007)

21 Yi, P., Dai, Z., Zhang, S., Zhong, Y.: A new routing attack in mobile ad hoc networks. International Journal of Information Technology 11, 83–94 (2005)

22 Yoo, Y., Agrawal, D.P.: Why does it pay to be selfish in a manet? IEEE Wireless Communications 13(6), 87–97 (2006)

23 Zhen, J., Srinivas, S.: Preventing replay attacks for secure routing in ad hoc networks. In: Pierre, S., Barbeau, M., An, H.-C. (eds.) ADHOC-NOW 2003. LNCS, vol. 2865, pp. 140–150. Springer, Heidelberg (2003)

Peers Feedback and Compliance Based Trust Computation for Cloud Computing

Jagpreet Sidhu and Sarbjeet Singh

Computer Science and Engineering, UIET, Panjab University, Chandigarh
jagpreet.pu@gmail.com, sarbjeet@pu.ac.in

Abstract. Cloud computing is a new computing model where software, platform and infrastructure resources are delivered as services using pay-as-you-go model. It gives an excellent way to lease numerous types of distributed resources but it also makes security problems further complicate and more important for cloud users than before. The key barrier to extensive usage of cloud computing is the lack of confidence (trust) in cloud services by potential cloud users. For critical business applications and other sensitive applications, cloud service providers must be selected based on high level of trustworthiness. In this paper, we present a trust model to evaluate service providers in order to help cloud users select the most reliable service providers and services in business. We have made an attempt to design a trust model which enables clients to determine trustworthiness of service providers by taking into account three different types of trust viz. interaction-based trust, compliance-based trust and recommendation-based trust. These types can be assigned appropriate weights to designate precedence among them in order to compute total trust. The model has been simulated using MATLAB. Simulation has been done to validate flexibility, robustness and scalability of the model. The proposed trust model is an attempt towards a model where diverse facets of trust contribute in formation of trust (confidence) in the mind of cloud user about service provider and its offered services.

Keywords: Trust, Trustworthiness, Confidence in Service Provider, Cloud Computing, Cloud Security.

1 Introduction

Cloud Computing is a technology which provides application, data and computing as service over the Internet. It is not a completely new architecture in computing instead it is a new computing model which includes other technologies coupled together to provide services over the network connection (Fig.1). As per NIST [1] definition of cloud, "Cloud computing is a model for enabling convenient, on-demand network access to a shared pool of configurable computing resources (e.g., networks, servers, storage, applications, and services) that can be rapidly provisioned and released with minimal management effort or service provider interaction".

NIST [1] also focuses on five essential characteristics of cloud computing viz. on-demand self-service, broad network access, resource pooling, rapid elasticity and measured service. Service models of cloud computing are Software as a Service

J. Lloret Mauri et al. (Eds.): SSCC 2014, CCIS 467, pp. 68–80, 2014.

(SaaS), Platform as a Service (PaaS) and Infrastructure as a Service (IaaS) and all the service are provided over the network which is generally Internet. NIST also defines four deployment models for cloud which are private cloud, public cloud, community cloud and hybrid cloud.

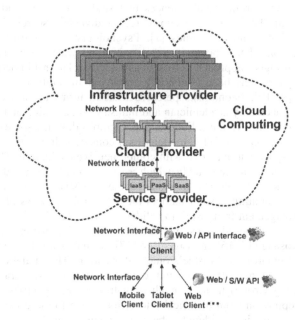

Fig. 1. General view of Cloud Computing

Although Cloud computing allows consumers to avoid initial capital expenses, diminish operating costs and enhance response times, still advantages of cloud restrict clients to migrate their businesses to cloud. One of the major reasons for this is security [2]. Cloud users feel less confident while migrating to cloud as they have apprehensions about the security and privacy of their data. From security perspective, number of unchartered risks and challenges come into picture resulting from relocation of data and shifting of control from client to service provider, fading much of the effectiveness of conventional protection mechanisms [3].

This paper aims to formulate and simulate a trust model for cloud computing systems. The paper is organized as follows: Section 2 describes pervious work on trust in cloud computing. Section 3 describes the proposed trust model. Section 4 presents simulation results and Section 5 is summary and conclusion.

2   Related Work

Trust is generally associated to "levels of confidence in something or someone" [4]. Trust is a fascinating subject and many social scientists have researched on the concept of trust and developed theories around it [4] but still there is no generally agreed definition of trust for cloud computing. The definition of trust given by "Diego Gambetta" is the most commonly used definition in the field of computing.

Diego Gambetta defines trust as "a particular level of the subjective probability with which an agent assesses that another agent or group of agents will perform a particular action, both before he can monitor such action (or independently of his capacity ever to be able to monitor it) and in a context in which it affects his own action" [5].

Trust had its origin from social sciences that study the nature and behavior of human societies [6]. Trust has been considered in diverse research fields such as psychology, sociology, and economics [7]. Psychologists study trust as a mental attitude and focus on what happens in a person's mind when he trusts or distrusts someone [8]. Sociologists approach to trust is as a social relationship between people. Social context of trust has been commonly employed in multi agent systems and social networks [9, 10]. Economists perceive trust in terms of utility [11]. Many efforts have been enacted by academician and industry on designing and developing a trust model for computing systems. Following paragraphs describe some of these.

Qiang Guo et al. proposed ETEC model which considers direct (time-variant) and recommendation (space-variant) trust with comprehensive evaluation. The model can be used to form peers alliance quickly which assists to make correct decisions. The model provide a helpful measure to enhance the robustness, fault tolerance and security of cloud computing. As per authors they are in the process of developing a complete trust management framework to validate their model [12].

C. Chaowen et al. proposed a trust model based on two dimensional measurements [13]. Beth [14], Jøsang [15, 16] and EigenRep [17] evaluate trust degree by history of interactions and reputations of trustee's outer information. The model evaluates trust by calculating both inner attributes and outer information as parameters. TCG (Trusted Computing Group) helps in evaluating trustees inner attributes which are combined with reputation from historical interactions. Due to these two dimensional evaluations, trust degree is considered to be more dynamic, reliable and flexible. As a result of trust accumulation, spoofing can be avoided with model. The model works for limited services in cloud computing [13].

Ko. Ryan KL et al., proposed a detective trust framework which shifted its concerns to integrity and accountability of data stored in cloud from conventional performance and system health issues. The framework aimed at a layer above conventional system-centric perspective to file-centric perspective. Authors were able to list several cloud accountability issues using their cloud trust framework. They aim at building a single point of view for accountability of cloud service provider based on their framework. They are currently researching and developing solutions for each accountability layer [18].

K Hwang et al., proposed integrated Cloud architecture to strengthen security and privacy in cloud applications. Several security mechanisms are suggested to reinforce public cloud which is crucial for widespread acceptance of cloud computing services. The proposed security architecture is still in the early development phase. Authors aimed at common cloud standards and interoperability which are still open problems [19].

A. Mohammed et al. proposed effective SLA (Service Level Agreement) to ensure agreed terms for services delivered by CSP (Cloud Service Provider). A SLA was defined on non-functional requirements in order to maintain a reliable protocol during client and cloud provider negotiations. Scenarios were illustrated to validate applicability of SLA frameworks to cloud computing service negotiations. They design SLA metrics and simulation activities to evaluate the proposed framework for cloud computing. Authors argue that result of this work will aid cloud client in choosing the most reliable service [20]. [21] discusses trust evaluation in cloud based on friends and third party's recommendations. In this paper trust has been evaluated based on a user's past experiences with service provider and based on friends and third party's recommendations. Authors have also simulated the model and results show that the model is workable.

There is need for trust model in cloud computing to build client's trust in cloud computing services. A trust model from client perspective is desired to build client's confidence to migrate to cloud computing services. Though many trust models and frameworks have been proposed for cloud computing systems, they address trust from limited service models and deployment models perspective. There is a need to formulate a generic trust model which is adaptable to all service and deployment models of cloud computing. We attempt to address this problem by designing and developing such a trust model which enables clients to determine trustworthiness of service providers by taking into account three different types of trust viz. interaction-based trust, compliance-based trust and recommendation-based trust and is adaptable to all service and deployment models of cloud computing.

3   Proposed Trust Model

The proposed trust model provides a mechanism to access trustworthiness of service providers in cloud environment. The model is applicable to all service models (IaaS, PaaS, SaaS) and deployment models (public, private and hybrid). A schematic highlighting interactions among major entities of the trust model to access trustworthiness is shown in Fig. 2. Table 1 briefly describes the major entities of the proposed trust model.

As per Fig. 2, a service provider first advertises its services in cloud service directory. These services are searchable by cloud users and if found suitable, a negotiation process is initiated. Finally when agreement is reached between service

Table 1. Entities of the Trust Model

Entity	Description
Cloud User	Cloud User is consumer of cloud services. A Cloud User can be a service, an application or an end user.
Service Provider	Service provider is the owner of the service being provided on cloud. Service provider can also acts as client when its services are hosted by cloud provider.
Cloud Service Directory	Directory service is a collection of service advertisement by service providers. It provides services & service providers selection on the basis of client's requirements.
SLA Agent	SLA Agent intermediates the formation of contract for services provisioning between service provider and cloud user.
Compliance Agent	Compliance Agent is a monitoring body which checks the performance of cloud services as per agreed SLAs for its clients.

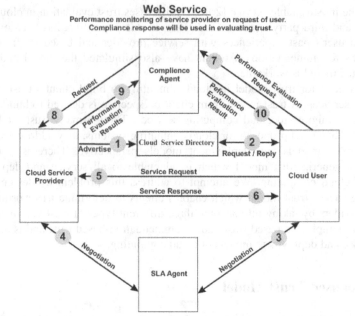

Fig. 2. Trust evaluation (Interaction among major entities)

Table 2. Different types of trust

Trust Type	Description
Interactions Based Trust (IBT)	Interaction based trust is the trust evaluated by a cloud user about a cloud service provider based on the historical interactions it had with the service provider. Interaction based trust is denoted by IBT.
Compliance Based Trust (CBT)	Compliance based trust is the trust evaluated by a compliance agent. Compliance agent is engaged by cloud user to evaluate compliance as per SLA agreement with service provider. Compliance based trust is denoted by CBT.
Recommendations Based Trust (RBT)	Recommendation based trust is the trust evaluated by recommenders of cloud user for a particular service or service provider. The information obtained from various recommenders is aggregated and the resulting trust is called recommendation based trust, denote by RBT.
Final Trust (FT)	Final trust is formed based on IBT, CBT and RBT. In other words final trust is formed by aggregating interaction-based, compliance-based and recommendation-based trust. Final trust is denoted by FT.

provider and cloud user, the SLA is finalized otherwise user selects another service provider. Cloud user starts accessing services of service provider and during any time, cloud user can engage a compliance agent to monitor QoS parameters as per agreed SLA. The compliance as per SLA is checked by compliance agent by monitoring services at service provider's end and a compliance report is generated which can be used by cloud user to form trust on service provider. The final trust computation process takes into consideration three types of trust which are described in Table 2.

The formulas to evaluate different types of trust are presented in Table 3.

Table 3. Formulas to evaluate IBT, CBT, RBT and FT

Type of Trust	Evaluation Formula
Interaction Based Trust (IBT)	$$IBT = T_s/(T_s + T_f) * e^{(P_t-S_t)^{T_d}} \qquad (1)$$ T_s: Successful transaction between service providers and cloud users T_f: Unsuccessful transaction between service providers and cloud users P_t: Present Time S_t : Starting time of transactions between service provider and cloud users T_d: Time decay factor
Compliance Based Trust (CBT)	$$CBT = \sum_{u=1}^{n} M_u * P_u \qquad (2)$$ $M_{(1...n)}$: Monitored parameters $P_{(1...n)}$: Precedence among parameters agreed in SLA
Recommendation Based Trust (RBT)	$$RBT = \sum_{u=1}^{p} R_p * RP_p \qquad (3)$$ R_p: Recommendation sent by peer RP_p: Reputation of peer sending recommendations
Final Trust (FT)	$$FT = IBT * P_{IBT} + CBT * P_{CBT} + RBT * P_{RBT} \qquad (4)$$ IBT: Interaction Based Trust CBT: Complaince Based Trust RBT: Recommendation Based Trust $P_{IBT}, P_{CBT}, P_{RBT}$: Precedence of Interaction – based, Compliance – based and Reputation – based trust

It is clear from the formulas described in Table 3 that IBT takes into consideration the results of previous interactions to form trust on service provider. Successful interactions increase IBT whereas unsuccessful interactions decrease IBT. Trust also decreases with time. To calculate CBT, compliance agent monitors QoS parameters as per agreed SLA. Preferences among monitored parameters can also be set. From the compliance levels of individual parameters, the overall compliance-based trust CBT is calculated. RBT makes use of peers' opinions to evaluate trust. The recommendations from peers are aggregated by setting preferences among them and RBT is calculated as per equation (3) described in Table 3. To calculate FT, the preferences among IBT, CBT and RBT are set and equation (4) is used to obtain FT.

4   Simulation Results

To test the validity of the proposed trust model, we designed and developed a prototype of the trust model in Matlab. The prototype has been developed to validate the proposed approach. The experimental runs were designed and executed to demonstrate realization of objectives and characteristics of design i.e. flexibility, robustness and scalability. The system and simulation configuration is presented in Table 3 and 4 respectively.

Table 4. System Configuration

Component	Description
Processor	Intel® Core™ 2 Duo processor E6850 3.00 GHz
Number of processors	1
Memory capacity	4 GB (4 x 1 GB)
Hard disk capacity	250 GB
Operating system	Genuine Windows 7 professional
Simulator version (Release name)	MATLAB 8 (R2012b)

Table 5. Simulation Configuration

Entity	Value
Number of cloud nodes	50
SLA agent	1
Cloud auditor	1
Cloud service directory	1

Table 6. Design Principle of Trust Model

Design Principles	Demonstration and Validation Criteria
Flexibility	Demonstrated and validated by varying number of QoS parameters, type of QoS parameter, priorities among QoS parameters, service models, deployment models and trust evaluation modules.
Robustness	Demonstrated and validated by computing final trust in case of non-availability of any one or two types of trust from IBT, CBT and RBT.
Scalability	Demonstrated and validated by increasing number of cloud users, service providers, recommenders, QoS parameters.

Test plans have been designed to demonstrate and validate the design principles of flexibility, robustness and scalability. Table 5 presents how design principles have been demonstrated and validated and Table 6 presents configuration of the test scenarios.

Table 7. Configuration of Test Scenarios

Test Scenario	Nodes	QoS Parameters	Final Trust (FT) assessment based on
T1	5	5	IBT, CBT, RBT
T2	5	5	IBT, CBT
T3	25	5	CBT, RBT
T4	50	5	IBT, RBT

In test scenario T1, final trust has been evaluated based on all types of trust (IBT, CBT and RBT) and all types of trust contributed equally (i.e. equal weighing factors were given to all types of trust) in the formation of final trust FT. The test inputs and the output results are shown in Fig. 3.

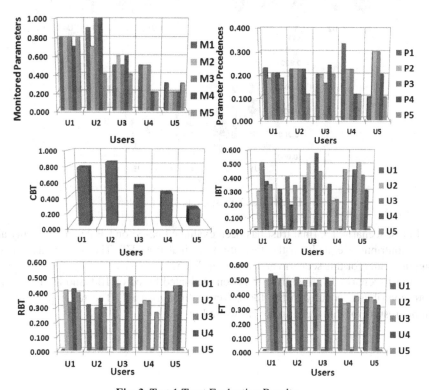

Fig. 3. Test 1 Trust Evaluation Results

In test scenario T2, final trust has been evaluated based on IBT and CBT only and both contributed equally in the formation of final trust FT. The test inputs and the output results for this scenario are shown in Fig. 4.

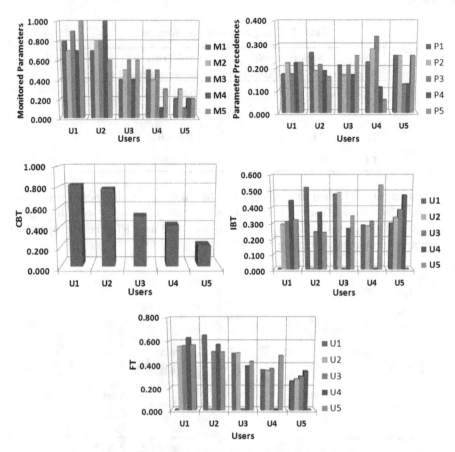

Fig. 4. Test 2 Trust Evaluation Results

In test scenario T3, final trust has been evaluated based on CBT and RBT only and both contributed equally in the formation of final trust FT. The test inputs and the output results for this scenario are shown in Fig. 5.

In test scenario T4, final trust has been evaluated based on IBT and RBT only and both contributed equally in the formation of final trust FT. The test inputs and the output results for this scenario are shown in Fig. 6.

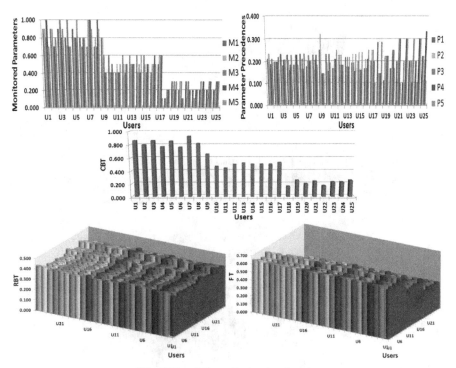

Fig. 5. Test 3 Trust Evaluation Results

These scenarios were designed to demonstrate the flexibility, robustness and scalability of the model. As the model can calculate final trust FT in the absence of any one or two types of trust, the proposed trust model is robust. It is flexible as any number and types of parameters can be used and different preferences among them can be specified depending on the need and requirements of the application in hand. The model is also linearly scalable.

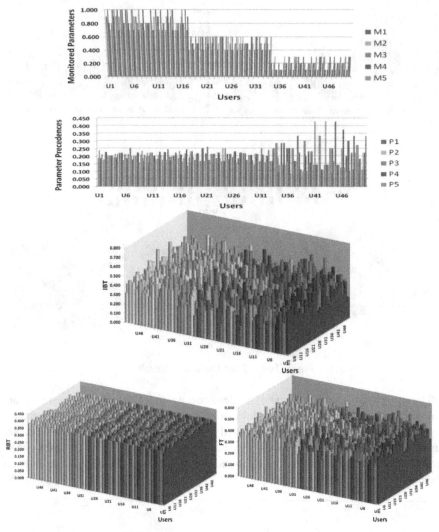

Fig. 6. Scenario 4 test Inputs and Results

5   Summary and Conclusion

Trust is the need of the hour at present for rapid adaptation and growth of cloud computing. Cloud user need to have confidence and faith on service provider to migrate its security critical information, data and resources to cloud computing. Trust issues need to be addressed on priority basis. Although there are many trust models and frameworks proposed for distributed computing, peer to peer and grid computing but the unique characteristics of cloud requires changes in proposed approaches. Most of the existing models and frameworks do not consider various types of trust to come up with final trust value. We believe that involvement of other types of trust will make trust assessment more accurate and reliable. In this paper we have made an attempt to design and evaluate a trust model which involves peers feedback (RBT), compliance results (CBT) in addition to user's past interaction with service provider (IBT). Simulation results show that model is robust, flexible and scalable and can be adopted for use in cloud based systems to determine trustworthiness of service providers.

References

1. Mell, P., Grance, T.: The NIST definition of cloud computing (draft). NIST special publication, 7 (2011)
2. Takabi, H., Joshi, J.B., Ahn, G.J.: Security and privacy challenges in cloud computing environments. IEEE Security & Privacy 8(6), 24–31 (2010)
3. Zissis, D., Lekkas, D.: Addressing cloud computing security issues. Future Generation Computer Systems 28(3), 583–592 (2012)
4. Firdhous, M., Ghazali, O., Hassan, S.: Trust and Trust Management in Cloud Computing– A Survey. InterNetWorks Research Group, University Utara Malaysia, Technical Report No: UUM/CAS/InterNetWorks/TR2011-01, http://www.Internetworks.my/pubs/techrep/TR2011-01.pdf
5. Gambetta, D.: Trust Making or Breaking of Cooperative Relations. Oxford, Blackwell (1990)
6. Yu, H., Shen, Z., Miao, C., Leung, C., Niyato, D.: A Survey of Trust and Reputation Management Systems in Wireless Communications. Proceedings of the IEEE 98(10), 1755–1772 (2010)
7. Gan, Z., He, J., Ding, Q., Varadharajan, V.: Trust relationship modelling in e-commerce-based social network. In: International Conference on Computational Intelligence and Security, Beijing, China, pp. 206–210 (2009)
8. McKnight, D.H., Chervany, N.L.: Conceptualizing Trust: A Typology and E-Commerce Customer Relationships Model. In: 34th Hawaii International Conference on System Sciences, Island of Maui, HI, USA (2001)
9. De Paoli, S., Gangadharan, G.R., Kerr, A., D'Andrea, V., Serrano, M., Botvich, D.: Toward trust as result: An interdisciplinary approach. Proceedings of ALPIS, Sprouts: Working Papers on Information Systems 10(8) (2010)
10. Akhoondi, M., Habibi, J., Sayyadi, M.: Towards a model for inferring trust in heterogeneous social networks. In: Second Asia International Conference on Modelling & Simulation, Kuala Lumpur, Malaysia, pp. 52–58 (2008)
11. Menkes, R.A.: An economic analysis of trust, social capital, and the legislation of trust. LLM Thesis, Ghent, Belgium (2007)
12. Guo, Q., Sun, D., Chang, G., Sun, L., Wang, X.: Modeling and evaluation of trust in cloud computing environments. In: 2011 3rd International Conference on Advanced Computer Control (ICACC), pp. 112–116 (2011)
13. Chaowen, C., Chen, L., Yuqiao, W.: A Subjective Trust Model based on two-dimensional measurement. In: International Conference on Computer Engineering and Technology, ICCET 2009, pp. 37–41 (2009)
14. Beth, T., Borcherding, M., Klein, B.: Valuation of trust in open networks. In: Gollmann, D. (ed.) ESORICS 1994. LNCS, vol. 875, pp. 3–18. Springer, Heidelberg (1994)
15. Jøsang, A.: An Algebra for Assessing Trust in Certification Chains. In: NDSS, 99, 6 (1999)

16. Jøsang, A., Ismail, R., Boyd, C.: A survey of trust and reputation systems for online service provision. Decision Support Systems 43(2), 618–644 (2007)
17. Kamvar, S.D., Schlosser, M.T., Garcia-Molina, H.: EigenRep: Reputation management in peer-to-peer networks. In: Proceedings of 12th International World Wide Web Conference, Budapest, Hungary (2003)
18. Ko, R.K., Jagadpramana, P., Mowbray, M., Pearson, S., Kirchberg, M., Liang, Q., Lee, B.S.: TrustCloud: A framework for accountability and trust in cloud computing. In: IEEE World Congress on Services (SERVICES), pp. 584–588 (2011)
19. Hwang, K., Kulkareni, S., Hu, Y.: Cloud security with virtualized defense and reputation-based trust mangement. In: Eighth IEEE International Conference on Dependable, Autonomic and Secure Computing, DASC 2009, pp. 717–722 (1999)
20. Alhamad, M., Dillon, T., Chang, E.: Conceptual SLA framework for cloud computing. In: 4th IEEE International Conference on Digital Ecosystems and Technologies (DEST), pp. 606–610 (2010)
21. Singh, S., Chand, D.: Trust evaluation in cloud based on friends and third party's recommendations. In: Recent Advances in Engineering and Computational Sciences (RAECS), pp. 1–6. IEEE (2014)

Fair-Trust Evaluation Approach (F-TEA) for Cloud Environment

Kandaswamy Gokulnath and V. Rhymend Uthariaraj

Anna University, Chennai, India

Abstract. The Main objective of the current work is to evaluate the trust of service provider in a fair manner. Fairness is introduced by considering the type of service(IaaS, PaaS and SaaS) accessed by the cloud user. While updating the trust value, the type of service accessed is not usually considered. Proposed approach identifies the type of service and updates the trust accordingly. In the literature several works exist for trust evaluation, but no attempt are made to evaluate trust in a fair manner. In this work,quantitative approaches are proposed to evaluate trust in a fair manner. Recursive nature of the proposed method restricts the time complexity to linear. Since cloud computing provides three types of services, it becomes vital to consider the type of service along with trust value. This enables the future users to access the precisely trusted providers according to their requirement. The dynamic nature of cloud computing challenges the trust evaluation by frequently changing the behavioral pattern. The quantitative metrics used in this work also addresses this problem. Simulation results showed good performance improvement over available methods towards QoS metrics.

1 Introduction

Cloud Computing defined by NIST in [14] as "Cloud computing is a model for enabling ubiquitous, convenient, on-demand network access to a shared pool of configurable computing resources (e.g., networks, servers, storage, applications, and services) that can be rapidly provisioned and released with minimal management effort or service provider interaction."

NIST in [14] also defines the characteristic, service models and deployment models of cloud computing. Inference from it yields abundant scope for security and trust. Since the service providers are not necessarily in the same premises(not even close in geography), believing the third party owned resources are unavoidable. This raises the notion of effective management of trust and security.Also, it is evident that cloud should be dynamic to cater the on-demand service provision. This dynamic nature of cloud enhances the complexity of the trust management. Normally, the trust management in distributed system is unease and dynamism of cloud environment makes trust management even complex.

Trust defined by [12] as entities level of assurance and dependence promised by it to behave all the time. Thus, trust is a continuous entity, since the level of trust of an entity continuously changes.

J. Lloret Mauri et al. (Eds.): SSCC 2014, CCIS 467, pp. 81–91, 2014.

Trust evaluation in literature shall be categorized as with and without prior experience. With prior experience is denoted by direct trust. Past transnational knowledge and its subsequent trust level obtained after evaluation shall be used to proceed current transaction. Without prior experience type of trust evaluation obtains the experience of other entities. Reputation of focused entity or recommendation of the particular entity shall be used for current transaction. Both the methods merits and demerits are discussed in the next section.

Cloud computing provides three types of services (IaaS, SaaS and PaaS). Hence, the user requirements vary form one service provider to another with respect to context. Thus, evaluation of trust unlike traditional method needs specificity towards context. This work deals with the fairness in evaluation of trust.

The organization of chapters in this article is as follows: Section 2 highlights the methods available in the literature for trust evaluation and their demerits. Section 3 discusses the proposed work The Fair Trust Evaluation Approach(F-TEA). Section 4 summaries the result obtained from simulation. Section 5 highlights the overview and achievement. Section 6 Concludes F-TEA and provides the future possible enhancements. References are quoted at the end.

2   Related Work

This section of work highlights some of the available work in the literature with their merits and demerits.

Direct method of trust evaluation was proposed by [6] considers past transaction experience. Computational complexity was better addresses by this approach because no external entities were involved. This method faces the problem when their is no direct encounters. There may be genuine resources which might not be encountered for past transactions. Thus, it fails to evaluate a may be genuine service provider. Space complexity increases as number of direct transaction entities are updated in the local storage.Similar kind of problem is faced by [11] [5] [20].

Recommendation based trust surveyed by [4] states, space complexity can be attenuated. This method aggregates the evaluated trust rate of the service providers from well known entities. Problem of communication cost gets involved when communicating with external entities. Since the scope of trust is relied upon an external entity, trustworthiness of the entity apart from the actual resource is to be evaluated by the system. Hence, a level of complexity is higher than the direct trust.

Agents based trust evaluation modeled by [18] based on Bayesian probability for generic distributed environment. These model designs the agents with more than one parameter for evaluation. Synonymous architecture was considered in this model, which makes a big set back of this model. Since the agents involved in any distributed environment may not be synonymous all the time. This method of trust evaluation comes under reputation based trust. EigenTrust based recommendation model was proposed by [11] and [20]. All the three approaches do not address the problem of fake recommendation and penalizing mechanisms were also not proposed.

Weight based feedback model was proposed by [24].According to this model, feedback from different agents had different level of weights. The same kind of model was extended by [23]. However both the models suffers computational and spacial overheads. On the other hand, [5] proposed a better solution, nevertheless lacks in space overhead.

SFTrust [25] proposed a service based weight assignment apart from feedback based model. Though it considers service type, it was still static. Hence, adapting the logic for dynamic environment like cloud is highly unachievable.

Almost all the models proposed in [6] [4] [11] [5] [20] [18] [23] [24] did not solve the problem of trust, and attenuation of trust over time. Attenuation factor of trust over a period of time was considered by [1]. It also considers various aspect of time related calculations for trust.

Cloud computing environment offers versatile service to diverse requirements of clients. Type of service accessed for evaluation of trust must be considered for fair evaluation. Different QoS metrics shall be requested by different type of clients.It was identified that the existing methods did not address the fairness factor for evaluating trust. Fairness among the service type oriented trust is mandatory for cloud computing environment. In this work a fairness approach is proposed, which considers the service type accessed by previous user. Thus, QoS specific trust shall be achieved.

3   Fair-Trust Evaluation Approach(F-TEA)

Prime focus of this work is to evaluate trust for cloud environment by considering the nature of service type preferred. Minimal parameters were considered for trust evaluation. This enables the performance improvement of evaluation approach with respect to time. The parameters discussed here are [25], [23], [5], [18], [20], [13], used for evaluation of trust without time consideration. The notion of time decay model introduced by [1] and also the recent values for evaluation. As stated earlier, trust is dynamic. Time is a key entity in identifying the trust rate metric. In this work, time is given a due attention as well as the service transacted earlier. A generic fair trust approach is proposed at last. Throughout the sections term **entity** will be used to represent the system providing cloud service.

3.1   Trust Value

Trust value denotes the assessed rate of trust for an entity on completion of a transaction.

$$T_V = \frac{t_v^{n-1} + t_v^n}{N} \tag{1}$$

$T_V \rightarrow$ Updated trust value

$t_v^{n-1} \rightarrow$ cumulative trust value upto previous $((n-1)^{th})$ transaction

$t_v^n \rightarrow$ trust value of latest (n^{th}) transaction.

$N \rightarrow$ total number of transactions.

Trust value for an entity shall be updated by the following range, as mentioned in [9].

$$t_v^n = \begin{cases} \geq 0.85, & \text{complete trust} \\ \in (0.7, 0.85), & \text{partial trust} \\ \in (0.55, 0.7), & \text{distrust} \\ \leq 0.55, & \text{complete distrust} \end{cases} \tag{2}$$

Here, percentage of promising level of entities are represented as probability values. "Promising" here denotes the degree of match between expectation to performance on completion of transaction. Entities with more than 85% promising level are considered as higher level trusted entities. Those falling between 70 to 85% level of promising considered to be modestly trusted. Lesser than 70% fails to gain the trust level and 55% lesser level are considered even distrusted.

3.2 Penalty Value

Penalizing is the process of subtracting the trust value of the entity by some degree with respect to error committed. Every transaction begins with Service Level Agreement(SLA) signed between the cloud user and cloud service provider. SLA carries the level of assurance by the service provider as the key component, δ value is used as the error tolerance, say, $\pm .01$.

If the transaction value does not fall within this limit, penalty will be applied over the overall trust value of that entity(service provider).

$$t_p = t_v^{n-1} - \frac{t_v^{n-1} - (1 - t_v^n)}{N} \tag{3}$$

Intention of penalty method is to penalize the erroneous entities, which do not perform to the level of promise.

3.3 Feedback Credibility

To assess the credibility of the parallel entities(peers), some level of quantification is mandatory. Also, it is necessary to filter the malicious entities. Following equation is used to estimate the credibility of the entities.

$$FC = \frac{\sum_{i=0}^{4} \sum_{j=1}^{m} t_v^{n-i}}{5} \tag{4}$$

where i $\rightarrow$ recent transactions,

j $\rightarrow$ entity number upto m.

if,

$$\tilde{FC} = \begin{cases} \frac{\sum_{i=0}^{4} \sum_{j=1}^{m} t_v^{n-i}}{5}, & \forall FC > 0.7 \\ 0, & \text{otherwise} \end{cases} \tag{5}$$

Feedback is the process of obtaining the trust value from external entities, if no direct transaction is available. Feedback is collected from those entities with estimated trust values with prior transactions. A minimum of 31 transactions are required to qualify any entity to be a feedback entity. 31 applied from generic Central Limit Theorem which states $n > 30$. Here, m entities are used to update the feedback with minimum of 31 transactions. As these 31 transactions are chosen to be recent updated trust value will be obtained. Thus, time sensitive trust values are reflected.

3.4   Direct Trust

Direct trust is a measure of trust rate from the committed past transactions by self entity. As in feedback, 31 transaction values are obtained to evaluate recent transaction updates. So the direct trust values are written as if,

$$\hat{(T_V)} = \frac{\sum_{i=0}^{4} \sum_{j=1}^{m} t_v^{n-i}}{5} > 0.7 \tag{6}$$

then,

$$DT_v = \frac{t_v^{n-1} + t_v^n}{N} \tag{7}$$

$$\implies DT_V = T_V$$

else,

$$d_{tp} = t_v^{n-1} - \frac{t_v^{n-1} - (1 - t_v^n)}{N} \tag{8}$$

3.5   Indirect Trust

Indirect trust obtains feedback from external entities and updates the trust value. As mentioned earlier minimum of 31 transactions are mandatory to evaluate the trust. Indirect trust is mentioned as,

$$ID_{TV} = \begin{cases} \frac{\sum_{i=1}^{31} \sum_{j=1}^{m} t_v^{n-i}}{M}, & \forall ID_{TV} > 0.7 \\ t_v^{n-1} - \frac{t_v^{n-1} - (1 - t_v^n)}{N}, & \text{otherwise} \end{cases} \tag{9}$$

In the above equation, feedback credibility is modified to 31 transactions and same m entities are preserved. This enables credible resources to take part in the feed back process.

3.6   Service Context

So far, existing approaches deals with the update of cumulative trust value as overall trust of any given entity. Here, in the current approach fairness factor is introduced by specifying the type of service accessed. Since, cloud computing uses three types of services(IaaS, PaaS and SaaS). To enable type of service requested by the cloud user, a set with three type of services used for evaluation. if IaaS is requested,

$$TC \in IS\hat{(TC)} = \begin{cases} T_V \, or \, ID_{TV}, \forall TC \in IS, \\ 0 \qquad \text{otherwise} \end{cases} \qquad (10)$$

Similarly for PaaS and SaaS.

3.7 Algorithm

Pseudo-code of the F-TEA is given in Algorithm 1,

Input: Entity(cloud service provider) n with previous one as $(n-1)$ with or with past history of transaction and cloud user.

Output: Evaluated trust value.

Algorithm 1. F-TEA

```
for each TC if service request == IaaS
If Prior relation exist
   for each n_i ∈ N
     If, TC ∈ IS
        trust ← D_TV
        compute D_TV
        If D_TV ≥ .70
          update D_TV
          else
             compute P_V^internal
          update D_TV
          else
          compute P_V^internal
          update D_TV
else,
   for each n_i ∈ N
       If, TC ∈ IS
       trust ← ID_TV
       compute ID_TV
       If ID_TV ≥ .70
          update ID_TV
          else
             compute P_V^internal
          update D_TV
             else
             compute P_V^internal
             update D_TV
             else
                return(0);
repeat TC for SaaS and PaaS.
```

---

4 Simulation Results

Cloudsim, a simulator for cloud environment, was used to test the performance of the proposed approach. Also, due comparison is made with the existing approaches like peertrust [24], ftrust [25], mastrsut. Configuration details of the simulation setup for the experiments has been tabulated in Table 1.

Table 1. Simulation Test-Bed

S.No	Entity	Quantity
1	Data Centre	1
2	Host	10
2	Virtual Machine	1200 per host
3	PE's	2-8 per vm
4	Job Length	50000
5	Application	Varying

Throughout the experiments conducted, it is assumed that initial trust over the past transactions are available. In the test-bed a single datacentre is designed to host ten host machines. Each host machines are assigned with a capacity of 100 virtual machines(vm's). Hence, a sum of 100000 vm's with cumulative 6000 processing elements were created. All other parameters were used as it is given in cloudsim.

4.1 Availability

For Experimental setup untrusted resources were created under simulational environment. Under following different conditions, a sum of 12000 virtual machines were tested against decreasing number of untrusted resources. Five instances are taken for consideration. In instance 1-2 2000 untrusted resources were deployed for IaaS. Results shows the number of trusted resources are higher within execution time(100msec) on comparison with other approaches. Instance 3-5 deployed with 1500 untrusted resources and identified with better performance as like previous instance.

4.2 Evaluation Overhead

Comparison of proposed work with other existing work over the time taken to evaluate in terms of milliseconds is shown in the below figure. An average of 10000 vm's (Min 8000 and Max 12000) were considered for execution time. All the vm's are tested with identical application with 50000 MI per sec. It is noted that the simulated results reads little overhead for F-Tea on comparison with other approaches. This is identified mainly because of the simple average method used for evaluation.

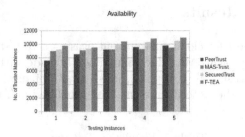

Fig. 1. Availability of Trusted Resources

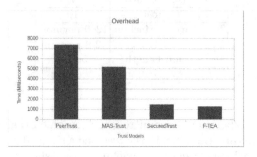

Fig. 2. Evaluation Time Comparison

4.3   Context Specificity

In the existing methods, trust was calculated against the cumulative past transaction behavior. Fairness is introduced in the current work by considering the type of service utilized in the past transaction. Context specificity was measured in a scale of 1-10 against the Infrastructure-as-a-service(IaaS). Different applications with same job length were given as input for all the methods. Inference of the study is highlighted in figure 3. Current method filters the type of service interacted from the past transaction. Also, because of this approach context specificity substantially increases.

4.4   Erroneous Identification

For experiment purpose, fixed number of malicious resources were created under simulation environment. Malicious resources were introduced by varying the number of vm's of a service provider. Here each type of service (IaaS, PaaS and SaaS) were assigned with 4000 vm's. While comparing the malicious resource identification with respect to overall performance, proposed work excels in constantly reducing the number of malicious entities. The below figure depicts the comparison.

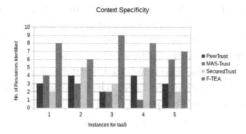

Fig. 3. Context Specific Trusted Resources

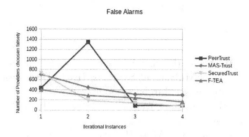

Fig. 4. False Resources identified as Genuine

5 Discussion

Throughout the work the term entity represents the cloud service provider. In this work a quantitative approach for trust evaluation together with service type request has been proposed. This work can also be extended for public, private and hybrid cloud environments.It can be extended for any kind of dynamic systems. It is designed for cloud computing, but any distributed environment can make use of this approach.

The proposed work is embedded together with time restricted evaluation. Hence, dynamic behavior of the malicious elements can be easily traced. Proposed work is simple, straight forward, and as portable as possible. Minimal computational time is involved in evaluating the trust.

Since, the recursive type of computation is used, time complexity is linear. Thus, avoids exponential complexity. Since simple averaging method is used, updating the trust value has less overhead. Also, misbehaving entities are penalized. Penalty levied is fair with respect to error.

6 Conclusion

In this work an attempt has been made to evaluate trust in a fair manner. Considering service type of the past transaction(s) helps to precisely evaluate the trust. Proposed expressions are estimating the genuine entities abiding the QoS parameters. It also shows some considerable performance improvement in identifying the service specific service provider. Penalizing the malicious entities ensures that trust value remains optimal. Penalizing can be further developed. Scope of this work could be extended to identify the trust at the beginning stage(boot-level) of the service provider. Also, the work could be tested with both the ends of the cloud environment (User and service provider).

Acknowledgments. Authors would like to thank Anna Centenary Research Fellowship(ACRF) for constant encouragement for this research by periodic stipend and contingency grants for years.

References

[1] Das, A., Islam, M.M.: SecuredTrust: A Dynamic Trust Computation Model for Secured Communication in Multiagent Systems. IEEE Transactions on Dependable and Secure Computing 9(2) (March/April 2012)

[2] Josang, A., Ismail, R.: The Beta Reputation System. In: 15th Bled E-Commerce Conference, Bled, Slovenia (June 2002)

[3] Bradai, A., Ben-Ameur, W., Afifi, H.: Byzantine Resistant Reputation-based Trust Management, pp. 269–278. IEEE conference Publications (October 2013)

[4] Govindan, K., Mohapatra, P.: Trust Computations and Trust Dynamics in Mobile Adhoc Networks: A Survey. IEEE Communications Surveys and Tutorials 14(2) (May 2011)

[5] Hu, J., Wu, Q., Zhou, B.: FCTrust: A Robust and Efficient Feedback Credibility-Based Distribution P2P Trust Model. In: Proc. IEEE Ninth Int'l Conf. Young Computer Scientist, pp. 1963–1968 (2008)

[6] Li, H., Singhal, M.: Trust in Distributed Systems. In: Network Security. IEEE Computer Society (February 2007)

[7] Huynh, T.D., Shadbolt, N.R., Jennings, N.R.: Developing an Integrated Trust and Reputation Model for Open Multi-Agent Systems. In: Proc. Seventh Int'l Workshop Trust in Agent Societies, pp. 65–74 (2004)

[8] Huynh, T.D., Jennings, N.R., Shadbolt, N.R.: An Integrated Trust and Reputation Model for Open Multi-Agent System. Autonomous Agents and Multi-Agent Systems 13(2), 119–154 (2006)

[9] Ishmanov, F., Kim, S.W.: A Secure Trust Establishment in Wireless Sensor Networks. In: 2011 International conference on Electrical Engineering and Informatics(ICEEI), pp. 1–6 (2011)

[10] Jennings, N.R., Huynh, T.D., Shadbolt, N.R.: FIRE: An Integrated Trust and Reputation Model for Open Multi-Agent Systems. In: Proc. 16th European Conf. Artificial Intelligence, pp. 18–22 (2004)

[11] Kamvar, S.D., Schlosser, M.T., Garcia-Molina, H.: The Eigen Trust Algorithm for Reputation Management in P2P Networks. In: Proc. 12th ACM Int'l World Wide Web Conf., pp. 640–651 (2003)

[12] Khan, K.M., Malluhi, Q.: Establishing Trust in Cloud Computing. IT Pro. (September/October 2010)

[13] Li, B., Xing, M., Zhu, J., Che, T.: A dynamic Trust Model for the Multi-agent Systems. In: Proc. IEEE Int'l Symp. Information Processing, pp. 500–504 (2008)

[14] Mell, P., Grance, T.: The NIST Definition of Cloud Computing, Special Publication 800-145 (September 2011)

[15] Sabater, J., Sierra, C.: REGRET: A Reputation Model for Gregarious Societies. In: Proc. Fourth Workshop Deception, Fraud and Trust in Agent Societies, pp. 61–69 (2001)

[16] Sabater, J., Sierra, C.: Social Regret, A Reputation Model Based on Social Relations. ACM SIGecom Exchanges - Chains of Commitment 3, 44–56 (2001)

[17] Sabater, J., Sierra, C.: Reputation and Social Network Analysis in Multi-Agent Systems. In: Proc. First Int'l Joint Conf. Autonomous Agents and Multi-Agent Systems, pp. 475–482 (2002)

[18] Wang, Y., Vassileva, J.: Bayseian Network-Based Trust Model. In: Proc. IEEE/WIC Int'l Conf. Web Intelligence, pp. 372–378 (October 2003)

[19] Wang, X., Wang, L.: P2P Recommendation Trust Model. In: Proc. IEEE Eighth Int'l Conf. Intelligent Systems Design and Applications, pp. 591–595 (2008)

[20] Wen, D., Huaimin, W., Yan, J., Peng, Z.: A Recommendation-Based Peer-to-Peer Trust Model. J. Software 15(4), 571–583 (2004)

[21] Wen, L., Lingdi, P., Kuijin, L., Xiaoping, C.: Trust Model of Users' Behavior in Trustworthy Internet. In: Proc. IEEE WASE Int'l Conf. Information Eng., pp. 403–406 (2009)

[22] Fan, W., Yang, S., Pei, J., Luo, H.: Building trust into cloud. International Journal of Cloud Computing and Services Science 1(3), 115–122 (2012)

[23] Xiong, L., Liu, L.: A Reputation-Based Trust Model for Peer-to-Peer Ecommerce Communities. In: Proc. Fourth ACM Conf. Electronic Commerce, pp. 228–229 (2003)

[24] Xiong, L., Li, L.: Peertrust: Supporting Reputation-Based Trust for Peer-to-Peer Electronic Communities. IEEE Trans. Knowledge and Data Eng. 16(7), 843–857 (2004)

[25] Zhang, Y., Chen, S., Yang, G.: SFTrust: A Double Trust Metric Based Trust Model in Unstructured P2P Systems. In: Proc. IEEE Int'l Symp. Parallel abd Distributed Processing, pp. 1–7 (2009)

Research on Access Control Techniques
in SaaS of Cloud Computing

Shabana Rehman[1] and Rahul Gautam[2]

[1] Department of Information System, Salman bin Abdul Aziz University,
Al-Kharj, KSA
shabana.infosec@gmail.com
[2] Department of Computer Science, Center of Development of Advanced Computing,
UP, India
rahulgautam9777@gmail.com

Abstract. Where the flexibility of Cloud Computing provides number of usage possibilities to the organizations, the security threats stop them in fully relying on it. Among all security threats, 'Unauthorized Access Threat' is one of the most important and difficult to manage. In SaaS, access control issues are of foremost concern. The aim of this paper is to explore the current trends that cloud providers are following in implementing access control measures in SaaS. In this article, a critical review of these measures is done and their advantages and drawbacks are discussed. On the basis of ongoing research, future research directions in the area of SaaS access control are also identified.

Keywords: Cloud Computing, SaaS, Access Control, Security, Research Directions.

1 Introduction

In information security, access control is considered as an essential and most important measure of information security assurance [1] and when it comes to cloud computing then it becomes more significant. Cloud Computing include different types of services e.g. SaaS (Software as a Service), PaaS (Platform as a service) and IaaS (Infrastructure as a Service). The National Institute of Standards and Technology [2] defines Software as a Service (SaaS) as *"The capability provided to the consumer to use the provider's applications running on a cloud infrastructure. The applications are accessible from various client devices through either a thin client interface, such as a web browser (e.g., web-based email), or a program interface."* The security issues related to each model is different. SaaS is considered as most vulnerable model of cloud computing, where security is of foremost concern. There is no doubt that access control is first step towards protection, therefore it become inevitable for the customers and CSP (Cloud Service Providers) to get well informed about best access control mechanism available and also their shortcomings. Now days, number of researchers are working in the direction of SaaS access control but still SaaS is vulnerable to many unauthorized

J. Lloret Mauri et al. (Eds.): SSCC 2014, CCIS 467, pp. 92–100, 2014.

access attacks. In this paper, access control measures related to SaaS model of Cloud Computing are covered along with vulnerabilities in these systems.

The rest of the paper is organized as follows: section 2 covers security threats and vulnerabilities in SaaS. Section 3 covers access control approaches in SaaS Model. In Section 4, SaaS Access Control software tools are presented and future directions are discussed in section 5. Conclusion is done in section 6.

2   Security Threats and Vulnerabilities

The dynamics of SaaS made security a challenging issue for security experts and CSP (Cloud Service providers). Unlike traditional systems, SaaS opens number of new surface areas for attacks. As the use of SaaS is increasing, experts are discovering new threats every day. SaaS threats can be originated by the provider as well as from SaaS architecture itself. As defined in [3,4,5] some of the common threats under "Originated by the provider" and "Originated from the SaaS architecture" categories are as follows:

Table 1. Threats of SaaS

S. No.	Originated by the Provider	S. No.	Originated from the SaaS Architecture
T1	Customer data violation by provider	T6	Manipulation of shared resources
T2	Unreliable computation by customer	T7	Network access threats
T3	Misbehavior hiding by customer	T8	Authentication threat
T4	Customer Data Disclosure by Provider	T9	Bad subcontractors
T5	Secondary Use	T10	Insecure or incomplete data deletion

The threats are the result of vulnerabilities in the system. Vulnerability is the probability that an asset will be unable to resist the actions of a threat agent [6]. There are number of databases that provide software vulnerabilities information. One such database is NVD (National Vulnerability Database) [7]. Before adapting proper security measures, security team has to search their software specific vulnerabilites available in various online databases. Once vulnerabilities are identified, SaaS specific threats can be classified under each category. One vulnerabilty can results in multiple threats. Common SaaS security vulnerability classes as identified in [8, 9, 10, 11] are shown in Table 2. Example of each type of vulnerability from NVD and severity is also shown in the table. Threats corresponding to each vulnerability class are shown in the last column of the table. As it can be seen, most of the vulnerabilities are related to the access control procedure of the software. To fight with these Access control issues there is an urgent need of new and improved access models and procedures that can be applied in cloud computing. Numbers of researchers are working in this direction and in the next section; we have covered a survey of most recent SaaS access control models and procedures.

Table 2. SaaS Security Vulneabilties with Correcponding Threats

S. No.	Vulnerability	Example from NVD	Severity (out of 10)	Correcpond ing Threats
V1	UNAUTHORIZED ACCESS TO INTERFACE	CVE-2013-4615	5.0	T1, T2, T7, T8, T10
V2	INTERNET PROTOCOL VULNERABILITIES	CVE-2013-1194	5.0	T7, T8
V3	DATA RECOVERY VULNERABILITY	CVE-2010-3061	5.0	T4, T5, T10
V4	SOFTWRAE LEVEL INJECTION	CVE-2014-2245	6.0	T2, T7, T8
V5	OS LEVEL INJECTION	CVE-2012-0175	9.5	T7, T8
V6	WEAK AUTHENTICATION SCHEMES	CVE-2013-6439	9.5	T8
V7	COOKIE VULNERABILITY	CVE-2014-1257	3.6	T7
V8	PATH TRAVERSAL	CVE-2013-6304	4.0	T7
V9	HYPERVISOR VULNERABILITIES	CVE-2014-1642	4.4	T7, T8
V10	INADEQUATE OR MISCONFIGURED FILTERING RESOURCES	CVE-2013-2400	5.8	T6, T10
V11	IMPROPER AUDIT AND LOGGING	CVE-2014-1948	2.6	T3, T5, T9

3   Access Control Approaches in SaaS Model

National Institute of Standard and Technology [12] defines access control as *"Access is the ability to do something with a computer resource (e.g., use, change, or view). Access control is the means by which the ability is explicitly enabled or restricted in some way (usually through physical and system-based controls)."* There are three basic forms of access control models: Discretionary Access Control, Mandatory Access Control, and Role Based Access Control. Among these, (RBCA) Role Based Access Control is most efficient and common these days as it establishes the relationship between users and their responsibility [13]. As SaaS is different from traditional software systems, current access control measures cannot be applied directly to cloud computing. According to Dancheng Li et al. [14], applying them directly can lead to following problems:

(a) Role name conflicts
(b) Cross-level management
(c) Isomerism of tenants' access control and
(d) Temporal delegation constraints.

To avoid these problems Dancheng Li et al. [14] proposed 'H-RBAC MODEL'. In their model, they divided the access control system into two parts, one is tenant level access control and other is system level access control. Where tenant-level part is origination-based, system-level is administrative role-based. Their model is basically based on classical ARBAC97 [15]. The advantages of this model includes good scalability, simplicity, flexibility, self-governance within tenant but more work still need to be done in optimization of efficiency of the model, as the permission assignment is a frequent process in SaaS. A similar work was also reported in [16] where they proposed S-RBAC (SaaS-Role Based Access Control). P-RBAC (Privacy-Role Based Access Control) proposed by Qun Ni and Elisa Bertino [17] is another promising research work that can be applied in SaaS. In P-RBAC another component is added in RBAC that takes care of privacy related information. In [18], author proposed 'Break The Glass' approach in RBAC (BTG-RBAC) that is used to control the service to the denied users. In this concept, the users, that are normally denied access, are allowed to access the resource in case of emergency. This concept is applied in SaaS by Rajesh. K et al. [19]. They presented the modified BTG-RBAC model for SaaS framework in which flexibility is provided to the SaaS users in case of emergency without compromising security. The measurement of resource utilization during the denied service use is a proposed future work by the authors.

SaaS security also depends on the security of APIs. In computer programming, an APIs application programming interface specifies how some software components should interact with each other. Sirisha et al. [20] proposed access control mechanism based on RBAC that provide two stage access control mechanism. Another extension of RBAC is 'Contract RBAC' model that is used to manage Intra-cross cloud service and Inter-cross cloud service. The model is proposed by Chen et al.(2013) [21] in which they compared their model with similar traditional models and found their model to be more effective than others in cloud management. Model also provides flexibility to the users to choose service from existing CSP (cloud provider) or to switch to different CSP. Proposed by Cao et al.(2013) [22], T_ARBAC (Tenant-Administrative Role Based Access Control) is another recent approach in the field of SaaS access control measures.

In cloud computing, many new techniques and paradigm are emerging day by day, one such relatively new paradigm is verifiable computing. In verifiable computing, relatively weak computational power computer, transfer its load to computationally powerful computer and powerful computer return the result with the proof that computation is correct. Due to the transmission of data form one computer to another, access control plays a very important role in this process. Xu et al. (2013) [23] proposed *verifiable computation with access control* (AC-VC) process in which, process of transferring the data from weak computer to outsourced powerful computer is controlled by proper access rights. They also formalize the notion of AC-VC and presents formal security definition.

Lots of research work is also taking place on access control of encrypted data stored on the outsourced cloud. Some of the prominent research work includes [24, 25, 26, 27]. Recently Wan et al. [27] proposed hierarchical attribute-set-based encryption (HASBE) in which they extended cipher text-policy attribute-set-based encryption (ASBE). They also formally proved that their scheme is based on the security of cipher text-policy attribute-based encryption (CP-ABE) by Bethencourt [24].

In the field of SaaS access control policies, Choi et al. [28] presented Onto-ACM (ontology-based access control model). In their model they used ontology reasoning and semantic analysis method for access control between the CSP (Cloud Service Provider) and the user. Onto-ACM, uses Jena inference engine for interfaces and SPARQL for query processing. The main advantage of the model is the convenience in the policy management. Oblivious access control policy evaluation (O-ACE) is another approach in policy management by Pervez et al. [29]. In their method, O-ACE evaluates the access control policy by not exposing any useful information to CSP (Cloud Server Provider) or users. Some notable access control approaches based on signature includes 'Slight Homomorphic Signature' by Wang et al. [30], and Software Service Signature (S3) by Xu et al. [31].

4   SaaS Access Control Software Tools

As researchers are developing new techniques and procedures for SaaS access control, numbers of software companies have been using these techniques to produce software tools. Now days there are large number of access control tool that are specially prepared after keeping in mind the security requirements of SaaS. Some of the prominent and popular tools are shown in Table 3. The sole purpose of mentioning these tools here is to provide some idea of SaaS access control tools to the readers. The authors do not recommend or advertise any of the mentioned tools.

Table 3. SaaS Access Control Tools

S. No	Software	Company
1.	Intel Expressway Cloud Access 360	L&T Infotech[32]
2.	Visual Guard	Novalys [33]
3.	Web Based (SaaS) IP access control	Double Vision Group Inc[34]
4.	SaaS-based Access Control Solutions	DORMA and Brivo [35]
5.	SaaS Security: Cloud Access Control	Safenet[36]
6.	Cisco Software-as-a-Service (SaaS) Access Control	Cisco [37]

The first tool i.e. 'Intel Expressway Cloud Access 360' is a software tool that is designed by L&T Infotech [32] to control the access control in cloud computing (specifically for SaaS Model). Visual Guardis another useful software tool for cloud service provider. It is developed by Novalys and its solution covers application security requirements and Access Management Solutions for SaaS. It has been initially developed in 1995 for a major European Banking Group. Now it is a tool that covers most of the security needs of cloud Provider [33]. Similarly Web Based (SaaS) IP access control, SaaS-based Access Control Solutions, SaaS Security: Cloud Access Control and Cisco Software-as-a-Service (SaaS) Access Control are the tools that are popular in the market for providing SaaS access control.

5   Research Directions in SaaS Access Control

After a thorough review of various access control techniques for SaaS, numbers of new directions are identified. Following is list of areas in which research is going on and need further investigations:

1. Access Control Models for SaaS
2. Signature based Access Control in SaaS
3. Access control Management in SaaS
4. Encryption of Access Control Data in SaaS
5. Access Control Policies in SaaS
6. Access control in Verifiable computing
7. Access Control Framework in SaaS
8. Software Tools for Access Control in SaaS

Figure 1 is showing the various research directions with the example of the research work that is already carried out. Detail of the example work is covered in section 4.

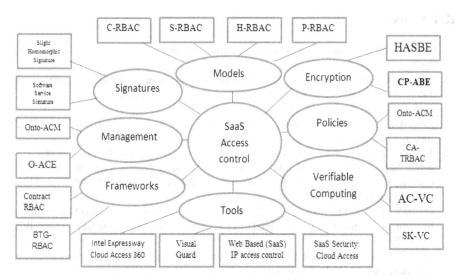

Fig. 1. SaaS Access Control Research Directions

Among all the access control models, RBAC is found to be most suitable for SaaS but with some modifications. In H-RBAC [Li, 2011], as a future work, authors suggest the integration of security in the early phase of the design itself, rather than incorporating it later. They also suggest efficiency measurement of H-RBAC as another future direction. P-RBAC authors [Ni, 2010] suggests that closing the gap between high-level policy and low-level policy is one of the immediate work that can be done by applying new types of policy elements, policy visualization techniques to better understand complex policy sets etc. Researchers of 'BTG-RBAC' [Rajesh, 2012] suggests, computing resource utilization and measurement during the access of denied service, as one of the future works.

6   Conclusion

There is no doubt that without effective access control measures; the benefits of SaaS technology cannot be derived. This paper is an approach to identify latest techniques and tools in the field of SaaS access control so that user or CSP can derive maximum benefit from SaaS. In this paper, first threats and vulnerabilities related to SaaS are identified then exhausted research is conducted on various tools, techniques, models etc. of access control procedures that can be used in the SaaS model of cloud computing. Although a good amount of research is already done in this area, still there is need of more accurate and efficient methods. After thorough review, it is discovered that RABC is the most prominent model of access control in SaaS and number of variants are emerging based on this model e.g. C-RBAC, P-RBAC, H-RBAC. In the last section numbers of future directions are also proposed for the researchers who want to peruse their research in this field.

References

1. Benantar, M.: Access Control Systems: Security, Identity, Management and Trust Models. Springer US (2009)
2. Mell, P., Grance, T.: The NIST Definition of Cloud Computing. Special Publication 800-145 (2011), http://csrc.nist.gov/publications/nistpubs/800-145/SP800-145.pdf
3. DORMA: Brivo to Introduce SaaS-Based Access Control Solution at ISC West (2012), http://www.securitysales.com/article/dorma-brivo-to-introduce-saas-based-access-control-solution-at-isc-west
4. Aime, M.D., Lioy, A., Pomi, P.C., Vallini, M.: Security Plans for SaaS. In: Agrawal, D., Candan, K.S., Li, W.-S. (eds.) Information and Software as Services. LNBIP, vol. 74, pp. 81–111. Springer, Heidelberg (2011)
5. Chou, Y., Levina, O., Oetting, J.: Enforcing Confidentiality in a SaaS Cloud Environment. In: 19th Telecommunications forum TELFOR, Serbia, Belgrade, November 22-24. IEEE Press (2011)
6. Risk Taxonomy, Technical Standard (2009), http://pubs.opengroup.org/onlinepubs/9699919899/toc.pdf
7. National Vulnerability Database (2014), http://nvd.nist.gov/
8. Grobauer, B., Walloschek, T., Stöcker, E.: Understanding Cloud Computing Vulnerabilities. Co-published by the IEEE computer and reliability societies (2011)
9. Wang, H., Liu, F., Liu, H.: A Method of the Cloud Computing Security Management Risk Assessment. In: Zeng, D. (ed.) Advances in Computer Science and Engineering. AISC, vol. 141, pp. 609–618. Springer, Heidelberg (2012)
10. Ganesan, R., Sarkar, S., Tewari, N.: An Independent Verification of Errors and Vulnerabilities in SaaS Cloud. In: 42nd International Conference on Dependable Systems and Networks Workshops (DSN-W). IEEE Press (2012)
11. Rehman, S., Mustafa, K.: Software Design Level Vulnerabilities Classification Model. International Journal of Computer Science and Security 6(4), 238–255 (2012)
12. National Institute of Standard and Technology/Information Technology Laboratory (NIST/ITL) Bulletin (December 1995), http://csrc.nist.gov/groups/SNS/rbac/documents/design_implementation/Intro_role_based_access.htm (retrieved on May 2014)
13. Demin, F., Xiaoming, W., Zongtao, Z.: An Expanded Role-Based Access Control Model. Computer Engineering and Applications (2003)

14. Li, D., Liu, C., Liu, B.: H-RBAC: A Hierarchical Access Control Model for SaaS Systems. I. J. Modern Education and Computer Science 5 (2011), http://www.mecs-press.org/
15. Sandhu, R., Bhamidipati, V., Munawer, Q.: The ARBAC97 Model for Role-Based Administration of Roles. ACM Transactions on Information and System Security (TISSEC) 2, 105–135 (1999)
16. Li, D., Liu, C., Wei, Q., Liu, Z., Liu, B.: RBAC-based Access Control for SaaS Systems. In: IEEE 2nd International Conference on Information Engineering and Computer Science, ICIECS (2010)
17. Ni, Q., Bertino, E.: Privacy-Aware Role-Based Access Control. ACM Transactions on Information and System Security 13(3), Article 24 (2010)
18. Ferreira, A., Chilro, D., Antunes, L.: How to Securely Break into RBAC: The BTG-RBAC Model. In: Proceedings of 25th Annual Computer Security Applications Conference, Honolulu, Hawaii (2009)
19. Rajesh, K., Nayak, A.: Modified BTG-RBAC Modelf or SaaS. In: Proceedings of International Conference on Cloud Computing, Technologies, Applications & Management (2012)
20. Sirisha, A., Kumari, G.: API Access Control in Cloud Using the Role Based Access Control Model. In: Trendz in Information Sciences & Computing, TISC (2010)
21. Chung, H., Chen, J., Violetta, M.A., Yang, C.Y.: Contract RBAC in cloud computing. Springer Science Business Media, New York (2013)
22. Cao, J., Li, P., Zhu, Q., Qian, P.: A Tenant-Based Access Control Model T-Arbac. Computer Science and Application (2013), http://www.hanspub.org/journal/csa.html
23. Xu, L., Tang, S.: Verifiable computation with access control in cloud Computing. Springer Science+Business Media, New York (2013)
24. Bethencourt, J., Sahai, A., Waters, B.: Ciphertext-policy attribute based encryption. In: Proc. IEEE Symp. Security and Privacy, Oakland, CA (2007)
25. Wang, G., Liu, Q., Wu, J.: Hierarchical attribute-based encryption for fine-grained access control in cloud storage services. In: Proc. ACM Conf. Computer and Communications Security (ACM CCS), Chicago, IL (2010)
26. Yu, S., Wang, C., Ren, K., Lou, W.: Achieving Secure, Scalable, and Fine-grained Data Access Control in Cloud Computing. In: IEEE INFOCOM (2010)
27. Wan, Z., Liu, J., Deng, R.H.: HASBE: A Hierarchical Attribute-Based Solution for Flexible and Scalable Access Control in Cloud Computing. IEEE Transactions on Information Forensics and Security 7(2) (2012)
28. Choi, C., Choi, J., Kim, P.: Ontology-based access control model for security policy reasoning in cloud computing. Springer Science+Business Media, New York (2013)
29. Pervez, Z., Khattak, A.M., Lee, S., Lee, Y., Huh, E.: Oblivious access control policies for cloud based data sharing systems. Springer (2012)
30. Wang, Z., Sha, K., Lv, W.: Slight Homomorphic Signature for Access Controlling in Cloud Computing. Springer Science+Business Media, New York (2013)
31. Xu, L., Cao, X., Zhang, Y., Wu, W.: Software Service Signature (S3) for authentication in cloud Computing. Springer Science+Business Media, New York (2013)
32. L&T Infotech: Selected to drive Cloud access security software to market. Express Computers (May 15, 2011), http://go.galegroup.com/ps/i.do?id=GALE%7CA257405511&v=2.1&u=sdl&it=r&p=CDB&sw=w&asid=b7f8961ca216c99 7f7384bc9c9c8c5f5

33. Visual-Gurad (2014), `http://www.visual-guard.com/EN/net-powerbuilder-application-security-authentication-permission-access-control-rbac-articles`
34. Double Vision (2014), `http://www.doublevision.ca/access-control-systems.html`
35. Dorma (2012), `http://www.prweb.com/releases/2012/2/prweb9225731.htm`
36. Safenet (2014), `http://www.safenet-inc.com/data-protection/virtualization-cloud-security/saas-security-cloud-access-control/`
37. Cisco (2014), `http://www.cisco.com/c/en/us/products/collateral/security/anyconnect-secure-mobility-client/white_paper_c11-596141.html`

Tag Digit Based Honeypot to Detect Shoulder Surfing Attack

Nilesh Chakraborty and Samrat Mondal

Computer Science and Engineering Department,
Indian Institute of Technology Patna,
Patna-800013, Bihar, India
{nilesh.pcs13,samrat}@iitp.ac.in

Abstract. Traditional password based authentication scheme is vulnerable to shoulder surfing attack. So if an attacker sees a legitimate user to enter password then it is possible for the attacker to use that credentials later to illegally login into the system and may do some malicious activities. Many methodologies exist to prevent such attack. These methods are either partially observable or fully observable to the attacker. In this paper we have focused on detection of shoulder surfing attack rather than prevention. We have introduced the concept of tag digit to create a trap known as honeypot. Using the proposed methodology if the shoulder surfers try to login using others' credentials then there is a high chance that they will be caught red handed. Comparative analysis shows that unlike the existing preventive schemes, the proposed methodology does not require much computation from users end. Thus from security and usability perspective the proposed scheme is quite robust and powerful.

Keywords: Authentication, Shoulder Surfing Attack, Honeypot, Partially Observable Scheme.

1 Introduction

In a bank ATM system password or PIN is a commonly used authentication scheme. Although it is a popular scheme but is vulnerable to shoulder surfing attack. In this, an attacker may obtain the login credentials just by observations of single or multiple login sessions. In this context, two well known types are *partially observable* [4] scheme and *fully observable* [17] scheme. In the first one attacker can partially observe the login session and in the later case everything of the login session can be observed by the attacker. Thus providing schemes which will resist fully observable shoulder surfing attack is really very challenging.

Now depending upon the security and skill level, the shoulder surfing attack can be further classified in two types– *Strong and Weak*. In strong shoulder surfing attack, the attacker has the highest level of cognitive skills and can use the smart gadgets like camera to record the multiple login sessions. Such schemes assume that multiple sessions can be observed by the attacker. Few recent schemes to avoid such attack are SLASS [4], ColorPass[3]. Another variant

J. Lloret Mauri et al. (Eds.): SSCC 2014, CCIS 467, pp. 101–110, 2014.

is known as *Weak Shoulder Surfing Attack* [11]. In this case, attacker is assumed to have limited cognitive skills and generally observes a single login session to get to know the password [11].

As password or PIN based authentication is a common choice for ATM card system, so shoulder surfing attack has become a major concern in many banking applications. Few years back it has been reported [5] that $217,000 has been stolen from *Long Island* banks of USA using the clone ATM cards from April to May 2010. Last year report [13] shows a very high existence of shoulder surfers in UK as cash-machine fraud was on the rise. Fig. 1 shows the evidences of the clone ATM cards found and how the number increased during first four months of a year in UK [13]. The clone ATM cards only come into play once the attacker gets to know the user's original PIN by performing shoulder surfing attack. Thus handling such attack has become a major objective for banking system.

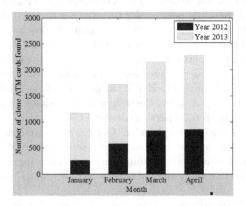

Fig. 1. ATM Card Fraud Jan-April 2012/13: Courtesy Sky News

Along with providing the necessary security, user friendliness is another important aspect that must be considered carefully in developing an authentication scheme. If a login scheme requires too much computation from users end then it will not be very useful as it may lead to more unsuccessful login attempt. But to prevent fully observable attack or strong shoulder surfing attack the schemes may require to include some computations that users have to perform. Thus those schemes may not be much applicable in a public domain. Thus a trade-off is required between the level of security and the level of usability. This makes defense against the shoulder surfing attack to be very challenging problem.

So far most of the work concentrate on prevention of shoulder surfing attack. But in this paper, we have focused on detection of shoulder surfing attack and take appropriate measure once it is detected. We have proposed a *honeypot* or a trap for shoulder surfers. The honeypot is developed using a concept of *tag digit* which is introduced in this paper. Compared to prevention schemes, the proposed detection scheme requires less effort from user end and can be implemented on top of the conventional PIN based ATM systems. The rest of the paper is organized as follows. In Section 2 a survey on the existing work is made. Section 3 describes our proposed methodology in details. The security and usability analysis are performed in Section 4 and Section 5 respectively. The conclusion and future work is provided in Section 6.

2   Related Work

Since 2002 researchers have focused to design scheme to resist shoulder surfing attack as International Standard for PIN management mandates the fact that PIN entered by the customer should be prevented from the observation attack [1] in public domain. One of the oldest (*Mod10*) methodology to prevent shoulder surfing attack proposed in 1998 [16] where user has to perform mathematical Mod operation while login. The complex nature of the proposed scheme has been simplified by Perkovic et.al. in the year of 2010 when he proposed *STL* method and reduces the error rate during login. Some partially observable login mechanisms like SLASS [4], ColorPass [3] were proposed to reduce error rate further. However, they still put some cognitive overheads on users. Methodologies implemented in fully observable environment demand even more complex cognitive operations from user end which is proven by Hopper and Blum [7] in 2001. Thus fully observable methodologies are more error prone with high login duration. For example, in S3PAS scheme [17] user needs to find 3 randomly scattered characters from a set of 94 characters and make a virtual triangle while login at each round. This kind of authentication procedures requires high cognitive skill of users and make the scheme almost impossible to be used by novice users. The other drawbacks of these schemes are long enough password to be remembered by user [12], many number of login rounds [11] [15] in a session etc.

To design an effective scheme against shoulder surfing attack which will reduce human cognitive effort to a great extend, we have focussed on detection technique rather than prevention technique. Recently Jules and Rivest [9] proposed a detection technique on password file maintained by the system . One of the closely related work prior to [9] was proposed by Bojinov et al. [2]. But the concept of *honey server* was missing in this work which slightly relaxes the security aspect of the detection mechanism. Genc et al. [6] proposed a direction driven approach which the authors claimed that it would improve the model proposed by Jules and Rivest [9]. The concept of honeyword has also been deployed in terms of password encryption of low entropy based password [8]. But detection of shoulder surfing attack using honeyword is absolutely new to the best of our knowledge and can be used by novice user with ease.

3   Proposed Methodology

The proposed methodology is based on *partially observable attack* model. So some part of login process will not be accessible to the attacker. The objective here is to detect the shoulder surfers. So we will assume that attacker already has some information about the user's password. Now using the proposed methodology the attacker may be identified as shoulder surfers not the genuine users. To achieve this we will create a honeypot consisting of some honeywords as described in the next subsection.

3.1 Overview of Honeypot and Honeyword

In general *honeypot* is used to refer to a trap. In this case we will create a honeypot which can be considered as a set of passwords. These are known as honeywords. Thus for a particular user, the system maintains a set of passwords which consists of the original one and some system generated passwords. Now the system generated passwords may be different [9] or may be very similar (proposed in this paper) to the original one but they are not exactly the same as the original one. Thus *honeyword* is nothing but the incorrect password that are attached with the user original password to fox the attacker. Suppose a user is u_i and his corresponding password is stored at the kth index position along with the honeywords. The original password of the user stored at k^{th} index position is denoted by P_{ik} and to confuse the attackers, another different $j-1$ numbers of passwords are stored in the system database along with P_{ik}. So for user u_i the following details are maintained.

$$u_i \implies P_{i1}, P_{i2}, ..., P_{ik}, ...P_{ij}$$

Now index position of original password (here k) is kept secret by the system by storing it in relatively higher secured place.

3.2 Tag Digit

In our proposed approach user remembers a five digit number as his PIN. Each digit can take values from $0...9$. During the creation of PIN user will also select an index position. Based on this we introduce the notion of tag digit. This is defined as below.

Definition 1. *Tag Digit: It corresponds to the PIN digit of the index position selected by the user during PIN creation.*

Our honeypot is defined on the basis this tag digit. For an example, user chosen PIN is 24632 and the index position selected by the user is 3. So the tag digit becomes 6. Thus user must remember this position in addition to the original PIN. Now the honeypot is created assuming that each index position can be a potential PIN. This is shown in Fig 2. The possible tag digits are encircled in the Figure. So in this case the third one is the correct PIN and others are used as honeywords. Attacker gets trapped if he enters any of the honeywords stored by the system.

②4632   2④632   24⑥32   246③2   2463②

Fig. 2. Virtual view of honeypot against Shoulder Surfing attack

3.3 Login Process

Our system is a partially observable system and at least one component of the login session should not be accessible to the attacker. For login sessions some challenges will appear to user and that is assumed to be secured. The challenges will be generated by the system and it will be available to the user though some audio system like ear phone which only user can listen.

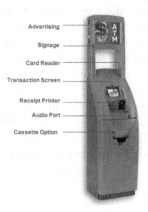

Fig. 3. Different parts of ATM machine

In modern ATM systems there is a provision of plug in the audio device. Fig. 3, shows the external parts of an ATM machine, in which there exists an *Audio Port* which can be used to listen to the challenge values by plug in an ear phone (cost of which is very much affordable). Thus our proposed methodology will work on existing ATM systems without any significant additional changes.

User chosen PIN is of length five. So for each digit there is a corresponding round. In each round user needs to enter one of the PIN digit, for example, user will enter his first PIN digit in the first round, second digit in the second round and so on. Now in each round user will get two audio challenges − "tag" and "not tag". The challenges will come with a gap of 3 seconds. User will enter his tag digit after listening to challenge "tag" and rest of the digits will be entered after listening to challenge "not tag".

After the second challenge comes, system will be waiting for the response from the user, this is because user will definitely response with either of the challenge value during a round, now if user does not response after listening to the first challenge in a round then it is obvious that user will response with the second challenge in that round. But waiting time by the system will definitely not exceed to the maximum session round time limit.

Appearance of the challenge values should always be in a way so that attacker does not able to guess the challenges. For example, if in each round challenge "not tag" always follows challenge "tag" then by analyzing the time taken to enter the response by a user, attacker can easily guess the user's tag digit. Thus the order of challenge "tag" and "not tag" will randomly vary for each round. This will also help in avoiding side channel attack [10].

3.4   Login Example

Now let's consider our earlier example i.e. the PIN is 24632 and the index position is 3. So the tag digit becomes 6. Now for the first round user will enter the digit 2 in response of the challenge "not tag". Similarly for second, fourth and fifth rounds also user will enter the digits in response of "not tag" challenge. Only in third round user will enter the digit in response of "tag" challenge.

If system finds that all the digits entered by a user are correct but user has not identified the tag digit properly then system will detect *shoulder surfing attack*. In Table 1 we have shown responses during a session by a user. The random sequence has been maintained by the machine for throwing the challenges in a round. In Table 1 first column corresponds with the round number during a session, *PD* signifies PIN Digit of user, *FC* and *SC* corresponds to first and second challenge during a round respectively and *RA* denotes the challenge after which user gave his response. The response time taken by user has been shown as *RT* column.

Table 1. Response during a session with tag digit 6

Round	PD	FC	SC	RA	RT (sec)
1	2	tag	not tag	not tag	4
2	4	tag	not tag	not tag	4
3	6	not tag	tag	tag	4
4	3	not tag	tag	not tag	2
5	2	not tag	tag	not tag	2

First row of the above table signifies that in round 1 user enters digit 2 after listening to the challenge "not tag" which comes after challenge "tag" and in that round, the response time of user was approximately 4 sec. As there is a 3 sec pause between first and second challenge and user enters the response after listening to the second challenge so the response time has been increased. But as attacker can not listen to the challenges (as they are coming through some secured media) and challenges are generated in random order so attacker will not be able to know after listening to which challenge user has given his response and thus information regarding tag digit will remain hidden from the attacker.

4 Security Analysis

In this section we will measure robustness of our methodology against password guessing and shoulder surfing attack from probabilistic point of view. Suppose A is the event corresponds to guessing actual password of the user and B is the event corresponding to guessing the position of the tag digit. One thing can be noticed here, as event A corresponds to knowing the password, so if any one knows the password then he knows all the digits chosen by the user along with the position of the tag digit. Position of tag digit is having impact on the password from structural point of view. Because while entering the password user needs to enter the tag digit information. So if an attacker knows the position of the tag digit then it will increase the probability against password guessing attack. So we can write the following probabilities :

- $P(A) = 1/(10^5 \times 5)$, as attacker needs to guess five digits along with the position of tag digit
- $P(B) = 1/5$, needs to choose the correct position of the tag digit from five possible options
- $P(A|B) = P(A \cap B)/P(B) = 1/10^5$

So remembering the tag digit strengthens the security of password against guessing attack by a factor of $1/5$. Tag digit has created a honeypot of cardinality 5 for attacker. Guessing the password digits correctly but not the position of the tag digit will detect shoulder surfing attack. As shoulder surfers have to guess (one) user original password from the *honeypot* having five (options of) passwords so detection chance of shoulder surfing attack is 80%, if attacker knows the digits in user password without knowing the position of the tag digit. Compared to the conventional four digit PIN, we have increased the PIN length by one. If conventional four digit long PIN is used then cardinality of honeypot becomes 4 instead of 5. So adding one extra digit increases chances of detecting shoulder surfing attack without putting any significant overhead to the user.

$$⑧8888 \quad 8⑧888 \quad 88⑧88 \quad 888⑧8 \quad 8888⑧$$

Fig. 4. Creating *honeypot* when all digits are same in user PIN

Few important notes regarding our proposed scheme for creating honeypot:

- Attacker only sees digits entered by the user, but tag digit information remains hidden to the attacker. This secret tag digit information creates honeypot for the attacker.
- If all the digits chosen by customer are same then also *honeypot* can be created depending upon the position of the tag digit. The reason is that the position of the tag digit plays a significant role for creating *honeypot*. Fig.4 shows that how *honeypot* can be created even if user chooses all the digits same in his PIN.

– Sometime the genuine users might give his tag digit information wrongly by mistake. In that case system will consider genuine user as an attacker. This type of situation is termed as *false detection of shoulder surfing* or *fdss*.

The above discussion shows shoulder surfing detection technique can be advantageous in many ways for providing security but user should be careful to avoid *fdss* while login.

5   Usability Analysis and System Evaluation

In this section we will discuss about different usability aspects related to registration process, login process etc.

Our methodology will fail if the information of the tag digit is available to the attacker. The tag digit is decided during the registration process only. So we assumed that during the registration process shoulder surfing is not allowed. To achieve this, registration may be done using a private system. If we use the conventional public system or ATM system then there is always a chance of shoulder surfing and hence we need to avoid that.

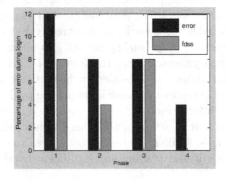

Fig. 5. Percentage of error and false detection of shoulder surfing during login

To check how our methodology works in public domain we have taken help from 25 people to login using our methodology. First we give them how our system works and also share the motivation behind the proposed work. We encourage them to give some trials after we demonstrated the login procedure in front of them. The workstation that we have used to conduct the experiment had 4 GB RAM, i3 core processor and processing speed of 2.4 GHz.

We conducted our experiment in four phases to analyze the login time and the percentage of error during login. In each phase all 25 users login with their corresponding PIN and tag digit. We have found that average time taken by the user to login is around 16 seconds and the error rate is significantly low. With every phase the users get habituated with the system and that result in reducing the error rate. In Fig 5, we have shown the login *error rate* vs *fdss rate*.

Table 2. A comparative analysis of error rate during login

	Mod10	STL	SLASS	THS
Max % of Error	18	18	16	12
Min % of Error	12	6	7	4
Trials	30	30	12	4

Here error refers to the unsuccessful login attempt using wrong PIN digit and *fdss* refers to unsuccessful login attempt using wrong tag digit. Fig. 5 shows that least login error is 4% in phase 4 and that of overall login error is 8%, considering all the phases.

We have also performed a comparative analysis of our proposed scheme with some of the existing shoulder surfing resilient schemes in terms of error rate during login. We have chosen three login methodologies − Mod10 [16], STL [14] and SLASS [4], that give protection against strong shoulder surfing attack and have been implemented in partially observable scenario like our tag digit based honeypot scheme (THS).

Mod10 method [16] requires mathematical skills of users. So novice users face difficulties in login using this scheme and thus error rate for this scheme goes high. STL [14] method relaxes the computational part of Mod10 method as user needs to follow a *look up* table during login. Though login using this scheme is much simpler than of Mod10 method but user needs to perform some cognitive shift operations (maximum $10 + 10$ and minimum $1 + 1$) during login. Here shift operation signifies moving from one cell to another in a table. As SLASS [4] requires less number of shift operations (maximum 3 and minimum 0) than that of STL so error during login is further decreased. The comparative result shows that though number of login trials by users are less in case of our proposed methodology but it resulted in least percentage of error during login period compared to others (as more cognitive skills are required for login). This shows that users can adopt more easily with the detection technique rather than the existing prevention techniques.

6   Conclusion and Future Work

In this paper we have proposed a novel methodology which can detect shoulder surfing attack. The proposed methodology can be built on top of conventional ATM system. Also it can even be used by a novice user as it does not require any significant computation from user end. Experimental analysis shows that our login process is less error prone but still quite effective in detecting the shoulder surfing attack. In future we would like to extend the detection scheme for a fully observable environment and also we will try to increase the number of honeywords to increase the security strength without putting much overhead on the users.

Acknowledgement. This work is partially supported by a research grant from the Science and Engineering Research Board (SERB), Government of India, under sanction letter no. SB/FTP/ETA-226/2012.

References

1. Banking- Personal Identification Number (PIN) Management and Security - Part 1: Basic Principles and Requirements for Online PIN Handling in ATM and POS Systems, Clause 5.4 Packaging Considerations, ISO 9564-1:2002 (2002)
2. Bojinov, H., Bursztein, E., Boyen, X., Boneh, D.: Kamouflage: Loss-resistant password management. In: Gritzalis, D., Preneel, B., Theoharidou, M. (eds.) ESORICS 2010. LNCS, vol. 6345, pp. 286–302. Springer, Heidelberg (2010)
3. Chakraborty, N., Mondal, S.: Color Pass: An intelligent user interface to resist shoulder surfing attack. In: 2014 IEEE Students' Technology Symposium (TechSym), pp. 13–18 (2014)
4. Chakraborty, N., Mondal, S.: SLASS: Secure login against shoulder surfing. In: Martínez Pérez, G., Thampi, S.M., Ko, R., Shu, L. (eds.) SNDS 2014. CCIS, vol. 420, pp. 346–357. Springer, Heidelberg (2014)
5. Gardiner, S.: $217,000 'Skimmed' from ATMs. The Wall Street Journal (June 2010)
6. Genc, Z.A., Kardas, S., Kiraz, M.S.: Examination of a new defense mechanism: Honeywords. IACR Cryptology ePrint Archive 2013, 696 (2013)
7. Hopper, N.J., Blum, M.: Secure human identification protocols. In: Boyd, C. (ed.) ASIACRYPT 2001. LNCS, vol. 2248, pp. 52–66. Springer, Heidelberg (2001)
8. Juels, A., and Ristenpart, T. Honey encryption: Security beyond the brute-force bound. IACR Cryptology ePrint Archive 2014, 155 (2014)
9. Juels, A., Rivest, R.L.: Honeywords: making password-cracking detectable. In: ACM Conference on Computer and Communications Security, pp. 145–160 (2013)
10. Kocher, P.C.: Timing Attacks on Implementations of Diffie-Hellman, RSA, DSS, and Other Systems. In: Koblitz, N. (ed.) CRYPTO 1996. LNCS, vol. 1109, pp. 104–113. Springer, Heidelberg (1996)
11. Kwon, T., Shin, S., Na, S.: Covert attentional shoulder surfing: Human adversaries are more powerful than expected. IEEE T. Systems, Man, and Cybernetics: Systems 44(6), 716–727 (2014)
12. Mahansaria, D., Shyam, S., Samuel, A., Teja, R.: A fast and secure software solution [ss7.0] that counters shoulder surfing attack. In: 13th International Conference on Software Engineering and Application, pp. 190–195 (2009)
13. Skynews. ATM 'shoulder surfing' card fraud on rise (June 2013), http://news.sky.com/story/1100203/atm-shoulder-surfing-card-fraud-on-rise
14. Perković, T., Čagalj, M., Saxena, N.: Shoulder-surfing safe login in a partially observable attacker model. In: Sion, R. (ed.) FC 2010. LNCS, vol. 6052, pp. 351–358. Springer, Heidelberg (2010)
15. Roth, V., Richter, K., Freidinger, R.: A PIN-entry method resilient against shoulder surfing. In: ACM Conference Computer Communication Security, pp. 236–245 (2004)
16. Wilfong, G.: Method and appartus for secure pin entry. Lucent Technologies, Inc., Murray Hill, NJ, U. S. Patent, ed. United States (1999)
17. Zhao, H., Li, X.: *S3PAS*: A scalable shoulder-surfing resistant textual-graphical password authentication scheme. In: 21st International Conference on Advanced Information Networking and Applications Workshops, pp. 467–472 (2007)

Cheating Prevention Using Genetic Feature Based Key in Secret Sharing Schemes

L. Jani Anbarasi[1], Modigari Narendra[2], and G.S. Anandha Mala[3]

[1] Research Scholar, Anna University, Chennai, India
[2] Sri Ramakrishna Institute of Technology, Coimbatore, India
[3] Easwari Engineering College, Chennai, India
jani_lj_2000@yahoo.com,
{narendramodigari,gs.anandhamala}@gmail.com

Abstract. Shamir proposed a t out of n secret sharing scheme where secrets are encrypted into scrambled images called shares or shadows. The secrets can be reconstructed when t or more participants pool their shares or shadow images together. Major drawbacks in such schemes are if a forged share is pooled then it leads to reconstruction of wrong secret. Cheating is also possible by some participants who can deceive the remaining participants by pooling forged shares. Many cheating prevention schemes have been proposed which uses authentication bits, hash codes etc. This paper proposes a new biometric personal authentication technique which prevents the cheating of participants. The results of the system and the security analysis shows that the proposed scheme gives secret sharing participants the confidence of the recovered original secret without the need to worry about forging of shadow images or dishonest participants.

Keywords: Image Processing, Threshold Secret Sharing, Biometrics.

1   Introduction

Security of multimedia information is of greater concern due to its huge storage and insecure transmission through a public network (for example, medical and satellite images). Confidentiality and Integrity are the major issues to be considered while the data is in insecure communication. The data should not be accessed or modified by unauthorized persons. Thus, the secret images can be securely shared by using secret sharing schemes, in which the Confidentiality and Integrity of the secrets are preserved. Secret sharing is the process of sharing the secrets among n participants as n secret shadows, where a qualified (threshold) set of t participants (t<n) can pool their shadows to recover the original secret, and participants less than t cannot recover the secret. In 1979, Blakley and Shamir [1] introduced the (t, n)-threshold secret sharing schemes, where a dealer can share the secret data into n shadows which are then distributed to n legitimate participants. Any t out of n, legitimate participants can cooperate, to retrieve the secret data with their consequent shadows. Wang and Su [2]

J. Lloret Mauri et al. (Eds.): SSCC 2014, CCIS 467, pp. 111–119, 2014.

and Chang et al. [3, 4, 5, 6, 7] discussed problems like pixel expansion, contrast, and meaningless shadows. Since eavesdroppers will be attracted towards meaningless shadows, these shadows are embedded into a cover image, and stego images are generated using the steganography technique. The meaningful cover image avoids the suspicion of intruders.

The subcutaneous vascular pattern that appears on the palm can accurately identify an individual. The vascular shape [8, 9] has enough information to authenticate individual to a reasonable level. Utilizing the prime feature of palm vein authentication we propose a biometric authentication to prevent cheating of dishonest participants. In this paper we present a palm-vein recognition authentication key for personal identification using Threshold based Feature Selection Algorithm (TFSA) and Probability based Genetic Feature Space Reduction algorithm. This authentication value is used as the key for every participants using who the secret is securely shared using Shamir secret sharing scheme. During reconstruction the secret authentication key is recovered from each participants which can be matched with the participant's vein by the dealer using which dishonest participants are identified and prevented from creating a wrong secret or cheating other participants.

2   System and Methodology

The overall system works in three stages identification of the participants authentication value using genetic space reduction algorithm , secret sharing using Shamir scheme, reconstruction of the secret and verification of the honesty of the participants.

2.1   Selection of Participants Authentication Value

A low cost NIR Charge Coupled Devices (CCD) camera is used to acquire palm images. Uniform and consistent images of good quality can be obtained with low cost. The resolution of the sensor was captured at 256X256 with 8 bit gray scale per pixel. Median filter is applied to enhance the images from low contrast and non uniform illumination. The preprocessed images are subjects to segmentation where it is divided into background and object using binarization. Otsu's Thresholding technique is implemented on the image to approximate the palm region. Comparison between the segmented hand shape with original shows that they are almost distinguishable as shown in Figure 2 a and b. If a small region is extracted from a palm image then it is important to fix the ROI to be in the same position to avoid this entire palm contour is chosen as the ROI in this paper.

Palm Vein Feature Extraction performs feature extraction using TFSA and the selected features are optimized using PGFSR. The optimized features are stored using tries structure which proves effective storage and retrieval.

Thresholding based Feature Selection Algorithm: The segmented palm contour is processed using TFSA which retrieves a binary encoded Generated True Sibling (GTS) feature subset. TFSA identifies the positions of possible feature veins based

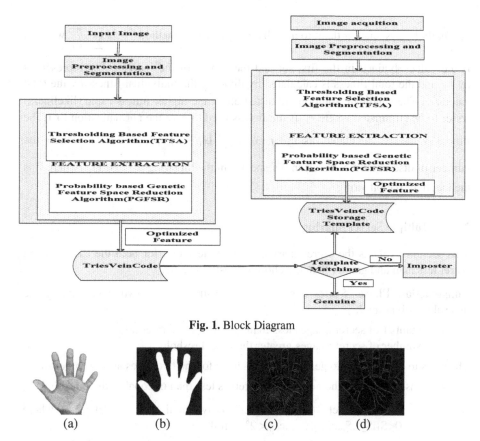

Fig. 1. Block Diagram

Fig. 2. Original palm vein image, Palm contour segmented using Otsu's method, Palm Feature obtained using TFSA and Optimized using PGFSR

on the threshold θ which lies between $\lambda < \theta < \gamma$. The retrieved or attained sibling bits strings are grouped to generate a binary encoded Generated True Sibling feature subset.

Probability based Genetic Feature Space Reduction Algorithm: Feature selection plays a major role in reducing the search space and is exponential to the number of features. Genetic algorithm is one of the widely used global search methods which results high quality solution even for complex techniques within a tractable time.GTS binary encoded bit string is subjected to fitness evaluation in comparison with nearest bit string, So that the difference between them will bring out the length of the encoded pattern .The filtering process for feature subset reduction progress, over the highest fitness than more the likeliness to sustain for next level (generation). The probability helps to retrieve the vein patterns which are having more chances to get filtered with the property of likeliness on its length i.e. presence of vein with more likely identifiable pattern.

The probability based selection strategy is performed to avoid premature convergence. The selected set of chromosomes i.e. retrieved bit strings are truncated optimally by associating them to a probability selection method. $P_i = \dfrac{f_i}{\sum\limits_{j=1}^{n} f_j}$ where n

is the value obtained in the first set and the fitness of the individual is represented by f_i and the total fitness is calculated by dividing the individual fitness by the total value f_j. The candidate solution are tested under the higher fitness value (likeliness) lesser to be eliminated where f_i is the fitness used to give the normalization to 1.The

fitness value is calculated using $f(x) = \sum\limits_{i=1}^{L-1} |x_i - x_{i+1}| \in (0, L-1)$ where the

number of discontinuities between 0's and 1's in the bit string $x \in (0,1)^L$ where L is the length of the bit string.

2.2   Multiple Secret Sharing

This section explains the secret sharing of multiple secret for both the cases having secret less than and greater than the chosen threshold value.

Construction Phase. Secret shadows are constructed for two cases, using the invertible polynomial,

- Number of secret images less than or equal to the threshold
- Number of secret images greater than the threshold

The steps to be followed to generate the shadows for the two cases are given below:

- Case p≤t where the number of secrets is less than or equal to the threshold

    1.   Construct $(t-1)^{th}$ degree polynomial h(x) mod 2^8, where $0 < S_1, S_2 ... S_p, c_1, c_2, \ldots, c_{t-p} < 2^8$ as follows

    $$h(x) = S_1 + S_2 x^1 + \ldots + S_p x^{p-1} + c_1 x^p + c_2 x^{p+1} + \ldots + c_{t-p} x^{t-1} \bmod 2^8 \tag{1}$$

    2.   Compute $Y_i(K^i)$ mod 2^8 for i=1,2...n where K_i is the Triesveincode of each participants
    3.   Distribute the Y_i to the participants
- Case p>t where the number of secrets is greater than the threshold

    1.   Construct $(p-1)^{th}$ degree polynomial h(x) mod 2^8, where $0 < S_1, S_2 ... S_p < 2^8$ as follows:

    $$h(x) = S_1 + S_2 x^1 + \ldots + S_p x^{p-1} \bmod 2^8 \tag{2}$$

    2.   Compute $Y_i(K^i)$ mod 2^8 for i=1,2...n
    3.   Computes h(i) mod 2^8 for i=1,2...p-t
    4.   Distribute the Y_i, h(i) to the participants.

2.3   Recovery Phase

Participants pool their shadows to recover the secret images S_1, $S_2 ... S_p$. Before pooling the shadows the Triesverincode is recovered from each participant vein using

Table 1. Algorithm for the generation of authentication key

Algorithm: Threshold based Feature Selection Algorithm (TFSA)
Input: B = { b_1, b_2, b_3....... b_n} Palm Images θ - Threshold Lower bound λ and Upper bound γ
Output: The abstract model with the maximum threshold value GTS = { c_1, c_2, c_3....... c_n} of feature subset

1.Generate an initial population of feature subset for B encoded with bit string based on a random threshold $\theta \geq \lambda$
 	
  Repeat
For each ¥ij$[B]$ where $i \in \{1,2\cdots r\}$, $j \in \{1,2\cdots c\}$
Perform
$$\begin{bmatrix} Pos\{B[i][j] \geq \theta\})thenB[i][j]=1 \\ Pos\{B[i][j] < \theta\})thenB[i][j]=0 \end{bmatrix}$$
Check $B[i][j]==0$ for all $B[i][j] \leq c$.
Until $Pos([i]==c) \& \& \theta \leq \gamma$
2. Generate skeleton structure from the retrieved bit string
For each ¥i,j Compare $(B[i][j]==1 \& \& B[i][j+1]==0)$
    Compute $Cx[i] = Cx[i] \cup \{i\}$, $Cy[j] = Cy[j] \cup \{j\}$
  $GTS((i, j),(i+1, j-1))$ // Generated true sibling pixels
3. To sustain the proposed model repeat the cycle with immediate neighbour   **Ignore** if
  $(B[i][j]==0 \& \& B[i][j+1]==0 \& \& B[i][j+2]==0)$
Compute if $(B[i][j]==1 \& \& B[i][j+1]==1)$,
$$\begin{bmatrix} Cx\ [i] = Cx\ [i] \cup \{i\} \\ Cy\ [j] = Cy\ [j] \cup \{j\} \end{bmatrix}$$
$GTS((i, j),(respective\ incremental\ values))$

Algorithm: Probability Based Genetic Feature Space Reduction Algorithm (PGFSR)
Input :   Generated GTS = {C_1,C_2, C_3....... C_n} Feature Subset.
Output: Optimized Feature SubsetXbest
BEGIN **Initialize**: Generated feature subset {GTS-binary string} from TFSA module is given as initial population to the   next stage for optimal feature space reduction. **While** (not computationally converged) **Perform** fitness evaluation for all generated feature {GTS-binary string} based on probability based selection strategy $f(x)$. **Calculate on** $P_i = \dfrac{f_i}{\sum_{j=1}^{z} f_j}$
X_{best} the probability Pi using a fitness function f(x) Where   n is the number of vein patterns captured in the TFSA and $$f(x) = \sum_{i=1}^{L-1} \left| x_i - x_{i+1} \right| \in (0, L-1)$$ **END**

which every participant are verified for their honesty and the secrets are reconstructed. The polynomial $h(x)$ mod 2^8 can be uniquely determined as follows:

- **Case P≤t**

$$h(x) = \sum_{i=1}^{t} Y_i \prod_{j=1, j\neq1}^{t} \frac{x - I_j^{'}}{I_i^{'} - I_j^{'}} \bmod 2^8 \qquad (3)$$

$$h(x) = S_1 + S_2 x^1 + \ldots + S_p x^{p-1} + c_1 x^p + c_2 x^{p+1} + \ldots + c_{t-p} x^{t-1} \bmod 2^8$$

- **Case P>t**

$$h(x) = \sum_{i=1}^{t} Y_i \prod_{j=1, j\neq i}^{t} \frac{x - I_j^{'}}{I_i^{'} - I_j^{'}} + \sum_{i=1}^{p-t} h(i) \prod_{j=1, j\neq i}^{p-t} \frac{x - j}{i - j} \bmod 2^8 \qquad (4)$$

$$h(x) = S_1 + S_2 x^1 + \ldots + S_p x^{p-1} \bmod 2^8$$

3   Simulation Results

The performance and simulation of the proposed system are detailed in this section. The experimental platform was programmed in Matlab 7.9. A simulation for the (3, 4) scheme is applied, where the threshold chosen is 3. For both the cases, consider the number of secrets P as 3 for (P ≤ t) and 4 for (P>t) respectively. Various medical images of size 256x256 are taken for simulation; few are given in Figure 3. The shares generated are shown in Figure 4.

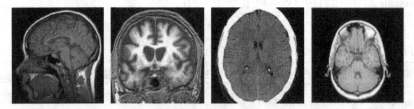

Fig. 3. Medical secret images

Fig. 4. Experimental results of Generated Shadows

4   Security Analysis

4.1   Correlation Analysis and Information Entropy

To resist a statistical attack, less correlation among two adjacent pixels is very essential and critical. The correlation coefficient of two adjacent horizontal and diagonal pixels in the original image and encrypted image is examined. In order to test the correlation between two adjacent pixels, 3000 pairs (horizontal and vertical) of adjacent pixels were selected in a random manner from the original secret and encrypted images. The correlation coefficient is calculated; they are given in Tables 2 and 3 for both the cases respectively.

Table 2. Correlation analysis for the case (P>t)

S. n o	Secret		Share 1		Share 2		Share 3		Share 4	
	HC	VC	HC	VC	HC	VC	HC	VC	HC	VC
1.	0.9658	0.9696	0.0707	0.0266	0.0212	0.0524	0.0032	0.0092	0.0309	0.0616
	0.9734	0.9787								
	0.9777	0.9889								
	0.9715	0.9830								
2.	0.9715	0.9830	00156	0.0435	0.0656	0.0066	0.0072	0.0004	0.0046	0.0703
	0.9591	0.9776								
	0.9373	0.9342								
	0.9884	0.9955								

Table 3. Correlation analysis for the case (P≤t)

S. n o	Secret		Share 1		Share 2		Share 3		Share 4	
	HC	VC	HC	VC	HC	VC	HC	VC	HC	VC
1.	0.9658	0.9696	0.0376	0.0097	0.0037	0.0302	0.0307	0.0347	0.0254	0.0173
	0.9734	0.9787								
	0.9777	0.9889								
2.	0.9715	0.9830	0.0056	0.0045	0.0656	0.0066	0.0872	0.0014	0.0146	0.0701
	0.9591	0.9776								
	0.9373	0.9342								

Information entropy is defined to express the degree of uncertainties in the system. Information entropy can measure the distribution of the grey value in the image; the results show that the greater the information entropy, the more uniform is the distribution of the grey value. For an ideally random image, the value of the information entropy is 8. The information entropies of the secrets and the encrypted shares for the case P≤t are shown in Table 4 and for the case P>t in Table 5, all of which are very close to 8. The functional performance of the proposed scheme is compared with few related schemes and is presented in the Table 6.

Table 4. Information Entropy of various shares for the case (P≤t)

S.No	Secrets Name	Secret	Share 1	Share 2	Share 3	Share 4
1	Medical1	6.4691	7.9815	7.9836	7.9811	7.9836
	Medical2	7.7178				
	Medical3	6.3921				
2	Medical4	6.4137	7.9328	7.9373	7.9218	7.9344
	Medical5	6.5042				
	Medical6	5.5344				

Table 5. Information Entropy of various shares for the case (P>t)

S. No	Secrets Name	Secret	Share 1	Share 2	Share 3	Share 4
1.	Medical1	6.4691	7.9527	7.9532	7.9495	7.9518
	Medical2	7.7178				
	Medical3	6.3921				
	Medical4	6.4137				
2.	Medical4	6.4137	7.9328	7.9373	7.9218	7.9344
	Medical5	6.5042				
	Medical6	5.5344				
	Medical8	6.9369				

Table 6. Functionality and computation quantity analysis

Functionality	Proposed	[12]	[10]	[11]
Verification	Yes	no	11	No
Authentication	Yes	No	yes	No
Meaningful shares	No	no	yes	Yes

5   Conclusion and Future Work

In this paper, multiple secret images are shared, using the Lagrange interpolation polynomial and the secret images are reconstructed without any loss by performing the calculations using GF (2^8). The proposed threshold multi-secret sharing has the verifiable property using biometric palm vein authentication key, by which cheating of the participants is prevented. The achieved size of the shadow is the same as that of the secret images. The simulation results and the security analysis prove that this algorithm provides high security, confidentiality and integrity for the communication of secret images over the public network.

References

1. Naor, M., Shamir, A.: Visual cryptography. In: De Santis, A. (ed.) EUROCRYPT 1994. LNCS, vol. 950, pp. 1–12. Springer, Heidelberg (1995)
2. Wang, R.Z., Su, C.H.: Secret image sharing with smaller shadow images. Pattern Recogn. Lett. 27, 551–555 (2006)
3. Chang, C.C., Hsieh, Y.P.: Sharing secrets in stego images with authentication. Pattern Recogn. 41, 3130–3137 (2008)
4. Lin, C.C., Tsai, W.H.: Secret Image sharing with steganography and authentication. J. Syst. Software 73, 405–414 (2004)
5. Wu, Y.S., Thien, C.C., Lin, J.C.: Sharing and hiding secret images with size constraint. Pattern Recogn. Lett. 37, 1377–1385 (2004)
6. Thien, C.C., Lin, J.C.: Secret Image sharing. Comput. Graphics 26(1), 765–770 (2002)
7. Lin, P.L., Chan, C.S.: Invertible secret image sharing with steganography. Pattern Recogn. Lett. 31, 1887–1893 (2010)
8. Chen, Y.C., Tsai, D.S., Hong, G.: A new authentication based cheating prevention scheme in Noar Shamir's visual cryptography. J. Vis. Commun. Image R. 21, 900–916 (2010)
9. Lin, P.U., Lee, J.S., Chang, C.C.: Distortion free secret image sharing mechanism using modulus operator. Pattern Recogn. 42, 886–895 (2009)
10. Ulutas, M., Ulutas, G., Nabiyev, V.V.: Medical Image Security and EPR hiding using Shamir's secret sharing scheme. J. Syst. Software 84, 341–353 (2011)
11. Anbarasi, L.J., Kannan, S.: Secured Secret Color Image Sharing With Steganography. In: IEEE International Conference on Recent Trends in Information Technology, pp. 44–48 (2012)
12. Yang, C.C., Chang, T.Y., Hwang, M.S.: A (t, n) multi-secret sharing scheme. Appl. Math. Comput. 151(2), 483–490 (2004)

Security Enhancement in Web Services by Detecting and Correcting Anomalies in XACML Policies at Design Level

M. Priyadharshini[1], J. Yowan[2], and R. Baskaran[1]

[1] Computer Science Department, Anna University, India
mpriya1977@gmail.com, baaski@annauniv.edu
[2] Department of Information Science and Technology, Anna University, India
jyowan@gmail.com

Abstract. The significance of XACML (Extensible Access Control Markup Language) policies for access control is immeasurably increasing particularly in web services. XACML policies are web access control policies which are used to permit the genuine users to access the resources and also deny the sham users. Generation of this XACML policy is very important task in order to avoid security seepage. Detecting and Correcting inconsistencies in access control policies are highly time consuming and tedious when size of XACML polices are high. The Process when done at execution time could even need more time and effort. The purpose of this work is to devise an anomaly detection and correction tool which could be used at the time of designing policies so as to reduce time and effort. Policy designer could easily discover and resolve the inconsistencies such as conflicts and redundancies in the XACML policies with the help of our XACML Policy Analyzer tool.

Keywords: Web Services, XACML, Access Control, Anomalies, Policy Analyzer.

1 Introduction

Extensible Access Control Markup Language(XACML) [1], which is a general purpose access control policy language drafted by the Organization for the Advancement of Structured Information Standards (OASIS), has been broadly used to specify access control policies for numerous applications, especially in the domain of Web Services [3]. XACML policy designer when creating XACML Policies may sometimes create it with inconsistencies [2]. Conflict and Redundancy are the two types of inconsistency that exist in XACML Policies. In the XACML policies redundancies occur, if one rule's content may be repeated in another rules with same effect such as permit or deny. Conflicts occur, if one rule's content may be repeated in other rules with different effect such as permit or deny. Redundancies in the policies increase the policy evaluation time. Conflicts in XACML Policies lead two kinds of problems. First, Security problem (e.g. permitting sham users).Second, accessibility

J. Lloret Mauri et al. (Eds.): SSCC 2014, CCIS 467, pp. 120–135, 2014.

problem (e.g. denying genuine users).The Policy designer can manually resolve these problems only for the policies which contain few rules. The Policy designer cannot manually resolve these problems for the policies which contain many rules.

XACML has four different combining algorithms [1] such as Deny-overrides, Permit-overrides, First-Applicable and Only-One-Applicable. Policy Designer cannot assign correct combining algorithm without correct conflict information about the XACML policies. Redundancy elimination is the solution for XACML policy optimization. Policy optimization can improve the performance of XACML Evaluation.

In this paper, we propose four algorithms for detecting and correcting anomalies in XACML policies. First, Redundancy Detecting Algorithm which finds the redundancies present in the policies. Second is the Redundancy Elimination Algorithm that eliminates the redundancies in the policies. Third, Conflict Detection Algorithm is used to identify the conflicts in the policies. Fourth, Conflict Correction Algorithm is used to resolve the conflicts in the policies.At present XACML conflict correction mechanisms use only one combining algorithm to resolve all detected conflicts within an XACML policy or policy set. Also, many other conflict correction methods are present [4], [5], [6], but they don't support XACML. Thus we provide a policy detection and conflict correction mechanism for XACML in this proposed work.

The rest of this paper is organized as follows. Section 2 describes the overview of XACML Policy and a discussion on the anomalies in the XACML Policy is also been presented. Section 3 presents the proposed methodology. In Section 5, we present the results and discussion of the proposed methodology. In Section 6 few related works are specified and finally conclusion and future work in Section 7.

2   Overview of XACML

The root of all XACML policies is PolicySet or a Policy. A PolicySet contains many Policies or other PolicySets and corresponding policy combining algorithm. A Policy contains a target, set of rules and also rule combining algorithm. The target defines a set of subjects, resources and actions. A rule set is a sequence of rules. Each rule consists of a target, a condition, and an effect.

The target of a rule determines whether an access request is applicable to the rule and it has a similar structure as the target of a policy or a policy set. Table 1 shows a sample XACML policy. The root policy set **pset1** contains two policies, **Pol1** and **Pol2**, which are combined using First-Applicable combining algorithm. The policy **Pol1** has two rules, **r1** and **r2**, and its rule combining algorithm is Deny-Overrides. The policy **Pol2** includes four rules **r3**, **r4**, **r5** and **r6** with Deny-Overrides combining algorithm. In this sample, there are three subjects: Assistant **Manager**, **Project Manager**, and **Site Engineer**; two resources: **Project Report** and **Contractor Details**; and two actions: **Read** and **Write**; one condition with time attribute: **8<=Time<= 18**.

Table 1. Sample XACML policy

```
<PolicySetPolicySetid="pset1" Policy Combining AlgId="First-Applicable">
 <Target/>
 <Policy PolicyId="pol1"   RuleCombiningAlgId="Deny-Overrides">
  <Target/>
  <Rule RuleId="r1"  Effect="Permit">
   <Target>
    <Subjects>
      <Subject>Project Manager</Subject>
    </Subjects>
    <Resources>
      <Resource>Project Report</Resource>
      <Resource>Contractor details</Resource>
    </Resources>
    <Actions>
      <Action>Read<Action>
      <Action>Write<Action>
    </Actions>
   </Target>
  </Rule>
  <Rule RuleId="r2"  Effect="Permit">
    <Target>
      <Subjects>
        <Subject>Project Manager</Subject>
        <Subject>Assistant Manager</Subject>
      </Subjects>
      <Resources>
        <Resource>Project Report</Resource>
        <Resource>Contractor details</Resource>
      </Resources>
      <Actions>
        <Action> Read<Action>
      </Actions>
    </Target>
  </Rule>
</Policy>
<Policy PolicyId="pol2" RuleCombiningAlgId="Permit-Overrides">
 </Target>
   <Rule RuleId="r3"  Effect="Permit">
    <Target>
     <Subjects>
        <Subject>Site Engineer</Subject>
     </Subjects>
     <Resources>
        <Resource>Contractor details</Resource>
     </Resources>
     <Actions>
        <Action> Read<Action>
     </Actions>
    </Target>
    <Condition>8 <=Time<=18</Condition>
```

```
    </Rule>
    <Rule Rule Id="rule4"  Effect="Permit">
      <Target>
        <Subjects>
            <Subject>Assistant Manager</Subject>
        </Subjects>
        <Resources>
            <Resource>Project Report</Resource>
        </Resources>
        <Actions>
            <Action>Read<Action>
        </Actions>
      </Target>
    </Rule>
    <Rule Rule Id="r5"  Effect="Deny">
     <Target>
        <Subjects>
            <Subject>Site Engineer</Subject>
        </Subjects>
        <Resources>
            <Resource>Contractor details</Resource>
            </Resources>
            <Actions>
                <Action>Read<Action>
            </Actions>
        </Target>
      </Rule>
      <Rule Rule Id="r6"  Effect="Deny">
        <Target>
          <Subjects>
              <Subject>Assistant Manager</Subject>
          </Subjects>
          <Resources>
              <Resource>Project Report</Resource>
          </Resources>
          <Actions>
              <Action>Read<Action>
          </Actions>
        </Target>
      </Rule>
    </Policy>
 </PolicySet>
```

2.1   Anomalies in XACML

Redundancy and Conflict are two anomalies that could exist between Policies and
Policy Sets which need to be resolved so as to enable taking smooth decision in case
of access control.

Anomalies at Policy Level
A Policy contains a target, set of rules and also rule combining algorithm and there is a possibility that two rules defined may lead to different decisions that is to permit or deny or else even they may have same redundant rule been defined thus leading to anomalies at Policy level.

Redundancies:
In Policy pol1, rule r1 is in redundant with rule r2 in Fig 1 where r1 allows the Project Manager (Subject) to read (Action) Project Report and Contract details (Resources) which is also permitted by r2.The complete set of redundancies in each policy of the sample XACML policy in Table 1 is shown in Table 2.

Table 2. Redundancy at Policy Level

S. no	Policy Id	Redundancy between the rules			
1	pol1	**Rule Id**	**r1**	**r2**	
		r1	-	yes	
		r2	yes	-	
2	pol2				
		Rule Id	**r3**	**r4**	**r5**	**r6**
		r3	-	no	no	no
		r4	no	-	no	no
		r5	no	no	-	no
		r6	no	no	no	-

Conflicts:
*In Policy **pol2**, rule **r3** is in conflict with rule **r5** and also **r4** is in conflict with **r6** in **Table 1** because **r3** allows the Subject **Site Engineer** to **read** (Action) the Resource **Contract details** in the time interval [8:00, 18:00] which are denied by **r5**. The complete conflicts in each policy of the sample XACML policy in Fig 1 is shown in Table 3.*

Anomalies at Policy Set Level
A Policy Set has a set of policies and there is a possibility that two policies defined could possess same target, set of rules and rule combining algorithm leading to different decisions that is to permit or deny or else even they may have same redundant policy been defined thus leading to anomalies at policy set level.

Table 3. Coflicts at policy level

S. no	Policy Id	Conflicts between the rules			
1	pol1	**Rule Id**	**r1**	**r2**	
		r1	-	no	
		r2	no	-	
2	pol2				
		Rule Id	**r3**	**r4**	**r5**	**r6**
		r3	-	no	yes	-
		r4	-	-	-	yes
		r5	yes	-	-	-
		r6	-	yes	-	-

Redundancies:

*Redundancies may also occur between policies or policy sets. Rule **r2** of Policy **pol1** is in redundant with rule **r4** of Policy **pol2** in Table 1because r2allows the **Assistant Manager** (Subject) to **read** (Action) **Project Report** (Resource) which is also permitted by **r4**. The complete redundancies between each policies of the sample XACML policy in Table 1 is shown in Table 4.*

Table 4. Redundancy in policy set level

S. no	Policy Ids	Redundancy between the rules			
		Rule Id	**r3**	**r4**	**r5**	**r6**
1	pol1 and pol2	r1	no	no	no	no
		r2	no	yes	no	no

Conflicts:

*Conflicts may also occur between policies or policy sets. Rule **r2** of Policy **pol1** is in conflict with rule **r6** of Policy **pol2** in Table 1 because **r2** allows the **Assistant Manager** (Subject) to **read** (Action) **Project Report** (Resource) which is denied by **r6**. The complete conflicts between each policies of the sample XACML policy in Fig 1 is shown in Table 5.*

Table 5. Conflicts at policy set level

S. no	Policy Ids	Conflicts between the rules			
		Rule Id	**r3**	**r4**	**r5**	**r6**
1	pol1 and pol2	r1	no	no	No	no
		r2	no	no	No	yes

3   Proposed Methodology

The proposed methodology consists of sequence of activities to construct the Boolean Expression followed by the Algorithms to detect as well as to correct the anomalies in the XACML Policy. The algorithms include redundancy detection algorithm, redundancy elimination algorithm, conflict detection algorithm and finally conflict correction algorithm as given in Fig. 1 below.

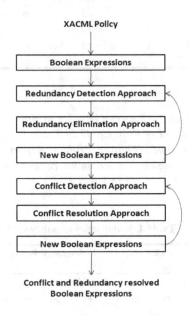

Fig. 1. Proposed Architecture

3.1   Construction of Boolean Expression

First, XACML policy is parsed to identify policy set id, policy id, rule effect, rule id and also attributes such as subjects, actions, resources and conditions. The parsed result is used to form Boolean Expression.

Second, After Parsing, a new Boolean variable should be assigned to each attributes. We assign each of the attributes values as a Boolean variable. For example, an attribute Subject="Project Manager" is assigned into a Boolean variable S1.

Table 6. Boolean Expressions of XACML Policy in Table 1

S. no	Rule	Effect	Boolean Expression
1	r1	Permit	$(S1) \wedge (R1 \vee R2) \wedge (A1 \vee A2)$
2	r2	Permit	$(S1 \vee S2) \wedge (R1 \vee R2) \wedge (A1)$
3	r3	Permit	$(S3) \wedge (R2) \wedge (A1) \wedge (C1)$
4	r4	Permit	$(S2) \wedge (R1) \wedge (A1)$
5	r5	Deny	$(S3) \wedge (R2) \wedge (A1)$
6	r6	Deny	$(S2) \wedge (R1) \wedge (A1)$

Third, we utilize the Variable Assigning technique to construct Boolean expressions in terms of Boolean variables for XACML rules. Each Boolean expression of a rule contains attributes combined by logical operator $\lor$ and $\land$. Boolean Expressions are used for anomaly detection, elimination and correction. Thus Table 6 shows the complete list of Boolean expressions for the XACML in Table 1.

3.2   Redundancy Detection Algorithm

Redundancy Detection Algorithm is used to find the redundancies present in the XACML Policies. Line 4-15 in Algorithm 1 contains redundancy_detection() method which can find the redundancies in the XACML Policies. Redundant rules have the following two properties:

1.   All rules are pair wise disjointed
          Rule id r_i ≠ Rule id r_j

2.   The effects of matched rules contain either "Permit" only or "Deny" only.

Line7 in Algorithm1 checks these properties. In **Table 6**, rule **r1** is in redundant with rule **r2** because Subject (S1), Resources (R1, R2), and Action (A1) are present in both the rules. So Subject_Match_r_i_r_j, Resource_Match_r_i_r_j, Action_Match_r_i_r_j and No_Condition_r_i_r_j from **Line 8-11** in Algorithm 1 are greater than zero.

Algorithm1. Redundancy Detection in XACML Policy

Input: Boolean Expression of rules with Effect

Output: Detected Redundancies between the rules

```
1      /*parsing the XACML Policy*/
2      /*Boolean Encoding*/
3      /*Boolean Expression of each rules*/
4      redundancy_detection()
5        for each rᵢ ∈ Bₑ
6          for each rⱼ ∈ Bₑ
7            if ∃ rᵢ∈ Bₑ, rⱼ∈ Bₑ,rⱼ≠rᵢ,rᵢ.Effect=rⱼ.Effect
8              if Subject_Match_rᵢ_rⱼ>0
9                if Resource_Match_rᵢ_rⱼ>0
10                  if Action_Match_rᵢ_rⱼ>0
11                    if ConditionMatch_of_ rᵢ_rⱼ>0
12                    ||No_Condition_Match_rᵢ_rⱼ=0
13                      Redundancy present between rᵢ and rⱼ
14                      redundancy_elimination();
15                      new_boolean_expression();
16                      redundancy_detection();
```

3.3   Redundancy Elimination Algorithm

After finding the redundancy, Redundancy Elimination algorithm identifies the redundancy type so as to find the different set of solutions to handle the redundancy.

Check Points for Redundancy Elimination

Redundancy Elimination Algorithm consist four Check points. The Check Points are Same, Different Equal, Different Subset and Different Superset. These Check Points analyse and find out the correct redundancy type. The Check Points for the redundancy elimination approach are shown in Fig 2.

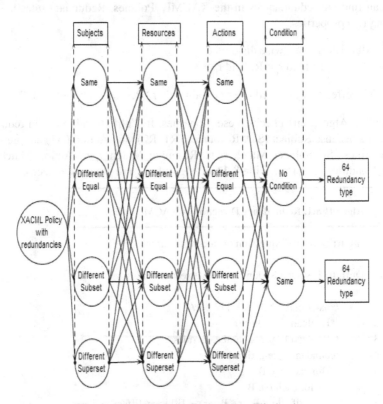

Fig. 2. Check Points for Redundancy Elimination

The Check points are briefly explained below:

Same: All the attribute values of same attribute group for rule r_i and r_j should be same. Consider rule r1 and r2 from the Boolean Expression Table, Here Resources R1 and R2 are present in both the rules. All Resources of r1 are not only same to the Resources of r2 but also the Resource length of r1 is equal to the Resource length of r2.Here Resource length of r1 and r2 is 2.

Different Equal: Few attribute values of same attribute group for rule r_i and r_j should be same and also the length of the attribute groups of the both the rules r_i and r_j should be same. Consider rule r1 and r2 from the Boolean Expression Table, For instance, if we change the Resource R2 of r2 to R3, now the Resources of rule r1 are R1and R3.Here only Resource R1 is present in both the rules. Few resources of r1 are not only same to the Resources of r2 but also the Resources length of r1 is equal to the Resource length of r2.Here Resource length of r1 and r2 is 2.

Different Subset: Few attribute values of same attribute group for rule r_i and r_j should be same and also the attribute group length of the rule r_i should be less than r_j. Consider rule **r1** and **r2** from the Boolean Expression Table. Here Subject S1 is present in both the rules. Subject **S2**of **r2** is not present in the rule **r1**.Few Subjects of **r1** are not only same to the Subjects of rule **r2** but also the Subjects length of **r1** is lesser than the Subjects length of **r2**.Here Subject length of **r1** is **1** and Subject length **r2** is **2**.

Different Superset: Few attribute values of same attribute group for rule r_i and r_j should be same and also the attribute group length of the rule r_i should be greater than r_j. Consider rule **r1** and **r2** from the Boolean Expression Table. Here Actions **A1** and **A2**are present in both the rules. Action **A2**of **r1** is not present in the rule **r2**.Few Actions of **r1** are not only same to the Actions of rule **r2** but also the Actions group length of **r1** is greater than the **r2**.Here Action group length of **r1** is **2** and length of **r2** is **1**.

The function redundancy_detection() in Algorithm 1 is invoked to find the redundancy between the rules. In Boolean Expression Table 6, rule **r1** is redundant with rule **r2**.The function redundancy_elimination() in Algorithm 2 uses Check point to eliminate the redundancy between the rules. The Check Points between these rules are Different Subset for Subjects, Same for Resources and Different Superset for Actions. The Solution for this redundancy type is to remove the Subject **S1** from the rule **r2**.Now new_boolean_expression() function in Algorithm 1 is called to assign new Boolean expression for rule **r1** and **r2**.The Boolean expression after redundancy elimination is shown in the Table 7.

Table 7. Boolean Expression after Redundancy Elimination

S. no	Rule	Effect	Boolean Expression
1	r1	Permit	$(S1) \wedge (R1 \vee R2) \wedge (A1 \vee A2)$
2	r2	Permit	$(S2) \wedge (R1 \vee R2) \wedge (A1)$
3	r3	Permit	$(S3) \wedge (R2) \wedge (A1) \wedge (C1)$
4	r4	Permit	$(S2) \wedge (R1) \wedge (A1)$
5	r5	Deny	$(S3) \wedge (R2) \wedge (A1)$
6	r6	Deny	$(S2) \wedge (R1) \wedge (A1)$

Again redundancy_detection() function is called to find the redundancy between the rules in the new Boolean expression. Now rule **r2** is redundant with rule **r4**. Again function redundancy_elimination() uses Check points to eliminate the redundancy between the rules. The Check Points between these rules are Same for Subjects, Different Superset for Resources and Different Superset for Actions. The Solution for this redundancy type is to remove the rule **r4** from the Sample XACML Policy. Now new_boolean_expression() function assign new Boolean expression for the new Sample Policy. This process continues until eliminate the redundancies in the XACML Policy completely. A complete list of Boolean encoding for the example XACML policy in Table 1 is shown in Table 2.

3.4   Conflict Detection Algorithm

Conflict Detection Algorithm is used to find the conflicts present in the XACML Policies. Line 4-25 contains conflict_detection() method which can find the conflicts in the XACML Policies.

Algorithm2. Conflict Detection in XACML Policy

Input: New Boolean Expression without redundancy

Output: Detect Conflicts present between the rules

1	/*parsing the XACML Policy*/
2	/*Boolean Encoding*/
3	/*Boolean Expression of each rules*/
4	conflict_detection()
5	for each r $\in$ nB$_e$
6	for each r $\in$ nB$_e$
7	if $\exists$ r$_i$∈nB$_e$, r$_j$∈nB$_e$,r$_i$≠r$_j$,r$_i$.Effect≠tr$_i$.Effect
8	if Subject_Match_r$_i$_r$_i$>0
9	if Resource_Match_r$_i$_r$_i$>0
10	if Action_Match_ r$_i$_r$_i$>0
11	if Condition_Match_r$_i$_r$_j$>0
12	‖No_Condition_Match_r$_i$_r$_j$=0
13	‖One_Condition_r$_i$_r$_j$>0
14	Conflict present between r$_i$ and r$_i$
15	if $\exists$ r$_i$∈ Ps, r$_j$∈ Ps,r$_i$≠r$_j$,r$_i$.Effect=r$_i$.Effect
16	if Subject_Match_r$_i$_r$_i$>0
17	if Resource_Match_r$_i$_r$_i$>0
18	if Action_Match_r$_i$_r$_i$>0
19	if One_Condition_r$_i$_r$_j$>0
20	Conflict present between r$_i$ and r$_j$
21	
22	
23	get_policy_designer_effect();
24	conflict_resolution();
25	new_boolean_expression();

Conflicting rules have the following two Conditions:

Condition1 has three properties
1. All rules are pair wise disjointed

        Rule id $r_i \neq$ Rule id r_j

2. The effects of matched rules should contain both "Permit" and "Deny"
3. If Condition attribute present in the rules then

        "NoCondition list length is greater than zero" or

        "ConditionMatch list length is greater than Zero"

        or "OneCondition list length is greater than Zero".

Line7-11 in the Algorith 2 checks these properties.

Condition2 has three properties
1. All rules are pair wise disjointed

        Rule id $r_i \neq$ Rule id r_j

2. The effects of matched rules contain either "Permit" only or "Deny" only.
3. If condition attribute present in the rules then "OneCondition list length should be greater than Zero".

Line17-21 of Algorithm 2 checks these properties.

In new Boolean Expression table, rule **r3** is in conflict with rule **r5** because Subject (S3), Resources (R2), and Action (A1) are present in both the rules and also Condition attributes is present only in the rule **r3**. So Subject_Match_r_i_r_j, Resource_Match_r_i_r_j, Action_Match_r_i_r_j and One_Condition_r_i_$r_j$size are greater than zero. Rule **r2** is in conflict with rule **r6**becauseSubject (S1), Resources (R1), and Action (A1) are present in both the rules and also So Subject_Match_r_i_r_j, Resource_Match_r_i_r_j, and Action_Match_r_i_$r_j$sizeare greater than zero.

3.5   Conflict Resolution Algorithm

First, the function conflict_detection() is called to find the conflicts between the rules. In Boolean Expression table, rule **r2** is in conflict with ruler**6**and also **r3** is in conflict with **r5**.

Second, get_policy_designer_effect() is called to get the rule effects of the conflicting rules and show that effects and conflicting segments to the Policy Designer. The policy designer should set the correct effects to those conflicting segments; to enable easy interpretation a grid based representation is used. Here the following three segments are the conflicting segments.

1. S2-R1-A1 from rule r2
2. S3-R2-A1-C1 from rule r3
3. S3-R2-A1 from rule r5

If the Policy Designer set the effect **Permit** to the conflicting segments S2-R1-A1 and S3-R2-A1-C1, the conflicting segment S3-R2-A1 will be hidden to the Policy designer for which the system provides a user interface to suggest the policy designer as in Fig. 3.

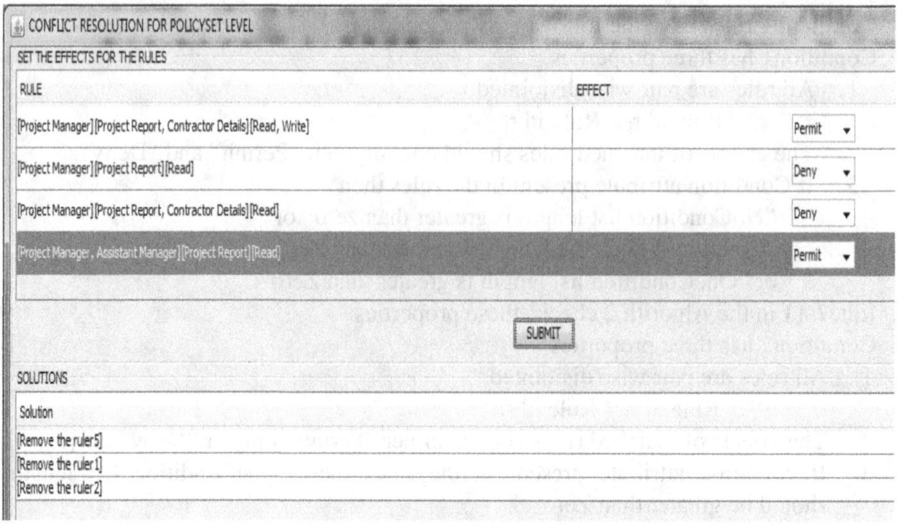

Fig. 3. User Resolution suggestion User Interface

Third, the function conflict_resolution() uses Check point to resolve the conflicts between the rules r2 and r6 and also between the rule r3 and r5. The Check Points between the rule r2 and r6 are Same for Subjects, Different Superset for Resources and Same for Actions. The Solution for this conflict type is to remove the rule **r6**.The Check Points between the rule **r3** and **r5** are Same for Subjects, Same for Resources, Same for Actions and one condition is present in **r3**. The Solution for this conflict type is to remove the rule **r5**.After the conflict resolution new_boolean_expression() function assign new Boolean expression we get new Refined Boolean Expression presented in Table 8.

Table 8. Refined Boolean Expression

S. no	Rule	Effect	Boolean Expression
1	r1	Permit	$(S1) \wedge (R1 \vee R2) \wedge (A1 \vee A2)$
2	r2	Permit	$(S2) \wedge (R1 \vee R2) \wedge (A1)$
3	r3	Permit	$(S3) \wedge (R2) \wedge (A1) \wedge (C1)$

4   Results and Discussion

The proposed methodology of conflict and redundancy elimination covers the already prevailing methodologies where only part of the methodology was implemented and analyzed.

Table 9 presents various tools(T) and approaches(A) that are used for detecting and resolving anomalies in XACML Policy, the features they support and hence the purpose of the proposed methodology to highly reduce the processing time of PDP is also solved resolving the anomalies.

Table 9. Listing of Tools and Approaches for Anamoly Detection and Resolution

S. no	Tools/Approach	Phase	Features Supported	Features Not Support
1	Margrave(T)	Implementation	Policy Verification	Anomaly Resolution
2	EXAM(T)	Implementation	Policy Analysis, Policy Verification, Policy Integration	Anomaly Resolution
3	PCL(A)	Implementation	Conflict Resolution	Without pre-defined combining algorithm in XACML Policy
4	XEngine(T)	Implementation	Conflict Resolution	Without predefined combining algorithms in the policy
5	SunPDP(T)	Implementation	Conflict Resolution	Without predefined combining algorithms in the policy
6	XAnalyzer(T)	Design	Redundancy Elimination and Conflict Resolution	Without predefined combining algorithms in the policy
7	XACML Policy Analyzer(T)	Design	Redundancy Elimination and Conflict Resolution without pre-defined combining algorithms	-

A sample policy with 6 Rules, 2 Policies and 1 Policy Set is taken as a sample and executed in our system and compared with that of XAnalyzer[2].Our approach is found to consume lesser time for redundancy removal as well as for conflict detection when compared to the other approaches and also this proves to be efficient since done at design level itself. The result of the experimentation is provided as follows in Table 10.

The other important aspect that could justify our approach is that our approach eliminates the process of applying rule combining algorithms during processing as done with other approaches which could raise the performance increase in total processing time.

Table 10. Comparision of Approaches in Conflict Resoultion and Redundancy Elimination

S. no	Tools/Approach	Phase	Conflict Resolution Time(s)	Redundancy Elimination Time (s)
1	XAnalyzer(T)	Design	0.82	0.87
2	XACML Policy Analyzer(T)	Design	0.80	0.84

5   Related Works

In [7], Dan Lin et al proposed a policy similarity measure for XACML policy similarity analysis. In [8], Lin et al designed a tool EXAM can be used for policy property analysis, policy similarity analysis and policy integration. Fisler et al. [9] designed a tool Margrave, which can verify policy properties and perform change-impact analysis. During runtime Sun PDP [10] and XEngine [11] detect the conflicts and resolve the conflicts by applying predefined combining algorithms in the policy. In [2], Hongxin Hu et al developed a tool XAnalyzer which can be used for policy analysis at policy design time. XAnalyzer can identify all conflicts within a policy and help policy designers to select appropriate combining algorithms for conflict resolution. Bauer et al. [12] adopted a data-mining technique to eliminate contradictions occurring between access control policies. Our tool XACML Policy Analyzer also concentrates on policy analysis at policy design time. XACML Policy Analyzer can identify all conflicts within a policy and finally it selects first - Applicable combining algorithm to resolve the conflicts.

Few other approaches which were concentrating on formalizing XACML policies were provided [13] and [14]. In [13] a process algebra named as Communication Sequential Process(CSP) is provided to verify the policy's properties as well as to compare access control policies. In [14] Ahn et al does the formalization using a declarative programming known as Answer Set Programming (ASP) which enables ASP reasoners to perform policy evaluation. In either methods of formalization no guarantee for the complete elicitation of policy properties and policy verification is provided.

6   Conclusions

We have proposed a mechanism that facilitates systematic detection and resolution of XACML policy anomalies eliminating the need to construct BDD. An efficient anomaly detection and resolution is done at the design level hence reducing the processing time of the PDP and this could be helpful in cases of larger XACML policies with more number of rules, policies and policy set. This also aims at security in terms of access control and to increase availability of the service. As a future extension this could be implemented for XACML3.0 and also could be included with handling obligations and user defined functions.

References

1. Godik, S., Moses, T.: Extensible Access Control Markup Language (XACML). version 2.0, OASIS Standard (2005)
2. Hu, H., Ahn, G., Kulkarni, K.: Discovery and Resolution of Anomalies in Web Access Control Policies, p. 11 (2013)
3. XACML. OASIS XACML committee website (2011), http://www.oasisopen.org/committees/xacml/
4. Jajodia, S., Samarati, P., Subrahmanian, V.S.: A logical language for expressing authorizations. In: IEEE Symposium on Security and Privacy, Oakland, CA, pp. 31–42 (May 1997)
5. Jin, J., Ahn, G., Hu, H., Covington, M., Zhang, X.: Patient-centric authorization framework for sharing electronic health records. In: Proceedings of the 14th ACM Symposium on Access Control Models and Technologies, pp. 125–134. ACM, New York (2009)
6. Li, N., Wang, Q., Qardaji, W., Bertino, E., Rao, P., Lobo, J., Lin, D.: Access control policy combining: theory meets practice. In: Proceedings of the 14th ACM Symposium on Access Control Models and Technologies, pp. 135–144. ACM (2009)
7. Lin, D., Rao, P., Bertino, E., Lobo, J.: An approach to evaluate policy similarity. In: Proceedings of the 12th ACM Symposium on Access Control Models and Technologies, pp. 1–10. ACM (2007)
8. Lin, D., Rao, P., Bertino, E., Li, N., Lobo, J.: Exam: A Comprehensive Environment for the Analysis of Access Control Policies. International Journal of Information Security 9(4), 253–273 (2010)
9. Hu, H., Ahn, E.: Enabling Verification and Conformance Testing For Access Control Model. In: Proceedings of the 13th ACM Symposium on Access Control Models and Technologies, pp. 195–204. ACM (2008)
10. http://sunxacml.sourceforge.net
11. Liu, A., Chen, F., Hwang, J., Xie, T.: XEngine: A Fast and Scalable XACML Policy Evaluation Engine. ACM SIGMETRICS Performance Evaluation
12. Bauer, L., Garriss, S., Reiter, M.: Detecting and Resolving Policy Misconfigurations In Access-Control Systems. ACM Transactions on Information and System Security (TISSEC) 1, 2–5 (2011)
13. Bryans, J.: Reasoning about XACML policies using CSP. In: Proceedings of the 2005 workshop on Secure Web Services, p. 35. ACM (2005)
14. Ahn, G., Hu, H., Lee, J., Meng, Y.: Representing and Reasoning about Web Access Control Policies. In: 34th Annual IEEE Computer Software and Applications Conference, pp. 137–146. IEEE (2010)

Design for Prevention of Intranet Information Leakage via Emails

Neenu Manmadhan[1], Hari Narayanan[1], Jayaraj Poroor[2], and Krishnashree Achuthan[1]

[1] Amrita Center for Cyber Security Systems and Networks
Amrita Vishwa Vidyapeetham, Amritapuri, Kollam – 690525
mneenusoorya@gmail.com, hari@am.amrita.edu, Krishna@amrita.edu
[2] Founding Minds Software, Inforpark, Kakkanad, India – 682030
jayaraj.poroor@gmail.com

Abstract. The ubiquitous presences of internet and network technologies have enabled electronic mail systems as the primary medium of communication. Both between and within organizations, sensitive and personal information often transits through the electronic mail systems undetected. Information leakage through this mode of communication has become a daunting problem in today's world. Often the mail volume within an organization is quite large making manual monitoring impossible. In this paper an integration of secure information flow techniques on intranet electronic mail systems is investigated. Categorization of emails based on the sensitivity is accomplished effectively using machine learning techniques. Analyzing the information flow and simultaneously mapping, categorizing and sorting emails in real time prior to receipt of emails has been characterized in this study. Defining security policies and application of lattice models for controlled exchange of emails is discussed. The paper proposed a secure architecture for an email web application. Experimental analysis on the accuracy of the application was determined using Enron email dataset.

Keywords: Email filtering, Secure Communication, Information Leakage Prevention.

1   Introduction

Electronic mails are the most widely adopted mode of communication. Approximately 929 million email accounts that exist today are related to businesses and this contributes to email traffic of over 100 billion emails sent or received every day [1]. Information leakage results from the unauthorized distribution of sensitive information deliberately by either a malicious user or inadvertently by a normal user. According to a recent survey [2] of business professionals, fifty six percent of them admitted to sending emails to wrong recipients inadvertently and over 53% had received unencrypted, sensitive information via email. Although emails provide the swiftness and flexibility with communication, these statistics portray large potential risks as well. When one compares the long term impact, perhaps the accidental leakage of

J. Lloret Mauri et al. (Eds.): SSCC 2014, CCIS 467, pp. 136–148, 2014.
© Springer-Verlag Berlin Heidelberg 2014

information is more severe than intentional attempts, as in the former case, the frequency is higher and the user could be completely oblivious of the impact from the data loss [3]. Today email clients are ubiquitously used within many business organizations. Since many organizations i.e. over 60% of them in a specific study [4] do not use preventative measures for email data leakages, the extent of damage from such leakages may be staggering.

Our focus in this paper is related to this exact problem i.e. data leakages that occur from emails. While most emphasis in the security industry is focused on emails sent or received between businesses, there are several sophisticated alternatives to prevent data leakages from and to a network [5]   such scrutiny for intranet emails is not widely adopted. With social engineering on the rise, manipulation to reveal information has become much more prevalent today than ever before [6]. Posing authenticity, a "need to know" attitude, or harmless pursuit, a malicious insider could exploit naïve colleagues or officials. We propose a multilevel architecture in screening email content that allows administrators to exercise more control on email broadcasts. The proposed solution automatically prevents circulation of emails it detects as sensitive through machine learning techniques that are integrated onto access control.

2   Related Works

Incidents of data loss pose a major threat to the reputation and competitiveness of organizations [7]. Although it is possible to forensically identify the perpetrator using various techniques [8], the impact from the loss of data cannot be annihilated with this approach. Various solutions exist for this problem. The semantic representations of business personnel, their roles within an organization etc. has been utilized to identify structural linkages in communication [9] and model the organizational behavior. Various email security products like McAfee, Liquid Machines and Voltage Security are commercially available to detect and secure sensitive data in email communications [5, 10]. Their proprietary solutions assist with preventing data loss. Most of these solutions are embedded in the network layer that will enforce some policies. Also these products focus only on the communication between networks and not within the same network. One of the most predominant ways to securing data is clustering information topically to allow better control of its access [11]. Fundamentally, these approaches rely on defining the sensitivity of data. However, they do not measure the degree of sensitivity of the information being communicated through emails.

Classification of emails using predefined categories is a useful methodology in its analysis. A comparative study of various machine learning techniques such as Naïve Bayes, Nearest Neighbour, Support Vector Machine (SVM), Decision Tree, and Multilayer Perceptron to classify content [12] found SVM and Naïve Bayes superior in their performances when Term Frequency (TF) representation is used with feature selection. Naive Bayes algorithm is used commonly in spam filtering for its efficiency and high precision [13]. The performance comparisons of Naïve Bayes Classifier with that of SVM, K-Nearest Neighbour and Decision Tree for document classification [14] found Naïve Bayes to be simpler and more efficient for training and classification. However, accuracy of the classification depends greatly on the pre-processing of the data. Even if the classification method is efficient the final result will be accurate only if there is data quality.

Classifiers use feature selection to make the classification process fast, accurate and cost effective. By using Discriminative Power Measure and GINI index as the feature selection metrics, it is found that TF based metric is better than document frequency based metric for smaller feature sets [15].Three indexing methods - TFIDF (Term Frequency Inverse Document Frequency), multiword and LSI (Latent Semantic Indexing) are compared and it is found that the performance of TFIDF and multiword are comparable but LSI's performance is poor [16]. Three metrics TFIDF, CBTW (Category Based Term Weights) and TFSLF (Term Frequency Sum of Local Frequencies) were compared for their performance [17]. An improved feature selection method named Distinguishing Feature Selector (DFS) was developed by Alper and Serkin in 2012 [18] whose performance is better with respect to accuracy and processing time but filter based methods do not consider feature dependencies. Zhihua et al. in their work on Naive Bayes Multi Label (NBML) classifiers that used a two-step feature selection strategy [19] which had comparable performance to commonly used algorithms such as Ada Boost and kNN. However, one of the weaknesses of NBML is that it cannot correlate between the labels. In a parallel attempt, Mark et al. [20] have used unsupervised learning techniques to automatically summarize the content of emails.

An intranet communication system can be visualized as a hierarchical structure allowing flow of information between multiple entities, with different security clearance at each level. Hence an adaptation of Denning's [21] lattice structure to formulate security requirements in this scenario becomes possible. A separation of right to access information from right to propagate information was proposed by Denning. Sandhu [22] discuss three access control models which either provide confidentiality or integrity to information, while extensions to his work to meet both the confidentiality and integrity requirements were done by Shen et. al [23].

This paper implements an integrated approach to intelligently classify information while enhancing its security by using access control. A characterization of the effectiveness of this integrated approach is presented using the Enron email corpus. Prior work indicated Enron's organizational structure before its debacle [24] and the analysis from clustering of keywords in this corpus [25] together with additional features like thread and email address groups showed increased accuracy.

3   SecIES: Multilevel Security Architecture

A multilevel secure content filtering architecture is proposed for an intranet email application - SecIES (Secure Intranet Email System). The email application allows exchange of emails between employees within an organization that may be at different levels of hierarchy. The architecture depicted in SecIES (Fig. 1) has three primary modules: 1) Pre-processing engine 2) Email content classification engine 3) Security enforcement engine.

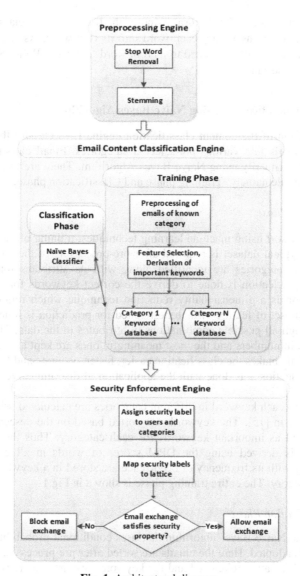

Fig. 1. Architectural diagram

These modules are elaborated as follows:

3.1   Pre-processing Engine

Pre-processing assists with extraction of the correct keywords for content classification. The pre-processing steps include execution of two critical functions namely "stop word removal, stemming". The first step i.e. Stop Word Removal is the process in which elimination of stop words such as 'is', 'are', 'am' etc. that doesn't convey any relevant information is removed from the content of the message. This helps to reduce the search space which in turn dwindles the time taken for classification. The second step i.e. stemming purges each word into its root word. As an example 'connection', 'connected' can be reduced to its root word 'connect'. Porter Stemmer algorithm is used for the same.

3.2   E-mail Classification Using Naïve Bayes Algorithm

The main function of the content classification engine is to classify the content and therefore the emails into various pre-selected categories. Email classification phase and this is done primarily using Naïve Bayes Algorithm. There are two main components to this module namely: Training phase and Classification phase.

1) Training Phase

To accurately sort using machine learning techniques, training of the classification engine with a typical dataset is required after pre-processing of the content. Prior to training certain categories are identified along with its attributes for this training dataset. Feature selection is done to derive the correct keywords for each category. Feature selection is a dimensionality reduction technique which removes the noise features. The subset of features which best suited for prediction is found out here by searching through all possible combinations of attributes in the data. These attributes can be reduced in numbers and the most meaningful ones are kept and irrelevant ones are removed. This makes the classification easier, faster, accurate and low cost. In this work feature selection was done with the application of discriminative power metrics (DPM) [15].

DPM score of each keyword in different categories are calculated using the methodology specified in [15]. The keywords are sorted based on the descending order of DPM considered as important keywords for each category. Thus the feature set of each category is derived using the DPM scores of words in all categories. The attributes along with its frequency of occurrence are stored in a keyword database for each of the category. The entire training phase is shown in Fig.1

2) Classification Phase

In this phase, Naive Bayes algorithm that uses conditional probability approach to classification is adopted. Here the emails are sorted after pre-processing to predefined categories. Each email is tokenized and the keywords are listed as K $\{k_1, k_2, k_n\}$. For each of the keyword in the keyword list, the probability of occurrence of that keyword in all the categories is found out using the keyword database. This is done for all the keywords in the email. Conditional probability of keywords in the email is multiplied and final probability is calculated for all the categories. Category with highest probability (P (cat|K)) is the category of the email which is computed as follows.

$$P(cat|K) = (P(K|cat) \times P(cat)) \div P(K).$$ (1)

for all categories where

$$P(K|cat) = P(k_1|cat) \times P(k_2|cat) \times P(k|cat).$$ (2)

3.3   Security Enforcement Engine Using Lattice Model

This section details a multi-level security enforcement engine using one of most efficient information flow control models namely the Lattice model. Information Flow is concerned with how information is disseminated or propagated from one object to another. According to Denning's Lattice Model [21], an information flow model consist of a set of objects like files, emails and set of subjects like employees in the organization who are the reason for this information flow. Security levels are assigned to 1) subjects i.e. the employees based on the organizational hierarchy and 2) the objects (i.e. emails with particular thematic topics). This assignment is mapped to a lattice structure and the email exchange is allowed only if it follows the simple security property as proposed by Bel LaPadula model (BLP) is satisfied. The sensitivity levels are classified as: top-secret, secret, confidential, and unclassified. An adaptation of BLP Model is used in this work. Here we make use of the security property that Alice can send an email to Bob, only if security level of category of the content of the email is less than or equal to the security level of recipient.

4   Case Study- Enron Corpus

For implementation and evaluation of the proposed architecture Enron corpus was used. The Enron email corpus is a large dataset containing 5000000 emails from 151 employees of 400 MB size. This data set is structured in that it provided ample opportunity to test the hypothesis of the proposed architecture. The hierarchical structure of Enron employees was adapted from [24]. This structure was used as the basis to identify the roles of employees. A set of 13,486 emails of 31 employees deemed critical in terms of their role in the organization and content of their communications were used in the present study. In this subset, emails that contain only 'thanks' were purged. Also none of the emails have any attachment. The experimental data for this work was extracted from the message body of the emails present in the inbox folder. The

Table 1. Category Security Levels

Category	Security Levels
Announcement	Unclassified
Business	Top Secret
Legal	Secret
Environment	Secret
Student	Confidential
Project	Confidential
Meeting	Unclassified
Personal	Unclassified

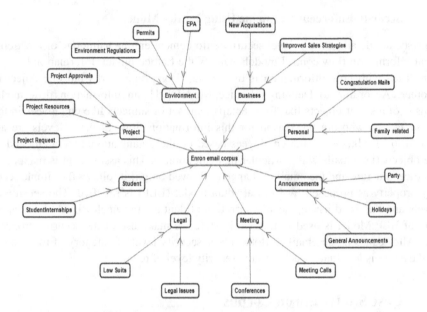

Fig. 2. Ontological Presentation of Categories

Table 2. Employee Descriptions

Employee Role	Employee Names	No of Emails	Security Level
Chairman	Kenneth Lay	1368	Top Secret
CEO	Jeffery Skilling, David Delainey	1274	Top Secret
Director	Robert Badeer, Robert Benson Matthew Motley, Michael Maggi Lawrence May, Andrew Lewis Sandra Brawner, Sean Crandall	2848	Secret
Vice President	John Arnold, Harpreet Arora Shelley Corman, Rod Hayslett Steven Kean, Danny McCarty Richard Shapiro, Rod Hayslett Jane Tholt	937	Secret
Specialist	Monika Causholli, Phillip Platter, Holden Salisbury, Cara Semperge	1755	Confidential
Trader	Eric Bass, Don Baughman, Craig Dean, Diana Scholtes, Ryan Slinger, Eric Saibi	2735	Unclassified

employee names, roles of employees, number of emails, and their security levels are described in Table 2. The security levels of employees were correlated to the roles of the employees in the organization. Eight categories were derived from the email corpus. The details of category description are shown in Fig. 2. Project category emails consist of Project Requests, Project Resources and Project approval emails. Student category includes Student Internship related emails. Law suits and Legal issues are incorporated in Legal category. Meeting category consists of conferences and meeting calls. Announcement category includes general announcements, holiday and party announcements. Family related and congratulation emails are included in personal category. New acquisitions and improved sales strategies come under business category. EPA, Environment Regulations and permits are categorized into Environment category. Categories and assigned security levels are detailed in Table 1.

5   Implementation and Analysis

A corporate intranet email application that contained 30 authenticated users was created using php, JavaScript, HTML with the data stored in MySQL database. In the process of email classification, train the model to identify different topics of emails in the inbox folders of employee described in Table 2 was carried out. Approximately 1000 emails were randomly chosen from a set of 13,486 emails to identify the topics of emails. Eight most common topics and 10 keywords relevant to each category were chosen using these 1000 emails. An ontological presentation of these emails is pictorially represented using Ontogen tool in Fig. 2.

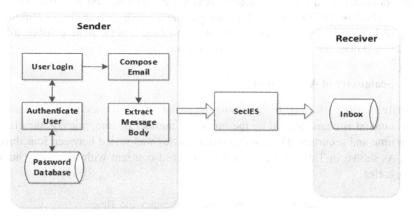

Fig. 3. Flow Diagram

For further analysis, initially identified keywords were used to extract more keywords of each category programmatically. The training aspects of classification module after pre-processing were implemented in java. Fig. 3 explains the process flow of the entire application. Whenever an employee tries to login to the application, he is authenticated by comparing user id and password entered by him, with that of password database. An authenticated employee can login to the application and can send an email to another employee. Before sending the email, the email content is extracted and passed it to three step processing i.e. pre-processing, classification and security enforcement as described in section 3. Once the message is termed cleared, and then it is forwarded as intended by the sender. Otherwise the email remains blocked.

5.1   Computation of Accuracy

To characterize the efficiency and performance of the application, the accuracy was characterized as a function of training size. Accuracy is defined as the ratio of number of emails correctly delivered to the total number of emails sent. When feature selection was not done as part of training, the accuracy was approximately 62%. With the implementation of feature selection algorithm i.e. DPM, accuracy improved considerably. As seen in Fig. 5, there is a modulation in accuracy as a function of feature size. A training set is defined as the number of keywords in each category that would be used to correctly classify the emails. The training set in this case used 6400 mails (which include 1000 mails initially taken for category identification and 5400 mails taken from 13,486 mails in Table2) and features were extracted from it using DPM. Emails which were not used for training were used for testing. The initial increase in accuracy up to 89.9% and then a decrease to 71.43% is due to over accumulation of key words with the inevitable inclusion of noise with increasing training size. In order to prevent this inclusion, an additional intervention was made and a new model was developed which use the feature space reduction algorithm called PCA. The new model thus had both TF-IDF followed by PCA. The resulting keywords were used to train the Naïve Bayes classifier. TF-IDF algorithm makes use of term frequency and inverse document frequency. Input to PCA is the matrix obtained with the words and its corresponding TF-IDF score. PCA reduces the number of features by eliminating the noise keywords. Figure 4 shows that this new model is far more consistent in its accuracy and does not vary as a function of feature size.

5.2   Scalability of Application

An analysis was performed to determine the scalability of the model. The scalability in this context is characterized by the impact of number of categories on the classification time and accuracy. The number of categories was varied between four through eight. As shown in Table 3, the accuracy remained constant with increasing number of categories.

Table 3. Category Count Vs Accuracy and Time

No of Categories	Accuracy(%)	Classification Time(secs)
4	72.4	0.1752
5	72.4	0.24293
6	72.4	0.27774
7	72.4	0.3266
8	72.4	0.34212

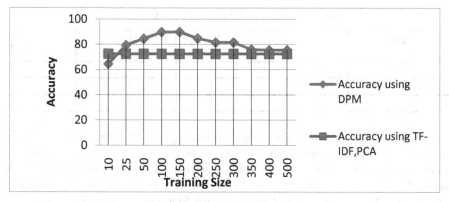

Fig. 4. Accuracy vs Training Size

5.3   Characterizing Misclassifications

Misclassification or errors are observed in typical predictive classification applications. However, it is important to characterize this to make further improvements. The confusion matrix for three categories from Table 2 namely -'Environment, Legal, Student' of this model based on the above mentioned test set is shown in Table 4. This matrix assists with identifying the gaps in classification. The shaded diagonal elements in the matrix show the correctly classified emails while others show the misclassifications. Based on the above confusion matrix a table of confusion was calculated for all the categories to find out the number of true positive, true negative, false positive and false negative for the above mentioned three categories. An example table of confusion say for category 'legal' is shown as Table 5.

Table 4. Confusion Matrix

	Environment	Legal	Student
Environ-ment	17	0	0
Legal	2	11	0
Student	0	0	13

Table 5. Table of Confusion

TP	FN
(Legal emails correctly classified as legal)	(Legal emails incorrectly marked under other non-legal categories)
FP	**TN**
(Non-legal emails incorrectly classified as legal)	(Non-legal emails correctly classified as not legal)

Accuracy of each category can be calculated by using equation (3). Number of TP, FP, TN and FN of each category with respective accuracies are tabulated in Table 6

$$\text{Accuracy}_{cat} = (TP_{cat}+TN_{cat})/ (TP_{cat}+TN_{cat}+FP_{cat}+FN_{cat}). \qquad (3)$$

Table 6. Accuracy, TP, FP, TN, FN for Categories

Category	Accuracy$_{cat}$ (%)	TP	FP	TN	FN
Environment	95.35	17	2	24	0
Legal	95.35	11	0	30	2
Student	100	13	0	30	0

The data in Table 6 is valid for a single operating point. Operating point here is the number of keywords considered for the categories which resulted in the above mentioned values. The values shown in Table 6 are for a single operating point of 800 keywords for each category. In order to understand the classifier performance in a wider perspective we make use of area under the ROC curve. True positive and false positive rates are shown in an ROC graph (Fig 5), where the y-axis represents the True Positive Rate (TPR) – the emails correctly classified to its original category and the x-axis represents the False-Positive Rate (FPR) - Emails incorrectly classified to any other category. The ROC graph indicates that the classifier can correctly classify the environment, student, and legal category with an accuracy of more than 90 percent. Student and legal categories achieved 100 percent TPR at certain operating points which is shown in Figure 5.The upper boundary of 100 percent is marked with solid line in Figure 5. The legal category gained 0 false positive rates at certain operating points. Also the false positive rates are comparatively low for all operating points for all categories. Hence this classifier is highly accurate on classifying the different categories using the selected operating points.

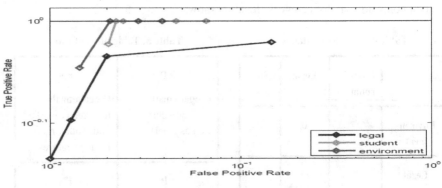

Fig. 5. ROC curves

6   Conclusion and Future Work

Leakage of sensitive information can cause irreparable losses to an organization. This paper has proposed an architecture i.e. SecIES to prevent information leakage through emails. The approach categorizes emails using Bayesian classifiers and provides a multi-level security using lattice construction for secure information flow using BLP model between the users and the thematic topics of their emails. The effectiveness of this model was assessed by first creating an email application, and measuring the model's accuracy on Enron email corpus. This was followed by generating the table of confusion for predominant themes. Judicious choice of thematic topics and defining the security levels is fundamental to this architecture. Optimization of accuracy was achieved using a combination of feature selection and feature space reduction algorithms. Characterization of accuracy revealed little sensitivity to increase in the classification categories indicating potential for robustness of this approach to secure email communication. Increasing the number of categories does proportionately increase the classification time. The architecture also demonstrated that it is capable of maintaining 72.4% accuracy, which means either the permissible emails are correctly delivered or non-permissible emails are blocked. While 27.6% emails were incorrectly classified and sent to wrong recipient. Although the proof of concept has been shown for three categories or name descriptors, it is important to explore the performance when other categories are introduced. Future work involves looking at local languages other than English, understand the email text semantics, and include email communications to the internet as well. We can further increase its scope of application by modifying the system so that it can efficiently run on mobile phones with resource constraints and provide an easy access to email accounts for mobile email users.

References

1. Email Statistics Report (2013-2017), http://www.radicati.com/wp/wp-content/uploads/2013/04/Email-Statistics-Report-2013-2017-Executive-Summary.pdf
2. Silver Sky Email Security Habits Survey Report (2013), https://www.silversky.com/knowledge-center/white-papers/silversky-email-security-habits-survey-report
3. Shabtai, A., Elovici, Y., Rokach, L.: A survey of data leakage detection and prevention solutions, pp. 1–46. Springer (2012)
4. Majority of Business Professionals Have Sent E-mails to the Wrong Person (2013), http://www.esecurityplanet.com/network-security/majority-of-business-professionals-have-sent-e-mails-to-the-wrong-person.html
5. Achieving End-to-End Email, http://www.voltage.com/wp-content/uploads/Voltage_DS_SecureMail.pdf
6. Which Disney© Princess are YOU? (2010), http://www.sans.org/reading-room/whitepapers/engineering/disney-princess-you-33328
7. Liu, S., Kuhn, R.: Data Loss Prevention. IEEE IT Professional 12, 10–13 (2010)
8. Agarwal, A., Gaikwad, M., Garg, K., Inamdar, V.: Robust Data leakage and Email Filtering System. In: International Conference on Computing, Electronics and Electrical Technologies (ICCEET), pp. 1032–1035 (2012)
9. Grobelnik, M., Mladenic, D., Fortuna, B.: Semantic technology for capturing communication inside an organization. IEEE Internet Computing, 59–67 (2013)

10. Mcafee Total Protection for Data Loss Prevention (2013), `http://www.mcafee.com/in/resources/solution-briefs/sb-total-protection-for-dlp.pdf`

11. Zilberman, P., Dolev, S., Katz, G., Elovici, Y., Shabtai, A.: Analyzing Group Communication for Preventing Data Leakage via Email. In: IEEE International Conference on Intelligence and Security Informatics (ISI), pp. 37–41 (2011)

12. Simanjuntak, D.A., Ipung, H.P., Lim, C., Nugroho, A.S.: Text Classification Techniques Used to Facilitate Cyber Terrorism Investigation. In: IEEE 2nd International Conference on Advances in Computing, Control, and Telecommunication Technologies, pp. 198–200 (2010)

13. Vira, D., Raja, P., Gada, S.: An Approach to Email Classification Using Bayesian Theorem. Global Journal of Computer Science and Technology Software Data Engineering 12(13) (2012)

14. Ting, S.L., Ip, W.H., Tsang, A.H.C.: Is Naïve Bayes a Good Classifier for Document Classification? International Journal of Software Engineering and Its Applications 5(3), 37–46 (2011)

15. Azam, N., Yao, J.: Comparison of term frequency and document frequency based feature selection metrics in text categorization. Elsevier 39(5), 4760–4768 (2012)

16. Zhang, W., Yoshida, T., Tang, X.: TFIDF, LSI and Multi-word in Information Retrieval and Text Categorization. In: IEEE International Conference on Systems, Man and Cybernetics, pp. 108–113 (2008)

17. Rahman, A., Babri, H.A., Saeed, M.: Feature Extraction Algorithms for Classification of Text Documents. In: International Conference on Computer and Information Technology, pp. 231–236 (2012)

18. Uysal, A.K., Gunal, S.: A novel probabilistic feature selection method for text classification. Knowledge-Based Systems 36, 226–235 (2012)

19. Wei, Z., Zhang, H., Zhang, Z., Li, W., Miao, D.: A Naive Bayesian Multi-label Classification Algorithm With Application to Visualize Text Search Results. International Journal of Advanced Intelligence 3(2), 173–188 (2011)

20. Dredze, M., Wallach, H.M., Puller, D., Pereira, F.: Generating Summary Keywords for Emails Using Topics. In: Proc. 13th ACM International Conference on Intelligent User Interfaces, pp. 199–206. ACM (2008)

21. Denning, D.E.: Lattice Model of Secure Information Flow. Communications of the ACM 19(5), 236–243 (1976)

22. Sandhu, R.S.: Lattice-Based Access Control Models. IEEEComputer 26(11), 9–19 (1993)

23. Ying, S., Lirong, X.: Lattice based BLP Extended Model. In: Second International Conference on Future Information Technology and Management Engineering, pp. 309–312 (2009)

24. Diesner, J., Frantz, T.L., Carley, K.M.: Communication networks from the Enron email corpus "It's always about the people. Enron is no different". Computational & Mathematical Organization Theory 11(3), 201–228 (2005)

25. Wang, M., He, Y., Jiang, M.: Text categorization of Enron email corpus based on information bottleneck and maximal entropy. In: IEEE 10th International Conference on Signal Processing (ICSP), pp. 2472–2475 (2010)

Ideal and Computationally Perfect Secret Sharing Schemes for Generalized Access Structures

Dileep Kumar Pattipati[1], Appala Naidu Tentu[2], and V.Ch. Venkaiah[1]

[1] School of Computer and Information Sciences,
University of Hyderabad,Hyderabad-500046, India
dileepkumar_p@outlook.com, venkaiah@hotmail.com
[2] CR Rao Advanced Institute of Mathematics, Statistics, and Computer Science
University of Hyderabad Campus, Hyderabad-500046, India
naidunit@gmail.com

Abstract. A secret sharing scheme is proposed in this paper. The scheme is ideal and uses computationally perfect concept. It uses a one way function and realizes generalized access structure. The scheme is useful for non-ideal access structures. For example, Stinson[14] has identified eighteen possible non-isomorphic monotone access structures with four participants. Fourteen of them admit ideal and perfect secret sharing schemes. The remaining four cannot be made both perfect and ideal. By making use of the computationally perfect concept, we propose ideal scheme for those four access structures.

Novelty of the scheme is that it is applicable for any number of participants and generates the least amount of public information. In fact, we show results that establish that the proposed scheme is optimal for access structures consisting of four or less number of participants. Our scheme can be extended to multiple secrets. Since some applications require that a secret sharing scheme designed for it be extended to the case of multiple secrets, our approach finds it useful in such scenarios.

Keywords: Computationally perfect, Ideal scheme, One-way function, Secret sharing.

1 Introduction

Secret sharing is a cryptographic primitive which is used to distribute a secret among a set of participants in such a way that an authorized subset of participants can uniquely reconstruct the secret, but an unauthorized subset cannot obtain any information about the secret. It is a fundamental technique used in secure multiparty computations where various distrusted participants cooperate and conduct tasks based on the private data they provide. Secret sharing was first proposed by Blakley [3] and Shamir [11]. The approach in [11] relies on Lagrange polynomial interpolation, whereas the scheme in [3] is geometric and uses the concept of intersecting hyperplanes.

J. Lloret Mauri et al. (Eds.): SSCC 2014, CCIS 467, pp. 149–161, 2014.

The family of authorized subsets is known as the access structure. An access structure is said to be monotone if a set is qualified implies that its superset is also qualified. Several access structures have been proposed in the literature. They include the (t, n)-threshold access structure and the generalized access structure. In a (t, n)-threshold access structure, there are n shareholders. An authorized group consists of any t or more participants and any group of at most $t - 1$ participants is an unauthorized group. Let U be a set of n participants and 2^U be its power set. Generalized access structure refers to the case where the collection of authorized subsets of U may be any subset Γ of 2^U, $\Gamma \subseteq 2^U$, having the monotonicity property.

A secret sharing scheme is a perfect realization of Γ [14] if for all authorized sets $A \in \Gamma$, the users in A can always reconstruct the secret, and for all unauthorized sets B not in Γ, the users in B collectively cannot obtain any information about the secret. Note that a scheme that satisfy this criteria is unconditionally secure. This is because no amount of computation would help to recover the secret by an unauthorized set. Such a scheme is referred in the literature as an information theoretic scheme [7, 19] or a perfect secret sharing scheme in the information theoretic sense [1, 8, 10, 13, 19] or unconditionally secure secret sharing scheme [4, 6].

The information rate, ρ_i, for participant i is defined as the ratio of the length of the secret, expressed in bits, to the length of the share, also expressed in bits i.e.

$$\rho_i = \frac{\log_2 |\text{secret}|}{\log_2 |\text{share}|}.$$

The information rate ρ of the scheme is defined as $\rho = \min\{\rho_i : i \text{ is a participant of the scheme}\}$.

A well known fact in secret sharing is that the size of a share is atleast the size of the secret. Therefore, the information rate of the participant and hence the information rate of the scheme are both bounded between 0 and 1. Schemes with maximum information rate are desirable[14]. A secret sharing scheme is ideal if its information rate is 1 [14]. Not all access structures admit ideal schemes. For example, Stinson [14] has shown that out of all possible generalized access structures with four participants, there are four non-isomorphic structures that do not admit an ideal and perfect secret sharing scheme. These access structures are given below.

- $P_1P_2 + P_2P_3 + P_3P_4$
- $P_1P_2 + P_2P_3 + P_2P_4 + P_3P_4$
- $P_1P_3P_4 + P_1P_2 + P_2P_3$
- $P_1P_3P_4 + P_1P_2 + P_2P_3 + P_2P_4$

The first access structure $\Gamma = P_1P_2 + P_2P_3 + P_3P_4$ denotes that the set of authorized sets are $\{\{P_1, P_2\}, \{P_2, P_3\}, \{P_3, P_4\}\}$. Similar notation is used for the access structures in the paper.

In case of access structures that do not admit ideal schemes, an optimal scheme can be defined. A secret sharing scheme is optimal if it has maximum permissible information rate.

Secret sharing schemes which are perfect and not ideal can be made computationally perfect and ideal. Note the tradeoff between perfect and ideal. A scheme is called computationally perfect if an authorized set can always reconstruct the secret in polynomial time whereas for an unauthorized set this is computationally hard [16–18]. A variation to this is known in the literature as a computational secret sharing scheme [19].

A computational secret sharing scheme [19] is a protocol π between a dealer D and a set of participants P to share a secret $s \in F_q$, with respect to an access structure Γ such that:

- The dealer D distributes a share $s_i \in S'$ to player P_i, $i = 1, 2, \cdots, n$. D retires from the protocol immediately afterwards.
- There is a polynomial-time algorithm π_{REC}, such that $\pi_{REC}(s_{i_i}, s_{i_2}, \cdots, s_{i_m})$ $= s$ with probability 1 if $\{P_{i_1}, P_{i_2}, \cdots, P_{i_m}\} \in \Gamma$.
- For any set of players $\{P_{i_1}, P_{i_2}, \cdots, P_{i_m}\} \notin \Gamma$ and any (possibly randomized) polynomial-time algorithm π_{ADV}, $Prob[\pi_{ADV}(s_{i_i}, s_{i_2}, \cdots, s_{i_m}) = s] \leq \frac{1}{|F_q|^c}$ for an arbitrary constant c.

Cachin et al. [4] and Vinod et al. [19] proposed ideal computational secret sharing schemes for generalized access structures. These techniques make use of either one-way or trapdoor one-way functions, and can be generalized to any number of participants. The Cachin et al. scheme creates an exponential amount of public information whereas the Vinod et al. scheme uses an exponential number of trapdoor one-way functions.

1.1   Our Contribution

In this paper we propose an ideal scheme for non-ideal access structures. The proposed scheme is computationally perfect. A novelty of the scheme is that the same ground field caters to both the secret space and the share space and it is applicable for any number of participants. Further, the amount of public information is not exponential. The scheme needs only one one-way function.

1.2   Outline of the Paper

The existing computational secret sharing schemes and their drawbacks are discussed in section 2. The basic idea of our scheme is to secure a set of numbers keeping one of them as the secret. Section 3 comes up with an implemetation to achieve this. Then we make use of the computationally perfect[16] concept and propose ideal schemes for a generalized access structure with any number of participants in section 4. The amount of public information created by our scheme is less than that of the Vinod et al. and Cachin et al. schemes. It is shown in section 5 that the proposed scheme creates a minimal amount of public information for all access structures with four participants.

2   Existing Ideal and Computational Secret Sharing Schemes

A scheme that uses the information dispersal algorithm and reduces the share size was proposed in [9]. The ground field for shares and secret are different in this approach. The scheme proposed in [4] requires that a unit of information be publicized for each authorized set. Since there can be an exponential number of authorized sets in a generalized access structure, the amount of public information can be exponential. A scheme that uses boolean functions and trapdoor one-way functions was proposed in [19]. The number of one-way functions that this scheme requires is comparable to the size of the field. Clearly this is very large and is not practical.

Computationally perfect concept is used to generate ideal schemes for several sub-classes of generalized access structures. Computationally perfect schemes are designed for conjunctive hierarchial [16, 17], and compartmental access structures with lower bounds[18] based on MDS(Maximum Distance Seperable) codes.

3   How to Secure a Set of Numbers Keeping One of Them as the Secret?

If a set of n numbers $a_1, \cdots, a_n$, chosen from a field F_q, are to be secured, then the amount of secret information would be $n * \log |F_q|$ bits. We hereby propose a method to secure this set of numbers under the computational model[19] explained above. This method relies on the intractability of one-way functions and reduces the public information to one unit.

In this method, one of the numbers, say a_1 is kept secret and its image $f(a_1)$ under the chosen one-way function, f, is computed. This image is subtracted from each of the other numbers to be secured. Let the resulting numbers be $I_1, \cdots, I_{n-1}$. Publish these numbers. Note that the following equations govern the relationship between the numbers to be secured and the numbers that are publicized.

$$a_2 = f(a_1) + I_1 \tag{1}$$

$$a_3 = f(a_1) + I_2 \tag{2}$$

$$\vdots$$

$$a_n = f(a_1) + I_{n-1} \tag{3}$$

Observe that information such as the difference of two secret numbers can be inferred from the above set of equations. This can be arrested if the numbers to be secured are expressed in the following way.

$$a_2 = f(a_1) + I_1 \tag{4}$$
$$a_3 = f^2(a_1) + I_2 \tag{5}$$
$$\vdots$$
$$a_n = f^{n-1}(a_1) + I_{n-1} \tag{6}$$

where $f^h(\bullet)$ denote the composition of the function f with itself h times. This later approach is used to secure the given set of numbers.

4 Proposed Scheme

Let F_q be the ground field from which the secrets and the shares are chosen, and f be a trapdoor one-way function. Also, let $P_1, \cdots, P_n$ be the participants and $A_1, \cdots, A_{|\Gamma|}$ be the $|\Gamma|$ authorized sets of the access structure Γ.

4.1 Overview of the Scheme

The distribution phase of the scheme consists of two steps. In the first step, a perfect secret sharing scheme is chosen based on the access structure. The chosen scheme is used to generate shares. Note that the scheme may generate more than one share for a participant depending on the access structure. In the second step, the number of shares are reduced to one for each participant and is secretly communicated to the participant .

Let k be the secret. Choose randomly the shares of participants and distribute one each so that the sum of the shares of an authorized set is the secret k. A participant may receive more than one share, because it can be a member of more than one authorized set. To make the scheme ideal, each participant is assigned only one of the previously allocated shares. The chosen one-way function is applied on the assigned share successively. Each of the resulting values are subtracted from one of the remaining shares and the resulting values are published.

4.2 Setup and Distribution Phase

Let k be the secret, A_i denote the ith authorized set.

1. For each authorized set A_i do the following
   Choose $|A_i|$ - 1 random numbers from the field F_q. Let these numbers be $k_1, k_2, \cdots, k_{|A_i|-1}$. Distribute these numbers one each among the $|A_i| - 1$ members of the authorized set. Assign $k - (k_1 + k_2 \cdots + k_{|A_i|-1})$ as the share for the remaining participant.

   Note: If a participant x is a member of a_x authorized sets, then x receives, as a result of step 1, a_x shares. Let these shares be denoted by $s_{x_1}, s_{x_2}, \cdots, s_{x_{a_x}}$.

2. For each participant x, do the following
   (a) Assign one of the many shares corresponding to the participant. That share, say s_{x_1}, is secretly communicated to x.
   (b) Compute s_{x_j} - $f^{i-1}(s_{x_1})$ for every share s_{x_j}, $2 \le j \le a_x$, and publish each one of these values against the participant's identity with the access structure as the index.

4.3   Recovery Phase

1. Collect the shares from each participant of the concerned authorized set. Let i be the corresponding index of the authorized set. Also let the collected shares be denoted by $s_{x_1}, s_{x_2}, \cdots, s_{x_j}$, where j is the cardinality of the authorized set.
2. For each share s_{x_p}, do the following
   (a) Based on the index of authorized set i and participant's identity, find the corresponding public information I_p. Add I_p with $f^{i-1}(s_{x_p})$ to find the actual share k_p.

3. Add all the shares of the members of the authorized set, $(k_1 + k_2 \cdots + k_j)$, to find the secret k.

4.4   Example

Let the access structure consists of authorized sets $A_{(1)} = \{P_1, P_2\}$, $A_{(2)} = \{P_2, P_3\}$, and $A_{(3)} = \{P_3, P_4\}$.the ground field be F_{197}, and the secret be 8.

Consider the first authorized subset $A_{(1)}$. Let the share given to P_1 be $k_1 = 4$. Then the share for P_2 will be $k - k_1 = 4$. Assigning 6 to participant P_2 corresponding to the authorized set $\{P_2, P_3\}$ and 7 to participant P_3 corresponding to the authorized set $\{P_3, P_4\}$, we have the following share distribution.

share(P_1) = $\{4\}$
share(P_2) = $\{4, 6\}$
share(P_3) = $\{2, 7\}$
share(P_4) = $\{1\}$

Let the one-way function be exponentiation of the primitive element 2 in F_{197}. Without loss of generality, assume that the first share is given as the actual share to each user so that P_1, P_2, P_3 and P_4 get 4, 4, 2 and 1 respectively. For P_1 and P_4, no public information need be published. For P_2, using his share, publish $6 - f(4) = (6 - (2^4 \mod 197) \mod 197) = 187$ as the public information. Similarly, for P_3, publish $7 - f(f(2)) = (7 - f(2^2 \mod 197) \mod 197) = (7 - (2^4 \mod 197) \mod 197) = 188$ as the public information.

Assume that the authorized set $\{P_2, P_3\}$ would like to reconstruct the secret. Then P_2 and P_3 submit their shares 4 and 2 respectively. The reconstruction algorithm then computes the corresponding share for P_2 using the corresponding published value, i.e., it computes $f(4) + 187 = (16 + 187) \mod 197 = 6$. Since the share of the participant P_3 is 2, the secret is then $(6 + 2) \mod 197 = 8$.

Note: To achieve the least amount of public information, any optimal scheme such as the scheme discussed in section 5.3 may be employed in step 1 of the proposed scheme

4.5 Complexity Analysis

This section analyzes the computational requirements of the proposed scheme. In the first step of the distribution phase, each participant receives a share corresponding to each authorized set in which the participant is a member. Thus, the time needed for the first step will be $O(n|\Gamma|)$, where n is the number of participants and $|\Gamma|$ is the length of the access structure, i.e., the number of authorized sets. Let l denote the size of the largest share, expressed in bits. Assuming that the one-way function to be used is exponentiation of a generator element in F_q, Step 2b requires $O(n|\Gamma| \log l)$ operations. The complexity of the distribution phase is then $O(n|\Gamma| \log l)$ operations. The complexity of the reconstruction algorithm is $O(n \log l)$ operations. This is because an authorized set consists of $O(n)$ members.

4.6 Correctness of the Scheme

The following theorems establish that the proposed scheme is ideal and always recovers the secret in polynomial time if and only if the set of participants is an authorized set.

Theorem 1. *The secret can be recovered by the recovery phase described above if and only if the set of participants recovering the secret is an authorized set.*

Proof. The only if condition is proved by contradiction, i.e., if the set of participants is an unauthorized set then the secret cannot be recovered. An unauthorized set can be either a proper subset of one of the authorized sets or not a proper subset of an authorized set. In either case, sum of all the shares of the set does not result in the required secret.

(if part). If the set of participants is an authorized set, they can recover the secret. Sum of the shares of an authorized set is the secret itself. Each share is in turn the sum of the published value and the image of the one of the shares of the participant under the composition of the one way function f.

Theorem 2. *The proposed scheme is ideal.*

Proof. In the proposed scheme, each participant is given only one share. Further, both the shares and the secret are chosen from the same ground field. Thus the proposed scheme is ideal.

Theorem 3. *The proposed scheme is computationally perfect.*

Proof. From the complexity analysis, it can be easily inferred that an authorized set can recover the secret in polynomial time.

For an unauthorized set, shares of other participants are required to reconstruct the secret. This may require the share of the other participants not present in the unauthorized set.

5   Comparison with Other Schemes

The amount of public information published by Vinod et.al. scheme is not discussed in their original paper[19]. Analysis of their scheme is required to compare with our scheme. Also a note on optimal schemes for access structures consisting of four participants is needed to know the optimal information rate for these access structures. So this section reviews Cachin's[4] and Vinod et.al.[19] schemes, analyzes Vinod et.al. scheme for the amount of public information it publishes, and carries out a comparative analysis of our scheme with these schemes.

5.1   Analysis of Cachin's Scheme

The shares are selected randomly and each participant is allocated exactly one share. A one-way function is applied on the sum of shares of each of the authorized set. The computed value is subtracted from the secret and the resulting values are then published. Mathematically,

$$\forall A \in \Gamma, \ I_A = k - (\sum_{P \in A} share(P)) \tag{7}$$

where Γ is an access structure, A is an authorized set of Γ, P is a participant in A, k is the secret, $share(P)$ is the share of the participant P and I_A is the public information associated with the authorized set A. So the amount of public information is the number of authorized sets within the access structure $|\Gamma|$.

5.2   Analysis of Vinod et.al. Scheme

Overview of Vinod et.al. Scheme. Let F_q be the ground field from which the secret and the shares are choosen. Also let $ENC_K : F_q \to F_q$ be a family of trapdoor one-way functions with index K over F_q, and $DEC_K : F_q \to F_q$ be the corresponding inverses.

The scheme requires that the access structure be expresssed in terms of a boolean circuit consisting of FANOUT, AND, and OR gates. The FANOUT gate has two outputs and one input; whereas the other gates have two inputs and one output. An example of such a circuit is given in Fig 1. The output wire of the circuit is assigned the secret. Then, in each iteration, the input wires of a gate are assigned values, for whose ouput gate has already been assigned a value, according to the following rules:

- If G is an OR gate, then the input wires are assigned the same as that of the output wire.
- If G is an AND gate and the value on the output wire is $V(W_O)$, then one of the input wires is assigned a random value, say x from the ground field. The other wire is assigned the value $x \oplus V(W_O)$.
- If G is a FANOUT gate and the output wires are W_1 and W_2, then select a random key K from F_q and assign it to the input wire. Publish $ENC_K(V(W_1))$ and $ENC_K(V(W_2))$.

The above process is repeated until all the wires have been assigned a value. The values on the input wires of the participants are the shares of the participants. As each user has only one input wire, the scheme is ideal. The amount of public information is discussed below.

Analysis. The following analysis of the scheme establishes that the amount of public information required by Vinod et.al. scheme is $2*(m-1)$, where m is the number of FANOUT gates.

If an input is required by only one gate, then the input wire of the gate is provided the input. No FANOUT gates are required.

If an input is required by two gates, then a FANOUT gate is needed. The outputs of the FANOUT gate are connected to other gates.

If an input is required by three gates, then two FANOUT gates are needed. The first output of the first FANOUT gate is connected to the circuit and the second output is connected to the second FANOUT gate. The two outputs of the second FANOUT gate are connected to the circuit.

Theorem 4. *If the share of the participant is required as input for m gates, then the amount of public information corresponding to the participant is* $2*(m-1)$.

Proof. As per the discussion above, if the share of the participant is required for m gates, then $m-1$ FANOUT gates are needed. As per their implementation of computational model, each FANOUT gate generates two units of public information. See the explanation given in the overview of the scheme. Hence the total amount of public information is $2*(m-1)$.

Total amount of public information is then the sum of the individual public information for each participant.

Remark: The amount of public information is optimum when the number of FANOUT gates used is mininum. The FANOUT gates can be minimized by efficiently grouping authorized sets. The following diagrams, meant to achieve the same functionality, provide an example for efficient grouping of authorized sets. The second circuit shows that efficient grouping of authorized sets reduces the number of FANOUT gates and hence reduces the amount of public information.

5.3 Optimal Schemes for Non Ideal Access Structures

As already mentioned in Section 1, there are access structures which cannot be both perfect and ideal. So any scheme designed to realize these access structures can atmost have optimal information rate. The access structures for which there exist no ideal scheme and has four participants are given below.

- $AS1 = P_1P_2 + P_2P_3 + P_3P_4$
- $AS2 = P_1P_2 + P_2P_3 + P_2P_4 + P_3P_4$
- $AS3 = P_1P_3P_4 + P_1P_2 + P_2P_3$
- $AS4 = P_1P_3P_4 + P_1P_2 + P_2P_3 + P_2P_4$

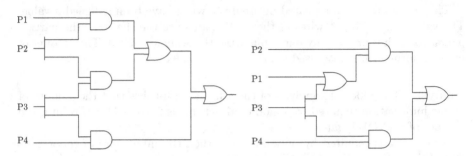

Fig. 1. Circuits for the Access Structure $P_1P_2 + P_2P_3 + P_3P_4$ illustrating Efficient Grouping

Any optimal secret sharing scheme for these four access structures must distribute five shares in total to the participants[5]. Optimal schemes are designed combining ideal decomposition approach[15] and an ideal secret sharing scheme.

For example $AS2$ is decomposed into $AS2_1 = P_2P_3 + P_2P_4 + P_3P_4$ and $AS2_2 = P_1P_2$. $AS2_1$ is solved using $(2,3)$-threshold scheme[11] and produces 3 shares. $AS2_2$ is solved using $(2,2)$-threshold scheme and produces two shares. Combining both the schemes give a total of 5 shares. Similarly $AS1$ can be solved by decomposing into $AS1_1 = P_1P_2$ and $AS1_2 = P_2P_3 + P_3P_4$. Similarly, the remaining two access structures $AS3$ and $AS4$ are solved using simmons geometric construction[12] and produces five shares[14].

5.4   Comparison with Other Computational Schemes

The amount of public information published by Cachin's scheme is $|\Gamma|$, cardinality of Γ, where Γ is an access structure. Public information required in the Vinod et al. scheme is analyzed above to be $2*(m-1)$, where m is the number of FANOUT gates. The amount of public information published by our scheme is zero for ideal access structures, whereas for non-ideal access structures, the amount of public information required is the total number of shares generated minus n, the number of participants. This can be seen to be minimum if an optimal information theoretic secret scheme is employed.

A brief comparison of the public information required by the proposed scheme with that of the Cachin et al. [4] and that of the Vinod et al. [19] schemes for the 18 permissible non-isomorphic access structures with four participants identified by Stinson[14] is given in table 1. Similar comparison for the number of one way functions is given in table 2.

Theorem 5. *The amount of public information produced by our scheme is optimal for access structures upto four participants.*

Proof. Stinson [14] has identified eighteen nonisomorphic montone access structures with four participants. Any generalized access structure with four participants can be shown to be equivalent to one of these eighteen access structures

Table 1. Public Information of the schemes

Access Structure Γ	Grouping of Γ	Cachin	Vinod	Our scheme
P_1P_2	P_1P_2	1	0	0
$P_1P_2 + P_2P_3$	$P_2(P_1 + P_3)$	2	0	0
$P_1P_2 + P_2P_3 + P_1P_3$	$P_2(P_1 + P_3) + P_1P_3$	3	4	0
$P_1P_2P_3$	$P_1P_2P_3$	1	0	0
$P_1P_2 + P_2P_3 + P_3P_4$	$P_2(P_1 + P_3) + P_3P_4$	3	2	1
$P_1P_2 + P_1P_3 + P_1P_4$	$P_1(P_2 + P_3 + P_4)$	3	0	0
$P_1P_2 + P_1P_4 + P_2P_3 + P_3P_4$	$(P_1 + P_3)(P_2 + P_4)$	4	0	0
$P_1P_2 + P_2P_3 + P_2P_4 + P_3P_4$	$P_2(P_1 + P_3) + P_4(P_2 + P_3)$	4	4	1
$P_1P_2 + P_1P_3 + P_1P_4 + P_2P_3 + P_2P_4$	$P_1(P_2 + P_3 + P_4) + P_2(P_3 + P_4)$	5	6	0
$P_1P_2 + P_1P_3 + P_1P_4 + P_2P_3 + P_2P_4 + P_3P_4$	$(P_1 + P_2 + P_3)P_4 + P_2(P_1 + P_3) + P_1P_3$	6	10	0
$P_1P_2P_3 + P_1P_4$	$P_1(P_2P_3 + P_4)$	2	0	0
$P_1P_3P_4 + P_1P_2 + P_2P_3$	$P_1(P_2 + P_3P_4) + P_2P_3$	3	4	1
$P_1P_3P_4 + P_1P_2 + P_2P_3 + P_2P_4$	$P_1(P_2 + P_3P_4) + P_2(P_3 + P_4)$	4	6	1
$P_1P_2P_3 + P_1P_2P_4$	$P_1P_2(P_3 + P_4)$	2	0	0
$P_1P_2P_4 + P_1P_3P_4 + P_2P_3$	$P_1P_4(P_2 + P_3) + P_2P_3$	3	4	0
$P_1P_2P_3 + P_1P_2P_4 + P_1P_3P_4$	$P_1(P_2(P_3 + P_4) + P_3P_4)$	3	4	0
$P_1P_2P_3 + P_1P_2P_4 + P_1P_3P_4 + P_2P_3P_4$	$P_1P_2(P_3 + P_4) + P_3P_4(P_1 + P_2)$	4	8	0
$P_1P_2P_3P_4$	$P_1P_2P_3P_4$	1	0	0

Table 2. Comparison of the proposed and other secret schemes

Scheme	No. of One-way Functions	Amount of Public Information
Cachin et al.	1	$|\Gamma|$
Vinod et al.	Field size	depends on the access structure
Our schemes	1	less than that of the Vinod et al. as well as Cachin et al. schemes

by graph isomorphism and monotone operations. So, it is sufficient to prove that the amount of public information is optimal for these access structures. Fourteen of them have ideal and perfect secret sharing schemes [14]. For these access structures, employ an ideal scheme corresponding to the access structure in step 1 of our method. This results in the zero public information of our scheme.

As discussed above, there are optimal schemes for the remaining four access strcutures which generate five units of shares. Employing these schemes in step 1 of our method, the amount of public information is one unit for our scheme. This is the minimum possible public information for these access structures. Hence our scheme publishes optimal public information.

6 Conclusion

An ideal secret sharing scheme, which makes use of computationally perfect concept is proposed in this paper. It uses one way function and realizes generalized access structure. Novelty of the scheme is that it is applicable for any number of participants and generates the least amount of public information. In fact, we showed results that established that the amount of public information is optimal for access structures consisting of four or less number of paticipants. Since some applications require that a secret sharing scheme designed for it be extended to the case of multiple secrets, our approach finds it useful in such scenarios.

The proposed scheme is not secure against cheating. A dishonest participant may gain illegal advantage by giving wrong share. To prevent such dishonest participants, robust schemes[2] have been introduced. A robust scheme calculates the correct secret, even if some of the participants sumbit wrong shares. We will try to bring robustness into our scheme as part of our future work.

References

1. Beimel, A.: Secret-sharing schemes: A survey. In: Chee, Y.M., Guo, Z., Ling, S., Shao, F., Tang, Y., Wang, H., Xing, C. (eds.) IWCC 2011. LNCS, vol. 6639, pp. 11–46. Springer, Heidelberg (2011), http://dx.doi.org/10.1007/978-3-642-20901-7_2

2. Ben-Or, M., Goldwasser, S., Wigderson, A.: Completeness theorems for non-cryptographic fault-tolerant distributed computation. In: Proceedings of the Twentieth Annual ACM Symposium on Theory of Computing, STOC 1988, pp. 1–10. ACM, New York (1988), http://doi.acm.org/10.1145/62212.62213

3. Blakley, G.R.: Safeguarding Cryptographic Keys. In: Proceedings of the 1979 AFIPS National Computer Conference, vol. 48, pp. 313–317 (June 1979)

4. Cachin, C.: On-line secret sharing. In: Boyd, C. (ed.) Cryptography and Coding 1995. LNCS, vol. 1025, pp. 190–198. Springer, Heidelberg (1995)

5. Capocelli, R., Santis, A., Gargano, L., Vaccaro, U.: On the size of shares for secret sharing schemes. Journal of Cryptology 6(3), 157–167 (1993), http://dx.doi.org/10.1007/BF00198463

6. Charnes, C., Martin, K.M., Pieprzyk, J., Safavi-Naini, R.: Secret sharing in hierarchical groups. In: Han, Y., Quing, S. (eds.) ICICS 1997. LNCS, vol. 1334, pp. 81–86. Springer, Heidelberg (1997), http://dl.acm.org/citation.cfm?id=646277.687203

7. Chor, B., Goldwasser, S., Micali, S., Awerbuch, B.: Verifiable secret sharing and achieving simultaneity in the presence of faults. In: Proceedings of the 26th Annual Symposium on Foundations of Computer Science, SFCS 1985, pp. 383–395. IEEE Computer Society, Washington, DC (1985), http://dx.doi.org/10.1109/SFCS.1985.64

8. Ding, C., Laihonen, T., Renvall, A.: Linear multisecret-sharing schemes and error-correcting codes. j-jucs 3(9), 1023–1036 (1997)

9. Krawczyk, H.: Secret sharing made short. In: Stinson, D.R. (ed.) CRYPTO 1993. LNCS, vol. 773, pp. 136–146. Springer, Heidelberg (1994), http://dl.acm.org/citation.cfm?id=646758.705700

10. Lin, C., Harn, L., Ye, D.: Ideal perfect multilevel threshold secret sharing scheme. In: Proceedings of the 2009 Fifth International Conference on Information Assurance and Security, IAS 2009, vol. 02, pp. 118–121. IEEE Computer Society, Washington, DC (2009), http://dx.doi.org/10.1109/IAS.2009.279

11. Shamir, A.: How to share a secret. Commun. ACM 22(11), 612–613 (1979), http://doi.acm.org/10.1145/359168.359176

12. Simmons, G.J.: How to (really) share a secret. In: Goldwasser, S. (ed.) CRYPTO 1988. LNCS, vol. 403, pp. 390–448. Springer, Heidelberg (1990), http://dx.doi.org/10.1007/0-387-34799-2_30

13. Stadler, M.: Publicly verifiable secret sharing. In: Maurer, U. (ed.) EUROCRYPT 1996. LNCS, vol. 1070, pp. 190–199. Springer, Heidelberg (1996), http://dx.doi.org/10.1007/3-540-68339-9_17

14. Stinson, D.: An explication of secret sharing schemes. Designs, Codes and Cryptography 2(4), 357–390 (1992), http://dx.doi.org/10.1007/BF00125203
15. Stinson, D.: Decomposition constructions for secret-sharing schemes. IEEE Transactions on Information Theory 40(1), 118–125 (1994)
16. Tentu, A.N., Paul, P., Venkaiah, V.C.: Ideal and perfect hierarchical secret sharing schemes based on mds codes. IACR Cryptology ePrint Archive 2013, 189 (2013), http://dblp.uni-trier.de/db/journals/iacr/iacr2013.html#TentuPV13
17. Tentu, A.N., Paul, P., Vadlamudi, C.V.: Conjunctive hierarchical secret sharing scheme based on MDS codes. In: Lecroq, T., Mouchard, L. (eds.) IWOCA 2013. LNCS, vol. 8288, pp. 463–467. Springer, Heidelberg (2013), http://dx.doi.org/10.1007/978-3-642-45278-9_44
18. Tentu, A.N., Paul, P., Venkaiah, V.C.: Computationally perfect secret sharing scheme based on error-correcting codes. In: Martínez Pérez, G., Thampi, S.M., Ko, R., Shu, L. (eds.) SNDS 2014. CCIS, vol. 420, pp. 251–262. Springer, Heidelberg (2014), http://dx.doi.org/10.1007/978-3-642-54525-2_23
19. Vinod, V., Narayanan, A., Srinathan, K., Pandu Rangan, C., Kim, K.: On the power of computational secret sharing. In: Johansson, T., Maitra, S. (eds.) INDOCRYPT 2003. LNCS, vol. 2904, pp. 162–176. Springer, Heidelberg (2003), http://dx.doi.org/10.1007/978-3-540-24582-7_12

An Approach to Cryptographic Key Exchange Using Fingerprint

Subhas Barman[1], Samiran Chattopadhyay[2], and Debasis Samanta[3]

[1] Govt. College of Engg. and Textile Technology, Berhampore, West Bengal, India
[2] Jadavpur University, Kolkata, West Bengal, India
[3] Indian Institute of Technology, Kharagpur, West Bengal, India

Abstract. Cryptography is the most reliable tool in network and information security. The security of cryptography depends on the cryptographic key management. It consists of key generation, key storing and key sharing. A randomly generated long key (of 128, 190 or 256 bits) is difficult to remember. As a consequence, it is needed to be stored in a secured place. An additional authentication like knowledge or token based authentication is used to control the unauthorized access to the key. It is found that password is easy to break and token can be damaged or stolen. Moreover, knowledge or token based authentication does not assures the non-repudiation of a user. As an alternate, it is advocated to combine biometric with cryptography, known as crypto-biometric system (CBS), to address the above mentioned limitations of traditional cryptography as well as enhance the network security. This paper introduces a CBS to exchange a randomly generated cryptographic key with user's fingerprint data. Cryptographic key is hidden within fingerprint data using fuzzy commitment scheme and it is extracted from the cryptographic construction with the production of genuine fingerprint data of that user. Our work also protects the privacy and security of fingerprint identity of the user using revocable fingerprint template.

1   Introduction

The rapid growth of information and communication technology demands more and more attention of information security. Cryptography is the most trustworthy measure in data security while storing or transmitting data. Cryptography ensures the information security using encryption-decryption algorithms along with cryptographic key(s) [1].

In cryptography, the encryption and decryption algorithms are public but the cryptographic keys are either totally secret (symmetric cryptography) or a pair of private and public keys (for asymmetric cryptography). As a consequence, the security of cryptography depends on security of cryptographic key. In general, knowledge based authenticator (e.g. password) or possession based authenticator (e.g. smart card) is used in cryptography to protect the key from unauthorized access. Knowledge or possession based authenticator is not associated with the user [3]. It is also found that the password based authentication can be guessed

J. Lloret Mauri et al. (Eds.): SSCC 2014, CCIS 467, pp. 162–172, 2014.
© Springer-Verlag Berlin Heidelberg 2014

by social engineering and dictionary attacks whereas, the smart cards can be stolen or damaged. Therefore, these authentications are not able to provide non-repudiation in information security [5].

Moreover, symmetric cryptography also requires an efficient key management and key distribution process to implement a proper data security with cryptography. The key management includes key generation and key storing for maintaining secrecy of cryptographic key. Key distribution process is used to distribute a key to its intended user before message transmission between two communicating parties [1].

Of late, to address the above shortcomings of cryptography, biometric based authentication is used with high degree of assurance in security system. Similarly, researchers are trying to integrate the most trustworthy authenticator, that is, biometric with traditional cryptography [4]. The biometric based cryptography (also known as CBS) uses biometric features to generate or protect the cryptographic key. In the first case, (that is, key generation technique) a stable binary string as cryptographic key is derived from biometric traits [8,12,13,16]. In the second case, cryptographic key is bound with biometric data using a cryptographic construction and it is known as key release scheme. Genuine biometric template is required to access the cryptographic key [9,11].

The key sharing of symmetric cryptography is carried out using asymmetric cryptography and messages are encrypted and decrypted using symmetric cryptography with a shared key. In the traditional crypto-system, third party certification is needed to check the authenticity of both communicating parties. Nevertheless, the traditional crypto-system does not satisfy the non-repudiation property of information security as the knowledge based authenticator is used in this type of protocols. Whereas, in CBSs, as the key is directly linked with user's biometric traits, it does not need to memorize a key and it also confirms the non-repudiation property [13].

However, CBSs have some issues [5]. The privacy of biometric identity must be protected such a way that the identity should not be revealed to others [7]. Secondly, biometric is inherent and it is not revocable like password or smart card. Whereas, cryptography demands revocable key for better security. Therefore, it is advocated to use transformed biometric data to provide diversification to the irrevocable biometric. Otherwise, biometric may become useless forever when compromised [6].

In this work, cryptographic key is generated randomly and the key is encoded with the biometric data. The client's fingerprint data is captured and features are extracted from the biometric. Cancelable template (C_T) of that biometric template is generated by the client and that C_T is enrolled with server. After enrollment process, client stores locked template which is encoded template of client with key and server stores C_T. This stored template is used to exchange a randomly generated cryptographic key between server and client.

The rest of the paper is organized as follows. A brief review of related research is given in Section 2. The proposed approach for cryptographic key exchange with fingerprint of client is given in Section 3. The experimental results and security analysis are discussed in Section 4. Finally, the paper is concluded in Section 5.

2   Related Work

Most of the crypto-biometric systems found in the literature are related to either key release or key generation using biometric data.

2.1   Key Release

In the key release schemes, cryptographic key is considered as a secret and biometric data is used to secure that secret key. The cryptographic key or secrets is released from the cryptographic construction after producing the genuine biometric. There are two ways to bind the cryptographic key with biometric namely, fuzzy vault [9] and fuzzy commitment scheme [18]. Hao et al. [4] proposed a biometric based fuzzy commitment scheme, where randomly generated cryptographic key K is protected by iris code. To release the secret key, that is, at the time of key regeneration, a fresh query instance of same iris is produced to release the same cryptographic key.

In the existing work of key release, researchers are also trying to protect a cryptographic key using fingerprint based fuzzy vault scheme [11]. In [11], coordinate of the minutiae points are used to hide a secret key (K) using a cryptographic construction (i.e., fuzzy vault). The K is released from the vault when the query instance of the same fingerprint is presented to the vault as input. Similarly, Nandakumar et al. [9] also proposed an approach of fingerprint based fuzzy vault where coordinate values along with orientation of the minutiae points are considered as fingerprint data to protect a key.

2.2   Key Generation

In literature, there are many work reported on cryptographic key generation from biometric data. Monrose et al. [12] proposed an approach of biometric based key generation from biometric traits. In this work, cryptographic key K is directly extracted from voice of user while speaking a pass-phase. Similarly, other biometric traits, like on-line handwritten signature [13], face [14], fingerprint of user [17], [16], iris feature vector [15] are used to extract a key for cryptographic use. Ratha et al. [6] discussed cancelable template generation from fingerprint template. In literature, most of the approaches are not able to revoke the generated key if it is compromised [8]. The existing work even do not address the problem of cryptographic key sharing. However, for secure transmission of data using symmetric cryptography, the key must be revocable and in session based communication, it is required to create unique keys for every session.

3 Proposed Methodology

In this section, we discuss our proposed approach in details.

3.1 Basic Key Regeneration Approach

The cryptographic key (K) is randomly generated and encoded with an error correction code (ECC) using XOR operation, that is, $K_{en} = K \oplus ECC$ as reported in [4]. Now, the user scans his fingerprint (I_F) and minutiae points (i.e., fingerprint features, $T_F = f_e(I_F)$) are extracted from it. User also generates cancelable template from original minutiae points applying an one way transformation function (f_c) with the help of user specific random transformation key t_p (i.e., $C_T = f_c(T_F, t_p)$). The C_T is XORed with K_{en} and generate a locked template $C_{T_{lock}}$ that is, $C_{T_{lock}} = C_T \oplus K_{en}$. In the locked template, both C_T and K are locked with each other where one is not unlocked without the other one. In key regeneration steps, another fingerprint instance is taken and the query cancelable template C'_T is generated. The C'_T is XORed with the locked template $C_{T_{lock}}$ and the key is extracted from the locked template with error (e), that is, $C'_T \oplus C_{T_{lock}} = K'$ where $K' = K + e$. Now the exact K will be decoded if the amount of error is removable by ECC.

3.2 Enrollment of Client's Fingerprint Data

In biometric based cryptographic system, enrollment is the first action by which the biometric of a user is registered to the system. In the enrollment process biometric template of client is stored in the server database with some other information of the client. There are two ways of enrollment of client with the biometric namely, on-line and offline. In the offline based enrollment process, both client and server meet in a secured location for the enrollment of biometric template of client. The steps related to the on-line based enrollment process of client are given in Fig. 1.

In the enrollment process, initially, client generates cancelable template from his fingerprint. Then the cancelable template is shared with server through a secured manner. Main function of enrollment is storing the cancelable template as well as cryptographic key to secure the key with cancelable template and vice-versa. Details steps of enrollment process are discussed below.

Cancelable Template Generation. Client scans his fingerprint (I_F) and minutiae points (i.e., fingerprint features, $T_F = f_e(I_F)$, f_e is a feature extraction algorithm) are extracted from fingerprint image (I_F). User also chooses a transformation key t_p which is a vector of random number and is used to transform the fingerprint template into cancelable template C_T (i.e., $C_T = f_c(T_F, t_p)$, f_c is the transformation function). We have used Cartesian transformation [6] to generate cancelable template from fingerprint template. To do that, total minutiae coordinates or fingerprint image area is divided into cells (C_i, i is the

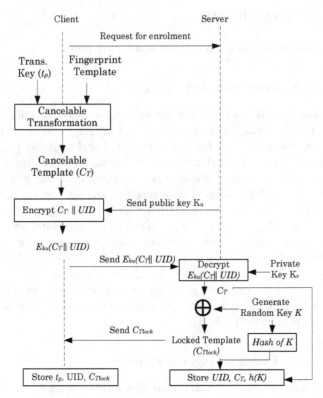

Fig. 1. Enrollment of client with biometric

cell number and $i = 1, 2, ..., n$) of equal size. Each cell contains m number of minutiae point(s) where $m = 0, 1, 2, ...$. Now, a t_p is generated from a password using pseudo random number generator (PRNG) and it has n elements (t_{p_j} and $j = 1, 2, ..., n$ and $1 \leqq t_{p_j} \leqq n$). A cell C_i is replaced by a cell number equal to the value of t_{p_j}. In this process, minutiae point of C_i will be replaced by the minutiae point of cell $C_{t_{p_j}}$. A sample Cartesian transformation is given in Fig.2. Before transformation, 4th and 8th cells do not contain any minutiae points but after transformation, 5th and 8th do not contain minutiae points whereas 4th cell is updated with the minutiae points of 1st cell. Third cell $C3$ is unchanged as the random vector provides similar cell no., i.e., $t_{p_3} = 3$.

Enrollment. After generation of cancelable template C_T, it is enrolled to server in the following way.

1. Client $\rightarrow$ Server: Client sends encrypted C_T and UID (i.e., $E_{K_u}(C_T \| UID)$ where K_u is the server's public key) to server.
2. $UID \| C_T = D_{K_v}(E_{K_u}(C_T \| UID))$; Server decrypts $E_{K_u}(C_T \| UID)$ with its private key (K_v) and separates C_T and UID.

Original cells	1	2	3	4	5	6	7	8	9
Random Vector	7	5	3	1	4	2	8	9	6

(a) Original cell vector and random vector

$C7(M_{11},M_{12})$	$C8(M_{13})$	$C9$
$C4$	$C5(M_7,M_8)$	$C6(M_9,M_{10})$
$C1(M_1,M_2)$	$C2(M_3)$	$C3(M_4,M_5,M_6)$

$C7(M'_{13})$	$C8(-)$	$C9(M'_9,M'_{10})$
$C4(M'_1,M'_2)$	$C5(-,-)$	$C6(M'_3)$
$C1(M'_{11},M'_{12})$	$C2(M'_7,M'_8)$	$C3(M_4,M_5,M_6)$

(b) Original minutiae points within assigned cells

(c) Displaced minutiae points within newly assigned cells as per random vector

Fig. 2. Cartesian Transformation using random vector given in (a)

3. $C_{T_{lock}} = C_T \oplus K$; Server generates a random key (K) and encodes C_T with K using exclusive-OR (i.e. XOR) operation.
4. Server computes $h(K)$ using a hash function h.
5. Server stores UID, C_T and $h(K)$.
6. Server $\rightarrow$ Client; Server transmits $C_{T_{lock}}$ to Client.
7. Client stores UID, t_p and $C_{T_{lock}}$.

After enrollment, client destroys his fingerprint information (i.e., fingerprint image I_F, fingerprint template F_T, cancelable template C_T) and server destroys the key K.

3.3 Cryptographic Key Exchange

In our work, enrolled template (i.e., C_T) is used to share the key K between server and client for data communication. Server and Client both can extract the key from $C_{T_{lock}}$ by exclusive-OR operation with a genuine cancelable template. Client can generate new C_T from his fresh fingerprint image, i.e, query instance of same fingerprint and server has the C_T in database. Therefore, server needs $C_{T_{lock}}$ to extract the key K and client transmits the encoded template $C_{T_{lock}}$ to server. The diagram of key sharing protocol is given in Fig.3.

Server and client establish a communication with the cryptographic key (K) in the way as discussed below.

1. Client requests server for communication.
2. Client generates a query template C'_T (cancelable) with the same transformation function (f_c) and transformation key (t_p).
3. Client extracts the key (say K') from $C_{T_{lock}}$, i.e., $K' = C_{T_{lock}} \oplus C'_T$.
4. Server computes $h(h(K))$ and sends it to client.

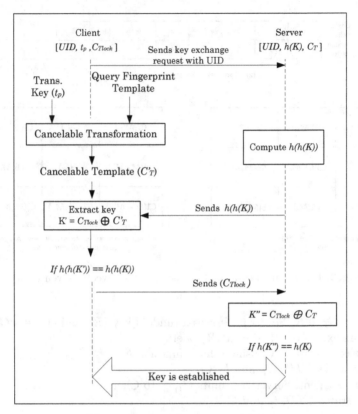

Fig. 3. Sharing of cryptographic key

5. Client computes $h(h(K'))$ and compares it with $h(h(K))$. If both are equal then, the extracted key is correct key.
6. Client sends $C_{T_{lock}}$ to server.
7. Server extracts the K" from $C_{T_{lock}}$ by XOR operation with stored cancelabe template C_T, that is, $K" = C_T \oplus C_{T_{lock}}$.
8. Server computes $h(K")$ and compares it with $h(K)$. If $h(K") == h(K)$ then the key is established successfully between server and client (i.e., $K = K' = K"$).

Similarly, server also can initiate to establish a secure communication. In that case, server requests for encoded template from client. Server can extract key from encoded template as stated above. Client follows the same process as discussed above to release the secret key K from encoded template.

4   Experimental Result

4.1   Database

In our work, fingerprint database from FVC2004 [19] is used for our experiment. In FVC2004, there are two sets (A and B) of fingerprint database. There are four databases (DB1, DB2, DB3, DB4) in each set. Set A consists of 800 fingerprint images of 100 persons and 8 instances of each person. We have considered only DB2, DB3 and DB4 databases in our experiment.

4.2   Experimental Setup

In our experiment, minutiae points of fingerprint image is used as features. The minutiae features are extracted from a fingerprint image using NBIS software (MINDTCT) of NIST [10]. From the features file, we have considered only those features having quality more than 50%. In our experiment, we have considered only x, y-coordinate values to generate cancelable template. Transformation key is generated randomly (using PRNG) from password. Minutiae points are divided into 25 cells. Cells are shuffled using transformation key and respective minutiae points are displaced according their new location. In our experiment, we have considered 256 bits long key as cryptographic key. First 256 bits of cancelable template are considered as template.

4.3   Result

An instance of a fingerprint is taken as genuine fingerprint of client and all other fingerprints with all instances are taken as imposter fingerprint. Now we assume that an impostor have to generate a cancelable template from his fingerprint to compromise the genuine cancelable template. In our expriment the genuine cancelable template is compared with all impostor cancelable templates and dissimilarities are measured with respect to Hamming distance. The minimum, average and maximum dissimilarities (i.e., Hamming distances) are plotted in Fig. 4. It confirms that at least 38% (minimum) bits of the genuine template need to be guessed by the impostor. Similarly, 47.6% (average) and 57% (maximum) bits of the genuine cancelable templates are distinct with respect to the impostors.

4.4   Security Analysis

Security of the proposed protocol is analyzed with respect to 1. privacy of fingerprint identity, 2. authentication, 3. session key generation and 4. secure sharing of cryptographic key.

Privacy of Fingerprint: In this work, the privacy of fingerprint identity of client is protected in three ways. Firstly, fingerprint template is transformed into a cancelable template (i.e., $C_T = f_c(T_F, t_p)$) which assures that it is one way transformation, that is, getting back the original template from cancelable template is not possible. Secondly, the cancelable template is stored in the server database and when the server database is hacked by any third party, he or she will not be able to know about the original fingerprint data (i.e., $T_F \neq f_c^{-1}(C_T, t_p)$). Thirdly, neither the raw biometric template nor the cancelable template is openly transmitted over network channel. Encoded cancelable template $C_{T_{lock}}$, which is locked and protected, is transmitted by client.

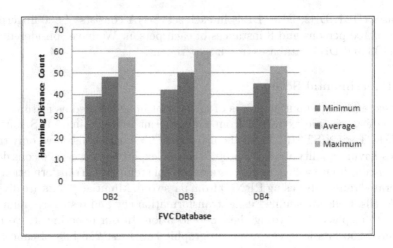

Fig. 4. Dissimilarity between genuine and impostor cancelable template

Authentication: Cryptographic key is encoded with biometric template and only genuine client can access the cryptographic key with its genuine fingerprint data. On the other end, only genuine server can extract the cryptographic key using stored cancelable template.

Session Key Generation: Symmetric cryptography demands unique session key for better security of data transmission through communication channel. In our work, server can generate random session key which can be shared with client using cancelable fingerprint template of client. The client can easily decode the session key using his own cancelable template generated from a new instance of fingerprint.

Secure Sharing of Cryptographic Key: Security of cryptography system depends on security of the cryptographic key (K). The key can be compromised during transmission over communication channel. In our work, security of K is affirmed in the following way.

1. The cryptographic key in our approach does not need to store in anywhere. Even, client does not has the overhead to remember K. Therefore, there is no chance to compromise K for an adversary from client end.
2. The key (K) is destroyed after locked it with biometric data (i.e., $K \oplus C_T$) and only a hash value of key (i.e., $h(K)$) is stored with the database of server. The K is transmitted over network within the protection of client's biometric data. An attacker does not have any chance to access the K without genuine fingerprint data (i.e., (I_F, t_p) or (T_F, t_p) or C_T) of client.
3. The locked template $C_{T_{lock}}$ (K and C_T are locked with each other) is stored with client and only client can extract the key K with his own biometric

data (C_T). An adversary does not able to unlock K even when he has a complete knowledge about the locked template $C_{T_{lock}}$.

5 Conclusion

In traditional symmetric cryptography, key management is an important issue. Key sharing between two communicating parties is the main challenge under key management system of symmetric cryptography. In this work, the key sharing problem is addressed using fingerprint data of a user. The third party or attacker is not able to attack the key without having knowledge about the fingerprint data of a user. We have also found in our experiment that, an impostor can not generate a genuine fingerprint template from his own fingerprint data.

This work also ensures the privacy of fingerprint identity of user using cancelable template.

References

1. Stallings, W.: Cryptography and Network Security: Principles and Practice, 5th edn. Prentice Hall (2010)
2. Advance Encryption Standard (AES), Federal Information Processing Standards Publication 197 United States National Institute of Standards and Technology (NIST) (November 26, 2001)
3. Maltoni, D., Maio, D., Jain, A.K., Prabhakar, S.: Handbook of Fingerprint Recognition. Springer, New York (2003)
4. Hao, F., Anderson, R., Daugman, J.: Combining Crypto with Biometrics Effectively. IEEE Transactions on Computers 55(9), 1081–1088 (2006)
5. Uludag, U., Pankanti, S., Prabhakar, S., Jain, A.K.: Biometric Cryptosystems: Issues and Challenges. Proceedings of the IEEE 92(6), 948–960 (2004)
6. Ratha, N.K., Chikkerur, S., Connell, J.H., Bolle, R.M.: Generating Cancellable Fingerprint Templates. IEEE Transactions on Pattern Analysis and Machine Intelligence 29(4), 561–572 (2007)
7. Jain, A.K., Nandakumar, K., Nagar, A.: Fingerprint Template Protection: From Theory to Practice. In: Security and Privacy in Biometrics. Springer
8. Jagadeesan, A., Duraiswamy, K.: Secured Cryptographic Key Generation from Multimodal Biometrics: Feature Level Fusion of Fingerprint and Iris. International Journal of Computer Science and Information Security 7(2), 28–37 (2010)
9. Nandakumar, K., Jain, A.K., Pankanti, S.: Fingerprint-Based Fuzzy Vault: Implementation and Performance. IEEE Transactions on Information Forensics and Security 2(4), 744–757 (2007)
10. Watson, C., Garris, M., Tabassi, E., Wilson, C., McCabe, M., Janet, S., Ko, K.: User's Guide to NIST Biometric Image Software (NBIS), National Institute of Standards and Technology (2007)
11. Yang, S., Verbauwhede, I.: Automatic secure fingerprint verification system based on fuzzy vault scheme. In: Proceedings of the IEEE International Conference on Acoustics, Speech, and Signal Processing (ICASSP 2005), vol. 5. IEEE (2005)
12. Monrose, F., Reiter, M.K., Li, Q., Wetzel, S.: Cryptographic key generation from voice. In: Proceedings of IEEE Symposium on Security and Privacy, pp. 202–213 (2001)

13. Feng, H., Wah, C.C.: Private key generation from on-line handwritten signatures. Information Management & Computer Security 10(4), 159–164 (2002)
14. Chen, B., Chandran, V.: Biometric Based Cryptographic Key Generation from Faces. In: Proceedings of 9th Biennial Conference of the Australian Pattern Recognition Society on Digital Image Computing Techniques and Applications, pp. 394–401 (2007)
15. Rathgeb, C., Uhl, A.: Context-based biometric key generation for Iris. IET Computer Vision 5(6), 389–397 (2011)
16. Gaddam, S.V.K., Lal, M.: Efficient Cancellable Biometric Key Generation Scheme for Cryptography. International Journal of Network Security 11(2), 57–65 (2010)
17. Lalithamani, N., Soman, K.P.: Irrevocable Cryptographic Key Generation from Cancelable Fingerprint Templates: An Enhanced and Effective Scheme. European Journal of Scientific Research 31(3), 372–387 (2009)
18. Juels, A., Wattenberg, M.: A Fuzzy Commitment Scheme. In: Tsudik, G. (ed.) Proc. 6th ACM Conf. Computer and Communications Security, pp. 28–36 (1999)
19. Fingerprint Verification Competition FVC2004 (2004), http://bias.csr.unibo.it/fvc2004

Cryptanalysis of Image Encryption Algorithm Based on Pixel Shuffling and Chaotic S-box Transformation

Pankaj Kumar Sharma[1], Musheer Ahmad[1], and Parvez Mahmood Khan[2]

[1] Department of Computer Engineering, Faculty of Engineering and Technology,
Jamia Millia Islamia, New Delhi 110025, India
[2] Department of Computer Science and Engineering, Faculty of Engineering,
Integral University, Lucknow 226026, India

Abstract. Recently Hussain *et al.* proposed an image encryption algorithm which has three independent phases: (1) total pixel shuffling performed, in spatial domain, with permutation sequences extracted from chaotic skew tent map, (2) diffusion carried out using random codes generated from same chaotic map, and (3) extra confusion induced with substitution-box transformation. Though, the encryption algorithm achieves optimal scores of NPCR/UACI and exhibits great encryption strength. But, a careful analysis unveils its inherent security flaws, leaving it vulnerable to cryptographic attack. In this paper, we analyze its security weaknesses and proposed a chosen plaintext-attack with inverse S-box to break the algorithm completely. It is shown that the plain-image can be recovered successfully without knowing the secret key. The computer simulation of attack highlights the ineptness of Hussain *et al.* algorithm and shows that it is not commendable to deploy it for practical encryption of digital images.

Keywords: Cryptanalysis, total shuffling, S-box transformation, chaotic tent map, confusion and diffusion.

1 Introduction

Digital image encryption has been a very active area of research in the field of information security over the last two decades. To restrict the unauthorized access of digital images while being transferred over insecure open networks, it is mandatory to encode them with secure and robust encryption algorithms. Besides being reliable, these algorithms must be fast, so that sharing and transmission in real time could be possible. Unlike texts, digital images have high spatial redundancy and bulk data capacity, that is, the adjoining pixels are extremely correlated to each other. The traditional encryption algorithms like Serpent, Blowfish, RC4, DES, IDEA, AES, etc, originally meant for texts, are found incompetent for the encryption of digital images. One of the reasons being they incur high computational overheads and encryption time [1, 2]. Consequently, researchers have come up with large number of image encryption techniques based on chaotic maps [3-15]. Chaotic maps are non-linear and pseudo-random in nature, and their system trajectories are greatly sensitive towards

J. Lloret Mauri et al. (Eds.): SSCC 2014, CCIS 467, pp. 173–181, 2014.

initial conditions and control factors, making them appropriate for image encryption. Most of the chaos-based image encryption algorithms use chaotic maps to execute effectively the significant (i) pixels shuffling, spreading the pixel values of plain-image by relocating them in random order to obtain visual effect of disorder, and (ii) pixels diffusion, masking shuffled pixel values in deterministic and reversible fashion. The initial conditions used to iterate chaotic maps, involved in encryption algorithms, served as essential part of secret key. The large key space of chaos-based algorithms makes it almost a herculean task to apply brute-force attack.

An image encryption algorithm is said to be insecure if it is vulnerable to any of the classical and other type of cryptographic attacks. The ultimate objective of an attacker is to find a way to recover the secret key in lesser time or storage than the brute-force attack [16]. The four classical attacks in cryptanalysis are (i) *ciphertext-only attack*: the attacker only have access to some ciphertext images, (ii) *known-plaintext attack*: the attacker can obtain some plaintext images and corresponding ciphertext images, (iii) *chosen-plaintext attack*: the attacker can have temporary access to encryption machine and choose some specially designed plaintext images to produce corresponding ciphertext images, and (iv) *chosen-ciphertext attack*: the attacker can have temporary access to decryption machine and choose some specially designed ciphertext images to obtain corresponding plaintext images. The careful security examinations of some, seemingly complex and secure, image encryption algorithms found that they are insecure and cryptographically weak. Their inherent inevitable flaws make them prone to even classical attacks and easily breakable with simple statistical methods. As a result, many image encryption algorithms have been successfully broken by cryptanalysts under these attacks [16-28]. Recently, Hussain *et al.* [15] proposed an encryption algorithm for gray scale images which makes use of chaotic skew tent map for total shuffling and diffusion of pixels. A nonlinear S-box transformation is applied on each diffused pixel to obtain final encrypted image. The algorithm has promising encryption strength with near optimal values of Number of Pixels Change Rate (NPCR) and Unified Average Changed Intensity (UACI) measures [15]. However, the security investigation and analysis exposes its flaw, which is utilized to break the algorithm with chosen plaintext attack and inverse S-box in this work.

The structure of rest of this work is arranged as follows: Section 2 provides Hussain *et al.* image encryption algorithm. Section 3 discusses the complete break of encryption algorithm under chosen plaintext-attack and simulation of cryptanalysis is demonstrated in same Section, which is followed by conclusions made in Section 5.

2   Review of Hussain *et al.* Algorithm

The Hussain *et al.* algorithm consists of three independent phases namely shuffling phase, diffusion phase and S-box transformation phase. The chaotic skew tent map given in eqn(1) is utilized during first two phases of algorithm. The map $F(x(n),p)$: $(0, 1) \rightarrow (0, 1)$ has positive Lyapunov exponent for all $p \in [0, 1]$ and thus exhibits chaotic behavior. The state of the map $x(n)$ visits the entire interval $(0, 1)$ [29]. The initial values of $x(0)$ and p, used to iterate the map (1), served as secret key of algorithm. To improve further the confusion and diffusion property, Hussain *et al.* used chaotic S-box, design by Khan *et al.* [30], as static look-up table for S-box transformation.

$$x(n+1) = F(x(n),\, p) = \begin{cases} \dfrac{x(n)}{p} & 0 < x(n) \le p \\[2ex] \dfrac{1-x(n)}{1-p} & p < x(n) < 1 \end{cases} \tag{1}$$

Table 1. Khan *et al.* [30] chaotic S-box as 16×16 look-up table

	0	1	2	3	4	5	6	7	8	9	A	B	C	D	E	F
0	3	167	29	139	249	80	34	165	250	251	238	110	33	38	140	17
1	0	41	135	164	236	71	16	209	99	143	151	70	188	184	252	242
2	60	120	231	105	49	66	128	121	125	218	178	196	89	154	244	192
3	155	82	162	185	138	97	213	50	10	113	54	237	183	22	202	194
4	208	191	129	136	197	137	26	152	168	103	13	65	132	39	79	61
5	119	160	44	207	102	175	95	72	74	235	55	63	247	144	203	20
6	8	177	223	92	254	90	228	118	224	219	117	240	7	6	19	147
7	21	186	241	48	1	216	122	93	69	73	5	15	158	114	106	187
8	88	130	87	68	78	98	245	47	84	234	176	141	255	51	149	53
9	225	214	123	35	28	166	233	220	248	211	101	45	198	115	77	52
A	94	193	86	133	76	85	67	200	226	14	62	4	40	146	239	126
B	36	230	148	150	11	75	56	153	96	215	30	145	25	100	58	174
C	181	172	190	57	163	64	171	124	217	111	18	131	31	243	195	253
D	246	182	201	104	221	27	109	107	232	157	199	83	161	42	227	112
E	179	159	12	210	169	127	170	189	2	206	108	204	173	23	81	116
F	229	91	24	37	32	43	134	222	59	142	180	205	9	46	156	212

The steps of Hussain *et al.* algorithm to encrypt a gray-scale image of size M×N are as following; the terms used have their usual meanings:

<Phase 1: Shuffling>

A.1. Reshape the image to vector $P = \{p_1, p_2, \ldots, p_{MN}\}$.

A.2. Iterate map (1) for L times with given $x(0)$ and p. Discard the values.

A.3. Further iterate the map for MN times to obtain the sequence $X = \{x_{L+1}, x_{L+2}, \ldots, x_{L+MN}\}$.

A.4. Let $Y = sort(X)$. Compute permutation sequence $T = \{t_1, t_2, \ldots, t_{MN}\}$ such that y_i coincides with x_{ti}.

A.5. Relocate the pixel from i-th position in vector P to t_i -th position.

A.6. Let the shuffled vector be $P' = \{p'_1, p'_2, \ldots, p'_{MN}\}$, $n = L + MN$ and $i = 1$.

<Phase 2: Diffusion>

A.7. Again iterate map (1) and compute the random code d_i as:

$$d_i = mod(floor(x(n) \times 2^{48}),\, 256)$$

A.8. Diffuse i-th pixel as:

$$c_i = p_i' \oplus mod(p_{i-1}' + d_i, 256)$$

A.9. Evaluate $k_i = 1 + mod(c_i, 2)$ then iterate map (1) for k_i times.
A.10. Set $i = i + 1$, $n = n + k_i$.
A.11. Repeat steps **A.7** to **A.10** to diffuse all pixels.

`<Phase 3: S-box transformation>`
A.12. Separate the lower and higher nibbles n_1 and n_2 of pixel c_i and convert them to decimal numbers.
A.13. Pick (n_1, n_2)-th element of S-box, given in Table 1, and substitute it for pixel c_i
A.14. Repeat above two steps to substitute for all pixels to get final encrypted image.

The successful decryption of encrypted image can be performed by applying above steps in reverse order with correct secret key. The algorithm provides excellent encryption strength and has merits of optimal scores of NPCR/UACI, secret key sensitivity, etc. The readers are advised to refer to Ref. [15] for a detailed explanation of algorithm.

3   Cryptanalysis with CPA Attack

In modern cryptography, there is a fundamental principle enounced by Auguste Kerckhoffs in 19-th century known as Kerckhoffs's principle. It says that "*A cryptographic system should be secure even if everything about the system, except the key, is public knowledge*" [1, 31]. The principle entails that the attacker knows complete design and working of encryption algorithm except the secret key, i.e. everything about encryption algorithm including its implementation is public except the secret key which is private. The sole objective of attacker is to recover the plaintext without knowing secret key. Recovering the plain-image is as good as knowing the secret key [22]. The following inherent flaws are found in encryption algorithm under scrutiny.

a.   In shuffling phase, the permutation sequence T is completely dependent to secret key and has no nothing to do with pending plain-image. As a result, same permutation sequence is generated every time when encrypting distinct plain-images.

b.   In diffusion phase, there is a dependency on the plain-image. The random code d_{i+1} is affected by value k_i (1 or 2), which in turn depend on the parity (even or odd) of diffused pixel c_i. The same random code sequence $D = \{d_1, d_2, ..., d_{MN}\}$ is generated if the parity of corresponding pixels of two encrypted images is same. The code d_1 is fixed and independent to pending plain-image.

c.   The value of L (public or private) in step **A.2** has no effect on the complexity of attack. Because, the attacker is interested in recovering the random codes and permutation sequence which are extracted after executing chaotic map for L number of times. The actual initial value for chaotic map is x_L and not $x(0)$.

d.   In S-box transformation phase, a single and static S-box is employed. Since, the attacker the has knowledge of S-box, he/she can computes corresponding inverse S-box to obtain state of encrypted image just before S-box transformation.

The attacker exploits above analytical information to execute break. The cryptanalysis of Hussain *et al.* algorithm provided in subsequent paragraphs is an extension of chosen-plaintext attack suggested by Wang *et al.* in [21]. The steps of extended attack are described as:

Let P be the plain-image which is to be recovered from its received encrypted image CP. Apply reverse S-box transformation on CP to get rCP. The reverse S-box transformation on encrypted image is performed by applying phase 3 of algorithm, mentioned in Section 2, with inverse S-box (of Khan *et al.* S-box) given in Table 2. We choose two plain-images $J = \{0, 0, 0, ..., 0\}$ and $E = \{1, 2, 3, ..., MN-1, MN\}$ of same size of CP. Chosen plain image J is designed to deduce random codes and plain-image E is framed to deduce permutation vector. Before proceeding further, consider the notations.

$P' = \{ p'_1, p'_2, ..., p'_{MN} \}$ is shuffled image P just after phase 1

$rCP = \{rcp_1, rcp_2, ..., rcp_{MN}\}$ is encrypted image P just before phase 3

$J' = \{ j'_1, j'_2, ..., j'_{MN} \}$ is shuffled image J just after phase 1

$rCJ = \{rcj_1, rcj_2, ..., rcj_{MN}\}$ is encrypted image J just before phase 3

$E' = \{ e'_1, e'_2, ..., e'_{MN} \}$ is shuffled image E just after phase 1

$rCE = \{rce_1, rce_2, ..., rce_{MN}\}$ is encrypted image E just before phase 3

B.1.   Take plain-images $J = \{0, 0, 0, ..., 0\}$ and $E = \{1, 2, 3, ..., MN-1, MN\}$ whose corresponding encrypted images are CJ and CE, respectively. Set $k = 1$.

B.2.   Apply reverse S-box transformation on CJ and CE to obtain rCJ and rCE images.

$$rcj_k = j'_k \oplus mod(j'_{k-1} + d_k , 256) = mod(j'_{k-1} + d_k , 256) \text{ since } j'_k = 0$$

The $mod(j'_{k-1} + d_k , 256)$ is known through rcj_k, it was used to encrypt the pixel p'_k which can be retrieved as

$$p'_k = rcj_k \oplus rcp_k$$

B.3.   Similarly, for rCE, we have the following

$$rce_k = e'_k \oplus mod(e'_{k-1} + d_k , 256)$$ Note: $j'_0 = e'_0 = p'_0$ is part of the key

Since $mod(e'_{k-1} + d_k , 256) (= mod(j'_{k-1} + d_k , 256))$ and rce_k are known, e'_k can be retrieved as $e'_k = rec_k \oplus rcj_k$ and t_k is exactly equal to e'_k due to the nature of chosen-image E. Hence, $p_{tk} = p'_k$

B.4.   Now, change the pixel in previous images J and E at position t_k with the last recovered pixel value of image P. Set $k = k + 1$ and move back to step **B.2** to recover all pixels of image P.

The mentioned attack is simulated with secret key $x(0) = 0.27$, $p = 0.4$, $p'_0 = 123$, $L = 100$. The description of cryptanalysis on an image of size 3×3 is provided in Table 3. Consider a plain-image P of size 3×3 which is encrypted with Hussain *et al.*

algorithm to get encrypted image **CP**. The result of the break algorithm is to recover the image **P** out of received encrypted image **CP**. The reverse S-box transform provides the image **rCP**. The pixels gray-values of images **P**, **CP** and **rCP** are provided as:

$$P = \begin{pmatrix} 100 & 36 & 55 \\ 67 & 23 & 176 \\ 231 & 1 & 60 \end{pmatrix} \qquad CP = \begin{pmatrix} 125 & 115 & 216 \\ 76 & 82 & 164 \\ 242 & 132 & 41 \end{pmatrix} \qquad rCP = \begin{pmatrix} 40 & 157 & 117 \\ 164 & 49 & 19 \\ 31 & 76 & 17 \end{pmatrix}$$

Simulation results of cryptanalysis of Hussain *et al.* algorithm, on *Baboon* image of size 256×256, are shown in Figure 1. Based on theoretical and simulation analyses, it can be said that the encryption algorithm under study is insecure and can be cryptanalyze successfully with extended chosen-plaintext attack.

Table 2. Inverse S-box of Khan *et al.* S-box

	0	1	2	3	4	5	6	7	8	9	A	B	C	D	E	F
0	16	116	232	0	171	122	109	108	96	252	56	180	226	74	169	123
1	22	15	202	110	95	112	61	237	242	188	70	213	148	2	186	204
2	244	12	6	147	176	243	13	77	172	17	221	245	82	155	253	135
3	115	36	55	141	159	143	58	90	182	195	190	248	32	79	170	91
4	197	75	37	166	131	120	27	21	87	121	88	181	164	158	132	78
5	5	238	49	219	136	165	162	130	128	44	101	241	99	119	160	86
6	184	53	133	24	189	154	84	73	211	35	126	215	234	214	11	201
7	223	57	125	157	239	106	103	80	33	39	118	146	199	40	175	229
8	38	66	129	203	76	163	246	18	67	69	52	3	14	139	249	25
9	93	187	173	111	178	142	179	26	71	183	45	48	254	217	124	225
A	81	220	50	196	19	7	149	1	72	228	230	198	193	236	191	85
B	138	97	42	224	250	192	209	60	29	51	113	127	28	231	194	65
C	47	161	63	206	43	68	156	218	167	210	62	94	235	251	233	83
D	64	23	227	153	255	54	145	185	117	200	41	105	151	212	247	98
E	104	144	168	222	102	240	177	34	216	150	137	89	20	59	10	174
F	107	114	31	205	46	134	208	92	152	4	8	9	30	207	100	140

(a) *P*   (b) *CP*   (c) *rCP*   (d) *P*

Fig. 1. Simulation of attack (a) plain-image *P* (b) encrypted image *CP* (c) image *rCP* after reverse S-box transformation and (d) recovered image *P*

Table 3. Detail description of attack on an image of size 3×3

J	CJ	rCJ	E	CE	rCE	p_k	t_k	Recovered
iteration k = 1								
$\begin{smallmatrix}0&0&0\\0&0&0\\0&0&0\end{smallmatrix}$	$\begin{smallmatrix}132&10&100\\103&201&228\\102&182&28\end{smallmatrix}$	$\begin{smallmatrix}76&56&189\\73&210&102\\84&209&148\end{smallmatrix}$	$\begin{smallmatrix}1&2&3\\4&5&6\\7&8&9\end{smallmatrix}$	$\begin{smallmatrix}39&197&18\\65&221&240\\207&227&143\end{smallmatrix}$	$\begin{smallmatrix}77&68&202\\75&212&107\\83&222&25\end{smallmatrix}$	100 (40⊕76)	1 (77⊕76)	$\begin{smallmatrix}100&0&0\\0&0&0\\0&0&0\end{smallmatrix}$
iteration k = 2								
$\begin{smallmatrix}100&0&0\\0&0&0\\0&0&0\end{smallmatrix}$	$\begin{smallmatrix}125&198&100\\103&201&228\\102&182&28\end{smallmatrix}$	$\begin{smallmatrix}40&156&189\\73&210&102\\84&209&148\end{smallmatrix}$	$\begin{smallmatrix}100&2&3\\4&5&6\\7&8&9\end{smallmatrix}$	$\begin{smallmatrix}125&28&57\\65&221&240\\207&227&143\end{smallmatrix}$	$\begin{smallmatrix}40&148&195\\75&212&107\\83&222&25\end{smallmatrix}$	1 (157⊕156)	8 (148⊕156)	$\begin{smallmatrix}100&0&0\\0&0&0\\0&1&0\end{smallmatrix}$
iteration k = 3								
$\begin{smallmatrix}100&0&0\\0&0&0\\0&1&0\end{smallmatrix}$	$\begin{smallmatrix}125&115&64\\50&53&102\\182&28&26\end{smallmatrix}$	$\begin{smallmatrix}40&157&197\\55&143&84\\209&148&70\end{smallmatrix}$	$\begin{smallmatrix}100&2&3\\4&5&6\\7&1&9\end{smallmatrix}$	$\begin{smallmatrix}125&115&57\\113&214&175\\175&251&211\end{smallmatrix}$	$\begin{smallmatrix}40&157&195\\57&145&85\\85&9&153\end{smallmatrix}$	176 (117⊕197)	6 (195⊕197)	$\begin{smallmatrix}100&0&0\\0&0&176\\0&1&0\end{smallmatrix}$
iteration k = 4								
$\begin{smallmatrix}100&0&0\\0&0&176\\0&1&0\end{smallmatrix}$	$\begin{smallmatrix}125&115&216\\189&53&102\\182&28&26\end{smallmatrix}$	$\begin{smallmatrix}40&157&117\\231&143&84\\209&148&70\end{smallmatrix}$	$\begin{smallmatrix}100&2&3\\4&5&176\\7&1&9\end{smallmatrix}$	$\begin{smallmatrix}125&115&216\\210&214&175\\175&251&211\end{smallmatrix}$	$\begin{smallmatrix}40&157&117\\227&145&85\\85&9&153\end{smallmatrix}$	67 (164⊕231)	4 (227⊕231)	$\begin{smallmatrix}100&0&0\\67&0&176\\0&1&0\end{smallmatrix}$
iteration k = 5								
$\begin{smallmatrix}100&0&0\\67&0&176\\0&1&0\end{smallmatrix}$	$\begin{smallmatrix}125&115&216\\76&71&3\\207&221&251\end{smallmatrix}$	$\begin{smallmatrix}40&157&117\\164&21&0\\83&212&9\end{smallmatrix}$	$\begin{smallmatrix}100&2&3\\67&5&176\\7&1&9\end{smallmatrix}$	$\begin{smallmatrix}125&115&216\\76&209&167\\182&77&197\end{smallmatrix}$	$\begin{smallmatrix}40&157&117\\164&23&1\\209&158&68\end{smallmatrix}$	36 (49⊕21)	2 (23⊕21)	$\begin{smallmatrix}100&36&0\\67&0&176\\0&1&0\end{smallmatrix}$
iteration k = 6								
$\begin{smallmatrix}100&36&0\\67&0&176\\0&1&0\end{smallmatrix}$	$\begin{smallmatrix}125&115&216\\76&82&49\\207&221&251\end{smallmatrix}$	$\begin{smallmatrix}40&157&117\\164&49&36\\83&212&9\end{smallmatrix}$	$\begin{smallmatrix}100&36&3\\67&5&176\\7&1&9\end{smallmatrix}$	$\begin{smallmatrix}125&115&216\\76&82&121\\182&77&197\end{smallmatrix}$	$\begin{smallmatrix}40&157&117\\164&49&39\\209&158&68\end{smallmatrix}$	55 (19⊕36)	3 (39⊕36)	$\begin{smallmatrix}100&36&55\\67&0&176\\0&1&0\end{smallmatrix}$
iteration k = 7								
$\begin{smallmatrix}100&36&55\\67&0&176\\0&1&0\end{smallmatrix}$	$\begin{smallmatrix}125&115&216\\76&82&164\\250&221&251\end{smallmatrix}$	$\begin{smallmatrix}40&157&117\\164&49&19\\8&212&9\end{smallmatrix}$	$\begin{smallmatrix}100&36&55\\67&5&176\\7&1&9\end{smallmatrix}$	$\begin{smallmatrix}125&115&216\\76&82&164\\38&77&197\end{smallmatrix}$	$\begin{smallmatrix}40&157&117\\164&49&19\\13&158&68\end{smallmatrix}$	23 (31⊕8)	5 (13⊕8)	$\begin{smallmatrix}100&36&55\\67&23&176\\0&1&0\end{smallmatrix}$
iteration k = 8								
$\begin{smallmatrix}100&36&55\\67&23&176\\0&1&0\end{smallmatrix}$	$\begin{smallmatrix}125&115&216\\76&82&164\\242&4&179\end{smallmatrix}$	$\begin{smallmatrix}40&157&117\\164&49&19\\31&171&224\end{smallmatrix}$	$\begin{smallmatrix}100&36&55\\67&23&176\\7&1&9\end{smallmatrix}$	$\begin{smallmatrix}125&115&216\\76&82&164\\242&40&197\end{smallmatrix}$	$\begin{smallmatrix}40&157&117\\164&49&19\\31&172&68\end{smallmatrix}$	231 (76⊕171)	7 (172⊕171)	$\begin{smallmatrix}100&36&55\\67&23&176\\231&1&0\end{smallmatrix}$
iteration k = 9								
$\begin{smallmatrix}100&36&55\\67&23&176\\231&1&0\end{smallmatrix}$	$\begin{smallmatrix}125&115&216\\76&82&164\\242&132&154\end{smallmatrix}$	$\begin{smallmatrix}40&157&117\\164&49&19\\31&76&45\end{smallmatrix}$	$\begin{smallmatrix}100&36&55\\67&23&176\\231&1&9\end{smallmatrix}$	$\begin{smallmatrix}125&115&216\\76&82&164\\242&132&49\end{smallmatrix}$	$\begin{smallmatrix}40&157&117\\164&49&19\\31&76&36\end{smallmatrix}$	60 (17⊕45)	9 (36⊕45)	$\begin{smallmatrix}100&36&55\\67&23&176\\231&1&60\end{smallmatrix}$

The presented cryptanalysis requires 2×M×N plain-images to recover permutation sequence and randomly generated values used to mask shuffled pixels. Contrarily, the brute-force attack is independent to image size and needs to try for $\frac{n_1 \times n_2 \times n_3 \times n_4}{\Delta x(0) \times \Delta p} \approx$ 2.56×10^{32} different keys, where n_1 is length of $x(0) = 1 - 0$, n_2 is length of $p = 1 - 0$, n_3 is length of $p_0 = 255 - 0$, n_4 is length of $L = 100 - 0$ and $\Delta x(0), \Delta p \geq 10^{-15}$ [16]. If trial of one key (through Hussain *et al.* algorithm) takes 1ms time then brute-force attack will require 2.56×10^{29} s $\approx 8.1177 \times 10^{21}$ years for all possible keys.

The algorithm could be made secure against mentioned attack by (i) applying round operations (greater than 2) so that the attacker will not be able to recover random codes or shuffled pixels at various round's stages, and (ii) modifying c_i (refer step **A.8** of encryption algorithm) with some secure mathematical transformation like circular left/right shift on bits of pixels c_i by some random number of positions before passing it to S-Box. These remedial suggestions improve overall algorithm's encryption strength and robustness against mentioned CPA attack at the cost of encryption time.

4   Conclusion

This paper analyzes a recent image encryption algorithm proposed by Hussain *et al*. The algorithm is based on much studied architecture of chaos-based image encryption i.e. permutation-diffusion architecture. It involves three independent phases such as total shuffling, diffusion and S-box transformation. The algorithm has advantages of high encryption strength and performance. However, it has been found that the algorithm has few inherent defects due to which it is susceptible to mentioned attack. The analytical information gained by the attacker about algorithm makes him capable of recovering the plain-image with chosen-plaintext attack and inverse S-box without knowing the secret key. Hence, the presented work demonstrates a complete break and concludes that the Hussain *et al*. algorithm is insecure and doesn't have the efficacy of providing sufficient security to sensitive digital images.

References

1. Schneier, B.: Applied Cryptography: Protocols Algorithms and Source Code in C. Wiley, New York (1996)
2. Menezes, A.J., Oorschot, P.C.V., Vanstone, S.A.: Handbook of applied cryptography CRC Press (1997)
3. Wang, Y., Wong, K., Liao, X., Xiang, T., Chen, G.: A Chaos-based Image Encryption Algorithm with Variable Control Parameters. Chaos, Solitons & Fractals 41(4), 1773–1783 (2009)
4. Ahmad, M., Farooq, O.: Chaos based PN sequence generator for cryptographic applications. In: International Conference on Multimedia, Signal Processing and Communication Technologies, pp. 83–86 (2011)
5. Wang, Y., Wong, K.W., Liao, X., Chen, G.: A new chaos-based fast image encryption algorithm. Applied Soft Computing 11(1), 514–522 (2011)
6. Ye, R.: A novel chaos-based image encryption scheme with an efficient permutation-diffusion mechanism. Optics Communications 284(22), 5290–5298 (2011)
7. Liu, H., Wang, X.: Color image encryption based on one-time keys and robust chaotic maps. Computers and Mathematics with Applications 59(10), 3320–3327 (2010)
8. Hermassi, H., Rhouma, R., Belghith, S.: Improvement of an image encryption algorithm based on hyper-chaos. Telecommunication Systems 52(2), 539–549 (2013)
9. Fu, C., Chen, J., Zou, H., Meng, W., Zhan, Y., Yu, Y.: A chaos-based digital image encryption scheme with an improved diffusion strategy. Optics Express 20(3), 2363–2378 (2012)
10. Seyed, M.S., Mirzakuchaki, S.: A fast color image encryption algorithm based on coupled two-dimensional piecewise chaotic map. Signal Processing 92(5), 1202–1215 (2012)
11. Kanso, A., Ghebleh, M.: A novel image encryption algorithm based on a 3D chaotic map. Communications in Nonlinear Science and Numerical Simulation 17(7), 2943–2959 (2012)
12. Ahmad, M., Farooq, O.: A Multi-Level Blocks Scrambling Based Chaotic Image Cipher. In: Ranka, S., Banerjee, A., Biswas, K.K., Dua, S., Mishra, P., Moona, R., Poon, S.-H., Wang, C.-L. (eds.) IC3 2010. CCIS, vol. 94, pp. 171–182. Springer, Heidelberg (2010)

13. El-Latif, A.A.A., Niu, X.: A hybrid chaotic system and cyclic elliptic curve for image encryption. AEU-International Journal of Electronics and Communications 67(2), 136–143 (2013)
14. Enayatifar, R., Abdullah, A.H., Isnin, I.F.: Chaos-based image encryption using a hybrid genetic algorithm and a DNA sequence. Optics and Lasers in Engineering 56, 83–93 (2014)
15. Hussain, I., Shah, T., Gondal, M.A.: Image encryption algorithm based on total shuffling scheme and chaotic S-box transformation. Journal of Vibration and Control (2013), doi:10.1177/1077546313482960
16. Hermassi, H., Rhouma, R., Belghith, S.: Security analysis of image cryptosystems only or partially based on a chaotic permutation. Journal of Systems and Software 85(9), 2133–2144 (2012)
17. Çokal, C., Solak, E.: Cryptanalysis of a chaos-based image encryption algorithm. Physics Letters A 373(15), 1357–1360 (2009)
18. Rhouma, R., Solak, E., Belghith, S.: Cryptanalysis of a New Substitution-Diffusion based Image Cipher. Communication in Nonlinear Science and Numerical Simulation 15(7), 1887–1892 (2010)
19. Li, C., Lo, K.T.: Optimal quantitative cryptanalysis of permutation-only multimedia ciphers against plaintext attacks. Signal Processing 91(4), 949–954 (2011)
20. Rhouma, R., Belghith, S.: Cryptanalysis of a spatiotemporal chaotic cryptosystem. Chaos, Solitons & Fractals 41(4), 1718–1722 (2009)
21. Wang, X., He, G.: Cryptanalysis on a novel image encryption method based on total shuffling scheme. Optics Communications 284(24), 5804–5807 (2011)
22. Ahmad, M.: Cryptanalysis of Chaos Based Secure Satellite Imagery Cryptosystem. In: Aluru, S., Bandyopadhyay, S., Catalyurek, U.V., Dubhashi, D.P., Jones, P.H., Parashar, M., Schmidt, B. (eds.) IC3 2011. CCIS, vol. 168, pp. 81–91. Springer, Heidelberg (2011)
23. Rhouma, R., Belghith, S.: Cryptanalysis of a new image encryption algorithm based on hyper-chaos. Physics Letters A 372(38), 5973–5978 (2008)
24. Özkaynak, F., Özer, A.B., Yavuz, S.: Cryptanalysis of a novel image encryption scheme based on improved hyperchaotic sequences. Optics Communications 285(2), 4946–4948 (2012)
25. Solak, E., Rhouma, R., Belghith, S.: Cryptanalysis of a multi-chaotic systems based image cryptosystem. Optics Communications 283(2), 232–236 (2010)
26. Wang, X., Liu, L.: Cryptanalysis of a parallel sub-image encryption method with high-dimensional chaos. Nonlinear Dynamics 73(1-2), 795–800 (2013)
27. Tu, G., Liao, X., Xiang, T.: Cryptanalysis of a color image encryption algorithm based on chaos. Optik-International Journal for Light and Electron Optics 124(22), 5411–5415 (2013)
28. Rhouma, R., Belghith, S.: Cryptanalysis of a Chaos-based Cryptosystem on DSP. Communication in Nonlinear Science and Numerical Simulation 16(2), 876–884 (2011)
29. Ahmad, M., Khan, P.M., Ansari, M.Z.: A Simple and Efficient Key-Dependent S-Box Design Using Fisher-Yates Shuffle Technique. In: Martínez Pérez, G., Thampi, S.M., Ko, R., Shu, L. (eds.) SNDS 2014. CCIS, vol. 420, pp. 540–550. Springer, Heidelberg (2014)
30. Khan, M., Shah, T., Mahmood, H., Gondal, M.A., Hussain, I.: A novel technique for the construction of strong S-boxes based on chaotic Lorenz systems. Nonlinear Dynamics 70(3), 2303–2311 (2012)
31. Kerckhoffs's principle, http://crypto-it.net/eng/theory/kerckhoffs.html (last access on May 12, 2014)

PWLCM Based Secure Measurement Matrix Generation for Secure Video Compressive Sensing

Abhishek Kolazi, Sudhish N. George, and P.P. Deepthi

Department of Electronics & Communication Engineering,
National Institute of Technology, Calicut

Abstract. In this paper, a new approach for encrypting the video data through compressive sensing is proposed. Even though, Orsdemir's cryptography key based measurement matrix (Φ_B matrix) generation technique [11] provides a robust encryption method for CS framework, this scheme can not provide large key space and security. Hence the aim of this work is to improve the security and keyspace of the compressive sensing paradigm without affecting the basic features of compressive sensing such as good reconstruction performance, robustness to noise characteristics and also a low encoder complexity. In order to improve the key space and security, piecewise linear chaotic map (PWLCM) based of Φ_B matrix generation technique is proposed. The PWLCM is run for random number of iterations to form a random array which is used as the initial seed for generating the secure Φ_B matrix. The initial & system parameter values and the number of iterations of PWLCM are kept as secret key. The proposed Φ_B matrix generation technique is validated with popular CS based video reconstruction techniques and it is found that the proposed method provides an improvement in the key space and security without affecting the basic features of compressive sensing.

1 Introduction

The compressive sensing (CS) is an emerging technology in signal processing society. The CS enables to sample a sparse data at a rate which is much less than the traditional Nyquist rates and allows us to reconstruct the original data with minimum number of measurements [1],[8]. Incorporating an encryption scheme through compressive sensing provides data security at the initial signal acquisition stage itself [11]. Recently block based compressive sensing (BCS) has proven to be effective while dealing with large sized image and video datato reduce the complexity of operation and huge storage requirements [9]. As far as reconstruction part is considered there are different block based reconstruction schemes. Block compressive sensing using smoothed projection ladweber (BCS-SPL) is the most advanced one [7],[6]. When multiple hypothesis (MH) based prediction is employed for block-based CS reconstruction the PSNR of the BCS-smoothed projected Landweber (BCS-SPL-DDWT) reconstruction approach is further improved. The MH reconstruction performed on video [2] incorporate motion compensation(MC) and motion estimation (ME) at the reconstruction stage to improve the reconstruction quality better than doing it on a frame by frame basis.

All the reconstruction technique demands the knowledge of the sampling operator Φ. In this paper, this idea is exploited to provide security to the video frames. The Φ

J. Lloret Mauri et al. (Eds.): SSCC 2014, CCIS 467, pp. 182–191, 2014.

matrix is kept hidden from the eavesdropper or an attacker using the secret key. In [11], Orsdemir *et al.* proposed a robust encryption system for CS data by designing crypto-graphic key based pseudorandom Φ matrix generation. In cryptographic key based Φ matrix generation, the entire security depends only on the size the secret key used. It is not possible increase the key size to a large value without affecting the reconstruction performance of the CS framework. This is based on the fact that when the size of the key is increased, Φ matrix shows the exact Gaussian nature only at higher orders. But the aim of CS operation is to reduce the number of the samples to a small number, which results a reduced order of Φ matrix. The degradation in the Gaussian nature results a reduced reconstruction performance. Thus, it is not possible to increases the key size of Φ matrix generation without affecting the reconstruction performance. Moreover, when BCS approach is adopted, the knowledge about one complete block is available to an attacker, he can retrieve the Φ matrix used by performing the Brute force trials. Thus, it is required to design a Φ matrix generation with improved key space and security with-out affecting the reconstruction performance of CS video system. This paper proposes a chaotic map based Φ matrix generation by effectively utilizing the key space of chaotic map in the CS based video encryption system.

This paper is organised as follows. Section 2 describes an overview of the funda-mental principles of block-based compressive sensing. Section 3 deals with the pro-posed PWLCM based secure measurement matrix generation for compressive sensing of video data. Section 4 discusses about the analytical and experimental analysis of the proposed encryption system in terms of cryptanalysis and reconstruction performance. The paper concludes in section 5.

2 Background

This section provides an overview about block compressive sensing and the multi-hypothesis-BCS-SPL reconstruction approach.

2.1 Block Based Compressive Sensing

This is the basic idea of CS is that if a signal has sparse representation in any one of the basis it can be recovered by smaller number of projection onto second basis [4]. When CS is applied to video/images it is more advantageous to perform block-based com-pressive sensing (BCS) [7]. BCS has the following main advantages 1) random matrix Φ can be easily be stored because of the smaller size, 2) encoder need not wait until the whole image is measured for starting the processing and 3) since each block is pro-cessed independently, initial guess is easy to obtain and this speeds the reconstruction process. The mathematical expression for sampling operation in the BCS framework is given below.

$$y_j = \Phi_B x_j \tag{1}$$

where x_j is the vectorized signal of $j^{th} B \times B$ block in raster scanned order of the input image/video frame, y_j is corresponding CS data and Φ_B is measurement matrix used. The Φ_B matrix must satisfy restricted isometric property (RIP) [1]. It is required to fix a sub-rate which decides the compression ratio of video frames. When we apply block based CS on to the video we sample the first video frame with higher sub-rate and all other frames in the GOP are sampled at very low sub-rate compared to the first frame [2]. The sub-rate will decide the amount of compression and also the reconstruction quality. The sub-rate for the BCS is given as, $S = M/B^2$, where M represents the number of CS samples for each block.

2.2 Reconstruction Algorithms

A number of reconstruction algorithms BCS video data were proposed in the last decade [3], [7]. The reconstruction process is like solving an optimization problem with incomplete observation [5]. Recovery of the original image can be performed by using any of the BCS algorithms [9], [6]. Recently a multiple hypothesis (MH) based approach was introduced in [2]. This algorithm mainly concentrates on improving the reconstruction quality of the BCS-SPL reconstructed data. The MH based approach uses the structural similarity index (SSIM) as the stopping criteria [13] for BCS reconstruction. The predicted video frame is taken as a weighted sum of all the predicted block with in the search window of the reference video frame. Linear combination of all the predictions are taken to obtain initial guess up on which the residual calculation an updating is performed. In all other reconstruction algorithms, the initial guess is a rough guess. But MH based reconstruction gives importance to initial guess by applying the before mentioned MH based initial prediction [13]. Basic idea of MH is that the blocks which are more similar to the targeted block in the reference frame search window are given more weight and dissimilar blocks are given less weights. In this paper MH based reconstruction is employed for a set of compressive sensed video frames [2].

The video frames are clubbed as a group to pictures(GOP) of P. In this GOP, the key frames is compressive sensed at very high sub-rate remaining frames are sampled at minimum possible sub-rate to achieve better compression. Instead of reconstructing the data frame by frame the reconstruction quality is improved if we include motion compensation and motion estimation technique at the decoder [2]. For employing ME/MC, we have to reconstruct initial frame using the normal MH-reconstruction which will have higher PSNR compared to normal BCS-SPL reconstruction. This initial frame x_{ref} is taken as reference frame for the set of GOP in which that frame is included. Then, as a second step the current frame is reconstructed from y_i using normal MH, where y_i is the ith CS frame in the GOP. The result is actually a rough guess of the current frame. This rough guess may be termed as $\hat{x}$. The ME/MC is performed between x_{ref} and $\hat{x}$. The result will be a motion compensated frame x_{mc} from the second frame. This x_{mc} is our initial guess for the current frame. Then the residue x_r is calculated using x_{mc}, Phi_B and y_i. The x_{mc} is updated by adding x_r to it. The over all process is repeated for n times to enhance the frames. For first half of the GOP, forward prediction is employed and for remaining half, backward prediction is used [10].

3 Secure Video Compressive Sensing Using PWLCM Based Φ Matrix

PWLCM is a chaotic sequence model, the bifurcation diagram shows it is less sensitive to external disturbance than normal logistic map as described in [12]. Each chaotic maps have some region of operation to show chaotic behaviour. The sensitivity of chaotic systems is decided by initial conditions/control parameters. The value of PWLCM at $(n+1)^{th}$ is given as,

$$c_{n+1} = F(c_n) = \begin{cases} c_n/\mu, & 0 \leq c_n < \mu \\ (c_n - \mu)/(0.5 - \mu), & \mu \leq c_n < 0.5 \\ F(1 - c_n), & 0.5 \leq c_n < 1 \end{cases} \qquad (2)$$

The initial condition ranges from $c_0 \in I = [0,1)$ and the system parameter ranges as $\mu \in (0, 0.5)$. These quantities act as a key in the proposed encryption process.

According to CS theory the measurement matrix must satisfy restricted isometric property (RIP)[1]. One of the more surprising aspects of compressive sensing is that one can generate a measurement matrix Φ matrix at random (where the entries are drawn from an appropriate distribution) and that matrix has an overwhelming probability to satisfy RIP. This can be proved using Johnson-Lindenstrauss (JL) lemma [7]. The most suitable candidate as Φ matrix is a Gaussian random matrix. The Φ matrix has equal importance in reconstruction part of compressive sensed data. If the Φ_B matrix can be hidden by using a secret key, we can have a good encryption scheme in our hand. The Φ matrix used as sampling operator can be generated as a pseudo random matrix with a seed value.

3.1 PWLCM Based Secure Measurement Matrix Generation

In the proposed method, the PWLCM is run for random number of iterations and the inter equivalent values of these chaotic values form a random array. This random array is considered as the initial seed for generating the sampling matrix of given size for the CS video paradigm. Any suitable standard algorithms can be used for such an application. In the proposed approach, the initial state value, system parameter value and number of iterations are kept hidden as the secret key. A small change in these values results a drastic change in the output values generated by the dual one dimensional chaotic map. Since the values of the Φ matrix depend on PWLCM array, there is no room for an attacker to have an inverse mapping and obtain Φ matrix back from the available values. This is how the security is brought in this algorithm. By this encryption scheme, the following advantages can be obtained.

1. Without knowing the initial condition, the system parameter value and number of iterations of the chaotic sequence generator, an attacker can never recover the signal back.
2. The measurement matrix Φ matrix need not be transmitted which results a reduced transmission complexity.
3. The proposed method offers large key space.

The algorithm description of generating the Φ matrix is given below.

1. Run the one dimensional PWLCM based on Eq. 2 for $N1$ iterations to form a chaotic array of size $N1$, where c_0, μ and $N1$ are derived from the secret key.

2. Convert the each chaotic value C_i to binary value of 8 bits by algorithm shown below, where C_i represents the ith value of the chaotic sequence.

$$for \quad i = 1 : N1$$
$$t = C_i$$
$$for \quad j = 1 : 8$$
$$t = t \times 2$$
$$If(y > Threshold)$$
$$B_i(j) = 1$$
$$else$$
$$B_i(j) = 0$$
$$t = t - 1$$
$$end$$
$$end$$

where B is an array of length 8 and threshold is 0.5.

3. Convert each binary number in B array to corresponding decimal number and obtain a random array **r** of size $N1$.
4. Generate Φ matrix by using **r** as the initial seed.

3.2   Algorithm Description of Secure Video Compressive Sensing

The steps for performing the secure video compressive sensing operation using the proposed PWLCM based measurement matrix generation technique is given below.

1. Divide the whole set of video frames as different GOPs where each GOP contains P video frames.
2. First video frame in each GOP is sampled with a higher sub-rate since the first frame is used as reference frame during reconstruction the remaining frames which are sampled at low sub-rate to achieve higher compression.
3. Generate Φ_{B_k} for key frame and $\Phi_{B_{nk}}$ for non-key frame using the proposed PWLCM based Φ matrix generation technique.
4. Apply BCS on each frames separately by fixing sub-rate for each subsequent video frame to generate CS vectors of video frames using the generated Φ matrices.

The following section deals with the analysis of the proposed video encryption method.

4   Analysis of the Proposed Encryption System

For analysis of the proposed encryption scheme, different standard test video frames of Susie, Foreman, Akiyo are considered. GOP is taken as set of 8 consecutive video frames. 32-bit representation of PWLCM is considered for random array generation. Reconstruction performance is compared between motion compensated BCS-SPL (MC-BCS-SPL) for block based video compression and MH based MC-BCS-SPL (MH-MC-BCS-SPL), Matlab 2010 is used for simulation of results.

4.1 Key Space and Key Sensitivity Analysis

The system parameter of PWLCM μ and the initial state c_0 are treated as 32 bits. They are kept as secret information. We can also hide the array length $N1$ (number of iterations used to generate PWLCM sequence) this is also represented as 32-bit data. If this three parameters are kept hidden. The overall key size system is 96 bit representation. The total key space then becomes 2^{96}. So for a brute force search method, it becomes all most impossible to get the combinations in the key space and to recover the original key.

An attempt is made as an attackers point of view to obtain the initial video frame by using a wrong key. From the result in Fig.1, it could be inferred that if the key is not correct we get a completely wrong data recovery. It can be also noted that the reconstructed video frame using correct key has good visual quality. Which is very important in case of video encoding.

(a)   (b)   (c)

Fig. 1. Reconstruction using MH-MC-BCS-SPL on third Susie video frame set sub-rates 0.2 (a) original video frame (b) reconstructed video frame using correct key (c) reconstructed video frame using wrong key

4.2 Statistical Properties of the Encryption

The statistical property of the proposed scheme is monitored by calculating the correlation between adjacent pixels in the video frame. We tried to reconstruct video frame using a wrong-key and compare the correlation plot between the original frame and the wrong key decrypted image as in Fig.2. The correlation plot is highly scattered in case of wrong key decrypted image and where as the original image has a proper pattern. The disordered pattern shows low correlation between pixels. Here the correlation results are shown for adjacent pixels which are taken horizontally. The results are almost same when correlation is taken vertically and diagonally. To evaluate the correlation between two adjacent pixels in horizontal and diagonal directions,the following procedure is carried out. Randomly select 2,000 adjacent pixel pairs from the original image and wrongly decrypted image, respectively. Let (x_i, y_i) denote the ith pixel intensity. Each pair is regarded as a coordinate and placed in the rectangular coordinate system.

A quantitative evaluation on correlation was listed in Table 1. In Table 1 the correlation coefficient between the adjacent pixels located horizontally and adjacent pixels located diagonally are calculated. The results are given for original video frame and wrong key decrypted video frame. The experiment is performed for initial frame only.

Since the consecutive frame in GOP are almost similar. Initial video frame are compressive sensed at 0.7 sub-rate. The correlation coefficient is calculated by using the relation $r_{xy} = \dfrac{|cov(x,y)|}{\sqrt{D(x)}\sqrt{D(y)}}$ where x and y stand for the intensities of two adjacent pixels and $cov(x,y) = \dfrac{1}{N}\sum_{i=1}^{N}(x_i - E(x))(y_i - E(y))$ where $D(x) = \dfrac{1}{N}\sum_{i=1}^{N}(x_i - E(x))^2$ and $E(x) = \sum_{i=1}^{N}x_i$.

Table 1. Correlation coefficient of adjacent pixels in different video frames

Image name	Direction	Test results	
		Original frame	**Wrong-key decrypted frame**
Akiyo	Horizontal	0.9835	0.0957
	Diagonal	0.9658	0.0330
Foreman	Horizontal	0.9838	0.1281
	Diagonal	0.9557	0.0803
Susie	Horizontal	0.9749	0.0174
	Diagonal	0.9149	0.0174

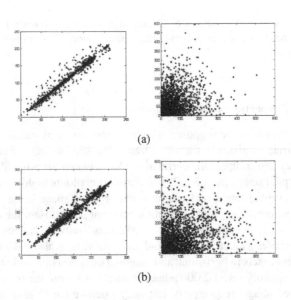

Fig. 2. Statistical properties of correct key decrypted vs wrong key decrypted video frames for proposed scheme (a) Correlation of adjacent pixel in Akiyo frame (b) Correlation of adjacent pixel in Foreman frame

4.3 Reconstruction Performance

The independent BCS-SPL-DDWT, MC-BCS-SPL-DDWT and MH-MC-BCS-SPL-DDWT reconstruction approaches are performed on Susie, foreman, Akiyo video sequences. Result in Table 2 indicates that there is no degradation in the video quality after performing encryption and decryption using PWLCM based measurement matrix generation techniques. The values used for performing experiment are system parameter $\mu = 0.365$ and the initial state $c_n = 0.1, N1 = 100$. In Table 2, the average PSNR value after reconstruction of CS video frames are given. The experiment is performed on 24 subsequent video frames of standard video sequences after embedding the proposed encryption. The result shows that MH-MC-BCS-SPL has very good PSNR compared to any other CS reconstruction scheme and has almost similar reconstruction quality of [2].

Table 2. Reconstruction performance of the proposed encryption system performed on different standard video frames using existing CS video recovery schemes.

Video	Reconstruction type	PSNR in dB				
		S = 0.1	S =0.2	S =0.3	S =0.4	S =0.5
Akiyo	BCS-SPL-DDWT	28.97	31.79	34.19	35.93	37.12
Akiyo	MC-BCS-SPL-DDWT	36.49	39.71	41.13	41.62	42.01
Akiyo	MH-MC-BCS-SPL-DDWT	35.55	38.39	39.15	39.58	39.98
Foreman	BCS-SPL-DDWT	25.65	28.70	30.67	32.21	33.59
Foreman	MC-BCS-SPL-DDWT	28.34	31.36	33.71	35.34	36.99
Foreman	MH-MC-BCS-SPL-DDWT	29.01	33.14	35.17	36.82	38.35
Susie	BCS-SPL-DDWT	31.12	33.78	34.99	37.03	38.09
Susie	MC-BCS-SPL-DDWT	34.20	36.25	37.68	38.82	39.94
Susie	MH-MC-BCS-SPL-DDWT	34.63	37.11	38.63	39.95	41.23

4.4 Robustness Characteristics

Consider the scenario where the exact encrypted image in the form of the measurements y is not available. A noisy $\hat{y}$ version of the measurements y is available instead of the original y. Even then the system gives a PSNR of above 30dB for subrates 0.1 and above. This test is performed for the set of foreman video frames. This test proves that the proposed algorithm shows good robustness to noise characteristics even if the data is altered by an attacker. The graph in fig.3 gives the performance of foreman video frames under different additive white Gaussian noise power. As the secured measurement Φ_B matrix is used the whole process is iterated with noise power varying from 0dB to 50dB. The performance is consistent up to a noise power up to 35dB which is very reasonable. The x-axis corresponds to the normalized noise perturbation. Noise perturbation is calculated by using the relation $nPERT = 10log_{10}\dfrac{\|\hat{y} - y\|^2}{\|y\|^2}$. The noise power varying from 0dB to 50dB corresponds to nPERT varying from -42 to -16 in Fig.3.

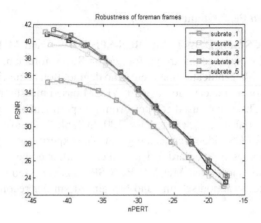

Fig. 3. Robustness to noise characteristics of the proposed encryption system for video data

4.5 Comparisons with Existing Method

Orsdemir's method proposed in [11] is less secure against brute force attack. The method uses only single key for generation of measurement matrix and we are hiding that measurement matrix. For BCS approaches, if the block size is chosen as 16×16, for a sub-rate of 0.5, the order of Φ matrix is 128×256. For such a matrix, if the key length is greater than 32, the Gaussian nature is of of the measurement matrix is degraded which results a reduced reconstruction quality. Thus, for comparison, we have chosen as 32-bit key for Orsdemir's key based measurement matrix generation technique. Thus, the key space of Orsdemir's method is 2^{32} and on an average, the attacker should try only 2^{31} operations to find out the correct Φ matrix used. But, in the proposed system there are three parameters which are kept hidden initial condition, system parameter and length of the vector. If each parameter is represented by 32-bits. The key space will improve to 2^{96}. For a brute force attack we require a total of 2^{95} operations which is a large number for CS video encryption.

Moreover, Orsdemir's measurement matrix is generated using a single key. The values of the measurement matrix depend upon on a single seed. In the proposed scheme each nominal value of the measurement matrix depend upon more than one value in the random array. This make it impossible for a attacker to have a valid mapping from the available set of information and get back the data. The proposed scheme is more robust against known-plain text attack than mentioned Orsdemir's method.

5   Conclusion

In this paper, piecewise linear chaotic map (PWLCM) based generation of measurement matrix for compressive sensing of video data is proposed to achieve improved security and key space. The PWLCM is run for random number of iterations to generate a random array. The generated random array is used as the initial seed for generating the random measurement matrix used in CS video framework. The proposed system is compared with the existing scheme and it is found that our method shows better security and key space than its counterpart. Moreover, the proposed low complexity encryption technique maintains the reconstruction and robustness to noise performance of CS system when compared with conventional CS video system. In addition to these features, the proposed measurement matrix generation technique avoids the burden in transmitting the measurement matrix in the compressive sensing paradigm.

References

1. Candes, E., Romberg, J.: Robust signal recovery from incomplete observations. In: 2006 IEEE International Conference on Image Processing, pp. 1281–1284. IEEE (2006)
2. Chen, C., Tramel, E.W., Fowler, J.E.: Compressed-sensing recovery of images and video using multihypothesis predictions. In: 2011 Conference Record of the Forty Fifth Asilomar Conference on Signals, Systems and Computers (ASILOMAR), pp. 1193–1198. IEEE (2011)
3. Do, T.T., Gan, L., Nguyen, N., Tran, T.D.: Sparsity adaptive matching pursuit algorithm for practical compressed sensing. In: 2008 42nd Asilomar Conference on Signals, Systems and Computers, pp. 581–587. IEEE (2008)
4. Do, T.T., Tran, T.D., Gan, L.: Fast compressive sampling with structurally random matrices. In: IEEE International Conference on Acoustics, Speech and Signal Processing, ICASSP 2008, pp. 3369–3372. IEEE (2008)
5. Figueiredo, M.A., Nowak, R.D., Wright, S.J.: Gradient projection for sparse reconstruction: Application to compressed sensing and other inverse problems. IEEE Journal of Selected Topics in Signal Processing 1(4), 586–597 (2007)
6. Fowler, J.E., Mun, S., Tramel, E.W.: Multiscale block compressed sensing with smoother projected landweber reconstruction. In: Proceedings of the European Signal Processing Conference, pp. 564–568 (2011)
7. Gan, L.: Block compressed sensing of natural images. In: 2007 15th International Conference on Digital Signal Processing, pp. 403–406. IEEE (2007)
8. Haupt, J., Nowak, R.: Signal reconstruction from noisy random projections. IEEE Transactions on Information Theory 52(9), 4036–4048 (2006)
9. Mun, S., Fowler, J.E.: Block compressed sensing of images using directional transforms. In: 2009 16th IEEE International Conference on Image Processing (ICIP), pp. 3021–3024. IEEE (2009)
10. Mun, S., Fowler, J.E.: Residual reconstruction for block-based compressed sensing of video. In: Data Compression Conference (DCC), pp. 183–192. IEEE (2011)
11. Orsdemir, A., Altun, H.O., Sharma, G., Bocko, M.F.: On the security and robustness of encryption via compressed sensing. In: IEEE Military Communications Conference, MILCOM 2008, pp. 1–7. IEEE (2008)
12. Wang, X.Y., Yang, L.: Design of pseudo-random bit generator based on chaotic maps. International Journal of Modern Physics B 26(32) (2012)
13. Wang, Z., Bovik, A.C., Sheikh, H.R., Simoncelli, E.P.: Image quality assessment: From error visibility to structural similarity. IEEE Transactions on Image Processing 13(4), 600–612 (2004)

A Mathematical Analysis of Elliptic Curve Point Multiplication

Ravi Kishore Kodali

Department of Electronics and Communication Engineering,
National Institute of Technology, Warangal,
Warangal, 506004 India

Abstract. This work presents a mixed-coordinate system based elliptic curve point multiplication algorithm. It employs the width-w Non-Adjacent Form (NAF) algorithm for point multiplication and uses the Montgomery trick to pre-compute the odd points $P_i = iP$ for $i = 1, 3, \cdots, 2^w - 1$ with only one field inversion.

Keywords: Non-Adjacent Form, Point Multiplication, Elliptic Curve.

1 Introduction

With the advent of the world wide web, huge amount of data by various applications/ nodes is being shared. With information sharing hitting unprecedented levels, security of the information being shared becomes paramount. While the data being exchanged among the nodes using the Internet it is necessary to make use of various cryptographic techniques and secure the data so as to reduce the risks associated. RSA, one of the asymmetric key cryptographic techniques, is being widely used over the Internet. However, this technique requires large key sizes and is compute intensive. Alternately, Elliptic Curve Cryptography (ECC)proposed by Koblitz [9] and Miller [13] can also be used as ECC provides similar security levels by making use of lesser key sizes as compared to the RSA. ECC, standardized by ISO [1], IEEE [15] and NIST [14], has been gaining its acceptance recently. However, ECC involves repeated application of compute intensive elliptic curve based point multiplication operation. This work primarily focusses on speeding up point multiplication.

2 Elliptic Curve Cryptography

ECC uses elliptic curves as given by equation 1.

$$y^2 = (x^3 + ax + b), \tag{1}$$

where $(a, b, x, y) \in F_p$, a prime field and p is a prime number and satisfying the condition $4a^3 + 27b^2 \neq 0$. Consider two points, P and Q lying on the elliptic curve (EC), $E_p(a, b)$ [10].

J. Lloret Mauri et al. (Eds.): SSCC 2014, CCIS 467, pp. 192–200, 2014.

The addition of these two points resulting in R, another point lying on the EC $E_p(a, b)$ is given by equation

$$R(x_R, y_R) = P + Q, \qquad (2)$$

where

$$x_R = (\lambda^2 - x_P - x_Q) \qquad (3)$$

$$y_R = (\lambda(x_P - x_R) - y_P) \qquad (4)$$

$$\lambda = \frac{y_Q - y_P}{x_Q - x_P} \qquad (5)$$

The point doubling operation may be considered as being P = Q, R = 2P, the λ is to be computed by

$$\lambda = \frac{3x_P^2 + a}{2y_P} \qquad (6)$$

The point multiplication can be achieved by using point addition and doubling operations repeatedly. One of the algorithms for point multiplication, double and add method is given by algorithm 1.

Algorithm 1. Double and add algorithm

Input: k (binary representation), P (a point on the EC)
Output $Q = k \times P$
A. $Q = \phi$ (point of infinity).
B. for $i = t - 1$ downto 0
   $Q = 2Q$.
   if $k_i = 1$, $Q = Q+P$.
C. Return Q

---

3   Related Work

For a given point, $P(x, y)$, the negative of P is given by $-P = (x, -y)$ for an elliptic curve over a prime field. The subtraction of points over a prime field may be considered as $R = P - Q = P + (-Q)$ [7]. In order to achieve efficiency while carrying out point multiplication, a sliding window method is used [17]. The window size, the corresponding computational complexity and Fuzzy optimization are given in [8]. While representing the scalar values, various radices have also been used such as radix -2 and radix -3 have been used [4]. A multibase non-adjacent form (mbNAF) technique is used to represent integers using different bases [12]. An improved method based on the width-w NAF multiplication, where $P_i = iP$ for $i = 1, 3, \cdots, 2^w - 1$ are pre-computed using double and add method and are stored, is presented. This method performs multiplication faster, when compared to the double and add method. This work focusses on addressing the cost issue of the odd point pre-computation and storage. In addition, as will be elaborated in the subsequent sections, the work focusses on representing the scalar k in various coordinate systems in order to achieve efficiency with point multiplication. The mixed coordinate system [5] is used in the reduction of computation cost of point multiplication. Another problem is field inversion while using the double and add algorithm. The same is overcome by applying the Montgomery trick, which trades inversions with multiplications [2]. The points are represented in mixed coordinate system to carry out point multiplication operations subsequently and obtain improved efficiency.

4   NAF Representation

The value of k is represented in its binary form is used by the double and add algorithm. When k is represented using $t-$ bits, the number of $1's$ can be $\frac{t}{2}$ and the cost of point multiplication $k \times P$ by using double and add method involves t point doubling operations and $\frac{t}{2}$ point addition operations. If k is a large value, the computational complexity is bound to be high. This complexity motivates the development of different decimal number representation schemes. The number of point addition operations can be reduced by minimizing the number of $1's$ while representing the values of k. In the signed digit representation, the value of k is represented by

$$k = \sum_0^{t-1} k_i 2^i, \tag{7}$$

where $k_i \in \{0, +1, -1\}$. In Non-Adjacent Form (NAF) representation, no two adjacent coefficients k_i can be non-zero.

Algorithm 2. Computing width-w NAF
___
Input: k
Output: width-w NAF of k
A. $i = 0$.
B. while k ≥ 1 do
    if k is odd
        $k_i = u$, where $u \equiv k(mod2^w)$
        $k = k - k_i$
    else $k_i = 0$.
C. $k = k/2$
D. $i = i + 1$
Return $\{k_{i-1}, k_{i-2}, \cdots, k_1, k_0\}$

In NAF, the average density of non-zero coefficients $= \frac{1}{3}$, resulting in the reduced requirement of point addition operations. In width-w NAF, the number of point addition operations is further reduced. In width-w NAF, each coefficient k_i is odd and satisfies the following:

- $k_i \leq (2^w - 1)$.
- at most one of any w consecutive coefficients is non-zero.

In this case, the average density of non-zero coefficients is approximately $\frac{1}{w+1}$.
Algorithm 3 provides width-w NAF point multiplication [17].

Algorithm 3. Width-w NAF Point Multiplication

Input: w, width-w NAF of k, P
Output: Q = kP
A. Compute $P_i = iP$ for $i = 1, 3, \cdots, 2^w - 1$.
B. $Q = \phi$.
C. for i = t-1 downto 0 do
$\quad$ $Q = 2Q$.
$\quad$ if $k_i \neq 0$ then
$\quad\quad$ if $k_i > 0$ then $Q = Q + P_{k_i}$.
$\quad\quad$ else $Q = Q - P_{k_i}$.
Return Q.

4.1 Examples

Let $k = 1234567$ and its binary representation contains 21- bits:
100101101011010000111. In this 11 1's and 10 0's can be found resulting in
20 doubling operations (D) and 10 point addition operations (A). The width-
4 NAF representation of 1234567 is 9 0 0 0 0 0 13 0 0 0 0 0 13 0 0 0 0 0 0 0 7. In this,
an increased number of 0's can be seen. The computational cost = $18D + 4A$,
assuming that the values $9P, 13P$ and $7P$ are computed before hand and stored.

5 Coordinate Systems

The point multiplication cost also depends on the coordinate system used for
representing the points on EC's. The same is compared with the help of few of
the coordinate systems namely: Affine, Projective, and Jacobian.

5.1 Affine Coordinate System

In the affine coordinate system [16], the equations 3, 4, 5, and 6 for point addition $(R = P + Q)$ and point doubling operations as given in section 2. The
computation cost of one point addition would be: 1 inversion (I), 2 multiplication (M) and 1 squaring (S) operations, or $I + 2M + S$. Note that addition,
subtraction and multiplication by a constant is neglected because they are usually faster than point multiplication and inversion. Similarly, the computation
cost of a point doubling operation would be $I + 2M + 2S$.

5.2   Projective Coordinate System

In projective coordinates [11], the following substitutions are made: $x = X/Z$ and $y = Y/Z$. The point addition formulae would be: $X_R = vA$, $Y_R = u(v^2 X_P Z_Q - A) - v^3 Y_P Z_Q$ and $Z_R = v^3 Z_P Z_Q$, where $u = Y_Q Z_P - Y_P Z_Q$, $v = X_Q Z_P - X_P Z_Q$ and $A = u^2 Z_P Z_Q - v^3 - 2v^2 X_P Z_Q$.

The point doubling formulae would be: $X_R = 2hs$, $Y_R = w(4B - h) - 8Y_P^2 s^2$ and $Z_R = 8s^3$, where $w = aZ_P^2 + 3X_P^2$, $s = Y_P Z_P$, $B = X_P Y_P s$ and $h = w^2 - 8B$.

5.3   Jacobian Coordinate System

In the Jacobian coordinate system [3], the following substitutions are made: $x = X/Z^2$ and $y = Y/Z^3$. The point addition formulae would be: $X_R = -H^3 - 2U_1 H^2 + r^2$, $Y_R = -S_1 H^3 + r(U_1 H^2 - X_R)$ and $Z_R = Z_P Z_Q H$, where $U_1 = X_P Z_Q^2$, $X_Q Z_1^2$, $S_1 = Y_P Z_Q^3$, $S_2 = Y_Q Z_P^3$, $H = U_2 - U_1$ and $r = S_2 - S_1$.

The point doubling formulae would be: $X_R = T$, $Y_R = -8Y_1^4 + M(S - T)$ and $Z_R = 2Y_P Z_P$, where $S = 4X_P Y_P^2$, $M = 3X_P^2 + aZ_P^4$ and $T = -2S + M^2$. Table 1 provides a comparison of the computation costs involved in these operations.

Table 1. Computational cost comparison for Point addition and Doubling operations in various coordinate systems

Operation	Affine	Projective	Jacobian
Point Addition	$I + 2M + S$	$12M + 2S$	$12M + 4S$
Point Doubling	$I + 2M + 2S$	$7M + 5S$	$4M + 6S$

5.4   Discussion

For prime p   100- bits in elliptic curve arithmetic, the cost of an inversion operation (I) ranges from 9M to 30M, where M is the cost of multiplication operation [5]. Hence, projective coordinate system extends a great reduction in the computation cost of point addition and doubling operations.

Table 2. Comparison of Computation costs for the example in section 4.1

Format	Affine	Projective	Jacobian
Binary	$645M + 50S$	$260M + 120S$	$200M + 160S$
Width-w NAF	$473M + 40S$	$174M + 98S$	$120M + 124S$

Table -2 provides a comparison of computational costs for the example considered. From Table -1 it can be noticed that the Jacobian coordinate system provides faster doubling operations when compared with the projective coordinate system, whereas the projective coordinate system facilitates faster addition operation. It is necessary to make use of appropriate coordinate system depending on the computational requirements.

6   Cost Analysis of Width-w NAF Point Multiplication Using Mixed Coordinates

Assume a $t-$ bit width-w NAF representation of the scalar k. The computational cost of algorithm 3 $= t$ point doubling operations and $\frac{t}{w+1}$ point additions. By using mixed coordinate system, additional overhead for converting points from one coordinate system to another is also involved. The entire cost analysis of algorithm 3 using mixed coordinates:

1. Assuming we input the original point in affine coordinates, we would have to convert it to Jacobian coordinates, for the first step in algorithm 3 is doubling, and according to the mixed coordinate system described above, we use the Jacobian coordinate system for doubling and Projective coordinate system for addition. The conversion cost from Affine to Jacobian $= S + 2M$.
2. Since $t-$ point doubling operations are performed, the cost $= t(6S + 4M)$.
3. While performing point addition operations $\frac{t}{w+1}$ times, the points are converted from Jacobian to Projective system. The conversion cost $= \frac{t}{w+1}(I + 2M)$.
4. Next, we perform point addition operation in projective coordinate system $\frac{t}{w+1}$ times. In this step, we also have to convert the pre-computed point P_{k_i} from affine to projective system. The net cost of this step $= \frac{t}{w+1}(12M + 2S + 2M)$.
5. Since we iterate from addition to doubling $\frac{t}{w+1}$ times, we would have to convert the result of addition, which is in Projective system, to the Jacobian system. The cost of this step $= \frac{t}{w+1}(2M)$.
6. Finally, we convert the result from Projective system to affine system, whose cost $= 2M$.

The total cost C_{mnaf} is given by equation 8.

$$C_{mnaf} = (4M + S) + t(6S + 4M) + \frac{t}{w+1}(I + 2S + 18M)$$

$$= I(\frac{t}{w+1}) + M(4 + 4t + \frac{18t}{w+1}) + S(6t + 1 + \frac{2t}{w+1}) \quad (8)$$

6.1   Evaluation

The cost of the mixed coordinate system width-w NAF point multiplication method is compared with the traditional double and add algorithm. The average cost C_{da} of the traditional double and add algorithm, based on affine coordinates is given by

$$C_{da} = t(I + 2M + 2S) + \frac{t}{2}(I + 2M + S) = I(\frac{3t}{2}) + M(3t) + S(\frac{5t}{2}) \quad (9)$$

The Case of Higher Bit Scalars. Consider a 160-bit and a 192-bit representations of scalar k. Assuming $t-$ to be almost same across both binary and NAF representations, and considering the average case of $I = 19.M$, a cost comparison of double and add method and the mixed coordinate based width-w NAF method is made. The same comparison is given in Table 3.

Table 3. Computation cost comparison - 160-bit k

Bit Width	C_{da}	w	C_{mnaf}
160	$5160M + 400S$	4	$1844M + 1025S$
		5	$1664M + 1014.3S$
		6	$1501.14M + 1006.7S$
		7	$1394M + 1001S$
		8	$1310.67M + 996.5S$
192	$6192M + 480S$	4	$2209M + 1229.8S$
		5	$1972M + 1217S$
		6	$1800.57M + 1207.85S$
		7	$1672M + 1201S$
		8	$1572M + 1195.67S$

7   Trading Field Inversions with Multiplications – The Montgomery Trick

In the previous sections, we have seen that a mixed coordinate system can provide best computational efficiency with the point multiplication operation. As established previously, a key step in the performance of the width-w NAF multiplication algorithm is the pre-computation of the points $P_i = iP$ for $i = 1, 3, \cdots, 2^w - 1$. In our work, we use the technique introduced by Dahmen *et al* in [6]. This technique determines $(2i - 1)P$ as

$$(2i - 1)P = 2P + (2i - 3)P$$

These points in affine coordinate system can be obtained by using the following formulae:

$$
\begin{array}{cc}
2P(x_2, y_2): & 3P(x_3, y_3): \\
x_2 = \lambda_1^2 - 2x_1 & x_3 = (\lambda_2^2 - x_2 - x_1) \\
y_2 = \lambda_1(x_1 - x_2) - y_1 & y_3 = (\lambda_2(x_2 - x_3)) - y_2 \\
\lambda_1 = \frac{3x_1^2 + a}{2y_1} & \lambda_2 = \frac{y_2 - y_1}{x_2 - x_1}
\end{array}
$$

$$
\begin{aligned}
(2i - 1)P(x_{i+1}, y_{i+1}): x_{i+1} &= (\lambda_i^2 - x_2 - x_i) \\
y_{i+1} &= (\lambda_i(x_2 - x_{i+1}) - y_2) \\
\lambda_i &= \frac{y_i - y_2}{x_i - x_2}
\end{aligned}
$$

From these formulae it may be noticed that the field inversion operation is critical while performing pre-computations. It is possible to compute all these den_i simultaneously by using the Montgomery trick [2].

The cost $C_{precomp}$ of pre-computing the points $P_i = iP$ for $i = 3, \cdots, 2^w - 1$ by using both Dahmen's method and Montgomery trick is given by

$$C_{precomp} = 10(2^{w-1} - 11)M + 2^{w+1}S + I \qquad (10)$$

7.1 Total Cost Analysis

The total cost of the mixed coordinate based width-w NAF method of point multiplication is given by: Total cost $= C_{precomp} + C_{mnaf}$. Table 4 presents the total cost comparison of both the methods.

Table 4. Total computation cost comparison for $k=$ 192- bits

C_{da}	w	Total Cost
$6192M + 480S$	4	$2307.5M + 1261.8S$
	5	$2140.5M + 1281S$
	6	$2129.07M + 1335.85S$
	7	$2320.5M + 1457S$
	8	$2860.5M + 1707.67S$

The pre-computation is done only once for a given w, and hence the total cost given in Table -4 includes one time cost.

8   Conclusions

The width-w NAF method based point multiplication provides improved performance over traditional double and add method. By using the mixed coordinate system in this width-w NAF method based multiplication results in further performance improvement. As the point multiplication is repeated applied in ECC, any improvement in the performance of multiplication operation yields in faster ECC encryption and decryption.

References

1. ISO/IEC 14888-3. Information Technology - Security Techniques - Digital Signatures with Appendix - Part 3: Certificate Based-Mechanisms (1998)
2. Avanzi, R.M., Cohen, H., Doche, C., Frey, G., Lange, T., Nguyen, K., Vercauteren, F.: Handbook of elliptic and hyperelliptic curve cryptography. Chapman and Hall/CRC (2005)
3. Chudnovsky, D.V., Chudnovsky, G.V.: Sequences of numbers generated by addition in formal groups and new primality and factorization tests. Advances in Applied Math 7, 385–434 (1986)

4. Ciet, M., Joye, M., Lauter, K., Montgomery, P.L.: Trading inversions for multi-plications in elliptic curve cryptography. Designs, Codes and Cryptography 39, 189–206 (2006)
5. Cohen, H., Miyaji, A., Ono, T.: Efficient elliptic curve exponentiation using mixed coordinates. In: Ohta, K., Pei, D. (eds.) ASIACRYPT 1998. LNCS, vol. 1514, pp. 51–65. Springer, Heidelberg (1998)
6. Dahmen, E., Okeya, K., Schepers, D.: Affine precomputation with sole inversion in elliptic curve cryptography. In: Pieprzyk, J., Ghodosi, H., Dawson, E. (eds.) ACISP 2007. LNCS, vol. 4586, pp. 245–258. Springer, Heidelberg (2007)
7. Hankerson, D., Hernandez, J.L., Menezes, A.: Software implementation of elliptic curve cryptography over binary fields. In: Paar, C., Koç, Ç.K. (eds.) CHES 2000. LNCS, vol. 1965, pp. 1–24. Springer, Heidelberg (2000)
8. Huang, X., Sharma, D., Cui, H.: Fuzzy controlling window for elliptic curve cryptography in wireless sensor networks. In: ICOIN (2012)
9. Koblitz, N.: Elliptic curve cryptosystems. Mathematics of Computation 48, 203–209 (1987)
10. Kodali, R.K., Karanam, S., Patel, K., Budwal, H.S.: Fast elliptic curve point multiplication for wsns. In: 2013 IEEE TENCON Spring Conference, pp. 194–198. IEEE (2013)
11. Koyama, K., Tsuruoka, Y.: Speeding up elliptic cryptosystems by using a signed binary window method. In: Brickell, E.F. (ed.) CRYPTO 1992. LNCS, vol. 740, pp. 345–357. Springer, Heidelberg (1993)
12. Longa, P., Miri, A.: New multibase non-adjacent form scalar multiplication and its application to elliptic curve cryptosystems. Cryptology e-print Archive, 052 (2008)
13. Miller, V.S.: Use of elliptic curves in cryptography. In: Williams, H.C. (ed.) CRYPTO 1985. LNCS, vol. 218, pp. 417–426. Springer, Heidelberg (1986)
14. National Institute of Standards and Technology. Digital signature standard
15. IEEE P1363. Standard Specifications for Public-Key Cryptography (2000)
16. Silvermann, J.H.: The Arithmetic of Elliptic Curves, ii edn. Graduate Texts in Mathematics. Springer (2009)
17. Solinas, J.: Efficient arithmetic on koblitz curves. Designs, Codes and Cryptography 19, 195–249 (2000)

Forensic Analysis for Monitoring Database Transactions

Harmeet Kaur Khanuja[1] and Dattatraya S. Adane[2]

[1] Department of Computer Engineering, MMCOE, Pune, India
harmeetkaurkhanuja@mmcoe.edu.in
[2] Department of Information Technology, RKNEC, Nagpur
dattaadane@yahoo.com

Abstract. Database forensics aids in the qualification and investigation of databases and facilitates a forensic investigator to prove a suspected crime which can be used to prevent illegitimate banking transactions. The banks deals in public money but unfortunately are becoming vulnerable by receiving illegal money in the form of legitimate business. The absence of any preventive measures in the banks to monitor such scam would be perilous some day. If they violate relevant laws and regulatory guidelines they can unknowingly keep raising Money Laundering practices in their system. In this article we propose a forensic methodology for private banks to have ongoing monitoring system as per Reserve Bank of India (RBI) guidelines for financial transactions which will check their database audit logs on continuous basis for marking suspected transactions if any. These transactions are then precisely analyzed and verified with Dempster Shafer Theory of Evidence to generate suspected reports automatically as required by Financial Intelligence Unit.

Keywords: Database Forensics, Database Transactions, Money Laundering, Dempster Shafer Theory.

1   Introduction

Databases have become an increasingly essential component of many organizations. Indeed, in today's business world, almost all applications use a database to manage data. Here the focus is on databases of banking transactions. Fraudulent banking activities are becoming more and more sophisticated which is threatening the security and trust of online banking business [1,2] resulting as a major issue for handling financial crimes. Moreover it is becoming challenging due to the Money Laundering (ML) practices carried over. Effective and efficient detection of Anti Money Laundering (AML) is regarded as a major challenge to all the banks and is an increasing cause for concern [4]. One way to ensure this is to keep end-to-end accountability of such information in banking databases through continuous assurance technology and transaction monitoring through Digital forensics methodology as mentioned in our earlier research papers [3, 18, 19]. In addition, Database forensics is a stream of Digital Forensics which has become an important field of study [5, 6, 7, 8, 9]. This technique identifies, preserves and analyzes digital information which can be used as evidences in civil and criminal legal proceedings.

J. Lloret Mauri et al. (Eds.): SSCC 2014, CCIS 467, pp. 201–210, 2014.
© Springer-Verlag Berlin Heidelberg 2014

Digital investigators can suspect the anomalous transactions during database monitoring process. To mark the suspicious transactions within audit log files we trail the customers' behavior pattern with respect to the published RBI (Reserve Bank of India) Rules and Regulations (http://www.rbi.org.in) [10, 11, 12]. This gives us the initial belief of a transaction to calculate the probability of suspiciousness along with information like date, time, and location etc. of a transaction. This information traced is then constructed as a Database Forensic XML (DFXML) file. The DFXML is used to create a training data set to further classify the transactions as suspicious. To give assurance of susceptibility some major support of evidences like Customer Profile, KYC forms etc. are congregate and analyzed with Dempster Shafer Theory (DST) of Evidence [15, 16, 17, 18]. Ongoing monitoring is an essential element of effective KYC procedures [13, 14]. Thus we developed an automated system for the banks which will be capable of generating automated Cash Transaction Report (CTR) and auto-populate Suspicious Transaction Reports (STR) for reporting of suspicious transaction reports as required by the Financial Intelligence Unit - India (FIU-IND) [28] as per law. Hence, we aim here is to determine what, when, where the suspected transactions are being carried out to help to counter Money Laundering process if any.

2   Related Work

According to RBI the STR [10, 11, 12] normally works on unusual activity carried out during financial banking transactions. The basic principle of suspiciousness relies on the nature of transactions which are inconsistent with what would have been expected from declared business transaction and corresponding to it, the value of transactions which may be inconsistent with the customers' apparent financial standing.

Thus diverse anomaly detection techniques have been reviewed in the literature to discover these suspicious financial transactions. Most of the AML approaches carry out clustering to identify inconsistency [22]. Few techniques employ artificial neural networks (ANN) [23], decision trees [24] and support vector machine [25] to identify suspicious transactions. In our system the transactions are being monitored using forensic methodology which on continuous basis traces the bank's database audit logs marking suspicious activity and creating DFXML for analysis. A novel approach is used to analyze and assure the suspected transactions using Dempster Shafer theory which helps to automate the process of generating CTR and STRs' XML files to report to FIU-IND. Here, initial belief is set on the basis of two parameters that are transaction amount (lower to higher value) and frequency of transactions (withdraw or deposit). These two parameters give the support of evidence for evaluating suspiciousness of the transaction. Secondly, a class is defined on Risk categories (Low, medium and high risk category) which classify the customers in a bank depending upon the Customer profile. It may contain information relating to Customer's identity, social/financial status, nature of business activity, information about his client's business and their location etc. This gives us additional support of evidence for evaluating the customer's transaction.

The system approaches to reduce false positives, without compromising on true positives, and ensures that high anomaly is raised only in transactions' which has enough conclusive evidences to support them.

3   Dempster – Shafer Theory of Evidence

Dempster - Shafer theory is based on the work of Arthur Dempster during the 1960's and in particular by Glenn Shafer's treatise A Mathematical Theory of Evidence (Shafer 1976). This particular theory is especially relevant for auditing and assurance as it focuses on evidence and evidential reasoning. This theory of evidence provides a framework to deal with a system with uncertain information. There are three basic functions that are important to understanding and applying DS theory: the basic belief mass function or basic probability assignment (bpa) function which specifies the belief mass distribution (e.g. m-values in our system) over all possible sub-sets of a frame of discernment (θ), the Belief function (Bel(s)), and the Plausibility function (Pl(s))[20,21,22]. A frame of discernment (also called a Universe of Discourse) in Dempster-Shafer is a set of mutually exclusive and exhaustive possibilities/evidence. The general procedure in DST is to collect the evidence, combine the evidence and interpret the evidence [18, 19].

3.1   Dempster-Shafer's Rule of Combination

One of the advantages of the Dempster-Shafer is the practical way to combine information. Individual evidences can be combined to form stronger evidences. Say, two evidences, represented in terms of the bpa, m_1 and m_2 such that,

$$\sum_B m_1 (B) = 1 \ and \ \sum_C m_2 (C) = 1 \tag{1}$$

We have,

$$1 = \sum_B m_1 (B) . \sum_C m_2 (C) = \sum_{B,C} m_1 (B) . m_2 (C) \tag{2}$$

$$= \sum_{B \cap C = \emptyset} m_1 (B) . m_2 (C) + \sum_{A \neq \emptyset} \left[\sum_{B \cap C = A} m_1 (B) . m_2 (C) \right] \tag{3}$$

Thus,

$$\sum_{A \neq \emptyset} \left[\frac{[\sum_{B \cap C = A} m_1 (B) . m_2 (C)]}{(1 - \sum_{B \cap C = \emptyset} m_1 (B) . m_2 (C))} \right] = 1 \tag{4}$$

The bpa, represented by 'm', is often thought of as Bayesian probability. In DST, the bpa is defined as a generalized Bayesian probability. Thus we can define the combination of basic probability assignments as

$$m_{12}(A) = \frac{[\sum_{B \cap C = A} m_1(B).m_2(C)]}{(1 - \sum_{B \cap C = \emptyset} m_1(B).m_2(C))} \tag{5}$$

for all $A \neq \emptyset$, and $m_{12}(\emptyset) = 0$. This satisfies $\sum_A = 1$.

The Belief function can be expressed in terms of the basic probability assignment, bpa:

$$Bel(A) = \sum_{B \in A} m(B) \tag{6}$$

Given the belief function, Bel(A), the degree of doubt then, is Bel(~A) which is known as Plausibility function and is given as

$$Pl(A) = 1 - Bel(\sim A) \tag{7}$$

In our system, bpa is defined as m(s) with various support of evidence as shown:

Table 1. Belief mass function, Belief function and Plausibility function

m(s)	Probability of Suspiciousness, Based upon fairly stated evidences w.r.t. occurrences of transactions and amount occurrences
m(~s)	Probability of Non-Suspiciousness, fairly stated evidences w.r.t. Risk category
m(s, ~s)	Represents the belief not assigned to any particular state, but assigned to the entire frame {s, ~s}, which represents ignorance.
Bel(s)	Total Belief function Bel(s) = m(s), Bel(~s) = m(~s) [from eqn. 6]
Pl(s)	Plausibility function , Pl(s) = 1 - Bel(~s) [from eqn. 7]

Pure positive evidence can be expressed as m(s) > 0, and m(~s) = 0, and pure negative evidence as m(s) = 0, and m(~s) > 0.

4   System Architecture

The Fig.1 outlines the proposed system architecture.

4.1   Design of Proposed System

As shown in Fig.1 Database forensic procedure is carried out to monitor ongoing transactions through database audit logs. The RBI rules are considered to filter and collect the suspicious set of transactions at this level. At the next level the analysis

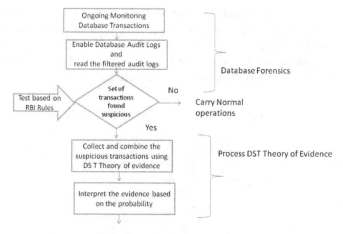

Fig. 1. Proposed System Architecture

is carried out based on Dempster Shafer Theory of evidence framework as described in Section 2.

The audit logs are basically used to gather inputs of multiple operations carried out during banking transactions. The detailed information like date, timestamp, account holders identification, amount transacted, etc. can be viewed in audit logs as shown in Fig. 2 below.

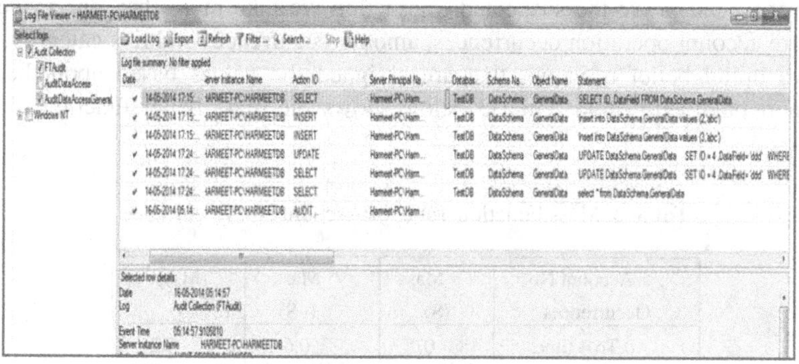

Fig. 2. Audit Log viewer

The transactions from the substantial audit logs are constructed to .xml file known as DFXML to generate structured required forensic information as per the evidences which is shown in fig. 3. And further analysis is carried out on DFXML file.

The published Regulations of Reserve Bank of India for Anti money Laundering (http://dor.gov.in/acts_rules, PML (Amendment) Act, 2012.pdf) are the rules used for our system. It says any activity violating the rules will be marked as suspicious. For example, if multiple or sudden increase of payment transactions is being made by an account holder or frequent transactions are made from an account then these are not the normal activities of the customer and will have high probability to be a fraud transaction and accordingly for genuine transactions the probabilities assigned are low. Level of suspiciousness is defined by assigning the probabilities on 0-1 scale. These probabilistic values give a degree of initial belief.

```
<?xml version="1.0" encoding="us-ascii" standalone="yes"?>
<Bank-log>
        <record>
                <Transaction_ID>14854</Transaction_ID>
                <Account_Number>101</Account_Number>
                <User_Name>sachin</User_Name>
                <Date_Time>18/01/2014 7:45:56 AM</Date_Time>
                <Operation_type>Deposit</Operation_type>
                <Amount>12000</Amount>
        </record>
        <record>
                <Transaction_ID>11086</Transaction_ID>
                <Account_Number>101</Account_Number>
                <User_Name>uday</User_Name>
                <Date_Time>18/01/2014 7:47:58 AM</Date_Time>
                <Operation_type>Deposit</Operation_type>
                <Amount>75000</Amount>
        </record>
        <record>
                <Transaction_ID>35525</Transaction_ID>
                <Account_Number>101</Account_Number>
                <User_Name>ajay</User_Name>
                <Date_Time>18/01/2014 7:48:19 AM</Date_Time>
                <Operation_type>Deposit</Operation_type>
                <Amount>80000</Amount>
        </record>
                <record>
                <Transaction_ID>27689</Transaction_ID>
                <Account_Number>88905678</Account_Number>
                .........
</Bank-log>
```

Fig. 3. DFXML file obtained from audit Log file

To verify and prove the suspected transaction we take more than one evidences. These are account operation occurrences, amount occurrences and risk category. Thus we have initial belief m-values that are assigned the values based upon the level of support obtained. Table 2 and 3 below shows the mass belief function Mass(S) or m(s).

Table 2. Mass Function Table of Account No. Occurrence

Account No Occurrences	Mass (S)	Mass (~S)	Mass (S, ~S)
0 To 4 times	0.2	0.6	0.2
4 To 8 times	0.4	0.5	0.1
8 to 12 times	0.6	0.4	0.1
12 To 16 times	0.8	0.1	0.1
16 To 20 times	1.0	0.0	0.0

Table 3. Mass Function Table of Amount Occurrence

Amount Occurrences	Mass (S)	Mass (~S)	Mass (S, ~S)
20 To 30 lakh	0.3	0.6	0.1
30 to 40 lakh	0.4	0.5	0.1
40 To 50 lakh	0.5	0.3	0.2
50 To 60 lakh	0.6	0.3	0.1
60 To 70 lakh	0.7	0.2	0.1
70 To 80 lakh	0.8	0.0	0.2

m(s) values : For Account occurrences and Amount occurrences
m(~s)values : For Risk category (Low, medium and high risk category is assigned)
It is the probability of occurrences' of Account and Amount.

5   Experimentation

Let us consider two items of evidence E1 and E2 pertaining to a frame θ. The corresponding belief masses represented as m_1 and m_2. The combined belief masses (m-values) for a subset A of the frame θ using Dempster's rule are given by

$$m_{12}(A) = \frac{[\sum_{B \cap C = A} m_1(B) . m_2(C)]}{(1 - \sum_{B \cap C = \emptyset} m_1(B) . m_2(C))} \qquad \text{From eqn. (5)}$$

Case 1:
Evidence 1 (E1): m(s) Account No. Occurrence 4 to 8 times,
m(~s): Risk category = medium

Evidence 2 (E2): m(s) Amount Occurrence is 20 To 30 Lakh,
m(~s): Risk category = Low

Case 2:
Evidence 1 (E1): m(s) Accnt No. Occurrence 12 to 16 times,
m(~s):Risk category = High

Evidence 2 (E2): m(s) Amount Occurrence is 60 To 70 Lakh,
m(~s):Risk category = High

Refer Table 2 and 3 in Section 3, we have

Table 4. Data Input

Evidence	m(s)	m(~s)	m(s,~s)	Bel(s)	Pl(s)
Case 1: E1	0.4	0.5	0.1	0.4	0.5
E2	0.3	0.6	0.1	0.3	0.4
Case 2 : E1	0.8	0.1	0.1	0.8	0.9
: E2	0.7	0.2	0.1	0.7	0.8

Combining the Evidence E1 and E2 for the above data set, we get

Table 5. Observation Combining two evidences E1 and E2

Case	Combined Belief mass function	Observation/ Results
Case 1	$m_{12}(A) = 0.31$ $m_{12}(\sim A) = 0.6833$	Since $m_{12}(A) < m_{12}(\sim A)$ The transaction is not suspicious.
Case 2	$m_{12}(A) = 0.9220$ $m_{12}(\sim A) = 0.00064$	Since $m_{12}(A) > m_{12}(\sim A)$ The transaction is suspicious.

The beliefs and plausibilities are: $Bel(A) = 0.31$ and $Bel(\sim A) = 0.6833$, $Pl(A) = 0.3167$, and $Pl(\sim A) = 0.69$. Thus, based on the evidences and analytical procedures for Case1 the investigator has 0.31 degree of belief for transactions to be considered as suspicious. There is 0.69 degree of plausibility for transactions to be genuine indicating less suspicious.

On the other hand in Case2, $Bel(A) = 0.9220$ and $Bel(\sim A) = 0.00064$, $Pl(A) = 0.9993$, and $Pl(\sim A) = 0.078$, the investigator has 0.9220 degree of belief for transactions to be considered as suspicious. There is 0.078 degree of plausibility for transactions to be genuine indicating more suspicious.

6   Conclusion

Identification of suspicious financial or banking transactions to discover money-laundering activities has always been indeed a complex problem. This complexity has been acknowledged by verifying the degree of Belief and Plausibility up to greater extent for a transaction to be suspicious. This study employed a model to monitor ongoing   transactions with database forensics to identify anomalies in sequence of transactions. These anomalies are qualified using Dempster Shafer Theory that quantifies the degree of anomaly for each incoming transaction. This model has been tested on synthetic dataset of financial banking transactions and is shown to have promising results. The model has to be verified on real world data set in future.

References

1. Bertino, E., Sandhu, R.: Database Security – Concepts, Approaches, and challenges. IEEE Transactions on Dependable and Secure Computing 2(1), 2–19 (2005)

2. Richardson, R.: CSI/FBI Computer Crime and Security Survey (2011), http://www.gocsi.com
3. Raghavan, S.: Digital forensic research: current state of the art. In: CSI Publications. Springer (2012)
4. Jun, T.: On Developing Intelligent Surveillant System of Suspicious Financial Transaction. IEEE (2010)
5. Pavlou, K.E., Snodgrass, R.T.: Forensic analysis of database tampering, ACM Transactions on Database Systems (TODS) 33(4), Article 30, 47+25 pages (2008)
6. Godbole, N., Belapure, S.: Cyber Security, Understanding Computer Forensics and Legal Perspectives. Wiley-India (2011) ISBN: 978-81-265-2179-1
7. Pavlou, K.E.: Database Forensics in the Service of Information Accountability/ SIGMOD/PODS PhD Poster Session, Poster Presented (2011)
8. Pavlou, K.E., Snodgrass, R.T.: Dragoon: An Information Accountability System for High-Performance Databases. In: Demonstration. International Conference on Data Engineering, ICDE (2012)
9. Olivier, M.S.: On metadata context in Database Forensics. Digital Investigation 5(3-4), 115–123 (2009), http://www.sciencedirect.com
10. RBI Rules, http://rbidocs.rbi.org.in/rdocs/content/Pdfs/68787.pdf
11. RBI Rules, http://rbidocs.rbi.org.in/rdocs/notification/PDFs/PM2212A_II.pdf
12. Sarbanes-Oxley (SOX) Compliance Checklist SOX-Compliance (2011), https://correlog.com/support-public/SOX-Compliance.pdf
13. Anti Money Laundering Rules, http://www.dor.gov.in/sites/upload_files/revenue/files/PML%20%28Amendment%29%20Act,%202012.pdf
14. Bhaskaran, R.: CEO, Indian Institute of Banking and Finance. Anti Money Laundering & Know Your Customer (KYC). Macmillan Publisher India (2012) ISBN 13: 978-0230-33196-9
15. Shafer, G.: Dempster–Shafer theory (2002)
16. Sentz, K., Ferson, S.: Combination of Evidence in Dempster–Shafer Theory. Sandia National Laboratories (2002)
17. Dempster, A.P.: Upper and lower probabilities induced by a multivalued mapping. The Annals of Mathematical Statistics 38(2), 325–339 (1967), doi:10.1214/aoms/1177698950
18. Khanuja, H.K., Adane, D.S.: Database Security Threats and challenges in Database Forensic: A survey. In: Proceedings of 2011 International Conference on Advancements in Information Technology, AIT 2011 (2011), http://www.ipcsit.com/vol20/33-ICAIT2011-A4072.pdf
19. Khanuja, H.K., Adane, D.S.: A Framework For Database Forensic Analysis. Published in Computer Science & Engineering: An International Journal (CSEIJ) 2(3) (2012)
20. Khanuja, H.K., Adane, D.S.: Forensic Analysis of Databases by Combining Multiple Evidences. International Journal of Computers & Technology. Council for Innovative Research 7(3) (2013)
21. Panigrahi, S., Sural, S., Majumdar, A.K.: Detection of Intrusive Activity in Databases by Combining Multiple Evidences and Belief Update. In: IEEE Symposium on Computational Intelligence in Cyber Security (2009)
22. Wang, X., Dong, G.: Research on Money Laundering Detection Based on Improved Minimum Spanning Tree Clustering and Its Application. In: Proceedings of the 2009 Second International Symposium on Knowledge Acquisition and Modeling, vol. 02, pp. 62–64. IEEE Computer Society (2009)

23. Lv, L.-T., Ji, N., Zhang, J.-L.: A RBF neural network model for anti-money laundering. In: International Conference on Wavelet Analysis and Pattern Recognition, ICWAPR 2008. IEEE (2008)

24. Wang, S.-N., Yang, J.-G.: A Money Laundering Risk Evaluation Method Based on Decision Tree. In: International Conference on Machine Learning and Cybernetics. IEEE (2007)

25. Tang, J., Yin, J.: Developing an intelligent data discriminating system of anti-money laundering based on SVM. In: International Conference on Machine Learning and Cybernetics, Guangzhou, China, vol. 6, pp. 3453–3457. IEEE (2005)

26. Srivastava, R.P.: The Dempster-Shafer Theory of Belief Functions for Managing Uncertainties: An Introduction and Fraud Risk Assessment Illustration. Australian Accounting Review 21(3), 282–291

27. Harrison, K., Srivastava, R.P., Plumlee, R.D.: 'Auditors' Evaluations of Uncertain Audit Evidence: Belief Functions versus Probabilities. In: Srivastava, R.P., Mock, T. (eds.) Belief Functions in Business Decisions. STUDFUZZ, vol. 88, pp. 161–183. Physica-Verlag, Springer-Verlag Company, Heidelberg (2002)

28. Financial Intelligence Unit- India (FIU-IND), http://fiuindia.gov.in/

Framework of Lightweight Secure Media Transfer for Mobile Law Enforcement Apps

Suash Deb[1], Simon Fong[2], and Sabu M. Thampi[3]

[1] Cambridge Institute of Technology, Ranchi, India
suashdeb@gmail.com
[2] University of Macau, Taipa, Macau SAR
ccfong@umac.mo
[3] Indian Institute of Information Technology & Management, Kerala, India
sabu.thampi@iiitmk.ac.in

Abstract. Law enforcement officers nowadays are usually equipped with some camera device which captures real time visuals on their duties. The footages would be used as evidence and they carry legal effects. However in the near future, civilians are encouraged to use their smart phone in recording footages in critical scenes; how could the video or pictures recorded by a normal cell phone from the hand of a civilian (that can be anybody) carried the same legal effect when it comes to authentication? In this paper we explore the possibility of an image processing technology which can hidden a secret message in each video frame for verification purpose – to prove that the footage is indeed taken by or belong to a particular user. In our design, the algorithm must be lightweight enough to be embedded into the use of a cell phone or compact camera device, the secrecy must be secured known to only the authenticator, and the watermarking process must be simple. Such digital water-marking technique is presented in this paper, backed with simulation experiments.

Keywords: Video, Security, Digital Watermarking.

1 Introduction

Multimedia data security is important for evidence-based law enforcement. It is foreseen in the near future law enforcing officers as well as civilian volunteers use their smart-phones in capturing crucial moments such as crimes, scenes of law violations, trespassing, road traffic accidents etc. conveniently using the cameras on their mobile phones. While encryption algorithms ensure that data is transmitted securely across the network, there is little restriction that the receiver cannot distort, forge the contents or authenticate the ownership of the captured multimedia data. To address this issue, digital watermarking is used. Digital watermarking of MPEG video must take into account two major factors, such as overheads due to watermark insertion and detection, and MPEG compression ratio. In this paper, we proposed an extension to the still image watermarking algorithm by Hsu and Wu [HW96]. Two variations of the MPEG watermarking algorithm are implemented under the

J. Lloret Mauri et al. (Eds.): SSCC 2014, CCIS 467, pp. 211–220, 2014.
© Springer-Verlag Berlin Heidelberg 2014

extension. We also found that the P-frame watermarking scheme performs better than the I-frame watermarking scheme in all the aspects. The P-frame watermarking scheme has the attractive feature that it does not reduce the compression ratio. At the same time the overheads due to the algorithm are minimal and the watermark can be completely recovered. On comparison with the original video no visual distortions could be observed for the P-frame watermarked video. Thus, the watermarking algorithms could be used to secure video distribution.

Being able to authenticate the ownership of a digital content against imposters is a key step toward a comprehensive information security infrastructure for law enhancement. Unless the owners or the users who actually captured the video are convinced that their footages do belong to them and have not been edited in anyway, few would willing to participate seriously in volunteering being an eye-witness of the crime scene. Data encryption and scrambling technology offers security for content delivery and means for controlling access and collecting revenues. The descrambling of data or the data decryption can be performed using a secret key, which the receiver obtains only from some trusted site. Unfortunately, there is little, if any, protection for decrypted or descrambled data, which can be freely redistributed or misappropriated. Digital watermarking is intended as the solution to the need to provide value added protection on top of data encryption and scrambling for content protection. A watermark is an invisible signal added to digital data that can be detected or extracted later to make an assertion about the data.

In this paper, we propose the extension of still image watermarking scheme for MPEG-1 video as a framework. The digital watermarking algorithm can be easily modified to work for other MPEG formats. The watermarking scheme proposed has the advantage that it adds minimal overhead to the MPEG-1 encoder/decoder during the watermark insertion and retrieval procedure. In addition it does not increase the MPEG-1 compression ratio. The rest of the paper is organized as follows: Section 2 discusses related work. Section 3 describes the proposed algorithms. Section 4 shows the experiment results. Finally, a conclusion is given at the end

2   Related Work

A variety of watermarking schemes had been proposed in the recent past. These techniques can be classified into one of the two categories: spatial-domain and transform-domain. The earlier watermarking schemes employed spatial-domain watermarking. The simplest spatial-domain watermarking is one in which the least significant bits in an image's pixel data are modified [STO94]. As opposed to spatial-domain watermarking that have relatively low bit capacity, transform-domain techniques can embed a number of bits without noticeable visual artifacts. They are also quite robust against lossy image compression, filtering and scanning. Transform domain watermarking techniques can be employed with the Discrete Cosine Transform, the Fast Fourier Transform, and the wavelet transform, etc.

Hsu and Wu [HW96] proposed a DCT based watermarking scheme for still images. In this paper, the algorithm is extended for MPEG-1 video sequences. The basic outline of their idea is as follows: It is well known that in MPEG-1 compression the DCT coefficient on the top left hand corner of the 8 x 8 blocks are most important as most of the signal energy is concentrated in this region by the DCT operation. These coefficients carry the low frequency components of the signal and modifications to these components are perceptible to the human eye. As the horizontal and the vertical frequency components increase, the changes to the DCT coefficients for these frequencies become imperceptible. Embedding the watermark in the high frequency components would be a good idea if no compression was used or if the compression used was lossless. However MPEG uses lossy compression, whereby the DCT coefficients are quantized. During quantization, most of the higher frequency components become 0, increasing the chances of the watermark being lost. As a compromise, for the two contradictory objectives the watermark should be embedded in the center frequencies of the 8x8 block.

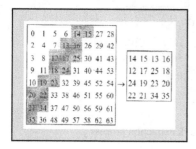

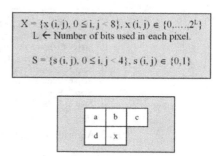

Fig. 1. Example of middle frequency coefficients in an 8 x 8 block

Fig. 2. The residual mask used

The choice of middle coefficients as shown in Figure 1 needs not be the only one. Other middle coefficients can also be defined. The next step is to choose a watermark that is to be embedded. The watermark or the signature data S can be represented as a sequence of 1's and 0's. The resolution of the image is 4x4 half of the original image X in both the horizontal and the vertical directions. The 4x4 signature data S, is then permuted according to some pseudo-random sequence to produce S', a permuted version of S. The DCT is then performed on a given 8x8 block. A 2-D block mask is used to compute the residual pattern from the chosen middle band coefficients. According to the algorithm, if $a = b = c = 0$, $d = -1$, $x = 1$, then the residual image R is the sub-block difference of the current and previous block [HW96].

Let FDCT be the operator for the Forward Discrete Cosine Transform and IDCT be the operator for the Inverse Discrete Cosine Transform. Then the following variables are defined for an 8 x 8 image block X.

$$Y_{m,n} = \{y_{m,n}(k, l), 0 \leq k, l < 8\}$$
$$Y_{m,n} = FDCT(X)$$
$$z_{m,n}(u, v) \leftarrow Re\text{-order}(y_{m,n}(k, l))$$
where $0 \leq u, v < 4$ and $(k, l) \in$ Middle band

$$R = \{r(i, j) = r_{m,n}(p, q), 0 \leq i, j \leq 8\}, 0 \leq p, q \leq 4,$$
$$i = m \times 4 + p, j = n \times 4 + q\}$$
$$r_{m,n}(p, q) = SGN[z_{m,n}(p, q) - z_{m-1,n}(p, q)], \text{ where}$$
$$SGN(x) = 1, \text{ if } x \geq 0 \text{ and } SGN(x) = 0 \text{ if } x < 0.$$

The middle band DCT coefficients are then modified for each marked pixel of the permuted signature data. A pixel in the signature data is marked if $s(i,j) = 1$. The modification of the DCT coefficient is done in such a way so that the residual value $r_{m,n}(p,q)$ is reversed. Mathematically, $\forall\ s(i,j) = 1$ in S, the DCT coefficients $y_{m,n}(k, l)$ and $y_{m-1,n}(k, l)$ are modified into $y'_{m,n}$ and $y'_{m-1,n}$ such that $r'(i, j) = 1 - r(i, j)$. Again $r'_{m, n}(p, q) = SGN\ [z'_{m, n}(p, q) - z'_{m-1, n}(p, q)]$.

The watermark can be extracted by using the original as well as the watermarked image. Both the images are DCT transformed and the residual pattern is obtained for both the images. The permuted watermark can be extracted by an XOR operation on the two residual patterns. The original watermark can be extracted from the permuted watermark as the pseudo-random sequence can be regenerated. The algorithm for the watermark extraction process can be defined as follows.

Step1: Compute $Y_{m,n} = FDCT\ (X)$
Step2: Compute $Y'_{m,n} = FDCT\ (X')$
Step3: Compute $z_{m,n}(p,q) \leftarrow$ Re-order($y_{m,n}(k,l)$)
Step 4: Compute $z'_{m,n}(p,q) \leftarrow$ Re-order($y'_{m,n}(k,l)$)
Step 5: Compute $r(i,j) = r_{m,n}(p,q)$
Step 6: Compute $r'(i,j) = r'_{m,n}(p,q)$
Step 7: $S' \leftarrow r_{m,n}(p,q) \oplus r'_{m,n}(p,q)$
Step 8: $S = ReversePermute\ (S')$

Fig. 3. Algorithm for the watermark extraction process

3   Proposed Solution

The desirable characteristics of a digital watermark for MPEG video were proposed in [HW98] and can be summarized as follows - Imperceptible, Statistically Undetectable, Robust to lossy compression, and Robust to signal manipulation and processing operations. As can be seen from the algorithm by Hsu and Wu [HW96], the main task in the watermark insertion process is the computation of the residual value and its reversal in order to insert the watermark. The reversal of the residual value produces a problem. If two consecutive blocks are considered, and the residual value $r(i, j)$ is to be changed to $r'(i, j) = 1 - r(i, j)$, the corresponding middle band coefficients need to be changed as well.

A simple way to change the coefficients would be to swap the corresponding coefficient between the two blocks. This would achieve the needed change in the residual value. The changed coefficients could propagate through to all the blocks in a given frame. However this scheme would add an overhead in the decoding phase during the watermark detection process since some of the coefficients may sink to the lower end blocks of the frame. Alternately the decoding process could be simplified at the cost of the encoding process. Also the number of changes needed for a frame with 'N' 8×8 blocks is 2N-2, as only the first and the last blocks would some of their coefficients be changed once. The remaining blocks would have some of their coefficients changed twice.

In another approach, the changes are made to only to the next 8×8 block without modifying the current block. The process is then continued for all the succeeding blocks. This method requires modifications of coefficients in only N-1 blocks reducing the number of computations from the previous case by a factor of 2. Also the overhead during encoding (while adding the watermark) and during decoding (while retrieving the watermark) is minimal. However the problem with this approach is that, if the sign of the $(i,j)^{th}$ coefficient in a series of successive blocks do not change then the modified coefficient has a tendency to either monotonically increase (for positive coefficients) or monotonically decrease (for negative coefficients).

To prevent the coefficients from monotonically increasing or decreasing and eventually leading to an overflow or underflow condition, the coefficients in alternate blocks could be changed. In other words, in every two blocks, one block is transmitted as it is and the some coefficients in the second block are modified depending upon the watermark as well as the corresponding coefficient in the previous block. This method has the advantage that the coefficients in only N/2 blocks get modified. The insertion and the detection of watermark adds minimal overhead by using this method. The pseudo-code for the watermarking process is expressed as:

```
procedure embed_watermark(
    watermark: character [4][4];
    mpeg_video: character [ ];
    water_mpeg_video: character [ ];)
begin procedure
        watermark_mode: integer;
        buffer: character [...];
        in,out: FILE;
        in := file_open(mpeg_video, "read");
        out := file_open(water_mpeg_video, "write");
        watermark_mode := 1;
        while (!eof(in)) {
            buffer = readfile(in);
            if (buffer = Start of GOP)
                watermark_mode := 1;
            if ((buffer != end of frame)&&(watermark_mode = 1)
                watermark_block(reference_block, block);
            if ((end of frame = TRUE)&&(watermark_mode = 1))
                watermark_mode := 0;
            write(buffer, out);
        }
        file_close(out);
        file_close(in);
end procedure;
```

Fig. 4. Pseudo-code for embedding watermark into MPEG-1 video

The watermarking scheme as described by the algorithm watermarks the first frame encountered after the GOP header is detected. In MPEG-1 this would correspond to an I-frame. The algorithm could be easily modified to do the watermarking on all I-frames or on selective P/B frames or all frames. The procedure watermark_block(reference_block, block) is the core watermarking procedure. Two variations of the watermarking algorithm were implemented. In the first, the I-frames were watermarked as described above. In the other, only the intra-coded blocks of the P-frames were watermarked.

The P-frame watermarking scheme is better than the I-frame watermarking scheme. The reason for this goes back to the nature of MPEG-1 coding. It is known that the I-frames are the most important frames in any GOP of an MPEG-1 bitstream. When I-frames are watermarked, information is added to these frames. Even though there are no drastic distortions, some distortion can be seen on careful inspection. Once distortions are introduced into I-frames, these distortions propagate into all other the other frames in the same GOP. The importance of P-frames in a GOP is much less than that of an I-frame. Thus distortions to a P-frame affect the quality of a video sequence to a much lower extent. Also, only intra-coded macroblocks of the first P-frame in each GOP was watermarked. This would reduce the encoding cum watermarking time when compared to the I-frame watermarking scheme, though in both schemes an equal number of frames were watermarked.

The watermarking scheme described in this report can be used for resolving the rightful ownership of video. The person distributing the video can embed his watermark into the video. Say Alicia embeds her unique watermark into the video. Now another person, Bob, claims ownership of the video. Alicia can prove her ownership of the video by extracting her watermark with the help of the watermarked video and the original video. Bob cannot do the same, as he does not have the original video. Let, Alicia's original video = V, Alicia's watermark = W, Alicia's watermarked video = V_W and Bob's watermark = F. Now assume, Bob obtains Alicia's watermarked video and adds his own watermark to it. The resulting video is V_{WF}. Now Bob can use V_W as his original and publish V_{WF} as his watermarked video. As the watermarking scheme do not create any visible distortions to the video sequence, $V \approx V_W \approx V_{WF}$. To resolve such a multiple ownership dispute, Alicia can ask for Bob's original and vice versa. Bob's original being V_W, Alicia can prove the presence of her watermark in it. Bob cannot do the same for Alicia's original. Thus the multiple ownerships dispute can be resolved in this case. However, Bob can add his own watermark to the video already watermarked by Alicia in the following way. It may be recalled that Bob does not have any knowledge of Alicia's original video (V) and Alicia's watermark (W). In such a case Bob can create his own watermark (F) and extract it from the already watermarked video (V_W). The resultant video after extraction of F from V_W is called V_F, for instance. Clearly, Bob can now claim ownership of V_W, using V_F as his original. This is possible because the watermarking scheme is not non-invertible. A watermarking scheme is invertible if there exists a mapping E^{-1}, such that: $E^{-1}(V_W) = (V_F, F)$ and $E(V_F, F) = V_W$, and the construction of E^{-1} should be computationally feasible. To resist this kind of an attack that is also known as the CMYY attack [CMYY98], non-invertible watermarking schemes must be used [QN98]. One approach is to make a strict requirement on the construction of the watermark and binding the watermark with the original video. To a large extent, this would limit the choices of the watermark F and the false original V_F for an attacker. Clearly if it is computationally infeasible for an attacker to find V_F and F such that $E(V_F, F) = V_W$, then the problem is solved. The present variation of the algorithm cannot the resist the CMYY attack.

4   Experiment and Results

The experiments were conducted on Sun Solaris Sparc Stations. 'C' was used as the programming language. The watermarking algorithm was incorporated into the Berkeley MPEG-1 encoder (mpeg_encode) [GR94] [BMRC] and the Berkeley MPEG-1 decoder (mpeg_play) [PSR93] [BMRC]. For watermark detection and visual display purposes, MATLAB Version 5 was used. The MATLAB engine was called from a 'C' program using header files provided by MATLAB.

The raw frame sequence *football.raw* with 30 frames was used for testing the watermarking schemes. The raw frame sequence was converted into an MPEG-1 file, *football.mpg* and the watermark was embedded into the file during its creation. Figures 5 and 6 show frame 22 and frame 11 of the watermarked video (I-frames / P-frames watermarked) compared to frame 22 and frame 11 of the original video.

The watermarking procedure adds an overhead to the MPEG-1 encoder and decoder. The test was performed on the football movie sequence with 30 frames. The results are tabulated in Table 1, Table 2 and Table 3, where bpp represents the bits per pixel and fps represents the frames per second.

Frame 22

Original video

I-frame watermarked video

P-frame watermarked video

Fig. 5. Original video compared to I-frame watermarked and P-frame watermarked video (Frame 22)

Frame 11

Original video   I-frame watermarked video

P-frame watermarked video

Fig. 6. Original video compared to I-frame watermarked and P-frame watermarked video (Frame 11)

Table 1. Comparison of compression ratios with and without watermarking

Experiment Number	Original video Compression ratio (bpp)	I-frame watermarked video compression ratio (bpp)	P-frame watermarked video compression ratio (bpp)
1	0.3971	0.398	0.3971
2	0.3971	0.398	0.3971
3	0.3971	0.398	0.3971
4	0.3971	0.398	0.3971
5	0.3971	0.398	0.3971

Table 2. Encoding time with and without watermarking

Experiment Number	Original video CPU time (fps)	I-frame watermarked video CPU time (fps)	P-frame watermarked video CPU time (fps)
1	0.300873	0.302541	0.301417
2	0.300812	0.302389	0.301477
3	0.300993	0.302297	0.302267
4	0.300903	0.302358	0.301205
5	0.300933	0.30245	0.301296

Table 3. Average CPU time for encoding original and watermarked video

Original video Avg. CPU time (fps)	I-frame watermarked video Avg. CPU time (fps)	P-frame watermarked video Avg. CPU time (fps)
0.3009028	0.302407	0.3015324

It can be seen from the Table 1 that the compression of watermarked video is slightly less than for the original video as the bits per pixel (bpp) increases for the watermarked video (I-frame watermarking case). This fact is also reflected in the size of these MPEG-1 files. The size of the original video was 125,807 bytes whereas the size of the watermarked video (I-frame watermarking) was 126,087 bytes, a difference of 280 bytes. From Tables 2 and 3, it can also be seen that the encoding operation is slowed down due the embedding of the watermark both watermarking schemes. However the increase in time for the P-frame watermarking scheme is not as much as the increase in time for the I-frame watermarking scheme. The P-frame watermarking scheme does not reduce the compression ratio. On careful inspection of Figure 5, it can be seen that distortions are less for the P-frame watermarked videos compared to I-frame watermarked videos. Considering the factors of encoding cum watermarking time, the compression ratio as well as the distortions introduced into the frames due to watermarking, the P-frame watermarking scheme is better than the I-frame watermarking scheme.

The embedded watermark can be recovered by running another program. When the MPEG-1 decoder is run in the watermark detection mode, a text file is created. If the original video and the watermarked video are played using the MPEG-1 player in the watermark detection mode, then the extracted watermark information is stored in a text file. The comparison program uses the generated text file, to display the retrieved watermark and the embedded watermark in the MATLAB environment. The watermark embedded in *football.mpg* was retrieved. Figure 7 shows the embedded as well as the retrieved watermark. As can be seen from the figure, the two watermarks are identical.

Fig. 7. Original watermark and retrieved watermark

5   Conclusion

In this paper, a digital watermarking scheme for MPEG-1 video was developed which is supposed to be useful for the development of evidence-based law enforcement application. The watermarking scheme is particularly attractive, as it does not reduce the MPEG-1 compression ratio. At the same time, the watermark insertion and retrieval algorithms add minimal overhead to the MPEG-1 encoder and decoder. The results obtained clearly indicate that P-frame watermarking is better than the I-frame watermarking scheme as it achieves higher compression ratio and has practically no visual distortions due to watermarking. Furthermore, for all the schemes the watermark could be recovered perfectly. The watermarking algorithms could be used for resolving ownership and in fingerprinting applications. In particular, it is believed that the watermarking algorithms could be also used in multimedia commerce applications such as secure video distribution. The present version of the algorithm however cannot resist the CMYY attack, which is still a drawback

Acknowledgments. The authors express gratitude to the Master graduate, Mr. Pratik Burman Ray for his contribution to the paper.

References

[BMRC] Berkeley Multimedia Research Center Web Site,
    http://bmrc.berkeley.edu/frame/research/mpeg/
[CMYY98] Craver, S., Memon, N., Yeo, B., Yeung, M.: Resolving Rightful Ownerships with Invisible Watermarking Techniques: Limitations, Attacks, and Implications. IEEE Journal on Selected Areas in Communications 16 (May 1998)
[Gall91] Le Gall, D.: MPEG: A Video Compression Standard for Multimedia Applications. Communication of the ACM 34(4), 46–58 (1991)
[GR94] Gong, K.L., Rowe, L.A.: Parallel MPEG-1 Video Encoding. In: Proceedings of the 1994 Picture Coding Symposium (1994)
[HW96] Hsu, C.T., Wu, J.L.: Hidden Signatures in Images. In: Proceedings of the International Conference on Image Processing, vol. 3, pp. 223–226 (1996)
[ISO/IEC93] ISO/IEC 11172-2, Information Technology – Coding of moving pictures and associated audio for digital storage media at up to about 1.5 Mbit/s – Part 2: Video
[MW98] Memon, N., Wong, P.W.: Protecting Digital Media Content. Communications of the ACM, 35–43 (1998)
[PSR93] Patel, K., Smith, B., Rowe, L.: Performance of a Software MPEG Video Decoder. In: Proceedings of ACM Multimedia, vol. 93 (August 1993)
[QN98] Qiao, L., Nahrstedt, K.: Watermarking Methods for MPEG Encoded Video: Towards Resolving Rightful Ownership. In: Proceedings of the International Conference on Multimedia Computing and Systems, pp. 276–285. IEEE (1998)
[STO94] Schyndel, R.G.V., Tirkel, A.Z., Osborne, C.F.: A Digital Watermark. In: Proceedings of the IEEE International Conference on Image Processing, pp. 86–90 (1994)
[VP99] Voyatzis, G., Pitas, I.: The Use of Watermarks in the Protection of Digital Multimedia Products. Proceedings of the IEEE, 1197–1207 (July 1999)

A Novel Comparison Based Approach for Fault Tolerance in Mobile Agent Systems

Richa Mahajan[1] and Rahul Hans[2]

[1] Dept. of Computer Science and Engineering, Guru Nanak Dev University,
Amritsar, 143005, India
[2] Dept. of Information and Technology, DAV Institute of Engineering and Technology,
Jalandhar, 144004, India
richamahajan12@ymail.com, rahulhans@gmail.com

Abstract. Mobile agent is an intelligent agent which acts on the behalf of user. In the area of distributing computing mobile agent is having a wide scope. Security and fault tolerance are the two main issues in the progress of mobile agent computing. Fault tolerance makes system versatile and provides reliable execution even in case of an occurrence of any fault. This paper proposes a novel fault tolerance approach for read only as well as read/write applications. To achieve fault tolerance use the concept of checkpointing and cloning of original agent and to make it suitable for write applications integrate it with a mechanism which preserves exactly once execution in it also integrated the mechanism with footprints approach which are helpful for location tracking of the agent. For the sake of implementation we need aglet mobile agent platform to run an agent successfully within its itinerary. The results have been evaluated on the basis of parameters like checkpointing, round trip time and exactly once mechanism. The evaluated results shows that our proposed approach is suitable for read as well as read/write applications.

Keywords: Checkpoint, Cloning, Exactly Once, Fault Tolerance, Mobile Agent.

1 Introduction

Mobile agents are software agents having a unique ability to migrate from one host to another in its itinerary. Mobile Agents can execute on those system which provides resources to it that are needed to complete its task [9, 10]. To accomplish their task mobile agent moves to remote host, can compute locally and only results can transfer through network, which results less congestion in network [11]. The main characteristics of mobile agent which differentiates it from other paradigms are given below [16]:

- Proxy: Mobile agents may act on the behalf of someone.
- Reactive: Ability to sense environment and act accordingly.
- Autonomous: It means have an ability to act without direct external interfaces.
- Migrate: It is the core property of mobile agent that it can migrate or transport itself.

J. Lloret Mauri et al. (Eds.): SSCC 2014, CCIS 467, pp. 221–229, 2014.
© Springer-Verlag Berlin Heidelberg 2014

Mobile agents have been developed as an extension to mobile code approach and its paradigm is different from others because not only data but the code acting on the data is also transported among the nodes which makes the developed application more flexible. Mobile agents could replace the traditional clients-server model and its architectures. In a client/server model, a server is a machine that provides some service and a client makes requests for those services through a communication channel Communication between the client and the server is usually through message passing. Thus, when a client needs a particular service, it usually sends a request message to the server that contains the needed service and may increase the networks traffic.

In mobile agent computing environment any component of the network machine, link, or agent may fail at any time, thus may preventing mobile agents from continuing their executions [13, 14]. Therefore, fault-tolerance is a vital issue for the deployment of mobile agent systems. Fault tolerance specifies an ability of a system to respond gracefully to an unexpected failure. Its aim is to provide reliable execution of agents even in case of failure. Two desire properties to achieve fault tolerance are Non-Blocking and Exactly Once [8]. The rest of the paper is organized as follow. Section 2 presents an overview of some techniques related to fault tolerance in mobile agent system. Section 3 will discuss about proposed approach for write applications. Section 4 describes the evaluation and analysis of our proposed approached. Section 5 examines the conclusion and future work.

2   Related Work

Fault Tolerant enables a system to continue its working, possibly at a reduced level, rather than blocking or failing completely, when some part of the system fails [3]. Various authors have proposed a number of fault tolerant techniques for mobile agent systems. Most of these are based on replication and checkpointing and the hybrid of these two. All of these existing techniques are having their own strength and weakness.

Replication based techniques, the replica of an agent is created and in case of an occurrence of a fault, instead of blocking the system, replica of an agent will start executing within its itinerary. Two type of replication techniques are there i.e. Spatial and Temporal replication [4]. In Spatial replication the agent is replicated and sent to several sites so that the agent can survive site failures. The Temporal approach is based on the check pointing the code and state of agent on the previous site [5, 7]. Spatial replication has a drawback that additional communication cost is added when move to next stage.

Checkpointing based techniques, helps to limit the rollback of an agent which results to reduce the total execution time of an agent [1, 17]. In this technique after a particular interval the partially collected data is stored at the originator host. In case of occurrence of fault there is no need to again visit those servers whose data is collected once and stored at originator [12]. It is one of the simplest and easiest ways to achieve fault tolerance. Almost all existing techniques use this concept to accomplish its aim to achieve fault tolerance of mobile agent.

In Novel Dynamic shadow approach for fault tolerance in mobile agent system hybrid the concept of replicated (shadow or cloning) agent and checkpointing. In this approach shadow of an agent moves with the original agent. If due to any fault original agent gets faulty then it can recover from its shadow [2, 6]. Checkpointing helps when both original agent and its shadow get destroy. In this case execution starts from the server immediate next to checkpointing. It helps to reduce the round trip time of an agent. This approach is suitable for read only application so we extended this technique also suitable for read/write applications as our proposed work and is discussed in next section.

3   Proposed Approach for Write Applications

3.1   Presumptions

- Doesn't consider server crash
- Home server always remain active
- Communication channels are trust worthy

3.2   Notations

- MA : Mobile Agent
- Si : Respective Server visited by MA in its itinerary
- RTT : Round Trip Time
- RTTWFT : Round Trip Time without fault tolerance
- RTTFT : Round Trip Time with fault tolerance approach

3.3   Proposed Approach

To describe proposed approach consider a scenario of e-shopping. Mobile agent is use to collect the price information of laptop from different servers and finally by comparing their cost returns back to home server with the lowest price. Mobile agent starts itinerary by dispatching from home server and the address of next server is picked by mobile agent autonomously.

In our proposed approach fault tolerance is achieved by cloning the original agent and checkpointing. After execution the original agent is dispatched from home server and also creates a copy of original agent as clone at originator. In case of occurrence of fault, original agent can recover itself from its clone. In this way cloning the original agent helps to provide fault tolerance in mobile agent systems.

Checkpointing saves the data of visited severs in its itinerary and also the address of last visited host [15]. Checkpointing is implemented after every four servers. In case when both original and clone agent get dispose of due to occurrence of any fault. In this situation a fault message is send to home server and in response home server sends a replicated copy of MA. Due to checkpointing instead of start execution from

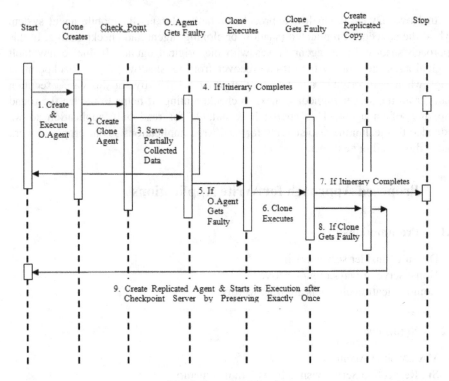

Fig. 1. Sequence Diagram

home server, it starts from checkpoint before the faulty. It helps to reduce the execution time in the itinerary as it reduces the rollback. Fig.1 represents the sequence of various actions which are performed in our proposed approach.

Exactly once is implemented by making a comparison mechanism at each server. Current status of an agent is residing in the local memory of respective server we can call it as footprint

Status	Agent_id	Time

Fig. 2. Format of Data Saved in local memory

Status tells whether the agent is executed or not, agent_id identifies the agent and time tells us the system time at which agent executed or not.

When clone arrives at server it follows a comparison mechanism. If status of original agent resides in the local memory of respective server is found faulty, only then clone executes otherwise it moves to next server. Same process repeats until its itinerary is not completed. In this way exactly once prevents clone to execute again if original agent has been executed once on that server. This property makes it suitable for both read only as well as read/write applications.

4   Evaluation and Analysis

To implement our proposed approach, consider its itinerary of 16 servers. All these servers should have aglet platform to execute agent successfully. Results are evaluated by various experiments and represented below in the form of tables and graph charts.

4.1   Experiment I: Evaluate Round Trip Time without Considering Fault with Checkpointing

Let's assume checkpointing is implemented after every 4th server and length of itinerary is 16. Checkpointing enhances the execution time as the partial results have to save on home server after a particular interval; it is well explained in fig. 3.

Table 1. Comparison of R_{TT} with Checkpointing

No. of Host	3	9	16
R_{TT} of Original Agent	3,000 ms	11,000 ms	19,000 ms
R_{TT} of Clone Agent	4,000 ms	12,0000 ms	20,000 ms

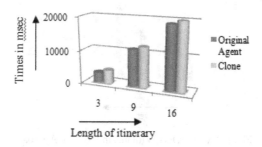

Fig. 3.   Comparison of RTT with Checkpointing

4.2   Experiment II: Evaluate Round Trip Time (RTT) by Considering Fault

In our proposed approach, to deal with agent failure, cloning of original agent and checkpointing is used. In table 2 experimental value shows that checkpointing helps to reduce the round trip time by limits the number of servers to visit again in case of occurrence of fault and it is implemented after every 4th server.

Table 2. Comparison of RTT by Considering Fault

Faulty Server	3	9	14
RTT_{WFT}	19,000 ms	25,000 ms	30,000 ms
RTT_{FT}	22,000 ms	19,000 ms	20,000 ms

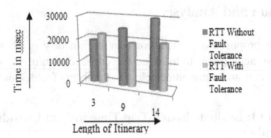

Fig. 4. Comparison of RTT by Considering Fault

4.3   Experiment III: Comparison of Existing and Proposed Approach

In fig. 5 and 6, assume checkpointing is implemented at 4th server and fault arises at 7th server. In earlier approach, both original agent and its clone get executed at each server. In this way they are contributing to violate exactly once execution of mobile agent. It is well explained in fig. 5.

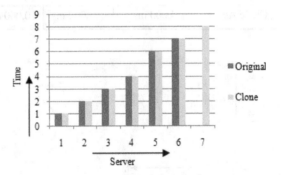

Fig. 5. Exactly Once Violates in Existing Approach

Acc. to our proposed approach, clone agent visits each server but executes only when original agent get destroyed or become faulty. In this way it helps to preserve exactly once property of mobile agent and make it suitable for read only as well as read/write applications, graphically it is represented in fig. 6.

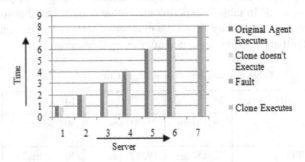

Fig. 6. Achieving Exactly Once in Proposed Approach

Each time when clone arrives at any server a comparison mechanism is followed. The clone agent checks the status of original agent from local memory of corresponding server. After reading the status it performs accordingly.

4.4 Experiment IV: Location Tracking Mechanism and Dealing with Server Crash

Location tracking is needed to stop a running agent or start a new agent, for the development of agent-based applications, in geographically distributed environment and to deal with server crash. As the agent moves to the next server it leaves its status, agent_id and time of execution on the current server. If due to server crash the original agent as well as clone gets lost and we don't receive any acknowledgement the replicated agent may also get lost due to server crash. To deal with this situation we send a search agent in the itinerary which checks out the local memory of the servers and gets us the time and status of agents executed and keeps in pinging the next server at the time which it pings the next faulty server it does not receive any acknowledgement it reports back to home server about which one is the faulty server and the next agent execution starts from the server next to faulty server.

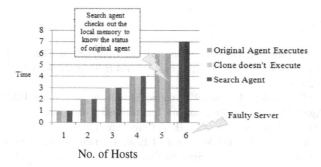

Fig. 7. Comparison mechanism and working of search agent for non blocking execution

In our proposed approach with the addition of checkpointing (after 4 servers) and comparison mechanism (consumes 1/5 of execution time) overheads also increase. The experimental results based on checkpointing time (CP), comparison time and total execution time mentioned in table V, shows that checkpointing and comparison time puts an overhead of about 15% and 29% which is endurable.

5   Conclusions and Future Work

In this paper we proposed a novel fault tolerant approach for mobile agent systems. Evaluated results show that our proposed approach works well with agent failure and server failure. To provide fault tolerance, we used the concept of cloning the original agent so that the faulty original agent can recover from its clone. Checkpointing is used to limit the rollback of replicated agent in case of failure of both original and clone agent. Earlier approach was suitable for read only applications as in this approach both original agent and its clone executes at each server and violate exactly once execution.

To make our proposed approach worth for both read only as well as read/write applications we have added the concept of exactly once execution in it. In our proposed approach along with the original agent its clone also visits each server but execute only in a case when original agent fails. After successful execution original agent updates its status as visited in local memory of respective server and moves to next server in its itinerary. When clone visits that server a comparison mechanism is followed, it reads the status of original agent from the local memory of corresponding server. If status is found as faulty only in this case clone executes otherwise moves to next server. In this way it helps to preserves exactly once execution of mobile agent and make it suitable for both read only and read/write applications. Also for the case of server failure which leads to blocking we have used the concept of location tracking and search agent which searches for the faulty server in the network and reports to the home server about the faulty server.

In future, work could be done for the multiagents system and also to reduce the overheads due to checkpointing and comparison and further this system can be developed to deal with network congestion problem.

References

1. Rajwinder, S., Mayank, D.: Antecedence Graph Approach to Checkpointing for Fault Tolerance in Mobile Agent Systems. Proc. of IEEE Transactions On Computers 62(2) (February 2013)
2. Rahul, H., Ramandeep, K.: Novel Dynamic Shadow Approach for Fault Tolerance in Mobile Agent Systems. In: Proc. of 6th International Conference on Signal Processing Communication Systems. Publication IEEE Conference (2012)
3. Mohammadi, K., Hamidi, H.: Modeling of Fault-Tolerant Mobile Agents Execution in Distributed Systems. In: Proc. of Systems Communications. Publication IEEE Conference (2005)
4. Choi, S.J., Baik, M.S., Kim, H.S., Yoon, J.W., Shon, J.G., Hwang, C.S.: Region-based Stage Construction Protocol for Fault tolerant Execution of Mobile Agent. In: Proc. of the 18th International Conference on Advanced Information Networking and Application. Publication IEEE Conference (2004)
5. Pleisch, S., Schiper, A.: Modeling fault-tolerant mobile agent execution as a sequence of agreement problems. In: Proc. of 19th IEEE Symposium of RDS. Publication IEEE Conference (2000)
6. Rahul, H., Ramandeep, K.: Fault Tolerance Approach in Mobile Agents for Information Retrieval Applications Using Check Points. Proc. of International Journal of Computer Science & Communication Networks 2(3), 347–353 (2012)
7. Linda, Z., Nadjib, B.: Optimistic Replication Approach for Transactional Mobile Agent Fault Tolerance. In: Proc. of 11th ACIS International Conference on Software Engineering, Artificial Intelligence, Networking and Parallel/Distributed Computing. Publication IEEE Conference (2010)
8. Rostami, A., Rashidi, H., Zahraie, M.S.: Fault Tolerance Mobile Agent System Using Witness Agent in 2-Dimensional Mesh Network. Proc. of International Journal of Computer Science Issues 7(5) (September 2010)

9. Budi, A., Alexei, I., Alexander, R.: On using the CAMA framework for developing open mobile fault tolerant agent systems. In: Proc. of International Workshop on Software Engineering for Large-scale Multi-agent systems. Publication IEEE Conference (2006)

10. Goutam, K.S.: Transient Fault Tolerance in Mobile Agent Based Computing. Proc. of INFOCOMP Journal of Computer Science 4, 1–11 (2005)

11. Pears, S., Xu, J., Boldyreff, C.: Mobile Agent Fault Tolerance for Information Retrieval Applications: An Exception Handling Approach. In: Proc. of 6th International Symposium on Autonomous Decentralized Systems (2003)

12. Beheshti, S., Movaghar, A.: Fault tolerance in Mobile Agent Systems by Cooperating the Witness Agents. In: Proc. of International Conference on Information and Communication Technologies, vol. 2, p. 3018-2. Publication IEEE Conference (2006)

13. Adel, A., Rees, J.S.: Mobile Agent Technology and Mobility. In: Proc. of 5th Annual Postgraduate Symposium on the Convergence of Telecommunications, Networking and Broadcasting, Liverpool, p.14-2, ISBN:1-9025-6010-8

14. Yousuf, F., Zaman, Z.: A Survey of Fault Tolerance Techniques in Mobile Agents and Mobile Agent Systems. In: Proc. of International Conference on Environmental and Computer Science, pp.454 – 458 (2009)

15. NaghshNilchi, A.R., Vafaei, A., Hamidi, H.: Evaluation of Security and Fault Tolerance in Mobile Agents. In: Proc. of International Conference on Wireless and Optical Communications Networks. Publication IEEE Conference (2008)

16. Lange, D.B.: Mobile Objects and Mobile Agents: The Future of Distributed Computing? This paper is based on a chapter of a book by Lange and Oshima entitled Programming and Deploying Java^{TM} Mobile Agents with Aglets^{TM}. Addison-Wesley (1998) ISBN: 0-201-32582-9

17. Ramandeep, K., Rama, C.K., Rajwinder, S.: Antecedence Graph based Checkpointing and Recovery for Mobile Agents. In: Proc. of International conference on Communication Control and Computing Technologies, pp. 419–424. Publication IEEE Conference (October 2010)

Watermark Detection in Spatial and Transform Domains Based on Tree Structured Wavelet Transform

Ivy Prathap and R. Anitha

Department of Applied Mathematics & Computational Sciences,
PSG College of Technology, Coimbatore, India
ivysaji@gamil.com, anitha_nadarajan@mail.psgtech.ac.in

Abstract. This paper presents an efficient, robust and blind approach to detect watermarks embedded in spatial and frequency domains of images. Spatial and transform domain energy features are extracted from the images using Tree Structured Wavelet Transform. An efficient classifier, Totalboost is used to classify the images as watermarked or unwatermarked. In addition to this, the proposed detector can be able to detect watermarks even after various image processing and signal processing attacks. Simulation results show the effectiveness of the proposed scheme in terms of specificity, sensitivity and accuracy. Comparison with state-of-the-art schemes demonstrate the efficiency of the proposed scheme.

Keywords: Tree Structured Wavelet Transform, Totalboost, watermark detector, robust, blind.

1 Introduction

Dramatic technological improvements in the production, manipulation, and circulation of digital media have transformed the practices of information processing, many of which are illegal and malignant. Copyright protection becomes vital in the view of large illegal duplication and piracy. Digital watermarking, which allows embedding information imperceptibly in an original multimedia object, has emerged as a widely approved method for copyright protection and ownership identification [1].

Image watermarking techniques can be classified into two broad categories based on the domain in which the watermark is inserted: spatial domain techniques and frequency domain techniques. In spatial domain techniques, the watermark is directly embedded into the unwatermarked image by altering the pixel values [2]. In contrast, frequency domain methods transform the representation of spatial domain into the frequency domain and then modify its frequency coefficients to embed the watermark[3].

A watermarking system consists of two modules, an embedding module that insert the watermark into the host data and a detection/extraction module that detects and retrieves the embedded watermark. Depending on whether the original data should be available or not during detection, watermarking methods are

J. Lloret Mauri et al. (Eds.): SSCC 2014, CCIS 467, pp. 230–238, 2014.

classified as blind or non-blind. Although the requirements of a watermarking system are relative to the specific application, a reliable detection of the embedded watermark is needed. An important property of watermark detection comparable with steganalysis [4] is that it should be robust against intentional or unintentional attacks.

In this paper, we propose an efficient, robust and blind approach to detect watermarks embedded in either spatial or transform domain. The spatial and transform domain energy features are extracted from the images using Tree Structured Wavelet Transform. Further watermark detection is accomplished using Totalboost, an efficient classification algorithm. Moreover, the proposed detector is able to detect watermarks even after various image processing and signal processing attacks. Simulation results show the effectiveness of the proposed scheme in terms of specificity, sensitivity and accuracy. The outstanding performance is compared with that of some state-of-the-art watermark detection schemes.

2   Related Works

Watermark detection plays a crucial role in multimedia copyright protection and can be traditionally tackled by using correlation based algorithms. Watermark detection can be generally achieved with the help of statistical detection methods[5]. Hence, how to select an appropriate statistical model or decision rule is one of the major issues in the watermark detection process. Many approaches for the optimal detection of additive watermarks embedded in transform domain coefficients are available in literature[6, 7]. The host transform coefficients are modelled as noise in these detection schemes. If the assumed noise is gaussian, the optimal detector is Linear Correlation (LC) detector [8]. Since the Discrete Cosine Transform (DCT) and Discrete Wavelet Transform (DWT) coefficients do not obey Gaussian law, the LC detector becomes sub-optimal and modelling the host image becomes critical for detection and the authors Hernandez et al.[7] derive an optimal detector for additive watermarking schemes in DCT domain following a Generalized Gaussian Distribution (GGD). The mid-frequency DCT coefficients are modeled by a family of symmetric alpha-stable distributions and a detector for Cauchy-distributed DCT coefficients[6]. Yet, both approaches are based on a strong assumption that the embedding power of the watermark is known to the detector and hence non-blind.

Another watermark detection scheme for GGD noise is proposed in [9], where the detector is asymptotically optimal. A Rao-Cauchy distribution based lightweight watermark detector is proposed in [10]. But, it deals with only transform domain watermark detections. A curvelet domain watermark detection is proposed by Deng et al.[11]. But, the authors do not deal with robustness to various image and signal processing attacks. A Bessel K-distribution based watermark detection by Bian and Liang [12] uses Bessel K probability density function to model the noise distribution. They derive a locally optiumum detector using the noise model and deals with transform domain watermarks only and is a non-blind scheme. A Naive Bayesian classifier based watermark detection scheme based on wavelet tansform domain is proposed in [13], but it is a semi-blind one.

There is a major need to design a new watermark detector which can detect watermarks irrespective of the embedding domains. We extract the relevant spatial and transform domain features from images using Tree-Structured Wavelet Transform [14] and create a training model using Totalboost algorithm which can classifiy the test images as either watermarked or unwatermarked. The remainder of the paper is structured as follows: In Section 2 we discuss the proposed watermark detector. Section 3 describes the experimental results along with a comparison with an existing watermark detection scheme. Conclusion is drawn in Section 4.

3   The Proposed Method

The watermark detection process can be treated as a 0/1 classification problem. We classify the unwatermarked images as class 0 and watermarked images as class 1. An effective classification algorithm based on Tree Structured Wavelet Transform (TSWT) and Totalboost is proposed for identifying watermarks. To build an effective classification algorithm, it is essential to choose robust and adequate features that can recognize the main characteristics of the image. The main contribution of this paper is to present an efficient scheme which consists of feature extraction and classification of watermarked and unwatermarked images. The experimental results show that the proposed watermark detection algorithm is robust to different image processing and signal processing attacks.

3.1   Feature Extraction

The ability of DWT to capture both the spatial and frequency domain information of a an image motivates us to use it for efficient feature extraction[15]. The conventional DWT recursively decomposes images into low frequency sub bands. But, the middle frequency bands of the image contain meaningful spatial and frequency domain information which makes conventional DWT inappropriate in this scenario. Since most of the spatial and frequency domain watermarks are imperceptibly embedded in the low frequency and middle frequency sub bands, we need a detection mechanism which can identify these watermarks efficiently. Hence, we approach the watermark detection problem using Tree Structured Wavelet Transform (TSWT)[14]. TSWT detects those sub bands that contain significant energy features and then selectively decomposes them further. This significant features can be able to efficiently detect watermarks embedded in both spatial and frequency domains.

Tree Structured Wavelet Transform is applied to each of the the test images and decomposition is done by comparing the average energy value, e of the sub image with the largest energy value e_{max} in the same decomposition level.

The average energy of each child node (sub band) is calculated as follows: If the decomposed image is $f(m,n)$ with $1 \leq m \leq M$ and $1 \leq n \leq N$, the mean energy is:

$$e = 1/(MN) \sum_{i=1}^{M} \sum_{j=1}^{N} |f(m,n)| \qquad (1)$$

where M and N are the pixel dimensions of the sub-image and $|f(m,n)|$ is the absolute value. The ratio of mean energy in the low frequency sub bands to the mean energy in the middle frequency bands is proposed by Porter and Canagarajah [16] as a criterion for optimum feature selection from the decomposed sub bands which emphasizes the spatial or frequency changes in the image. The average energy ratio is

$$e_r = e/e_{max} \qquad (2)$$

where e_{max} is the maximum of the average energy of each sub-image for one level of decomposition.

From the final level of decomposition, average energy features are extracted and corresponding energy ratios are computed. In the case of four-level decomposition of an image of size 256×256, sixteen energy features $e_1, e_2, ..., e_{16}$ and corresponding twelve average energy ratios from each of the four levels, $er_1, er_2, ..., er_{12}$ are extracted. The energy feature set generated is , $F = \{e_1, e_2, ..., e_{16}, er_1, er_2, ..., er_{12}\}$. Since this unique energy feature set represents the spatial and frequency domain significant information, it can be able to correctly detect whether an image is watermarked or not.

A part of the three level two-dimensional TSWT decomposition of an image is shown in figure 1. The rounded nodes contain significant information. So, they undergo further decomposition. The sub bands are decomposed until the size of the smallest sub band comes to 16×16. Note that in the level 2 nodes (1.1), (1.3), and (2.3), there is more meaningful information and the decomposition is carried to the next higher level ("high" is down in the figure).

3.2 Classification Using Totalboost

The significant feature set, F which can detect both spatial and transform domain watermarked images is generated. The next step is to classify the test images into unwatermarked or watermarked. The design of classifier is another important factor in analyzing unwatermarked and watermarked images, because it affects the performance of the watermark detector in terms of accuracy. This is accomplished with the help of a machine learning algorithm such as Totalboost. Totalboost performs multiclass classification by attempting to maximize the minimal margin in the training set. The margin of a classification is the difference between the predicted soft classification score for the true class, and the largest score for the false classes.

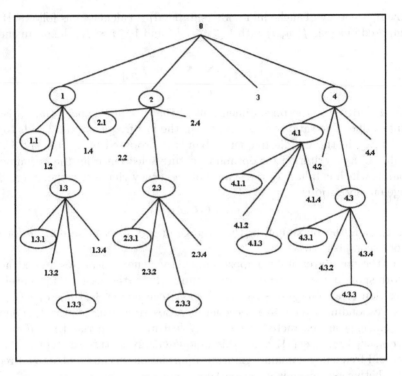

Fig. 1. Three level two-dimensional wavelet decomposition of an image

4   Experimental Results and Performance Evaluation

We conducted several experiments to show the effectiveness of the proposed method under different scenarios. The proposed watermark detector is implemented using MATLAB R2013a with Matlab scripts. Different types of images such as GIF, JPEG, BMP and PNG images of standard size 256×256 to analyze the performance of the proposed scheme from computer vision test images [17]. We have done Tree Structured Wavelet Transform with decomposition up to 4 levels. The 28 features mentioned in Section 3.1 are extracted from each image and are used for training and testing.

4.1   Simulation Results

Experiments were conducted with the extracted feature set and different well known classifiers such as Naive Bayes, decision tree and Totalboost. The performances of the watermark detector with different classification algorithms are shown in Table 1. From the table one can see that Totalboost detects watermarked images efficiently with an accuracy of 0.89, sensitivity of 0.892 and specificity 0.881. We can see that the sensitivity, specificity and accuracy of Totalboost is better compared with other classifiers such as Naive Bayes [18] and decision tree[19].

Specificity, sensitivity and accuracy are used to evaluate the performance of the proposed scheme.

True Positive (TP) = Number of samples correctly predicted as watermarked

False Positive (FP) = Number of samples incorrectly predicted as watermarked

True Negative (TN) = Number of samples correctly predicted as not watermarked

False Negative (FN) = Number of samples incorrectly predicted as not watermarked

Sensitivity, specificity and accuracy are defined as below:

$$Sensitivity(TPR) = \frac{TP}{(TP + FN)} \tag{3}$$

$$Specificity(TNR) = \frac{TN}{(FP + TN)} \tag{4}$$

$$Accuracy = \frac{(TP + TN)}{(TP + FP + TN + FN)} \tag{5}$$

Table 1. Performance of different classifiers against watermark detection

Classifier	Sensitivity	Specificity	Accuracy
Total Boost	0.892	0.881	0.890
Decision Tree	0.820	0.666	0.800
Naive Bayes	0.840	0.260	0.670

We have used five different watermarking algorithms, two spatial domain algorithms namely, LSB1[20], LSB2 [21] two transform domain schemes, using DWT[22], Contourlet Transform[23], and an online watermarking tool, Batchwatermark Tool[24], which is the available freely. The accuracies of classification of watermarked and unwatermarked images are given in Table 2. It is obvious from the table that the accuracy of detection of LSB1 and LSB2 watermarked images is 0.85 and 0.83 respectively. The detector performs well with better accuracy of 0.91 and 0.89 for Transform domain watermarked images compared to that of spatial domain watermarks. Also, it detects the images watermarked with Batchwatermarker tool with an accuracy of 0.88.

The most challenging issue of a watermark detector is that it could be able to correctly detect watermarks even after various attacks. This is achieved with the help of the efficient energy feature set generated. The percentage of detections against various image processing and signal processing attacks of the proposed watermark detector is given in Table 3. One can see that the watermark is detected with high percentage even after performing various image processing and signal processing attacks.

Table 2. Detection Accuracy against various watermarking domains

Watermarking domains	Watermarking scheme used	Accuracy
Spatial	LSB 1 [20]	0.85
	LSB 2[21]	0.83
Transform	Contourlet[23]	0.91
	Wavelet [22]	0.89
Online watermarking tool	Batch watermarking [24]	0.88

Table 3. Percentage of detection for different images against attacks

Attacks	Lena	Peppers	Harbour
Median filter (2x2)	96.5	93.21	95.6
Averaging filter (7x7)	95.5	84.90	95.03
Gaussian Filtering	97.5	96.50	95.60
Gaussian noise (scale=0.50)	95.40	92.53	98.20
JPEG Compression(CR=50)	93.5	97.20	97.23
Rotation(50%)	94.32	92.37	91.50
Scaling	93.15	90.10	91.20
Translation	95.5	92.20	93.45
Contrast Adjustment	95.14	96.01	95.90
Histogram Equalization	94.50	96.50	97.10

4.2   Performance Comparison

We have compared the performance of the proposed method with that of two other watermark detection schemes. The comparison results given in Table 4 reveals that our method is a better watermark detection compared to the laplacian model[25]. Also, we compare the performance of the proposed scheme with the available Naive Bayesian classifier based detection scheme[13] in Table 5. It can be seen from the table that the performance of our scheme is better in terms of improved accuracy. Moreover, the scheme in [13] is a semi-blind scheme which is designed to detect wavelet domain watermarks, whereas our scheme is blind and can detect watermarks in both spatial and frequency domains.

Table 4. Comparison with the laplacian model based detection scheme [25]

Images	Proposed detection(%)		Laplacian model based detection[25](%)	
	JPEG (50 %)	Gaussian noise (0.50)	JPEG (50 %)	Gaussian noise (0.50)
Lena	93.5	97.20	91.41	96.23
Pepper	95.40	92.53	91.45	89.26

Table 5. Comparison with the Naive Bayes watermark detection scheme

Images	Proposed method(%) Accuracy	Naive Bayes based detection(%) Accuracy
Lena	98.1	95.3
Barbara	98.5	88.7
Cameraman	98.2	94.8

5 Conclusion

An efficient watermark detector is developed to detect watermarks embedded in both spatial and frequency domains. The unique energy feature set is generated from the test images are used to classify the unwatermarked and watermarked images using Totalboost which can be able to detect watermarks even from the attacked images. Comparison with the existing transform domain watermark detection schemes shows the improved performance of our method.

References

[1] Tian, H., Zhao, Y., Ni, R., Pan, J.-S.: Geometrically invariant image watermarking using scale-invariant feature transform and K-means clustering. In: Pan, J.-S., Chen, S.-M., Nguyen, N.T. (eds.) ICCCI 2010, Part I. LNCS, vol. 6421, pp. 128–135. Springer, Heidelberg (2010)

[2] Nasir, I., Weng, Y., Jiang, J., Ipson, S.: Multiple spatial watermarking technique in color images. Signal, Image and Video Processing 4(2), 145–154 (2010)

[3] Lu, W., Sun, W., Lu, H.: Novel robust image watermarking based on subsampling and dwt. Multimedia Tools and Applications 60(1), 31–46 (2012)

[4] Natarajan, V., Anitha, R.: Universal steganalysis using contourlet transform. In: Wyld, D.C., Zizka, J., Nagamalai, D. (eds.) Advances in Computer Science, Engg. & Appl. AISC, vol. 167, pp. 727–735. Springer, Heidelberg (2012)

[5] Hernández, J.R., Pérez-González, F.: Statistical analysis of watermarking schemes for copyright protection of images. Proceedings of the IEEE 87(7), 1142–1166 (1999)

[6] Briassouli, A., Tsakalides, P., Stouraitis, A.: Hidden messages in heavy-tails: Dct-domain watermark detection using alpha-stable models. IEEE Transactions on Multimedia 7(4), 700–715 (2005)

[7] Hernandez, J.R., Amado, M., Perez-Gonzalez, F.: Dct-domain watermarking techniques for still images: Detector performance analysis and a new structure. IEEE Transactions on Image Processing 9(1), 55–68 (2000)

[8] Kay, S.: Fundamentals of Statistical Signal Processing: Detection theory. Prentice Hall Signal Processing Series. Prentice-Hall PTR (1998)

[9] Nikolaidis, A., Pitas, I.: Asymptotically optimal detection for additive watermarking in the dct and dwt domains. IEEE Transactions on Image Processing 12(5), 563–571 (2003)

[10] Kwitt, R., Meerwald, P., Uhl, A.: A lightweight rao-cauchy detector for additive watermarking in the dwt-domain. In: Proceedings of the 10th ACM Workshop on Multimedia and Security, pp. 33–42. ACM (2008)

[11] Deng, C., Zhu, H., Wang, S.: Curvelet domain watermark detection using alpha-stable models. In: Fifth International Conference on Information Assurance and Security, IAS 2009, vol. 1, pp. 313–316. IEEE (2009)

[12] Bian, Y., Liang, S.: Image watermark detection in the wavelet domain using bessel k densities. IET Image Processing 7(4), 281–289 (2013)

[13] Elbasi, E., Eskicioglu, A.M.: Naïve bayes classifier based watermark detection in wavelet transform. In: Gunsel, B., Jain, A.K., Tekalp, A.M., Sankur, B. (eds.) MRCS 2006. LNCS, vol. 4105, pp. 232–240. Springer, Heidelberg (2006)

[14] Chang, T., Kuo, C.C.: Texture analysis and classification with tree-structured wavelet transform. IEEE Transactions on Image Processing 2(4), 429–441 (1993)

[15] Sani, M., Ishak, K., Samad, S.: Classification using adaptive multiscale retinex and support vector machine for face recognition system. Journal of Applied Sciences 10(6) (2010)

[16] Porter, R., Canagarajah, N.: A robust automatic clustering scheme for image segmentation using wavelets. IEEE Transactions on Image Processing 5(4), 662–665 (1996)

[17] Computer vision test images, http://www.cs.cmu.edu/~cil/v-images.html/

[18] Zhang, H.: The optimality of naive bayes. American Association for Artificial Intelligence 1(2), 3 (2004)

[19] Cha, S.H., Tappert, C.: A genetic algorithm for constructing compact binary decision trees. Journal of Pattern Recognition Research 4(1), 1–13 (2009)

[20] Dehkordi, A.B., Esfahani, S.N., Nasiri Avanaki, A.: Robust lsb watermarking optimized for local structural similarity. In: 2011 19th Iranian Conference on Electrical Engineering (ICEE), pp. 1–6. IEEE (2011)

[21] Bamatraf, A., Ibrahim, R., Salleh, M.N.B.M.: Digital watermarking algorithm using lsb. In: 2010 International Conference on Computer Applications and Industrial Electronics (ICCAIE), pp. 155–159. IEEE (2010)

[22] Zhang, L., Li, A.: Robust watermarking scheme based on singular value of decomposition in dwt domain. In: Asia-Pacific Conference on Information Processing, APCIP 2009, vol. 2, pp. 19–22. IEEE (2009)

[23] Prathap, I., Natarajan, V., Anitha, R.: Hybrid robust watermarking for color images. Computers & Electrical Engineering 40(3), 920–930 (2014)

[24] Batchwatermarking tool, https://www.batch-photo-processing.com/

[25] Ng, T., Garg, H.: Maximum-likelihood detection in dwt domain image watermarking using laplacian modeling. IEEE Signal Processing Letters 12(4), 285–288 (2005)

Category Based Malware Detection for Android

Vijayendra Grampurohit[1], Vijay Kumar[2],
Sanjay Rawat[3], and Shatrunjay Rawat[4]

International Institute of Information Technology, Hyderabad

Abstract. Android, being the most popular operating system for the mobile devices, has attracted a plethora of malware that are being distributed through various applications (apps). The malware apps cause serious security and privacy concerns, such as accessing/leaking sensitive information, sending messages to the paid numbers, etc. Like traditional analysis and detection approaches for desktop malware applications, there have been many proposals to apply machine learning techniques to detect malicious apps. However unlike classical desktop applications, Android apps available on the "Google Play" [1] have a feature in "category" of app. In this initial work, we propose and investigate the possibility of improving the efficiency of machine learning approach for android apps by exploiting the category information. Experiment results performed over a large dataset, are encouraging which shows the effectiveness of our simple yet productive approach.

Keywords: mobile security, Android, malware detection, machine learning, data mining.

1 Introduction

Android is an open source Linux-based mobile operating system distributed by Google. According to the latest statistics, android powers hundreds of thousands mobile devices over 190 countries [2]. Google Play [1] is the official android centralized market place maintained by Google, where any independent application developer can submit his/her android app and make it available to the users. The growing popularity of this android ecosystem also is becoming a worthy target for security and privacy violations. Highly sensitive and confidential information such as text messages, private and business contacts, calendar data, etc may be leaked through an application. Sensors such as GPS present in the phones allow applications to provide context-sensitive user experience. But this also creates serious privacy concerns, as the data could be exploited for tracking or monitoring the user. Apart from these issues, smart phones are also susceptible to various malware threats such as viruses, Trojan horses, worms, etc. [3].

Android security model relies highly on permission-based mechanism. There are about 130 permissions that govern access to different resources. Whenever an user tries to install a new application, he/she is prompted to approve or reject all the permissions requested by the application. The application will be installed only after the user accepts all the necessary permissions requested by it.

J. Lloret Mauri et al. (Eds.): SSCC 2014, CCIS 467, pp. 239–249, 2014.

In this paper, we use the permissions and api level information from the apps as the features to detect malicious applications. Further we observe that, android store [1] defines a category for every published application. We have done extensive studies and discovered that, certain categories are highly prone to malicious acts compared to other categories. We explicitly incorporate this information in our model and learn a naive bayes classifier for each category using the features that encode information about permissions and api calls. Given a new test application with a known category, we apply an appropriate classifier to detect if the application is malicious. We created a large data set of android applications and achieve an improvement of 3 − 4% by incorporating category level information.

The rest of the paper is organized as follows: We discuss the Preliminary background in section 2. section 3, describes proposed method. section 4, contains experimental results and discussions. In section 5 we describe related works and finally conclude in section 6.

2   Preliminary Background

In this section we discuss Android architecture and basics of android application in brief.

2.1   Android Architecture

Android platform is an open source software stack for building and running applications with various layers running on top of each other with lower-level layers providing services to upper level layers. It consists of an operating system, native libraries, application framework, and core applications.

The kernel derived from linux kernel is the first layer of software that interacts with the device hardware. Android kernel handles power and memory management, device drivers, process management, networking and security. It also ensures certain separation between applications by creating different processes for different applications.

On top of the kernel are the native libraries. The libraries component acts as a translation layer between kernel and application framework. The library component shares its space with the runtime. Some of the core libraries include the Surface Manager (responsible for graphics on the devices screen), 2D and 3D graphics libraries, WebKit (the web rendering engine that powers the default browser) etc.

The run-time component consists of the Dalvik virtual machine that interacts and runs an application. The virtual machine is an important part of the Android operating system and executes system and third-party applications.

The next layer in the stack is the application framework. The framework provides a suite of services to the developers for writing applications. The layer supports entities such as the Package Manager for managing applications on the phone, and the Activity Manager for loading activities and managing the activity stack.

Finally, at the top of the stack resides the user applications. These include applications that is written by developers. Applications such as Contacts, Phone, Messaging, and Angry Birds apps are executed in this space by using the api libraries and the Dalvik virtual machine.

2.2 Android Application Basics

Android applications or simply apps are written in Java programming language. The Android SDK tools compile the source code, any data and resource files into an Android package - an archive file with an *.apk* suffix. A single *.apk* file which contains all the necessary code of an application is used to install the application in the Android powered devices.

An app must declare its components in a *manifest* file which must be at the root of the application project directory. The manifest file also states the user permissions that the application requires, such as internet access, read-access to the user's contacts, access to user's location, etc. We show an example of manifest file in listing 1.1. The example manifest file provides information about required permissions to read phone state, SMS, Internet access, etc. We extract and encode the information from the manifest file as features to detect the malicious applications.

Listing 1.1. Overview of Manifest file

```
1<manifest android:versionCode="15" android:versionName="1.3.1"
       android:installLocation="auto" package="com.oe.crazycorns"
2   xmlns:android="http://schemas.android.com/apk/res/android">
3   <uses−sdk android:minSdkVersion="8"/>
4   <uses−permission android:name="android.permission.INTERNET"/>
5   <uses−permission android:name="android.permission.ACCESS_NETWORK_STATE"/>
6   <uses−permission android:name="android.permission.READ_PHONE_STATE"/>
7   ............................................................
8   ............................................................
9</manifest>
```

3   Proposed Method

In this section, we explain the feature extraction and our proposed Naive Bayes classifier which exploits the category information of an application.

3.1 Reverse Engineering Android App

Reverse Engineering is a process by which one can discover and understand the complete working of an application by learning its operation, structure and functions. In this work, we use tools like ApkTool [4], Smali/Baksmali [5], Dex2Jar [6] and Android SDK for reverse engineering a Android Application.

The ApkTool [4] is a 3rd party tool that is used to analyze closed Android application binaries. We show the steps involved in Figure 1. To parse the .dex file, we use a tool called Baksmali [5] which is a disassembler for the dex format used by Dalvik. Baksmali disassembles .dex files into multiple files with

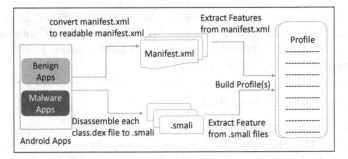

Fig. 1. Different Stages in Feature Extraction

.smali extensions. Each .smali file contains only one class information which is equivalent to a Java .class file.

3.2 Static Feature Extraction and Refinement

In order to build features for an application, we extracted the (binary) APK file using ApkTool [4] and Smali disassembler [5]. We extracted all the relevant api invocations in the Android application along with the permissions in the manifest file. Instead of using all the api calls, we use only a subset of them namely sensitive api calls, which are governed by an Android permission settings. To obtain the set of sensitive api's, we relied on the work of Felt *et al.* [7], who identified and used the mapping between permissions and Android methods. Further, a sensitive api is considered only if it is declared in the binary and if its corresponding permission is requested in the manifest file. This resulted in the elimination of large number of api calls. We used the Android Asset Packaging Tool (aapt) to extract and decrypt the data from the AndroidManifest.xml file, provided by the Android SDK.

3.3 Application Categories

When a developer publishes an application in Google Play, one needs to picks the category under which the application will be published. Currently, Google play has around 30 categories which are shown in Table 1. For each category, applications are ranked based on a combination of ratings, reviews, downloads, country, and other factors. We have done extensive study and found out that number of malwares is not uniform across all the categories. Certain categories such as Entertainment, Games, Tools, etc. are highly prone to malwares while categories such as medical, social have few malwares. In our work, we explicitly learn a model that exploits this information.

3.4 Bayesian Classification Model

One of the simplest and powerful machine learning techniques is Bayes classifier. This is probably due to its simplicity, linear computational complexity and accuracy. It is also referred as *Naive Bayesian Classifier* because of the naive assumption it makes, that all the features representing the data are independent for a particular choice of the behavior one is trying to learn.

The naive bayesian classifier consists of training and testing phases. In the training phase, a model learns from sufficient number of training data containing both benign and malicious android apps. Then during testing or detection phase, the model infers whether the given test app is benign or malign using the model learnt during the training.

We extract the desired features from each application in the corpus. The feature set is further reduced by a feature reduction function. Each application X is represented as a vector $X = [x_1, \ldots, x_m]$, where $x_i \in \{0, 1\}$, $\forall i = 1, \ldots, m$ are the random variables indicating a particular characteristic feature of the android application. We consider the api calls and permission as the characteristic features. If a particular api call/permission is present in the application then the corresponding feature x_i is defined as 1 otherwise as 0.

Let Y denote the label of each application suspicious, $Y \in \{malign, benign\}$. We define the application category as $C \in \{1, 2, \ldots, K\}$ where K denote the number of categories available in the android store. We exploit the information from both api calls and categories and thus we define the posterior density of Y using bayes rule as,

$$P(Y = y_i | X = x_j, C = c_k) = \frac{P(X=x_j|C=c_k,Y=y_i)P(C=c_k|Y=y_i)P(Y=y_i)}{P(X=x_j|C=c_k)P(C=c_k)}$$

(1)

where the probabilities, $P(X|C,Y)$, $P(C|Y)$, $P(C)$, $P(X|C)$ and $P(Y)$ are estimated from the training data.

During inference, any test app is classified as malign if P(Y=malign|X,C) > P(Y=benign|X,C). Since the category of a test application will be known apriori, we classify the app using the classifier trained on the corresponding category. This makes sense because apps belonging to similar category use similar kind of api calls and permission.

4   Experiment Results and Discussions

In this section, we describe the dataset and discuss the experimental results.

4.1   Data Set

Our data set consists of 25865 apps collected from Google Play [1] and Android Malware Genome Project [8]. We collected 24335 apps from Google Play and 1530 applications from Genome Project as shown in Table 1. We collected only the top free apps in each category for creating a benign set. For the benign applications, we used VirusTotal [9] to make sure that they are genuinely benign. Each of these benign and malware applications belong to 30 categories as defined in android market (Table 1).

Table 1. Benign & Malware App Categories

Category	Geniune	Malware	Category	Geniune	Malware
Arcade	1409	123	Medical	499	5
Books & References	884	10	Music & Audio	1287	30
Brain	1342	117	News & Magazine	545	20
Business	574	13	Personalization	2131	16
Cards	545	21	Photography	324	37
Casual	1658	140	Productivity	728	85
Comics	517	19	Racing	615	90
Communication	280	83	Shopping	169	10
Education	959	30	Social	683	5
Entertainment	1546	173	Sport	800	4
Finance	403	20	Sport Games	633	30
Health & Fitness	703	27	Tools	1227	275
Libraries & Demo	564	32	Transportation	397	17
Lifestyle	1112	26	Travel & Local	602	23
Media & Video	827	37	Whether	404	12

4.2   Evaluation Measures

To evaluate the effectiveness of proposed approach, we calculate true positive, true negative, false positive and false negative rates, precision and recall rates and F-measure in our experiments. These measures are defined as follows. Let TP (true positive) be the number of Android malware apps that are correctly detected, FN (false negative) be the number of malware apps that are detected as benign, TN (true negative) be the number of benign apps that are correctly classified, and let FP (false positive) be the number of benign app that are incorrectly detected as Android malware. In terms of classification error, two cases can occur: (a) A benign app may be misclassified as suspicious and (b) a suspicious app may be misclassified as benign. For our problem, the latter case is more crucial as it is more important to prevent a malicious app in reaching the end device than excluding a benign app from the distribution chain. We use the following measures to check the performance of our proposed approach.

$$\text{True Positive Rate (TPR)} = \frac{TP}{TP+FN} \qquad \text{False Positive Rate (FPR)} = \frac{FP}{TN+FP}$$

$$\text{Recall (Rec)} = \frac{TP}{TP+FN} \qquad \text{Precision (Prec)} = \frac{TP}{TP+FP}$$

Figure 2 shows the frequently occurring api calls and permissions in the Android application. We consider only the api calls and permission that are highly frequent as features. We adopted a ten-fold cross validation strategy for our experiments. We trained our model using 9 folds and tested on remaining fold. We repeat the experiment 10 times and report the average accuracy. This ensures a wider range of samples for the testing the classifier.

We also conducted our experiments as Aafer et al. [10] but with four different set of top features. These top features are selected based on frequently occurring

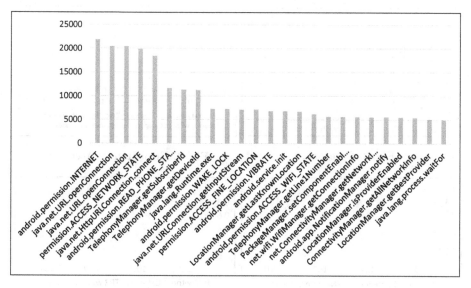

Fig. 2. Frequently occurring permissions & api calls

features in our samples as shown in Figure 2. We refer top 10, 15 and 25 ranked features as $10Tf$, $15Tf$ and $25Tf$ respectively and five lowest ranked features as $5Lf$.

Figure 4 shows the average error rates and accuracy for different feature sets with and without category information. We observe an increasing accuracy and decreasing error rates when larger number of features are used to train the classifier. It is also evident, by exploiting the category information, there is a clear improvement in the accuracy and error rates. Also, note that there is almost a difference of 20% in the performance using $5Lf$ and $10Tf$ feature sets indicating the importance of feature ranking based on the frequency of api calls.

Figure 5 shows the true negative and false positive rates and Figure 6 shows the true positive and false negative rates using different sets of features. We can observe in both the cases, that there is a improvement in the performance when the category information is included in the model. Finally, we show the precision and recall in Figure 7 and 8 with varying number of features. As the features are increased, both precision and recall improved and when the category information is included in the model, the performance is even better.

We summarize the results of various measures without category information in Table 2 and with category information in Table 3. It can be observed from the Table 3 that an average improvement of $3 - 4\%$ across all the categories is achieved.

We also report the measure Area under Curve (AUC) which defines the total area under the Receiver Operation Characteristic (ROC) curve, for different number of features. We can see that AUC for $10f$, $15f$, and $25f$ is very close to 1 implying a very good performance.

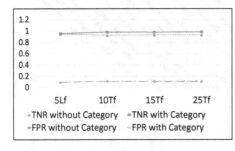

Fig. 3. Category

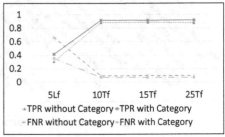

Fig. 4. Error Rate & Accuracy

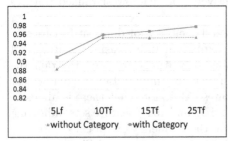

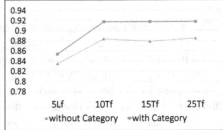

Fig. 5. True Negative & False Positive Rate

Fig. 6. True positive & False Negative Rate

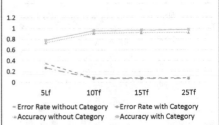

Fig. 7. Precision

Fig. 8. Recall

5   Related Work

In this section, we describe some of the previous approaches employed by researchers for detecting the malacious applications. There are various methods in the literature adapting different strategies to detect the malware applications. These can be roughly grouped into static and dynamic analysis. Below, we give a brief review of various approaches belonging to these categories.

One of the important methods for analysing the malware is through static analysis which performs detection of malware applications before installation or run on the device. There are various approaches proposed for malware detection based on static analysis. Comdroid was proposed by Chin *et al.* [11] for

Table 2. Various measures for different feature sets without Category

	5fL	10f	15f	25f
ERR	0.35	0.082	0.079	0.079
ACC	0.734	0.913	0.922	0.923
TNR	0.944	0.922	0.929	0.927
FPR	0.09	0.11	0.107	0.104
TPR	0.305	0.883	0.885	0.878
FNR	0.665	0.094	0.096	0.094
Prec	0.884	0.953	0.952	0.953
Rec	0.835	0.884	0.879	0.885
AUC	0.58	0.907	0.9	0.914
F-Mes	0.858	0.917	0.917	0.918

Table 3. Various measures for different feature sets with Category

	5Lf	10Tf	15Tf	25Tf
ERR	0.27	0.075	0.071	0.071
ACC	0.781	0.959	0.967	0.977
TNR	0.954	0.979	0.977	0.979
FPR	0.1	0.113	0.113	0.114
TPR	0.415	0.918	0.915	0.918
FNR	0.355	0.071	0.069	0.069
Prec	0.91	0.959	0.967	0.977
Rec	0.854	0.918	0.928	0.928
AUC	0.635	0.956	0.956	0.959
F-Mes	0.881	0.938	0.941	0.958

detecting application communication based vulnerabilities in Android. Profile-Droid [12] and Risk Ranker [13] leverages static analysis for profiling and analyzing Android applications. ScanDroid [14] proposed by Fuchs *et al.* analyses the data policies in application manifest and data flows across content providers. Barrera *et al.* [15] propose a methodology for identifying application clusters based on requested permissions. Dicerbo *et al.* [16] uses Android permissions in the manifest file to identify malicious Android applications. Zhou *et al.* [17] proposed a permission-based behavioral footprinting scheme and heuristics based filtering scheme to detect the malware. Other static analysis approaches exploit the information present in bytecode of the android application to predict its behavior [18]. Using the bytecode, they retrieve information ranging from coarse-grained levels as packages to fine-grained levels as instructions. However, this approach is computationally expensive and we thus focus on extracting permissions and api level information in our work, as they clearly capture the applications behavior.

A different direction for detecting Android malware relies on dynamic analysis where the malwares could be detected in run time. Zhao *et al.* [19] propose AntiMalDroid to detect Android malware that use logged behavior sequence as the feature and construct the models for further detecting malware and its variants effectively in runtime. Enck *et al.* [20] perform dynamic taint analysis to track the flow of private and sensitive data through third party applications and detect any leakage to remote servers.

Signature-based approaches detect the malwares by the sets of rules or policies. The advantage of such methods is that they can precisely detect the Android malware if matching any of signatures. Kim *et al.* [21] build a power consumption history from the collected samples, and generate a power signature from the constructed history for power aware malware detection. Enck *et al.* [22] proposed Kirin, security service that perform the certification of applications. They define a variety of potential dangerous permission combinations as rules to block the installation of potential unsafe applications. Our approach is different in a way that, these techniques are not adaptive to a new Android malware and they require continuous update of the signatures.

In [23], authors extract the function calls from binaries of applications and apply their clustering mechanism, called Centroid, for detecting unknown malware. In contrast, our approach is based on automated analyses of Android packages. A recent paper by Sahs and Khan [24] proposes a machine learning approach to Android Malware detection based on (SVM). They use the Android permissions in the Manifest files as the features and learn a single-class (SVM) model using benign samples alone. This is contrast to our approach which uses api calls, permissions and categories as features for training the naive-Bayes model.

Samsung Knox, a enterprise mobile security solution is meant to create a virtual partition on Android devices that would insulate apps and data from attack.

6   Conclusion

In this paper, we proposed a naive-Bayes approach for detecting Android malware application. Unlike the previous approach which uses only api calls for prediction, we combine various information from api calls, permissions and category information of an application. This is based on observation that, every application in the android market has a category assigned to it. We created a large dataset of 25865 applications from Google Play and Genome Project. We demonstrated the effectiveness of our approach on the dataset and showed that exploiting category information indeed improves the performance. As future work, we plan to explore if the static analysis can be combined with dynamic analysis to achieve better performance.

References

1. https://play.google.com/store?hl=en
2. http://developer.android.com/about/index.html
3. http://en.wikipedia.org/wiki/Mobile-virus
4. http://code.google.com/p/android-apktool/
5. http://code.google.com/p/smali/
6. https://code.google.com/p/dex2jar/
7. Felt, A.P., Chin, E., Hanna, S., Song, D., Wagner, D.: Android permissions demystified. In: ACM Conference on Computer and Communications Security (2011)
8. Zhou, Y., Jiang, X.: Dissecting android malware: Characterization and evolution. In: Security and Privacy (2012)
9. https://www.virustotal.com/
10. Aafer, Y., Du, W., Yin, H.: DroidAPIMiner: Mining API-level features for robust malware detection in android. In: Zia, T., Zomaya, A., Varadharajan, V., Mao, M. (eds.) SecureComm 2013. LNICST, vol. 127, pp. 86–103. Springer, Heidelberg (2013)
11. Chin, E., Felt, A.P., Greenwood, K., Wagner, D.: Analyzing inter-application communication in android. In: International Conference on Mobile Systems, Applications, and Services (2011)

12. Wei, X., Gomez, L., Neamtiu, I., Faloutsos, M.: Profiledroid: Multi-layer profiling of android applications. In: International Conference on Mobile Computing and Networking (2012)

13. Grace, M., Zhou, Y., Zhang, Q., Zou, S., Jiang, X.: Riskranker: scalable and accurate zero-day android malware detection. In: International Conference on Mobile Systems, Applications, and Services (2012)

14. Fuchs, A.P., Chaudhuri, A., Foster, J.S.: Scandroid: Automated security certification of android applications. Manuscript, Univ. of Maryland (2009), http://www.cs.umd.edu/~avik/projects/scandroidascaa

15. Barrera, D., Kayacik, H.G., van Oorschot, P.C., Somayaji, A.: A methodology for empirical analysis of permission-based security models and its application to android. In: ACM Conference on Computer and Communications Security (2010)

16. Di Cerbo, F., Girardello, A., Michahelles, F., Voronkova, S.: Detection of malicious applications on android OS. In: Sako, H., Franke, K.Y., Saitoh, S. (eds.) IWCF 2010. LNCS, vol. 6540, pp. 138–149. Springer, Heidelberg (2011)

17. Zhou, Y., Zhang, X., Jiang, X., Freeh, V.W.: Taming information-stealing smartphone applications (on android). In: McCune, J.M., Balacheff, B., Perrig, A., Sadeghi, A.-R., Sasse, A., Beres, Y. (eds.) Trust 2011. LNCS, vol. 6740, pp. 93–107. Springer, Heidelberg (2011)

18. Hao, H., Singh, V., Du, W.: On the effectiveness of api-level access control using bytecode rewriting in android. In: ACM SIGSAC Symposium on Information, Computer and Communications Security (2013)

19. Zhao, M., Ge, F., Zhang, T., Yuan, Z.: AntiMalDroid: An efficient SVM-based malware detection framework for android. In: Liu, C., Chang, J., Yang, A. (eds.) ICICA 2011, Part I. CCIS, vol. 243, pp. 158–166. Springer, Heidelberg (2011)

20. Enck, W., Gilbert, P., Chun, B.G., Cox, L.P., Jung, J., McDaniel, P., Sheth, A.: Taintdroid: An information-flow tracking system for realtime privacy monitoring on smartphones. In: OSDI (2010)

21. Kim, H., Smith, J., Shin, K.G.: Detecting energy-greedy anomalies and mobile malware variants. In: International Conference on Mobile Systems, Applications, and Services (2008)

22. Enck, W., Ongtang, M., McDaniel, P.: On lightweight mobile phone application certification. In: ACM Conference on Computer and Communications Security (2009)

23. Schmidt, A.D., Bye, R., Schmidt, H.G., Clausen, J., Kiraz, O., Yuksel, K.A., Camtepe, S.A., Albayrak, S.: Static analysis of executables for collaborative malware detection on android. In: ICC (2009)

24. Sahs, J., Khan, L.: A machine learning approach to android malware detection. In: Intelligence and Security Informatics Conference (2012)

Design and Analysis of Online Punjabi Signature Verification System Using Grid Optimization

Ankita Wadhawan and Dinesh Kumar

Department of Information Technology, DAV Institute of Engineering & Technology,
Jalandhar, Punjab, India

Abstract. Signature verification is the major research topic in the area of biometric authentication. Signature is a behavioral attribute based on ones behavior. In this a given input is examined and is either rejected as forgery or accepted as genuine. To the best of our knowledge no work has been done on online signature verification of Indian Languages. This paper deals with the on-line signature verification of Punjabi signatures. A digitizing tablet with stylus is used for acquiring signatures online. Support vector machines were used for recognition of Signatures. The performance of the system was explored by radial basis function in which grid optimization is used. Numbers of experiments are performed by increasing the number of samples and it has been found that the accuracy of the system increases as more and more number of samples are trained. Experiments were performed by using different gamma values to obtain error rates.

Keywords: online signature verification, support vector machines, false acceptance rate, false rejection rate.

1 Introduction

Currently, personal certification is important to provide security to any individual. A biometric characteristic like fingerprints, retina, handwriting, voiceis a biological or behavioural property of an individual which is used to identify individuals automatically from which distinguishing, repeatable biometric features can be extracted.

During last years, passwords and PIN based methods were used to identify a person. For this the person has to be physically present during the time-of-identification. Biometrics authentication is used to remove the need of passwords and PIN. Signature verification is divided into two: off-line and on-line signature verification. In off-line verification system static data is used for verification which mainly includes shape of the signature. Meanwhile in on-line signature verification system dynamic data is used for verification like writing speed, writing pressure, time duration, azimuth angle etc. On-line signatures are more robust as compared to the off-line signatures because an expert can duplicate the shape of a signature, but it is impossible to copy the timing changes in x, y co-ordinates and pressure.

J. Lloret Mauri et al. (Eds.): SSCC 2014, CCIS 467, pp. 250–262, 2014.

The word signature means to sign a written document with one's own hand. Its need is to authenticate writing and to bind the individual with the temper contained in the document

1.1   Characteristics of On-line Signature Data

Various characteristics are used for on-line signature recognition in the analysis of an individual's handwriting. These characteristics vary in use from individual to individual and are collected using sensitive technologies, such as PDAs or digitizing tablets. Common dynamic characteristics are:

- the velocity,
- acceleration,
- timing,
- pressure,
- direction of the signature strokes
- pen up/down

The dynamic features of one's signature are captured by using some special graphic pen tablet device for verification. The signature is represented by multiple features like x co-ordinate, y co-ordinate, writing forces i.e. the pressure applied. Local features are calculated at each position in the time sequence (e.g. distance between two consecutive points) whereas the global features calculate the properties of the whole signature (e.g. total signing time) [1].

Nowadays various signature verification technologies like hidden markov model, dynamic time warping, neural networks, support vector machines, vector quantization etc have been proposed to classify signatures.

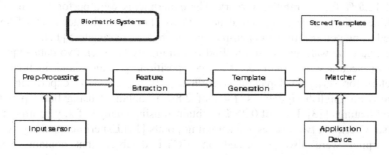

Fig. 1. Biometric Recognition System

In this research on-line signature verification system for Punjabi signatures is proposed. Signatures are classified by using support vector machines (SVM).Support vector machines are machine learning models through which patterns are recognized and data is analysed. SVM is used to solve classification and regression problems [2].

The paper is outlined as follows: In section 2 the work done in previous years is described. Section 3 describes the properties of Punjabi language. The proposed system for Punjabi on-line signature verification is described in section 4. Section 5 describes the experimental results obtained from different experiments. The conclusion and the future research directions are explained in the last section.

2   Related Work

The first signature recognition system was developed in 1965 [3]. Research in online signature verification was started in the 1970's [4] [5] [6].

In [2] an approach based on support vector machine (SVM) and using tablet to verify input signature is proposed. The experiments carried out were based on the x, y coordinates and the pressure applied. This system has the capability to verify signatures within the range of acceptable capability due to low rate of FRR and FAR.The integration of genetic algorithm and SVM results in the memory efficient method for online signature verification. 75 features were derived from SVC2004 database and were used to generate six different feature sets. The experimental results showed that the shape, dynamics and time features have better performance as compared to the other group of features [7]. In [8] off-line and on-line features of Japanese signatures were combined together and signatures were classified using support vector machines. A series of coordinates and time was used to generate pen velocity movement. The accuracy of 92.96% was achieved.The authors of [9] have proposed an online signature verification system for western and Chinese signatures.The signature samples were classified by using support vector machines and random forests. Different combinations of features used were: pen coordinates; incremental variation of pen coordinates and pen pressure. The performance for both the Dutch and Chinese data is improved by combining the pen pressure with the other time functions.

Neural networks consist of input layer, hidden layer and output layer. Numbers of neurons present in each layer are connected to other neurons by using weights. The overall handwritten recognition rate achieved in [10] using pressure patterns is between 71.2 % and 95.5 %. The false acceptance rates vary from a low of 5 % to a high of 12.5 % for the random forgery. The experiments were performed on English and Chinese signatures using neural network as classifier. The accuracy of 95% is achieved using pen-position and pen-movement angle as parameters [11].

Dynamic time warping is used to find the similarity between two data sequences. 97.6% of accuracy is obtained using pen-position, pressure, and inclination as parameters for verifying Japanese signatures [12]. In [13] [14] experiments were performed on English signatures. FRR of 2.8% is obtained using both spatial and temporal features [13]. FRR of 0.25% is obtained using change of x, y coordinate and p, pressure between two successive sampling points [14].Experiments using dynamic time warping were also performed on MCYT database that contains Spanish signatures [15] [16] [17].

In hidden markov model the system is assumed to have unobserved states that are hidden in nature. HMM is governed by a finite number of states and a set of random functions, associated with the output observation of each state. Experiments on MCYT database were performed having x, y coordinates, pen pressure, vector angle and vector length [18] and x, y coordinate, pressure, path tangent angle h, path velocity magnitude v, log curvature radius q, and total acceleration magnitude [19] as parameters and the EER of 1.2% and 4.5% is obtained respectively.Online signature verification of Chinese signatures results in EER of 17% using x: velocity along x axis, y: velocity along x axis, p: tool-tip pressure, pen-up/down state duration as parameters [20].

Number of techniques for on-line signature verification in various languages has been observed and it has been found that no work has been done in online signature verification for Indian languages. The great amount of work has been performed with foreign languages like Chinese, Japanese, Spanish, and English etc. Some amount of work has been done in Indian languages on off-line signature verification of Bengali and Hindi signatures [21] [22] [23].

In this research an online signature verification system for verifying Punjabi signatures is proposed. The signatures are classified using support vector machines. Support vector machines are preferred as it provides kernel functionality which helps in building an expert knowledge about the problem and is defined by optimization problem.

3   Importance of Punjabi Language

Punjabi is an Indo-Aryan language. Punjabi is the official language of the state of Punjab in India and is written in 'Gurmukhi' script in eastern Punjab (India), and in 'Shahmukhi' script in western Punjab (Pakistan) [24]. Punjabi language has various dialects that include Majhi, Doabi, Malwai, Powadhi, Pothohari, and Multani, spoken in the different sub-regions of greater Punjab. Punjabi's prestige dialect is Majhi, spoken in Amritsar, Lahore, TaranTaran, and Gurdaspur.

Some of the major properties of the Gurmukhi script are:

- Gurmukhi has forty-one consonants (vianjan),
- nine vowel symbols (lāgamātrā),
- two symbols for nasal sounds (bindī and ṭippī), and one symbol which duplicates the sound of any consonant (addak).
- Four conjuncts used are: three subjoined forms of the consonants Rara, Haha and Vava, and one half-form of Yayya.

Three horizontal zones are there which divides a word written in Gurmukhi script. These three horizontal zones are shown in Fig.2.

Fig. 2. Three zones and headline in University word

ੲ	ਅ	ੲ	ਸ	ਹ
ਕ	ਖ	ਗ	ਘ	ਙ
ਚ	ਛ	ਜ	ਝ	ਞ
ਟ	ਠ	ਡ	ਢ	ਣ
ਤ	ਥ	ਦ	ਧ	ਨ
ਪ	ਫ	ਬ	ਭ	ਮ
ਯ	ਰ	ਲ	ਵ	ੜ

Fig. 3. Character set of Gurmukhi script

4   System Design

The proposed on-line Punjabi Signature verification system consists of following six phases:

- Data acquisition
- Feature vector generator
- Enrolment
- Database development and collection
- Verification
- Prediction

The algorithm of the proposed system is as follows:

Step I: Input signature on USB tablet

Step II: Generate feature vector of the signature having format

$$[label][index1]:[value1][index2]:[value2]...[indexN]:[valueN]$$

In this feature vector is represented as:

+1 1: minimum pressure 2: average pressure 3: maximum pressure 4: signature length 5: total signing time 6: total pen down count

Step III: Enrol users and save their signatures as template for future use.

Step IV: Collect dataset D, containing all the Punjabi signature samples.

Step: V Divide the entire dataset D into two subsets that aretraining set and testing set

Step: VITrain system with signature samples

Step: VIICreate model file for each user present in the database, which contains the support vectors that are needed to classify the testing data.

1.txt   2.txt   ...   n.txt

Step VIII: Classifier compares these vectors with the vectors contained in each model file.

StepIX: If testing signature matches and belongs to specified model, then value in the result file is positive, otherwise it is negative.

StepX: The outputs generated are compared by the comparer and the Punjabi test signatures are verified with the file containing positive value.

4.1   Data Acquisition

Data acquisition is the process of acquiring the inputs from the digitizing tablet and stores them in the database for processing.

USB Pen Tabletwith working area of 4 x 3 inches, 1024 pressure levels having cordless digital stylus pen with a pen tip and two barrel buttons is used to provide hardware interface. Universal Serial Bus (USB) is a way of providing communication that gives a personal computer (PC) the ability to interconnect different devices. Devices are configured by USB protocols during system start up or when they are plugged in at run time.

For the accomplishment of the routing and retrieval of data the descriptors of the human interface device (HID) and the data it provides are examined. A VID and PID are 16-bit vendor identity number (Vendor ID) and product identity number (Product ID) respectively.

4.2   Feature Extraction

The main function of feature extraction is to find out the most reliable features from the collected sample.In on-line signature verification system the dynamic properties from the signature are extracted. A collection of some of the features that have been used studied and reported [25] [7] [26].

The raw data of each signature contains the following information:

- Pen-up status
- Pen-down status
- X co-ordinate
- Y co-ordinate
- Pressure value at a particular point
- Button status of pen

Vector representation of the signature that is used as a training set is represented by:

$$+1\ 1:0\ 2:1.241\ 3:1.0079\ 4:34\ 5:08\ 6:189$$

Features used for vector representation are:

- Minimum pressure: it is the minimum pressure value applied by the signer while writing.
- Average pressure: it is calculated by finding out the average of all the pressure values.
- Maximum pressure: it is the strongest pressure applied by the signer while signing.
- Signature length: it represents the length of all lines drawn in the signature.
- Total signing time: it is the total time needed to get a person to sign, since the beginning of the signature. It is obtained in seconds.
- Total pen down count: this feature shows how many times the signer touched a pen on the surface during signing.

4.3   Enrolment

The enrolment data record consists of six biometric features that are minimum pressure, average pressure, maximum pressure, signature length, total signing time and total pen down count and arbitrary non-biometric data such as user ID, name, age, gender.

4.4   Database

The Gurumukhi script employed by Punjabi is characterized by bars on top of the symbols. As Punjabi is the official language of the state of Punjab in India, this research is based on the collection of Punjabi signatures. The database consists of 500 genuine Punjabi signatures collected from 20 individuals out of which 13 are females and 7 are males. The database also contains 100 forged Punjabi Signature samples that are used for testing. Raw data consists of: x and y pen co-ordinates, pen pressure and pen up/down status. Each data set is divided into two sets: training set and testing set.

4.5   Verification

For verifying on-line signatures support vector machines are used, which is a supervised learning method based on the concept of decision boundaries that are defined by decision planes which separates a set of objects having different class memberships [1]. SVM is a learning machine first proposed by V. Vapnik [27]. A support vector machine constructs a hyper plane in a high dimensional space. A good separation is achieved by the hyper plane that has the largest distance to the nearest training data points of any class. The kernel is the part of the SVM that maps the input data to the very high-dimension feature space[28].

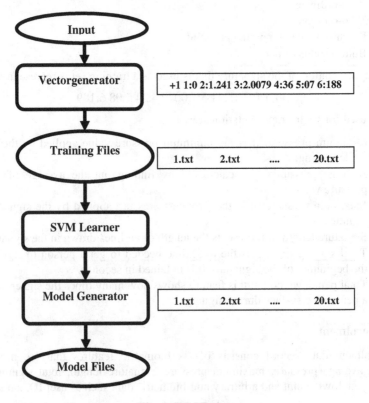

Fig. 4. SVM Trainer

In this research the radial basis kernel functions and the grid method is used. Grid search is the standard way of performing hyper parameter optimization. Radial basis function kernel consists of two hyper parameters first is regularization constant C which is a trade-off between training error and the flatness of the solution and second is a kernel hyper parameter γ.Grid search is used to estimate the better C before the final training is performed. An SVM is trained with each pair (C, γ). The settings that achieve the highest point in the validation procedure are used [29] [30].

A very important task in this system is to choose the correct feature vector from the raw data. First a pre-processing is done to remove the irrelevant information. In this pressure is mapped by its maximum value to achieve better results.

1) *SVM Trainer:* SVM trainer is used to train the system with training set.
2) *SVM Loader:* SVM loader is used to load the model files generated after training the system. Model files for each user are generated and are used to perform the verification task.

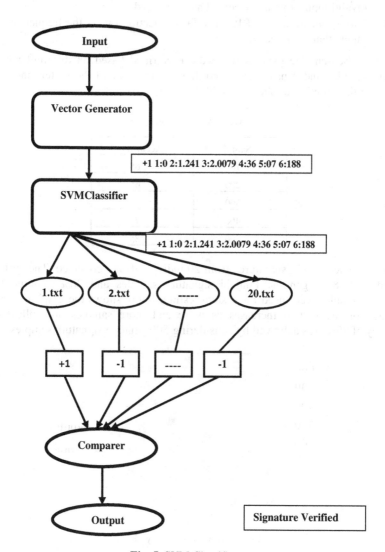

Fig. 5. SVM Classifier

3) *SVM Classifier:* For classification, Punjabi signatures are used for testing and are converted to vectors. Classifier compares these vectors with the vectors contained in each file. If testing signature matches and belongs to specified model, then its value is positive, otherwise it is negative.

5   Experimental Results

The effectiveness of biometric authentication system is usually measured by:

- False acceptance rate (FAR): The false acceptance rate is the frequency of invalid inputs that are accepted as authorized.
- False rejection rate (FRR): The false rejection rate is the frequency of valid inputs that are rejected.

In this research five experiments were performed based on different number of training samples and it has been found that the accuracy of the system increases by increasing the samples, as shown in table1.

Table 1. Verification results

Samples	Accuracy %
100	65
200	65
300	73.3
400	78
500	85

500 genuine Punjabi signatures from 20 individuals are collected. The system was trained with 80% genuine Punjabi signature samples and 20% genuine Punjabi signature samples were used for system testing. Fig.6. shows the graph in which the accuracy of the system increases as more and more samples are collected. The accuracy of 85% was achieved by considering 500 genuine signature samples.

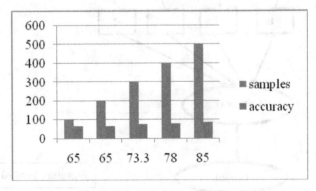

Fig. 6. System Accuracy Graph

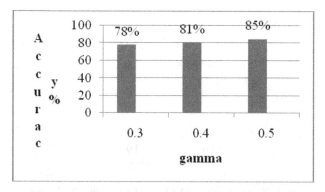

Fig. 7. Comparison of results using different values of gamma for the SVM classifier

Table 2. Values of FAR and FRR

Gamma	FRR	FAR
0.5	0.16	0.49
0.4	0.19	0.65
0.3	0.22	0.72

The FRR and FAR rates changed as the value of gamma used in SVM classifier changes as shown in table2.

The comparison of error rates using different values of gamma used as for training SVM classifier are shown in Fig.8.

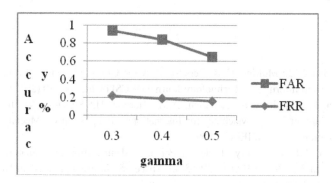

Fig. 8. Comparison of different values for FRR and FAR for different Gamma values

Receiver operating characteristic (ROC) curves provides comprehensive way for assessing accuracy of prediction. This curve is obtained by plotting FAR against the FRR of the experiments. The system performance by ROC curve and the intersection of FAR and FRR for different gamma values are shown in Fig.9.

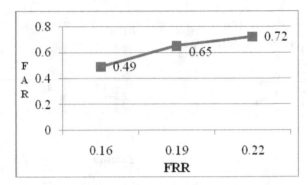

Fig. 9. Representation of FAR and FRR by the ROC curve

6   Conclusion and Future Scope

This research is regarding the development of online Punjabi signature verification system, as excess of work has been done in languages like English, Japanese, Chinese, and Spanish etc. and no work has been done in Indian languages for online signature verification. For signature verification support vector machines are used. Various experiments show that the accuracy of the system increases as the system is trained with more number of samples. FRR and FAR error rates are used to measure the authenticity and reliability of the system.

For futuristic work this research can be extended for the verification of signatures in other Indian languages. There is a necessity for finding a more comfortable pen tablet USB devices at cheaper costs from which more and more dynamic features can be extracted.

References

[1] Alhaddad, M.J.: Multiple Classifiers to verify the Online Signature. World of Computer Science and Information Technology Journal (WCSIT) 2(2), 46–50 (2012)

[2] Azlina, F., Mardiana, B., Zahariah, A.M., Haroon, H.: Signature Verification System using Support Vector Machine. In: International Symposium on Mechatronics and its Applications, pp. 1–4. IEEE (2009)

[3] Mauceri, A.J.: Feasibility Studies of Personal Identification by Signature Verification. Report no. SID 65 24 RADC TR 65 33, Space and Information System Division, North American Aviation Co., Anaheim, USA (1965)

[4] Sternberg, J.: Automatic signature verification using handwriting pressure, 1975 Wescon Tech Papers, Paper No. 31/4, Los Angeles (1975)

[5] Herbst, N.M., Liu, C.N.: Automatic signature verification based on accelerometry. IBM J. Res. and Devel. 21, 245–253 (1977)

[6] Lin, C.N., Herbst, N.M., Anthony, N.J.: Automatic signature verification: System description and field test results. IEEE Trans. Syst. Man, Cybern. SMC-9(1), 35–38 (1979)

[7] Kour, J., Hanmandlu, M., Ansari, A.Q.: Online signature verification using GA-SVM. In: International Conference on Image Information Processing (ICIIP), pp. 1–4. IEEE (2011)

[8] Ito, T., Ohyama, W., Wakabayashi, T., Kimura, F.: Combination of signature verification techniques by SVM. In: International Conference on Frontiers in Handwriting Recognition, pp. 430–433 (2012)

[9] Parodi, M., Gómez, J.C., Liwicki, M.: Online Signature Verification Based on Legendre Series Representation. Robustness Assessment of Different Feature Combinations. In: International Conference on Frontiers in Handwriting Recognition, pp. 379–384 (2012)

[10] Tseng, L.Y., Huang, T.H.: An Online Chinese Signature Verification Scheme Based on the ART1 Neural Network. In: International Conference on Neural Networks, vol. 3, pp. 624–630 (1992)

[11] Fahmy, M.M.M.: Online handwritten signature verification system based on DWT features extraction and neural network classification. Ain Shams Engineering Journal 1(1), 59–70 (2010)

[12] DSakamoto, Morita, H., Ohishi, T., Komiya, Y., Matsumot, T.: On-line Signature Verification Algorithm Incorporating Pen Position, Pen Pressure and Pen Inclination Trajectories. In: Proc. Acoustics, Speech, and Signal Processing (ICASSP), vol. 2, pp. 993–996 (2001)

[13] Jain, A.K., Griess, F.D., Connell, S.D.: On-line signature verification. Journal of Pattern Recognition Society (12), 2963–2972 (2002)

[14] Daramola, S.A., Ibiyemi, T.S.: Efficient on-line signature verification system. International Journal of Engineering & Technology IJET-IJENS 10 (2004)

[15] Putz-Leszczyńska, J., Kudelski, M.: Hidden Signature for DTW Signature Verification in Authorizing Payment Transactions. Journal of Telecommunications and Information Technology, 59–67 (2010)

[16] TalalIbrahim, M., Khan, M.A., Alimgeer, K.S., Khan, M.K., Taj, I.A., Guan, L.: Velocity and pressure-based partitions of horizontal and vertical trajectories for on-line signature verification. Pattern Recognition 43, 2817–2832 (2010)

[17] Qiao, Y., Wang, X., Xu, C.: Learning Mahalanobis Distance for DTW based Online Signature Verification. In: Proc. of the IEEE International Conference on Information and Automation, Shenzhen, China, pp. 333–338 (2011)

[18] Muramatsu, D., Kondo, M., Sasaki, M., Tachibana, S., Matsumoto, T.: A Markov Chain Monte Carlo Algorithm for Bayesian Dynamic Signature Verification. IEEE Transactions on Information Forensics and Security 1(1), 22–34 (2006)

[19] Fierrez, J., Ortega-Garcia, J., Ramos, D., Gonzalez-Rodriguez, J.: HMM-based on-line signature verification: Feature extraction and signature modeling. Pattern Recognition Letters 28, 2325–2334 (2007)

[20] Zhang, D., Inagaki, S., Kanada, N., Suzuki, T.: Online Signature Verification System with Antiforgery Provision Based on Segmentation and Structure Learning of HMM. In: IEEE international conference on Systems man and cybernetics (SMC), pp. 2834–2840 (2010)

[21] Pal, S., Alireza, A., Pal, U., Blumenstein, M.: Off-line Signature Identification Using Background and Foreground Information. In: International Conference on Digital Image Computing Techniques and Applications (DICTA), pp. 672–677 (2011)

[22] Pal, S., Blumenstein, M., Pal, U.: Hindi Off-line Signature Verification. In: International Conference on Frontiers in Handwriting Recognition, pp. 373–378 (2012)

[23] Pal, S., Pal, U., Blumenstein, M.: Off-line verification technique for Hindi signatures. IET Biometrics 2(4), 182–190 (2013)

[24] Ethnologue. Indo-Aryan Classification of 221 languages that have been assigned to the Indo Aryan grouping of the Indo-Iranian branch of the Indo-European languages

[25] Lei, H., Govinaraju, V.: A study on the consistency of features for online signature verification. In: SSPR/SPR, p. 444 (2004)

[26] Sonawane, R.C., Patil, M.E.: An effective stroke feature selection method for online signature verification. In: Third International Conference on Computing Communication & Networking Technologies, pp. 1–6. IEEE (2012)

[27] Vapnik, V.N.: The Nature of Statistical Learning Theory. Springer (1995)

[28] Vapnik, V.: Statistical Learning Theory. John Wiley & Sons, New York (1998)

[29] Bergstra, J., Bengio, Y.: Random Search for Hyper-Parameter Optimization. J. Machine Learning Research 13, 281–305 (2012)

[30] Hsu, C.-W., Chang, C.-C., Lin, C.J.: A practical guide to support vector classification.Technical Report, National Taiwan University (2010)

Internal Hardware States Based Privacy Extension of IPv6 Addresses

T.R. Reshmi, Shiney Matilda Manoharan, and Krishnan Murugan

Ramanujan Computing Centre,
Anna University, Chennai, India, 600025
{reshmi.engg,shineysunil6}@gmail.com, murugan@annauniv.edu

Abstract. The Internet Protocol Version 6 (IPv6) usage is booming up in recent years due to the address scarcity of existing protocol. This protocol faces various security threats and is under research for few decades. Although IPsec is mandated for security over IPv6 end-to-end communication, it does not support link local communication. Link local security issues are considered to be important during autoconfiguration. The existing mechanism SeND used to provide security during autoconfiguration faces issues related to algorithmic complexity, router functionality implications, key generation etc. The paper proposes a privacy extension method for link local address generation by using the internal hardware states of the system, thus overcoming the existing issues. The prototype is implemented in a real time system and compared with SeND. The proposed method has proven to outperform the existing methods in terms of algorithmic strength and thereby reduce the complexity and time delay during implementation.

Keywords: Autoconfiguration, IPv6, SeND, Privacy extension, Link local address.

1 Introduction

IPv6 provides a mechanism where hosts and routers can find each other automatically; this is the feature of IPv6 which replaces ARP protocol in IPv4. Thus through this feature each machine can automatically identify and determine their default routers. Hosts are allowed to communicate with nodes both internally and externally nodes in this mechanism named Neighbor Discovery (ND). This functionality is achieved through the Neighbor Discovery Protocol. Neighbor Discovery Protocol (NDP) allows nodes in a network to perform the following functionalities [2].

  a) Determine the link layer address of the neighboring nodes that are known to be attached to the same link.
  b) Identify neighboring routers through which packets can be forwarded on its behalf.
  c) Constantly track the reachability of neighbors
  d) Identify alternate routers when there is a failure in the router path.

J. Lloret Mauri et al. (Eds.): SSCC 2014, CCIS 467, pp. 263–271, 2014.

The neighbor discovery is protected through some basic protective features offered by NDP. The NDP being a link local protocol, must have its hop limit set to 255, its source address should be either unspecified or link-local. The routers do not forward these link local addresses. Therefore the messages of NDP cannot be injected into the infrastructure of the network beyond the directly connected second layer access networks. This protective shield does not completely protect IPv6 local networks thus posing serious security threats. IPv6 neighbor discovery is prone to spoofing, Denial-of-Service (DoS), replay, redirect, and rogue router attacks [3].

The threats mentioned above should be eradicated for the normal functioning of Neighbor Discover. The solutions to these threats are offered by the Secure Neighbor Discover Protocol (SeND) [4] .The SeND protocol uses digital signature, cryptographically generated addresses (CGAs), and X.509 certification mechanism to enable its enhanced protective feature. The SeND protocol ensures integrity of messages, prevents thefts of IPv6 address and replay attacks. It also provides a feature where the router's authority can be verified ensuring safe communication. Although SeND is a technique with promising features that would protect NDP and make IPv6 a safe protocol, its implementation and deployment is not an easy task. Thus SeND does not fulfill the mature implementation needs that are expected by various network device manufacturers and operating system developers. The SeND is computationally intensive and consumes more bandwidth [5]. This paper discusses the implementation and deployment challenges of SeND and also provides some directions and proposals for facilitating the enhancement of security using the internal hardware states of machines during the autoconfiguration process.

2   Background

In stateless address autoconfiguration mechanism [1], the hosts can enable to determine their own addresses. Router advertisements that contain subnet prefixes associated with a link along with the unique identifier (known as the interface identifier) generated through the information available at the host locally are used to generate the address. Nodes attached to a same link can communicate using their self-generated link local addresses. The stateless mechanism unlike the stateful approach does not require configuration of a host's address manually. The addresses are automatically generated by the hosts themselves in the stateless mechanism eliminating the need of additional servers. This mechanism has strong benefits over the usage of DHCP and is known as one of the major advancements over IPv4

There are two approaches through which stateless address autoconfiguration of nodes can be performed. The first being the MAC based address generation, where the EUI-64 based interface identifier (ID) is generated using a node's MAC address. This mechanism is described as hardware address based address generation. The address generation is as follows. The 48 bit MAC address of a host is split into two halves of 24bit .One of the 24 bits block is named as OUI (Organizationally Unique Identifier) and the other is known to be network interface card specific. There exists a 16-bit value (0xFFFE) reserved by IEEE for this MAC based address generation which is inserted between the OUI and the network interface specific blocks. The Fig.1 below depicts the format of IPv6 address generated using the EUI-64 mode of generation

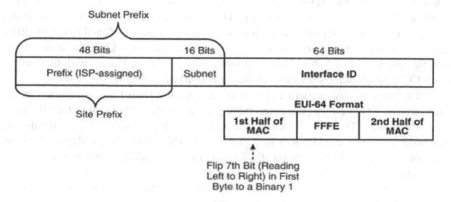

Fig. 1. IPv6 Address Format with Interface ID and EUI-64

As per the IPv6 addressing standards, there exists a left most 7th bit which determines if the address are locally or globally administered .This bit is named as the Universal/Local bit. If the bit value is set to 1 then it configured as the locally administered address else in case of bit value 0 then they are termed as globally unique address

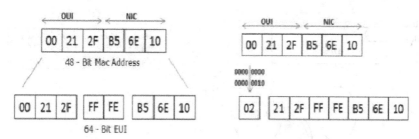

Fig. 2. Generation of EUI-64 Based IPv6 Address

The second approach used for stateless address autoconfiguration mechanism is a security enhanced approach, wherein the IPv6 address generation is protected by various measures e.g. involving binding of a public key signature to the address. This mechanism of address generation is a major offering of the Secure Neighbor Discovery protocol and is known as the cryptographically generated address (CGA) approach. The CGA's[6] addresses that involve hashing techniques over predetermined data structures known as CGA parameters to produce secure addresses for the host .This address generated is purely associated with the public key which is in Distinguished Encoding Rules (DER) encoded format. The interface identifier is generated by hashing the public key and CGA parameters, the receiver can verify the integrity of the sender by re-computing the hash with the available key and CGA option, thus enabling authentication of address without the need of an external third party intervention.

The generation of CGA's involves determining the public key of the owner address, selecting the appropriate security-level (Sec) value and generation of a random 128 bit modifier at its first step. These are then subjected to SHA-1 hashing. This process is then looped continuously with various values assigned to the modifier until 16 × security parameter leftmost-bits of hash2 equals zero. Once this condition is satisfied the loop terminates. This final modifier value is used along with the various other CGA parameters as the input to the hash 1(shown in Fig 3).

The leftmost 64 bits is extracted from the resultant of hash 1 and is assigned as the Interface ID. The security parameter value is then inserted into the interface ID's left most three bits. The u bit (universal/ local bit) value is set to 1 to indicate the universal scope of the address or to 0 to indicate local scope of the address. The g bit is known the individual/group bit. Performing duplicate address detection at the end of this process assures that there is no collision of address over the network. The Fig.3 gives an overview of the CGA generation process and describes diagrammatically the steps involved in the unique address generation

The cost of generating a new CGA depends exponentially on the security parameter Sec, which can have values from 0 to 7. Though CGA based mode of stateless address autoconfiguration enhances the security level of the process, it is also subjected to various risks and issues that pose a threat to the usage of SeND protocol.

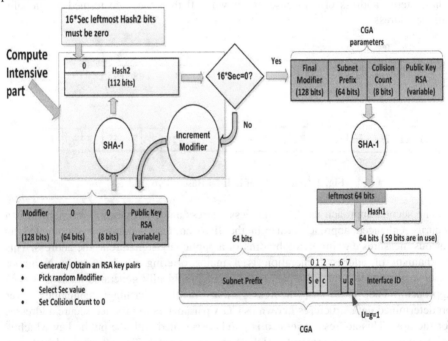

Fig. 3. CGA generation

3   Proposed Work

The paper presents a novel privacy extension of IPv6 addresses using internal hardware states of the machines. The **HA**rdware **V**olatile **E**ntropy **G**athering and Expansion (HAVEGE) algorithm used for empirically strong random number generation is the inspiration for the extended algorithmic design of the proposed work. The various issues related to the existing SeND as per references [5], [7-10] that has motivated for the new proposal has been discussed below.

3.1   Issues Related to SeND

1. *Security Issues*: An attacker to facilitate address stealing will have to compute the cryptographic hash value (hash1) collision when an address is generated through the CGA mechanism. This computing is infeasible thus posing a strong shield against address stealing. Thus the CGA mechanism is used widely to prevent stealing/theft of another node's address However, CGA can't provide a promising assurance on a node's identity, and cannot guarantee/prove that the address is the original address of the associated node. Since there are no certifications over the CGA's, attackers can always generate a new valid addresses from their own public keys and impersonate other nodes.
2. *Technical Issues*: Majority of the operating systems support implementation of NDP whereas SeND has always lacked support from them. Although some major vendors and manufactures like Juniper, Cisco provides support for SeND in their routers at various levels, no major operating system is known to provide a considerably good level of support. Current implementations of SeND in various OS distribution like Debian Linux are still proofs of concept, there have been no production ready softwares that enable implementation of SeND for achieving ND security.
3. *Complexity Issues:* The average CGA address generation time depends on the security parameter used in the CGA data structure. However, it's impossible to tell exactly how much time CGA generation will take when Sec isn't zero; it could vary significantly. Theoretically, the computational complexity of hash2 consumption increases by 2^{16} for each security parameter value. For higher values of security parameters the address generation process involves highly intense computations. This directly implies to higher cost of address generation when there is a need of high security parameter. Almost all network devices manufactures look for highly secure mechanism and in CGA this expectation is met by increasing Security parameter values as per need, but owing to the higher cost of address generation deprives the usage of CGA's in various sectors. This challenge drives the need for a more feasible and implementable security solution for the autoconfiguration process.

3.2   Privacy Extensions Using Hardware Volatile Entropy Gathering and Expansion

A random number generator is empirically strong if a random number sequence generated as its output cannot be judged or guessed from a uniformly distributed independent sequence of numbers. The heuristic approach named HAVEGE

(HArdware Volatile Entropy Gathering and Expansion), that enables generation of random numbers that are empirically strong [12].

There are numerous global states of a microprocessor that are purely invisible through instruction sets like caches, buffers etc. Any external event like an operating system interrupt affects these internal states of a processor directly inducing modifications to their existing status. These events introduce a considerably large amount of change / modifications in bits of the internal states. This feature is used as the basis for the HAVEGE algorithm. This algorithm holds good for almost all systems, since every personal or general purpose computers are built upon processors that ensure high performance ratios. This high performance is achieved by using microprocessors that possesses complex hardware mechanisms.Several hundreds of thousands of bits are derived randomly from these internal states that are subjected to change every time an external event occurs in the system. These randomly collected bits are empirically strong. The entropy/ uncertainty that have been induced due to these internal states are calculated in the HAVEG algorithm using the system's hardware clock cycle [13].

The HAVEGE Algorithm is the extension to the HAVEG. It is an algorithm that was constructed to state an approach where the entropy gathering mechanism of HAVEG is combined along with random number generation to ensure generation of unpredictable random numbers. The HAVEGE generator is known to comprise of data that are usually thousands of volatile internal states, as discussed above. These are the micro-architectural internal states that are prone to changes due to any external event. Even the user who performs the random number generation possesses no idea of the changes in the internal hardware states. This feature makes the random number generated through this algorithm strong empirically, where in the generator cannot be set to a state where the same sequences of bits are generated again.

The volatile internal states present in the HAVEGE generator are listed below,

DATA TLB: The translation look-aside buffer is a table consisting of information of the pages in the memory that is accessed by the processor. As per the HAVEGE algorithm each entry of a page in the TLB possesses 129 states. The HAVEGE algorithm is constructed with a loop that accesses 128 pages of memory.

Level 1 Data Cache: The Level 1 cache also known as the primary cache is a memory along with the processor core possessing information of the latest information acceded by a processor. In the HAVEGE Generator, the cache lines of the level 1 data cache are assured to be in one of the possible seven states. This data is usually mapped in the WALK table between any one of the possible 32 byte block available. The L1 cache is in one of the 7512 possible states. The processor might additionally possess L2, L3 cache which are not used in HAVEGE generator.

Level 1 Instruction Cache: The Level 1 instruction cache consists of 256 sets in which from HAVEGE perspective each possesses 7 possible states. The HAVEGE algorithm is made of a loop body that performs self-modifying walks over the level 1 instruction cache.

The HAVEGE Algorithm is used to generate random numbers that replace the CGA during the IPv6 address generation. The link local addresses using the new privacy extension method generates 64-bit random address using the internal states of L1 caches and Data TLB. The extraction of internal states and bit randomness is completely unknown to the system users which ensure the security and integrity of address generation. The generation of highly random addresses is the sole purpose of integrating HAVEGE with SeND.

4   Performance Analyses

The proposed prototype is implemented in Linux kernel version 2.6.34 and the currently implemented IPv6 privacy extensions are modified .The modified kernel per [11] uses different system control parameters which can be read and written by user based on the requirements and thereby controlling the operation of IPv6 privacy extensions. The internal states based privacy extension method and existing SeND are implemented and compared in the same environment. The tests are conducted over 50 times and each time the generated addresses are recorded to calculate the performance metrics listed below.

1) **Address generation delay:** The time taken for address generation in real time scenario has been calculated using a timer function. The time includes the key generation, key verification and address generation delay. The time denoted the runtime of the algorithms.
2) **Algorithmic complexity:** Algorithmic complexity estimates the complexity in processing the algorithmic steps. It determines the hastiness and resource utilization of the algorithmic steps. Complexity is defined as a numerical function T (n) - time versus the input size n.
3) **Entropy level:** The entropy level depicts the measure of randomness of the algorithm generated addresses. The security level of the algorithm is determined by the entropy. The more random the address generation the stronger will be the algorithm. The formula for the entropy calculation is as given in equation 1.

$$Entropy(S) = \sum_{i=1}^{C} P_i \, log_2 \, P_i \qquad (1)$$

5   Result Analyses

The results obtained from the experiments and quantitative analysis is compared for the algorithms. The results derived from the performance analysis are given in Table 1.

Metric	EUI-64 Address	Cryptographically Generated Address (sec = 1)	HAVEGE based generated IPv6 address
Address Generation delay(in microseconds)	1	89003	1
Algorithmic Complexity	$log(n) + (n \, log(n))$	$2^s (O(n) + O(log \, n)) + O(n \, log \, n)$	$log(n) + n \, log \, n$
Entropy Level (Entropy Derived in terms of Security)	0.31	0.52	0.91

The results obtained, clearly distinguishes the various level of security provided in each mechanism.

Address generation delay: The time consumed in generating the interface ID through the CGA based address generation results in considerably very high even for smaller security parameter. The HAVEGE based address generation and MAC based stateless address autoconfiguration takes very minimal and negligible amount of time. The runtime of these algorithms are very less compared to CGA. The HAVEGE based autoconfiguration provides high level security but takes minimal address generation time.

Algorithmic Complexity: Comparing the algorithmic complexity for the various address generation mechanisms, it can be concluded that the complexity level of CGA based address generation is very high. The complexity of CGA varies with the Sec value. The complexity of HAVEGE based address generation is even less compared when compared to the Sec-0 level of CGA.

Entropy Level: The entropy level of the address autoconfigured through the MAC based method is very low (very low randomness), thus impacting security. The CGA on the other hand possesses a considerably good entropy level ensuring security, but, the mechanism using HAVEGE algorithm which ensures unpredictable random number generation offers higher degree of randomness ensuring greater security levels.

Thus HAVEGE with minimal computational complexity, negligible time delay along with higher security levels will be a reliable approach for autoconfiguration of IPv6 addresses.

6   Conclusion

The IPv6 suite provides a feature where each device can automatically generate its own addresses. This feature is achieved securely through CGA's which is a commendable feature of the SeND protocol. The CGA provides various protective mechanisms where the sender's integrity is promised without relying on any external their party. However, the CGA's proves to be complex in computations that result in higher cost of address generation. Thus various systems and manufactures refrain from using CGA's to secure their neighbor discovery. The robust mechanism using the hardware states for generating addresses has been proposed in this paper. The HAVEGE based address possesses high rate of randomness with minimized computations thus ensuring highly secure stateless address autoconfiguration process. The test results conclude that the proposed mechanism outperforms SeND. The RSA key used in SeND is again used in the proposed mechanism. The efficient key distribution mechanism can be a future work for the secured autoconfiguration schemes.

References

1. Thomson, S., Narten, T., Jinmei, T.: IPv6 Stateless Address Autoconfiguration. RFC 4862, Internet Engineering Task Force (September 2007)

2. Narten, T., Nordmark, E., Simpson, W., Soliman, H.: Neighbor Discovery for IPversion 6 (IPv6). RFC 4861, Internet Engineering Task Force (September 2007)
3. Nikander, P., Kempf, J., Nordmark, E.: IPv6 Neighbor Discovery (ND) Trust Models and Threats. RFC 3756 (Informational), Internet Engineering Task Force (May 2004)
4. Arkko, J.: Kempf, Ed., J., Zill, B., Nikander, P.: SEcure Neighbor Discovery (SEND).RFC 3971, Internet Engineering Task Force (March 2005)
5. Supriyanto, Hasbullah, I.H., Murugesan, R.K., Ramadass, S.: Survey of Internet Protocol Version 6 Link Local Communication Security Vulnerability and Mitigation Methods. IETE Technical Review 30 (2013)
6. Aura, T.: Cryptographically Generated Addresses (CGA). RFC 4982, Internet Engineering Task Force (July 2007)
7. AlSa'deh, A., Meinel, C.: Secure Neighbor Discovery: Review, Challenges, Perspectives, and Recommendations. IEEE Security & Privacy Magazine 10(4), 26–34 (2012)
8. Groat, S., Dunlop, M., Marchany, R., Tront, J.: The privacy implications of stateless IPv6 addressing. In: Proceedings of the Sixth Annual Workshop on Cyber Security and Information Intelligence Research, CSIIRW 2010, pp. 52:1–52:4. ACM, New York (2010)
9. Gelogo, Y.E., Caytiles, R.D., Park, B.: Threats and Security Analysis for Enhanced Secure Neighbor Discovery Protocol (SEND) of IPv6 NDP Security. International Journal of Control and Automation 4(4), 179–184 (2011)
10. Caicedo, C.E., Joshi, J.B.D., Tuladhar, S.R.: IPv6 Security Challenges. Computer 42(2), 36–42 (2009)
11. http://www.linux.org/ (accessed on January 2014)
12. Seznec, A., Sendrier, N.: HAVEGE: a user-level software heuristic for generating empirically strong random numbers. ACM Transaction on Modeling and Computer Simulations (TOMACS) 13(4) (October 2003)
13. Seznec, A., Sendrier, N.: HArdware Volatile Entropy Gathering and Expansion: generating unpredictable random numbers at user level, INRIA Research Report, RR-4592 (October 2002)

An Improved EMHS Algorithm
for Privacy Preserving in Association Rule
Mining on Horizontally Partitioned Database

Rachit Adhvaryu and Nikunj Domadiya

Computer Science and Engineering Department,
B.H. Gardi College of Engineering and Technology
{rvadhvaryu,domadiyanikunj002}@gmail.com

Abstract. The advances of data mining techniques played an important role in many areas for various applications. In context of privacy and security issues, the problems caused by association rule mining technique are recently investigated. The misuse of this technique may disclose the database owner's sensitive information to others. Hence, the privacy of individuals is not maintained. Many of the researchers have recently made an effort to preserve privacy of sensitive knowledge or information in a real database. In this paper, we have modified EMHS Algorithm to improve its efficiency by using Elliptic Curve Cryptography. We have used ElGamal Cryptography technique of ECC for homomorphic encryption. Analysis of the experiment on various datasets show that proposed algorithm is efficient compared to EMHS in terms of computation time.

Keywords: Data Mining, Elliptic Curve Cryptography, ElGamal Cryptography, EMHS, Privacy, Privacy Preserving Association Rule Mining.

1 Introduction

Data mining or knowledge discovery techniques such as association rule mining, classification, clustering, sequence mining, etc. have been most widely used in today's information world[1]. Successful application of these techniques has been demonstrated in many areas like marketing, medical analysis, business, Bioinformatics, product control and some other areas that benefit commercial, social and humanitarian activities. These techniques have been demonstrated in centralized as well as distributed environments. In centralized environment, all the datasets are collected at central site (data warehouse) and then mining operation is performed, as shown in Fig 1a, where in distributed environment, data may be distributed among different sites which are not allowed to send their data to find global mining result. There are two types of distributed data considered. One is horizontally partitioned data and another is vertically partitioned data. As shown in Fig 1b And Fig 1c Data are distributed among two sites which wish to find the global mining result. The horizontal partitioned data shown in Fig 1b and Fig 1c shows vertical partitioned data. In horizontal partitioned

J. Lloret Mauri et al. (Eds.): SSCC 2014, CCIS 467, pp. 272–280, 2014.

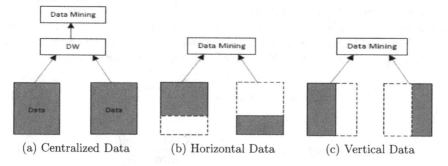

(a) Centralized Data   (b) Horizontal Data   (c) Vertical Data

Fig. 1. Different Database Environment

data, each site contains same set of attributes, but different number of transactions wherein vertical partitioned data each site contains different number of attributes but same number of transactions[1]. Recently these techniques are investigated in terms of privacy and security issues and it is concluded that these techniques threat to the privacy of individuals information. That means one (e.g. adversary or malicious user) can easily infer someone's sensitive information (or knowledge) by mining technique. So, sensitive information should be hidden in database before releasing. For distributed mining it should be protected from the involving parties (or sites) who wish to find global mining result[2]. Therefore, to preserve privacy for sensitive knowledge, privacy preserving data mining (PPDM) become a hot directive in data or knowledge engineering field.

2   Association Rule Minng

Association Rule Mining is a popular technique in data mining for discovering interesting relations between items in large databases. It is purposeful to identify strong rules discovered in the databases using different available measures. Based on the concept of strong rules, Rakesh Agrawal et al[3]. described association rules for discovering similarities between products in large-scale transaction data in supermarkets. For example, the rule (Bread, Butter) $\Rightarrow$ (Milk) found in the sales data of a shop would indicate that if a customer buys bread and butter together, he or she is likely to also buy milk. Such information can be used in decision making about marketing policies such as, e.g., product offers, product sales and discount schemes. In addition to the above mentioned example association rules are used today in many application areas including Web usage mining, Intrusion detection, Continuous production, and Bioinformatics[3]. As opposed to sequence mining, association rule learning typically does not consider the order of items either within a transaction or across transactions.

The problem of association rule mining[3] is defined as: Let I= $\{i_1, i_2, \ldots, i_n\}$ be a set of n binary attributes called items. Let D=$\{t_1, t_2, \ldots, t_m\}$ be a set of transactions called the database. Each transaction in database D has a unique transaction identity ID and contains a subset of the items in I[3]. A rule is defined as an implication of the form X ⇒ Y where X,Y is subset of I and X ∩ Y = ∅. The sets of items X and Y are called antecedent (left-hand-side or LHS) and consequent (right-hand-side or RHS) of the rule respectively. The Support and Confidence[3] of the rule X ⇒ Y is calculated using following equation:

$$Support(X \Rightarrow Y) = \frac{(X \cup Y).count}{n} \tag{1}$$

$$Confidence(X \Rightarrow Y) = \frac{(X \cup Y).count}{X.count} \tag{2}$$

The most famous application of association rules is its use for Market Basket Analysis[4]. Association Rules are helpful in many fields like Telecommunication and Medical records for retrieving some desired results. Association rules has been used in mining web server log files to discover the patterns that accesses different resources continuously or accessing particular resource at regular interval. Association rules are also useful in mining census data, text document, health insurance and catalog design[4].

3   Related Work

To understand the background of privacy preserving in association rule mining, we present different techniques and algorithm in the following subsections.

3.1   Secure Multiparty Computation with Trusted Third Party

This technique worked as a client server system where one site is a server responsible for the generating global result and all remaining sites are client sites which sends its encrypted data to the server to retrieve global result[5].

An example to SMC with trusted third party was PPDM-ARBSM algorithm[6]. This algorithm has mainly two servers: Data Mining Server and Cryptosystem Management Server[6]. A disadvantage of this algorithm was that the failure of third party fails the communication.

3.2   Secure Multiparty Computation with Semi Honest Model

This technique assumes all the sites as honest. One site acts as an initiator[7] and all others as sites. All the sites send their encrypted data to the next site in queue. Finally the last site sends all data to initiator which finds the global result[7].

An example to SMC with semi honest model was Fast Private Association Rule Mining for Securely Sharing algorithm[8]. The detailed description is mentioned in[8]. The limitation of this algorithm was the increase in computation time with the increase in the number of sites.

3.3   MHS Algorithm for Privacy Preserving on Horizontal Partitioned Database

MHS algorithm worked on minimum 3 sites. One site acts as an Initiator, one site acts as Combiner[9]. This algorithm used RSA cryptosystem. All sites find its frequent itemsets, encrypt it using RSA public key and send it to Combiner. The task of the combiner is to merge all the data with its own data and send it to the initiator. The task of the initiated was to decrypt all the data and generate global results[9]. As this algorithm was based on the concept of frequent itemsets, the limitation was the increase in computation time with the increase in the database size and number of sites.

3.4   EMHS Algorithm for Privacy Preserving Association Rule Mining on Horizontally Partitioned Database

1. Maximal Frequent Itemset: A Frequent Itemset which is not a subset of any other frequent itemset is called MFI. By using MFI, communication cost is reduced[10]. FI was replaced by MFI.
2. RSA Algorithm: One of the widely used public key cryptosystem. It is based on keeping factoring product of two large prime numbers secret. Breaking RSA encryption is tough[10]. This was used in the first phase.
3. Homomorphic Paillier Cryptosystem: Paillier cryptosystem is an additive homomorphic cryptosystem, meaning that one can compute cipher texts into a new cipher text that is encryption of sum of the messages of the original cipher texts. For E.g. Let m1, m2 be the two messages[10]. Then Encryption= E (m1+m2) =E (m1) *E (m2) and Decryption= D (E (m1) *E (m2)) =m1+m2 i.e. the sum of m1 and m2. Also, if the size of the public key is to (bit) then the size of cipher text c is 2*t (byte)[10].

EMHS algorithm was implemented in 3 phases. In the first phase, RSA cryptosystem was used. While in the second and third phase Homomorphic Paillier cryptosystem was used. The results showed better performance in the mining process as compared to other algorithms.

4   Proposed New Algorithm

4.1   Basic Concepts of New Algorithm

Suppose database D is distributed among n sites (S1,S2,..,Sn) in such a way that database Di ($1 \leq i \leq$ n) containing site Si consists of same set of attributes but different number of transactions. All sites are considered as semi honest. Now the problem is to mine valid global association rules satisfying given minimum support threshold (MST) and minimum confidence threshold (MCT) in unsecured environment, which should fulfill following privacy and security issues.

1. No any involving party should be able to know the contents of the transaction of any other involving parties.

2. Adversaries should not be able to affect the privacy and security of the information of involving parties by reading communication channel between involving parties.

4.2   Elliptic Curve Cryptography

Elliptic curve provides public cryptosystem based on the discrete logarithm problem over integer modulo a prime. Elliptic curve cryptosystem requires much shorter key length to provide a security level same as RSA with larger key length. A detailed overview of elliptic curves and an elliptic curve cryptosystem is given in[11]. We used ElGamal Cryptography[11] in our proposed algorithm. In the following, we give an overview of ElGamal cryptography.

ElGamal Cryptography

(a) A wishes to exchange message M with B.
(b) B first chooses Prime Number p, Generator g and private key x.
(c) B computes its Public Key $Y = g^x$ mod p and sends it to A.
(d) Now A chooses a random number k.
(e) A calculates one time key $K = Y^k$ mod p.
(f) A calculates C1 $= g^k$ mod p and C2 $=$ M*K mod p and sends (C1,C2) to B.
(g) Now, B calculates $K = C1^x$ mod p.
(h) B calculates $K^{-}1 =$ the Inverse of K mod p.
(i) B recovers M $= (K^{-}1$*C2) mod p.
(j) Thus, Message M is exchanged between A and B securely.

ElGamal Cryptography Example

(a) A wishes to exchange message 100 with B.
(b) B first chooses Prime Number p $= 139$, Generator g $= 3$ and private key x $= 12$.
(c) B computes its Public Key $Y = 3^{12}$ mod 139 $= 44$ and sends it to A.
(d) Now A chooses a random number k $= 52$.
(e) A calculates one time key $K = 44^{52}$ mod 139 $= 112$.
(f) A calculates C1 $= 3^{52}$ mod 139 $= 38$ and C2 $= 100$*112 mod 139 $= 80$ and sends (38,80) to B.
(g) B calculates $K = 38^{12}$ mod 139 $= 112$ (same as one time key of A)
(h) B calculates $K^{-1} = 112^{-1}$ mod 139 $= 36$
(i) B recovers M $= (36 * 80)$ mod 139 $= 100 =$ M
(j) Thus, message 100 is exchanged between A and B securely.

4.3   Proposed Communication Protocol

The proposed communication protocol is defined in Fig. 2. Suppose there are 5 sites (namely Site 1, Site 2, Site 3, Site 4, Site 5) which contains datasets D1, D2, D3, D4 and D5. Among them, there are 2 sites, namely Initiator and Combiner. All the parties are semi-honest. Suppose that they want to find the global results without revealing their information to other sites. The proposed communication protocol is same as EMHS algorithm.

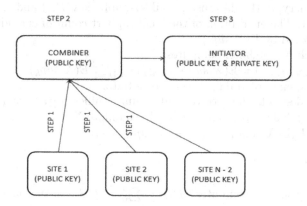

Fig. 2. Proposed Communication Protocol

We first show how to use Paillier cryptosystem to compute global support counts.

Lemma 1. *With itemset X and (n-1) sites, the global support counts can be done as follows:*

Encryption: $E(X.sup_1 + \ldots + X.sup_{n-1}) = E(X.sup_1) * \ldots * E(X.sup_{n-1})$.

Decryption: $D(E(X.sup_1) * \ldots * E(X.sup_{n-1})) = X.sup_1 + \ldots + X.sup_{n-1}$.

After decryption, the result is the sum of support counts of X at sites (n-1).

The detailed description of our proposed algorithm is as follows:

Phase 1:

1. The initiator shares ElGamal public key E_{pu} and Paillier public key P_{pu} with all the sites. It also generates Elgamal private key E_{pk} and Paillier private key P_{pk}. The keys are generated using ElGamal and Paillier Cryptography.
2. Each site computes its local MFI. Then, all the sites except Initiator and Combiner encrypts it local MFI using ElGaml public key(E_{pu}) and sends it to the Combiner.

3. The Combiner merges the received data with its own data and sends the union of all data to the Initiator.
4. Initiator decrypts the received data using ElGamal private key(E_{pk}). Then it adds its own data and computes the Global MFI. Then, final Global MFI is shared to all other sites.

Phase 2:

1. Based on global MFI, Each site finds Frequent Itemsets and its Local Support Count, encrypts the data using Paillier public key(P_{pu}) and sends it to the Combiner. The encryption of the local support count of candidate X at site S_i is denoted by $E(X.sup_i)$
2. With each X, combiner computes:
$E(X.sup_{Combiner}) = E(X.sup_{Combiner}) * \prod_{k=1}^{n-2} E(X.sup_k)$
After this, encrypted data is sent to Initiator.
3. Initiator decrypts the received data using Paillier private key(P_{pk}). It generates a global support count of each candidate X as:
$X.sup = D(E(X.sup_{Combiner})) + X.sup_{Initiator}$

Phase 3:

1. Each site together computes $\mid DB \mid = \sum_{i=1}^{n} \mid DB_i \mid$ in the same way used in phase 2.
2. Finally, Initiator generates the global association rules and sends the result to all other sites.

5   Analysis of the Proposed Algorithm

In this section, we evaluate EMHS and Proposed algorithm in terms of privacy and computation time.

5.1   Comparison in Terms of Privacy

EMHS and our Proposed algorithm both satisfies semi-honest model. The smaller key size of ECC provides equivalent security as compared to RSA. Thus the privacy remains the same in EMHS and our proposed algorithm.

5.2   Comparison in Terms of Computation Time

Both EMHS and newly Proposed Algorithm are executed with the number of sites, increasing from 3 to 7 on four real datasets: Chess[12], Connect[12], Mushroom[12], and Pumsb[12]. All these datasets have different features as explained in Table 1.

Based on the experimental results on 4 different datasets and the number of sites increasing from 3 to 7, the computation time is less as compared to EMHS algorithm. The comparison results of EMHS and Proposed Algorithm is shwon in Fig 3a, Fig 3b, Fig 3c and Fig 3d respectively.

Table 1. Detailed Description of Database[12]

DATABASE	ROWS	COLS
CHESS	3196	37
CONNECT	5000	46
MUSHROOM	8124	23
PUMSB	6000	776

5.3 Experimental Results

In implementation, each dataset is divided into 3 to 7 parts on the basis of
the records. We implemented using **Frequent Pattern Mining Framework
(FPMF)**. We have set Minimum Support Threshold(MST) = 80% and Minimum Confidence Threshold(MCT) = 40%. **CharmMFI** algorithm is used to
find local MFI at each site. **Eclat Algorithm** is used to find local frequent
itemsets from the global itemsets at each site in the proposed algorithm.

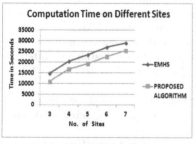

(a) CHESS Database

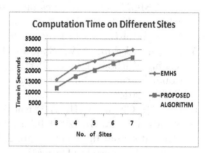

(b) CONNECT Database

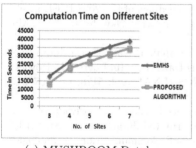

(c) MUSHROOM Database

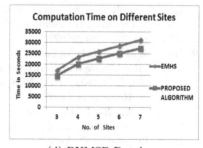

(d) PUMSB Database

Fig. 3. Comparison on Different Databases

6   Conclusion

In this paper, we proposed an algorithm to improve privacy and performance of
EMHS when increasing the number of sites. We maintain the model of EMHS

and apply ElGamal Cryptography in the first phase and Paillier cryptosystem in the second phase.

From the experimental results we conclude that the proposed algorithm has better performance than EMHS in dense datasets when increasing the number of sites. In future, we will try to solve the problem of collusion between Initiator and Combiner.

References

1. Atallah, M., Elmagarmid, A., Ibrahim, M., Bertino, E., Verykios, V.: Disclosure limitation of sensitive rules. In: Proceedings of the 1999 Workshop on Knowledge and Data Engineering Exchange, KDEX 1999, pp. 45–52. IEEE Computer Society, Washington, DC (1999)
2. Clifton, C., Kantarcioglu, M., Vaidya, J.: Defining privacy for data mining. In: National Science Foundation Workshop on Next Generation Data Mining, pp. 126–133 (2002)
3. Agrawal, R., Srikant, R.: Privacy-preserving data mining. In: Proceedings of the ACM SIGMOD Conference on Management of Data, pp. 439–450 (2000)
4. Verykios, V.S., Bertino, E., Fovino, I.N., Provenza, L.P., Saygin, Y., Theodoridis, Y.: State-of-the-art in Privacy Preserving Data Mining (March 2004)
5. Muthu Lakshmi, N.V., Sandhya Rani, K.: Privacy Preserving Association Rule Mining Without Trusted Party For Horizontally Partitioned Databases. International Journal of Data Mining and Knowledge Management Process (IJDKP) 2(2) (March 2012)
6. Gui, Q., Cheng, X.-H.: A Privacy-Preserving Distributed Method for Mining Association Rules. In: 2009 International Conference on Artificial Intelligence and Computational Intelligence, pp. 294–297 (2009)
7. Han, J., Kamber, M.: Data Mining: Concepts and Techniques, pp. 227–245. Morgan Kaufmann Publishers Inc., San Francisco (2001)
8. Estivill-Castro, V., Hajyasien, A.: Fast Private Association Rule Mining by a Protocol Securely Sharing Distributed Data. In: Proceedings of the 2007 IEEE Intelligence and Security Informatics (ISI 2007), New Brunswick, New Jersey, USA, May 23-24, pp. 324–330 (2007)
9. Hussein, M., El-Sisi, A., Ismail, N.: Fast Cryptographic Privacy Preserving Association Rules Mining on Distributed Homogenous Data Base. In: Lovrek, I., Howlett, R.J., Jain, L.C. (eds.) KES 2008, Part II. LNCS (LNAI), vol. 5178, pp. 607–616. Springer, Heidelberg (2008)
10. Xuan, C.N., Hoai, B.L., Tung, A.C.: An enhanced scheme for privacy preserving association rules mining on horizontally distributed databases. In: 2012 IEEE RIVF International Conference on Computing and Communication Technologies, Research, Innovation, and Vision for the Future (RIVF), pp. 1–4 (2012)
11. Stallings, W.: Cryptography and Network Security, 5th edn. (2011)
12. http://fimi.ua.ac.be/data/

Secure Communication
Using Four-Wing Hyper-Chaotic Attractor

Arti Dwivedi[1,*], Ashok Kumar Mittal[1,2], and Suneet Dwivedi[2]

[1] Physics Department, University of Allahabad, Allahabad, UP, India – 211002
[2] K Banerjee Centre of Atmospheric and Ocean Studies,
University of Allahabad, Allahabad, UP, India – 211002
arti2dwivedi@gmail.com

Abstract. It is shown how a four-wing hyper-chaotic attractor can be used for secure communication using parameter convergence. Using some variables for complete replacement and some for feedback control and unknown parameter adaptation, two hyper-chaotic attractors are synchronized in a time less than the time scale of their chaotic oscillations. This synchronization is used for and secure communication of digital messages. The coding parameter of the transmitting system changes so rapidly that an intruder cannot infer any information about the attractors corresponding to the two coding parameters. The scheme presented in this paper is more secure as compared to other similar schemes. This is demonstrated by comparison with an existing scheme based on parameter adaptation and Lyapunov stability theory.

Keywords: Synchronization, Hyper-chaotic systems, Parameter Adaptation, Chaos shift keying, Secure Communication.

1   Introduction

Chaos synchronization was first proposed by Pecora and Carroll [1-2] in 1990. The Communication by synchronized chaotic circuits was demonstrated by Cuomo and Oppenheim [3], Kocarev and Parlitz [4].The secret message is encoded in the chaotic variables of the transmitter system and transmitted to the receiver system. As the transmitted signal is chaotic it is difficult to extract the message from this irregular signal by any third party. Only the bona-fide recipient, who has enough knowledge about the transmitter system, can achieve synchronization and thereby decode the hidden message.

A widely used scheme proposed for communication of binary messages using chaotic carrier is Chaos-Shift Keying (CSK) [4-6]. In this scheme the two distinct symbols '0' and '1' of the binary message are coded in the form of two distinct values p_0 and p_1 of a parameter of the transmitter system. To transmit the bit '0' ('1') the parameter value of the transmitter is held constant at p_0 (p_1) for time T_d , called the

---

* Corresponding author.

J. Lloret Mauri et al. (Eds.): SSCC 2014, CCIS 467, pp. 281–290, 2014.

bit-duration or parameter switching time. A signal based on the chaotic variables of the transmitter drives an identical receiver system. The parameter of the receiver system remains fixed at the value p_0. If the parameters of the two systems are identical, they synchronize; if they are different, synchronization does not take place. Thus the receiver can infer which bit was transferred by observing whether the two systems synchronized or not in time T_d.

Later parameter adaptation schemes were proposed. In these schemes the parameter of the receiver, instead of remaining fixed, was allowed to evolve at a rate dependent on the synchronization error. This allowed the receiver parameter to synchronize with the transmitter parameter. In this way it is possible for the receiver to decode the message coded in the transmitter parameter.

In this paper, we combine the techniques of complete replacement [1-2,7], feedback control and parameter adaptation [8-11] for achieving very rapid synchronization of two identical modified four-wing chaotic attractors [12] in a time less than the average time period of chaotic oscillations. Due to lower switching time, this scheme provides not only faster but also more secure communication. As the bit duration time is smaller than the typical chaotic oscillation time, an intruder cannot collect enough information about the attractor to decode any bit.

In section 2, we show how the transmitter and receiver systems can be synchronized rapidly, in a time smaller than the chaotic oscillation time-scale of the transmitter, by combining the techniques of complete replacement, feedback control and parameter adaptation. In section 3, we show how a digital message can be coded at the transmitting end and decoded at the receiving end. In section 4, we explore the effect of noise and time delay. In section 5, we present a security analysis Section 6 provides comparison with an existing scheme. In section 7 the potential advantage of our scheme for secure transmission of images is discussed. Conclusions are summarized in section 8.

2   Parameter Adaptation Using Complete Replacement

Master-slave systems consist of two chaotic systems, in which the master system evolves independently, whereas the slave system is driven by a signal from the master system. The two systems are described by same set of differential equations with same set of parameter values, but the initial conditions may be different. The complete replacement technique [7] of Pecora and Carroll (PC) [1-2] is illustrated in Fig. 1. The master system is decomposed into subsystems u and v, governed by the equations: $\dot{u} = f(u,v)$ and $\dot{v} = g(u,v)$. The variables of the subsystem u drive the slave subsystem: $\dot{v}' = g(u,v')$. The master and slave systems synchronize if all the conditional Lyapunov exponents of the slave subsystem v' are negative.

In [1], the Lorenz system with parameters $\sigma = 10$, $b = 8/3$, $r = 60$ was taken as the master system. It was found that all the conditional Lyapunov exponents were negative for two choices of the slave v system: (i) $v = \{y, z\}$ and (ii) $v = \{x, z\}$.

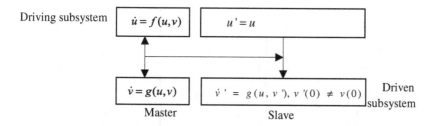

Driving subsystem

$\dot{u} = f(u,v)$ $u' = u$

$\dot{v} = g(u,v)$ $\dot{v}' = g(u, v'), v'(0) \neq v(0)$ Driven subsystem

Master   Slave

Fig. 1. PC master-slave system divided into two subsystems

We consider as the master system, a modified hyper-chaotic four-wing system [12] where F is a constant and parameters are chosen as $a = 4$, $b = 6$, $c = 10$, $d = 5$, $e = 0.5$. This system is hyper-chaotic with Lyapunov exponents 0.891, 0.148, 0, -12.024 respectively. All the four variables are transmitted; the variables x and w are used for driving the slave system by complete replacement, whereas the variables y and z are used for providing feedback control and parameter adaptation. Thus the master and slave systems are governed by equation (1) and (2) respectively

$$\dot{x} = ax - byz, \; \dot{y} = -cy + xz - w + F, \; \dot{z} = x + xy - dz, \; \dot{w} = y - exy \quad (1)$$

$$\dot{y}' = -cy' + xz' - w + F' + u_1, \dot{z}' = x + xy' - dz' + u_2 \quad (2)$$

where u_1, u_2 are the feedback controllers. Our design goal is to choose these controllers and a parameter adaptation law for F' in such a way that the synchronization error evolution equations becomes linear with time independent coefficients.

$$u_1 = -xe_z - k_1 e_y + ce_y - k_2 e_z, \; u_2 = -xe_y + k_3 e_y + de_z - k_4 e_z, \; \dot{F}' = -se_z (3)$$

Here $k_1=9$, $k_2=1.99$, $k_3=1400$, $k_4=96$, $s=30$ and e_x, e_y, e_z denote the synchronization error between master and slave variables. Combining equations (1), (2) and (3) we get

$$\dot{e}_z = -k_1 e_y - k_2 e_z + e_F, \; \dot{e}_w = k_3 e_y - k_4 e_z, \; \dot{e}_F = -se_z \quad (4)$$

where $e_y = y' - y$, $e_z = z' - z$, $e_F = F' - F$

Equation(4) are linear equations with constant coefficients, the matrix of coefficients having large negative eigenvalues: -40, -35, -30. Hence the errors vanish smoothly and rapidly.

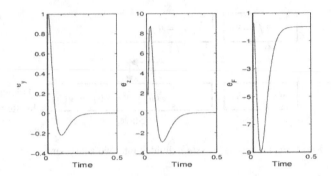

Fig. 2. Synchronization error as a function of time for the augmented error system governed by equation (5)

Fig. 2. shows that response system synchronizes with the drive system and parameter F' converges rapidly to F in a time as small as 0.3. In this simulation the parameter F of the drive system was taken as 1 and the initial conditions $(x, y, z, w, y', z' F')$ were chosen as $(0, 1, 1.2, 2, 2, 3, 1.3)$.

3   Secure Communication Using Parameter Adaptation

This convergence can be used for coding a binary message by making the parameter F a piecewise constant function of time. If C denotes the bits '0' or '1', corresponding to the bit C, the value of F is taken to be $F_C = (0.5C + 1)$. The transmitter system remains chaotic for this range of F. In order to communicate the bit C, F is held at a constant value Fc for a time T_d.

The synchronization time scale T_s, which is governed by the eigenvalues of (4), is independent of the oscillation time scale T_c of the chaotic drive system. Therefore T_s can be made much less than T_c by appropriate choice of parameters. It is possible to choose the parameter switching time T_d to lie between these two values so as to achieve two objectives: (i) the receiver parameter can synchronize with the transmitter parameter before it is switched to a new value and (ii) the parameter switching is so rapid that an intruder cannot decode the message by identifying any property of the different attractors, for example by using a return map technique [13].

Since the switching time T_d is greater than the synchronization time T_s, the value of F' will converge sufficiently close to F_c so that the binary symbol of the message can be deciphered. After the switching time interval T_d the value of F is changed to a value corresponding to the next bit in the message. In this way the receiver can decipher the nth bit by determining the integer nearest to $C_n = (F'_n - 1)/0.5$, where F'_n is the value of F' at time nT_d.

Large initial error in the variable z causes a large and rapid overshoot in F'. To overcome this problem, the operation of the adaptation law is suspended for time T_d before transmission of the message. During this period the value of F is kept constant at a pre-decided value known to the receiver. For this duration, the parameter F' of the response system is also kept constant. This leads to a reduction in the synchronization error of the z variable at time $t = 0$ when the transmission of the message is started. Fig.3. shows how the receiver can recover the message by observing F' at integral multiples of the switching time T_d. The horizontal line before the time $t = 0$ corresponds to the pre-agreed value $F = F' = 1$ to prevent overshooting as explained earlier.

Fig. 3. shows that the receiver message converges rapidly and smoothly to a value very close to the transmitter value. This rapid and smooth convergence will not, in general, be possible for nonlinear parameter modulation, as that would make the coefficients of the augmented error equations depend on the chaotic variables. This in turn would make the synchronization time more than the chaotic oscillation time, limiting the speed and reducing the security. Fig. 3. shows that if the error equations are linear with constant coefficients, a switching time as small as 0.3 can be used for communicating a binary message. The switching time is less than the average chaotic oscillation time (about 0.8). Therefore, each instance of a bit presents only a small fragment of the attractor corresponding to the parameter, which represents the bit.

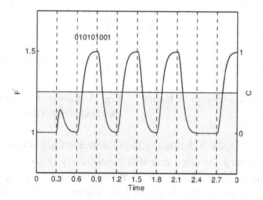

Fig. 3. Recovery of the binary message {010101001} at the receiving end from the values of the receiver parameter F' observed at integral multiples of the switching time

Different occurrences of the same bit will present different portions of the attractor. Because of smooth convergence of the unknown parameter, the method can be easily extended to communication of digital messages composed of more than two symbols. This will make it even more difficult for an intruder to identify the different attractors.

4   Effect of Noise and Time Delay

In the real world all the variables transmitted through the communication channel get distorted due to the presence of noise. In conventional communication it is easy to filter the noise because the signal occupies a narrow band. The problem of noise is a bigger challenge for chaotic communication. It is therefore necessary to investigate the effect of noise in the proposed scheme.

For low intensity noise below the threshold value of 0.01 it is still possible to decode the system as is evident from Fig. 4. For larger noise, it is necessary to use de-noising (or filtering) schemes [14-20].

In most of the proposed schemes the recipient makes use of the transmitted master variables and the slave variables that correspond to the same time. Due to time delay the observed synchronization error will be

$$e_y = y_R(t) - y_T(t-\tau) \quad , \quad e_z = z_R(t) - z_T(t-\tau) \tag{6}$$

where τ is identical channel delay in all the variables.

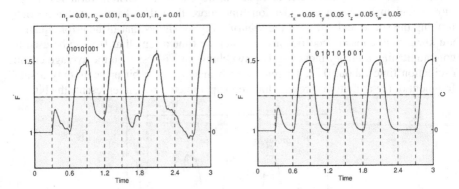

Fig. 4. Effect of noise on recovery of binary message {010101001}

Fig. 5. Recovery of binary message with identical channel delay $\tau = 0.05$

It can be seen from figure 5 that using the communication scheme proposed in this paper an error free binary message can still be correctly decoded if all the variables suffer the same time-delay. However, synchronization is destroyed and binary message decoding becomes difficult if different channels suffer different time delays. But this problem can be overcome by increasing the separation level between the parameter values used for coding and also, if needed, by increasing the switching time. Another way to overcome this problem is to transmit three variables corresponding to same time sequentially using a single channel, which are then deciphered at the receiving end to be treated as having arrived simultaneously.

5   Security Issues

In conventional communication, a sinusoidal carrier is used so that the transmitted power is concentrated in a narrow band. An intruder can easily detect and intercept such signals and decode the message because the carrier profile is quite simple.

Chaos based communication systems offer a potential solution to this problem. When chaotic variables are used as carriers, the signal is broad-band and noise-like so it is difficult for an intruder to detect the signal.

In conventional communication the problem of narrow band concentration of power is solved by using spread spectrum techniques. These techniques require complex circuitry. In contrast, chaotic signals require simple circuitry and therefore provide a potentially cost-effective solution.

However, several cryptanalysis techniques were soon proposed demonstrating the vulnerability of chaotic schemes. These techniques relied on identifying properties that could be used for making distinctions between the different attractors for the different parameter values used for encryption.

But such cryptanalytic techniques cannot be used against our scheme because of rapid parameter switching. As the coefficients of the synchronization error equations are linear with time independent coefficients, the synchronization time can easily be made much smaller than the chaotic oscillation time. This greatly enhances the security of the transmission because the chaotic system switches from one attractor to another much before it traverses a significant part of any attractor. As a consequence any cryptanalytic technique based on distinguishing the attractors corresponding to different parameters will fail. We demonstrate this by showing that an intruder cannot decode the message by applying cryptanalysis techniques like power analysis [21] or return maps [13].

An intruder who intercepts the transmitted signal x in our scheme, and tries to apply the power analysis technique [21], will obtain Fig. 6. after filtering the squared signal. It is evident from the figure that there is no pattern which can help distinguish the bits 0 and 1 of the signal.

An intruder, who uses the return map technique [13] will obtain Fig. 7. and fail to discover any property that can be used to decipher the message. Because of rapid switching between the parameters, most of the points on this map are obtained from values of successive maxima and minima that correspond to different parameter values. Hence they do not reflect any property of either of the parameter values.

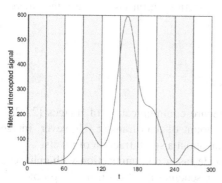

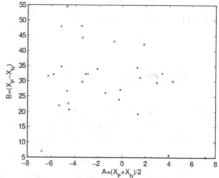

Fig. 6. Power analysis [21] fails to reveal any pattern to distinguish bits 0 (grey) and 1 (white)

Fig. 7. Return map for transmitter with bit duration time 0.3 helps distinguish between the two bits

6   Comparison with an Existing Scheme

In this section we demonstrate the advantages of our scheme by comparing it with an existing [9] parameter adaptation scheme based on the Lyapunov stability method. In this reference a binary message was communicated using Lorenz systems at the transmitter and receiver ends with a bit duration time of 5.0 while the typical oscillation time of the transmitter system is about 0.65. We have argued above that for secure communication it is desirable to have the bit duration time much smaller than the typical oscillation time. However, in this scheme it is not possible to reduce the bit duration time significantly without causing decoding errors. Even for a bit duration time as large as 1.0 the message is not decoded correctly as is evident from Fig. 8.

The return map for the scheme of reference [9] as obtained by the technique of reference [13] is shown in Fig. 9. This clearly shows that the points of the return map fall on two quasi-distinct branches corresponding to the two parameter values used for coding. Thus the return map can be used to decode the message.

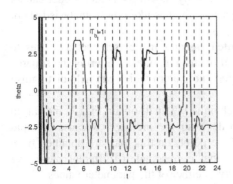

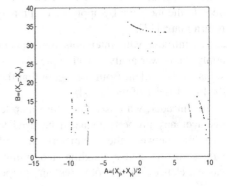

Fig. 8. The scheme of reference [9] will incorrectly decode the binary message {0000110010100011100100000}

Fig. 9. Return map for scheme [9] reveals a pattern to distinguish between the different bits

7   Secure Transmission of Images

Chaotic systems have also been used for secure communication of images [22-25]. Transmission of an image entails a large amount of data transfer. However, image transmission can tolerate errors in information about a small fraction of pixels.

We have seen that our approach can provide faster communication with enhanced security. But like other chaotic communication schemes it suffers from the problem of errors due to noise. This suggests that our approach can be very useful for secure transmission of images.

8   Conclusions

We have proposed a faster and more secure communication scheme based on complete replacement, feedback control, and parameter adaptation. In this scheme a binary message is communicated by switching a forcing parameter of a four-wing hyper-chaotic system. This scheme enables correct decoding of a message even with the parameter switching time much smaller than the average chaotic oscillation time, leading to faster and more secure communication. The scheme is also robust against small noise and time-delay in the transmission channel.

Because of rapid and smooth convergence, closer values of parameters can be used for coding. This will allow use of several symbols for coding messages, further increasing the speed of communication as well as security.

Acknowledgments. AD thanks CSIR(SRF) for providing fellowship. AKM and SD thank DST/MOES/ISRO/CSIR for financial assistance in the form of research project.

References

1. Pecora, L.M., Carroll, T.L.: Synchronization in chaotic systems. Phys. Rev. Lett. 64, 821–825 (1990)
2. Pecora, L.M., Carroll, T.L.: Driving systems with chaotic signals. Phys. Rev. A. 44, 2374–2384 (1991)
3. Cuomo, K.M., Oppenheim, A.V.: Circuit implementation of synchronized chaos with applications to communications. Phys. Rev. Lett. 71, 65–68 (1993)
4. Kocarev, L., Parlitz, U.: General approach for chaotic synchronization with applications to communication. Phys. Rev. Lett. 74, 5028–5031 (1995)
5. Kennedy, M.P., Kolumban, G.: Digital communication using chaos. Signal Processing 80, 1307–1320 (2000)
6. Dedieu, H., Kennedy, M.P., Hasler, M.: Chaos Shift Keying: Modulation and Demodulation of chaotic carrier using self-synchronizing Chua's circuit. IEEE Transaction on Circuit and System-II Analog and Digital Signal Processing 40, 634–642 (1993)
7. Pecora, L.M., Carroll, T.L., Johnson, G.A., Mar, D.J., Heagy, J.F.: Fundamentals of synchronization in chaotic systems, concepts and applications. Chaos 7, 520–543 (1997)
8. Dwivedi, A., Mittal, A.K., Dwivedi, S.: Adaptive synchronization of diffusionless Lorenz systems and secure communication of digital signals by parameter modulation. IET Communications 6, 2016–2026 (2012)
9. Feki, M.: An adaptive chaos synchronization scheme applied to secure communication. Chaos, Solitons and Fractals 18, 141–148 (2003)
10. Adloo, H., Roopaei, M.: Review article on adaptive synchronization of chaotic systems with unknown parameters. Nonlinear Dyn. 65, 141–159 (2011)
11. Chen, S., Lu, J.: Synchronization of uncertain unified chaotic system via adaptive control. Chaos, Solitons and Fractals 14, 643–647 (2002)
12. Dong, E., Chen, Z., Yuan, Z., Chen, Z.: A New Four-wing Hyper-chaotic Attractor and Its Circuit Implementation. In: International Workshop on Chaos-Fractal Theory and its Applications (2010)
13. Perez, G., Cerdeira, H.A.: Extracting messages masked by chaos. Phys. Rev. Lett. 74, 1970–1973 (1995)

14. Jovic, B., Unsworth, C.P., Berber, S.M.: De-noising Initial Condition Modulation Wideband Chaotic Communication Systems with Linear & Wavelet Filters. In: Proceedings of the First IEEE International Conference on Wireless Broadband and Ultra Wideband Communications (Aus Wireless 2006), Sydney, Australia, pp. 1–6 (2006)
15. Grzesiak, M.: Wavelet filtering of chaotic data. Nonlinear Processes in Geophysics 7, 111–116 (2000)
16. Broomhead, D., Huke, J., Muldoon, M.: Linear Filters and Nonlinear Systems. Journal of the Royal Statistical Society 54, 373–382 (1992)
17. Roy, M., Kumar, V., Kulkarni, B., Sanderson, J., Rhodes, M., Stappen, M.: Simple denoising algorithm using wavelet transform. AIChE Journal 45, 2461–2466 (1999)
18. Constantine, W., Reinhall, P.: Wavelet-based in-band denoising technique for chaotic sequences. International Journal of Bifurcation and Chaos 11, 483–495 (2000)
19. Boccalleti, S., Guiaquinta, A., Arecchi, F.: Adaptive recognition and filtering of noise using wavelets. Physical Review E 55, 5393–5397 (1997)
20. Carroll, T.L.: Approximating chaotic time series through unstable periodic orbits. Physical Review E 59, 1615–1621 (1999)
21. Alvarez, G., Montoya, F., Romera, M., Pastor, G.: Breaking parameter modulated chaotic secure communication system. Chaos, Solitons and Fractals 21, 783–787 (2004)
22. Yin, P., Min, L., Li, P.: A text encryption scheme based generalized discrete chaos synchronization for image communication. In: International Conference on Environmental Engineering and Technology. Advances in Biomedical Engineering, vol. 8, pp. 310–316 (2012)
23. Yau, H.-T., Pu, Y.-C., Li, S.-C.: Application of chaotic synchronization system to secure communication. Information Technology and Control 41, 274–282 (2012)
24. Huang, C.K., Liao, C.W., Hsu, S.L., Jeng, Y.C.: Implementation of gray image encryption with pixel shuffling and gray-level encryption by single chaotic system. Telecommunication Syst., 1–9 (2011)
25. Sengodan, V., Balamurugan, A.: Efficient signal encryption using chaos based system. International Journal of Electronics Engineering 2, 335–338 (2010)

DDoS Detection System Using Wavelet Features and Semi-supervised Learning[*]

V. Srihari and R. Anitha

Dept. of Applied Mathematics and Computational Sciences
PSG College of Technology, Coimbatore, India
srihari.sse@gmail.com, anitha_nadarajan@mail.psgtech.ac.in

Abstract. Protection of critical information infrastructure is a major task for the network security experts in any part of the globe. There are certain threats that will never evade away despite sophisticated advancements in defense strategy. Among them, Distributed Denial of Service (DDoS) attacks have witnessed continual growth in scale, frequency and intensity. The impact of DDoS attacks can be devastating such that it creates severe ripples to the cyberworld. Nowadays, attackers are advancing towards different variants of DDoS attacks to escape from the detection mechanisms. In this paper, a new DDoS Detection system is proposed. Initially, wavelet based features are extracted and classified using semi-supervised learning to detect the DDoS attacks. Different wavelet families are studied and the combination of them seems to be robust and efficient and hence used as features. Machine learning algorithms are highly appreciated in many classification problems. There is a considerable demand for labeled dataset and hence to bridge the gap between them and unlabeled dataset, semi-supervised learning algorithm is employed to classify the attack from normal traffic. Extensive analysis is performed by conducting experiments and by using real-time dataset. Results obtained are convincing and hence can be modeled for real-time approach.

Keywords: Distributed Denial of Service attacks, Wavelets, Semi-Supervised learning, Tri-training.

1   Introduction

In the era of global connectivity, the usage of internet has become a prosaic task of everybody's life. Advancement in internet and associated technologies are always disrupted by the dark centric elements that almost look opaque to the user. These elemental threats convey severe loss to the corporate and social world. Among those threats, Distributed Denial of Service (DDoS) attacks stand ahead of others due to its impact and circumvention. Initially, flooding was done with a single machine (DoS attack) to stop the service provided to a legitimate user. In case of DDoS attack,

---

[*] This work is funded by Department of Atomic Energy, India through Society for Electronic Transactions and Security (SETS), Chennai, India.

J. Lloret Mauri et al. (Eds.): SSCC 2014, CCIS 467, pp. 291–303, 2014.
© Springer-Verlag Berlin Heidelberg 2014

attacker gains control of vulnerable machines and utilize them as agents (*bots*) to flood the target machine. Since the source IP addresses are geographically distributed, detection of DDoS attacks is a very challenging task. Attacker can perform various flooding attacks based on the protocols such as UDP flood, SYN flood, ICMP flood, HTTP flood and FTP flood. IP spoofing also performs simple DDoS attack by forging the fields of incoming packets to conceal the identity of the user.

In spite of the expertise and acumen of security experts and researchers, DDoS attacks continue to evolve threatening the cyberworld. Arbor Networks, DDoS solution provider [1] analyzed network traffic collected from more than 270 service providers and estimated that 54% of DDoS attacks are over 1 Gb/sec. This signifies the global threat of DDoS attack with steady increase every year. The statistics also indicate that the attack reached the peak at 191 Gbps. Couple of years back, South Korean government faced a massive and technically well advanced DDoS attack [2]. Entire architecture followed two-tier C&C servers to enhance the scalability and resiliency and the communication between the bots and C&C server used multiple encryption ciphers to thwart reverse engineering. Understanding the growing threat and sophisticated complexity of DDoS attacks, RioRey [3] has written the taxonomy of 25 different attack vectors of DDoS attacks. Based on the proposed attack vectors and to countenance the DDoS attack challenge, a robust and vibrant DDoS detection and defense mechanisms are needed. This paper proposes an efficient detection technique based on wavelet transform based features.

Some of the major characteristics of network traffic are self-similarity, long range dependence and multifractality. Wavelet analysis is well suited to study the network traffic since they decompose the signal into both time and frequency domains with variable window sizes. In our work, three different wavelet families (Daubechies, Symlets and Coiflets) are applied to make the system robust and efficient.

In reality, there is a vast availability of unlabeled data and a limited availability of labeled data related to DDoS. Hence, cost-expensiveness and low detection rates are associated with supervised and unsupervised learning respectively. Semi-supervised learning provides reasonable justice and trade-off between the above mentioned classifiers such that unlabeled data can be labeled with the limited set of labeled data related to DDoS. The choice of algorithm depends on the compatibility with the proposed architecture. Tri-training [4] uses three independent algorithms: two for classifying the unlabeled data and based on their agreement, the newly labeled data is added to the trained model of third classifier. Hence tri-training enhances the accuracy of classification and surmounts the cost expensiveness of labeled dataset. Thus the detection model is built based on the wavelet families as features and semi-supervised based tri-training as classification algorithm.

The major contributions are summarized as follows:

- Extraction of three different wavelet families i.e Daubechies, Symlets and Coiflets to form a feature set. Scrutinized study is made on the orders of the wavelets and decided ones are db4, sym2 and coif3. To the best of our knowledge, this combination of wavelets provides efficient detection.
- The application of tri-training based semi-supervised learning to classify the data as normal or attack data. Semi-supervised learning provides realistic approach to the problem since it uses both labeled and unlabeled data and hence offers accuracy and reduces cost-expensiveness.

- Extensive study on both normal and attack dataset to evaluate the performance of the system. The focus is also on the emerging attack vectors that challenges the capability of the existing systems.

The paper is organized as follows: Related work concerned to the proposed DDoS detection scheme and the state-of-the-art defense mechanisms are briefed in section 2. Section 3 describes the proposed detection framework with the description of functionalities of each block. Section 4 explains the dataset generated and collected to conduct experiments. Section 5 illustrates the performance evaluation of the proposed system and comparison with some of the existing schemes. Section 6 concludes the overall work.

2   Related Work

DDoS Detection system is a highly acclaimed area in the research community. Application of wavelet for the detection of DDoS attacks has brought significant attention to many people. REN et al. [5] proposed DDoS detection system based on the self-similarity of network traffic. This paper is considered to be one of the pioneering work using wavelets for DDoS detection. Daubechies family of wavelets is used and the mechanism is limited to off-line mode of attacks. Lu and Ghorbani [6] proposed anomaly detection model by extracting features based on traffic flow and then applied Discrete Wavelet Transform (DWT). The major advantages of these methods are full usage of DARPA dataset in terms of network perspective and achieved noteworthy accuracy for the same.

Palmieri et al. [7] proposed a solution for card-sharing traffic, by decomposing the traffic signal and performing wavelet analysis. The proposed system performed the tasks based on the multi-resolution analysis of Daubechies wavelets. Considering the fact that the combination of wavelets and SVM is highly successful in generic detection problem approach, YANG and WANG [8] framed the model to detect DDoS attacks. They fine tuned the model by adding wavelet kernel in support vector machine (WSVM). Also, authors adopted Morlet and Mexico hat wavelet functions to design WSVM. KDDCUP99 dataset was used for experiments and the system could able to achieve an accuracy of about 95% which is better than the conventional SVM.

Since there is a continual revision of DDoS attacks to hide from the radar, the focus of literature survey is on the recent DDoS defense systems. Agrawal et al. [9], Subbulakshmi et al. [10] and Ramamoorthi et al. [11] addressed the usage of SVM and enhanced SVM to classify DDoS attack from normal traffic. Rahmani et al. [12] described the DDoS detection mechanism based on divergence technique namely F-divergence. Also, Rahmani et al. [12] stated certain pragmatic constraints to verify the real-time congestion traffic.

One of the pragmatic issues with machine learning algorithms is the unavailability of labeled real-time dataset and if so they are fairly expensive [13-14]. This raises ambiguity about the performance of supervised learning, since it requires a sufficient amount of labeled data to train the classifier. In case of unsupervised learning, large number of uncertainty is associated to model the dataset. Semi-supervised training provides reasonable trade-off between the two such that it uses both labeled and unlabeled data to model the classifier. Chapelle et al. [15] have organized semi-supervised learning algorithms into four classes based on functionality: Generative models, Graph-based models, Low density separation and Change of representation.

Zhou and Li [4] proposed new tri-training approach based on co-training method representing the change of representation class. Henceforth in the first phase of the proposed mechanism, we use three classifiers: two to classify unlabeled dataset from the labeled dataset separately and based on their agreement, third classifier is used to classify the provided data using the previously obtained trained model.

3   Proposed Detection Model

Fig.1 depicts the proposed detection system to defend DDoS attacks. Wavelet families are used as feature set and modeled with tri-training based semi-supervised learning. In tri-training, Naïve Bayes (NB) and Decision Tree (DT) are used to classify unlabeled entities and based on their agreement, they are provided as trained model to Support Vector Machine (SVM).

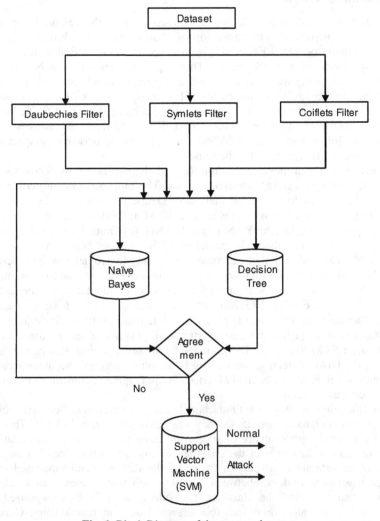

Fig. 1. Block Diagram of the proposed system

3.1   Feature Extraction

Application of wavelets to identify DDoS attack from the normal traffic is governed by the following factors.

Self-similarity [16] is considered to be one of the predominant characteristics exhibited by normal traffic of network. Self-similarity denotes the scale invariance property i.e., any attribute displays similar behavior when observed at any scale (usually time). Logics behind self-similarity in network traffic are governed by three factors: network infrastructure and protocols associated with them, nature of communication between network entities and user behavior. There are some tools and techniques to generate self-similar DDoS traffic but still state-of-the-art research work can detect even minute intricate difference between self-similar normal traffic and self-similar DDoS attack. Self-similarity in network traffic can be captured by almost all of the wavelet families by performing wavelet decomposition

Multi-resolution analysis aids wavelets to decompose the signals with respect to the provided scaling function. In the scenario of DDoS attacks, certain low-level DoS (LDoS) attacks are completely invisible in large scale analysis. By applying multi-resolution, frequency bands are divided into sub-levels and hence can detect stealth or spiked LDoS attacks.

The above mentioned characteristics of wavelets are available in the wavelet families discussed below and hence used in the detection scheme. Apart from that there are certain specific features of these wavelets that suit the detection model.

Daubechies wavelets generally provide compact support, orthonormalitiy and sharp filter transition bands. Apart from that, time invariance, faster computation and good classification accuracy [17] are suited for robust and dynamic DDoS attacks.

Symlets are very much similar to that Daubechies but are more symmetric and hence applied in multipath channel parameter estimation techniques. Also the major characteristics of Symlets such as variation trend estimation of signal and exceptional signal detection [18] can be used as effective feature for the proposed problem.

Coiflets have symmetric scaling functions which exhibit interpolating characteristics and hence produce good approximation even at different resolutions [19]. These attributes influenced to use Coiflets for the detection scheme.

Wavelet features. In general, low-dimensional decomposition and reconstruction and high-dimensional decomposition and reconstruction detail coefficients are applied and coefficients along the horizontal, vertical and diagonal are extracted. Now the sum and average of horizontal and vertical coefficients are retrieved and used as wavelet features. Extensive analysis is made on the orders of wavelets with respect to robustness, running time and efficiency of the system.

Order of Daubechies wavelet used is db4 and Dh_{sum} and Dh_{avg} represent the sum and average among the horizontal coefficients and Dv_{sum} and Dv_{avg} represent the sum and average among the vertical coefficients.

$$D = \{Dh_{sum}, Dh_{avg}, Dv_{sum}, Dv_{avg}\} \tag{1}$$

Order of Symlets wavelet used is sym2 and Sh_{sum} and Sh_{avg} represent the sum and average among the horizontal coefficients respectively and Sv_{sum} and Sv_{avg} represent the sum and average among the vertical coefficients respectively.

$$S = \{Sh_{sum}, Sh_{avg}, Sv_{sum}, Sv_{avg}\} \tag{2}$$

Order of Coiflets wavelet used is coif3 and Ch_{sum} and Ch_{avg} represent the sum and average among the horizontal coefficients respectively and Cv_{sum} and Cv_{avg} represent the sum and average among the vertical coefficients respectively.

$$C = \{Ch_{sum}, Ch_{avg}, Cv_{sum}, Cv_{avg}\} \tag{3}$$

Combined Wavelet Feature Set (WFS) for the detection method is

$$WFS = D \cup S \cup C \tag{4}$$

3.2   Semi-Supervised Learning

Learning based algorithms are continually striving to benchmark their application in network security as they provide sensible justice to discriminate the attack traffic from normal traffic. The traditional approaches used in learning are supervised and unsupervised learning. Nowadays, semi- supervised learning is becoming a highly pertinent area as they provide reasonable trade-off between supervised and unsupervised learning. Also in reality, there exists limited labeled data and abundant unlabeled data. As the name implies, semi-supervised learning has the advantage of using both the large amount of unlabeled data and small amount of labeled data. Based on the analyzed network traffic and efficient way to handle the robust wavelet features, semi-supervised learning is applied in the proposed work.

Tri-Training. Tri-training is a modified version of co-training algorithm. In case of co-training, the system is trained with two different classifiers with labeled data on two independent set of attributes. Then each classifier classifies the unlabeled data and the obtained labels of examples are used to augment the training set of another. The main disadvantages of co-training are time consumption to cross validate and to produce final hypothesis.

To overcome the pitfalls of co-training learning, Zhou and Li [4] proposed a modified version named tri-training algorithm. Tri-training removes the ambiguity of using different views of attributes to train the labeled dataset. Also, the algorithm uses three classifiers instead of two and hence enhancing the clarity to produce final hypothesis.

The algorithm is explained as follows: Let $l_1, l_2, l_3 \dots l_n$ denote labeled examples of a Labeled set L labeled set, $ul_1, ul_2, ul_3 \dots ul_n$ denote the unlabeled examples of unlabeled set UL and C_1, C_2 and C_3 are the three classifiers used. Initially, two classifiers, C_1 and C_2 are used to build the trained model with the labeled dataset L. Then the examples in the unlabeled dataset UL are classified using the two trained model. If the predicted outcome is same for both the classifier then the concerned examples are added to the trained model. The cycle is repeated until there is mutual agreement between two classifiers. Then the obtained final and labeled dataset is trained with third classifier, C_3. Now the dataset UL is mapped to L and test example data can be provided to classify.

3.3   Algorithms Used in Tri-Training

This section briefs the three classifiers used in the proposed tri-training.

Naïve Bayes (NB). NB is a supervised algorithm based on Bayesian theorem typically suited when the dimensionality of provided features is high. NB works on principle such that presence or absence of feature is unrelated to the presence or absence of any other feature provided the class label. Some of its advantages are it performs well even if the dataset is not clearly independent and small number of features is sufficient to build the model.

Decision Tree (DT). Decision Tree is a set of classification rules that are organized in a hierarchical tree-like manner in such away that output of a classifier can be determined based on the conditions that are fulfilled. The major advantages of Decision Tree are non-parametric and easy to interpret but their main drawback is they can easily overfit the data.

Support Vector Machine (SVM). SVM is a bilinear supervised learning algorithm that transforms data to a higher dimension space. SVM has good generalization ability and uses the principle of structural risk minimization. Some of the advantages of SVM are high accuracy and are extensile for data that are not easily separable in the feature space. Let two feature vectors X and Y be the two disjoint sets of points in R^n, then SVM constructs the hyperplane determined by a vector w that produces the linearly separable plane.

3.4   Outline of the Proposed Detection System

As the typical classification problem, the proposed system contains two phases: training and testing. In the training phase, there are three types of data entities: Normal, Attack and Unlabeled. For the provided dataset, three of the above mentioned wavelet families (Daubechies, Symlets and Coiflets) are extracted. Dataset containing WFS along with labels (0-Normal, 1-Attack and 2-Unlabeled) is formed. Now, the labeled data entries are used to train the models: Naïve Bayes and Decision Tree separately. Unlabeled data entries are provided as test data and classified with these models. If there is mutual agreement (predictions of the model are same) for both the classifier then the classified data is added as an entry in the trained model. Now the disagreed data entry is again classified with the two classifiers and the experiment is repeated until mutual agreement is obtained for all the entry in dataset. Since all the entries are classified, the obtained dataset is used as a dataset for training SVM. SVM provides lot of advantages and hence it is used as a major classifier in the proposed system. Now any test data is provided as input to SVM and the output is obtained.

To design an efficient detections scheme, packet based sliding window with dynamic threshold is used in this work. In general, DDoS attack can happen at any instant and its impact will be severe within a fraction of second. So the conventional time-based sliding window is unrealistic as the computational overhead will be high when computed for every unit seconds. Number of packets for each window is determined by dynamic threshold based mechanism. Threshold is determined based on the incoming traffic flow and the memory size of the data payload.

4   Experimental Results and Analysis

Experiments are done by using both normal dataset and various attack datasets. Table.1 displays the summary of different datasets used in our experiments.

Table 1. Summary of Dataset used in the proposed system

Name of the trace	Nature	Type	Flooding used	Size	No of files
CAIDA	Collection	Attack	ICMP TCP SYN HTTP	21 GB	1870
NETRESEC	Collection	Normal	NA	16 GB	2060
LOIC	Generation	Attack	TCP SYN UDP HTTP	10 GB	36
HOIC	Generation	Attack	HTTP	7 GB	32
Blackenergy Bot	Generation	Attack	TCP SYN UDP HTTP ICMP	10.8 GB	34

4.1   Collection of Dataset

CAIDA Dataset. Cooperative Association for Internet Data Analysis (CAIDA dataset) collects several different types of data at geographically and topologically diverse locations and makes them available to research community. For our experiments, DDoS attack dataset containing one hour of anonymized traffic traces with the total size of 21 GB is considered. This one hour traffic is split up into 5 minute pcap files and non-attack traffic traces are removed. To perform meticulous study on the traces, packet based sliding is performed on obtained pcap files. After performing packet based sliding, a total of 1870 files are generated. Fig. 2(a) shows the traces of the CAIDA dataset used in our experiment.

NETRESEC. NETRESEC is an independent software vendor specializing in network security monitoring and network forensics. They also maintain pcap repository files collected from various sources of internet. For our experiments, traces of normal files are collected and packet sliding window is used to obtain 2060 files. Fig. 2(b) depicts the traces of the normal data used.

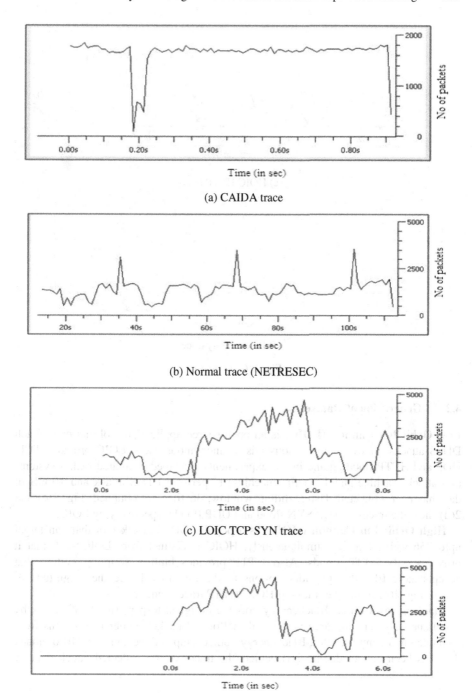

(a) CAIDA trace

(b) Normal trace (NETRESEC)

(c) LOIC TCP SYN trace

(d) LOIC UDP trace

Fig. 2. Traces of various dataset after performing packet sliding window

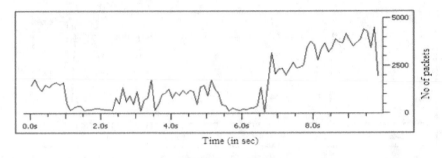

(e) HOIC HTTP trace

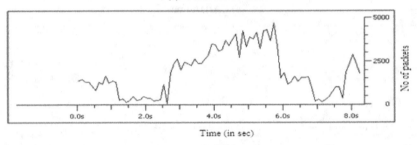

(f) Blackenergy trace

Fig. 2. (*continued*)

4.2   Generation of Dataset

Low Orbit Ion Cannon (LOIC) is an open-source application tool that can launch DDoS attacks on websites by thousands of anonymous users. LOIC provides TCP, UDP and HTTP flooding and in our experiments, a testbed is created with 5 systems (4 - attack machine and 1- victim machine) to perform DDoS attack and 10 GB of data has been collected. Using sliding window, 36 files are obtained. Fig. 2(c) and 2(d) show the traces of TCP SYN flood and UDP flood respectively by LOIC.

High Orbit Ion Cannon (HOIC) is a popular DDoS attack tool that can target upto 256 web addresses simultaneously. HOIC is distinct from LOIC such that it provides only HTTP floods. Also HTTP provides built-in scripting system that accepts .hoic files that provides options to the user to enhance the magnitude of attack. Fig. 2(e) shows the traces of HOIC HTTP traces generated.

Blackenergy Botnet. Blackenergy bots are designed to perform DDoS attack by simultaneously sending large number of malformed packets under instructions from command and control center. Blackenergy botnet setup is done and 10.8 GB of attack data has been collected. Fig. 2(f) depicts the traces of the collected attack data by blackenergy botnet.

5   Performance Analysis

A total of 2060 and 1972 windows of normal and attack data respectively are obtained from the dataset. Exactly half of them are split up to form training and testing set (Normal: Training - 1030 and Testing - 1030 and Attack: Training - 986 and Testing - 986).

5.1   Accuracy of the System

Experiments are conducted to detect the accuracy of the proposed system. Trained model is build by clubbing all the collected and generated attack entities in one group and the dataset concerned to normal entity in another group. As discussed, testing traces for both normal and attack are validated with the trained model. Support Vector Machine (SVM) is used as a classifier because of its advantages that are already conferred. Table 2 depicts the obtained result for the proposed system. Detection rate for normal and attack are 98.25% and 97.66% respectively and the average efficiency is 97.955%

Table 2. Performance of the proposed system

Category	Detection Rate P_D	False Positive Rate P_{FP}	False Negative Rate P_{FN}
Normal	98.25	1.75	NA
Attack	97.66	NA	2.34

5.2   Detection Time

Detection Time T_D is another important metric that measures the performance feasibility of the proposed technique. In the proposed scheme, T_D comprises of time taken to perform packet based sliding window T_{PW} for the given trace, time taken to extract the features T_{WFS} and the Classification Time T_{CL}. Attacks are performed on Windows storage server 2003 with Intel Xeon processor and 12GB RAM configuration. While conducting experiments, time taken for the mentioned parameters is observed. The average detection time(T_D) is found to be 1.5 sec.

5.3   Performance Comparison

Comparison with the existing mechanisms is performed that are using CAIDA dataset. Table 3 shows the comparison of Detection Rate (DR), False Positive Rate (FPR), False Negative Rate (FNR) obtained using CAIDA dataset. Liu et al. [20] proposed a method based on the traffic flow with an opinion that credit score is proportional to the diversification of flow. Detection Accuracy Ratio (DAR) is proposed to estimate the accuracy and the value obtained by the same is about 95%. An identifier/locator [21] scheme is presented based on separating customer networks from provider networks. Also, identifier/locator mapping is introduced to prevent DDoS attacks and the accuracy obtained is almost 95%. Greedy algorithms such as

Matching Pursuit and Orthogonal Matching Pursuit algorithms [22] are proposed to detect DDoS attacks. Also, all the above mentioned research works have used CAIDA dataset. Comparison of performance of the proposed scheme with that of the above mentioned papers are shown in Table 3.

Table 3. Performance Comparison among the existing systems using CAIDA dataset

Method	Performance Metrics		
	DR	FPR	FNR
Traffic flow [20]	95%	NA	NA
Identifier/location separation [21]	94.87%	3.85%	1.28%
Greedy Algorithm [22]	93.20%	12.1%	NA
Proposed Method	97.955%	1.75%	2.34%

6   Conclusion

A DDoS detection mechanism is proposed in this work. Extensive study on DDoS is made and three families namely: Daubechies, Symlets and Coiflets are applied in the work. Combination of these wavelets with specific orders is used as they are more novel, robust and efficient. The demand for unlabeled dataset is considered and semi-supervised learning algorithm is employed to provide trade-off between labeled and unlabeled dataset. Tri-training based semi-supervised learning algorithm is applied based on the feasibility with the proposed features. Naïve Bayes and Decision Tree algorithms are used as initial classifier to label the unlabeled dataset. Dataset are both generated and collected to study the efficiency of the proposed system. Different flooding attacks that are used in the dataset are TCP SYN, UDP, HTTP and ICMP. The success rate or detection rate of the system is found to be 98.25% for normal and 97.66% for attack. Comparison of the performance of the proposed system with that of some of the recent research in the domain of DDoS indicates the effectiveness of the proposed method.

References

1. The Enterprise guide to DDoS Protection. Technical Report, Arbor White paper (2013)
2. Ten Days of Rain. Technical Report, McAfee White paper (2011)
3. RioRey Taxonomy of DDoS attacks. Technical Report, RioRey White paper (2011)
4. Zhou, Z.H., Li, M.: Tri-training: Exploiting unlabeled data using three classifiers. IEEE T. on Knowledge and Data Mining 17(11), 1529–1541 (2005)
5. Ren, X., Wang, R., Wang, H.: Wavelet analysis method for detection of DDoS attack on the basis of self-similarity. Frontiers of Electrical and Electronics Engineering in China 2(1), 73–77 (2007)
6. Lu, W., Ghorbani, A.A.: Network anomaly detection based on wavelet analysis. EUROSIP J. on Advances in Signal Processing 4 (2009)
7. Palmieri, F., Fiore, U., Castiglione, A., Santis, A.D.: On the detection of card-sharing traffic through wavelet analysis and Support Vector Machines. J. on Applied Soft Computing 13(1), 615–627 (2013)

8. Yang, M.H., Wang, R.C.: DDoS Detection based on wavelet kernel support machine. The Journal of China Universities of Posts and Telecommunications 15(3), 59–94 (2008)

9. Agrawal, P.K., Gupta, B.B., Jain, S.: SVM Based Scheme for Predicting Number of Zombies in a DDoS Attack. In: IEEE Intelligence and Security Informatics Conference, pp. 178–182. IEEE (2011)

10. Subbulakshmi, T., Shalinie, S.M., Ganapathi Subramanian, V., Bala Krishnan, K., Anand Kumar, D., Kannathal, K.: Detection of DDoS attacks using Enhanced Support Vector Machines with real time generated dataset. In: 3rd IEEE International Conference on Advanced Computing, pp. 17–22. IEEE (2011)

11. Ramamoorthi, A., Subbulakshmi, T., Shalinie, S.M.: Real time detection and classification of DDoS attacks using Enhanced SVM with string kernels. In: Recent Trends in Information Technology, pp. 91–96. IEEE (2011)

12. Rahmani, H., Sahli, N., Kamoun, F.: DDoS flooding attack detection scheme based on F-divergence. J. Computer Communications 35(11), 1380–1391 (2012)

13. Li, K., Zhang, W., Ma, X., Cao, Z., Zhang, C.: A novel semi-supervised SVM based on tri-training. In: 2nd IEEE International Symposium on Intelligent Information Technology Application, pp. 47–51. IEEE (2008)

14. Li, Y., Li, Z., Wang, R.: Intrusion detection algorithm based on semi-supervised learning. In: IEEE International Conference on Information Technology, Computer Engineering and Management Sciences, pp. 153–156. IEEE (2011)

15. Chapelle, O., Scholkopf, B., Zien, A.: Semi-Supervised Learning, 2. MIT Press, Cambridge (2006)

16. Xiang, Y., Lin, Y., Lei, W.L., Huang, S.J.: DDoS detection based on traffic self-similarity. IEE Proceedings-Communications 151(3), 292–295 (2004)

17. Satiyan, M., Hariharan, M., Nagarajan, R.: Comparison of Performance using Daubechies Wavelet family for facial Expression Recognition. In: 6th International Colloquium on Signal Processing and its Applications (CSPA), pp. 1–5. IEEE (2010)

18. Xian, G., Wang, Z.: An effective technique of wavelet transform for optical signal real-time processing. In: Proceedings on Communications, Circuits and Systems, pp. 653–657. IEEE (2005)

19. Haung, S., Hsieh, C.T.: Coiflet Wavelet transform applied to inspect power system disturbance - generated signals. IEEE T. on Aerospace and Electronic Systems 38(1), 204–210 (2000)

20. Liu, H., Sun, Y., Valgenti, V.C., Kim, M.S.: TrustGuard: A flow level reputation based DDoS defense mechanism. In: Consumer Communications and Network Conference (CCNS), pp. 287–291. IEEE (2011)

21. Luo, H., Lin, Y., Zhang, H.: Preventing DDoS attacks by means of identifier locator separation. IEEE Networks (2013)

22. Andrysiak, T., Saganowski, Ł., Choraś, M.: DDoS attacks detection by means of greedy algorithms. In: Choraś, R.S. (ed.) Image Processing and Communications Challenges 4. AISC, vol. 184, pp. 303–310. Springer, Heidelberg (2013)

An Integrated Approach of E-RED and ANT Classification Methods for DRDoS Attacks

P. MohanaPriya, V. Akilandeswari, G. Akilarasu, and S. Mercy Shalinie

Department of Computer Science and Engineering,
Thiagarajar College of Engineering,
Madurai-625 015, Tamil Nadu, India
{mohanapriyatce,akilavembu,akilgva}@gmail.com, shalinie@tce.edu

Abstract. The main objective of this paper is to detect the Distributed Reflector Denial of Service (DRDoS) attack based on a protocol independent based detection technique. The proposed system applies Enhanced-Random Early Detection (E-RED) algorithm and Application based Network Traffic (ANT) classification method in order to detect and classify the DRDoS attack according to their types. In the experimental analysis, the performance of the proposed system is evaluated by the Transmission Control Protocol (TCP) and Domain Name System (DNS) response packets. It detects the DRDoS attacks with 99% true positives and 1% false positive rates and classifies the types of attacks with 98% classification accuracy. The results and discussions show that the proposed method detects and classifies the highest probability of reflected response traffic as compared to the traditional methods.

Keywords: DRDoS attack, E-RED algorithm, Protocol independent detection, Attack traffic classification, TCP reflected attack, DNS reflected attack.

1 Introduction

With an intention to degrade the valuable Quality of Service (QoS), attacker launches the simple Denial of Service (DoS) attack [1] by exploiting the various types of protocols such as Transmission Control Protocol (TCP), User Datagram Protocol (UDP), and Internet Control Message Protocol (ICMP) etc. Later, attacker uses the extendable versions of DoS attacks such as Distributed Denial of Service (DDoS) attack [2] and Distributed Reflector Denial of Service (DRDoS) attack [3] to spread the attack range severely for the target servers. In case of DRDoS attack, the attacker spoofs the source IP address as same as target server and use reflectors to multiply and spread the attack range by means of response packets to the target server in order to utilize the total bandwidth of the target server. The most common target of an attacker relies on high profile based web servers such as bank, government educational institutions, finance services, online gaming [10] and research labs in order to bring down their services to all its intended users.

Most of the traditional countermeasures for DDoS attacks are insufficient to prevent DRDoS attack. Though ingress filtering [11] is the possible solution for block

J. Lloret Mauri et al. (Eds.): SSCC 2014, CCIS 467, pp. 304–312, 2014.
© Springer-Verlag Berlin Heidelberg 2014

the DDoS [5] flooding attack, it is difficult to implement in real time for DRDoS [4] attack as the attack originates from several reflectors. Researchers show a keen interest in defeating these attacks either at source, intermediate network (or) target side by proposing an algorithm by overcoming the fixed IP spoofing.

The remainder of this paper is organized as follows: Section 2 briefly discusses the existing detection methods for DRDoS attack. Section 3 insights the proposed E-RED detection algorithm. Section 4 explains the proposed ANT classification method. The experimental network structure is explained in Section 5. In Section 6, the performance analysis of the proposed algorithm is explained. Finally, Section 7 concludes this paper with possible future works.

2   Related Works

In this section, the existing DRDoS attack detection techniques are discussed. Some of them are discussed below.

In Request-Response based relationship method [7], the detector can monitor both the request and response packets and it stores potential response packets in its buffer for each request packet. When a response packet sent to the victim is monitored the response packets stored in the buffer is compared. If there is a match, the monitored response packet is considered as valid. Otherwise, the monitored response packet is considered as an invalid packet and it gets dropped without reaching the target server.

The Pairing based Filtering (PF) [8] scheme is proposed to validate incoming replies packets by pairing them in a distributed manner, with the corresponding request packets. This pairing is performed at the edge routers of the ISP perimeter that contains the victim rather than the edge router to which the victim is directly connected which leads to the bandwidth exhaustion attacks in addition to the protection from victim's resource exhaustion attacks.

In Rank Correlation based Detection (RCD) [3], the content of legitimate packet is stored as a flow in a router nearby to the victim. The incoming unmatched flows are called as suspicious flows and they are located at the upstream router of the victim server. In this method, once an attack alarm raises sampling is done for the suspicious flows per time unit T which provides a value sequence for each flow. These sequences are submitted to the detection center which divides the flows into pairs. The next step is to calculate the spearman rank correlation coefficient. If the calculated rank value is 1, then these flows are considered as a pure attack flows

The Continuous and Random Dropping (CARD) method [6] is an advanced queue method that drops the packets when it reaches the certain probability. A maximum threshold has been set to block the incoming packets. When the proposed method identifies the reflected response packets, alert counter will trigger an alarm to indicate that the incoming packets are from malicious origins.

Some of the anticipation methods [9] to detect DRDoS attack are done by protecting a client, protecting a server and to safeguard the sole Internet Service Provider (ISP) responsibility. In case of TCP SYN-ACK response packets, protection of client is done by blocking the high numbered service ports.

3   Enhanced – Random Early Detection (E – RED) Algorithm

In this section, E-RED algorithm is depicted with two main modules namely PACKMAT and THRESCOM which is used for attack detection.

Let consider Average queue length as $AVQlen$,

Incoming Packet Structure as $Struct[INpack]$,

Incoming Packet as $[INpack]$,

Packet Structure in Existing Queue as $PackStruct[EXISqueue]$,

Minimum threshold as $(minthres)$

Maximum threshold as $(maxthres)$,

Target Server as T_s,

Token Bucket as TB,

Borrow Bucket as BB.

Phase 1: Packet Matching (PACKMAT)

IF $(Struct[INpack]) \equiv PackStruct[EXISqueue]$

{

    Pass $[INpack]$ to **THRESCOM**

}

ELSE

{

    Drop $[INpack]$

}

Phase 2: THREShold COMparison (THRESCOM)

IF $(AVQlen) < minthres$ THEN

    No action is needed.

ELSE IF $minthres \leq ((AVQlen)\ [INpack]) \leq (maxthres)$ THEN

    $[INpack]$ forwarded to TB.

ELSE $((AVQlen)\ [INpack]) > (maxthres)$

Drop $[INpack]$ and passes to BB.

Algorithm 1. Enhanced RED Algorithm

Fig. 1 shows the process of Enhanced RED algorithm. The first phase of E-RED algorithm is dealt with PACKet MATching (PACKMAT). In this phase, the packet structure of incoming packet is compared with the contents of legitimate packet in the existing queue. The matched packets are allowed to enter into the second phase named THREShold COMparison (THRESCOM). In THRESCOM phase, RED algorithm is used to detect the attack packets with default threshold values. The RED algorithm monitors the average queue length and drops the packet based on the comparison with the default threshold values. If the average queues length of incoming packet is lesser than the minimum threshold value, then RED remains in a static state (i.e. taking no action). If the average queue length of incoming packet lies between the minimum and maximum threshold values, then those packets are allowed to enqueue with the existing queue present inside the token bucket. If the average queue length of incoming packet is greater than the maximum threshold value, then those packets are dropped without entering the token bucket. The dropping attack packets are allowed to pass into the Borrow Bucket (BB) which prevents unnecessary packet loss.

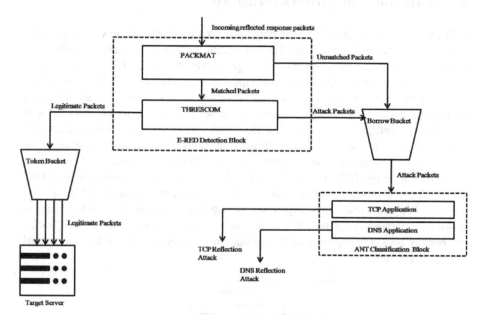

Fig. 1. Scenario of Enhanced –Random Early Detection (E-RED)

4   Application Based Network Traffic (ANT) Classification Method

The packet structure contains the following sequence of information such as *Packet Size, Source IP address, Source Port number, Destination IP address, Destination Port number.*

Table 1. Different Applications on the Network Traffic

Application	Port Numbers	Number of Packets
TCP	20	933777
DNS	53	179960

Table 1 refers the different applications on the network traffic. The first step towards classification is to determine the classes to which the network traffic ((i.e.) the packet structure) that are categorized. Here, the classification is done on the three numbers of classes. The classes are the applications such as TCP and DNS. For classification, the input data is collected from the borrow bucket. From the header information of all the packets available in borrow bucket, the source and destination port numbers are compared with the actual port numbers of the applications.

5   Experimental Network Structure

In this section, the simulated experimentation is explained. Fig. 2 shows the simulated experimental network structure. The simulated network structure contains two networks such as campus network and target server network. The reflected attack traffic data are collected between the campus network and the reflector network for one day time duration. The various nodes involved in this attack generation process are attacker node, normal user node, reflector node. All these nodes are installed with GNU/Linux operating system. During the attack, the proposed system extracts the features of a packet such as source IP address, source port number, destination IP address and destination port number. In the reflector network, DNS server is configured with the GNU/Linux OS in that kernel 2.6.9. It is employed with Intel Xeon 3.20 Hz quadruple SMP system, 16 GB core memory and Intel 1000 Mbps and Ethernet Pro Network. This experimental network is connected to the campus network to obtain normal traffic. The two new data structures such as token bucket and borrow bucket is deployed at the simulation setup in order to collect the normal and attack packets.

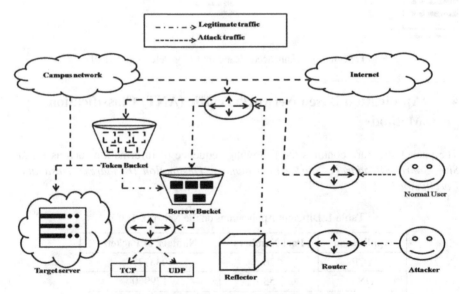

Fig. 2. Simulated Experimental Network Structure

6   Results and Discussions

Fig. 3 shows the number of TCP packets entering into the target server. When compared to DRDoS attack, the number of reflected attack packets entering during the DDoS attack is comparatively low. Fig. 4 represents the amount of legitimate traffic entering during attack.

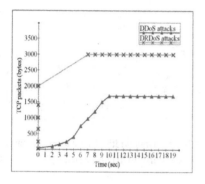
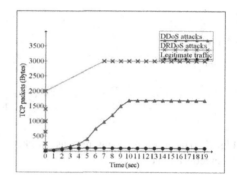

Fig. 3. TCP Packets arrival rate during DDoS and DRDoS Attack

Fig. 4. Traces of legitimate traffic during attack

Fig. 5 shows the traces of TCP-SYN request that has been originated by the attacker. The attacker spoofs the source IP address same as target server and sends the TCP-SYN request to the set of compromised machines named as "zombies". Fig. 6 shows the multiple outgoing request packets from the zombie network since it involves master and slave machines to process the instructions given by the attacker.

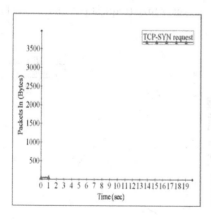
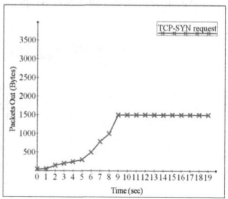

Fig. 5. Traces of incoming TCP-SYN request entering into zombie network

Fig. 6. Traces of outgoing SYN request from zombie network

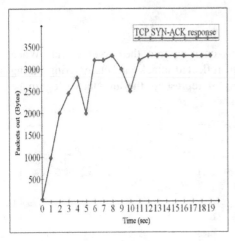
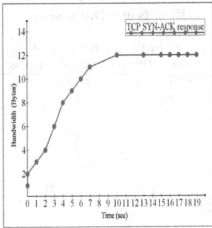

Fig. 7. Traces of outgoing response packets From reflector networks

Fig. 8. Bandwidth Utilization of target server during DRDoS attack

Fig. 7 represents the outgoing (or) generated TCP SYN-ACK response packets from the reflector network nodes. The small sized TCP-SYN request packets are reflected when it reaches the reflector components. Fig. 8 shows the bandwidth utilization of target server during DRDoS attack.

Fig. 9 represents the ratio between the number of response packets generated with the number of request packets originated which is referred as amplification factor. In reflection attack, the amplification factor is three times higher than the number of request packets originated and it is given by Equation (1).

$$\text{Amplification Factor} = \text{Size (response packet) / Size (request packets)} . \qquad (1)$$

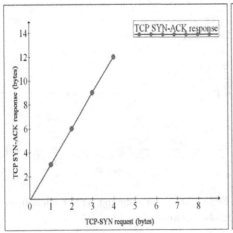
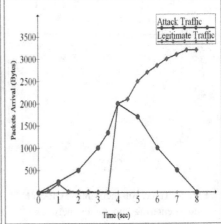

Fig. 9. Amplification Factor

Fig. 10. Performance of proposed E-RED Algorithm

Fig. 10 shows the arrival of legitimate and attack traffic with and without the proposed algorithm. In the initial stage, the arrival of attack traffic is high and then it gets reduced while the proposed E-RED algorithm begins. Hence, the proposed algorithm effectively reduce the arrival of response packets with high (98%) true positive rate and low (2%) false positive rate.

Table 2. Application Network based Traffic (ANT) Classification Method

Attack	Classification Accuracy
TCP reflected attack traffic	97%
DNS reflected attack traffic	98%

Table 2 shows the performance of proposed ANT classification method by classifying TCP and DNS reflected attack traffic with 98% of classification accuracy. The average classification accuracy obtained in analysis is 98% which is comparatively high when compared to other existing classification methods.

7   Conclusion and Future Work

The proposed E-RED algorithm completely based on queuing theory and it identifies the SYN reflected attack packets. This reflected attack packets degrade the performance of network server by crashing application and operating system. The proposed method can manage the high packet arrival rate because of additional data structure named "Borrow Bucket". In the performance evaluation, it provides high detection rate and low false positive rate for SYN reflection attack traffic. However, the proposed E-RED algorithm is developed to perform protocol independent detection for all types of protocol both in large volume and low volume of attack traffic. Finally, this method achieves 99% of true positive rates and low false positive rate of 1% before the reflected responses mount at the target server. In the extension of this methodology, a protocol independent mitigation algorithm will develop for reflected Distributed Denial of Service attacks by considering additional parameters in the E-RED algorithm. The proposed ANT classification model well classifies the types of reflected attacks based on the applications and their respective port numbers.

Acknowledgements. The authors would like to thank our institutional authorities to their kind hearted cooperation and to their all support in education and infrastructure. Further, we submit our hearty thanks to TCS, Chennai for their unremarkable financial assistance.

References

1. Jiang, X., Yang, J., Jin, G., Wei, W.: RED-FT A Scalable Random Early Detection Scheme with Flow Trust against DoS Attacks. IEEE Communication Letters 17, 1–4 (2013)

2. Ben-Porat, U., Bremler-Barr, A., Levy, H.: Vulnerability of network mechanisms to sophisticated DDoS attacks. IEEE Trans. Comp. 62, 1031–1043 (2013)
3. Wei, W., Chen, F., Xia, Y., Jin, G.: A Rank Correlation based Detection against Distributed Reflection DoS attacks. IEEE Communication Letters 17, 173–175 (2013)
4. Thandeeswaran, R., Asha, A., Jeyanthi, N.: Novel Survey on Detection of DDoS Attack Using Traceback Technique in VoIP Networks. Mathematical Archive 2, 2229–5046 (2011)
5. Beitollahi, H., Deconinck, G.: Analyzing well-known counter measures against Distributed Denial of Service Attacks. Computer Communications 35, 1312–1332 (2012)
6. Rani, R., Vatsa, A.K.: CARD (Continuous and Random Dropping) based DRDOS Attack Detection and Prevention Techniques in MANET. Engineering and Technology 2, 1449–1456 (2012)
7. Tsunoda, H., Ohta, K., Yamamoto, A., Ansari, N., Waizumi, Y., Nemoto, Y.: Detecting DRDoS attack by a simple response packet confirmation mechanism. Computer Communications 31, 3299–3306 (2008)
8. Al-Duwairi, B., Manimaran, G.: Distributed packet pairing for reflector based DDoS attack mitigation. Computer Communications 29, 2269–2280 (2006)
9. Reeta, M.: Anticipation methods from DRDoS Attack. Computer Science and Information Technology 2, 890–894 (2012)
10. Larry, E.D., Lars, E.D.: Multiplayer Online games. In: Digital Forensics for Legal Professionals, pp. 301–308 (2012)
11. Shahabeddin, G., Mahmood, A.: Bloom Filter Applications in network security. Computer Networks 57, 4047–4064 (2013)

Low Complex System for Physical Layer Security Using NLFG and QCLDPC Code

Celine Mary Stuart and P.P. Deepthi

Department of Electronics and Communication
National Institute of Technology, Calicut
celinemarystuart@gmail.com, deepthi@nitc.ac.in

Abstract. In practical communication applications, the channels for intended users and eavesdroppers are not error-free and Wyner's wiretap channel model deals with the scenario. Using this model, the security of a stand-alone stream cipher can be strengthened by exploiting the properties of physical layer. In this paper, a joint channel coding and light weight cryptography for setting a Gaussian wiretap channel is proposed. The scheme is based on a keyed Quasi Cyclic Low Density Parity Check (QCLDPC) encoder and light weight stream cipher based on Linear Feedback Shift Register (LFSR). The significant contribution is that, highly complex non-linear function that provides security in a Non-Linear Filter Generator (NLFG) is replaced by a simple non-linear function without compromising security. Enhanced security with lesser complexity is achieved by embedding security in channel encoder. Results show that attacker cannot extract the secret key because of the errors introduced in the physical layer due to unknown structure of the channel encoder.

1 Introduction

In a traditional communication system, security is implemented by cryptographic means at higher layers. In the emerging computing and communication prototypes, there are challenges for installing security solutions in resource-constrained devices such as wireless sensor nodes, Radio-Frequency identification (RFID) tags, smart cards etc. The main challenges are requirement for minimum overhead and power consumption and reasonable security to support application and end-user requirements. To address these challenges, light-weight cryptography has been established [1]. Non-linear filter generator [2],[3] is a popular light-weight stream cipher made of LFSR and a non-linear filtering function. The security of NLFG depends on how complex the non-linear function is. The advantage of using stream cipher is that with the pre-computation of key stream, encryption and decryption can be extremely fast. Also the same hardware can be used for both encryption and decryption operations if it is designed as a binary additive one. In this work, very secure and extremely hardware efficient stream cipher designed using simple non-linear Boolean functions is incorporated for light weight encryption.

J. Lloret Mauri et al. (Eds.): SSCC 2014, CCIS 467, pp. 313–324, 2014.
© Springer-Verlag Berlin Heidelberg 2014

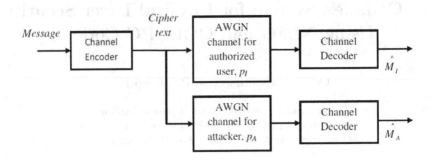

Fig. 1. Gaussian Wiretap Channel

With the introduction of wiretap channel [4],classical error correction codes are used for both error correction and privacy amplification [5]. In wiretap channel model, authorized users share information over a main channel and passive attacker observes the information through a degraded channel as shown in Fig.1. Both channels are assumed to be discrete and memory less. They are treated as binary symmetric channel (BSC) with bit-flipping probability of p_I and p_A respectively. Another assumption is that the quality of wiretap channel is less than that of main channel; i.e. $p_I < p_A$. Encoding techniques are to be chosen such that a good reliability is provided for intended user and also a good amount of security against attacker. Some previous works for achieving physical layer security by exploiting the differences between the channels experienced by the intended and un-intended users are reported in [6],[7],[8],[9],[10].The difficulty in breaking an LFSR based cryptographic system by considering tandem channel coding and cryptography is reported in [6],[7]. In [8], the messages are transmitted over punctured bits, with secrecy rate chosen less than the design rate to satisfy the constraints of reliability and security. Non-systematic transmission based on scrambling of information bits is exploited in [9]. A joint framework of physical layer and application layer security for wireless multimedia applications is investigated in [10]. In our work, QCLDPC codes [11],[12] that ensure low complexity are used to achieve secrecy capacity, considering a practical scenario of AWGN wiretap channel.

The purpose of our work is to increase the difficulty of attacker even when low complex channel encoder and light weight encryption block are used. In this work, methods are investigated to achieve a high level of security when both the intended and un-intended users are having access to channels that are corrupted by Additive White Gaussian Noise (AWGN). The message $\hat{M}_I$ estimated by intended user is with probability of error much lesser than $\hat{M}_A$ estimated by the attacker. The security gap is provided so that the probability of error in estimating $\hat{M}_A$ is approximately around 0.5. The main contributions of this work are: (i) methods for embedding security in the construction of QCLDPC code is explored; (ii) the increased security of the low complex stream cipher by incorporating secure channel code is analyzed; (iii) the increased security is quantified in terms of probability of correlation and BER performance.

The outline of the paper is as follows: Section 2 introduces the stream cipher and the fundamentals of QCLDPC code. In section 3, the proposed low complex NLFG based cryptographic system is explained and section 4 focuses on the analysis and simulation of the proposed system. Finally conclusions are drawn in section 5.

2 Preliminaries

2.1 Non Linear Filter Generator

Non-linear filter generator (NLFG) [2],[3] is one of the most popular and efficient LFSR based non-linear stream ciphers with low complexity. It consists of a maximal length LFSR and the linearity present in the output is masked by a non-linear Boolean function f called the filtering function. A Boolean function that characterizes the cryptographic properties of non-linearity, balancedness, correlation probability and algebraic degree are selected for masking. The selected Boolean function maps one or more binary input variables to a binary output variable. The key stream $Z = f(x_1, x_2, ..., x_{L_1})$ where x_1, $x_2, ..., x_{L_1}$ are the outputs of different stages of maximal length LFSR with L_1 stages. The period of the resulting key stream is exactly same as that of the underlying LFSR; i.e. 2^{L_1-1}, if the LFSR feedback polynomial is primitive and of degree L_1 and the non-linear filter function is balanced. Non-zero initial state results in a key stream with ones and zeros occurring uniformly in one period. Randomness properties, statistical properties and cryptographic strength of the resulting key stream depend on the primitive characteristic of the feedback polynomial used and the properties of the non-linear filter function. The linear complexity of Z is given as $L_m = \sum_{i=1}^{m} \binom{L_i}{i}$, where m is the algebraic order of the non-linear Boolean function.

2.2 QCLDPC Code

QCLDPC code [11],[12],[13]is a structured LDPC code whose parity check matrix is constructed as an array of sparse circulant matrices. Each circulant matrix is derived from identity matrix by permuting either rows or columns. The circulant sub-array gives the code a Quasi-Cyclic (QC) property, which facilitates efficient encoder implementation [14],[15]. The sparseness of parity check matrix H guarantees low encoding complexity and low decoding complexity, which grow linearly with block length. The codeword is defined by the generator matrix, G having dimension $K \times N$, where K is the length of message and N is the length of the codeword of rate K/N obtained by the null space of parity check matrix. For a K bit message, number of parity bits that provide the error correction capability of channel code is $M = N\text{-}K$. The K bits of information, $u = (u_1, u_2, ..., u_K)$ are encoded by multiplying it with the generator matrix G to generate an N bit codeword as $v = u*G = (v_1, v_2, ..., v_N)$. The generator matrix in systematic circulant form is obtained from non-systematic H matrix using the method given in [14]. As the generator matrix is in systematic form, encoding is done with an array of shift registers, ensuring the encoding complexity varying linearly with the number of parity check bits of the code.

The most commonly used iterative decoding algorithm to decode QCLDPC codes is Sum Product Algorithm (SPA) or Belief Propagation Algorithm (BPA) [16],[17]. Out of the various modified versions, Modified Min Sum Algorithm (MMSA) [18] shows an approximate BER performance approaching that of SPA and it only contains additions and comparisons that suits simple hardware implementation. Also MMSA converges faster when compared to other decoding algorithms. Therefore in this work, to design high speed and less complex secure channel coder, MMSA is used.

3   Proposed System For Physical Layer Security

3.1   Mathematical Model

Stream ciphers have attracted much attention for use in secure communication because of high throughput, less complex hardware circuitry and very little error propagation. Important classes of stream ciphers are based on a mixture of LFSR, non-linear filter generators and clock-controlled generators. Usually practical stream ciphers are designed with large period and high linear complexity to resist the known styles of attack. The linear complexity of the stream cipher based on NLFG depends on the length of the underlying LFSR and the algebraic order of the Boolean function chosen. As the algebraic order increases, the hardware complexity also increases. This paper introduces a low complex secure encryption strategy for shielding the data from unauthorized access. The proposed method helps to increase the security of the system with less overhead and less complexity by introducing secrecy in the channel coder. In the proposed system, the message, u is added with a random key stream, Z generated from NLFG with low complex Boolean function. The encrypted message ($c = u + Z$) is encoded by a secure channel encoder with generator matrix G, to obtain a vector y.

$$y = (u + Z)G = uG + ZG \tag{1}$$

The vector ZG of length N has arbitrary hamming weight and is not correctable in ordinary sense. As the hamming weight is not predictable, they cannot be computed by known algorithms, such as information-set decoding algorithm [19]. However, the error vectors can be computed by an intended user and can be subtracted from the encrypted vector. The transmitted code word y may be corrupted by channel noise and the received code word can be expressed as $r = y + e'$, where e' represents the channel noise. As the intended user knows the parity check matrix and initial state of NLFG, decoding and decryption can be done as follows:

- Decode the received sense word r using MMSA to obtain c'
- Decrypt c' to get u'.

3.2   Structural Model

The block diagram of the proposed low complex system for physical layer security is shown in Fig. 2. It comprises a key stream generator that produces a pseudorandom key sequence Z generated by a non-linear Boolean function of less algebraic order and a secure channel encoder based on QCLDPC code. The initial state of underlying LFSR for non-linear filter generator acts as key, K_1 of length L_1 bits. The parameters selected to generate the parity check matrix of secure channel code forms the key K_2 of length L_2 bits.

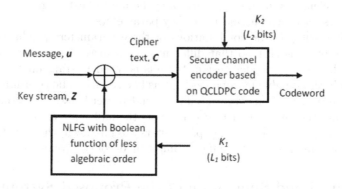

Fig. 2. Proposed system for physical layer security

As all the data sequences are assumed to be binary, cipher text is obtained by bit-wise *xor* operation of message sequence and key stream. The cipher text is encoded and transmitted using secure channel encoder made of QCLDPC code. By embedding security in the design of H matrix of QCLDPC code, we can achieve high security and reliability together even with a less complex NLFG.

3.3   Design of Secure Channel Code

Secure channel encoder is constructed by designing H matrix as in [11] using the key K_2. The various steps involved in the design of secure H matrix are as follows:

1. For a given code rate and dimension, select the size of generator matrix G as $K \times N$.
2. Choose an appropriate Galois field GF(q).
3. Select two integers $x, y \in Z_q = \{0,1,...,q\text{-}1\}$ such that $x^i = y^j = 1 \bmod(q)$, where $i = N/q$ and $j = K/q$.
4. Obtain the position matrix P of size $j \times i$ whose $(a, b)^{th}$ element $P_{a,b} = y^a x^b$; where $0 \leq a \leq j\text{-}1$ and $0 \leq b \leq i\text{-}1$.

5. Construct H matrix of size $(N\text{-}K) \times N$ as an array of circulant sub-matrices, each of size $q \times q$; $N\text{-}K = jq$ and $N = iq$. Each circulant sub-matrix is obtained by shifting identity matrix of size $q \times q$ according to the entries in position matrix P.

Based on different Galois fields, QCLDPC codes of various lengths, rates and minimum distances can be constructed. The parameters [11] that determine the dimension and position of ones in the H matrix of the QCLDPC code are tuned to make the channel encoder configurable according to the requirement. The non-zero entries in various positions of H matrix are decided by the circulant blocks obtained from the chosen non-zero integer values of a set Z_q. If q is prime, the nonzero elements in this field form a cyclic multiplicative group and the H matrix differs for each combination of key parameters.

Many different possible combinations of these parameters produce different H matrices of same size, so that different code spaces of same dimension can be obtained. For the decoder design, there is no need to transmit the entire H matrix. Only the tunable parameters kept as key K_2 are to be transmitted, thus reducing the transmission overhead. The intended user knows the actual field of operation and the integer pair that constructs the null space of the code. For an unintended receiver, since the key parameters are unknown, the structure of H matrix is also unknown and the data cannot be decoded properly.

4   Analysis and Simulation of the Proposed System

The proposed system can be analyzed in terms of security, BER performance and data complexity.

4.1   Security

The proposed system can be perceived as either a secure channel coding model or as an enhanced secure stream cipher model. Perceiving as a secure channel coding model, the main attack strategy is *information-set decoding* [18]. In the second perspective, the proposed system offers an improvement over stand-alone stream cipher based system and a well documented attack against such scenario is *fast correlation attack* [19],[20]. In the worst case, the cryptanalytic attack against any computationally secure system is *brute-force attack* [21] that would involve, searching the entire key space. The cryptanalytic strength of the proposed system against all these attacks is being analyzed in this section.

Information Set Decoding. In a cryptosystem, if the message is hidden by adding a random vector of length N and constant weight t, the random vector can be computed by classical information-set decoding algorithms such as Lee-Brickell's algorithm or Stern's algorithm [18]. The idea is to find a set of K error-free coordinates of a distorted vector such that a $K \times K$ sub-matrix of G denoted as G_J restricted to these coordinates is invertible. Then by multiplying the encrypted vector by the inverse of the sub-matrix will give the message.

In our proposed scheme, the transmitted word is $y = (u + Z) G$. The random vector Z added to message is of constant weight due to properties of stream cipher. But the random vector ZG having random weight is added to codeword uG. NLFG of large period is chosen to add error vectors of random weight to the message, so that the secret code structure of our system is protected. Since the key parameters are unknown, attacker cannot obtain a valid representation of the secure QCLDPC code. Also, he cannot collect K linearly independent error-free code words since intentional errors are present in the message. As the correlation provided by the proposed system is around 0.5, the attacker cannot collect K error-free coordinates. Also information set decoding cannot be performed successfully on this proposed scheme.

Fast Correlation Attack. Most commonly used and well known attack on non-linear filter generator is fast correlation attack [19],[20]. It is based on the statistical dependence between the key stream generated through the non-linear filter function, f and the sequence obtained through f_l, the best affine (linear) approximation of f. In the attack, the observed segment of the key stream sequence is considered as a noisy version of a linear transform of the unknown underlying LFSR sequence. Then the problem is viewed as decoding of a Linear Block Code (LBC) over Binary Symmetric Channel (BSC) as in [20],[22]. The model for correlation attack is given in Fig. 3. For an attacker, NLFG is reduced to a linear system (target system) by replacing f with f_l, such that the actual key stream Z can be considered as a noisy version of the output V of the target system, i.e. $Z = V + e$.

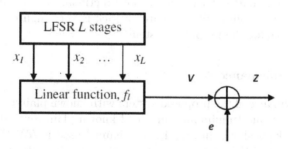

Fig. 3. Model for correlation attack

Here L is the length of underlying LFSR and let u_0 be the initial state and N_L be the length of observed key stream. Then the target system shown in Fig.3 can be modeled as a linear block code, C_1 of message length L and code length N_L. i.e. C_1 is an (N_L, L) code with generator matrix G_1 to produce a code word $V = u_0 G_1$, where $G_1 = (g_1 g_2 ... g_{N_L})$; g_i is i^{th} column of G_1. Since even the best designed Boolean function leaves around 65% correlation between Z and V, getting V from Z can be considered as a normal error decoding for this channel coder. Due to unknown structure of the channel code, the received message appears to be random for an attacker, in almost all cases. The mathematical model between message bits (u) and transmitted bits (y) on the channel can be written as $y = (u + u_0 G_1 + e) G = uG + u_0 G_1 G + eG$. In a known plain text attack, only known parameters are u and G_1. The received vector $r = y + e' = uG + u_0 G_1 G + eG + e'$. At high SNR, $e' \simeq 0$. Then received vector $r = uG + u_0 G_1 G + eG$. Since G is unknown, fast correlation attack fails in this scenario and the probability of correlation comes around 0.5 resulting in a cryptographically strong system.

Brute Force Attack. It is an extensive key search attack to find the key that will unlock the encryption, where the attacker tries every possible key combination. In the proposed system, for practical code lengths (say $K \geq 812$), the total key size, $L_t = L_1 + L_2$, corresponds to a large key space, too big for an exhaustive key search. For L_t bit key, an attacker can deduce the key in $2^{L_t - 1}$ operations on average. There are mainly three types of brute force attacks: Dictionary attack, Search attack and Rule-based search attack. In dictionary attack, the attacker tries keys from a pre-compiled list of possible values; i.e. to guess user names and passwords by trying hundreds of likely possibilities, such as words in a dictionary. This attack tries only those possibilities which are most likely to succeed. If the keys are not predictable, this attack is not successful. Search attack tries to cover all possible combinations of key and cannot reach a solution in polynomial time because of large space of possible candidates. Rule-based attack is to generate possible combinations, by creating certain rules for password generation. Since the key for the proposed scheme is not derived from any password and the key doesn't demand any particular property, both dictionary attack and rule-based attack fail here. The complexity of search attack is very high due to the large key space available for the proposed system.

4.2   Error Performance

The BER performance of the proposed system with known plain text bits greater than a threshold value (minimum number of known plain text bits required to mount the attack) is shown in Fig. 4. The channel used is AWGN with binary phase shift keying (BPSK) modulation. Simulation results indicate that the proposed secure scheme achieves a very good BER performance for intended user and provides high error rate for attacker.

The following observations are also made from the simulation results. When NLFG alone is made secure, due to the correlation existing between the computed key sequence and the original key stream, probability of error is around 0.25. But when security is provided both in NLFG and channel code, probability of error could reach 0.5 even under high SNR conditions. When known plain text bits are less than a threshold, even if K_1 alone is unknown, the probability of error approaches 0.5 as shown in Fig. 5.

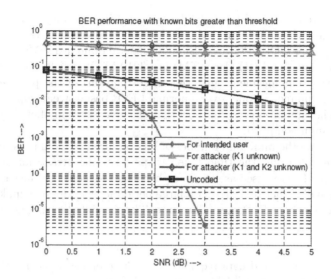

Fig. 4. BER performance of (1624, 812) QCLDPC code with known plain text bits greater than a threshold when K_1 alone is unknown and when both K_1 and K_2 are unknown

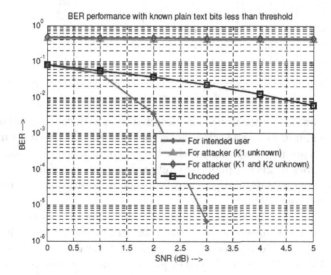

Fig. 5. BER performance of (1624, 812) QCLDPC code with known plain text bits less than a threshold when K_1 alone is unknown and when both K_1 and K_2 are unknown

4.3   Data Complexity

Simulations are conducted to verify the data requirement and correlation of the received data with the transmitted data by using low complex Boolean function along with secure QCLDPC code. Simulations are done using Matlab with system specifications Intel (R) Core (TM) i5 - 3210 M CPU @ 2.5 GHz with 4 GB RAM. Security enhancement (in terms of correlation) of the proposed system due to secure channel encoder over a normal LFSR based stream cipher system is analyzed. The simulation results show that the given system offers high security with less system complexity.

Table 1 shows the minimum number of bits required to mount fast correlation attack (threshold) and the time taken to perform the attack for a given key length, when NLFG is used as stream cipher. Here we consider the case of error-free reception of cipher text. To get a large period for the key stream, key length, L_1 of the underlying LFSR should be large. The simulated results are for smaller key lengths.

Table 1. Attack time and data requirement of the proposed system with NLFG as stream cipher and known QCLDPC encoder as channel coder

Length of key K_1 (L_1 bits)	Period of key stream	Minimum number of bits required to mount the attack	Time to attack QCLDPC coded system with security in encryptor alone (seconds) i.e. key used in NLFG is unknown
4	15	5	0.01
7	127	29	0.027
9	511	66	0.21
10	1023	68	0.33
17	131071	96	2.15
20	1048576	117	4.53

Table 2 shows the correlation of the decoded data with the original data when key K_1 alone is unknown and when both the keys K_1 and K_2 are unknown. If the parameters are unknown, an attacker has to go for a thorough search of key. When the number of known plain text bits is less than threshold or if both the keys are unknown, the data appears to be random resulting in the reception of highly un-correlated data.

A comparison based on the probability of correlation with increase in number of iterations for the proposed system and a system available in the literature [6] is shown in Table 3. Even after a good number of iterations, the correlation is more than 67% for the original system [6], assuming a bit-flipping probability of 0.2 for the Binary Symmetric Channel (BSC) considered. Under the same assumption, due to wise implementation of secure channel coder in the proposed system, the output resulted in a probability of correlation of around 0.5, which is the requirement of any secure system.

Table 2. Correlation of the decoded data with the original data when key K_1 alone is unknown and both the keys K_1 and K_2 are unknown

SNR (in dB)	(1624,812) code Threshold $\geq$ 68		(1624,812) code Threshold $<$ 68	
	Probability of correlation (K_1 unknown)	Probability of correlation (K_1 and K_2 unknown)	Probability of correlation (K_1 unknown)	Probability of correlation (K_1 and K_2 unknown)
0	0.5479	0.5238	0.5246	0.5244
1	0.6564	0.5393	0.5445	0.5286
2	0.7537	0.5345	0.5447	0.5187
3	0.7537	0.5286	0.5386	0.5274

Table 3. Probability of correlation with number of iterations

Number of iterations	5	10	15	30	50
Original system [6]	0.733	0.73	0.69	0.67	0.67
Proposed system	0.5293	0.5317	0.543	0.5488	0.5486

5   Conclusion

In this work, a secure channel coding system that achieves physical layer security with less structural complexity has been proposed. A light weight stream cipher based on simple non-linear Boolean function has been chosen along with structured QCLDPC code to provide enhanced security with low complexity. Tunability of parity check matrix could be achieved without compromising hardware simplicity, because of the circulant nature of the code chosen. Results show that improved security could be achieved by light-weight stream ciphers along with a secure channel encoder. By incorporating secure channel code, probability of correlation could be forced down to 0.5 (approx.), which is a major achievement of the proposed scheme.

References

1. Fan, X., Mandal, K., Gong, G.: WG-8: A Light-Weight Stream Cipher for Resource-Constrained Smart Devices. In: Singh, K., Awasthi, A.K. (eds.) QShine 2013. LNICST, vol. 115, pp. 617–632. Springer, Heidelberg (2013)
2. Dichtl, M.: On nonlinear filter generators. In: Biham, E. (ed.) FSE 1997. LNCS, vol. 1267, pp. 103–106. Springer, Heidelberg (1997)
3. Teo, S.-G., Simpson, L.R., Dawson, E.: Bias in the nonlinear filter generator output sequence. International Journal of Cryptology Research 2, 27–37 (2010)
4. Thangaraj, A., Dihidar, S., Calderbank, A.R., McLaughlin, S.W., Merolla, J.M.: Applications of LDPC codes to the wiretap channel. IEEE Transactions on Information Theory 53, 2933–2945 (2007)

5. Wong, C.W., Wong, T.F., Shea, J.M.: LDPC code design for the BPSK-constrained Gaussian wiretap channel. In: IEEE GLOBECOM Workshop (2011)
6. Harrison, W.K., Mclaughlin, S.W.: Physical-layer security: Combining error control coding and cryptography. In: Proc. IEEE Int. Conf. Communications, Dresden, Germany, pp. 1–5 (2009)
7. Harrison, W., Almeida, J., Bloch, M., McLaughlin, S., Barros, J.: Coding for secrecy: An overview of error-control coding techniques for physical-layer security. IEEE Signal Processing Magazine 30(5), 41–50 (2013)
8. Klinc, D., Ha, J., McLaughlin, S.W., Barros, J., Kwak, B.J.: LDPC codes for the Gaussian wiretap channel. IEEE Transactions on Information Forensics and Security 6, 532–540 (2011)
9. Baldi, M., Bianchi, M., Chiaraluce, F.: Coding with scrambling, concatenation, and HARQ for the AWGN wire-tap channel: A security gap analysis. IEEE Transactions on Information Forensics and Security 7, 883–894 (2012)
10. Zhou, L., Wu, D., Zheng, B., Guizani, M.: Joint physical-application layer security for wireless multimedia delivery. IEEE Communications Magazine 52(3), 66–72 (2014)
11. Tanner, R.M., Sridhara, D., Sridharan, A., Fuja, T.E., Costello Jr., D.J.: LDPC block and convolutional codes based on circulant matrices. IEEE Transactions on Information Theory 50, 2966–2984 (2004)
12. Fossorier, M.P.: Quasicyclic low-density parity-check codes from circulant permutation matrices. IEEE Transactions on Information Theory 50, 1788–1793 (2004)
13. Costello, D., Lin, S.: Error Control Coding. Pearson Higher Education (2011)
14. Li, Z., Chen, L., Zeng, L., Lin, S., Fong, W.H.: Efficient encoding of quasi-cyclic low-density parity-check codes. IEEE Transactions on Communications 54, 71–81 (2006)
15. Biasi, F.P., Barreto, P.S., Misoczki, R., Ruggiero, W.V.: Scaling efficient code-based cryptosystems for embedded platforms. Journal of Cryptographic Engineering 4(2), 123–134 (2014)
16. Fossorier, M.P., Mihaljevic, M., Imai, H.: Reduced complexity iterative decoding of low-density parity check codes based on belief propagation. IEEE Transactions on Communications 47, 673–680 (1999)
17. Chen, J., Dholakia, A., Eleftheriou, E., Fossorier, M.P., Hu, X.Y.: Reduced-complexity decoding of LDPC codes. IEEE Transactions on Communications 53, 1288–1299 (2005)
18. Peters, C.: Information-set decoding for linear codes over F_q. In: Sendrier, N. (ed.) PQCrypto 2010. LNCS, vol. 6061, pp. 81–94. Springer, Heidelberg (2010)
19. Meier, W., Staffelbach, O.: Fast correlation attacks on certain stream ciphers. Journal of Cryptology 1, 159–176 (1989)
20. Jonsson, F., Johansson, T.: A fast correlation attack on LILI-128. Information Processing Letter 81, 127–132 (2002)
21. Menezes, A.J., Van Oorschot, P.C., Vanstone, S.A.: Handbook of applied cryptography. CRC Press (1996)
22. Chepyzhov, V.V., Johansson, T., Smeets, B.: A simple algorithm for fast correlation attacks on stream ciphers. In: Schneier, B. (ed.) FSE 2000. LNCS, vol. 1978, pp. 181–195. Springer, Heidelberg (2001)

Authentication of Trusted Platform Module
Using Processor Response

Vikash Kumar Rai and Arun Mishra

Department of Computer Engineering, Defence Institute of Advanced Technology
Pune, India
raionway@gmail.com, arundoes@yahoo.co.in

Abstract. Authentication is the process which allows both the communicating entities to validate each other. Authentication is the base for the trust between the two communicating party if both party wants to properly communicate. Trusted Platform Module (TPM) can be used to securely store artifacts like passwords, certificates, encryption keys or measurements required to authenticate the platform. In the present scenario there is no concrete mechanism to authenticate the TPM chip. In this project, a method has been proposed to enable user of a system to authenticate the TPM chip of the communicating system. The proposed system uses public endorsement key of the TPM chip and the unique response the processor gives while executing a program with predefined set of step delays.

Keywords: authentication, attestation, endorsement key, processor response, measurement, trusted platform module.

1   Introduction

In current scenario of computing world, numerous critical activities like financial transactions, secret data exchange are being carried out. So for all these platform integrity is highly required. By saying platform integrity we mean that the known and trusted software are only installed on the system. Authentication i.e. ensuring that the platform can prove that it is what it claims to be [1] and attestation, which is a process use to prove that a platform is trustworthy and has not been breached [2], are necessary steps to ensure trusted computing in all computing environments. A Trusted Platform Module (TPM) is a specialized chip on a computer system that plays an important role to build the trustworthiness of the system. TPM can be used to store platform measurements that help to ensure that the platform remains trustworthy. TPM securely stores a series of measurements in Platform Configuration Registers (PCRs) [3]. The TPM also stores cryptographic keys and other sensitive data in its shielded memory, and provides ways for platform software to use those keys to achieve security goals [4]. Trusted platform module consist of three kind of keys those are storage root key (SRK), endorsement key (EK) and authentication identity key (AIK). AIK has two parts private and public. The public portion is known as

J. Lloret Mauri et al. (Eds.): SSCC 2014, CCIS 467, pp. 325–334, 2014.
© Springer-Verlag Berlin Heidelberg 2014

public AIK. Platform authentication, certification of keys and platform attestation can be done using AIK.

An AIK supports to confer privacy when used to authenticate the platform in transactions, but there is no procedure to know which TPM the AIK is linked to. Endorsement key (EK) an RSA Key pair composed of a public key (pub EK) and private (pr EK). The EK is used to identify a faithful TPM. Storage root key (SRK) always resides in the TPM's memory. SRK is generated for every new owner, whenever owner calls the take ownership operation of the TPM.

To verify the platform integrity, a verifier asks the attester to attest the system. Then, the attester provides measurement values stored in the platform configuration register. Verifier checks the measurement value and based on the obtained values the decision about the integrity of the attester machine will be taken. So the entire trust for the attester machine depends on the trusted platform module chip but what if the TPM is not genuine. Existing attestation scheme has no way so that verifier can authenticate the attester TPM [2]. An attacker can install malicious software on attester machine so the measurement values will be changed and the system will not remain a genuine one. But instead of changed measurement value of the system, the malicious software will send a different measurement value to the verifier that is of a genuine machine (attacker machine). So ideally, verifier should be able to identify that the measurement values are coming from a different TPM (attacker machine's TPM) and not from the attester TPM.

In our approach we have developed software that takes the unique response from the processor. This response along with the endorsement key of the trusted platform module is used to authenticate the attester machine. Our software contains piece of code and a set of step delays for an attester system. In the attestation process first the verifier sends the set of step delays to the attester machine. The attester machine then executes the binary code using the step delay received from verifier. This execution generates a unique response string based on the execution time. This response string is used for uniquely identifying the trusted platform module chip.

The rest of the paper is organized as follows: Section 2 discusses existing trusted platform module based attestation scheme and its limitations. Section 3 describes related work carried out by various researchers. Section 4 talks about the proposed approach. Experiments and results are shown in Section 5. Finally we conclude with some future works in section 6.

2   Existing Scheme

Attestation is a process use to prove that a platform is trustworthy and only genuine software is installed on it.

The Fig.1 given below describes the existing attestation scheme use to attest a system

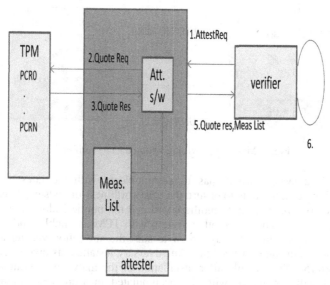

Fig. 1. TPM based attestation [2]

As shown in the Fig. 1 there are two systems one is verifier and other is attester. Verifier wants to communicate with attester but before that it checks the platforms integrity of the attester system. This process is known as attestation. Passing of information between the remote verifier and the TPM is the responsibility of dedicated software installed on attester system. TPM would generate Attestation Identity Key pair (AIK). The attestation process involved following steps [2]:

- A nonce will be supplied by the verifier to the attester to guarantee the freshness and request for attestation.

- The attester then gives the instruction to the TPM for the generation of the quote.

- The TPM will calculate the quote and sends back to the attestation software. The Quote is a digital signature containing the nonce provided by the verifier and the present measurement kept securely in the trusted platform module's Platform Configuration Registers (PCRs).

- The attester then takes the accumulated measurements from the measurement list.

- Attester dispatches both the quote and measurement to the verifier for verification.

- To verify the authenticity of measurement list, the hash of measurement list would be generated by the verifier and compared this with the aggregate unsigned TPM Quote. The quote will be unsigned with the public AIK. If both are equal then attestation is successful otherwise the attester system is not trusted.

The problem related to this approach is described with the help of Fig.2 given below

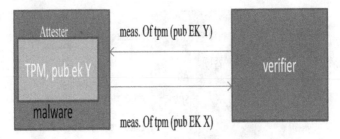

Fig. 2. Malware providing wrong data to verifier [5]

Verifier is a system which has to communicate with the attester but before communication verifier wants to ensure the trustworthiness of attester. Attester system has a TPM chip deployed on its motherboard and the public endorsement key of the TPM chip is Y (say). There is another system with TPM and public endorsement key of this adversary system is X (say). Now to start the attestation verifier asks for the attestation data to the attester machine. An adversary installed his own malware on the attester system[5]. Now ideally after installation of the malware, the quote generated by the TPM will not match with the accumulated measurement obtain from the measurement list. But since adversary wants to verifier that verifier talk to the malware infected system, the malware will send quote and measurement list generated by the TPM of adversary system (TPM with public EK X). The verifier will think that the quote and measurements are coming from the attester system with public EK Y but in reality it is generated from adversary system with public EK X. Now since quote is generated from the genuine machine with public EK X, after comparison verifier will find it correct. So verifier start further communication with attester machine considering it as a genuine system, although in actual it is malware infected. So finally the result of this is that verifier communicates with a untrusted machine thinking it as a trusted. This happens because there is no way to link the TPM with the machine and authenticate the TPM who is sending the data. So in our work we are solving this problem by authenticating TPM chip. Once TPM chip will be authenticated the wrong data cannot be provided to the verifier.

3   Related Works

Some works have been carried out in the field. McCune, J.M., Perrig, A., Reiter, M.K in the paper [6] discussed a camera base approach. It requires the computer's manufacturer to encode a hash of the platform's identity in a 2-D barcode and put this barcode to the system's case. This is to be noted that this step will only be performed by the manufacturer and not by the current owner. Using a camera-equipped smart phone, the user can take a picture of the 2-D barcode and the same smart phone can be used to process the computer's attestation. The benefits of using such approach are that it is an attractive solution, because it needs comparatively less effort from the manufacturer, and taking picture is also easy and interesting job for the people. The disadvantages of the approach are, it needs a vendor change, so it will not help current platforms. User should also own a smart phone should install the relevant software. Trusting the smart phone is also a problem. The 2-D barcode may be changed or hide by an attacker in a kiosk setting.

Lang, P. discussed about the concept of trusted BIOS in his paper [7]. In his paper he explained that if the user trusts the machine's BIOS, they can reboot the machine and have the trusted BIOS output the platform's identity. The trusted BIOS must be kept secure from malicious updates. User does not need any custom hardware and this is the main advantage of this approach. Simultaneously some disadvantages are also there like the user should reboot the machine, this can be harmful. It is the responsibility of the user to only give access to the verifier after rebooting; if it is not the case then the verifier may be faked by local malicious software. One big issue is that much of the motherboards do not keep the required protections to guarantee the trustworthiness of the BIOS, and also there is no indicative measure to convey the user about the trustworthiness of the BIOS on the local computer.

Pirker M., Toegl R., Hein D., Danner, P.l in his paper [8] discussed about the use of trusted third Party. The TPM can be equipped with a certificate provided by a trusted third party associating with a particular machine's TPM. Now the verifier can use the trusted third party's public key to verify the certificate and establish trust in the TPM's public key. The advantages with this approach is the verifier only requires to keep the public key for the trusted third party and perform basic certificate checks. Also one advantage is that no hardware changes are required .But some disadvantages are also there like it is not clear that how the verifier could communicate the TPM's location as specified in the certificate to the user in a clear and unambiguous fashion. Binding the certificate to the computer's serial number is a problem. This solution also raises the issue of creating a TPM's identity to the third party.

4   Proposed Approach

We propose a TPM authentication scheme for the attestation process. In our proposed approach we make use of the processor and get a unique response from the processor. We provide set of step delays to the processor and get the various responses. These responses in combination will form the unique Id of the processor. We use this processor unique response with the public Ek of the TPM to link the TPM with a processor. Our Approach consist of two phases

4.1   Registration

Registration is a onetime process and we assume that at the time of registration attester system is a trusted system and no malware is installed on the system.

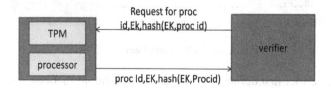

Fig. 3. Registration of attester at verifier

The following steps will be carried out at registration phase:

- The verifier first defines a set of step delays and instructions to be run on the attester system.
- The verifier then sends the step delays and instructions to the attester system and requests attester for the Processor unique ID (Unique response), Public EK and hash of processor unique ID and Pub EK.
- The attester system executes the received instructions and generates the processor unique Id.
- The attester sends Processor unique Id, Public EK and hash of (Processor ID and Pub EK) to the verifier.
- On receiving all this information, verifier will prepare a database which will be used during authentication process.

Below table shows the format of database securely stored at verifier system:

Table 1. Secure database at verifier

Step delay	Proc Id	Pub Ek	Hash(EK,Procid)
d1d2d3d4	01101100	X	Hash1
d5d6d7d8	11100001	Y	Hash2
d9d10d11d12	01100011	Z	Hash3

4.2   Authentication

Authentication will take place every time when a verifier wants to communicate with a attester. The following steps will be carried out during authentication process:

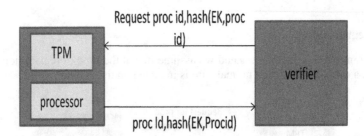

Fig. 4. Authentication of attester TPM

- The verifier first defines a set of step delays and instructions to be run on the attester system and requests for the Processor unique ID and hash of processor unique ID and Pub EK from the attester.

- The attester system executes the selected instructions and generates the processor unique Id.
- The attester sends Processor unique Id, hash of (Processor ID and Pub EK) to verifier.
- On receiving this information, verifier will take the Public EK, Corresponding to Processor ID getting from attester, from the stored database and generate its hash.
- Verifier then compares the generated hash value with received hash value. This comparison will ensure the integrity of received data during transmission.
- If the generated Hash value and received hash value will match then the verifier will compare generated hash value with stored hash value.
- If both values are matched then authentication of the TPM chip is successful.

In Fig.5 we have shown the authentication steps performed at the verifier side with the help of flow chart.

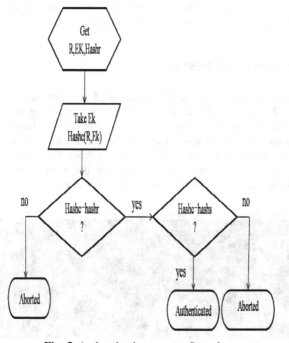

Fig. 5. Authentication process flow chart

4.3   Getting Processor Unique Response

Following steps will be followed in order to get the processor unique response:

- Verifier will decide the set of step delays and instructions to be run on the attester machine and sends it to the attester.
- Attester executes the instruction with a specific step delay received from verifier and has a specific execution time based on that delay.
- Same instruction will be executed iteratively; each time with a different step delay so it will take different execution time.
- Based on the execution time we calculate the responses.
- We combine these responses to get the unique Id of the processor.

To calculate the response from the execution time we apply the following rule: Response will be

$= 00$ if 0s <execution time<2s

$= 01$ if 2s <execution time<4s

$= 10$ if 4s <execution time<6s

$= 11$ if 6s <execution time<8s

We can make this interval of execution time even smaller and can also take responses in three bits or more to make it more precise.

5   Experiments and Results

The experiment was conducted on HP Desktop of configuration Intel® core™ i5-2430M CPU @ 2.40 GHz with, ubuntu 12.04 (64 bit operating system) installed. A 'Trusted Platform Module (Infenion TPM V1.2)' chip was embedded on the mother board of the computer. For the experiment of the our authentication scheme we have taken two above mentioned system and connects both the system through socket programming. Then we execute our code to get the responses from the attester machine. The figure shows the response for a specific delay.

Fig. 6. Response from processor based on delay

Fig.6 shows the response from the attester system after executing the code because with 20 millisecond step delays. The code consists of some basic mathematical calculations. The execution time lies between 0 to 2 seconds. In the similar way we executed our code four times and further responses comes as 10, 01, and 11and get combined to get a processor Id as 00100111.On getting this processor Id, attester generated the Public EK, and hash of both, then sent it to verifier. Verifier then stored all these information and prepares a database. For authentication we followed the same steps described in authentication phase.

Fig.7 shows authentication failure when incorrect data is provided to verifier.

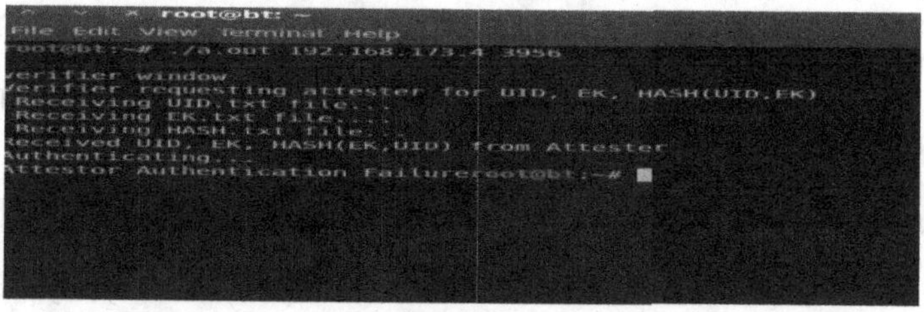

Fig. 7. Authentication failure at verifier

In Fig.8,it is shown that authentication is successful when correct information is given to verifier.

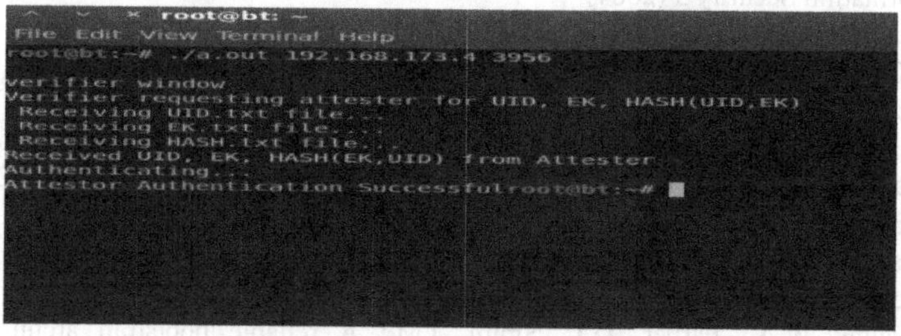

Fig. 8. Authentication failure at verifier

6   Conclusion and Future Work

Attestation of a trusted platform module is an important process in order to get the notion of trust for a computer.TPM based attestation is the one of the method for remote attestation. Authentication of TPM may play an important role during the attestation process. In the present work, a software has been developed for trusted platform module chip authentication using processor response.

The proposed work can be extended to get the processor unique identification based on some physical properties of the processor. These physical properties can be clock frequency, variations in integrated circuits.

References

[1]   Design of secure authentication and transaction protocol: In: Proceeding of International Conference on Computer Science and Service System (CSSS) (2011)
[2]   Parno, B., McCune, J.M., Perrig, A.: Bootstrapping Trust in Modern Computers

[3]   Trusted Computing Group: Trusted Platform Module Main Specification. Version 1.2, Revision 116 (2011)

[4]   Trusted Computing Group: PC client specific TPM interface specification (TIS). Version 1.21, Revision 1.00 (2011)

[5]   Sailer, R., Zhang, X., Jaeger, T., van Doorn, L.: Design and implementation of a TCG-based integrity measurement architecture. In: Proceedings of the USENIX Security Symposium (2004)

[6]   McCune, J.M., Perrig, A., Reiter, M.K.: Seeing-is-believing: Using camera phones for human-verifiable authentication. In: Proceedings of the IEEE Symposium on Security and Privacy (2005)

[7]   Lang, P.: Flash the Intel BIOS with confidence. Intel Developer UPDATE Magazine (2002)

[8]   Pirker, M., Toegl, R., Hein, D., Danner, P.: A PrivacyCA for anonymity and trust. In: Chen, L., Mitchell, C.J., Martin, A. (eds.) Trust 2009. LNCS, vol. 5471, pp. 101–119. Springer, Heidelberg (2009)

[9]   http://www.kcchao.wikidot.com/tpm (2014)

[10] Smith, S.W.: Outbound authentication for programmable secure coprocessors. Journal of Information Security 3 (2004)

[11] http://www.ma.rhul.ac.uk (2014)

[12] McCune, J.M.: Flicker: Minimal TCB Code Execution

[13] http://www.grounation.org/?post/2008/07/04/8-

[14] Gasser, M., Goldstein, A., Kaufman, C., Lampson, B.: The digital distributed system security architecture. In: Proceedings of the National Computer Security Conference (1989)

[15] Trusted computing and trusted network connect in a nutshell

[16] http://www.trust.f4.hs-hannover.de (2014)

[17] Arbaugh, W.A., Farber, D.J., Smith, J.M.: A reliable bootstrap architecture. In: Proceedings of the IEEE Symposium on Security and Privacy, pp. 65–71 (1997)

[18] Maiti, A., Schaumont, P.: A novel microprocessor intrinsic physical uncloneable function. In: 2012 22nd International Conference on Field Programmable Logic and Applications (FPL), pp. 380–387 (August 2012)

[19] Challenger, et al.: A Practice guide to trusted computing. IBM Press (2008)

[20] Trusted Computing Group (TCG), TPM main part 1.2.3, Design, principles, specifications version 1.2 (2011)

[21] Das, M.L., Saxena, A., Gulati, V.P.: A dynamic ID-based remote user authentication scheme. IEEE Transactions on Consumer Electronics 50(2), 629–631 (2004)

[22] Liu, J.-S.: A TPM Authentication Scheme for Mobile IP. In: International Conference on Computational Intelligence and Security Workshops (2007)

[23] Lee, H., Choi, D., Lee, Y., Won, D., Kim, S.: Security Weaknesses of Dynamic ID-based Remote User Authentication Protocol

[24] Wang, Y., Liu, J., Xiao, F., Dan, J.: A more efficient and secure dynamic ID-based remote user authentication scheme. Computer Communications 32(4), 583–585 (2009)

[25] Li, L., Li, C., Zhou, Y.: A Remote Anonymous Attestation Scheme With improves CA. In: International Conference on Multimedia Information Network and Security (2009)

Results on (2, *n*) Visual Cryptographic Scheme

Kanakkath Praveen and M.Sethumadhavan

Amrita Vishwa Vidyapeetham
Amrita Nagar P.O, Ettimadai,Coimbatore-641 112
praveen.cys@gmail.com, m_sethu@cb.amrita.edu

Abstract. In the literature a lot of studies were carried out on (2, *n*) visual cryptographic scheme (*VCS*) using either XOR or OR operation. A scheme on ideal contrast (2, *n*) *VCS* with reversing using combined OR and NOT operations was reported. In this paper, a construction on an ideal contrast (2, *n*) *VCS* using combined XOR and OR operations with less amount of transparencies than ideal contrast (2, *n*) *VCS* with reversing using OR and NOT operations is proposed. This paper also shows a construction of (2, *n*) *VCS* with pixel expansion one which perfectly reconstruct the white pixels and probabilistically reconstruct the black pixel using XOR operation.

Keywords: Visual Cryptography, Secret sharing, Perfect Reconstruction, Probabilistic scheme.

1   Introduction

Secret sharing scheme is a method of generating shares from a secret, and the generated shares are distributed to a group of participants. The dealer distributes shares to each participant in such a way that, while combining sufficient number of shares (k or more) the participants can reconstruct the secret but fewer than k participants are not allowed to reconstruct. Such a system is called as (k, n) threshold scheme. Naor and Adi Shamir in 1994 developed a (k, n) OR based visual cryptographic scheme (*VCS*) [1] for sharing secret images. The basic parameters for a *VCS* are pixel expansion and contrast. The pixel expansion is a measure of number of sub pixels used for encoding a pixel of secret image while contrast is the difference in grey level between black pixel and white pixel in the reconstructed image. Droste [3] in 1998 proposed a *VCS* with less pixel expansion than Naor's *et al.* scheme. In 2006 Bose et.al [7] proposed an optimal (2, *n*) *VCS*. In 2008 Sreekumar *et al.* [8] proposed a Uniform Secret Sharing Scheme for (2, *n*) *VCS*. In 2010 Liu *et al.* [9] proposed an XOR based (2, *n*) *VCS* with optimal pixel expansion but the contrast is not ideal. A *VCS* for general access structure was introduced by Ateniese *et al.* [2] in 1996. Adhikari *et al.* [4] in 2004 also constructed a *VCS* for general access structure. In 2005 Tylus *et al.* [5] proposed a *VCS* based on XOR operation. The (k, n) *VCS* and (2, *n*) *VCS* are special cases of general access structure constructions. Cimato *et al.* [10] in 2005 proposed an ideal contrast general access structure *VCS* with reversing using OR and NOT operations. An ideal contrast (2, *n*) *VCS* can be constructed using Cimato *et al.* construction.

J. Lloret Mauri et al. (Eds.): SSCC 2014, CCIS 467, pp. 335–340, 2014.
© Springer-Verlag Berlin Heidelberg 2014

In this paper, we propose a construction of an ideal contrast $(2, n)$ VCS using combined XOR and OR operations with optimal amount of transparencies. This scheme is better than the method proposed by Cimato et.al in the amount of transparencies. In 2004 Yang et al. [6] constructed a probabilistic non expandable VCS with same contrast level of the expandable VCS using OR operation. In this paper we show a construction of non expandable $(2, n)$ VCS which perfectly reconstruct the white pixel and probabilistically reconstruct the black pixel.

Let $P = \{P_1, P_2, P_3,\ldots, P_n\}$ be the set of participants, and 2^P denote the power set of P. Let us denote Γ_{Qual} as qualified set and Γ_{Forb} as forbidden set. Let $\Gamma_{Qual} \in 2^P$ and $\Gamma_{Forb} \in 2^P$ where $\Gamma_{Qual} \cap \Gamma_{Forb} = \emptyset$. Any set $A \in \Gamma_{Qual}$ can recover the secret image whereas any set $A \in \Gamma_{Forb}$ cannot leak out any secret information. Let $\Gamma_0 = \{A \in \Gamma_{Qual}: A' \notin \Gamma_{Qual}$ for all $A' \subseteq A, A' \neq A\}$ be the set of minimal qualified subset of P. The pair $\Gamma = (\Gamma_{Qual}, \Gamma_{Forb})$ is called the access structure of $(2, n)$ VCS. Let S be an $n \times m$ Boolean matrix and $A \subseteq P$, the vector obtained by applying the Boolean XOR operation to the rows of S corresponding to the elements in A is denoted by S_A. Let $w(S_A)$ denotes the Hamming weight of vector S_A. Definition for the basis matrix of $(2, n)$ VCS using XOR operation is given in [9]. In the next section an existing ideal contrast $(2, n)$ VCS is discussed.

2   Cimato's Ideal Contrast $(2, n)$ VCS

Let $P = \{P_1, P_2,\ldots P_n\}$ be the set of participants. The share generation and decryption phase is given below.

1. Let K be the secret binary image of size $(p \times q)$. For each participant u, $1 \leq u \leq n$ the share construction is given as.

    $$Sh_{(u,j)}(g,h) = \begin{cases} (u, j)^{\text{th}} \text{ element of } S^0 & \text{if } K(g,h) = 0 \\ (u, j)^{\text{th}} \text{ element of } S^1 & \text{if } K(g,h) = 1 \end{cases} ;1 \leq g \leq p,$$

    $1 \leq h \leq q$ and $1 \leq j \leq m$. Each participant u will have m transparencies with same size of the secret image. S^0 and S^1 are the basis matrices which can be constructed using perfect black pixel reconstruction scheme [2, 11].

2. Let us define a function $f(x) = \begin{cases} 1 & \text{if } x == 0 \\ 0 & \text{if } x == 1 \end{cases}$.

3. In the decryption phase, the stacking of any 2 of the n shares of the participants is done using the following steps. Apply steps from a) to c) for all pixels.

    a. Let $\lambda_j(g,h) = $ OR-ing any pairs $(Sh_{(x,j)}, Sh_{(y,j)})$ for all $j = 1,..,m, x \neq y$ and x, y are $\in \{1, 2, 3\ldots n\}$.

    b. $\sigma(g,h) = $ OR all $f(\lambda_j(g,h))$ for $j = 1,.., m$.

    c. Find $K = f(\sigma(g,h))$ for $1 \leq g \leq p, 1 \leq h \leq q$.

3   Proposed Ideal Contrast (2, n) VCS using Liu's Construction

Let $P = \{P_1, P_2, P_3,..., P_n\}$ be the set of participants. The share generation and decryption phase is given below

1. From the Construction 1 in [9] generate a matrix M with distinct rows of size $n \times m$, $m = \lceil \log_2 n \rceil$.

2. Two collections of $n \times m$ Boolean matrices S^0 and S^1 is given as $S^1 = \{C(i) : C(i)$ be the $n \times m$ matrix obtained by a cyclic shift on the rows of M over (i) positions$\}$ and all the rows in the matrix S^0 is same and are generated by randomly selecting a single row from M.

3. Let K be a binary secret image of size $(p \times q)$.For each participant u, $1 \le u \le n$ the share construction is given as.

$$Sh_{(u,j)}(g,h) = \begin{cases} (u, j)^{\text{th}} \text{ element of } S^0 & \text{if } K(g,h) = 0 \\ (u, j)^{\text{th}} \text{ element of } S^1 & \text{if } K(g,h) = 1 \end{cases} ; 1 \le g \le p,$$

$1 \le h \le q$ and $1 \le j \le m$. Each participant u will have m transparencies with same size of the secret image.

4. In the decryption phase, the stacking of any 2 of the n shares of the participants is done using the following steps. Apply steps from a) and b) for all pixels $(p \times q)$.

    a) Let $\lambda_j(g,h) = $ XOR-ing any pairs $(Sh_{(x, j)}, Sh_{(y, j)})$ shares for all $j = 1,....,m$, $x \ne y$ and x, y are $\in \{1,2,3,....n\}$.

    b) $\sigma(g, h) = $ OR-ing all $\lambda_j(g,h)$ for $j = 1,...., m$; where $1 \le g \le p$, $1 \le h \le q$, $\sigma(g, h)$ is the reconstructed secret which is same as that of K.

The number of transparencies of the proposed scheme using Liu's construction is $\lceil \log_2 n \rceil$ which is better than $2^{(n-1)}$ (resp. n) transparencies of ideal contrast (2, n) VCS using Ateniese et al. (resp. Blundo et al.) scheme.

3.1   Example

Let $P = \{P_1, P_2, P_3, P_4\}$ be the set of participants. The basis matrices S^0 (resp.S^1) for a

(2, 4) VCS is constructed as follows. Let $M = \begin{bmatrix} 0 & 0 \\ 0 & 1 \\ 1 & 1 \\ 1 & 0 \end{bmatrix}$, then according to the construction the randomly selected row from M is $(0, 1)$. Then $S^0 = \begin{bmatrix} 0 & 1 \\ 0 & 1 \\ 0 & 1 \\ 0 & 1 \end{bmatrix}$ and

$S^1 = \begin{bmatrix} 0 & 0 \\ 0 & 1 \\ 1 & 1 \\ 1 & 0 \end{bmatrix}$ .Suppose the secret matrix is given as $K = \begin{bmatrix} 1 & 0 \\ 0 & 1 \end{bmatrix}$. Two transparencies

of each participant are given as follows.

$$P_1 \Rightarrow Sh_{(1,1)} = \begin{bmatrix} 0 & 0 \\ 0 & 0 \end{bmatrix}, Sh_{(1,2)} = \begin{bmatrix} 0 & 1 \\ 1 & 0 \end{bmatrix}, P_2 \Rightarrow Sh_{(2,1)} = \begin{bmatrix} 0 & 0 \\ 0 & 0 \end{bmatrix}, Sh_{(2,2)} = \begin{bmatrix} 1 & 1 \\ 1 & 1 \end{bmatrix},$$

$$P_3 \Rightarrow Sh_{(3,1)} = \begin{bmatrix} 1 & 0 \\ 0 & 1 \end{bmatrix}, Sh_{(3,2)} = \begin{bmatrix} 1 & 1 \\ 1 & 1 \end{bmatrix}, P_4 \Rightarrow Sh_{(4,1)} = \begin{bmatrix} 1 & 0 \\ 0 & 1 \end{bmatrix}, Sh_{(4,2)} = \begin{bmatrix} 0 & 1 \\ 1 & 0 \end{bmatrix}.$$

In the decryption phase if P_2 and P_3 combines the two transparencies obtained are
$\lambda_1 = \begin{bmatrix} 1 & 0 \\ 0 & 1 \end{bmatrix}$ and $\lambda_2 = \begin{bmatrix} 0 & 0 \\ 0 & 0 \end{bmatrix}$, then $\sigma = \begin{bmatrix} 1 & 0 \\ 0 & 1 \end{bmatrix}$, which ideally reconstruct the

secret K.

4   Proposed Probabilistic Non Expandable $(2, n)$ VCS

Let $P = \{P_1, P_2, P_3, \ldots, P_n\}$ be the set of participants. The basis matrices S^0 (resp.S^1) of size $n \times 1$ is given as $S^0 = \{$"either" n tuple column vector with all zeros "or" n tuple column vector with all ones$\}$ and $S^1 = \{$any n tuple column vector with r ones where r

$= \left\lfloor \dfrac{n}{2} \right\rfloor$ or $\left\lceil \dfrac{n}{2} \right\rceil \}$.The reconstruction is done by XOR-ing any two shares. The patters

$\begin{bmatrix} 0 \\ 0 \end{bmatrix}$ and $\begin{bmatrix} 1 \\ 1 \end{bmatrix}$ in a matrix S^0 will give a white pixel during reconstruction and the

patters $\begin{bmatrix} 0 \\ 1 \end{bmatrix}$ and $\begin{bmatrix} 1 \\ 0 \end{bmatrix}$ in a matrix S^1 will give a black pixel during reconstruction. It is

clear that during reconstruction the white pixels will reconstruct perfectly in white region but the reconstruction of black pixel in black region is probabilistic. In order to increase the probability of occurrence of black pixel in black region we need to increase the number of patterns of $\begin{bmatrix} 0 \\ 1 \end{bmatrix}$ and $\begin{bmatrix} 1 \\ 0 \end{bmatrix}$ in a matrix S^1. In the paper [9] it is

given that if we are selecting a *n* tuple column vector with *r* ones the occurrence of

the patterns $\begin{bmatrix} 0 \\ 1 \end{bmatrix}$ and $\begin{bmatrix} 1 \\ 0 \end{bmatrix}$ reaches its maximum when $r = \left\lfloor \dfrac{n}{2} \right\rfloor$ or $\left\lceil \dfrac{n}{2} \right\rceil$. The

probability of occurrence of black pixel in the black region is observed as Prob(*b/b*) =

$$\dfrac{\left\lfloor \dfrac{n}{2} \right\rfloor \times \left\lceil \dfrac{n}{2} \right\rceil}{\dbinom{n}{2}}$$ .The probability of occurrence of black pixel in the white region is

observed as Prob(*b/w*) =0. The relative contrast is given as Prob(*b/b*) - Prob(*b/w*).

4.1   Example

Let us define two sets D^0 and D^1 as $D^0 = \left\{ \begin{bmatrix} 0 \\ 0 \\ 0 \\ 0 \end{bmatrix}, \begin{bmatrix} 1 \\ 1 \\ 1 \\ 1 \end{bmatrix} \right\}$ and $D^1 = \left\{ \begin{bmatrix} 0 \\ 0 \\ 1 \\ 1 \end{bmatrix}, \begin{bmatrix} 1 \\ 1 \\ 0 \\ 0 \end{bmatrix}, \right.$

$\left. \begin{bmatrix} 0 \\ 1 \\ 1 \\ 0 \end{bmatrix}, \begin{bmatrix} 1 \\ 0 \\ 0 \\ 1 \end{bmatrix} \right\}$, $S^0 \in D^0$ and $S^1 \in D^1$. Let S^0 and S^1 be the second matrix from D^0 and D^1

respectively. The possible pairs of patterns from the matrix S^0 is $\left\{ \begin{bmatrix} 0 \\ 0 \end{bmatrix}, \begin{bmatrix} 1 \\ 1 \end{bmatrix} \right\}$ and S^1 is

$\left\{ \begin{bmatrix} 0 \\ 0 \end{bmatrix}, \begin{bmatrix} 1 \\ 1 \end{bmatrix}, \begin{bmatrix} 1 \\ 0 \end{bmatrix}, \begin{bmatrix} 1 \\ 0 \end{bmatrix}, \begin{bmatrix} 1 \\ 0 \end{bmatrix}, \begin{bmatrix} 1 \\ 0 \end{bmatrix} \right\}$.The white pixel 0 will be reconstructed perfectly

but black pixel 1 will be reconstructed with a probability of 4/6.So the contrast of the scheme is 4/6.

5   Conclusion

Cimato *et al.* proposed an ideal contrast (2, *n*) VCS using the basis matrices of Ateniese *et al.* and Blundo *et al.* perfect black construction scheme. In this paper we proposed an ideal contrast (2, *n*) VCS using Liu's construction. The number of transparencies of the proposed scheme is better than that of existing construction. The contrast of the probabilistic schemes completely depends up on the basis matrices used, except in case of random grid constructions. The proposed probabilistic non expandable $(2, n)$ VCS has better contrast than that of existing schemes.

References

1. Naor, M., Shamir, A.: Visual Cryptography. In: De Santis, A. (ed.) EUROCRYPT 1994. LNCS, vol. 950, pp. 1–12. Springer, Heidelberg (1995)
2. Ateniese, G., Blundo, C., Santis, A.D., Stinson, D.R.: Visual Cryptography for general access structures. Information and Computation 129, 86–106 (1996)
3. Droste, S.: New results on visual cryptography. In: Koblitz, N. (ed.) CRYPTO 1996. LNCS, vol. 1109, pp. 401–415. Springer, Heidelberg (1996)
4. Adhikari, A., Dutta, T.K., Roy, B.: A New Black and White Visual cryptographic scheme for general access structures. In: Canteaut, A., Viswanathan, K. (eds.) INDOCRYPT 2004. LNCS, vol. 3348, pp. 399–413. Springer, Heidelberg (2004)
5. Tylus, P., Hollman, H.D.L., Lint, J.H.V., Tolhuizen, L.: XOR based visual cryptographic schemes. Design Codes and Cryptography 37(1), 169–186 (2005)
6. Yang, C.N.: New Visual secret sharing scheme using probabilistic method. Pattern Recognition Letters 25(4), 481–494 (2004)
7. Bose, M., Mukerjee, R.: Optimal $(2, n)$ Visual Cryptographic scheme. Design Codes and Cryptography 40(3), 255–267 (2006)
8. Sreekumar, A., Babusundar, S.: Uniform secret sharing scheme for $(2, n)$ threshold using Visual Cryptography. International Journal of Information Processing 2(4) (2008)
9. Feng, L., Wu, C.K.: Optimal XOR based $(2, n)$ Visual Cryptographic scheme. IACR Cryptology eprint Archives (2010)
10. Cimato, S., Santis, A.D., Ferrara, A.L., Masucci, B.: Ideal contrast Visual Cryptographic scheme with reversing. Information Processing Letters 93, 199–206 (2005)
11. Blundo, C., Bonis, A.D., Santis, A.D.: Improved schemes for Visual Cryptography. Design Codes and Cryptography 24, 255–278 (2001)

A Heuristic Model for Performing Digital Forensics in Cloud Computing Environment

Digambar Povar and G. Geethakumari

Department of Computer Science and Information Systems, BITS Pilani, Hyderabad Campus,
Jawaharnagar, Rangareddy Dist., Andhra Pradesh – 50078, India
{powar.d,geetha}@hyderabad.bits-pilani.ac.in

Abstract. Cloud computing is a relatively new model in the computing world after several computing paradigms like personal, ubiquitous, grid, mobile, and utility computing. Cloud computing is synonymous with virtualization which is about creating virtual versions of the hardware platform, the Operating System or the storage devices. Virtualization poses challenges to implementation of security as well as cybercrime investigation in the cloud. Although several researchers have contributed in identifying digital forensic challenges and methods of performing digital forensic analysis in the cloud computing environment, we feel that the requirement of finding the most appropriate methods to evaluate the uncertainty in the digital evidence is a must. This paper emphasizes on the methods of finding and analyzing digital evidence in cloud computing environment with respect to the cloud user as well as the provider. We propose a heuristic model for performing digital forensics in the cloud environment.

Keywords: Virtualization, cloud computing, cybercrime, digital evidence, digital forensics, cloud forensics.

1   Introduction

Cloud computing is maturing and continues to be the latest, most hyped concept in IT. Cloud computing evokes different perceptions in different people. Cloud computing has the potential to become one of the most transformative developments in the history of computing, following the footsteps of mainframes, minicomputers, PCs (Personal Computers), smart phones, and so on (Perry et al., 2009). Gartner estimates that there are currently about 50 million enterprise users of cloud office systems, which represent only 8 percent of overall office system users (excluding China and India). Gartner, however, predicts that a major shift toward cloud office systems will begin by the first half of 2015 and reach 33 percent penetration by 2017 and 60 percent by 2020 (Gartner, 2013). According to an IDC IT Cloud Services User Survey, 74 per cent of IT executives and CIOs have cited security as the top challenge preventing their adoption of the Cloud services model [2].

Some recent attacks on cloud computing platforms strengthen the security concern. For example, a botnet attack (running of "Zeus botnet controller" on an EC2 instance)

J. Lloret Mauri et al. (Eds.): SSCC 2014, CCIS 467, pp. 341–352, 2014.

on Amazon's cloud infrastructure was reported in 2009 [3]. This implies that an adversary can rent any number of virtual machines (VM's) to launch a Distributed Denial of Service (DDoS) attack on other systems including where the VMs are running. Also, due to the remote storage facility provided by cloud computing platforms such as Google Drive, Dropbox, Windows SkyDrive, etc., cyber criminals can keep their secret files (e.g., pornography pictures, forgery documents, etc.,) in cloud storage and can destroy all digital evidence from their local storage to get undetected during investigation. To investigate these kinds of cybercrimes involving cloud computing platforms, Investigators have to carry out digital forensic investigation in the suspected client device as well as cloud computing environment itself. The way of performing forensic investigation in cloud environment is explained in section 2.3. The remaining part of the paper is organized in three sections: Section 1 provides introduction to cloud computing, digital forensics and cloud forensics. Section 2 describes the phases of cloud forensics by proposing a heuristic model for performing forensic investigation in the cloud environment by applying appropriate methods of traditional digital forensic investigation in each phase. Section 3 provides conclusion and future work.

1.1   Cloud Compuing

There is no unique definition available for cloud computing that is acceptable to the world community of users. The most widely used definition of the cloud computing model is introduced by NIST [4] as "a model for enabling ubiquitous, convenient, on - demand network access to a shared pool of configurable computing resources (e.g., networks, servers, storage, applications and services) that can be rapidly provisioned and released with minimal management effort or service provider interaction". The authors agree on the definition, "An Internet based computing paradigm that delivers on-demand software and hardware computing capability as a 'service' through virtualization where the end user is completely abstracted from the computing resources". The working of whole cloud computing is based on 3-4-5 rule, in which, it provides 3 – unique services, 4 – unique deployment models and 5 – unique characteristics according to NIST [4]. Three services named according to the abstraction level of the capability provided and the service models of providers are: 1- Infrastructure as a Service, 2- Platform as a Service, and 3- Software as a Service [5].

Infrastructure as a Service (IaaS). This service model provides the user the facility of renting processing power and storage to run his or her own virtual machine in the cloud. User can access the launched virtual machine through the web browsers in computers or mobile devices. Users will be charged based on the resources the virtual machine consumes from the cloud. Amazon provides IaaS through its EC2 (Elastic Compute Cloud) facility. Many other vendors like Microsoft, Rackspace, GoGrid, terremark, etc., provide the same facility.

Platform as a Service (PaaS). This service model provides the user the facility of renting a platform to develop and deploy the user applications in the cloud environment. It is basically an application middleware offered as a service to developers, integrators, and architects. Users will be charged according to the platform (e.g., Database, .Net) used and bandwidth consumed. The well-known example of PaaS is Google App Engine. There are number of other PaaS providers like Windows Azure, Force.com, Drupal, Wolf Frameworks, Cloud Foundry, IBM Bluemix, Eccentex, AppBase, LongJump, SquareSpace, WaveMaker, etc., to name few.

Software as a Service (SaaS). This service model provides the user the facility of using cloud service provider's software application running on cloud infrastructure. User can access the application through the web browsers in computers or mobile devices. Users will be charged based on the usages of the application. Examples of SaaS include applications like Salesforce, QuickBooks, GoToMeeting, Zoho Office Suite, Microsoft Office 365, Google docs, Google calendar to name few.

According to the deployment model, cloud computing can be categorized into four categories – private cloud, public cloud, community cloud, and hybrid cloud [4].

Private Cloud. In this model, the cloud infrastructure is fully operated by the cloud owner organization. It is the internal data center where the infrastructure is located at the organization's premises. One can set up this kind of cloud computing environment using solutions like OpenStack, Eucalyptus, VMWare, etc. [6], [7], [8].

Public Cloud. Cloud Service Providers owns the cloud infrastructure and they make it available to the general people or a large industry group. Amazon, Microsoft and Google are the major public cloud service providers in the current IT industry.

Community Cloud. Similar to grid computing model in which several organizations with common concerns (e.g., mission, security requirements, policy, and compliance considerations) share cloud infrastructure. Different private cloud data centers can be connected to form this kind of computing model.

Hybrid Cloud. This model is a composition of two or more clouds (private, community, or public). Hybrid Cloud architecture requires both on-premises resources and off-site (remote) server based cloud infrastructure. Eucalyptus, VMWare, etc., are examples of Hybrid cloud deployment solutions.

5 - Unique characteristics of cloud computing according to NIST are [4]:

On-Demand Self-Service. A client can provision computer resources without the need for interaction with cloud service provider personnel.

Broad Network Access. Access to resources in the cloud is available over the network using standard methods in a manner that provides platform-independent access to clients of all types.

Resource Pooling. A cloud service provider creates resources that are pooled together in a system that supports multi-tenant usage. Physical and virtual systems are dynamically allocated or reallocated as needed.

Rapid Elasticity. Resources can be rapidly and elastically provisioned. The system can add resources by either scaling up systems (more powerful computers) or scaling out systems (more computers of the same kind), and scaling may be automatic or manual. From the standpoint of the client, cloud computing resources should look limitless and can be purchased at any time and in any quantity.

Measured Service. The use of cloud system resources is measured, audited, and reported to the customer based on a metered system.

1.2   Digital Forensics

Digital forensics is a relatively new sub-discipline of forensic science when compared to other common forensic science disciplines. Digital forensics has a number of synonyms including forensic computing, computational forensics, computer forensics and cyber forensics [9]. One of the first definitions of digital forensics was provided by McKemmish in 1999 as "the process of identifying, preserving, analyzing and presenting digital evidence in a manner that is legally acceptable by court of law". A widely used definition given by NIST (Kent et al., 2006) share some similarities with McKemmish is given as follows:

1. Collection discusses identifying relevant data, preserving its integrity and acquiring the data;
2. Examination uses automated and manual tools to extract data of interest while ensuring preservation;
3. Analysis is concerned with deriving useful information from the results of the examination; and
4. Reporting is concerned with the preparation and presentation of the forensic analysis.

There are many well-known tools available for performing forensic analysis like FTK (Forensic Tool Kit), EnCase, X-Ways Forensics, The Sleuth Kit (TSK), CyberCheck, etc. [19], [20], [21], [22].

1.3   Cloud Forensics

As there is no unique definition available for cloud computing, it is too early to expect a definition of emerging area like cloud forensics. According to Ruan et al., Cloud computing is based on broad network access. Network forensics deals with forensic investigations of networks. So, Cloud forensics is a subset of network forensics. Also, they view it as a cross discipline of cloud computing and digital forensics. Shams et al. [10], define cloud forensic as "the application of computer forensic principles and procedures in a cloud computing environment".

The "Cloud crime" can be defined as a crime that involves cloud computing in a sense that Cloud can be the object, subject or tool of crimes (Object - CSP is the target of the crime; Subject - Cloud is the environment where the crime is committed; Tool - Cloud can also be the tool used to conduct or plan a crime) [32].

According to the services and deployment models of cloud computing environment, the forensic analysis methods would have to vary. In the case of SaaS and PaaS, the control over process or network monitoring is very limited. In the case of IaaS, the cloud user will have more control over computing resources [14]. Apart from reporting step, the first 3 steps of computer forensics will vary for different services and deployment models in cloud computing. For example, the collection procedure of SaaS and IaaS will not be same. In SaaS model, the CSP (Cloud Service Provider) will have control over application logs and related data, while in IaaS, cloud user will have control over data generated by virtual machine instance. On the other hand, in the private deployment model, we have physical access to the digital evidence data, but we merely can get physical access to the data in public deployment model. Fig. 1 shows the management of cloud services in typical cloud data centers by CSP [14].

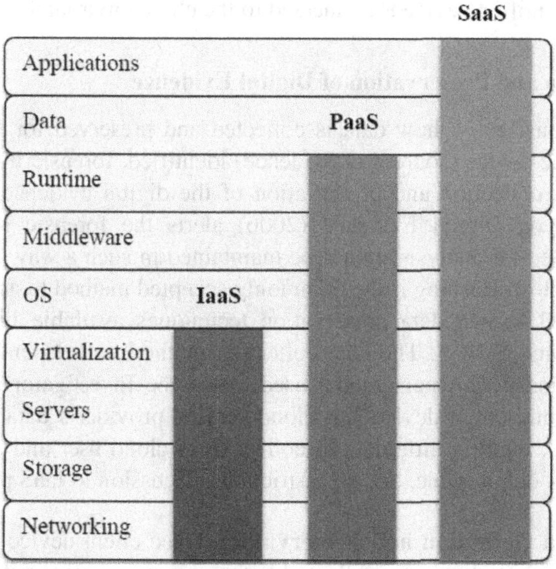

Fig. 1. CSP's control over multiple layers in three service models [14]

2 Methods of Digital Forensics in Cloud Computing

Incident response and computer forensics in a cloud computing environment require fundamentally different tools, techniques, and training [16]. A draft report from the National Institute of Standards and Technology (2011, p.64) noted that "little guidance exists on how to acquire and conduct forensics in a cloud environment" and suggested that the existing best practices and guidelines still apply to digital forensics in the cloud computing environment.

In this research work, we propose a heuristic model for performing digital forensics in Cloud computing environment (as shown in figure 2) which is based on the phases of models suggested by McKemmish (1999) and NIST (Kent et al., 2006). The model we proposed is self-explanatory which would enable forensic Investigators to perform investigation and tool developers to come up with forensic tools specifically for the cloud environment. In the following sub sections, we analyze importance of each stage of the proposed model by applying appropriate methods of traditional digital forensic investigation.

2.1 Identification of Digital Evidence

This phase describes the way of identifying the sources of evidence in a digital forensics investigation in the cloud environment as an entry point. As shown in Fig. 2, the sources of evidence could be desktop computers, laptops, mobile devices, or any device using which one can access cloud services (called as client device). After a reported cloud crime, client device can be identified using network forensic techniques. The identification phase may also be required during the analysis phase to know how the identified device is connected to the cloud environment.

2.2 Collection and Preservation of Digital Evidence

This phase emphasizes on how data is collected and preserved for further analysis. Irrespective of the device (sources of evidence) identified, forensic Investigators need to ensure proper collection and preservation of the digital evidence. The Scientific Working Group on Digital Evidence (2006) alerts the forensic Investigator that evidence submitted for analysis should be maintained in such a way that the integrity of the data is not lost. Hashing is the commonly accepted method to achieve this.

There are well known data preservation techniques available like MD4, MD5, SHA-1, SHA-2 and SHA-3. The data collection method will depend on the type of cloud platform and deployment model used. Also, the Investigator needs to collect data from the cloud client device and cloud service provider's data center. In SaaS and PaaS models, there is little data to collect from cloud user and service provider for provenance of cloud crime. So, we restrict our discussion to IaaS platform.

Client Side Data Collection and Preservation. Once client device is identified, its physical memory data should be collected before powering off the device. There are numerous tools available for memory acquisition (FTK imager, OSForensics, dd - data duplication, LiME, etc). The data from powered off device can be collected using software tools (FTK imager, EnCase Forensic Imager, TrueBack, etc) or hardware tools (Tableau forensic duplicator, HardCopy 3P, etc). Many of the above tools have the capability of forensically sound data acquisition, i.e., preservation.

Cloud Side Data Collection and Preservation. In case of private deployment model, Investigator can use remote acquisition methods to get the virtual disk data and physical memory data pertaining to a particular VM (for example Investigator can use dd - data duplication utility of Unix to acquire virtual disk image as well as physical memory image). Unfortunately, the provenance of cloud crime not only depends on analysis of virtual disk and memory of a VM used by a criminal but also logs generated by the virtual machine during its operation. Such logs are categorized as

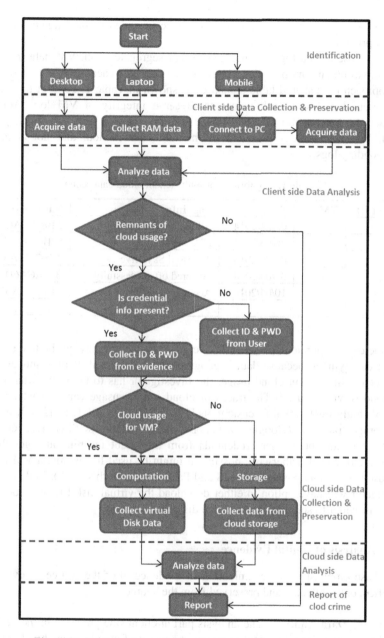

Fig. 2. Digital forensics model for cloud computing environment

API logs (logs start, end and life activity of a VM) and Host logs (also called as firewall logs, used to log network activity of a VM).

Private cloud data centers (any cloud data center for that matter) run as many VMs as possible depending on their computational capacity and the data generated by all the VMs are stored in a log file that cannot be provided to Investigator due to the issue of privacy.

We propose a data logging mechanism that segregates each VM data in a multi-tenant environment and provides a query based facility to acquire VM logs remotely. Our approach uses shared table database (as shown in Table 1) concept to store logs of different VMs with hash values to preserve integrity of VM logs. With this approach the Investigator or cloud user can query for logs of a VM for a specified period. The hash values provided in the table are random and not actuals for corresponding logs.

Table 1. Log format for multi-tenant cloud data center

Tenant ID	VM ID	Date	Log Info	Hash (MD5)
1	1	05/04/2014	Admin provisioning	AB87FCA6....3D
1	2	08/04/2014	FTK installed	87HCA6124...BC
2	1	09/04/2014	Accessed SkyDrive	A58C431A6....37
1	2	09/04/2014	Powered off successfully	B87ACA6D1...34
2	1	10/04/2014	Access request from x.y.z.t	AB87BCA65...6D
....	....	....	....	....

In the case of public deployment model, data collection may not be that simple as private deployment, because data is geographically dispersed. If remnants are found in client machine about cloud usage, the Investigator has to know for what purpose the cloud service is used. The traces of cloud service usage can be analyzed using available traditional digital forensic tools [17], [18], [19], [20], [21], [22]. If it is used for storage purpose (Google Drive, Dropbox, Windows SkyDrive, etc.), the Investigator can obtain user credentials from the client machine and get the data stored in cloud [12]. Otherwise, possibly it might be used for owning a VM in cloud (because we are not considering SaaS and PaaS models in this work). In this case, the Investigator will have option to either download the virtual disk file or request cloud service provider to ship his or her virtual disk data [24].

2.3   Analysis of Digital Evidence

This phase emphasizes on examination of evidence after the source of evidence is identified, data collected and preserved from the source.

Client Side Data Analysis. The analysis part at client side proceeds in the traditional digital forensic way by keeping a view on the usage of cloud service by client device in any way. We also agree with the Locard's Exchange Principle ("Every contact leaves a trace") that every chance of possible remnants in client device if criminal is not aware of anti-forensic techniques (Darik's Boot and Nuke (DBAN) [26]. Investigator may need to use traditional digital forensic tools [17], [18], [19], [20], [21], [22] to analyze cookies, logs, database files, registry, prefetch files, browser history, pagefile, link files, physical memory, network traffic (incoming and outgoing network packets from the client machine) etc., to get the possible evidence that proves the uses of cloud service. Darren Quick, et al., identified the types of terrestrial artifacts that are likely to remain on a client's machine when one of the cloud services is launched from it [12]. The procedure to perform the analysis to know about these artifacts is not unique due to a variety of operating systems like Windows, Ubuntu, Mac OS, Android, etc.

Cloud Side Data Analysis. The extensive study we conducted on the existing work on cloud forensics suggests that there is no cloud computing architecture that provides in-built forensic facility for data analysis. Once data is collected from cloud environment, analysis phase is very much similar to traditional digital forensics irrespective of the cloud deployment model. Based on the user's cloud service usage, either the VM data has to be analyzed or the set of files that are stored in the cloud have to be analyzed. Depending on the nature of cloud crime, VM logs has to be analyzed to know the VM activities over a period of time. Vassil Roussev et. al., have emphasized on real-time data processing in digital forensics in their paper "Real-time digital forensics and triage" [13]. According to them, the ability of forensic tools to employ a bigger "computational hammer" has not grown appreciably. Also, they have defined Digital forensic triage as "a partial forensic examination conducted under (significant) time and resource constraints". Our experimentation on data acquisition phase reveals that the average time required is about 20MB/sec for Hard disk and 12MB/sec for USB drives using software tools [19], [20], [22]. The actual processing time (includes indexing, carving files and analysis) is always greater than acquisition time. Thus, it may be derived that:

Total time (from evidence acquisition to reporting) = Acquisition + Processing time.

As 2TB Hard disks are common in the industry, it is difficult to pin point the processing time of such huge digital media due to the nature of the committed crime. Also, cloud service providers are offering large capacity virtual disk for a given VM (for example VMware vSphere5.5 provides 62TB [31]).

Subsequently we aim at minimizing the processing time of evidence which in turn would minimize the total (latency) time by using parallel programming model (MapReduce) on a distributed computing platform like Hadoop [30]. The approach that we propose would answer the queries of Investigator in real-time by searching user specified patterns in given evidence by distributing parts of evidence to clusters of commodity machines with local store and processing them in parallel. This approach can also be used for indexing search patterns (for example - headers and footers of files) to carve files from evidence data [15].

The implementation details of pattern matching algorithm using MapReduce in Hadoop cluster would form part of our further work comprising performance results. We have also contributed in designing a signature based virtual machine detection algorithm that detect VMs hidden using alternate data streams (ADS) in private cloud environment based on hosted hypervisors [27].

2.4   Reporting of Digital Evidence

This phase provides a way to document and present the evidence found during analysis before the court of law to enforce punishment to cybercriminal depending on nationwide policies. As per our knowledge is concerned, there is no major change required in reporting evidence other than following forensic aware Daubert principles (Marsico, 2004). The Investigators may need to focus on the technical aspects of forensic investigation and presentation of evidence to a court, assuming LEA (Law Enforcement Agency) is already aware of cloud computing deployment and service models.

3   Conclusion and Future Work

Adaptation of digital forensic techniques to the cloud environment is termed as cloud forensics. Cloud forensics is challenging in many ways. Cloud as a business model presents a range of new challenges to digital forensic Investigators due to its unique characteristics. It is necessary that forensic Investigators and/or researchers adapt existing traditional digital forensic practices and develop new forensic models which would enable Investigators to perform digital forensics in cloud computing environment.

The proposed framework - a heuristic model for performing digital forensics in the cloud computing environment, exemplifies some the challenges and provides bases for further research in this emerging computing paradigm. The model emphasizes on the requirements of changes needed in data collection, preservation, and analysis. It is not possible to detect cloud service usage without analyzing client devices. Once cloud service is identified, data collection from cloud environment will commence (based on the cloud deployment model). To address the challenges of multi-tenancy in cloud, we proposed a logging mechanism that isolates tenant logs and provides a facility to query for a particular tenant's VM logs over a period of time.

The term 'triage' is used in digital forensics recently by researchers to alarm digital forensic practitioners for speeding up computation that results in minimizing the total time of processing of digital evidence. Inspired with this, we are working towards "real-time digital forensics" which will hammer the computational processing in the analysis phase to have the initial screening of potential evidence that will lead to further processing in the large evidence file.

Acknowledgement. Our sincere thanks to Department of Computer Science and Information Systems of BITS Pilani, Hyderabad Campus, India, for providing us with the research environment.

References

1. Martini, B., Choo, K.-K.R.: Cloud storage forensics: ownCloud as a case study. Digital Investigation 10, 287–299 (2013)
2. http://www.clavister.com/Documents/resources/white-papers/clavister-whp-cloud-security-en.pdf (accessed April 25, 2014)
3. http://aws.amazon.com/security/security-bulletins/zeus-botnet-controller (accessed April 25, 2014)

4. Mell, P., Grance, T.: The NIST Definition of Cloud Computing - NIST Special Publication. 800-145 (September 2011)
5. Velte, T., Velte, A., Elsenpeter, R.: Cloud Computing, A Practical Approach. McGraw Hill Computing, New York (2009)
6. Open Source Private Cloud software, https://www.openstack.org
7. Open Source Private and Hybrid Cloud software, https://www.eucalyptus.com/eucalyptus-cloud/iaas
8. VMware Private Cloud Computing Solution, https://www.vmware.com/cloud-computing/private-cloud.html
9. Martini, B., Choo, K.-K.R.: An integrated conceptual digital forensic framework for cloud computing. Digital Investigation 9, 71–80 (2012)
10. Zawoad, S., Hasan, R.: Cloud Forensics: A Meta-Study of Challenges, Approaches, and Open Problems. arXiv:1302.6312v1[cs.DC] (February 26, 2013)
11. Federici, C.: AlmaNebula: A computer forensics framework for the Cloud. Procedia Computer Science 19, 139–146 (2013)
12. Quick, D., Choo, K.-K.R.: Digital droplets: Microsoft SkyDrive forensic data remnants. Future Generation Computer Systems 29, 1378–1394 (2013)
13. Roussev, V., Quates, C., Martell, R.: Real-time digital forensics and triage. Digital Investigation 10, 158–167 (2013)
14. Povar, D., Geethakumari, G.: Digital Evidence Detection in Virtual Environment for Cloud Computing. ACM Digital Library (2012), 978-1-4503-1822-8
15. Povar, D., Bhadran, V.K.: Forensic Data Carving. In: Baggili, I. (ed.) ICDF2C 2010. LNICST, vol. 53, pp. 137–148. Springer, Heidelberg (2011)
16. http://csrc.nist.gov/groups/SMA/ispab/documents/minutes/2011-07/Jul13_Cloud-ISIMC-Cloud-Security-ISPAB.pdf
17. The Volatility Framework, https://code.google.com/p/volatility (accessed April 25, 2014)
18. Memory forensics, http://www.mandiant.com/resources/download/memoryze (accessed April 25, 2014)
19. Forensic Toolkit, http://www.accessdata.com/products/digital-forensics (accessed April 25, 2014)
20. EnCase Forensic v7.09, http://www.guidancesoftware.com/products/Pages/encase-forensic/overview.aspx?cmpid=nav (accessed April 25, 2014)
21. X-Ways Forensics, http://www.x-ways.net (accessed April 25, 2014)
22. CyberCheck, http://www.cyberforensics.in (accessed April 25, 2014)
23. Daryabar, F., Dehghantanha, A.: A Survey about Impacts of Cloud Computing on Digital Forensics. IJCSDF (2013)
24. Dykstra, J., Sherman, A.T.: Acquiring forensic evidence from infrastructure-as-a-service cloud computing: Exploring and evaluating tools, trust, and techniques. Digital Investigation 9, 590–598 (2012)
25. Wolthusen, S.D.: Overcast: Forensic Discovery in Cloud Environments. In: Fifth International Conference on IT Security Incident Management and IT Forensics. IEEE (2009), 978-0-7695-3807-5/09
26. Anti-forensic tool, http://www.dban.org
27. Povar, D., Geethakumari, G.: A Novel approach to Detect Cloud Virtual Machines hidden using Alternate Data Streams. In: International Multi Conference on Automation, Computing, Control, Communication and Compressed Sensing (iMac4s 2013). IEEE XPlore (2013)

28. Birk, D.: Technical Issues of Forensic Investigations in Cloud Computing Environments. In: Workshop on Cryptography and Security in Clouds (2011)
29. Marty, R.: Cloud Application Logging for Forensics. In: Proceedings of the ACM SAC (2011)
30. http://hadoop.apache.org/docs/r1.2.1/hdfs_design.html
31. http://www.vmware.com/pdf/vsphere5/r55/vsphere-55-configuration-maximums.pdf
32. Ruan, K., et al.: Cloud forensics: An overview. IBM Tech. Journal (2010)
33. Garfinkel, S.L.: Digital forensics research: The next 10 years. Digital Investigation 7, 564–573 (2010)
34. http://www.forensicswiki.org (accessed April 25, 2014)
35. Brain Carrier: File System Forensic Analysis (2005)
36. http://www.theforensicacademy.com/Forensic.html (accessed April 25, 2014)

Detection of Active Attacks on Wireless IMDs Using Proxy Device and Localization Information

Monika Darji[1] and Bhushan H. Trivedi[2]

[1] L.J Institute of Computer Application, Ahmedabad, India
monikadarji79@gmail.com
[2] GLS Institute of Computer Technology, Ahmedabad, India
bhtrivedi@yahoo.com

Abstract. Implantable Medical Devices (IMDs) are used to monitor and treat physiological conditions within the body. They communicate telemetry data to external reader/programmer device and receive control commands using wireless medium. Wireless communication for IMDs increases cost effectiveness, flexibility, ease of use and also enables remote configuration and monitoring. However, it makes the IMDs vulnerable to passive and active attacks. While passive attacks on IMDs can be addressed using encryption techniques, active attacks like replay, massage injection and MITM need more advanced techniques to be detected and prevented. In case of other wireless devices one can deal with these security issues by installing one or more security mechanisms, but the same cannot be applied to IMDs. This is due to their positioning inside human body which makes replacement and power charging extremely difficult, their miniaturization which makes them storage, processing and power scarce, their unusual access requirements during device or patient emergency and their incapability of renewing shared secrets. It is advisable to use the resources of IMDs for life critical medical care and minimalist communication. This leads to the implied option of using an external proxy device which can offload security related processing from IMDs. Therefore, to address the problem of active attacks, we propose use of RF-signal based localization technique which leverages multi-antenna Proxy Device to profile the directions at which reader/programmer signal arrives and use of triangulation techniques to construct a signature that uniquely distinguishes an authorized reader/programmer from unauthorized one.

Keywords: IMDs, security, triangulation techniques, Angle of Arrival, TDOA, POA, RTOF, active attacks.

1 Introduction

Implantable Medical Devices like pacemakers, insulin pumps, cardiac defibrillators and nerve stimulators are deeply embedded systems support wireless connectivity that enables remote monitoring and post implementation adjustment. Adding wireless connectivity to IMDs has enabled remote monitoring of patients vital signs improving health care professionals ability to provide timely treatment, leading to a better health

J. Lloret Mauri et al. (Eds.): SSCC 2014, CCIS 467, pp. 353–362, 2014.

care system [1]. IMDs are miniaturized, battery powered, capable of a limited amount of processing, and have a small amount of storage [3]. Due to these constraints, they cannot support traditional security and privacy enhancing technologies. This lack of security between IMD and IMD reader/programmer is a vulnerability which might be exploited by either actively issuing queries to IMD or passively eavesdropping on existing IMD-reader communications. Therefore there is a stringent need of security in these devices.

Security refers to the basic provision of security services including confidentiality, authentication, integrity,   authorization, non-repudiation, and availability, and some augmented services, such as duplicate detection and detection of stale packets (timeliness) [2].

While security mechanisms like authentication and encryption are must, they alone are unable to fight active attacks like Man-in-the-Middle (MITM), Replay and Message Injection and needs to be handled using some additional technique. As IMDs resource constrained, many researchers have proposed to shift the security related processing to a tightly coupled device Trusted External Device which works as an intermediary [11]-[15] and verifies incoming requests. This approach can also protect the IMD against battery-draining attacks by shifting power-intensive computation and some of the protection mechanisms on to Trusted External Device.

To detect and prevent active attacks we propose to use a Proxy Device which is capable of performing secure communication with IMD and of relaying messages between reader/programmer and IMD after authenticating it. Such a device is envisioned to have a wide applicability as a centralized security solution for different classes of Implantable Medical Devices which are implanted in a patient's body.

In this model reader/programmer propagates an RF signal that is received by the Proxy Device (as shown in figure 1) which tries to estimate a location-dependent parameters like time difference of arrival (TDOA), received time of flight (RTOF), phase of arrival(POA) and angle of arrival(AOA). We assume an authentication mechanism in place with the Proxy Device for differentiating an authorized reader from an unauthorized one as presented in [11]-[15]. Once authentication phase is over, then in the next step, the collection of the estimated parameters is used to generate a unique signature which is used to distinguish authorized reader/programmer from unauthorized one. Our proposed model uses a proxy device which is capable of calculating localization parameters from received signal.

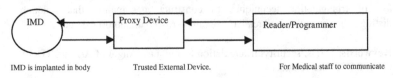

IMD is implanted in body   Trusted External Device.   For Medical staff to communicate

Fig. 1. Model showing Proxy Device for preventing active attacks to IMDs

The rest of the paper is organized as follows: Section 2 discusses the possible attacks on IMDs in wireless networking environment, section 3 discusses the related work proposed in literature to achieve security goals, section 4 discusses the RF based localization techniques, section 5 provides an overview of the components of our model, section 6 discusses the proposed Protocol design in Proxy Device, and section 7 concludes the paper by giving some future directions.

2   Possible Attacks on IMDs in Wireless Networking Environment

A passive or active adversary may misuse the vulnerability of unprotected wireless channel using standard or custom equipments like off-the-shelf software radio or Universal Software Radio Peripheral (USRP) to pose an attack on IMD [9]. Attacks on IMDs have been described in [3], [9], [10], [11]. Attacks on IMDs can be classified as following types:

Eavesdropping Attack: If wireless communication channel is not strongly protected, an eavesdropper may sniff the channel and threaten confidentiality.

Man-in-the Middle Attack: An adversary may be present during authentication session between programmer and IMD or when keying material between IMD and reader is exchanged in clear. Recently, two such protocols have been broken as illustrated in [15].

Impersonation and Injection Attack: A spoofed reader may declare itself a legitimate one and perform unauthorized communication threatening confidentiality, integrity and availability.

Denial-of-Service Attack: Attacker may continuously send request to exhaust the scarce resources like draining the battery on which the IMD is running. This can pose a severe threat to availability and can lead to a life threatening condition for the patient.

Replay Attack: Even if encryption is used, the older authorized packets can be trapped and replayed which may compel the IMD to disclose private information or exhibit abnormal behavior. Such an attack threatens integrity and availability.

We propose the use of a Proxy Device which mediates the communication between IMD and programmer. In this paper we are not considering the emergency situations where IMD should be accessible without any authentication to allow fail-openness [11] the proxy device can be switched off to allow this.

3   Related Work on IMD Security

The criticality of security issues related with wireless telemetry of IMDs has attracted many researchers to propose different solutions to this important problem. Confidentiality based approaches includes ultraviolet-ink micro pigmentation to create UV-visible Tattoos [7] and Access Tokens [8]. Access Control Based Approaches include use of proximity-based access control [9] wherein proximity-based device pairing protocol was proposed based on ultrasonic distance bounding allowing access to only those devices which are in close proximity; the utility of this approach relies on implementation ultrasonic distance bounding features on IMD which makes it invasive and also this approach may not work well in case on noisy channels. Another solution is proposed as Patient Notification and Access Control using RFID which provides Zero-power notification by harvesting induced RF energy to wirelessly power a piezo-element that audibly alerts the patient of security-sensitive events at no cost to the battery; Zero-power authentication that uses symmetric cryptographic techniques to prevent unauthorized access; Sensible key exchange that combines techniques from both zero-power notification and zero-power authentication for vibration-based key distribution that a patient can sense through audible and tactile feedback[10]. Some invasive techniques which propose changes in IMD are also mentioned here. A scheme [19] makes use of rolling code cryptography between IMD and reader to provide confidentiality. Scheme [20] presents a lightweight wireless protocol for IMDs that emphasizes on low-energy computation. Scheme [21] explores the use of block ciphers in IMD security. Another set of solution involves used of trusted external device like Communication Cloaker [11], Sheild [12], IMDGuard [13], Amulet [14] and SVM on Mobile Phone [15]. Communication Cloaker [15] provides a defensive countermeasure and controls access to the IMD by making it invisible to all unauthorized queries. It encrypts all communications to and from the IMD and checks them for authenticity and integrity. The shield [12] acts as a jammer-cum-receiver to jam the IMDs messages and unauthorized commands preventing others from decoding them while being able to decode them. The channel between Shield and legitimate programmer uses encryption. IMDGuard [13] utilizes the patient's electrocardiography signals for key extraction. Using the biometric exchange, it pairs with an IMD and use radio jamming to defend against eavesdropping and unauthorized commands. Amulet [14] is a vision which is dedicated to secure communications with wearable Medical Devices. Scheme [15] presents SVM based technique to battle against battery depletion attack. Our solution also uses a similar external proxy and presents detailed protocols for preventing active attacks in proxy environment. The scheme given in [22] also uses RF signal characteristics for physical anomaly detection by use of a passive monitoring device.

4   RF Based Localization Techniques

For wireless communication, transmitted signals characteristics can be used for deriving location information. A detailed survey of wireless indoor positioning techniques is presented in [5], interested users may refer that. Here, we are interested specifically in triangulation technique which uses geometric properties of triangles to estimate a wireless device location either by lateration or angulation. TDOA technique comes under lateration which estimates the position of wireless device by measuring its distances from multiple reference points and calculates the difference in time at which signal arrives. RTOF is a lateration technique used to measure the time-of-flight of signal from measuring device and back. POA is a lateration technique that uses phase differences to calculate the range in conjunction with TDOA. Angulation locates a wireless object by computing angles relative to multiple reference points to determine the location of transmitter. AOA can be used to estimate the location of a wireless device by the intersection of several pairs of angle direction lines, each formed by the circular radius from a receiving station.

SecureAngle [4] uses AOA signature in general wireless environment for providing a "virtual fence" and to prevent MAC spoofing. AOA-based signatures are used in [17, 18] to aid systems that detect network anomalies and miss-configurations.

5   Overview of Components

5.1   System Configuration

Our model has three components, the IMD, a Proxy Device and reader/programmer. The IMD inside patient's body performs sensing, computation, actuation and communicates telemetry data for an extended period of time. The programmer/reader is an outside controller used by medical staff to send commands to IMD or to read telemetry data using wireless channel. Proxy Device is trusted and tightly coupled with IMD and can mediate secure communication as proposed in [11]-[15]. Proxy authenticates the reader/programmer on behalf of IMD. After initial pairing between IMD and Proxy, IMD acts only on those requests that are sent though the Proxy Device. Only in the absence Proxy Device it performs direct communication with Reader/Programmer.

5.2   Adversary Model and Assumptions

Our Adversarial Model assumes presence of an active adversary during reader/programmer to IMD communication with capability of posing replay, message injection or MITM attacks. Moreover we assume that both active adversary during reader/programmer and adversary cannot transmit from the same location thereby differing in signal characteristics which is a realistic assumption. We also assume proper authentication mechanism in place for the Proxy to authenticate a reader/programmer before allowing it to access the IMD. We assume authenticated reader/programmer is in close proximity to Proxy Device and that adversary does not possess information to get authenticated. We use a combination of more than one type of triangulation based positioning technique for our signature generation scheme to make it more precise. Proxy Device as an antenna array using which it can sense the direction from which a signal is received.

5.3   Proxy Device Overview

The proxy device acts as a measuring unit which uses different types of signal measurements like time difference of arrival (TDOA), received time of flight (RTOF), phase of arrival(POA) and angle of arrival(AOA) .This information is used to generate a signature that is unique to the reader/programmer. In order to forge this signature attacker needs to have the location information of authorized reader/programmer, Proxy device and also the locations of all obstacles in the vicinity of authorized reader/programmer which is extremely difficult to obtain. This technique is useful to allow only authorized reader/programmer in vicinity of Proxy Device to have wireless access to IMD and to detect active attacks.

For two reader/programmers located at different locations, their signatures are very unlikely to be the same. Signatures change to some degree when obstacles in the environment or reader/programmers or Proxy Device move, and therefore this must be tracked and updated. We assume it is easy to discriminate valid reader/

programmers signature from an attacker's signature as there is a significant difference between the two.

5.4   Signature Generation

The proxy device first pairs with IMD and waits for communication request from reader/programmer. After authenticating the reader/programmer, proxy measures time difference of arrival (TDOA), received time of flight (RTOF), phase of arrival (POA) and angle of arrival (AOA) and uses these values to generate a signature unique to authorized device as shown in (1). To generate the signature, a secure hash function like SHA-256 may be used.

The Signature is calculated as:

$$S=\text{Hash (TDOA}\|\text{RTOF}\|\text{POA}\|\text{AOA)} \qquad (1)$$

The calculated signature is used to verify whether the communicating entity is the authentication one or a forged reader. Figure 2 shows the complete signature verification process.

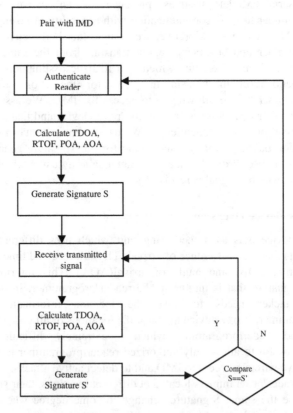

Fig. 2. Flowchart showing signature verification in Proxy Device

6   Protocol Design for Proxy Device

We assume that the IMD and Proxy Device have already paired with a shared secret key and Proxy Device is ready to handle any request from the reader/programmer. In the first phase, Proxy receives request from reader/programmer for communication with IMD. Proxy after authenticating reader/programmer, generates signature S and stores it and then grants access to the IMD. For every subsequent request from reader/programmer, proxy recalculates signature as S' and compares it with stored signature S. If there is a significant discrimination in signature, it asks reader/programmer to get re-authenticated (as either reader/programmer or intermediate obstacle has changed position). If reader/programmer successfully gets re-authenticated, it is granted access and its signature is modified. If instead of authorized reader/programmer, a spoofed device T sends any request the signature thus generated is S_T, which will not match with stored S and it will trigger the re-authentication process which will fail due to unavailability of required credentials with T therefore T will be denied access. When the re-authentication process fails, Proxy Device generated a response which can either be a Warning message configured to warn the patient or producing a jamming signal to disrupt further communications. This protocol is successful in preventing active attacks as any message from T will not get accepted unless the signature is verified. As mentioned earlier, it is very difficult for T to spoof the signature as T needs to have the location information of both authorized reader/programmer and Proxy device, and also obstacles in the path. Table 1 summarizes the notations used:

Table 1. Table of Notations used in protocol

Symbol	Represents
Alice	Proxy Device
Bob	Authenticated Reader/Programmer
Trudy	Adversary Reader/Programmer
S_B	Signature of Bob
S	Signature calculated for each subsequent request
$S_{B'}$	Modified Signature of Bob
S_T	Signature of Trudy

The protocol is summarized in below given figure 2 in the form of a sequence diagram:

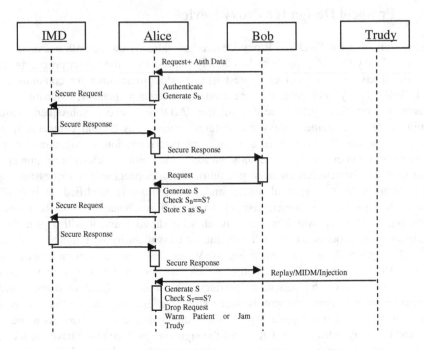

Fig. 3. Sequence Diagram for Protocol used by Proxy Device

7   Conclusion and Future Work

In this paper, we propose to use triangulation techniques based signature calculated by a Trusted Proxy Device, to provide a security scheme for protecting IMDs against active attacks like Replay, Man-in-the-Middle and Message Injection. As a future scope of work we propose use of RF-based scene analysis which can estimate location of an object by matching actual measurements with predefined location fingerprints which are collected (features of a scene) during training phase. This will be used when IMDs are accessed at a particular indoor location only.

References

1. Maisel, W.H.: Safety issues involving medical devices. Journal of the American Medical Association (August 2005)
2. Garcia-Morchon, O., Keoh, S., Kumar, S., Hummen, R., Struik, R.: Security Considerations in the IP-based Internet of Things, draft-garcia-core-security-02 (work in progress) (July 2011)
3. Li, C., Raghunathan, A., Jha, N.K.: Hijacking an insulin pump: Security attacks and defenses for a diabetes therapy system. In: Proceedings of the 13th IEEE International Conference on e-Health Networking, Applications, and Services, Healthcom 2011 (June 2011)

4. Xiong, J., Jamieson, K.: SecureAngle: improving wireless security using angle-of-arrival information. In: Proceedings of the 9th ACM SIGCOMM Workshop on Hot Topics in Networks (Hotnets-IX). ACM, New York (2010)
5. Liu, H., Darabi, H., Banerjee, P., Liu, J.: Survey of Wireless Indoor Positioning Techniques and Systems. IEEE Transactions on Systems, Man and Cybernetics, Part C (Applications and Reviews) (2007)
6. Lieckfeldt, D.: Efficient Localization of Users and Devices in Smart Environments. Dissertation, University of Rostock (2010)
7. Schechter, S.: Security that is Meant to be Skin Deep: Using Ultraviolet Micro-pigmentation to Store Emergency-Access Keys for Implantable Medical Devices. In: USENIX Workshop on Health Security and Privacy (2010)
8. Bergamasco, S., Bon, M., Inchingolo, P.: Medical data protection with a new generation of hardware authentication tokens. In: Mediterranean Conference on Medical and Biological Engineering and Computing (MEDICON), Pula, Croatia, pp. 82–85 (2001)
9. Rasmussen, K.B., Castelluccia, C., Heydt-Benjamin, T.S., Capkun, S.: Proximity-based access control for implantable medical devices. In: CCS 2009: Proceedings of the 16th ACM Conference on Computer and Communications Security, pp. 410–419. ACM, New York (2009)
10. Halperin, D., Heydt-Benjamin, T.S., Ransford, B., Clark, S.S., Defend, B., Morgan, W., Fu, K., Kohno, T., Maisel, W.H.: Pacemakers and Implantable Cardiac Defibrillators: Software Radio Attacks and Zero-Power Defenses. In: IEEE Symposium on Security and Privacy (2008)
11. Denning, T., Fu, K., Kohno, T.: Absence Makes the Heart Grow Fonder: New Directions for Implantable Medical Device Security. In: HotSec (2008)
12. Gollakota, S., Hassanieh, H., Ransford, B., Katabi, D., Fu, K.: They Can Hear Your Heartbeats: Non-Invasive Security for Implanted Medical Devices. In: ACM SIGCOMM (2011)
13. Xu, F., Qin, Z., Tan, C.C., Wang, B., Li, Q.: IMDGuard: Securing implantable medical devices with the external wearable guardian. In: Proceedings of the 30th IEEE International Conference on Computer Communications, INFOCOM 2011, pp. 1862–1870 (April 2011)
14. Sorber, J., Shin, M., Peterson, R., Cornelius, C., Mare, S., Prasad, A., Marois, Z., Smithayer, E., Kotz, D.: An amulet for trustworthy wearable mHealth. In: Proceedings of the Twelfth Workshop on Mobile Computing Systems & Applications (HotMobile 2012). ACM, New York (2012)
15. Hei, X., Du, X., Wu, J., Hu, F.: Defending resource depletion attacks on implantable medical devices. In: Proc. of the IEEE Globecom 2010, pp. 1–5 (2010)
16. Rostami, M., Burleson, W., Koushanfar, F., Juels, A.: Balancing security and utility in medical devices? In: Proc. of Automation Coference, pp. 1–6 (2013)
17. Bahl, P., Chandra, R., Greenberg, A., Kandula, S., Maltz, D., Zhang, M.: Towards highly reliable enterprise network services via inference of multi-level dependencies. In: Proc. of ACM SIGCOMM (2007)
18. Kandula, S., Mahajan, R., Verkaik, P., Agarwal, S., Padhye, J., Bahl, P.: Detailed diagnosis in enterprise networks. In: Proc. of ACM SIGCOMM (2009)
19. Li, C., Raghunathan, A., Jha, N.K.: Hijacking an insulin pump: Security attacks and defenses for a diabetes therapy system. In: Proc. IEEE Int. Conf. e-Health Networking, Applications and Services (June 2011)

20. Hosseini-Khayat, S.: A lightweight security protocol for ultra-low power ASIC implementation for wireless implantable medical devices. In: Proceedings of the 5th International Symposium on Medical Information Communication Technology, ISMICT 2011, pp. 6–9 (March 2011)
21. Beck, C., Masny, D., Geiselmann, W., Bretthauer, G.: Block cipher based security for severely resource-constrained implantable medical devices. In: Proceedings of 4th International Symposium on Applied Sciences in Biomedical and Communication Technologies, ISABEL 2011, pp. 62:1–62:5. ACM (October 2011)
22. Zhang, M., Raghunathan, A., Jha, N.K.: MedMon: Securing medical devices through wireless monitoring and anomaly detection. IEEE Trans. Biomedical Circuits and Systems (2013)

Vulnerability of MR-ARP in Prevention of ARP Poisoning and Solution

Mukul Tiwari[1] and Sumit Kumar[2]

[1] DIT University Dehradun India
mukultiwari1987@gamil.com
[2] ABB Global Industries and Services, India
ksiiitm@gmail.com

Abstract. In this paper we are discussing ARP poisoning and its solution over Local Area Network. As we know that Enhanced ARP (MITM-Resistant Address Resolution Protocol (MR-ARP)) is the prevention of ARP poisoning in which two tables are used, for cross checking any ARP request and if any new request arises then it uses voting process. First table is long term table which is updated for 60 minutes and other one is short term table which is same as normal ARP table. In some cases update policy of the long term table of MR-ARP causes the attack over LAN and ARP poisoning can be possible. MITM is quite possible over MR-ARP when any node become offline for some time and any other node wants to perform attack over that node. Here we will discuss the attack over MR-ARP and some corrective measures.

Keywords: ARP, Enhanced ARP, MITM, MR-ARP.

1 Introduction

In LAN environment systems are connected through switch or hub which understands only physical address of systems which is called MAC address but only logical address is known to other nodes that is IP address. To communicate over LAN it is necessary to find out the MAC address corresponding to the IP address. Address Resolution Protocol (ARP) [7] is used to bind MAC address with the corresponding IP address. In ARP security does not exists. In ARP whenever a request arises it is directly stored in ARP table without checking that the binding of request is genuine or fake. ARP poisoning is the attack where a user sends a malicious ARP request with forge IP, MAC binding and gets ARP table of victim updated. This ARP poisoning can lead MITM attacks over victim. To prevent ARP poisoning MR-ARP is the latest approach known till now but there are some issues and gaps which will be discussed in this paper.

2 Literature Review

The Address Resolution Protocol (ARP) is used to bind IP address and MAC address to perform communication over LAN as the connecting device over LAN can

J. Lloret Mauri et al. (Eds.): SSCC 2014, CCIS 467, pp. 363–369, 2014.
© Springer-Verlag Berlin Heidelberg 2014

understand only MAC address. If any system sends requests with fake IP address then that system get associated with other systems with that IP and everyone communicate with that system considering that they are communicating to the IP which is associated with that MAC. This kind of situation is called ARP poisoning and this can lead Man in the Middle (MITM) attack. MITM came into the focus in 1989 [2] and till now we do not have any full proof solution for that [4].

To make secure communication over LAN and prevent ARP poisoning many approaches came into focus. First of all the idea came into the picture was Dynamic ARP Inspection (DAI) [1] on Ethernet switch. This approach is quite useful but the portion of LAN which is far from the reach of ARP inspection remains still vulnerable. Apart from this approach some cryptographic and non cryptographic approaches introduced. In cryptographic approach S-ARP [3] and Ticket-Based ARP (TARP) [5] are the major name.

S-ARP and Ticket Based ARP both are centralised approach and have a centralised server to control the mechanism as Authoritative Key Distributer (AKD) for S-ARP and Local Ticket Agent (LTA) for TARP. Both the algorithms have high computational cost and single point failure problem with difficulties in up gradation [6].

The latest approach for prevention of ARP poisoning is MR-ARP [6]. MR-ARP is a non cryptographic approach. It works based on backward compatibility phenomena. MR-ARP is the most secure approach for prevention of ARP poisoning. In MR-ARP there are two types of ARP tables one is short term table and other one is long term table. Short term table is similar to normal ARP table but the main weapon of MR-ARP is its long term table. In MR-ARP if any new IP, MAC binding request comes then the authenticity of that request is checked by voting and if more than 50% reply comes into the favour of that binding then only the binding is to be stored in both the tables. If no reply comes then we consider that this binding is genuine that's why any other node is not voting against that node and the binding will be accepted. When any ARP request arises for which entry is not existed in short term table but exists in long term table then short term table automatically gets updated. One more feature is associated with long term table is timer that is by default set for 60 minutes as any entry is stored in long term table then it would be stored for 60 minutes if there is no communication takes place or any conflict arises. When any request arises in which IP matches with the long term table entry but MAC does not matches then system will send 50 random packet to the MAC which is stored in table and if any response will not come then new request will be accepted and updated into both the tables and timer will be set for 60 minutes but if response of any of the packets comes then new request would be declined by the system and reset the timer for 60 minute more for the old entry.

3   Issue and Gaps

MR-ARP works extremely well for prevention of ARP poisoning and makes secure LAN communication from MITM attack but there exists some condition where its long term table leads open the door for attackers. Its voting process for adding new request into the table is quite fine and it is very helpful for preventing any node to accept any malicious binding request when its ARP table is empty. Besides these situations there is one more condition which may lead ARP poisoning and MITM over MR-ARP.

Attack over MR-ARP can be performed in three phase. To perform ARP poisoning the weakest node is the systems which is offline and till the time it is offline meanwhile attack can be performed. The three phases are as follows:-

A. Phase 1

If any user is offline and any other wants to perform ARP poisoning over that node then he can send ARP request to any other node of network, in given example we named it as voter, with fake binding of IP and MAC in which IP belongs to the victim system and MAC should be attacker's MAC as shown in fig.1. Now because in voter's long term table that IP is associated with other MAC which is victim's MAC so conflict occurs then to resolve that according to MR-ARP algorithm voter will send 50 random packets to the MAC address which is stored. Victim is offline so he will not respond any of the packet so voter declines the previous binding and updates his both tables with the new IP, MAC binding.

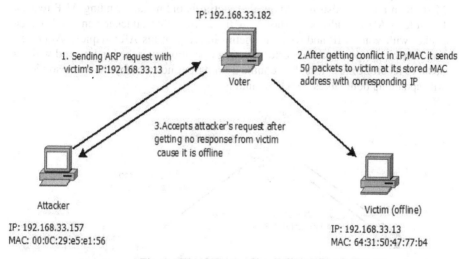

Fig. 1. Phase 1 of attack over MR-ARP

B. Phase 2

When victim become online he will broadcast his IP, MAC with ARP request for the MAC address of voter. Again voter will get a conflict that in his long term table the MAC which is stored with victim's IP belongs to attacker so voter will send 50 packets to attacker's MAC and attacker will immediately send response for these packets. In this way voter will know that the binding which is stored in his table is a genuine binding and the new request is fake so it will decline the new request which is genuine and send by victim.

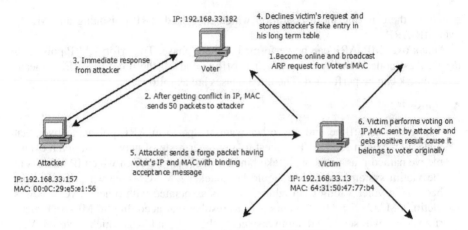

Fig. 2. Phase 2 of attack over MR-ARP

In this way when voter sends 50 packets to attacker and victim broadcasts its IP, MAC then attacker also may know that victim is online and sending ARP request for voter's MAC address as shown in fig 2.After that attacker can send a fake packet with voter's IP and MAC to victim in reply of his ARP request. After getting new binding victim will perform voting operation over the binding and will get positive result because it is the genuine binding but not send by the voter so victim will update its both tables with this binding.

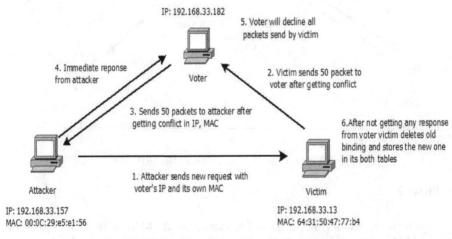

Fig. 3. Phase 3 of attack over MR-ARP

B. Phase 3

In 2nd phase attacker has only captured victim's IP and get associated with the voter but in this phase he will perform full MITM. After sending genuine IP, MAC of voter to victim attacker now sends other request with voter's IP and his own MAC. Now victim will get a conflict between the existing MAC and the

MAC of new request so to resolve this he will send 50 packet to voter's original MAC. Still voter is having attacker's MAC with the IP of victim so he will decline all the packets and will not send any response to victim.

After not getting any response from voter, victim will accept the new fake binding sent by attacker in which the MAC is attacker's MAC as shown in fig 3.

In this way full MITM can be perform over MR-ARP.

4   Possible Solution

Over MR-ARP attack is possible because of two reasons:

1. In MR-ARP when any entry is stored in long term table it can only be modified when system will not get response for the 50 packets which is send only when any conflict occurs.
2. When any request arise on any node and by voting or sending 50 packets to other node is can be proved that the binding is not genuine then request must be decline without sending any message to the node who made the ARP request.

In the given scenario also the attack can be possible because of these two reasons as when voter drops the victim's request then victim does not know that request has been declined by the voter and he considers that packet sent by the attacker as a genuine packet but that packet is fake and only having the genuine IP, MAC address of voter. In this way when attacker again sends a fake request then victim will send 50 packets to voter and voter rejects all the packets because in voter's long term table attacker's MAC is already saved for 60 minutes and attacker is continuously responding to those packets which is sent by the voter.

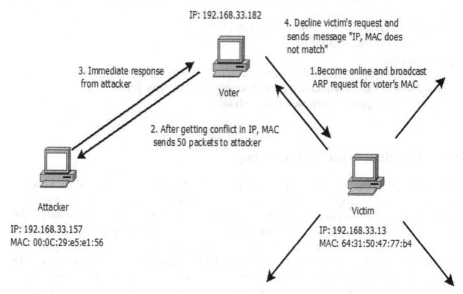

Fig. 4. Solution of attack over MR-ARP

If voter sends a message to victim before declining his request that "IP, MAC does not match" as shown in fig. 4 then victim may know that something going wrong. In this way he can immediately change its IP. If attacker's acceptance messages comes first over victim then also after getting messages from voter to change the IP victim may get a hint of ARP spoofing and MITM and can change his IP address. In this way ARP poisoning can be reduced over MR-ARP.

After performing that change in MR-ARP [6] the algorithm would be as follows:-

```
/* (IPa, MACa): the sender protocol (IP) and hardware (MAC) address of the re-
ceived ARP request or reply packet */
    if (IPa is registered in the short-term cache) {
            no action; /* in case of conflict, preserve existing mapping*/
    }
    else if ((IPa, MACa) is registered in the long-term table) {
            register (IPa, MACa) in the short-term cache;
            set the long-term table timer to 60 minutes;
    }
    else if (IPa is in the long term table, but registered MAC is not MACa) {
    /* conflict on IP and MAC mapping*/
            send 50 ARP request to existing MAC through unicasting at random inter-
            vals with an average of 10 msec;
    if (at least one ARP reply arrives)
            send message to (IPa, MACa) "IP, MAC does not match";
            retain the existing (IP, MAC) mapping and drop the new one;
    else
            accept the new mapping;
            The accepted mapping is registered in the short-term cache, too.
    }
    else {/* IPa is not in short-term/long-term tables */
            Send voting request for IPa;
    if (no response)
            The mapping (IPa, MACa) is registered in both tables;
    else if (there exist a MAC that polls over 50% of votes for IPa)
            That mapping is registered in both tables;
    }
```

5   Conclusion and Future Scope

MR-ARP is the best solution for prevention of ARP poisoning and MITM till now but it has some sort of loop hole with the algorithm. With the help of that flaw ARP poisoning was possible there but with the slight change of algorithm we made MR-ARP more secure and with the help of these changes ARP poisoning over LAN can be restricted too much. The new algorithm is also not containing any cryptographic method to make secure the ARP poisoning due to which complexity is not increasing. In this any centralized server technique is also not used which has a single point failure problem which can damage the whole system so we can say this approach is less complex and more powerful approach than any other existing approach.

In MR-ARP we have just included a message before declining the ARP request that "IP, MAC does not match". This is an informative message which represents that previous IP which was using by user has given to other system so IP must be changed by the user. We can use some authenticity for this message as any other user can not send this message in place of the requested system. If any other system may forge this message this may lead user to change his IP address again and again.

References

1. Bhaiji, Y.: Network Security Technologies and Solutions. Cisco Press (2008)
2. Bellovin, S.M.: Security problems in the tcp/ip protocol suite. Computer Communications Review 2(19), 32–48 (1989)
3. Bruschi, D., Ornaghi, A., Rosti, E.: S-ARP: a secure address resolution protocol. In: Proc. Annual Computer Security Applications Conference, ACSAC (2003)
4. Bellovin, S.M.: A look back at "security problems in the tcp/ip protocol suite". In: 20th Annual Computer Security Application Conference (ACSAC), pp. 229–249 (December 2004)
5. Lootah, W., Enck, W., McDaniel, P.: TARP: ticket-based address resolution protocol. Computer Networks 51, 4322–4337 (2007)
6. Nam, S.Y., Kim, D., Kim, J.: Enhanced ARP: Preventing ARP Poisoning-Based Man-in-the-Middle Attack. IEEE Communication Letters 14, 187–189 (2010)
7. Plummer, D.C.: An Ethernet address resolution protocol or converting network protocol addresses to 48.bit Ethernet address for transmission on Ethernet hardware. RFC 826 (November 1982)

Analyzer Router: An Approach to Detect and Recover from OSPF Attacks

Deepak Sangroha and Vishal Gupta

Department of Computer Science at AIACT&R, Delhi, India
deepaksangroha@yahoo.in, vishalgupta@aiactr.ac.in

Abstract. Open Shortest Path First (OSPF) is the most widely deployed interior gateway routing protocol on the Internet. We here present an approach to detect the attacks to which OSPF is vulnerable. As security feature, OSPF uses "fight-back" mechanism to detect false LSA flooded in network and take appropriate action. But few attacks have been proposed which bypass/overtake this mechanism to inject false LSA. And few attacks that are out of range of this mechanism. We will try to implement our approach to detect and mitigate these attacks. This approach is reactive so it may take small interval of time to detect and recover network from attack but is effective in doing so and securing the infrastructure.

Keywords: Autonomous System (AS), Link State Advertisement (LSA), Analyzer Router (AR), Backup Designated router (BDR), Attack detection, Link verification, Recovery.

1   Introduction

Open Shortest Path First (OSPF) [1] is the most popular and commonly used interior gateway routing protocol (IGP) on the Internet. IGP allow routers within a single autonomous system (AS) to construct their routing tables, while dynamically adapting to changes in the autonomous system's topology. OSPF is currently used within most autonomous systems on Internet as the other IGP available - Enhanced Interior Gateway Routing Protocol (EIGRP) is Cisco proprietary and works only on Cisco devices. OSPF was developed and standardized by the IETF's OSPF working group [1]. Our work is concerned with version 2 of the protocol which was specifically designed for IPv4 networks. Version 3 has been standardized to accommodate IPv6 networks in which the fundamental mechanisms of version 2 have been kept.

OSPF is a link-state routing protocol which means that each router advertises its links, networks and link cost also to neighboring routers. These advertisements are called Link State Advertisements (LSAs) [1]. Designated Router (DR) and Backup DR are mainly responsible for transmitting LSAs to each router in specific area. The cost of a link is usually statically configured by the network administrator or it depends on the bandwidth it holds. Higher the bandwidth of link, lower is the cost (delay) it have [1]. Means, route is selected with lower cost. Each LSA is flooded

J. Lloret Mauri et al. (Eds.): SSCC 2014, CCIS 467, pp. 370–378, 2014.

throughout the AS where a router receiving an LSA from one of its neighbors resends it to all its other neighbors. Every router compiles a database of the LSAs of all routers in the AS. The databases become identical on all routers after network stabilization. Using this database a router obtains a complete view of the AS topology. This allows it to employ Dijksatra's algorithm [2] (an algorithm used to calculate shortest path between source and destination) to calculate the least cost paths between it and every other advertised network or router. As a result, a next hop is derived for each destination, which forms the router's routing table.

There are several attacks that are proposed by different researchers, like Falsifying LSA, phantom router attack, remote false adjacency etc. [5, 9]. In this paper we present a new approach to detect these attacks. Our concept is based on analysis of LSAs flowing in network with which we try to catch or detect the attack and the attacker. This job is supposed to be done by a router which will be elected and called as Analyzer Router (AR), explained later.

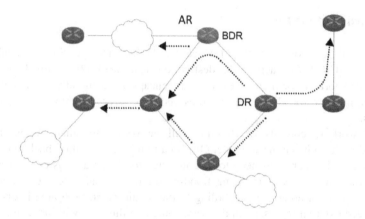

Fig. 1. A network topology with DR, BDR & AR showing LSA flooding

Above figure (Figure1 (a)) is showing network components in OSPF topology. All are explained in coming portions of the paper.

OSPF itself has some security features [4,7] that it uses to stop these attacks. Firstly, per-link authentication, OSPF doesn't allow any router to share LSA with unauthorized neighbor. But this happen only when, link-authentication is configured for OSPF instance. Authentication may be null (i.e. no authentication, type0), plain text authentication (key resides in router in plain text, type1) and cryptographic authentication (MD5 of message is appended with each LSA that need to be verified on the other end, type2) [7][4]. Secondly, each LSA is flooded in the whole network which protects the router from becoming victim silently. Finally, fight-back mechanism, this mechanism allows a router to flood correct LSA whenever it hears any false LSA. For example, if a router R1 hears a LSA about any link which actually possessed by itself (R1) from other router then it suddenly correct it by sending correct LSA [5].

When an attack happens on routing protocol, it can do certain damages to the network. Some of these are as below:

- **Link overload:** Diverting large volume of traffic thorough a limited capacity link.
- **Long routes:** Diverting traffic over unnecessarily long routes while wasting network resources.
- **Black Hole:** Large amount of traffic are directed to a specific router that can't handle the increased level of traffic and drops many packets.
- **Starvation:** Data traffic can be routed to a part of the network that doesn't include the target machine.
- **Churn:** Rapid change in traffic that can affect the congestion control techniques.
- **Instability:** OSPF becomes unstable so that convergence happening frequently and links don't reach to forwarding state.

2   Basics of OSPF

OSPF is a link state routing protocol which uses Dijksatra's algorithm to calculate the minimum cost path for each of the destination in network [2]. OSPF does not use TCP/IP transport protocol; its messages are encapsulated directly in IP datagrams with port number 89 [1]. OSPF handles its own error detection and correction functions.

OSPF working consists of dividing full network into small Areas that are numbered with 16 bit numeric value. One area numbered 0, called backbone area is core area and all other areas need to be connected to this area. This concept helps in easy network management, reducing flooding (of LSAs) and reducing routing table by making some of areas stub according to the requirement. Stub area is one which doesn't need external routes, so in that case routers in this area will just communicate with Designated Router (DR) (described below) and it's his responsibility to make communication possible with external network.

OSPF topology consists of many routers that are divided into several types on the basis of their working and responsibilities are as follows [1]:

- **Area Border Router (ABR):** A router that is connected at least two different areas, including back-bone area. ABR hold topology data for each area and advertise routes among each other after computing them.
- **Backbone router:** Any router present in backbone area.
- **Internal router:** Router that is connected to only single area.
- **Designated router (DR):** One router is elected as DR to perform special functions in the area. Its functions include generation of LSAs representing the subnets and playing a key role in the database exchange processes.
- **Backup Designated router (BDR):** A router that monitors and becomes prepared to take over when DR fails.

Security features like per link authentication, Fight-back mechanism are already introduced in introduction part. OSPF sends periodic updates in each 30 min [1], just to update entries on all routers in case any router hasn't received triggered update.

Some approaches have been introduced before this but they are with limited effect. Like Attack detection with Honeypot router [8] but that approach is not effective in lots of attacks.

3   Proposed Attack Detection Technique

This section presents, attack detection technique and in next part same will be implemented on some known attacks. The idea behind discussing technique first before the attacks is to make everybody aware about the concept as the technique works differently with different attack. So it will be easier to understand the working while detecting attack if we already have knowledge of it.

This is a reactive technique, so we are proceeding with an assumption that the attack has been occurred. The impact of attack may be targeted to single device or multiple but in each case, LSAs with false information are transmitted by the routers in network. It will trigger an update in the network to flood new changes throughout the network and routers updates their information accordingly.

From the network, one router is elected which performs special tasks. As this technique is based on analysis of LSAs so we will name this router performing special task as Analyzer Router (AR). We recommend electing BDR for this purpose. Special task is that it won't update its information (either Link state Database (LSDB) or routing table) instantly, but wait till the verification of the update that is flooded in the network. AR (Analyzer Router) will hold old topology and create a new copy also that will result after accepting the change. Now, two things will be checked, either the link/route really exists or not and secondly if exists, whether it really possess the things it is claiming. For example, if LSA flooded for new link, AR will verify whether this link is actually present in the network by finding reachability to such link. Second about its claims, like if it states that it holds better path, then AR will check if new path is actually better or not by comparing both.

Why BDR is recommended to do this task because DR and BDR are two routers in the network which have full knowledge of network topology and are responsible for sharing updates. DR router already has different tasks and network performance depends a lot on DR router. But BDR router monitors DR and keep it updated to become DR when original one fails. Generally, router with better performance or hardware configuration is elected as DR and the following as BDR. So BDR router will be much appropriate to do the task and also it has same copy of network topology as DR. So, from here we will use AR (Analyzer Router) to indicate this special router.

3.1   How it Works

Whenever any change occurs in network, the originating router is triggered to flood LSAs regarding the change to its neighbors and neighbors further flood it. This is the way how a change is made known to every router in network. Now when a router gets new LSA, it will update its topology table in process to work with Dijksatra's algorithm. This table is further used to calculate optimum routes.

Here is the difference in working, unlike normal routers in network; AR will be having two copies of topology table. One is identical to other routers but second one is without latest updates i.e. First is after the changes have been made in table and second is as before changes. This approach of having two tables will help AR to compare results before and after changes and also helpful while recovering from any bad LSA. Here we want to clear that generally a router have small amount of memory, usually around 60-70MB in total. High range router may have much more but it remains within 200MB. Having two copies of topology information may seem consumption of memory but the topology table or file created would be of small size, may be within few hundred of KB. So, it must not be consuming more memory and harming other works of router.

Now whenever a new LSA is flooded in the network, it may be due to new adjacency or any change. All routers will receive LSAs. By normal procedure every router will update its topology according to LSA but AR will be having two tables. Now it's time to verify the LSA update. First case is that LSA is for new subnet/link then AR will verify the existence of new subnet/link with ping. If it gets response then the LSA is real and table can be updated with it. Second case when LSA is regarding existing subnet/link but claiming to have different and better path [6] in terms of cost. In this the AR will first verify the existence of old connection. If it's not available then the existence of new one will be verified otherwise if it's available then AR need to compare both in terms of delay and cost. Tracing the path can also be used with which AR can try to reach each hop and check where the delay is happening if the delay is found for any subnet/link.

Above is the process of detection. In next portion of the paper, this concept is applied on few of the known attacks and will try to explain how it secures the network from false routing or other attacks.

4   AR with Some Known Attacks

This section tries to explain our concept of AR to secure against some known attacks.

4.1   Remote False Adjacency Attack [3]

In this attack, attacker establishes a fake adjacency with victim router by sending Hello and other messages required for adjacency establishment. This attack works because the victim router won't need any information from phantom router & the process works good even if attacker sends empty packets on behalf of phantom router to victim and keep requesting updates from victim. Phantom router is non-existing router which is not actually present in network but attacker compromises victim to assume presence of that router. Fight back security mechanism won't work here as this attack is not against any existing subnet instead it is for new link. Below figure2 (a) is showing the pictorial view of the attack. [3]

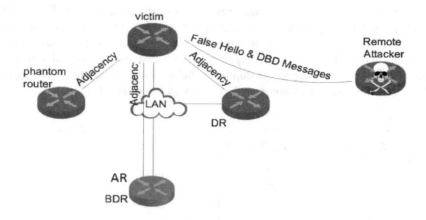

Fig. 2(a). Remote False Adjacency attack

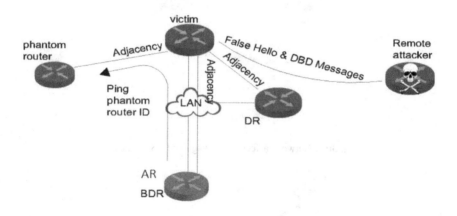

Fig. 2(b). Link verification by AR

Now when the victim router floods the new link info in the network, all routers will receive update via LSA. AR will verify the link on receiving the link LSA by trying to ping it. As this is a fake link (with phantom router) and don't exist in real so AR will not receive any response from it. Figure2 (b) shows the pictorial view of detection. In this way this fake adjacency will be caught.

4.2   Disguised LSA Attack [3]

Two LSAs are considered same if they have same sequence number & checksum and have age field having difference less than 15 minutes. So in this attack, the attacker keep monitoring for LSA flooding in the network. Then it starts sending its own LSA by guessing the sequence and checksum. Other nodes will drop LSAs from attacker if they get these LSAs after original ones by considering them as duplicate. But if attacker sends LSAs just before the real ones then other routers will consider LSAs from attacker as real and LSAs from original router will be considered as duplicate. The fight back will also not be triggered in this case as the original router may consider LSAs from attacker as duplicate. Below Figure3 (a) shows the network affected by this attack. Red nodes are having updates from attacker.

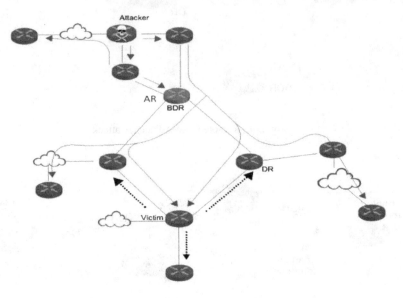

Fig. 3(a). Network affected by Disguised LSA attack

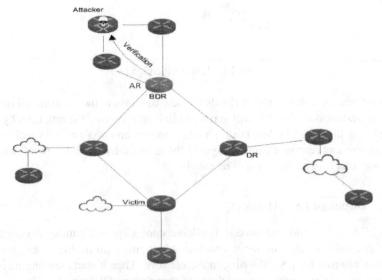

Fig. 3(b). LSA verification by AR

When AR will verify LSAs, ones that are received from original will be verified as AR will receive proper response from the subnets but in case of LSAs from attacker AR will not get response as the subnets are not present there in actual. Below figure3 (b) show the verification of LSAs from attacker.

4.3   Max Age Attack

In this, the attacker sends a copy of an existing LSA with maxage set. The original router will send a fresh copy of LSA with new age as a port of fight back mechanism. If the attacker keeps doing it, then it creates instability in network and causes performance degradation.

AR in this case will be monitoring and judge which router is sending fight back LSAs against which router's LSAs. The attacker will be detected as each time the maxage LSAs will be coming from same router.

4.4   Sequence++ Attack

The attacker keep sending false LSAs for any particular subnet with higher sequence number to indicate it as freshest update. Original router will send LSAs with higher sequence number in process of fight back mechanism. If this keeps happening then it creates instability in the network.

AR in this case will detect which router is sending fight back LSAs against which router same as in maxage attack. Secondly, AR can verify which router is having the subnet for which routers are sending LSAs. This will help in detecting which router is attacker and which one is victim.

4.5   Max Sequence Attack

The attacker sends LSA with maximum sequence number 0x7FFFFFFF. Theoretically original router must send fight back LSA but practically this LSA remains in network for 30min (1800 sec) and replaced when periodic update happens in network. So for one hour, the network will be using this fake LSA.

AR for this case works as in previous attack and will try to verify the LSA. AR will not get expected response as LSA is false. So the attack will be detected.

Thus in this section we have presented few known attacks on OSPF protocols and tried to detect them with the proposed new technique of selecting one router as Analyzer Router (AR) and performing some verification tasks for LSAs.

5   Recovery from Attacks

After detecting these attacks must be stopped and their effect must be nullified. With this detection technique we are already aware about the attacker router. Now there are few options that can be implemented to stop them from attacking further.

First, the attacker router can be declared as selfish or attacking one by flooding some update in the network. After receiving this update from AR, all other router in network will reject further updates from that router. Also will discard previous updates and send fresh LSAs regarding those subnets/links which were received from that attacker router.

Another approach is that AR itself takes responsibility to distribute verified LSAs and LSAs from AR will be having highest priority. In this way AR will become powerful asset in network to have control over LSAs.

6   Conclusion

In this paper, basic concepts of OSPF, its working, packets and security is studied. New concept to detect any attack that occurs in the network against OSPF is presented. One router in network will be elected as AR and it will verify each update in the network. Then this technique is implemented on some proposed attacks on OSPF. AR seems capable of detecting these attacks and can help network to recover from this. Presence of AR makes a network powerful against lots of attacks and makes the network much reliable

References

1. Moy, J.: OSPF version 2: IETF RFC 2328 (April 1998)
2. Dijkstra, E.W.: A note on two problems in connexion with graphs. Numerische Mathematik 1, 269–271 (1959)
3. Nakibly, G., Boneh, D.: Persistent OSPF attacks. In: Proceedings of the 19th Annual Network & Distributed System Security Conference, NDSS 2012 (2012)
4. Wang, F., Felix Wu, S.: On the Vulnerabilities and Protection of OSPF Routing Protocol. U.S. Department of Defense Advanced Research Projects Agency (1998)
5. Jones, E., Moigne, O.L.: OSPF Security Vulnerabilities Analysis. Internet-Draft draft-ietf-rpsec-ospf-vuln-02, IETF (June 2006)
6. Mahajan, R., Spring, N., Wetherall, D., Anderson, T.: Inferring link weights using end-to-end measurements. In: ACM SIGCOMM Internet Measurement Workshop (IMW) (November 2002)
7. Wang, F., Vetter, B., Wu, S.F.: Secure Routing Protocols: Theory and Practice. Technical report. North Carolina State University (May 1997)
8. Ghourabi, A., Abbes, T., Bouhoula, A.: Honeypot Router for routing protocols protection. Department of Computer Science and Networks, 2083 Cité El Ghazala, Tunisia. IEEE (2009)

Attack Graph Generation, Visualization and Analysis: Issues and Challenges

Ghanshyam S. Bopche[1,2] and Babu M. Mehtre[1]

[1] Center for Information Assurance & Management (CIAM),
Institute for Development and Research in Banking Technology (IDRBT), India
{bsghanshyam,bmmehtre}@idrbt.ac.in
[2] School of Computer and Information Sciences (SCIS),
University of Hyderabad, India

Abstract. In the current scenario, even the well-administered enterprise networks are extremely susceptible to sophisticated multi-stage cyber attacks. These attacks combine multiple network vulnerabilities and use causal relationship between them in order to get incremental access to enterprise critical resources. Detection of such multi-stage attacks is beyond the capability of present day vulnerability scanners. These correlated "multi-host, multi-stage" attacks are potentially much more harmful than the single point/ isolated attacks. Security researchers have proposed an Attack Graph-based approach to detect such correlated attack scenarios. Attack graph is a security analysis tool used extensively in a networked environment to automate the process of evaluating network's susceptibility to "multi-host, multi-stage" attacks. In the last decade, a lot of research has been done in the area of attack graph- generation, visualization and analysis. Despite significant progress, still there are issues and challenges before the security community that needs to be addressed. In this paper, we have tried to identify current issues and important avenues of research in the area of attack graph generation, visualization and analysis.

Keywords: Asset, Vulnerability, Threat, Risk, Exploit, Adversary, Network Security, Attack Graph.

1 Introduction

With the advent of Internet technologies, today's computer networks have grown exponentially in terms of both size and complexity. These networks hold critical resources/ assets and play a crucial role in most enterprises, including financial data system, health care system, power grids, and emergency communication systems. Because of extreme importance, these networks are increasingly vulnerable and always a soft target of sophisticated cyber attacks from potential adversaries such as hackers, corporate competitors, disgruntled employees, government agencies etc. These sophisticated attacks, no more exploiting *isolated* vulnerabilities (i.e. vulnerabilities that are local to a system only). Rather, they combine multiple vulnerabilities present across the network and use causal relationship between them to penetrate the enterprise network. Such kind of attacks is called as "*multi-host, multi-stage*" attacks. These attacks are so advanced and sophisticated that they can target- systems behind firewalls, protected by multiple

J. Lloret Mauri et al. (Eds.): SSCC 2014, CCIS 467, pp. 379–390, 2014.

layers of security, or hidden in a company network and have a capability to circumvent detection. Even the well-monitored networks are susceptible to such multi-stage attacks.

In order to capture the global picture of the network security, administrator should focus on correlated attacks. Attack graph is such a tool that depicts different correlated multi-stage attacks in a network. Attack graph forms the logical formalism and correlation among the vulnerabilities within a host or across multiple hosts. The series of exploits executed by an adversary constitute an attack path and a set of such attack paths form an attack graph. This resultant attack graph reveals various ways an attacker can leverage vulnerabilities in a network in order to incrementally penetrate the network and violate a security policy. In other words, the attack graph concisely represents all paths available to an adversary that end in a state where he/ she can successfully achieve his/ her goal.

Researchers and commercial organizations developed different approaches of the attack graph generation- an annotated review of many of these approaches is presented by Lippmann and Ingols in [18]. Each of the approach generates and represents an attack graph very differently. The whole research in the area of attack graph is centers on its efficient generation, scalable representation, and efficient analysis. Substantial improvement is already achieved in each of these sub areas, but even then, there are some issues and challenges before the security community.

Organization of rest of the paper is as follows: section 2 provides the overview of the generic workflow of the attack graph construction and analysis. Section 3 describes the issues and challenges in each phase of attack graph workflow, i.e., generation, visualization and analysis. Finally, we conclude the paper in section 4.

2   Workflow of Attack Graph Construction and Analysis

Attack Graphs have been proposed for years as a formal modeling tool to detect complex multi-stage attack scenarios [17]. To obtain the complete understanding of how attack graphs are constructed and utilized, a generic workflow is proposed in the literature (as shown in figure 1). This workflow consists of three dependent phases, namely, (1) *Information Gathering*, (2) *Attack Graph Construction*, and (3) *Attack Graph Visualization & Analysis*. For the construction of an attack graph, some initial information is required: including information about the systems under attack (i.e., information about individual hosts, network connectivity between hosts and the services functioning on these hosts) and the information about the vulnerabilities exploited by an adversary during attack attempts. This input information is separately collected from different sources and then unified/ merged in an information-gathering phase. In the second phase, an attack graph is constructed from the gathered input information. Finally, processing of attack graph is done in the visualization and analysis phase. This phase consists of two sub phases, namely, visualization and analysis, which are independent of each other and need to be performed repeatedly. Issues and challenges with each of these individual phases are described in section 3.

3   Issues and Challenges

Issues pertaining to each of the three dependent phases of attack graph construction and analysis (i.e., (1) Information Gathering, (2) Attack Graph Construction, and (3) Attack Graph Visualization & Analysis) are depicted in figure 2.

3.1   Issues with Information Gathering Phase

Obtaining quality information about the system or network under attack is the pre-requisite for the construction of attack graph [31]. This information must include- the configuration detail of each single host, type of services they run, network topology, security policies, adversary model, trust relationship and description of host-specific vulnerabilities that likely to be exploited by an adversary. This information is gathered from wide variety sources such as scanners (for e.g., port/ topology/ vulnerability scanners), policy parsers, vulnerability databases (VDBs), firewall configuration files and user inputs. This input information is gathered both automatically (using existing tools) and manually. The more qualitative and detailed the input information is, the resulting attack graph is more meaningful. Among all sorts of information, gathering vulnerability description and network reachability information is a challenging task and poses great difficulty.

3.1.1   Extraction of Vulnerability Information from Vulnerability Databases (VDBs)

Description of host-specific vulnerabilities, particularly *precondition* and *postcondition* is prerequisite for modeling correlated attacks. These descriptions include information on what resources must be available to an attacker before launching any attack and what are the resources available to him after the successful execution of the attack. These descriptions are useful in linking single attacks into a chain of multi-step attacks. Today, many commercial and non-commercial VDBs are available which provide vulnerability descriptions on reported vulnerabilities. However, there are some issues with the use of these VDBs as follows:

- Earlier, because of the lack of common criteria for vulnerability description, there is no unified view on vulnerability descriptions provided by the different VDBs. Various efforts have been made to resolve this issue and resulted into the meta vulnerability database called Common Vulnerabilities and Exposures (CVE) which provides the common identifier for reported vulnerabilities across various VDBs. In the context of attack graphs generation, there is a need of new unifying methodology for vulnerability description [6].
- There are no publicly available VDBs which *exclusively* maintains a repository for vulnerability preconditions and postconditions. Without these VDBs, it is undesirable to identify or evaluate the effects of host-specific vulnerabilities.
- Even though some VDBs exist, but they are either *proprietary* or does not provide the vulnerability description in a machine-readable format (for e.g., XML format). Even these VDBs are not maintaining uniformity in vulnerability attributes. Most

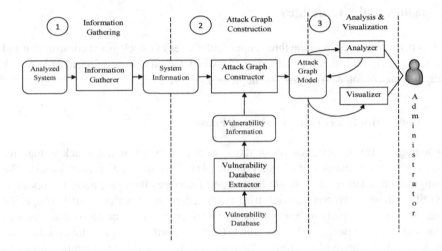

Fig. 1. Generic Workflow of Attack Graph Construction and Analysis

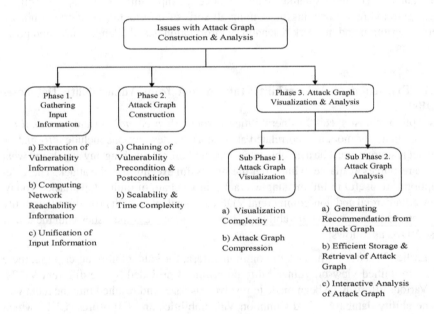

Fig. 2. Issues & Challenges with Attack Graph Construction & Analysis

of the present day attack graph generation tools depend on hand-generated vulnerability input and consider very few vulnerability attributes during attack graph generation. This raises the question about correctness and utility of the resulting attack graph. If the vulnerability description is readily available in a machine-readable format, it can be directly fed into an attack graph construction tool. This improves the time-complexity and correctness of the resulting attack graph.

3.1.2 Computing Network Reachability Information

Network topology determines which other hosts on a network can be reachable from the given host. This information is very useful to attack graph generation tools in relating different hosts to one another and thereby deriving possible attack paths. Possible sources of network topology details are network scan reports, firewall rules and file-based description of the network structure. Model checking-based approach of attack graph construction (i.e., [12]) assumes network reachability information is available prior to attack graph generation. TVA-based approach [17] obtained reachability information for each subnet using vulnerability scanners. Logic-based approach [3] uses firewall management tools such as Smart Firewall [32] to obtain network configuration information. For enterprise network with reasonably large size and containing many firewalls, computing reachability between all hosts is a computationally complex task. Each of these firewalls contains hundreds to thousands of rules for e.g., access control rules, NAT rules, network objects that represent groups of IP addresses. Single scan from one IP address exercise only a few of these rules and likely to miss the rules that apply to the other IP addresses or to destination IP addresses. In reality, it is very difficult to know which source and destination addresses treated differently by the firewall. For such networks, use of vulnerability scanners severely underestimates the reachability information. Again, single vulnerability scan cannot detect the effect of time-dependent firewall rules on the network reachability. Lippmann and Ingols in [18] pointed out the need of downloading and analyzing configuration files of network infrastructure devices that do filtering (for e.g., firewalls, routers, switches, and so forth) in order to accurately determine the reachability between hosts in a separate subnets. Hence, there is a need to develop scalable topology scanners, which perform such kind of analysis and facilitate network reachability information to the existing attack graph generation tools.

3.1.3 Unification of Input Data

Each piece of input information required for the attack graph generation is coming from different sources and is semantically different from the other piece of information. Even though each piece of information describing different aspects of the system security, we need to link all pieces together. In doing this we need a good data structure. Gathered input information may be static or dynamic in nature. For example, there may be a change in network topology whenever a host joins or leaves a network, there is always a possibility of new software installed, removed or reconfigured. Description of reported vulnerability is usually seen as a static kind of information. Hence, a *unified* data structure is required to manage *temporal* data. Again, these different pieces of information can be tightly or loosely coupled with each other, this aspect is also need to be considered while choosing data structure for input information. Combining all, we need a good, flexible, modifiable and unified data structure to model input information required for the attack graph generation.

3.2 Issues with Attack Graph Construction Phase

Once the input information (i.e., system information and vulnerability description) required for attack graph construction is gathered and unified, attack graph is constructed.

First, *reachability matrix* is computed to determine a set of network hosts that are reachable from every other host. Alongside, the host specific vulnerabilities and their respective descriptions are integrated together resulting, in an attack graph. Heberlein et al., in [40] identified a number of important features for e.g., *Type of exploits (Monotonic/ Non-monotonic Exploits), Number of attack paths (Single Path/ All Path), Chaining of exploits (Forward/ Backward Chaining)*, and so forth, for comparing and contrasting various attack graph efforts. They discussed issues with each of above features during attack graph construction. Some more issues pertaining to the attack graph construction phase are as follows:

3.2.1 Chaining Together Precondition and Postcondition of Attacks into a Sequence of Attacks

For the execution of an exploit adversary must have access to network preconditions and once executed successfully some new conditions called postconditions added to the network. Here precondition implies to *"what privileges available to an attacker on a networked host before launching any attack"*. Postcondition implies to *"what are the resources available to attacker after the successfully carrying out an attack, and the privilege level on acquired resources"*. In attack graph, each postcondition of one attack act as a precondition for another attack, thereby enabling sequence of attacks. Incorrect chaining of precondition and postcondition leads to completely wrong result. Hence chaining together attack precondition privilege level and attack postcondition privilege level is a big issue in attack graph generation research [8].

3.2.2 Scalability & Time Complexity

Early approaches of attack graph generation for e.g., [39], [9], [11], [38], [13] relied on state enumeration and generate full attack graphs. These approaches do not scale to the real network. Noel and Jajodia [28] introduced the concept of an exploit-dependency graph that in turn uses the concept of *"monotonicity [15]"* in order to overcome the scalability issue. This approach scale well to network containing tens or hundreds of hosts (e.g. [17], [26]), or even to thousands of hosts (e.g. [21], [20]), but the generated attack graph is too complex for humans to understand. Predictive attack graph [24] and multi-prerequisite attack graph [21] (developed at MIT) are scalable and provide more efficient representation. Ou et al., [20] proposed a scalable logic-based approach for attack graph generation, but the generated attack graph is large and difficult to understand. Two commercial tools for attack graph generation are from [2] and [1]. All of the above approaches having poor scalability and none of them scale *linearly* or *quadratically* in the number of hosts.

3.3 Issues with Attack Graph Visualization Phase

Once attack graph is constructed, it is made available to an administrator for understanding possible multi-step intrusions within enterprise network. Even though an attack graph is used for network security analysis, current approaches of its visualization have several practical weaknesses. Some of them are listed below:

- Since, today's enterprise networks are highly interconnected and complex, resulting attack graphs are quickly overloaded with large amount of data.
- Usually, a single exploit involves a source host, a destination host and one or more intermediate hosts. Hence, the number of vertices and edges grows *combinatorially*, at least quadratic in the number of hosts multiplied by number of vulnerabilities [7]. Therefore, for an enterprise network with reasonably large size, the attack graph is very complex and incomprehensible to human eyes. Manual analysis of such a big and complex graph is nearly impossible and hence hinders the process of extracting useful information out of it. For an enterprise network with thousands of hosts, even the computation of the attack graphs is infeasible and the explosion in its size is completely unavoidable.
- Another trouble with an attack graph is their inadequacy in representing network topology and reachability among the hosts. Hence, it is really difficult to relate an attack graph to the underlying network. Without reachability information one can not able to analyze *"why certain attack paths are possible?"* and to determine *"which filtering devices allow these attack steps?"*.
- Traditionally, complete attack graphs [24] are generated that depicts all possible attack scenarios, i.e., both successful attacks as well as those attacks which does not end up with the attackers goal state [5]. These complete attack graphs contain *redundant* nodes and edges and are so complex that it is very hard to an administrator to visually comprehend and analyze. The decision makers (i.e., the administrators) intent only rested in the successful attack scenarios, the residue of the scenarios are not meaningful to him. A real-world enterprise network, usually contains hosts with similar configuration and connected by similar kinds of access control rules. This again introduces redundancy in the resultant attack graph. Even the minimal attack graph of an enterprise network with reasonable size is incomprehensible to human eyes. Finally, we can, say attack graph carries lot of redundant information. Such redundancy, make the attack graph incomprehensible, and the generation, analysis, and management process difficult.

Producing an effective visualization for an attack graphs is essential to their utility [36]. Previous approaches produce complex displays. In literature, there are numerous ways to represent an attack graph. Alhomodi and Reed discussed the former work on attack graph representation in [34]. More or less of these representatives come out of the need of the scalable generation of an attack graph and some are to facilitate risk analysis. To make the attack graph comprehensible, various approaches based on different techniques such as (i) *Grouping* [10], [21], [25] (ii) *Aggregation* [28], (iii) *Clustering* [26], [27] (iv) *Treemaps* [29], [1] (v) *Graph Compression* [7] and (vi) *Prioritization* [22] [37] are proposed in the literature. Altogether, the above approaches first generate an attack graph and then treat them in order to minimize their visual complexity. Improvement is achieved to some extent by using algorithms that compute subgraphs via ranks or graph cliques, subnets via reachability, by grouping vulnerabilities per host, grouping hosts with similar configuration, and also by using compression algorithms. Even with these simplified views, one can not relate attack graphs with underlying network because network topology i.e., firewalls, network hierarchy, logical grouping of hosts such as subnet, Local Area Network (LAN) and Virtual LAN (VLAN) are not represented in the attack graph itself. Graph compression-based techniques are used for minimizing visual complexity of an attack graph by holding back in mind following things:

- Compressed attack graph must be meaningful to the security analyst and convey the similar threat information like an original attack graph.
- Compression must be lossless. In other words, it should recover all attack sequences, as they can be from original attack graphs.

The issues discussed above open new avenues of research in the area of developing scalable solutions for the attack graph generation and visualization. Such attack graph display would enhance the administrator's ability to leverage the data held within an attack graph and take proactive actions to effectively secure enterprise network. Therefore, techniques need to be developed to summarize and work with condensed representations of the attack graph.

3.4   Issues with Attack Graph Analysis Phase

In an enterprise network, an administrator perform a series of analysis over the attack graph to draw some valuable results such as, number of attack paths, the shortest attack path, the likelihood of successful attack etc. The outcomes of such analysis are applied to get some defensive steps to secure the network. Doing an analysis of the complex attack graph is difficult for an administrator. To make graph analysis easier a suite of metrics proposed by researchers. The detail of complete metric suite for attack graph analysis is given in [33]. Even though complete metric suite is there for attack graph analysis, decision makers are facing some more issues with attack graph analysis as follows:

3.4.1   Generating Recommendations from Attack Graph

In order to support administrator in addressing security issues pertaining to the enterprise network, an attack graph should generate some security recommendations. Such recommendations could be suggestions of the type for e.g., change in network topology, patches for the installed software's, blocking of unnecessary open ports/ services etc. which results in a fewer number of changes [18]. Noel et al. in [16] used an exploit-dependency attack graph to generate such security recommendation that guarantees the security of critical resources. NetSPA [24] generates a set of prioritized recommendations that suggest set of vulnerabilities that should be patched. Automatically generating recommendations from the attack graph is a fertile area of research in the field of network security.

3.4.2   Efficient Storage and Retrieval of Attack Graph

Once attack graph is generated for an enterprise network, an administrator has to store it for future analysis. Attack graph for an enterprise network with thousands of hosts could be massive in size. This attack graph needs to be stored and retrieved efficiently so that the process of subsequent analysis become easier and can be done on the fly. Barik and Mazumdar [30] used graph database for the efficient generation, storage and retrieval of attack graph to enhance existing analysis techniques. Most of the existing approaches of attack graph generation and analysis are silent about the issue of efficient storage and retrieval of attack graphs. This opens new opportunities for research.

3.4.3 Interactive Analysis of Attack Graphs

Attack graph helps administrator in performing security analysis of enterprise network and in interpreting/ understanding the diverse nature of multistage security threats. This asks for the scalable solution for the attack graph generation and its analysis. Most of the existing approaches of attack graph analysis usually make use of proprietary algorithms and their implementation cause delay in the availability of new analysis results. In case of *dynamic* networks, there is a frequent change in the network topology as hosts may join or leave the network at any point of time. Again, in some, real time networks, there may be frequent change in hosts/ network configurations and/ or security objectives as well. In such scenarios, *temporal* aspect of network security needs to be taken into account. Once the attack graph is available to an administrator, he has to analyze it as soon as possible. For doing this proprietary algorithms need to be adopted more frequently, which is not possible in real time. Hence, at this point of time administrator feel the need of techniques that facilitate interactive analysis of attack graph. Wang et al., are the first who addressed this issue in [19], [35]. They proposed a *relational model* for representing input information needed for attack graph construction, i.e., system/ network configuration and domain knowledge. The attack graph is generated as a relational view from these inputs. These relational views support different type of search operations and these operations are realized as a relational queries. These queries are built dynamically, revised at run time and used for interactive analysis. Because of the lack of graph data structures and supported operations in relational databases, proposed solution is not proved practical and scalable for the large enterprise network. The second approach in this direction came from [30]. They proposed a graph data model to represent input information required for the attack graph generation. For doing this, they used the *Neo4j* graph database. They showed how the *Cypher* graph queries are used for attack graph generation and for performing typical analysis over the generated attack graph. Therefore, generating scalable techniques for interactive attack graph analysis is the fertile area of research.

4 Conclusion

Attack graph help security analyst in modeling adversary behavior, identifying critical network weaknesses, evaluating network security and suggesting changes to improve security in a networked environment. It models how an adversary combines multiple vulnerabilities present across the network in order to compromise critical resources. Generating attack graph for today's highly connected and a sophisticated enterprise network is a challenging task. Although a lot of work published on attack graph construction and analysis, there are some open issues and challenges. Early research on attack graphs is centered around its scalable and efficient generation. At the very beginning, Red Teams used to construct an attack graph manually for determining vulnerability of networked systems. This approach of drawing attack graphs by hand is laborious, error-prone and almost impractical for a network with large number of systems. Later on, numerous automated approaches of attack graph generation for e.g., [39], [9], [10], [11], [38], [15], [13], [28], [17] [3], [24], [21], [2], [1], [5], etc. are proposed. These approaches have poor scalability and none of the approach scale linearly or quadratically in the number of hosts. The subject of scalability and time-efficient generation of an attack graph still open for research to the security community. The focus of attack graph research is then shifted from its scalable generation to effective visualization. A significant amount of progress is achieved in this direction using techniques called Grouping [10], [21], [25], Aggregation [28], Clustering [26], [27], Treemaps [29], [1], Graph Compression [7] and Prioritization [22] [37] etc. Yet the problem of comprehensible and scalable visualization of an attack graph persists in an enterprise containing thousands of hosts. Since, the resulting attack graph has been very complex and very big in size; administrator encountered a problem of interactive analysis. The field of interactive analysis of attack graph is less explored area and there is a scope of research in this direction. In this paper, we have tried to identify current issues and challenges encountered in each phase of the attack graph construction and analysis. This suggests future areas of research in the area of attack graph.

References

1. RedSeal Networks, http://www.redsealnetworks.com/
2. Skybox Security, http://www.skyboxsecurity.com/
3. Ou, X., Govindavajhala, S., Appel, A.: MulVAL: A Logic-based Network Security Analyzer. In: 14th USENIX Security Symposium, Baltimore, Maryland, U.S.A. (August 2005)
4. Jha, S., Sheyner, O., Wing, J.: Two Formal Analysis of Attack Graphs. In: Proc. of the 15th IEEE Workshop on Computer Security Foundations (CSFW 2002). IEEE Computer Society, Washington, DC (2002)
5. Ghosh, N., Ghosh, S.K.: A planner-based approach to generate and analyze minimal attack graph. Applied Intelligence 36(2), 369–390 (2012)
6. Schuppenies, R.: Automatic Extraction of Vulnerability Information for Attack Graphs. Master Thesis, Potsdam (March 2009)
7. Long, T.: Attack Graph Compression. Master Thesis, Concordia University, Montreal, Canada, USA (March 2009)
8. Kap, G., Ali, D.: Statistical Analysis of Computer Network Security, KTH Royal Institute of Technology, Sweden (October 2013)
9. Phillips, C., Swiler, L.: A graph-based system for network-vulnerability analysis. In: Proc. of the 1998 Workshop on New Security Paradigms (NSPW 1998), Charlottesville, Virginia, USA, pp. 71–79 (September 1998)
10. Swiler, L., Phillips, C., Ellis, D., Chakerian, S.: Computer attack graph generation tool. In: DARPA Information Survivability Conference and Exposition II (DISCEX 2001), vol. 2, pp. 307–321 (2001)
11. Ritchey, R.W., Ammann, P.: Using Model Checking to Analyze Network Vulnerabilities. In: Proc. of the IEEE Symposium on Security and Privacy (S&P 2000), pp. 156–165. IEEE Press, New York (2000)
12. Sheyner, O., Haines, J., Jha, S., Lippmann, R., Wing, J.M.: Automated generation and analysis of attack graphs. In: Proc. of the IEEE Symposium on Security and Privacy (S&P 2002), pp. 273–284. IEEE Press, Oakland (2002)
13. Sheyner, O., Wing, J.: Tools for Generating and Analyzing Attack Graphs. In: de Boer, F.S., Bonsangue, M.M., Graf, S., de Roever, W.-P. (eds.) FMCO 2003. LNCS, vol. 3188, pp. 344–371. Springer, Heidelberg (2004)

14. Sheyner, O.: Scenario Graphs and Attack Graphs. Ph.D. Thesis, Carneige Mellon University (CMU), Pittsburgh, USA (2004)

15. Ammann, P., Wijesekera, D., Kaushik, S.: Scalable, graph-based network vulnerability analysis. In: Proc. of the 9th ACM Conference on Computer and ommunications Security (CCS 2002), Washington, DC, USA, pp. 217–224 (November 2002)

16. Noel, S., Jajodia, S., O'Berry, B., Jacobs, M.: Efficient Minimum-cost Network Hardening via Exploit Dependency Graphs. In: Proc. of the 19th Annual Computer Security Applications Conference (ACSAC 2003), Las Vegas, NV, USA, pp. 86–95 (December 2003)

17. Jajodia, S., Noel, S., O'Berry, B.: Topological Analysis of Network Attack Vulnerability. In: Managing Cyber Threats: Issues, Approaches, and Challenges, pp. 247–266. Springer US (2005)

18. Lippmann, R., Ingols, K.W.: An annotated review of past papers on attack graphs. Project Report ESC-TR-2005-054, MIT Lincoln Laboratory (March 2005)

19. Wang, L., Yao, C., Singhal, A., Jajodia, S.: Interactive Analysis of Attack Graphs Using Relational Queries. In: Damiani, E., Liu, P. (eds.) Data and Applications Security 2006. LNCS, vol. 4127, pp. 119–132. Springer, Heidelberg (2006)

20. Ou, X., Boyer, W.F., McQueen, M.A.: A scalable approach to attack graph generation. In: Proc. of the 13th ACM Conference on Computer and Communications Security (CCS 2006), Alexandria, Virginia, USA, pp. 336–345 (November 2006)

21. Ingols, K.W., Lippmann, R., Piwowarski, K.: Practical Attack Graph Generation for Network Defense. In: Proc. of the 22nd Annual Computer Security Applications Conference (ACSAC 2006), Washington, DC, USA, pp. 121–130 (December 2006)

22. Mehta, V., Bartzis, C., Zhu, H., Clarke, E., Wing, J.: Ranking Attack Graphs. In: Zamboni, D., Kruegel, C. (eds.) RAID 2006. LNCS, vol. 4219, pp. 127–144. Springer, Heidelberg (2006)

23. Malhotra, S., Bhattacharya, S., Ghosh, S.K.: A Vulnerability and Exploit Independent Approach for Attack Path Prediction. In: Proc. of the IEEE 8th International Conference on Computer and Information Technology, Sydney, Australia, pp. 282–287 (July 2008)

24. Lippmann, R., Ingols, K., Scott, C., Piwowarski, K., Kratkiewicz, K., Artz, M., Cunningham, R.: Validating and restoring defense in depth using attack graphs. In: Proc. of the IEEE Conference on Military Communications, pp. 981–990. IEEE Press, Piscataway (2006)

25. Homer, J., Varikuti, A., Ou, X., McQueen, M.A.: Improving Attack Graph Visualization through Data Reduction and Attack Grouping. In: Proc. of the 5th Int. Work. on Vis. for Comp. Sec. (VizSEC 2008), Cambridge, MA, USA, pp. 68–79 (September 2008)

26. Noel, S., Jacobs, M., Kalapa, P., Jajodia, S.: Multiple coordinated views for network attack graphs. In Proc. of IEEE Workshop on Visualization for Computer Security (VizSEC 2005), Minneapolis, USA, pp. 99–106 (October 2005)

27. Noel, S., Jajodia, S.: Understanding complex network attack graphs through clustered adjacency matrices. In: 21st Annual Computer Security Application Conference, vol. 10 (December 2005)

28. Noel, S., Jajodia, S.: Managing attack graph complexity through visual hierarchical aggregation. In: Proc. of ACM Workshop on Visualization and Data Mining for Computer Security (VizSEC 2004), GMU, Fairfax, USA, pp. 109–118 (October 2004)

29. Williams, L., Lippmann, R., Ingols, K.W.: An interactive attack graph cascade and reachability display. In: Proc. of the 2007 Workshop on Visualization for Computer Security (VizSEC 2007), Sacramento, CA, USA, pp. 221–236 (October 2007)

30. Barik, M.S., Mazumdar, C.: A Graph Data Model for Attack Graph Generation and Analysis. In: Martínez Pérez, G., Thampi, S.M., Ko, R., Shu, L. (eds.) SNDS 2014. CCIS, vol. 420, pp. 239–250. Springer, Heidelberg (2014)

31. Cheng, F., Roschke, S., Meinel, C.: An integrated network scanning tool for attack graph construction. In: Riekki, J., Ylianttila, M., Guo, M. (eds.) GPC 2011. LNCS, vol. 6646, pp. 138–147. Springer, Heidelberg (2011)
32. Burns, J., Cheng, A., Gurung, P., Rajagopalan, S., Rao, P., Rosenbluth, D., Surendran, A.V., Martin Jr., D.M.: Automatic management of network security policy. In: Proc. of DARPA Information Survivability Conference & Exposition II, vol. 2, pp. 12–26 (2001)
33. Noel, S., Jajodia, S.: Metrics Suite for Network Attack Graph Analytics. In: 9th Ann. Cyb. and Info. Sec. Res. Conf. (CISRC), Oak Ridge National Laboratory, Tennessee (April 2014)
34. Alhomidi, M.A., Reed, M.J.: Attack graphs representations. In: 4th Computer Science and Electronic Engineering Conference (CEEC), pp. 83–88 (September 2012)
35. Wang, L., Yao, C., Singhal, S., Jajodia, S.: Implementing interactive analysis of attack graphs using relational databases. Journal of Computer Security 16(4), 419–437 (2008)
36. Williams, L.: GARNET: A Graphical Attack Graph and Reachability Network Evaluation Tool. Master Thesis, Massachusetts Institute of Technology (May 2008)
37. Sawilla, R., Ou, X.: Googling Attack Graphs. Technical Report TM-2007-205, Defense Research and Development Canada (September 2007)
38. Ramakrishnan, C.R., Sekar, R.: Model-based analysis of configuration vulnerabilities. Journal of Computer Security 10(1-2), 189–209 (2002)
39. Dacier, M., Deswarte, Y., Kaâniche, M.: Models and tools for quantitative assessment of operational security. In: Information Systems Security, pp. 177–186. Chapman & Hall, Ltd., London (1996)
40. Heberlein, T., Bishop, M., Ceesay, E., Danforth, M., Senthilkumar, C., Stallard, T.: A Taxonomy for Comparing Attack-Graph Approaches (July 5, 2014)

CAVEAT: Credit Card Vulnerability Exhibition and Authentication Tool

Ishu Jain, Rahul Johari, and R.L Ujjwal

USICT, Guru Gobind Singh Indraprastha University, Sec-16C, Dwarka, Delhi, India
ishujain100@gmail.com, {rahul,rlujjwal}@ipu.ac.in

Abstract. Online banking (or Internet baking or E-banking) makes people capable to do financial transactions on a secured website. It allows users to manage their money without going to their respective banks. Today, the users can do the financial transactions of their daily life like bill payments, shopping, booking movie, train, air and various other event tickets through online banking. Since the online banking involves circulation of money so it should be secured but as the use of online banking is increasing, the security threats to the banking applications are also increasing. In this paper, we have designed a Java based tool to show the exploitation of Injection (OWASP Top 10-2013 A1 Vulnerability) using SQL Injection attack and Broken Authentication(part of OWASP Top 10-2013 A2 Vulnerability) using Brute Force Attack and Dictionary Attack and the prevention of all these attack by storing the data in our database in encrypted form using AES algorithm.

Keywords: SQL Injection Attack, Brute Force Attack, Dictionary Attack, AES Encryption Algorithm, Credit Card Validation.

1 Introduction

Web applications have become the essential part of the daily life of internet users. Security is one of the most important part of web application because the security is one of the critical aspect used in assessing the quality of software. A web application is said to be secured if the web application developers are able to prevent their application from unauthorized access and modification, data theft and communication eavesdropping. Continuous efforts have been made by web developers to improve the security of the web applications. Though too many efforts have been made but still the applications are not 100% secure. In simple language, loop holes are known as vulnerabilities. In technical terms, loop holes in the web application that allows malicious users to breach the security of web application. The reason behind the vulnerabilities in a web application is either due to imperfection in design or any defect in implementation. Common examples of vulnerabilities in an application are unclosed database connections and improper input validations et al. The way through which malicious user exploits the different vulnerabilities of the application is known as attack. Examples of attack are SQL

J. Lloret Mauri et al. (Eds.): SSCC 2014, CCIS 467, pp. 391–399, 2014.

injection attack, Brute Force Attack, Dictionary attack. We demonstrate the exploitation of Injection (OWASP Top 10-2013 A1 Vulnerability) using SQL Injection attack and Broken Authentication (part of OWASP Top 10-2013   A2

Vulnerability) using Brute Force Attack and Dictionary Attack and the prevention of all these attack. To show the demonstration, we have designed a Java based credit card validation application tool where we performed SQL injection attack on CVV (Credit Card Verification Value Number) number field and Brute force attack and dictionary attack on one time password field. After successful deployment of attacks, we also prevented the SQL injection attack by properly validating the field and Brute force attack and Dictionary attack by storing the encrypted form of character string entered by the user using AES encryption algorithm.

1.1   SQL Injection Attack and Vulnerability Exploited by This Attack

SQL query insertion or injection in an application via input provided by the user is known as SQL Injection attack. Through SQL injection attack, a user can perform insert/delete/update/select/ alter table/drop database/create database/ create user on the database of application. After successful deployment of SQL injection attack an attacker can become the database administrator, tamper the data of database, spoof identity and cause repudiation such as making changes in accounts of different users. By deploying SQL Injection attack, malicious user can exploit the injection vulnerability in an application [5][11].

Examples of Injection are SQL, OS and LDAP injection. When a user transmits un-trusted data to interpreter as a part of query or command then it results into Injection vulnerability. The data entered by the attacker makes the interpreter through trick to execute unintended commands or access the data without authorization [8].

1.2   Brute Force Attack

Brute force attack is an application of brute force search approach. It simply means making all the possible combinations of given input. In Brute force attack, all the possible combination are made and checked till the correct one is found. In web applications, Brute force attacks are commonly made on password field, one time password field. Through Brute force attack, a malicious user can exploit the broken authentication vulnerability in an application and then can access all the application [6].

1.3   Dictionary Attack

Dictionary attack is a method to exploit the broken authentication vulnerability of an application by entering or trying all words of dictionary as an input. Dictionary attacks are commonly made on password field, one time password field. To perform dictionary attack, an attacker requires a dictionary and he applies all the words of dictionary as an input. Through dictionary attack, attacker is able to break the authenticity of the application [6]. By breaking authenticity, an attacker can access the confidential data of an application.

1.4   AES Encryption Algorithm

AES stands for Advanced Encryption Standards. It is a block cipher whose block length is 128bit. AES is a variation of rijndael cipher which was invented by Belgian cryptographers. Their names were Joan Daemen and Vincent Rijmen. To perform encryption using AES, it requires 14 round of processing for 256 bit key, 12 rounds for 192 bit key and 10 rounds for 128 bit key. In every case, every round is same but the last round is different [7].

1.5   Broken Authentication Vulnerability

Broken authentication vulnerability stand at second position under the OWASP top 10 application security risks-2013. An authentication is the process to determine how the application validates the identity of the user. The authentication function enables the application to identify a request as originating from a known user, as opposed to being anonymous. When functions of an application which are related to authentication are not implemented correctly results into broken authentication vulnerability. This vulnerability can be exploited in an application using brute force attack and dictionary attack. Authentication vulnerability generally occurs due to improper implementation authentication procedure in the web application [9].

2   Related Work

Huluka and Popov [1] use Root Cause Analysis (RCA) in session management and broken authentication Vulnerabilities and identify the way to improve different aspect of security of web applications. Through RCA they found 9 root causes that lead to broken authentication vulnerability and 11 root causes that lead to session management vulnerability and they also provide deep detailed view of vulnerabilities, which results into effective solutions. These solutions are used to minimize the recurrence of attacks on web applications.

Fonseca et. Al. [2] Present a prototype tool and methodology for the evaluation of security mechanism of web applications. The idea behind their methodology is that they assess the existing mechanisms of security and tools in different scenarios by injecting realistic vulnerabilities in an application and attacking them. They also proposed the Vulnerability & Attack Injector Tool (VAIT) which automates the entire process. They have shown the effectiveness of proposed methodology by running the tool on set of experiments. The results of their research proved that the methodology proposed by them is an effective way not only for the evaluation of weakness of security mechanism but also helps in identifying the ways of its improvement.

Sadeghian et al. [3] presents a comprehensive review of different types of SQL injection detection and prevention techniques. They made the detailed analysis of all the techniques and provide the strengths and   weaknesses of each technique. The structural classification of the SQL injection detection and prevention techniques assists other researchers in the adoption of correct technique for their studies.

Scholte et al.   [4] Represents IPAAS, a novel technique. This technique is based automated detection of data type of input parameters which successfully prevents the exploitation of XSS and SQL injection vulnerabilities. They implemented this technique for PHP applications and also analyze the performance of this technique by running this technique on five real-world web applications. Their technique successfully prevented 65% of XSS vulnerabilities and 83% of SQL injection vulnerabilities.

Sharma et al. [12]presents a detailed review on various types of Structured Query Language Injection attacks, Cross Site Scripting Attack, vulnerabilities, and prevention techniques. The Author(s), also propose future expectations and possible development of countermeasures against Structured Query Language Injection attacks.

Gupta et al. [10] discuss and analyze the current developments in online authentication procedures including biometrics, one-time-password systems and use of mobile device and Public Switched Telephone Network for cardholder authentication. The author(s) propose a complete new framework for both onsite and online (Internet shopping) credit card transactions.

Sharma et al. [13] present an integrated model to prevent reflected cross site scripting attack and SQL Injection attacks in applications which are made in PHP. There model works in two modes which are production and safe mode environment. They create sanitizer model for reflected cross site scripting attack and security query model for SQL Injection attack in safe mode. They validate user input text against sanitizer model and input entries which create SQL queries are validated against security query model in production mode.

3   Experimental Set up and Methodology Used

We have designed our credit card validation application tool using Java Programming Language and more specifically using the advanced open source Java MVC (Model View Controller) architecture driven technologies : JSP in the View tier, Servlets in the Controller tier and MS ACCESS Database in the back end.

3.1   Exploitation of Broken Authentication Web Vulnerability (Part of the OWASP Top 10-2013 A2 Vulnerability) Using Brute Force Attack and Dictionary Attack

1.   On the execution of application, Fig.1 will appear which will ask user to enter his credit card details.

    1)   If user is registered on this application then after successful submission of details, user will be forwarded to Fig. 5.

    2)   If user is not registered on this application then user will be forwarded to Fig. 2. This page will display a message "The Credit Card Holder does not Exist. Please Register" with a link. On clicking the link, the user will be forwarded to Fig.3 which will ask to enter his personal details to get registered on this application. After the successful submission of details, user will be forwarded to Fig. 4.This page will display the message "The Registration is successful. Please Login Here" with a link. On clicking the link user will be forwarded to Fig. 1.

2.   On successful submission of details in Fig. 1, user will be forwarded to Fig. 5 which will show his personal details and asks user to enter his One Time Password in OTP field.

3.   On the successful submission of one time password in OTP field, there are two cases :-

Case 1: In case of Brute Force Attack, user will be forwarded to Fig. 6 which will show the results of Brute force attack. This page will show the password entered by user and all the possible combinations of character string entered by user in OTP field on console.

Case 2: In case of Dictionary attack, user will be forwarded to Fig. 7 which will show the results of Dictionary attack. This page will show the password entered by user and either the password exist in the dictionary or not. If the password exists it will display the message that "This password exists in our dictionary" and if the password does not exist then it will display the message "This password does not exist in our dictionary".

3.2   Exploitation of Injection Web Vulnerability (OWASP Top 10-2013 A1 Vulnerability) Using SQL Injection Attack

We have shown the deployment of SQL injection attack on CVV number field of Fig.1.

1.   Enter the universal condition „OR""=" in CVV Number field and registered user details in the remaining fields of Fig. 8.

2. On successful submission of details, user will be forwarded to Fig. 9 which displays the result of SQL injection attack. This page will display the set of records fetched by the SQL query based on input made by the user.

3.3   Prevention of SQL Injection Attack

The prevention of SQL injection attack has been made in our application by putting two validations on CVV number field. First validation will not allow user to enter more than 3character and second validation will not allow entering any other character except digits.

3.4   Prevention of Brute Force attack and Dictionary Attack

To prevent the Brute force attack and Dictionary attack in our application, we store the one time password in our database by using AES encryption algorithm [7]. After the successful storage of encrypted one time password, if we made brute force attack then it will start making the combination of 16 bit long string, which is not the actual password, so on the basis of any combination of 16 bit long string user cannot exploit the OTP field and if we made dictionary attack then it will search for 16 bit long pattern of actual password in our dictionary, which will not exist in our dictionary because the dictionary stores only the actual passwords not their encrypted form and its results have been shown in Fig. 10.

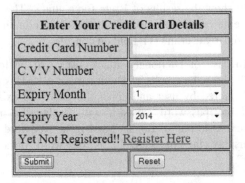

Fig. 1. Login Page

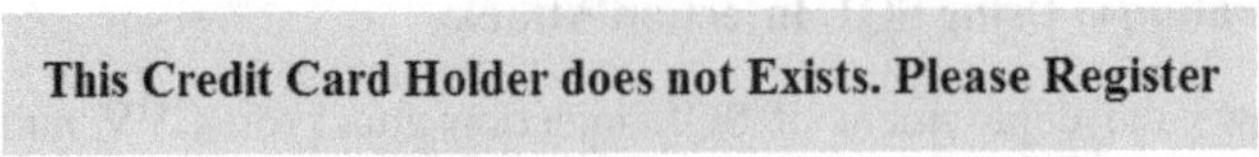

This Credit Card Holder does not Exists. Please Register

Fig. 2. Error Message if the user is not registered

Enter Information Here	
First Name	
Last Name	
Email	
Credit Card Number	
C.V.V Number	
Expiry Date: Month	1
Expiry Date: Year	2014
Submit	Reset
Already registered!! Login Here	

Fig. 3. Registration Page where user enter its personal detail

Registration is Successful. Please Login Here Go to Login

Fig. 4. Successful registration message

Please enter OTP

[   ] submit

Personal Details:						
First Name	Last Name	Email	Credit Card Number	CVV Number	Expiry Month	Expiry Year
xyz	abc	abc@gmail.com	4532783730970209	411	10	2020

Fig. 5. Detail Page showing personal details of user

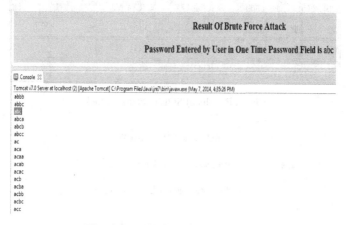

Result Of Brute Force Attack

Password Entered by User in One Time Password Field is abc

Fig. 6. Results of Brute Force Attack

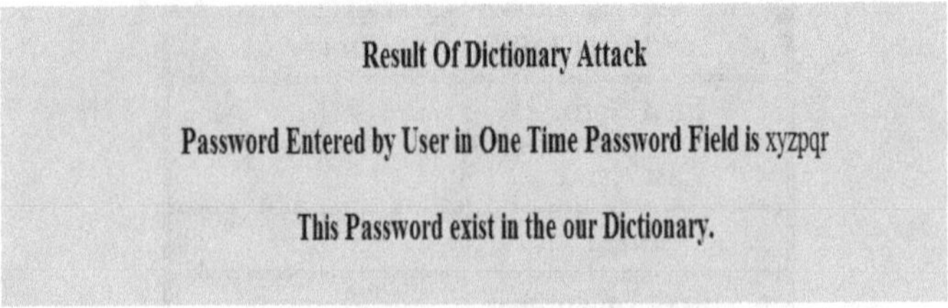

Result Of Dictionary Attack

Password Entered by User in One Time Password Field is xyzpqr

This Password exist in the our Dictionary.

Fig. 7. Results of Dictionary Attack

Enter Your Credit Card Details	
Credit Card Number	4532783730970209
C.V.V Number	'OR"='
Expiry Month	10
Expiry Year	2020
Yet Not Registered!! Register Here	
Submit	Reset

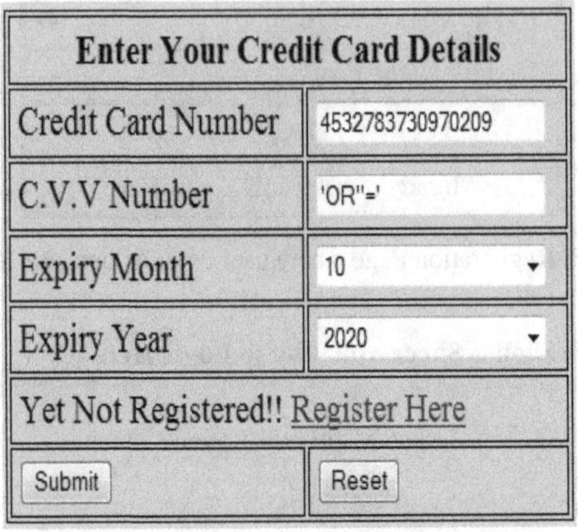

Fig. 8. Input for SQL Injection Attack

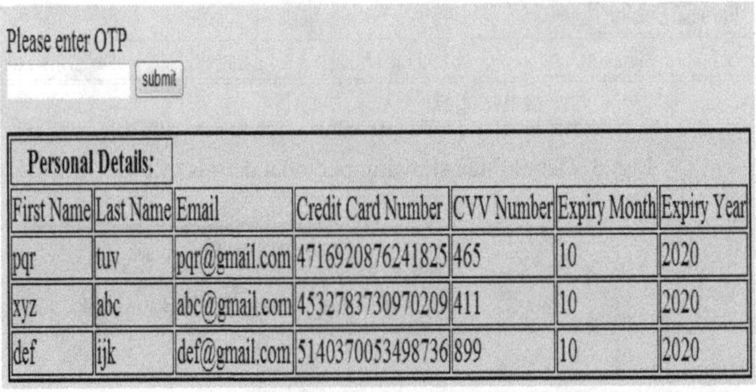

Please enter OTP

[submit]

Personal Details:						
First Name	Last Name	Email	Credit Card Number	CVV Number	Expiry Month	Expiry Year
pqr	tuv	pqr@gmail.com	4716920876241825	465	10	2020
xyz	abc	abc@gmail.com	4532783730970209	411	10	2020
def	ijk	def@gmail.com	5140370053498736	899	10	2020

Fig. 9. Results of SQL Injection Attack

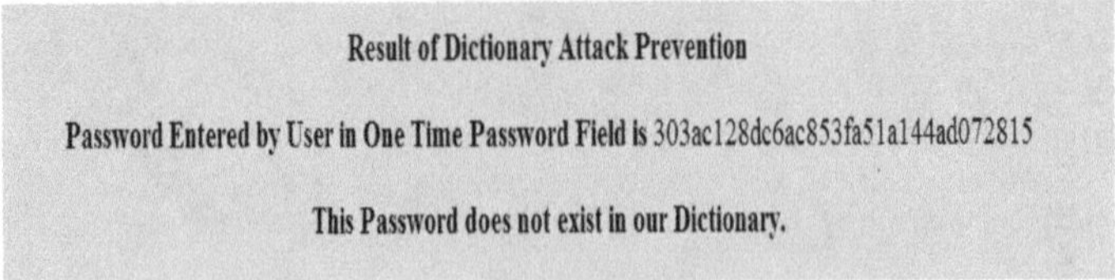

Result of Dictionary Attack Prevention

Password Entered by User in One Time Password Field is 303ac128dc6ac853fa51a144ad072815

This Password does not exist in our Dictionary.

Fig. 10. Results of dictionary attack prevention

4   Conclusion and Future Work

When we started developing the credit card validation application, our objective was to demonstrate the exploitation of Injection(OWASP Top 10-2013 A1 Vulnerability) using SQL Injection attack and Broken Authentication(part of OWASP Top 10-2013 A2 Vulnerability) using Brute Force Attack and Dictionary Attack and the prevention of all these attack. So we have successfully achieved our objective. In future we will try to exploit the remaining vulnerabilities of OWASP Top 10-2013 on our application by performing different attacks and will also give there preventions. After successful exploitation of other vulnerabilities we will deploy our application in open source through multiple vendors so that other people can take the benefit of our work.

References

1. Huluka, D., Popov, O.: Root Cause Analysis of Session Management and Broken Authentication Vulnerabilities, pp. 82–86. IEEE (2012)
2. Fonseca, J., Vieira, M., Madeira, H.: Evaluation of Web Security Mechanisms using Vulnerability and Attack Injection. IEEE (2013)
3. Sadeghian, A., Zamani, M., Manaf, A.A.: A Taxanomy of SQL Injection Detection and Prevention Techniques, pp. 53–56. IEEE (2013)
4. Scholte, T., Robertson, W., Balzarotti, D., Kirda, E.: Preventing Input Validation Vulnerabilities in Web Applications Through Automated Type Analysis. In: IEEE 36th International Conference on Computer Software and Applications, pp. 233–243 (2012)
5. https://www.owasp.org/index.php/SQL_Injection
6. https://www.owasp.org/index.php/Brute_force_attack
7. http://en.wikipedia.org/wiki/Advanced_Encryption_Standard
8. https://www.owasp.org/index.php/Top_10_2013-A1-Injection
9. https://www.owasp.org/index.php/Top_10_2013-A2-Broken_Authentication_and_Session_Management
10. Gupta, S., Johari, R.: A New Framework for Credit Card Transactions involving Mutual Authentication between Cardholder and Merchant. In: 2011 International Conference on Communication Systems and Network Technologies (CSNT), pp. 22–26. IEEE (2011)
11. Johari, R., Gupta, N.: Secure query processing in delay tolerant network using java cryptography architecture. In: 2011 International Conference on Computational Intelligence and Communication Networks (CICN), pp. 653–657. IEEE (2011)
12. Johari, R., Sharma, P.: A survey on web application vulnerabilities (SQLIA, XSS) exploitation and security engine for SQL injection. In: 2012 International Conference on Communication Systems and Network Technologies (CSNT), pp. 453–458. IEEE (2012)
13. Sharma, P., Johari, R., Sarma, S.S.: Integrated approach to prevent SQL injection attack and reflected cross site scripting attack. International Journal of System Assurance Engineering and Management 3(4), 343–351 (2012)

SQL FILTER – SQL Injection Prevention and Logging Using Dynamic Network Filter

Jignesh C. Doshi[1], Maxwell Christian[2], and Bhushan H. Trived[2]

[1] LJ Institute of Management Studies, Ahmedabad
doshijig@gmail.com
[2] GLS Institute of Computer Technology, Ahmedabad
{max4sall,bhtrivedi}@gmail.com

Abstract. Web has become buzz word for business in recent times. With the increase in attacks, web database applications become more vulnerable. Structure Query Language is most commonly used for database attack. As per the Open Web Application Security Project (OWASP) the top 5 attacks out of 10 are related to Structured Query Language (SQL). Database attack solutions fall into two category: Defensive coding and filters. The focus of such attacks is on data manipulation, steal and by pass authorization. In this paper authors have prepared a Dynamic Network filter to detect and prevent database attacks.

Keywords: SQL, SQLI, Firewall, Network filter.

1 Introduction

Today web applications are most commonly used for any business growth. Different types of web based applications are in use (like Data warehouse (DW), Business Intelligence (BI), etc.) with various types of database architectures (like Distributed Database (DDBMS), FDBMS etc.).

As per netcraft survey, the attacks have increased in numbers drastically in past few years. As per CERT approx. 59% of cyber security incidents are related to web applications [3]. As per OWASP the top 5 attacks out of 10 are related to information theft and database security [2].

Database is an integral part of any information system and they often hold sensitive data. As a result databases are often target in attacks. Major three reasons why Web Database applications are used popularly by attacker in SQLI are: i) accepts user input from user ii) concatenates input with hardcoded SQL and iii) concatenates query output with HTML code [6]. SQL Injection most commonly occurs where attacker modify SQL statements [1][2][3][5][6][7]. Major focus of SQLI is data manipulation and data theft, as SQLI works at application level and so it is handled quite easily.

Researchers have proposed various solutions for SQLI. They fall into two categories: 1) Defensive coding (coding is developed to protect data from SQLI attacks) and 2) Hardening (Filters/Firewalls).

In this paper, we present a simple, flexible, dynamic and secure network filter mechanism for preventing database from SQLI. The model is developed using JAVA and can work on multiple databases.

J. Lloret Mauri et al. (Eds.): SSCC 2014, CCIS 467, pp. 400–406, 2014.
© Springer-Verlag Berlin Heidelberg 2014

This paper is organized as follows: In section 2, we define SQL and Filter solutions of SQL attacks. In Section 3, we discuss proposed filter, In section 4, we discuss experiment of proposed filter. Conclusion and future work is provided in section 5 & 6 respectively.

2   Literature Survey

2.1   Related Work

One of the major vulnerabilities to data is SQL Injection (SQLI), SQLI is a code injection techniques that exploits database layer of an application and most popular among attackers[2]. An attacker uses SQLI for gaining database access, manipulate (add/modify/delete) data or steal information. In SQL injection attacker craft or modify or supplement SQL statements to gain access of database and retrieve data.

Several solutions exist to detect and prevent SQLI. These solutions can be categorized into two categories: defensive coding and hardening (Filters).

Existing solutions proposed by various researchers under defensive coding are implemented at coding level. These solutions are difficult to implement, requires developing efforts and developing skill and is not much flexible.

We summarize existing solutions [11],[12],[13],[14],[18] found under hardening category as below:

Table 1. SQLI Filter Solutions for hardening category

Solutions	Description	Observation
Apache Scalp [24]	**Type:** Log Analyzer **Implemented** : Application Level Apache generate log for any data sent request HTTP/GET. Scalp analyze these log files.	Apache does not log the data sent through HTTP/POST. So, attacks sent through the post variable are not detected by Scalp.
Snort [23]	**Type:** Open Source IDS/IPS **Implemented** : Network Level Contains the signatures of attacks in the form of rules, and based on these rules it detects the web application attacks.	Support only one database
GreenSQL [22]	**Type:** Open Source Security **Implemented** : Database Level It intercepts the communication between the application and database.	Not support all databases e.g. Oracle and operating systems e.g. Linux
ModSecurity [21]	**Type:** Firewall **Implemented** : Application Level provides protection from a range of attacks against web applications and allows for HTTP traffic monitoring and real-time analysis with little or no changes to existing infrastructure.	Difficult and require different setup for different application e.g. PHP

2.2   Problem Statement

Existing solutions [7][12][13] rely on complex static analysis in order to find potential vulnerabilities in the code. Some techniques are also based on dynamic negative tainting that focuses on un-trusted data.

Problems with existing solutions are [6],[7],[9],[12],[13] as follows:

- Conservative static analysis can generate high rates of false positives
- Can have scalability issues when applied to large complex applications Involve extensive human efforts
- Require deployment of extensive infrastructure
- Involve complex configurations

As a summary it is seen that all existing solutions have a static methodology with rigidness in user interface.

2.3   Research Question

Research Question	Objective	Variables studied	Resources
Which concepts are to be implemented to prevent SQLI?	Dynamically prevent SQLI without performance loss	SQLI, Application and Database Security, Network Packets	Data Base, Users

3   Proposed Solution

The architecture and profile of solution is as below:

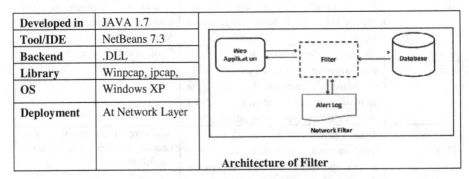

Developed in	JAVA 1.7
Tool/IDE	NetBeans 7.3
Backend	.DLL
Library	Winpcap, jpcap,
OS	Windows XP
Deployment	At Network Layer

Architecture of Filter

Fig. 1. Architecture and Tools used for Filter

We propose a highly dynamic and flexible automated approach to detect and prevent SQLI. Proposed solution is developed using open source technologies and will be deployed at network level. It will work for database as well as for any other network application.

Steps implemented in the experimental tool are as follows:

- **Configure Profile and Setting**
  The tool provides mechanism for maintaining information for the users who desire to capture the packets and check the possibilities of SQLI attacks in those packets. Each and every user can set his own preferences and information like the name, user name, etc
- **Configure ports**
  Tool also has a mechanism to list down the ports which are desired to be looked upon for packet capturing and filtering.
- **Configure filters**
  The tool also has a facility to set the filter preferences according to which the packets will be scanned traveling to and fro via the configured ports. Here we also specify all the possibilities of different vulnerable SQL strings
- **Monitor: Activate Monitoring**
  Once the preferences are set for the filters and ports, the monitoring can be activated
- **Log the captured information**
  The active monitors capture the traffic data and log them into appropriate logs as per the preferences of filters and ports

The key feature of this tool is that we can dynamically enable/disable the filters, as and when required.

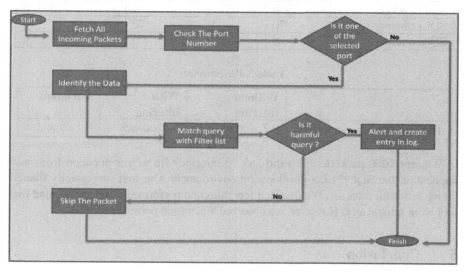

Fig. 2. How Proposed Solution will work?

Whenever any packet send matches with configured filter (i.e. port and data), toll will create log and skip packet execution.

How Proposed Solution is different from Existing Solutions?
For following reasons proposed filtering solution is different from existing ones.

- One can set / add / modify rules dynamically
- It can work for more than one data bases
- It filters data sent to database from any sources

4   Experiment: Testing of Proposed Solution

We wish to test proof of concept in this paper. For that we have tested proposed solution on web application hosted from local host with multiple instances of oracle database.

For testing this tool we used a small sized web application. We tested tool with different filtering rules (known SQLI attack rules and unknown rules) on different ports(oracle database instances). We monitored the traffic at the desired ports. The summarized result is as below:

Table 2. Result Summary

	Total Packets	With matching vulnerabilities	Logged by tool
Total Packets	1000	70	70
Valid Packets	930	0	0
SQLI filtered	70	70	70
SQLI omitted	0	0	0

Table 3. Performance

	Without filtering	With filtering	Variation
Time for execution per filter	0.2 seconds	0.3 seconds	0.1 seconds

We sent 1000 packets (930 valid and 70 injected) via web application from web application and SQL*PLUS development environment. Our tool successfully filtered 70 packets with rules set. We disabled few rules and performed testing and found that tool work satisfactory. However, we observed a marginal performance loss.

5   Conclusion

SQLI vulnerabilities are one of the major and commonly used attack methodologies in web domain. In this paper we proposed an architecture with supported experimented model to monitor and prevent the web based application from different SQLI attacks.

Our tool is based on monitoring and filtering of SQL queries based on their semantics and is completely dynamic in nature. This enriches this tool to work with a wide flavor of queries and filtering preferences.

The major highlight of this tool comes from its area of execution. As this tool works on the network layer, it does not imply any over head to the database for which it is capturing, monitoring and logging the information.

Key Benefits
1. It is a tool developed using open source technology
2. Always open ended to new additions with negligible modifications
3. Platform independent and hence works every where
4. Dynamic as per user preferences
5. Endless filter configurations and logging which helps in reducing human efforts
6. It does not require any specialized infrastructure for implementations

6   Future Work

In this paper, our intension is to test proof of concept. We are working on comparing proposed tool results with existing solutions. We are also planning to test tool on live web applications.

References

1. OWASP   Top   Ten   projects,   `https://www.owasp.org/index.php/Category:OWASP_Top_Ten_Project` (accessed May 31, 2014)
2. Godbole, N., Belapure, S.: Cyber Security – understanding Cyber Crimers, Computer Forensics and Legal Perspectives, pp. 495–499, 165–170. Wiley, India (2011)
3. The 2013 Data Breach Investigations Report: `http://www.verizonenterprise.com/DBIR/2013/, Verizon`
4. Lesov, P.: How the database security controls adapted to threats over the last 30 years. University of Minnesota, CS 8701 (Fall 2008)
5. Internet User World Statistics: http://www.internetworldstats.com/stats.htm (visited September 5, 2013)
6. Tajpour, A., Masrom, M., Heydari, M.Z., Ibrahim, S.: SQL injection detection and prevention tools assessment. In: Proc. of ICCSIT 2010, July 9-11, vol. 9, pp. 518–522 (2010)
7. Halfond, W.G., Viegas, J., Orso, A.: A Classification of SQLInjection Attacks and Countermeasures. In: Proc. of the Intl. Symposium on Secure Software Engineering (March 2006)
8. Martin, M., Livshits, B., Lam, M.S.: Finding Application Errors and Security Flaws Using PQL: A Program Query Language. In: Proceedings of the 20th Annual ACM SIGPLAN Conference on Object Oriented Programming Systems Languages and Applications (OOPSLA 2005), pp. 365–383 (2005)

9. Tajpour, A., Ibrahim, S., Sharifi, M.: Web Application Security by SQL Injection DetectionTools. IJCSI International Journal of Computer Science Issues 9(2(3)) (March 2012)
10. Halfond, W.G., Orso, A.: AMNESIA: Analysis and Monitoring for NEutralizing SQL-Injection Attacks. In: Proceedings of the IEEE and ACM International Conference on Automated Software Engineering (ASE 2005), Long Beach, CA, USA (November 2005)
11. Abdoulaye, D., Pathan, A.-S.K.: A Survey on SQL Injection: Vulnerabilities, attacks AND Prevention Techniques. In: IEEE 15th International Symposiam on Consumer Electronics (2011)
12. Tajpour, A., Massrum, M., Heydari, M.Z.: Comparison of SQL Injection Detection and Prevention Techniques. In: 2nd International Conference on Education Technology and Computer, ICETC (2012)
13. Sunitha, K.V.N., Sridevi, M.: Automated Detection System for SQL Injection Attack. IJCSS 4(4)
14. Sravanthi, A., Jayasree Devi, K., Sudha Reddy, K., Indira, A., Satish Kumar, V.: Detecting sql injections from web applications. [IJESAT] International Journal of Engineering Science & Advanced Technology 2(3), 664–671
15. Johri, R., Sharma, P.: A Survey on Web Application Vulnerabilities (SQLIA and XSS) Exploitation and Security Engine for SQL Injection. IEEE (2012)
16. Alneyadi, S., Sithirasenan, E., Muthukkumarasamy, V.: Word N-Gram Based Classification for Data Leakage Prevention. In: 2013 12th IEEE International Conference on Trust, Security and Privacy in Computing and Communications (TrustCom), pp. 578–585 (2013)
17. Singh, N., Purwar, R.K.: SQL Injections – A Hazard to Web Applications. IJARCSSE 2(6) (June 2012) ISSN: 2277 128X
18. Shabtai, A., et al.: A Survey of Data Leakage Detection and Prevention Solutions. Springer Briefrs in Computer Science (2012), doi: 10.1007/978-1-4614-2053-8_1
19. http://www.cert.org
20. http://www.netcraft.com
21. http://www.modsecurity.org
22. http://www.greensql.com
23. http://www.snort.org
24. https://code.google.com/p/apache-scalp/

Zero Distortion Technique: An Approach to Image Steganography Using Strength of Indexed Based Chaotic Sequence

Shivani Sharma[1], Virendra Kumar Yadav[1], and Saumya Batham[2]

[1] Computer Science Dept.,
[2] MCA Dept., ABES-EC, Ghaziabad,
Uttar Pradesh, India
{shivanisharma2804,virendrashines,saumyabatham003}@gmail.com

Abstract. Steganography is an art of hiding information. There are several existing approaches, of which LSB is the popular known technique. While performing image steganography, there are certain limitations, in terms of time, robustness, distortion, quantity of data to hide etc. A common major limitation involved in these approaches is: altering the pixel value of the image which leads to distortion in the cover image. It can be easily detected by histogram and PSNR value. Zero Distortion Technique (ZDT) is proposed to overcome the limitation, as no changes are reflected in the histogram and PSNR value of the cover and the stego image. Experimental results on certain images shows that the proposed algorithm gives refine results. The proposed technique is robust, fast and helpful in providing security to our confidential data.

Keywords: Steganography, Zero Distortion Technique (ZDT), steganalysis, LSB technique, cryptography, chaotic sequence, logistic maps.

1 Introduction

In today's era of internet it is difficult to provide privacy while sending any confidential information. There are many existing techniques which helps individuals in providing security to their data but only up to some extent. In the era of digital world, we have to think twice while sending our data to the other end, as there are many third parties in between, who are trying to retrieve data by unauthorized means. On the other hand, these techniques have their own limitations. Some of them are: quantity of data, robustness, distortion, time constraint and many more. One of the famous techniques known is LSB technique but it has its own limitations. It is bounded by the quantity of data we can send. In this technique we focus on the last bit only for hiding our data. Data hiding can be broadly classified into three categories i.e. steganography, watermarking and cryptography [1]. Cryptography is basically used to encrypt data so that it can't be understood by the intruder while steganography and watermarking is done to hide data. Watermarking make data authenticated by making a special mark to show owner's identity. It is mainly used for copyright purpose [2].

J. Lloret Mauri et al. (Eds.): SSCC 2014, CCIS 467, pp. 407–416, 2014.

Steganography is derived from a Greek word meaning 'concealed writing'. It has been widely used in ancient times also viz. tattoo, wax coating etc [9]. It is used to provide confidentiality to our data. Steganography is an emerging field for information security which is booming because of its vast features and techniques [10]. One of the advantages of steganography is that it does not attract the attention of steganalyst. Steganalysis is a technique of detecting hidden message from the stego image and steganalyst is the person which performs steganalysis. When steganography is applied on the cover image, it becomes stego image (an image containing hidden data).The image in which we are hiding data is known as cover image. In this technique we can use any image i.e. color, grey, black and white as the cover image. We can hide data in any of the 3 mediums - image, audio and video. While applying steganography, we must assure that distortion in the original image will be less so that it can't be detected by the steganalysis attack. The technique we are using should also emphasize on achieving optimal amount of data to be hidden in the stego image.

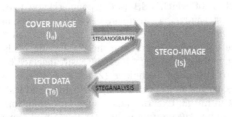

Fig. 1. Schematic diagram of Steganography

This work is organized as follows: In section 2, we have discussed a brief overview of related work done in the area of steganography. In section 3, we have discussed the proposed section 3.1, section3.1, section 3.2, section 3.3 which describes about Zero Distortion Technique, Encryption Technique, technique for embedding and extracting text from image using Zero Distortion Technique, Execution of algorithm for embedding text data into image and extracting text data from image using Zero Distortion Technique respectively and Section 4 presents figures and tables of proposed work. In last we have presented the experimental results.

2   Related Work

2.1   LSB Technique

Alaa A. Jabbar Altaay [9] in this paper author has categorized steganography techniques into two major types like Fragile Steganography, Robust Steganography. Fragile method means insertion of information in a medium in such a way that modification in the host file will destroy the whole embedded information. In contrast bits manipulation of robust methods will not easily be removed from host file.

There are several techniques used in steganography one most the most simple and widely used technique known is LSB [3]. In LSB (Least Significant Bit) as the name suggests we make changes in the least significant bit only. The LSB is chosen for steganography because there will be a slight change in the cover image as only the last significant bit is replaced by the data bit. It has been widely used because of its simplicity.LSB technique has some limitations also, as the resultant image become distorted [4]. The distortion in the cover image is visible to human eye and can also be seen with the help of histogram and PSNR value, we can hide a very little amount of data as we are making changes in the LSB only [5].LSB is mostly associated with the format JPEG, and steganalyst can extract our message very easily i.e. vulnerable to attacks.

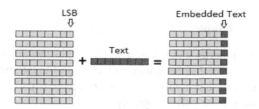

Fig. 2. Implementation of LSB Technique

3   Proposed Work

3.1   Zero Distortion Technique

In this paper we suggest a technique which leads to zero distortion. In other words we can say that we are extracting bits from the cover image in order to generate the text which we want to hide. We are storing the location bits which are matched with the data bit of the text which we want to hide. These location bits are in matrix form consists of binary bits i.e. 0 and 1, we than convert these binary bits into decimal format by which we get the ASCII value of the characters. Converting these ASCII value to characters we get our text data. There is no need to draw histogram and to calculate the PSNR value as we are not changing a single bit of the cover image. PSNR value is used to calculate the ratio between the signal (i.e. original image) and the noise involve during the compression of image. But as we are not compressing the image so we don't have to calculate it. Histogram is the representation of distribution of data on graph. Through histogram we can easily detect the changes done in the cover image. As this technique involves zero distortion it will be highly efficient while passing confidential data to the other end. Another feature of this technique is that we can hide a large amount of data, as we don't restrict ourselves to a particular row or column. To provide more security, encryption of the matrix of the location has been performed, which will randomize the value of matrix, so that it cannot be detected by the steganalysis. The stego image, chaotic sequence and the value of X_0 and μ will be passed to the receiver end from which text data will be extracted.

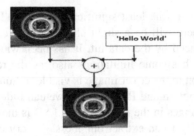

Fig. 3. Embedding of text into image

3.2 Encryption Technique

Chaos is a state of irregularity and disorder which makes the situation more complex to handle .Chaotic sequence has been used in the field of cryptography for providing randomness to the data so that it will become more secure [6]. Chaotic sequences and the word random can be used interchangeably.

Properties of chaotic sequence which makes it more powerful are:

- Unpredictability
- In decomposability
- Element of regularity

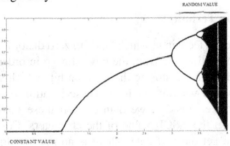

Fig. 4. Bifurcation Diagram for logistic map

The system shows different behavior for different range of μ. Some of them are shown below:

- For $0 < \mu < 1$ the output of the system is zero irrespective of the initial condition.
- For $1 < \mu < 3$ the system reaches a steady state.
- For $3 < \mu < 1+\sqrt{6}$ (approximately $\mu = 3.45$) the system oscillates between two values.

- For $\mu > 1+\sqrt{6}$ the system oscillates between infinite values and shows chaotic behavior.
- Beyond $\mu = 4$, the values eventually leave the interval [0,1] and diverge for almost all initial values.

Thus logistic map acts as an excellent chaotic system [8]. A chaotic system exhibits a great sensitivity to initial conditions. The logistic map shows this chaotic behavior for values of μ between 3.57 and 4. Chaotic sequence is so random that changing a single bit varies the sequence up to a large extent. The value generated by the chaotic sequence varies in the time interval of [0, 1].

$$\text{Chaotic sequence} = \begin{cases} 0 \\ 1 \end{cases}$$

Calculation of the values of the sequence will be carried out by using the following equation.

$$X_{n+1}=\mu * X_n * (1-X_n) \tag{1}$$

Here the value of μ is constant. Initially we fix the value of X_0 in the range of [0, 1].

$$X_0 = \begin{cases} 0 \\ 1 \end{cases}$$

We had randomized the matrix of locations by using chaotic sequence [7].

3.3   Techniques for Embedding and Extracting Text from Image Using Zero-Distortion Technique

With contrast to the earlier technique of LSB, we suggested this technique so that no distortion will be there in the image as it happens in the LSB technique.

3.3.1 Proposed Algorithm for Embedding Text into Image

This technique will embed the input text input image without changing any pixel value of the image.

INPUT: A cover image (grey) (I_0), an input text (T_0).
OUTPUT: Chaotic sequence (C_0s) and stego-image (I_s).
1) Read the cover image (I_0) and the input text (T_0).
2) Convert the cover image (I_0) into binary format and text data (T_0) to ASCII format and then into binary format.
3) Convert the matrix of text data (T_0) into a column vector.
4) For all i=1 to 8 repeat steps 4 to 8
5) Match the bits of text data (i.e. column vector) with the bits of the cover image (I_0).

6) If matched then save the location value in a matrix of n rows and 8 columns is the length of the text.
7) Increase count variable and location by 1.
8) Else increase the location.
    // resulting is the matrix of location (L_{0S}). Perform encryption on L_{0S} by using chaotic sequence approach [7].
    Calculate the dimension of matrix of location (L_{0S}) m x n, where m is the rows and n is the column.
9) Set X_0 value in the range of 0-1, and value of μ in the range of 3.5–4
10) For i=1 to m x n
11) Apply the equation (1) for generating chaotic sequence
12) Sort the values generated by the above formula and extract the index of the sequence.
13) Reshape the indexes into m x n matrix same as the dimension of matrix of location (L_{0S}).
    //This is the chaotic sequence i.e. C_{0S} which will be passed to the decryption side.
14) If count equals length of the text then text has been successfully embedded into image.
15) Else text has not been successfully embedded into image.
16) Display the stego-image (I_S).

3.3.2 Proposed Algorithm for Extracting Text from Image

This algorithm will extract the hidden text (T_0) from the stego image (Is).

INPUT: Chaotic sequence $(C_0 s)$, value of X_0 and μ , stego image (Is).
OUTPUT: Embedded input text (T_0)
1) Extract the matrix of location (L_{0S}) from the chaotic sequence by using the same formula.
    //Decryption has been performed
2) Convert the stego image (I_s) pixels into binary format.
3) For i=1 to length of the image Repeat step from 3 to 5.
4) Match the image location and value of the matrix of locations of stego image $(L_0 s)$.
5) If matched then save the value at that location of the image in an array.
6) Else the location of the image is increased.
7) Convert the array into decimal format i.e. the ASCII value of the embedded text.
8) Convert the ASCII value into characters and transpose it.
9) Embedded text will be displayed i.e. T_0.

4   Figures and Tables

4.1   Figures Shows the Schematic Diagram of the Zero Distortion Technique

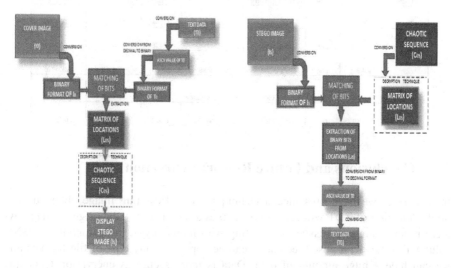

Fig. 4(a). Schematic diagrams (embedding text)   **Fig. 4(b).** Schematic diagrams (extracting text)

4.2   Comparision of LSB and ZERO – Distortion Technique

Comparison is based on the text length that we can hide in the image and time elapsed in hiding the text data. It is performed on various types of formats like jpg, png, tif etc.

Table 1. LSB technique

IMAGE	ORIGINAL-SIZE	FORMAT	ROWS X COLUMNS	TEXT LENGTH	STEGOIMAGE SIZE	TIME(seconds)
Tire	41.7 KB	tif	205X232	5800	41.9 KB	9.632069
cameraman	52.6 KB	jpg	256X256	8192	52.8 KB	17.649408
rice	59.4 KB	png	256X256	8192	59.5 KB	18.743116
coins	51.5 KB	jpg	246X300	9000	52.5	20.074579
moon	114 KB	tiff	537X358	23986	117 KB	146.803198

Table 2. ZDT technique

Image	Original-Size	Format	ROWS X COLUMNS	Image dimension	Text Length	StegoImage Size	Time(seconds)
Tire	41.7 KB	tif	205X232	<47560x8>	11856	41.7 KB	1.008306
cameraman	52.6 KB	jpg	256X256	<65536x8>	20338	52.6 KB	2.684668
rice	59.4 KB	png	256X256	<65536x8>	22905	59.4 KB	3.064316
coins	51.5 KB	jpg	246X300	<73800x8 uint8>	19552	51.5 KB	4.878285
moon	114 KB	tiff	537X358	<192246x8 uint8>	41922	114 KB	146.803198

5   Conclusions and Future Research Direction

In this paper we have presented a technique ZDT. Resulting image obtained after implementation of ZDT will reflect no changes as compared to the original image. As there is no changes, no issue of detecting with human eyes, by histogram or PSNR value will reflect. Proposed technique can be applied to any type of file formats and we can hide a huge amount of data. Data is more secure as encryption technique chaotic sequence has been used. ZDT algorithm can be considered as efficient algorithm in terms of time, capacity in comparison to LSB technique.

Future scope in this direction includes developing efficient algorithms in terms of time, space and of course in terms capacity of hiding and their strength to conceal the data within it.

References

1. Stalling, W.: Cryptography and network security: Principles and Practices, 4th edn. Prentice (2006), ISBN – 978-81-775-8774-6
2. Das, S., Bandyopadhyay, P., Paul, S.: A New Introduction towards Invisible Image Watermarking on Color Images. In: IEEE International Advance Computing Conference (IACC 2009) (2009)
3. Neeta, D., Snehal, K., Jacob, D.: Implementation of LSB Steganography and its evaluation for various bits
4. Juneja, M., Sandu, P.S.: Designing of Robust Image Steganography Technique Based on LSB Insertion and Encryption. In: International Conference on Advances in Recent Technologies in Communication and Computing (2009)
5. Alam, S., Zakariya, S.M., Rafiq, M.Q.: Analysis of modified LSB Approaches of Hiding Information in Digital Images. In: 5th International Conference on Computational Intelligence and Communication Networks 2013 (2013)

6. Acharya, A.K.: Image Encryption Using A Chaos Base Encryption Algorithm. In: International Conference on Commmunication, Computing and Security (ICCCS 2011) (2011), http://dl.acm.org/citation.cfm?id=1948060
7. Batham, S., Acharya, A.K., Yadav, V.K., Paul, R.: A New Video Encryption Algorithm Based on Index Based Chaotic Sequence. In: Confluence 2013 (2013)
8. Soni, A., Acharya, A.K.: A Novel Image Encryption Approach Using an Index Based Chaos and DNA Encoding and its Performance Analysis. IJCA (0975-8887) 47(23) (June 2012)
9. Altaay, A.A.J., Sahib, S.B., Zamani, M.: An Introduction to Image Steganography Techniques. In: International Conference on Advanced Computer Science Applications and Technologies 2012 (2012)
10. Gupta, S., Goyal, A., Bhushan, B.: Information Hiding Using Least Significant Bit Steganography and Crptography. I. J. MECS 2012 (2012)
11. Paul, R., Acharya, A., Yadav, V.K., Batham, S.: Hiding Large Amount of Data using a New Approach of Video Steganography. In: CONFLUENCE 2013, IET digital library (2013)

Experimental Results

Table 3. Coins .jpg

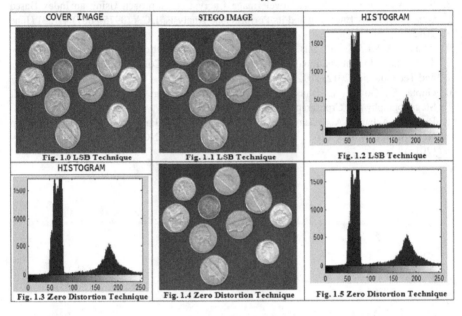

COVER IMAGE	STEGO IMAGE	HISTOGRAM
Fig. 1.0 LSB Technique	Fig. 1.1 LSB Technique	Fig. 1.2 LSB Technique
HISTOGRAM		
Fig. 1.3 Zero Distortion Technique	Fig. 1.4 Zero Distortion Technique	Fig. 1.5 Zero Distortion Technique

Table 4. Rice.png

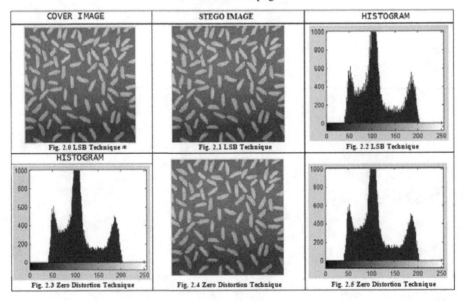

COVER IMAGE	STEGO IMAGE	HISTOGRAM
Fig. 2.0 LSB Technique	Fig. 2.1 LSB Technique	Fig. 2.2 LSB Technique
HISTOGRAM		
Fig. 2.3 Zero Distortion Technique	Fig. 2.4 Zero Distortion Technique	Fig. 2.5 Zero Distortion Technique

Piracy Control Using Secure Disks

Jitendra Lulla[1] and Varsha Sharma[2]

[1] Chelsio Communications, Bangalore, India
[2] Wipro Technologies, Bangalore, India
jlulla@chelsio.com, varsha.sharma@wipro.com

Abstract. A lot of money and efforts have been invested in controlling unauthorized sharing of copyrighted contents but still the problem persists. This paper introduces a method to control and limit the disk duplication. Confidentiality and authenticity measures have been employed in this method to ensure that the disk if copied will result in an unusable and unauthentic copy. It also ensures that any attempt to tamper the contents on the disk while copying will also result in an unusable copy of the disk. The method however requires 2 constraints to be fulfilled: first, the disk will be playable on special physical drives and the disk will be made available to the authorized end user in a restricted manner. This paper also mentions that the approach being described is a generic one and different disk and disk player vendors can surely have compatibility.

Keywords: Piracy Protection, Digital Rights Management, Secure Disks, Secure Disk Players.

1 Introduction

It is well known that copyright piracy is a serious crime which not only causes economic losses to all those who had invested their money in bringing out copyrighted materials in various forms for use by end-users but also adversely affects the creative potential of the society by denying the creators their legitimate dues. A lot of measures have been adopted to control the same. Though there has been a significant expenditure on its research and development the problem still exists and seeks stricter and tighter ways to achieve the same. The solution to the problem should not prevent the legitimate end users from accessing those materials without ease. This paper presents a solution to this problem.

2 Related Work

SONY DADC developed a disk copy protection method called SecuROM. It was for game installation control on PCs. [16, 17]. It limits the number of PCs activated at the same time with the same key. However the problem with SecuROM was unclean un-installation. Software Tempering was another method to change the behavior of the software upon detection of the piracy. [10] However it was annoying for legitimate

J. Lloret Mauri et al. (Eds.): SSCC 2014, CCIS 467, pp. 417–430, 2014.

users. Content Scrambling System was another DRM method which used an encryption algorithm to encrypt the DVDs. But this method was broken soon and an application called DeCSS was able to play the DVDs. [11, 12, 13] Blu Ray disks were being protected by AACS (Advanced Access Content System) but that also failed as the hackers soon published keys on the internet that enabled unrestricted access to AACS protected HD blu ray contents. [14, 15]

3   Solution

The solution is based on Manufacture On Demand method of disk business. The disk is prepared when a request for the same is made. The end user places a request. The content owner receives the request and prepares a secure disk which requires to be played in a given time duration to become usable for ever. This secure disk also ensures that its unauthorized copies will not play in the disk players. This disk is a crypto processed multisession disk which requires that the disk player when successfully plays the disk, writes a special datum (HwId, described later) on it. This disk accompanies a memory card and a PIN. The memory card contains encrypted and scattered security material to reverse crypto transform the original content on the disk. The requester requires to have a special disk player which has a keypad, a card reader and internet connectivity. Only when the disk is played for the first time, the requester or the end user is required to enter the PIN. The disk can be played any number of times on the same player if it has played successfully once. The copies cannot be played on any other player.

The above mentioned process mainly involves the following two objects: a: the end user, b: the content owner .

Figure 1 below depicts the process at content owner. The content owner, having received an order or request from the end user, prepares three deliverables for the end user:

- A secure disk
- A memory card
- A PIN

These three articles are dispatched to the end user. The end user is required to have a special disk player which also has a card reader and a numeric keypad in it.

3.1   Secure Disk

The Secure disk contains a. the crypto transformed original copy righted material, b. a digitally signed executable called "Reverse Processing Binary" and c. a hash computed on a and b above on it. This hash ensures the integrity of the disk contents and the digital signature on the "Reverse Processing Binary" ensures the authenticity of the executable. This leaves no room for any virus or tempered contents on the disk. This disk is a multisession disk and it can be "finalized" (i.e. its session can be closed) by the requester's disk player. When the requester successfully plays this disk on his disk player for the first time, a unique identification number of the disk player will get written on the disk which will be checked every time the disk is played next.

The ciphering key (will be referred to as "master cipher key" from now on in this document) used for encryption and decryption of the original copyrighted material (i.e. "a" on the disk) themselves are encrypted and stored on the crypto processed memory card being shipped with the disk.

3.2   Memory Card

The crypto processed memory card contains encrypted master cipher key at random locations.

3.3   PIN

The PIN (or Key) serves three main purposes, 1. It authenticates the user, 2. It fetches the master cipher key from the memory card, 3. It decrypts the master cipher key.

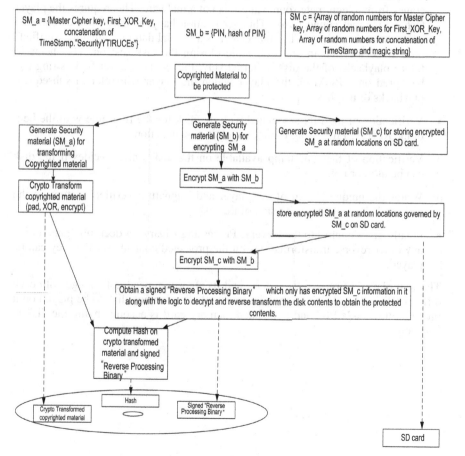

Fig. 1. Actions at Content Provider

The "Reverse Processing Binary" above is required for doing crypto operations required for PIN verification, fetching the ciphered master cipher key from the memory card and deciphering it, deciphering the protected copyrighted contents and doing any other required transformations on the protected copyrighted material so that it may be finally played on the player. The SM_a, SM_b and SM_c are crypto material generated at the content owner's site and are detailed in next section.

Figure 1 below shows how the disk and the memory card are prepared.

The process at the content requester's site requires a special disk player which has a keypad and a memory card reader also. Figure 2 below depicts a high level view of the actions at the player. The disk player's firmware and the "Reverse Processing Binary" together facilitate the playback of the protected contents.

The disk player's firmware is required for the following tasks:

- Verification of the hash available on the disk to ensure that the disk contents have not been modified.

- Verification of the sign of the Reverse Processing Binary to ensure that it comes from a legitimate source and it is not a malware. This requires the player to have internet connectivity. This verification happens only for the first time when the disk is played. The player writes a special datum "signature_verified" on a fixed location in the disk while closing the disk session. This helps in future playbacks of the disk. Alternatively, the "signature_verified" string can be stored on a ROM on the player which the player will refer in subsequent playbacks of the disk.

- Verification of the PIN associated with the disk for the first time with the help of the Reverse Processing Binary which is now in action.

- Verification of the timestamp available on the disk which decides if the disk can be used or not.

- Writes the unique Hw Id of the player and "signature_verified" datum on the disk and closes the write session of the disk.

- Finally gives control to the Reverse Processing Binary for decrypting and doing any other reverse transformations on the protected contents so that they can be played.

The disk player's firmware is generic and its algorithm need not change with each different disk. The algorithm remains constant allowing any disk to be played on it provided the disk's PIN and associated memory card is accompanying the disk in question.

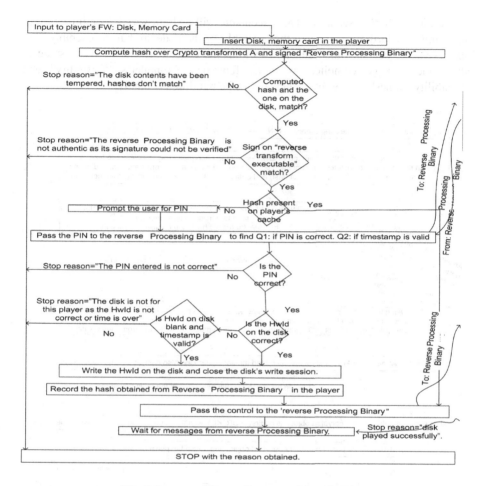

Fig. 2. Process at Content Requester (Player's FW)

Figure 3 below depicts the actions the Reverse Processing Binary performs. The Reverse Processing Binary is a custom program written and built for specifically the copyrighted contents available on the same disk. It cannot be used for any other disk's transformed contents even if the original contents are indeed same. This binary has been prepared considering the security aspects in mind to prevent it from disassembly and reverse engineering. This binary does not require internet connectivity. This binary also does not contain the master cipher key, the time stamp or any other security material which is used to decrypt and reverse-transform the copyrighted contents. All such security material is stored ciphered and scattered on the memory card. The Reverse Processing Binary will not contain the section header in it as it is not used for execution of it and its removal helps in preventing information leakage of the binary executable. Its symbols maybe stripped. The binary will be self-contained and will not need any shared objects (.so or DLL) to run. This will prevent symbol relocation at run time. The Reverse Processing Binary can also employ address obfuscation to further secure it. This executable will be built with O3 optimization or any similar to further complicate the assembly of the code so that disassembly may not reveal the details. Small functions within the executable can be made static to allow them to be compiled as inline functions. Compiler's "fvisibility" and "fvisibility-inlines" can be set to "hidden" while building the binary.

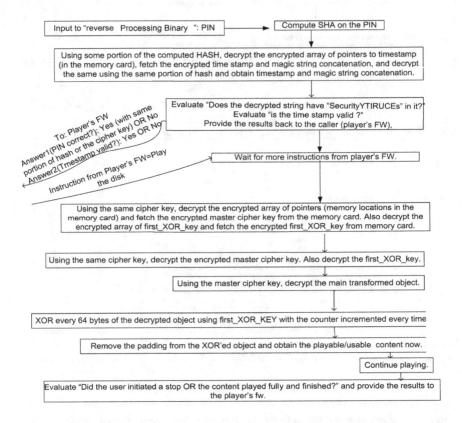

Fig. 3. Process at Content Requester (Reverse Processing Binary)

The main tasks performed by the Reverse Processing Binary are the following:

- Verification of the PIN.
- Checking the timestamp and the time-validity of the disk
- Reading and decrypting the scattered ciphered security material from the memory card
- Using the security material to finally decrypt and reverse process the original protected contents.

The algorithm for the Reverse Processing Binary is supposed to remain same to ensure compatibility with any hardware vendor's disk player. Every original disk (of any copyrighted material from any vendor) must contain the Reverse Processing Binary prepared in the same standard way so as to ensure that the disk is usable with any hardware disk player.

4   Detailed Solution

4.1   List of Objects Used in Disk Preparation

The disk preparation requires some crypto processing on the material to be protected. Figure 4 below lists the names given to various objects involved in the process of preparing the disk and memory card contents.

A: Original Copyrighted File
B: Padded Original Copyrighted File
C: Timestamp (Its concatenation with K becomes a part of Security material SM_a)
D: Master Cipher Key (part of Security material SM_a)
E: XORed Padded Original Copyrighted File
F: Encrypted XORed Padded Original Copyrighted File
G: Signed "Reverse Processing Binary".
H: SHA of F and G.
I: PIN (part of Security material SM_b)
J1: SHA of PIN (part of Security material SM_b)
J2: 1st 32 Bytes of J1.
K: Magic String : SecurityYTIRUCEs (Its concatenation with C becomes a part of Security material SM_a)
L: Concatenation of C and K
M: Encrypted concatenated timestamp and magic string
N: Encrypted Master Cipher Key
O: Encrypted First XOR Key
P: Key Array of random numbers to work as pointers (in the sd card) to the 32 byte Encrypted master Cipher key (part of Security material SM_c)
Q: Timestamp Array of random numbers to work as pointers (in the sd card). Each pointer points to a byte of Encrypted concatenated timestamp and magic string. (part of Security material SM_c)
R: First_XOR_KEY Array of random numbers to work as pointers (in the sd card) to the Encrypted First_XOR_Key (part of Security material SM_c)
S: Memory Card
T: Encrypted Fisrt_XOR_Key array
U: Encrypted Time stamp array
V: Encrypted Master Cipher Key array

Fig. 4. Names of Objects involved in Disk Preparation

The copyrighted material to be protected may first be padded to align it to 64 byte boundary.

4.2   Objects for Managing Expiry of Unused Disk

The timestamp (C): a timestamp value chosen for a particular request. This timestamp governs the period during which the prepared disk has to successfully start playing at least once. Please note that it is not mandatory to play it in full during this time period. Every disk being prepared will have its own timestamp depending on when the disk is being prepared. If the timestamp dictates a value of 72 it means that the disk has to start playing once in first 72 hours since the disk was made ready. The timestamp can be set to any realistic value depending on when it is reaching the end user and a comfortable time period for the end user during which she is expected to use the disk.

This timestamp is not kept on the disk. So, its validity cannot be changed with unintended end user. It is first encrypted and then stored at random places on the memory card accompanying the disk.

4.3   Master Cipher Key and the XOR Keys

The Master Cipher Key (D): A 256 bits encryption key is chosen for encrypting the copyrighted contents. The encryption algorithm can be AES 256 or any other depending on the hardware of the player and the costs involved. Correspondingly the key size will change. Please note that this key is not stored on the disk so any hacker cannot easily get it. It is first encrypted and then stored at random places on the memory card accompanying the disk.

There is a running counter which starts with a value same as the timestamp. The copyrighted material to be protected is first XORed (before encryption) with a set of special words each of which is a concatenation of the timestamp, the master cipher key and the running counter. As the counter is not fixed but it is changing, the concatenated word will be different and every 64 bytes of the main copyrighted material will be XORed with a different word.

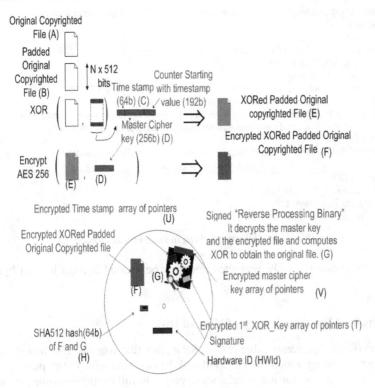

Fig. 5. Disk Contents Preparation (Part 1)

The first word to be used for XORing is called First_XOR_Key. The remaining words can be derived using First_XOR_Key as only the counter is changing in each word and the change is just a static constant increment in its value. This First_XOR_Key is not stored on the disk. It is first encrypted and then stored at random locations on the memory card. This XORed file is finally encrypted using the master cipher key.

4.4   Objects Managing Integrity Protection of the Disk

SHA2 on crypto transformed file (i.e. F) and Reverse Processing Binary (i.e. G):(H): It's a SHA 512 digest computed over F and G. This digest is stored on the disk in plaintext. The player's Firmware validates this message digest when the disk is inserted in the player to ensure the disk contents have not been modified.

Another object for ensuring the integrity of the disk contents is the Magic String (K) which is described later.

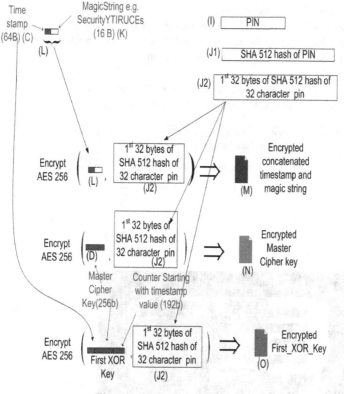

Fig. 6. Disk Contents Preparation (Part 2)

4.5   Objects Managing Confidentiality Protection of the Disk

PIN (I): It is a small key composed of numbers which is generated at the time of disk preparation. This key is shipped to the user along with the disk and memory card. The user is prompted to input only once for the first time when the disk is inserted. This PIN is not needed every time the disk is played. This PIN once verified by the player's firmware and the Reverse Processing Binary is stored in a more appropriate form in the player itself for future playbacks.

Interim Cipher Key (J2): It is a part of the SHA512 digest computed over the PIN. It is needed for decrypting and encrypting the intermediate objects. This key is not stored on the disk. It is also not stored on the memory card. It is computed when the disk is inserted for the first time. This key is stored on the player itself for subsequent use of the same disk.

Magic String (K): There exists a magic string "SecurityYTIRUCEs" which is concatenated with the timestamp. This concatenation is then ciphered using the Interim Cipher Key (J2). This encrypted concatenation is named M. When the disk is prepared, the M is kept in the Reverse Processing Binary. When the end user enters the PIN, this Interim Cipher Key is computed by the Reverse Processing Binary and the concatenated timestamp and the magic string is decrypted with the Interim Cipher Key.

Only if the decrypted concatenation is found to contain the magic string in it at the end user's site, the PIN is considered correct.

Array of Master Cipher Key byte Locations (P): It is an array of memory pointers. These pointers are locations in the memory card. Each memory pointer points to a byte of the encrypted master cipher key on the memory card.

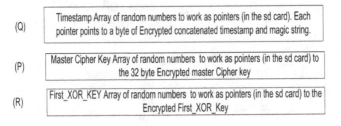

(Q)   Timestamp Array of random numbers to work as pointers (in the sd card). Each pointer points to a byte of Encrypted concatenated timestamp and magic string.

(P)   Master Cipher Key Array of random numbers to work as pointers (in the sd card) to the 32 byte Encrypted master Cipher key

(R)   First_XOR_KEY Array of random numbers to work as pointers (in the sd card) to the Encrypted First_XOR_Key

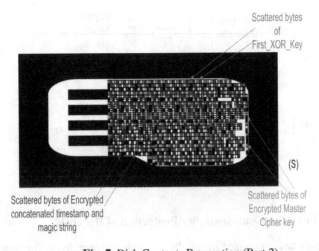

Scattered bytes of First_XOR_Key

(S)

Scattered bytes of Encrypted concatenated timestamp and magic string

Scattered bytes of Encrypted Master Cipher key

Fig. 7. Disk Contents Preparation (Part 2)

Array of Timestamp Byte Locations (Q): This is an array of memory pointers. These pointers are locations in the memory card. Each memory pointer points to a byte of the encrypted time stamp on the memory card.

Array of First_XOR_Key byte locations (R): This is an array of memory pointers. These pointers are locations in the memory card. Each memory pointer points to a byte of the encrypted First_XOR_Key on the memory card.

Each of the R, Q and P above is encrypted using Interim Cipher Key (J) to obtain T, U and V respectively. T, U and V are kept in the Reverse Processing Binary when the disk is prepared. When the disk is played at the end user's site, after successful verification of the PIN, the Interim Cipher Key is obtained by the player and the Reverse Processing Binary. After obtaining the Interim Cipher Key, the Reverse Processing Binary decrypts V, U and T to obtain P, Q and R. Using P, Q and R, the encrypted security material (M, N and O) is read from the memory card. This encrypted security material (M, N and O) is decrypted to obtain the master cipher key, timestamp and the Fisrt_XOR_Key.

The Reverse Processing Binary uses the decrypted security material to finally decrypt the original protected material and XOR's it with the XOR words derived from First_XOR_Key.

HwId: Each player must have a unique hardware ID. This ID is written on the disk when the disk starts to play successfully for the first time. For subsequent uses, this hardware ID on the disk ensures that the disk is played any number of times on the same player. The same disk cannot be played on any other player as the HwId would be different. This may appear as a usability issue but it can be relaxed by allowing a limited number of HwID's to be written on the disk. In that case, the disk will play on

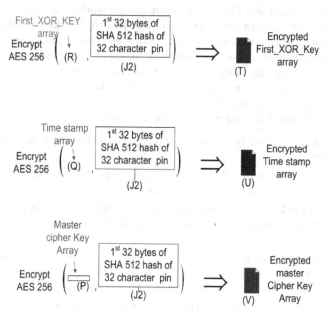

Fig. 8. Disk Contents Preparation (Part 4)

more than 1 players but all those players' HWID must be present on the disk. This can be done by making the disk's allowable wirte sessions to e.g. 3. This will allow a user to use the disk on 3 of his players.

The entire process of preparing the disk can be understood using figure 1, 5, 6, 7 and 8.

The entire reverse process at the user's site can be understood using Figure 2 and Figure 3.

5   Compatibility Among Different Disks and Disk Players

A successful solution should be generic enough and workable with different disk player hardware smoothly. The objective is to protect the contents and at the same time allow any disk to be played on any vendor's disk player. Here the main pieces of software are the firmware on the disk player and the Reverse Processing Binary on the disk. The algorithm for each of these software pieces has been mentioned in previous sections. The execution environment on the disk player should be kept same and a standard has to be followed by all the disk player vendors. Similarly the Reverse Processing Binary prepared for each copyrighted content should adhere to the same algorithm mentioned in previous sections.

6   Pros of The Approach

The piracy problem is tough and DRM is found not to be working as expected and there have been law suits against DRM enforcers e.g. Real Networks or Sony. The existing DRM solutions also have employed networking and crypto processing in the software and hardware for protection of copyrighted material. The solution presented in this paper proposes a new idea along with slightly detailed design.

There are certain usability issues with this approach but it is well known that security and usability cannot stay together:

The approach presented in this paper ensures the following:

- The disk contents cannot be modified. If any such attempt is made, the hash check will fail

- The disk contents are from authentic sources and no room for virus or malware exists as the binary executable on the disk is signed.

- The master cipher key or any ciphering material (which can directly be used to decrypt and reverse transform the protected contents) is not available on the disk.

- The executable on the disk is built with software security techniques mentioned in "high level view of the approach" section. These techniques genuinely attempt to make the disassembly and reverse engineering tough.

- The PINs associated with the disks ensure a controlled use of the disk.

- The idea of having a separate card reader on the player is novel. The fact that the disk cannot be played without the memory card ensures an extra hurdle to the piracy.

- The core security material is not on the disk but it is on the memory card. The security material is encrypted and scattered on the memory card. Extraction of this material from the memory card is impossible if the PIN is not known or if the disk is not available.

- The disk, the Pin and the memory card all three are needed for successful playing of the disk for the first time.

- The same disk cannot be played on any other player . This is ensured by the fact that the HwId of the player is written on the disk when the disk starts to play for the first time.

- There is a time restriction as well. The timestamp on the memory card ensures that the disk is played successfully by the legitimate users only. Once the disk is played successfully on a player, the HwId of the player is written on the disk making the disk usable only with the same player. If the disk is attempted to play after the elapsed given time period, only if the HwId is correct the disk will be played. Otherwise the disk will not play.

- If the disk clones/copies are made, they will not be usable as the HwID restricts the disks to be played on the same player.

- If the disk clones/copies are made, they will not be usable if they are attempted to play after the given time period.

- If the disk clones/copied are made, they will not be usable if they don't have the corresponding PIN "and" the memory card.

- After the decryption, a set of XOR keys is also needed each of these XOR keys will be different because of the counter. The counter may be chosen to increment differently depending on any further custom algorithm.

7   Cons of the Approach

As mentioned above, the security and usability cannot stay together, the usability issues with the approach are being acknowledged here:

- The player needs to be crypto capable. The crypto processes require powerful CPUs/ASICs.

- Addressal of reissuance of the disk/memory card and the PIN for new players if the end user buys a new player after he has played the disk on a different player.

- The disks cannot be made available off the shelf. But this is becoming a trend now and vendors have started the "Manufactured on Demand" kind of business models where a request is made first followed by the delivery of the disks.

- Addressal of genuine memory card/ PIN losses.

8   Conclusions

The unauthorized copy/cloning of the disks is not an easy problem to solve. It requires an approach which is a combination of hardware and software. This approach involves the hardware and software both. There are usability issues with the approach but when compared with the security we are getting, this approach appears viable.

References

1. News – Analog Free Media, http://www.analogfree.com/news/?paged=5
2. Litman, J.: Antibiotic Resistance. Cardozo Arts & Entertainment Law Journal 30(2) (2012)
3. Von Lohmann, F.: Unintended Consequences: Twelve Years under the DMCA. Electronic Frontier Foundation (2010)
4. Iyer, L., Arora, N.: Hollywood in India: Protecting Intellectual Property (A). Harvard Business School BGIE Unit case 711-017 (2011)
5. Hurkała, A., Hurkała, J.: Authentication System for Websites with Paid Content: An Overview of Security and Usability Issues. International Journal of Computer Science & Network Security 13(7) (2013)
6. LeVine, R.B., et al.: Systems and methods for preventing unauthorized use of digital content. U.S. Patent No. 8,261,359 (September 4, 2012)
7. Maes, M., et al.: Digital watermarking for DVD video copy protection. IEEE Signal Processing Magazine 17(5), 47–57 (2000)
8. Bell, A.E., Lotspiech, J.B., Traw, C.B.S.: Content guard system for copy protection of recordable media. U.S. Patent No. 6,832,319 (December 14, 2004)
9. Bharathan, V., et al.: Cloning protection scheme for a digital information playback device. U.S. Patent No. 6,158,005 (December 5, 2000)
10. Digital Rights Management, http://en.wikipedia.org/wiki/Digital_rights_management
11. Camp, L.J.: DRM: doesn't really mean digital copyright management. In: Proceedings of the 9th ACM Conference on Computer and Communications Security. ACM (2002)
12. Samuelson, P.: DRM {and, or, vs.} the law. Communications of the ACM 46(4), 41–45 (2003)
13. Camp, L.J.: First principles of copyright for DRM design. IEEE Internet Computing 7(3), 59–65 (2003)
14. Myska, M.: The True Story of DRM. Masaryk UJL & Tech. 3, 267 (2009)
15. Henry, K., Sui, J., Zhong, G.: An Overview of the Advanced Access Content System (AACS). Centre for Applied Cryptographic Research (CACR) (2007)
16. Fry, D.: Circumventing Access Controls Under the Digital Millennium Copyright Act: Analyzing the SecuROM Debate. Duke L. & Tech. Rev., 1 (2009)
17. Blanck, C.: The State of Digital Rights Management in Computer Games

Design of Security System of Portable Device: Securing XML Web Services with ECC

Gopinath V.[1] and Bhuvaneswaran R.S.[2]

[1] Sathyabama University, Department of Sciences and Humanities, Chennai, India
[2] Anna University, Department of Computer Science & Engineering, Chennai, India
vguru007@gmail.com

Abstract. In this paper, a design of a security system for portable drive is proposed using ECC to secure XML web service and associated application. An XML web service component is integrated with existing VPN gateway to provide security solution for both the XML web service and traditional network-based application. Both share the same digital ECC key, which is utilized by the XML Web Service security component. The high level design of the SSL VPN on a portable device helps in connecting the peer to peer network. It secures the data transmission over the entire network route from the client to the remote server, and effectively improves the data processing speed of the server. The design is experimented with customized java coding and its performance is analyzed and compared with existing scheme in which the RSA is used. The design is found to be more secure and faster based on the preliminary results

Keywords: SSL VPN; XML, Web Services security, Elliptic Curve Cryptography; Portable device.

1 Introduction

In this modern world secure communication is a significant need to perform high end data transfers. Employees of an organization who are away their office can connect to enterprise network with SSL (Secure Socket Layer) based remote access solution, through an internet connection. The security policies set by the enterprise administrator are applied accordingly to the incoming request. The connection is established seamlessly whenever a user tries to connect to his enterprise VPN with respect to his access privileges, management and security controls [1]. Multiple access modes like Clientless Mode and Thin Client Mode are provided with support system. Various web-based and Citrix applications are accessed using the multiple modes and software related to these multiple modes as well as preload of the client on the PC are not required to be downloaded as the small client is dynamically loaded[2].

The XML-based interoperable characteristics create a lot of challenges to enforce security for Web Services over the internet. To meet the requirements for Web Services security, many efforts have recently been made. Among them [2], [3] are noteworthy.

J. Lloret Mauri et al. (Eds.): SSCC 2014, CCIS 467, pp. 431–439, 2014.

Portable devices like USB thumb drive are vulnerable to security issues because of their mechanism as an attacker can easily acquire the private information in the thumb drive.

The proposed system provides Web service security [3]. Portable device level security has been provided; here the Portable device uses AES-256 – bit security key, which is flexible and cost-effective. It helps to keep everything, i.e. from documents to passwords, safer by encrypting the entire drive in which the data resides. Once the portable device is turned on, any file which is saved in that drive is encrypted automatically [5].ECC algorithm require only a small sized RSA and has fast processing speed. It occupies small storage space. The key size and system parameters of ECC are much smaller than those of RSA. 160-bit ECC and 1024-bit RSA have the same strength and so does 210-bit ECC and 2048-bit RSA. It means that ECC needs much smaller storage space and low bandwidth. It has higher flexibility, rich multi-group structure and selectivity for different curves can be obtained by changing the parameters [4].

Major aspects of this paper are,

- AES security key is established to avoid the mishandling or loss of data, when the Portable device is connected.
- Existing algorithm i.e. ANSI X9.62 [6] is being used for the VPN establishment and no new algorithm is used.
- When web services are established the same ECC digital key has been utilized.

The rest of this paper is organized as follows. Section 2 discusses about the related works. Section 3 is the proposed framework of secure portable VPN. Section 4 gives the details about the analysis and the experimental results. Section 5 concludes with future work.

2   Related Works

The growth of USB devices in recent years has created a major revolution in accessing, transferring and storing data. An approach for a secure solution of USB flash drives was proposed in [7]. When an USB flash drive reaches a wrongdoer, private information stored in them are vulnerable to exposure as they do not have a security mechanism. What happens when the data in an USB drive is stored with encryption? Persons other than the owner cannot open it without a key. With the rapid growth in technology, these thumb drives are also used in connecting with enterprise networks, taking slides for presentation etc.

In [2], web services and traditional network based applications utilize the same digital ECC key, SOAP message security, ECC algorithm and other supporting functions. This security scheme addresses authentication, authorization, confidentiality, integrity and non-repudiation issues. In [3], ECC encryption helps in increasing the speed of encryption and decryption and shortening the CPU execution cycle. The algorithm pointed in [6] depends on an analytical computation which is harder for intruders to attack than the current encryption with a minimal key size.

Aforementioned algorithms have some limitations. Web service security system is not available in the framework. Security is provided only when the connection is established and RSA algorithm has inbuilt SSL feature. Here the SSL uses RSA 128-bit security key. Algorithms involving public key tend to reuse the session frequently for transaction, which accounts for cost whereas encryption and message hashing amounts for the data transferred. Portable device level security is not offered, which means the security is not obtained when the device is lost or stolen.

In this paper limitation of the existing algorithm are addressed and proposing new security framework with ECCS.

3   Design of Security System of Portable Device with ECC

The proposed system is aimed at providing a high level design of the SSLVPN, which is applied on an USB based Application. It helps in connecting the peer to peer network through an Elliptic Curve Cryptography based on ANSI X9.62. The proposed security concept improves the level of protection that currently supports the Portable drive VPN and facilitates the realization of Peer to Peer Network. Figure. 1 shows about the high level design of the system.

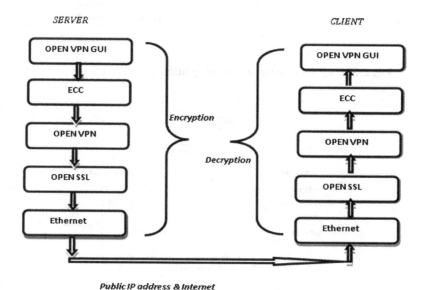

Fig. 1. SSL VPN Secure framework with portable device

With the idea of portable security, the design target is as follows: (1) Ensuring data security and privacy protection of different users. To Launch the ECC based SSL VPN, the USB should be plugged in to the system. (2) Providing customized security for Data packets which will be encrypted by ECC; (3) Implementing risk assessment and security monitoring on TCP and UDP based protocols; (4) Implementing a 2 layer security system to safeguard the integrity and confidentiality of user's private data to create a key that is difficult to decrypt and thereby making it impossible to hack the network. Figure 2) SSL VPN Secure framework with portable device for Client system 3.3) SSL VPN Secure framework with portable device for Server system.

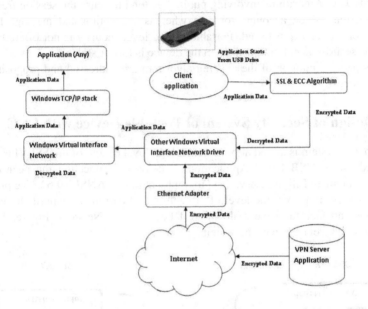

Fig. 2. SSL VPN Secure framework with portable device for Client system

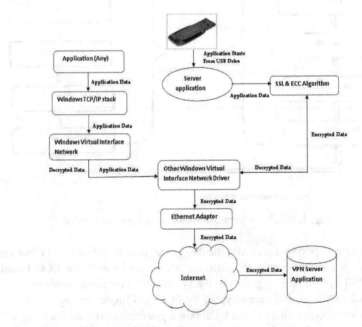

Fig. 3. SSL VPN Secure framework with portable device for Server system

3.1   Security Management in Portable Drives

The growth of USB devices in recent years has created a major revolution in accessing, transferring and storing data. An approach for a secure solution of USB flash drives was proposed in [7]. When an USB flash drive reaches a wrongdoer, private information stored in them are vulnerable to exposure as they are with no security mechanism. What happens when the data in an USB drive is stored with encryption? Persons other than the owner cannot open it without a key. With the rapid growth in technology, these thumb drives are also used in connecting with enterprise networks, taking slides for presentation etc.

3.2   ECC Encryption in VPN

ECC encryption method helps in overcoming the weakness of RSA encryption in public key structure by increasing the speed of encrypting and decrypting, shortening the CPU execution cycle and improves the data processing speed of the server [4].

The modified ECC is more secure and difficult for hackers to attack than the current encryption; it can offer equivalent security with substantially smaller key sizes [5].

The operation of an ECC-based SSL handshake, as specified in [6], the client and server works on an agreed ECC-based cipher set. ECC algorithm based on ANSI X9.62 standards.

3.3   Web Services Security and Framework Component

VPN Server Web service application is used by the client. The client dynamically loads the XML Web services security component to provide integrated security solution. It secures both web services and traditional network based application. Both utilize the same digital ECC key, SOAP message security, ECC algorithm and other supporting functions [2].

The XML web services with ECC component is added to the existing VPN to provide integrated security solution for securing both XML web service and traditional network applications, it uses the same digital ECC key that is used by the VPN Server. Both VPN and web services share the same key and the same access control mechanism. Web service security unit strictly applies more measures if the requests are from outside the VPN; whereas requests from the VPN require no such measures. This component has been built with Microsoft (MS) packages of XML security, SOAP security, and ECC algorithm, other supporting function based on MS Framework 4.0

3.4   Dataflow in the Integrated System

VPN has SSL and ECC. VPN client receives the network traffic from network tap (TAP) adapter [16]; After receiving the network traffic, application traffic is redirected to TAP adapter, it searches whether the traffic needs to be sent through tunnel, if network traffic needs to be tunneled then the VPN client applies the encryption algorithm to the network traffic. Finally it sends the encrypted network traffic to VPN server via the physical adapter. When the thumb drive is connected, connection is done automatically without the requirement for any pre-installed software and it enables the secured generation of public key and encryption and decryption. That is, we establish the secure data transmission when the portable device is connected, otherwise gets disconnected automatically.

4   Analysis and Experimental Results

This section presents the evaluation of Portable VPN replacing RSA with ECC in the SSL protocol. ECC is a public key cryptographic technique providing 160- bit security key. Algorithms involving public keys tend to reuse the session frequently for transaction, which accounts for cost whereas encryption and message hashing amounts for the data transferred. Below, RSA decryption is analyzed using OpenSSL speed program and also different key sizes are measured by ECDH operation. Results for the proposed system, shown in Figure 4 advantages of ECC over RSA with different key sizes

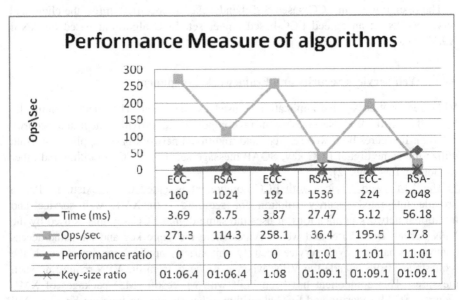

Performance Measure of algorithms

	ECC-160	RSA-1024	ECC-192	RSA-1536	ECC-224	RSA-2048
Time (ms)	3.69	8.75	3.87	27.47	5.12	56.18
Ops/sec	271.3	114.3	258.1	36.4	195.5	17.8
Performance ratio	0	0	0	11:01	11:01	11:01
Key-size ratio	01:06.4	01:06.4	1:08	01:09.1	01:09.1	01:09.1

Fig. 4. Performance Measure of public key algorithms

An interesting phenomenon is observed in case of Apache, where the network Pipe gets saturated for ECC-160 and RSA-1024, ECC-192 and RSA-1536 but the CPU utilization limits reach the highest level RSA-2048. In IIS, the CPU utilization limits reach all the three levels. The results of the experiment achieved in regards with the performance ratio and key-size ratio are listed as in Table 1

Table 1. Performance Measure of public key algorithms

	ECC-160	RSA-1024	ECC-192	RSA-1536	ECC-224	RSA-2048
Performance ratio	2.4 : 1	2.4 : 1	7.1 : 1	11:01	11:01	11:01
Key-size ratio	1 : 6.4	1 : 6.4	1:08	01:09.1	01:09.1	01:09.1

Portable devices use the key agreement procedure that is based on an AES 256 bit encryption scheme, which enables the Peer to Peer network to initiate the VPN establishment, while shifting the complex key negotiation to the network infrastructure. Table 4 shows the VULNERABILITY ANALYSIS OF SECURE PORTABLE DRIVE.

Table 2. Vulnerability Analysis of Secure Portable Drive

Vulnerability Analysis	Existing method	Proposed method
	X	O
Confidentiality	File encryption not provided	Symmetric key
	X	O
Authentication	Not provide	Password-based
	X	O
Access Control	Exposure to the normal area	Encryption of security area information
	X	O
Impersonation Attack	No impersonation	Two stages of user authentication
	O	O
Efficiency	Easy to implement	Easy to implement

[O: Provide, Secure, X: Not provide, Insecure]

The deployed VPN operates transparently to the Portable drive users' movement. Required enhancements for security service provision are integrated in the existing network infrastructure. The proposed security scheme is employed as an add-on feature to the portable drive standard. It can be applied on various parts like connecting enterprise network from home, accessing remote from client, host-to-host network.

5   Conclusion

The above analysis suggests that the use of Portable devices with ECC offer significant performance benefits to SSL clients and especially the servers as security needs rise. The proposed security scheme improves the Level of protection currently supported in portable drive. It secures data transmission over the entire network route by utilizing the default P2P network over the portable device. The potential incompatibilities that arise from the simultaneous use of ECC, as well as the impact of user mobility on VPN operation is considered, and detailed solutions are proposed. Also, we have focused on security aspect of web services and Integration of the Web Services security component with the Application server is proved to be feasible and efficient.

References

1. Enomoto, N., Yoshimi, H., Sai, C.: A secure and easy remote access technology. In: 6th Asia-Pacific Symposium on Information and Telecommunication Technologies, APSITT 2005 Proceedings, pp. 364–368 (2005), doi: 10.1109/APSITT.2005.203686
2. Goldberg, A., Buff, R., Schmitt, A.: Secure Web Server Performance Dramatically Improved by Caching SSL Session Keys. In: Proc. of Workshop on Internet Server Performance, SIGMETRICS 1998, pp. 1–4 (June 1998)
3. Liu, Y., Yeap, T.H.: Securing XML Web Services with Elliptic Curve Cryptography. In: Electrical and Computer Engineering, CCECE 2007, pp. 974–977 (2007)
4. Chen, W.S., Liu, C.: The Applied Research of ECC Encryption Algorithm in VPN Technology. In: Internet Technology and Applications (iTAP), pp. 1–4 (2011)
5. Junru, H.: The improved elliptic curve digital signature algorithm. In: 2011 International Conference on Electronic and Mechanical Engineering and Information Technology (EMEIT), vol. 1, pp. 257–259 (2011), doi: 10.1109/EMEIT.2011.6022868
6. Zhang, Q., Li, Z., Song, C.: The Improvement of digital signature algorithm based on elliptic curve cryptography. In: 2011 2nd International Conference on Artificial Intelligence, Management Science and Electronic Commerce (AIMSEC), pp. 1689–1691 (2011), doi: 10.1109/AIMSEC.2011.6010590
7. Lee, S.-H., Yim, K.-B., Lee, I.-Y.: A Secure Solution for USB Flash Drives Using FAT File System Structure. In: 2010 13th Network-Based Information Systems (NBiS), pp. 487–492 (2010)
8. Jeong, H., Choi, Y.: Vulnerability analysis of secure USB flash drives. In: Memory Technology, Design and Testing, MTDT 2007, pp. 61–64 (2007)
9. Savas, E., Naseer, M., Gutub, A.A.-A., Koc, C.K.: Efficient unified Montgomery inversion with multibit shifting. IEE Proceedings - Computers and Digital Techniques 152(4), 489–498 (2005)
10. Koblitz, N.: Elliptic curve cryptosystems. Mathematics of Computation 48, 203–209 (1987)
11. Fernandes, F.R., Machado, R.J.S., Ferreira, J.M., Gericota, M.G.: Gatewaying IEEE 1149.1 and IEEE 1149.7 test access ports. 2012 IEEE 18th International On-Line Testing Symposium (IOLTS), pp. 136–137 (June 2012)
12. Coarfa, C., Druschel, P., Wallach, D.: Performance Analysis of TLS Web Servers. In: Network and Distributed Systems Security Symposium 2002, San Diego, California (February 2002)
13. Adreozzi, S., Ciancarini, P., Montesi, D., Moretti, R.: Towards a model for quality of web and grid service. In: Proc. 13th IEEE international Workshops on Enabling Technologies: Infrastructure for Colloborative Enterprises (WET ICE 2004), pp. 271–276 (2004)
14. Gouscos, D., Kalikakis, M., Georgiadis, P.: An approach to modeling Web service QoS and provision price. In: Proceeding of the 3rd International Conference on Web Information Systems Engineering Workshops, pp. 121–130 (2003)

15. Thomas, J.P., Thomas, M., Ghinea, G.: Modeling of Web service flow. In: Proceeding of the IEEE International Conference on E-Commerce (CEC 2003), pp. 391–398 (2003)
16. Cardellini, V., Casalicchio, E., Colajanni, M.: A performance study of distributed architectures for the quality of Web services. In: Proceeding of the 34th Annual Hawaii International Conference on System Sciences (2001)
17. Badia, L.: Real World SSL Benchmarking. Rainbow Technologies Whitepaper (September 2001),
    http://www.rainbow.com/insights/whitePDF/RealWorldSSLBenchmarking.pdf
18. Certicom Research, SEC 2: Recommended Elliptic Curve Domain Parameters. Standards for Efficient Cryptography, Version 1.0 (September 2000)
19. Gupta, V., Blake-Wilson, S., Moeller, B., Hawk, C.: ECC Cipher Suites for TLS. IETF internet draft <draft-ietf-tls-ecc-03.txt>, work in progress (June 2003)
20. Kaliski, B.: TWIRL and RSA Key Size. RSA Laboratories Technical Note (May 2003),
    http://www.rsasecurity.com/rsalabs/technotes/twirl.html
21. Kent, S., Atkinson, R.: Security Architecture for the Internet Protocol. RFC 2401 (November 1998)
22. Koblitz, N.: Elliptic curve cryptosystems. Mathematics of Computation 48, 203–209 (1987)
23. MasterCard International and Visa International, Secure Electronic Transaction Specification, Version 1.0 (May 1997), http://www.setco.org/
24. Miller, V.S.: Use of elliptic curves in cryptography. In: Williams, H.C. (ed.) CRYPTO 1985. LNCS, vol. 218, pp. 417–426. Springer, Heidelberg (1986)
25. NIST, Advanced Encryption Standard (AES) (December 2001), http://csrc.nist.gov/CryptoToolkit/aes
26. ANSI X9.62, Public Key Cryptography for the Financial Services Industry: The Elliptic CurveDigital Signature Algorithm (ECDSA) (1999)
27. ANSI X9.63, Public Key Cryptography for the Financial Services Industry: Elliptic Curve Key Agreement and Key Transport Protocols, working draft (October 2000)
28. NIST, Special Publication 800-57: Recommendation for Key Management. Part 1: General Guideline, Draft (January 2003)
29. OpenSSL Project, http://www.openssl.org/
30. Ramsdell, B.: S/MIME Version 3 Message Specification, RFC 2633 (June 1999)

Author Index